Challenges for a
Service System in Transition

Challenges for a Service System in Transition

Ensuring Quality Community Experiences for Persons with Developmental Disabilities

edited by

Mary F. Hayden, Ph.D.
Research Director

and

Brian H. Abery, Ph.D.
Project Director

Research and Training Center
on Residential Services
and Community Living
Institute on Community Integration (UAP)
University of Minnesota

·P·A·U·L·H·
BROOKES
PUBLISHING CO.

Baltimore • London • Toronto • Sydney

Paul H. Brookes Publishing Co.
P.O. Box 10624
Baltimore, Maryland 21285-0624

Copyright © 1994 by Paul H. Brookes Publishing Co., Inc.

Typeset by Brushwood Graphics, Inc., Baltimore, Maryland.
Manufactured in the United States of America by
The Maple Press Company, York, Pennsylvania.

Library of Congress Cataloging-in-Publication Data
Challenges for a service system in transition : ensuring quality community experiences for persons with developmental disabilities / edited
by Mary F. Hayden and Brian H. Abery.
    p.   cm.
Includes bibliographical references and index.
ISBN 1-55766-125-1
1. Developmentally disabled—Services for—United States.
2. Developmentally disabled—United States. I. Hayden, Mary F.
II. Abery, Brian H.
HV1570.5.U6BC48   1993
362.1′968—dc20   93-30857
                                                                  CIP

British Library Cataloging-in-Publication data are available from the
British Library.

Contents

Contributors vii
Preface xi

**PART I   ISSUES AND METHODOLOGICAL APPROACHES TO
COMMUNITY LIVING RESEARCH**

Chapter 1   An Overview of the Community Living Concept
*K. Charlie Lakin, Mary F. Hayden, and
Brian H. Abery* 3
Chapter 2   Research Perspectives and the Community Living
Experience
Glenn T. Fujiura 23
Chapter 3   Qualitative Research Methods and Community
Living
Steven J. Taylor and Robert Bogdan 43
Chapter 4   A Multidimensional Approach to the Measurement
of Community Adjustment
Kevin S. McGrew and Robert H. Bruininks 65

**PART II   PROMOTING COMMUNITY INTEGRATION AND
SOCIAL RELATIONSHIPS**

Chapter 5   Enhancing the Social Inclusion of Persons with
Developmental Disabilities
Brian H. Abery and Maurice Fahnestock 83
Chapter 6   Facilitating Integration in Recreation Environments
*Stuart J. Schleien, John E. Rynders, and
Frederick P. Green* 121
Chapter 7   Distinguishing Between Socially and Nonsocially
Motivated Challenging Behavior: Implications for
the Selection of Intervention Strategies
*Jeff Sigafoos, Joe Reichle, and
Cheryl Light-Shriner* 147

PART III   COMMUNITY SERVICES AND SUPPORT ISSUES

Chapter 8   Waiting for Community Services: The Impact on
Persons with Mental Retardation and Other
Developmental Disabilities
Mary F. Hayden and Paris DePaepe 173

Chapter 9   Assessment and Enhancement of Quality Services
             for Persons with Mental Retardation and Other
             Developmental Disabilities
                 K. Charlie Lakin, Sheryl A. Larson, and
                 Robert Prouty 207
Chapter 10   Costs of Community-Based Residential and Related
             Services to Individuals with Mental Retardation
             and Other Developmental Disabilities
                 Darrell R. Lewis and Robert H. Bruininks 231
Chapter 11   State Agency and Community Provider Perspectives
             on Financing Community Services
                 Richard Hemp 265
Chapter 12   Compensation and Turnover of Direct Care Staff:
             A National Survey
                 Dale Mitchell and David Braddock 289
Chapter 13   Residential Services Personnel: Recruitment,
             Training, and Retention
                 Sheryl A. Larson, Amy Hewitt, and
                 K. Charlie Lakin 313

PART IV   ENHANCING INDEPENDENCE AND AUTONOMY

Chapter 14   A Conceptual Framework for Enhancing
             Self-Determination
                 Brian H. Abery 345
Chapter 15   "A Home of Our Own": Homes, Neighborhoods,
             and Personal Connections
                 Julie Ann Racino and Susan O'Connor 381
Chapter 16   Community Living: A Multicultural Perspective
                 Rannveig Traustadottir, Zana Marie Lutfiyya, and
                 Bonnie Shoultz 405
Chapter 17   Legal Guardianship: The Implications of Law,
             Procedure, and Policy for the Lives of Persons with
             Developmental Disabilities
                 C. David Flower 427
Chapter 18   Supported Employment: Program Models,
             Strategies, and Evaluation Perspectives
                 David R. Johnson and Darrell R. Lewis 449

Index 483

Contributors

Brian H. Abery, Ph.D.
Research and Training Center on
 Residential Services and Community
 Living
Institute on Community Integration (UAP)
University of Minnesota
107 Pattee Hall
150 Pillsbury Drive SE
Minneapolis, MN 55455

Robert Bogdan, Ph.D.
Division of Special Education and
 Rehabilitation
Syracuse University
805 South Crouse Avenue
Syracuse, NY 13244-2280

David Braddock, Ph.D.
University Affiliated Program in
 Developmental Disabilities
University of Illinois at Chicago
1640 West Roosevelt Road
Chicago, IL 60608

Robert H. Bruininks, Ph.D.
College of Education
University of Minnesota
104 Burton Hall
Minneapolis, MN 55455

Paris DePaepe, M.S.
Department of Educational Psychology
University of Minnesota
211 Pattee Hall
150 Pillsbury Drive SE
Minneapolis, MN 55455

Maurice Fahnestock, M.Ed.
Institute on Community Integration (UAP)
University of Minnesota
104-B Pattee Hall
150 Pillsbury Drive SE
Minneapolis, MN 55455

C. David Flower, B.A.
Department of Human Services
Division for Persons with Developmental
 Disabilities
444 Lafayette Road
St. Paul, MN 55155

Glenn T. Fujiura, Ph.D.
University Affiliated Program in
 Developmental Disabilities
University of Illinois at Chicago
1640 West Roosevelt Road
Chicago, IL 60608

Frederick P. Green, Ph.D.
School of Human Performance &
 Recreation
University of Southern Mississippi
Southern Station, Box 5142
Hattiesburg, MS 39406

Mary F. Hayden, Ph.D.
Research and Training Center on
 Residential Services and Community
 Living
Institute on Community Integration (UAP)
University of Minnesota
214-D Pattee Hall
150 Pillsbury Drive SE
Minneapolis, MN 55455

Richard Hemp, M.A.
University Affiliated Program in
 Developmental Disabilities
University of Illinois at Chicago
1640 West Roosevelt Road
Chicago, IL 60608

Amy Hewitt, M.S.W.
Research and Training Center on
 Residential Services and Community
 Living
University of Minnesota
214-B Pattee Hall
150 Pillsbury Drive SE
Minneapolis, MN 55455

David R. Johnson, Ph.D.
Research and Training Center on
  Residential Services and Community
  Living
University of Minnesota
12 Pattee Hall
150 Pillsbury Drive SE
Minneapolis, MN 55455

K.Charlie Lakin, Ph.D.
Research and Training Center on
  Residential Services and Community
  Living
University of Minnesota
214-A Pattee Hall
150 Pillsbury Drive SE
Minneapolis, MN 55455

Sheryl A. Larson, M.A.
Research and Training Center on
  Residential Services and Community
  Living
University of Minnesota
214-B Pattee Hall
150 Pillsbury Drive SE
Minneapolis, MN 55455

Darrell R. Lewis, Ph.D.
Educational Policy and Administration
University of Minnesota
136 Burton
Minneapolis, MN 55455

Cheryl Light-Shriner, B.A.
Research and Training Center on
  Residential Services and Community
  Living
University of Minnesota
207 Pattee Hall
150 Pillsbury Drive SE
Minneapolis, MN 55455

Zana Marie Lutfiyya, Ph.D.
Center on Human Policy
Syracuse University
200 Huntington Hall
Syracuse, NY 13244-2340

Kevin S. McGrew, Ph.D.
Department of Applied Psychology
St. Cloud University
720 4th Avenue South
St. Cloud, MN 56301

Dale Mitchell, Ph.D.
University Affiliated Program in
  Developmental Disabilities
University of Illinois at Chicago
1640 West Roosevelt Road
Chicago, IL 60608

Susan O'Connor, M.S.
Center on Human Policy
Syracuse University
200 Huntington Hall
Syracuse, NY 13244-2340

Robert Prouty, M.S.
Research and Training Center on
  Residential Services and Community
  Living
University of Minnesota
214-A Pattee Hall
150 Pillsbury Drive SE
Minneapolis, MN 55455

Julie Ann Racino, M.A., P.A.
Community and Policy Studies
2103 South Geddes Street
Syracuse, NY 13207

Joe Reichle, Ph.D.
Department of Communication Disorders
University of Minnesota
47 Shevlin Hall
Minneapolis, MN 55455

John E. Rynders, Ph.D.
Department of Educational Psychology
University of Minnesota
255 Burton Hall
Minneapolis, MN 55455

Stuart J. Schleien, Ph.D.
School of Kinesiology & Leisure Studies
University of Minnesota
1900 University Avenue SE
Minneapolis, MN 55455

Bonnie Shoultz, M.A.
Center on Human Policy
Syracuse University
200 Huntington Hall
Syracuse, NY 13244-2340

Jeff Sigafoos, Ph.D.
Fred and Eleanor Schonell Special
  Education Research Centre
University of Queensland
Brisbane, Qld 4072
AUSTRALIA

Steven J. Taylor, Ph.D.
Center on Human Policy
Syracuse University
200 Huntington Hall
Syracuse, NY 13244-2340

Rannveig Traustadottir, Ph.D.
Department of Social Sciences
University of Iceland
Odda v/Sudurgotu
101 Reykjavik
ICELAND

Preface

More than 30 years ago, President John F. Kennedy called for a national plan to combat mental retardation and directed his newly created President's Panel on Mental Retardation to develop this plan. The panel's report documented the substandard care and treatment of persons with mental retardation who lived in state-operated facilities and, in addition, proposed major policy changes and new services for this population.

In his address to Congress in February 1963, President Kennedy challenged the United States' current practices in the treatment and care of persons with mental retardation. He urged the following actions:

- bestow the full benefits of our society to those who suffer from mental disabilities;
- prevent the occurrence of mental illness and mental retardation wherever and whenever possible;
- provide for early diagnosis and continuous and comprehensive care, in the community, of those suffering from these disorders;
- stimulate improvements in the level of care given the mentally disabled in our State and private institutions, and reorient those programs to a community-centered approach;
- reduce, over a number of years, and by hundreds of thousands, the persons confined to these institutions;
- retain in and return to the community the mentally ill and mentally retarded, and restore and revitalize their lives through better health programs and strengthened educational and rehabilitation services; and
- reinforce the will and capacity of our communities to meet these problems, in order that the communities, in turn, can reinforce the will and capacity of individuals and individual families.
- We must promote—to the best of our ability and by all possible and appropriate means—the mental and physical health of all our citizens. (Kennedy, 1963, pp. 13–14)

This speech, which 30 years later still challenges society, greatly contributed to what was then a fledgling movement toward deinstitutionalization, community living opportunities, and fuller recognition of the citizenship of persons with mental retardation. This movement eventually revolutionized the service delivery system. In the 1960s and 1970s, this change was most evident in decreasing public institution populations. The average daily population of state-operated institutions decreased from 195,000 in 1967 to 128,000 in 1980 and has continued to decrease to 81,200 people in 1991 (Lakin, Prouty, Blake, Mangan, & White, 1993). During the 1960s and 1970s, the limited but growing body of research on deinstitutionalization and community living primarily focused on the topics of community placement and community tenure (often referred to as "adjustment"). This focus was reflected in an American Association on Mental Deficiency (AAMD) monograph published in 1981 (Bruininks, Meyers, Sigford, & Lakin, 1981), which presented an overview of some of the best research being conducted on these topics throughout the country. (AAMD later changed its name to the American Association on Mental Retardation, and has been known as AAMR since 1987.)

Yet, even as the AAMD monograph was in press, the mental retardation and developmental disabilities field had already started to shift its focus from community placement and tenure to the content of the community living experience. In the early 1980s, people began to look beyond the physical presence of people with mental retardation and other developmental disabilities in residential neighborhoods and toward the relationships, skills, and experiences of these persons that contributed to more meaningful participation and membership in their communities. The research focused on how to contribute to expanding the number and the quality of opportunities for persons with mental retardation and other developmental disabilities to live and participate as valued members of their communities. Most important, individuals with mental retardation and their families became valued contributors to this applied, value-driven focus on research for community inclusion.

This book derives from the second wave of community living research in which researchers view themselves not as passive observers of the phenomenon of community living, but as co-involved participants in the discovery of how to make inclusion a reality for growing numbers of persons with mental retardation. It represents an accumulation of research and demonstration activities of the Rehabilitation Research and Training Center (RRTC) on Residential Services and Community Living, a collaborative program involving the Institute on Community Integration at the University of Minnesota, the Center on Human Policy at Syracuse University, and the University Affiliated Program (UAP) on Developmental Disabilities at the University of Illinois at Chicago.

The RRTC started in 1988 with the goals of providing research information, demonstration of effective practices, technical assistance, and training to assist and support individuals with mental retardation and other developmental disabilities in order to increase their presence, participation, and empowerment within the community. This book also describes what has been learned in pursuit of this goal. RRTC participants examine: 1) the evolving concept of community living and the goals of inclusion and empowerment for community residents with mental retardation; 2) the status, trends, and barriers in the realization of inclusion and empowerment; 3) the conceptual and methodological aspects of community living research; and 4) the current state of knowledge and best professional practices in achieving positive consequences of the community living experience for persons with mental retardation.

Based upon the RRTC's goal, the editors would like to dedicate this book to those individuals with developmental disabilities who had the courage to envision full community inclusion, to identify problems in the implementation of this vision, and to work tirelessly to ensure that the vision would become a reality.

REFERENCES

Bruininks, R.H., Meyers, C.E., Sigford, B.B., & Lakin, K.C. (Eds.). (1981). *Deinstitutionalization and community adjustment of mentally retarded people*. Washington, DC: American Association on Mental Deficiency.

Kennedy, J.F. (1963, February). Message from the President of the United States. *Congressional Record*, 13–14.

Lakin, K.C., Prouty, R.W., Blake, E.M., Mangan, T., & White, C.C. (1993). *Residential services for persons with mental retardation and related conditions: Year ending June 30, 1991*. Minneapolis: University of Minnesota, Research and Training Center on Residential Services and Community Living, Institute on Community Integration.

PART I

ISSUES AND METHODOLOGICAL APPROACHES TO COMMUNITY LIVING RESEARCH

_ *Chapter 1* _____

An Overview
of the Community
Living Concept

K. Charlie Lakin,
Mary F. Hayden, and Brian H. Abery

The Rehabilitation Research and Training Center (RRTC) on Residential Services and Community Living is a collaborative program involving the Institute on Community Integration (UAP) at the University of Minnesota, the Center on Human Policy at Syracuse University, and the University Affiliated Program on Developmental Disabilities at the University of Illinois at Chicago. The goal of the Center is to assist and support persons with developmental disabilities in increasing their presence, participation, and self-determination in their communities. The Center's staff is committed to the belief that all persons with developmental disabilities can not only live in our communities, but that they can also be a valued part of those communities. The Center focuses on finding ways to better understand and promote opportunities for persons with mental retardation and other developmental disabilities to be accepted and included in valued social and cultural roles. This focus is maintained throughout the Center's coordinated programs of interdisciplinary research, program development and evaluation, training, technical assistance, and dissemination.

Soon after its initiation, the RRTC staff and its advisory committee met to establish a conceptual framework that would describe the meaning of community living. This framework provided the basis to develop the RRTC's mission and, consequently, to structure its parameters and priorities for research, demonstration, technical assistance, and training activities. The remainder of this chapter provides an introduction to that conceptual framework and to some of the most apparent accomplishments, issues, and pressing problems identified in the RRTC activities within that framework.

Preparation of this chapter was supported by a cooperative agreement (#H133B89948) between the National Institute on Disability and Rehabilitation Research (NIDRR) and the Rehabilitation Research and Training Center on Residential Services and Community Living at the University of Minnesota (College of Education) located within the Institute on Community Integration (UAP). The opinions expressed are those of the authors.

3

THE COMMUNITY LIVING CONCEPT

In its most simplistic sense, the concept of community is viewed in terms of population and organization, that is, shared space. In its most complex form, the concept tends to focus on aspects of mutuality and reciprocity and, in addition, includes shared interests, interpersonal relationships, interdependent roles and involvements, and common expectations and standards. For the purpose of this chapter, being part of a community means to share physical space with people who have mutual interests, enjoy relationships, develop interdependencies, and share common expectations. In the work of the RRTC, community living has been viewed as the effort to improve one's quality of life within collectives called communities. There are numerous aspects of quality of life, at least six of which have been identified. These include: 1) presence in the community; 2) health, safety, and basic comfort; 3) opportunity for personal growth and development; 4) social relationships; 5) valued community participation; and 6) personal self-determination.

Community presence refers to the physical presence of persons with mental retardation and other developmental disabilities in typical societal communities. *Health, safety, and comfort* include: a) the basic ingredients of good medical and mental health care; b) the recognition of rights and dignity; c) the provision of physical safety and comfort; d) the freedom from physical, emotional, and sexual abuse; and e) the provision of environments that have physical, sensory, aesthetic, and social characteristics. *Personal growth and development* implies opportunities to gain knowledge and develop new skills that add to one's personal competence and fulfill one's interests, as well as to the opportunity and ability to develop and express one's individuality. *Social relationships* entail a range of activities that include opportunities to meet and interact with new people and to maintain current friendships and family relationships. *Valued community participation* involves expanding opportunities for participation in roles valued by the larger community. *Personal self-determination* means being able to affirm one's personhood through choice, self-representation, and empowerment. The remainder of this chapter reviews these six aspects of community living within the context of the RRTC's activities and products.

Community Presence

Shift from Institutions to the Community   The initial step toward community integration of persons with mental retardation and other developmental disabilities is the opportunity for a physical presence in the community. Research shows that there has been a clear shift from people living in large, segregated institutions to people living in community settings. Increasingly, institutions are not only being depopulated, but are being closed. A recent study of institution closures nationwide showed that 33 institutions were closed in the 25 years between 1960 and 1985, a total of 72 have been or are projected to close in the 10 years between January 1986 and December 1995 (White, Prouty, Lakin, & Blake, 1992).

Although the United States has experienced a quarter of a century of de-institutionalization, there has been great variation across the states in rates of state institution depopulation (Braddock, Hemp, Fujiura, Bachelder, & Mitchell, 1990). For example, although the nation's overall institutional populations declined between 1977 and 1988 by 39%, Michigan's population declined 79%, Arkansas and Tennessee saw declines of less than 5%, and Nevada experienced an increase of 51% (Hemp, 1992). Since 1988, the state of New Hampshire and the District of Columbia have closed their only large public institutions for persons with mental retardation and other developmental disabilities.

The early years of state efforts to reduce the populations of large public institutions involved the development of many large private institutions and the transfer of tens of thousands of persons with mental retardation and other developmental disabilities to nursing homes. The populations of persons with mental retardation in these alternative institutions grew rapidly, fueled not only by the strong commitment to reduce public institution populations but also by the availability of Medicaid to fund them (Lakin, Hill, & Bruininks, 1989). Unfortunately, they have been particularly slow to decrease. By 1977, large private institutions (16 or more people living at the residence) housed 51,650 people. By June 30, 1991, their populations had only decreased to 44,700 (Lakin, Blake, Prouty, Mangan, & Bruininks, 1993).

Still in all, about 80,000 fewer persons with mental retardation and other developmental disabilities were residing in large institutional settings in 1991 than had resided in 1977. Conversely, between 1977 and 1991, the number living in community residences containing six or fewer people increased from 20,400 to 108,800, while the number of people living in community settings of 15 or fewer residents increased from 40,400 to 153,237 (Lakin, Blake, et al., 1993). In sum, much has been accomplished and much is left to be accomplished in assuring community living opportunities to a person with mental retardation. With respect to providing such opportunities to all persons with mental retardation, two groups reflect particularly notable current challenges. These groups are persons with severe impairments and persons who are currently awaiting services. In a recent state survey, it has been further estimated that between 1987 and 1990 another 16,900 fewer persons with mental retardation and other developmental disabilities will be in public and private residential facilities of 16 or more residents (Lakin, Menke, Jaskulski, Hill, & Wright, 1993). Presumably, under the Consolidated Omnibus Budget Reconciliation Act of 1987 (OBRA) (PL 100-262), nursing home populations will be considerably reduced as well.

Persons with Severe Disabilities   Individuals with severe developmental, behavioral, and physical disabilities can be found in community residences (Hayden & DePaepe, 1991; Hayden, Lakin, Hill, Bruininks, & Chen, 1992; Lakin, Hill, Chen, & Stephens, 1989; Shoultz, 1990). Research shows that their numbers are rapidly growing (Amado, Lakin, & Menke, 1990). For example, in 1982, approximately 6,000 persons with mental retardation lived in community residential settings (Lakin, Hill, & Bruininks, 1989), and by 1989, there were approximately three times that number (Lakin, Bruininks, & Larson, 1991). Providing adequate access to community services for persons with physical and behavioral needs, however, still often presents a challenge (Hayden & DePaepe, 1991; Reichle & Light, 1992). In fact, the approximately 167,000 people with mental retardation and other developmental disabilities who lived in residential institutions and nursing homes in June 1991, were primarily people with severe intellectual, medical, and behavioral disabilities (Feuerstein, Rand, & Rynders, 1989; Lakin, Bruininks, et al., 1991; Lakin, Hill, & Anderson, 1991; Lakin, Jaskulski, Hill, et al., 1989).

Although there are increasing numbers of persons with severe disabilities living in the community, residents of community facilities are distinctly different, as a group, from residents of large institutions. Smaller facilities are likely to have more people with relatively mild cognitive impairments than residents of larger facilities. In the 1987 National Medical Expenditure Survey, it was estimated that 14% of the persons who lived in residential facilities with 15 or fewer residents had rather severe mental retardation as opposed to 47% of residents of all larger facilities (Lakin, Hill, Chen, & Stephens, 1989). A national study of persons who live in small (six or fewer people) residential facilities estimated that approximately 20% of the residents of intermediate care facilities for persons with mental retardation (ICFs/MR) had severe mental retardation, as did about 9% of the foster home residents and 13% (another 10,000 people) of the non–ICF/MR group home residents (Hill et al., 1989).

The challenge of continuing to develop community services for state institution residents will rely on continuing focus on services that meet the needs of persons with mental retardation. On June 30, 1991, nearly two-thirds (65%) of state institution residents were reported to have mental retardation (Lakin, Blake, et al., 1993). Similar patterns exist for persons with medical or behavioral impairments. Substantial community presence currently exists, but institutional placement still prevails (Lakin, Hill, Chen, & Stephens, 1989). Systematic discrimination against persons with severe disabilities, despite evidence that they greatly benefit from community living (Larson & Lakin, 1989), continues to be common practice. There is a necessity to acknowledge current barriers that prevent the provision of services, to determine what services are needed, and to develop strategies and assurances that quality services are available in the community.

Waiting for Community Services Another group currently being commonly denied community services are those persons who live at home with their families. The findings of a recent national study found that persons with mental retardation and other developmental disabilities in the United States are currently waiting for 181,835 individual categories of residential and vocational services and/or other types of supports (Hayden, 1992). These findings were consistent with previous research that found long waiting lists for needed community services (Davis, 1987). These two studies noted that reported numbers were underestimates of the actual magnitude of persons needing community services.

The most serious problems with respect to service and program access appear to be for families who have kept their adult children at home beyond the age that most young adults typically leave to reside in the community (Hayden, Spicer, DePaepe, & Chelberg, 1992). Many of these people need only minimal assistance to live independently in the community (Wieck & McBride, 1990). Some persons, for example, may need only training in certain skills to acquire independence, while others may need a personal care attendant to assist them with day-to-day physical care and mobility. Increasingly, such assistance is made available to persons with all types of disabilities under the label of supported living.

Supported Living Supported community living is a new way of thinking about living in the community (O'Brien, 1991; O'Brien & O'Brien, 1991; Racino, 1991a). Within this model, services are viewed as being dependent upon the unique abilities, circumstances, desires, and needs of each individual. The approach begins with the premise that everyone wants a home to return to at the end of a day that is more than a physical space. Like others, persons with mental retardation and other developmental disabilities want homes of their own, where they can be themselves and choose to do what they want, when they want, and with whom they want (O'Brien, 1991; Skarnulis & Lakin, 1990). The fundamentally important part of this concept is personalization. The determination of what supports a person receives because of a disability would not determine the individual's life circumstances, but would be used to shape and balance those circumstances to reflect the individual's desires and preferences (O'Connor & Racino, 1989; Racino, Walker, O'Connor, & Taylor, 1993).

Supported community living includes several basic premises that are based on the following assumptions: 1) all persons need and deserve a home of their own (Racino, 1991a, 1991b); 2) funding for housing should be separated from the funding for services so that people can live where and with whom they want; 3) services should support persons' personal preferences and desired life-styles (O'Connor, 1991); 4) natural supports available to people through family, community, and friends should be sustained and fostered (Traustadottir, 1991); 5) people should have a choice in the services they receive and from whom they receive them; 6) services should be deliverable in numerous ways to different people in a variety of places; 7) service providers should find less intrusive ways to bring services and supports into people's homes and be more sensitive and respectful of being in other persons' homes; and 8) service providers need to be able to adjust to a "market" in which "clients" and revenues are determined by demand for specific services, not by the total number of people who desire to be provided with comprehensive care (O'Brien & O'Brien, 1991; Skarnulis & Lakin, 1990; Taylor, Bogdan, & Racino, 1991). Each of these premises implies significant changes from the traditional facility-based service delivery system, presenting an enormous challenge to redesign the system, from basic reimbursement to quality assurance and enhancement (Prouty & Lakin, 1991).

Supported living affects a relatively small fraction of persons with mental retardation and other developmental disabilities. Nationally, only about 28,000 people were reported as having received either supported or semi-independent living services in June 1991 (Lakin, Blake, et al., 1993). Still, the spread of the supported living concept can only foster the continuing decentralization and personalization of residential services. As an ideal, the concept brings heightened attention to basic aspects (e.g., independence, choice, autonomy, and relationships) of the quality of life of persons with mental retardation and other developmental disabilities. These aspects will also affect expectations for residential services in congregate settings.

Health, Safety, and Basic Comfort

Medical Care   People with mental retardation and other developmental disabilities need opportunities to test and to extend their abilities to live as independently as possible in their communities. As they do so, they should be assured of appropriate attention to their health. National and state studies have shown that persons with mental retardation and other developmental disabilities in community residential facilities almost universally receive annual (if not more) medical and dental services (Hill et al., 1989). Careproviders and family members usually report these services as being at least satisfactory (Lakin, Burwell, Hayden, & Jackson, 1992). Although there is a limited body of research, persons with very extensive health needs are already living in community settings with generally positive reviews of their health-related services (Lakin et al., 1992), but the research does indicate that persons with mental retardation and other developmental disabilities may need a few specialized services. However, it is important to note that the type and range of medical care and services needed to support most people with mental retardation and other developmental disabilities are similar to those utilized by the general public (Hayden & DePaepe, 1991). Yet, some people still have problems obtaining medical care and services and, as a result, may be placed at risk of reinstitutionalization. To improve access to medical services, supporters of full community inclusion need to develop strategies that enable the service delivery system to become more responsive to the needs of people with mental retardation and other developmental disabilities, ranging from managed care enrollment incentives to improved orientation and training of primary health care providers.

Basic Safety   There are typically three methods employed to assure the basic safety and well-being of persons with mental retardation and other developmental disabilities. These methods are staff training, technical assistance, and monitoring, and they challenge people to assure safety for several reasons. First, community residential services are provided in over 40,000 different sites (Lakin, White, Prouty, Bruininks, & Kimm, 1991). Second, there is increasing development of living arrangements with less than full-time oversight (Amado et al., 1990). Third, average caseloads for case managers in the middle 50% of states providing Medicaid Home and Community Based Services (HCBS) were 30–70 individuals per manager (Prouty & Lakin, 1991).

Responding to the challenges of an increasingly disbursed, deregulated, and diverse service delivery system through new ways of thinking about and designing quality assurance and other quality enhancement activities is of growing importance. These new ways include the development of a variety of alternative, supplemental quality enhancement activities at the state and local levels (Blake, Mangan, Prouty, & Lakin, 1993). Although comprehensive government quality assurance programs will endure in some form to assure basic scrutiny of the health and safety of individuals, quality enhancement activities are increasingly being built around the establishment of and the maintainence of ongoing relationships and mutual commitments among persons with mental retardation and other developmental disabilities, their families and friends, advocates, and others who are actively and frequently involved in each others' lives. These relationships and commitments are increasingly recognized as the single best means of protecting the individuals' basic well-being, while also contributing other important dimensions to their quality of life (O'Brien & O'Brien, 1991; O'Brien, O'Brien, & Schwartz, 1990; Taylor, Racino, & Walker, 1990).

Basic Rights Basic protection for persons with mental retardation and other developmental disabilities also means the assurance of basic rights and of freedom from abuse, exploitation, and neglect. Such projections begin by assuring that the rights provided for persons without disabilities are also recognized for persons with disabilities. Negative societal attitudes toward persons with mental retardation and other developmental disabilities and their ability to contribute frequently hinder recognition of their basic rights. Certainly, the low expectations and high degree of stigma faced by citizens with mental retardation provide substantial barriers to this group's ability to fully benefit from the Americans with Disabilities Act of 1990 (ADA) (Lakin & Jones, 1993), at least until society recognizes that the ultimate protection from abuse and neglect is derived from their being accepted and valued as full members of society. Persons with mental retardation and other developmental disabilities will be denied the ability to grow, develop, and fulfill valued roles as neighbors, coworkers, family members, and friends as long as expectations about their capacities remain low.

For children in this culture, the basic right to live in a family should be recognized and respected. The full commitment to this right is reflected in the policy of permanency planning (Rosenau, 1990). The United States has made great strides in reducing the number of children and youth with mental retardation who are living outside natural or adoptive homes; from about 91,000 in 1977 to 48,500 in 1987 (Hill, Hayden, Lakin, Menke, & Novak-Amado, 1990; Taylor, Lutfiyya, & Musgrave, 1989). Still, significant challenges remain in assuring a family home for all children and youth. These challenges range from the provision of needed supports to families (Wieck & McBride, 1991) to the assurance that the permanency planning process, which is required for children who receive child welfare services, is also extended to children with mental retardation and other developmental disabilities who receive services funded by other programs (Taylor, Lakin, & Hill, 1989).

Freedom from Discrimination Basic protection means freedom from discrimination in community participation that is based on severity of impairment

(Taylor, 1988); from discrimination in guardianship standards, which frequently deny people control over the most basic aspects of their lives (Flower, chap. 17, this volume) and from discrimination that occurs in repressive and punitive environments that exist in the name of habilitation and training (O'Brien, 1989; Reichle & DePaepe, 1991; Reichle & Light, 1992). New promises of programmatic access to activities sponsored by public agencies under the ADA offer the opportunity to reduce discrimination in community participation, especially with training and technical assistance coinvolvements that help such agencies meet their challenges and responsibilities (Schleien, Meyer, Heyne, & Biel, in press).

In 1989, the RRTC cosponsored a national conference on positive approaches to the management of excess behavior (Reichle & Light, 1992; Research and Training Center on Residential Services and Community Living, 1990). Conference participants generated recommendations focused on issues such as assessment, intervention, staff development, and technical assistance. Progress has also been made in the recognition of the rights of persons with challenging behavior to enjoy less restricted, less punitive lives in community environments. However, the momentum of this progress will again be lost unless significant resources are directed toward the needs of community agencies in the areas of assessment and intervention, prevention, and training and technical assistance. As services to these persons become increasingly dispersed across community settings, there is a critical need to integrate ongoing training, technical assistance, and crisis support activities. Doing so will ensure that both assessment and intervention technology meet the necessary social validity standards in the form of a lifestyle of maximum interest, preference, and autonomy for individuals with mental retardation.

Opportunity for Personal Growth and Development

Like most people, persons with mental retardation and other developmental disabilities need to learn new skills that add to their competence, fulfill their interests, and develop their individuality. Research consistently and convincingly shows that the functional skills of living in our society are better developed in community settings than in institutions (Larson & Lakin, 1991). The most obvious explanation of this well-established outcome is that learning is not an internal process but an interactive process, which involves both the individual and his or her environment. In other words, an individual learns the skills of the society by participating in that society.

Increasingly, the focus of developmental instruction and supported participation for persons with mental retardation and other developmental disabilities is being derived from the individual interests of the person and from analyses of what the person needs to know to increase his independence and to fulfill his personal interests. The concept of "personal futures planning" and other person-centered planning processes often subsume both general and specific approaches for considering such outcomes within the context of a person's desired housing, family involvement, social relationships, favorite recreation activities, and other circumstances of importance to the individual (Lutfiyya, 1990; Wieck & McBride, 1991). However, the growth of such efforts does not withstand the expectations of the potential of persons with mental retardation and other developmental disabilities to achieve levels of personal independence and participation in daily community life in areas such as leisure and general life-style (Abery, Thurlow, Bruininks, & Johnson, 1989; Hayden, Lakin, Hill, Bruininks, & Copher, 1992; Schleien, Meyer, Heyne, & Biel, in press); recreation and outdoor adventure (McAvoy, Schatz, Stutz, Schleien, & Lais, 1989; Schleien, 1990a, 1990b; Schleien, McAvoy, Lais, & Rynders, 1992; Schleien, McAvoy, Lais, & Rynders, in press; Schleien & Rynders, 1989); functional communication (Reichle, Piche-Cragoe, Sigafoos, & Doss, 1989; Reichle, York, & Sigafoos, 1991); art (Schleien, Rynders, & Mustonen, 1988); and use of community resources (Abery & Erickson, 1992; Lakin et al., 1991; Lakin et al., 1992; Schleien & Larson, 1986; Schleien & Ray, 1988).

A growing body of research is demonstrating that effective integration and productive participation can be obtained with appropriate teaching and environmental accommodations for persons with all levels and types of impairments in the full range of typical community activities (Abery & Lange, 1990; Abery, Thurlow, Johnson, & Bruininks, 1990; Reichle, Sigafoos, & Piche, 1989; Rynders, Schleien, & Mustonen, 1990; Schleien, Cameron, Rynders, & Slick, 1988; Schleien & Light, in press). Doing so, however, requires attention to the commitment and capacity of agencies, with respect to the overall quality of the integration effort for individuals with and without disabilities (Schleien, Heyne, Rynders, & McAvoy, 1990) and to the details of physical accessibility (Schleien, Ray, & Johnson, 1989).

Realizing the potential of persons with mental retardation and other developmental disabilities in community settings is dependent on the quality, preparation, and stability of the persons providing personal support and instruction to them. Clearly, the recruitment, training, and retention of staff, particularly direct care staff, will present one of the greatest challenges in the area of community services in the next decade and, therefore, is a much needed area of focus (Lakin, 1989a; Wallace, Larson, & Hewitt, 1992). The rate of annual staff turnover among the more than 100,000 full-time equivalent, paraprofessional, direct care staff in community residential settings averages 55%–75% nationwide (Lakin & Larson, 1992). The highest educational attainment of the vast majority of individuals in these roles is a high school diploma or its equivalent, and few have had any specialized training other than that provided by the agencies for which they work (Hill et al., 1989). Thus, there is a substantial need for the development of systematic approaches to train persons for such roles. Requirements for training and systems for delivering it, however, are currently limited (Prouty & Lakin, 1991). Although demonstrably effective and promising training practices and curricula exist, a great amount of general improvement is needed if the people who have the most direct involvement in the lives of persons with mental retardation are to be able to contribute as fully as needed to the enhancement of their skills and to community participation (Wallace et al., 1992).

Social Relationships

Social relationships are key factors in the achievement of quality of life for all people. Of any individual's relationships, those with family members usually represent some of the most important. For persons with mental retardation and other developmental disabilities, there are especially compelling reasons to promote sustained family involvement. Frequently, involvement entails far more than the typical support and nurturance provided by families, including important projections, monitoring, and individual advocacy provided by family members (Lutfiyya, 1991a). Family involvement in the lives of persons living in the community is notably higher than for persons in institutions (Hill et al., 1989). Still, many families are dissatisfied with the extent of communication between community settings and family and the extent to which the family involvements are facilitated (Larson & Lakin, 1991).

Social relationships with people other than family members are as important for persons with mental retardation and other developmental disabilities as for others (Abery et al., 1989; Abery et al., 1990; Lutfiyya, 1991b, 1991c). Similarly to most people, these individuals derive most of their social relationships from people who share their residence, workplace, and day program with them. Most other social relationships for persons with mental retardation and other developmental disabilities are with paid staff (Abery et al., 1990; Green & Schleien, 1991; Hayden, Lakin, Hill, Bruininks, & Copher, 1992). Many people in community settings can be as isolated as their counterparts who live in institutions. In fact, a recent independent assessment of Minnesota's Medicaid HCBS waiver program showed that, while HCBS recipients were actually engaged in recreation and leisure activities, only about 5% of recipients participated in these activities with people other than family members, people in their residential or day programs, or paid staff members (Lakin, Burwell, Hayden, & Jackson, 1992).

Other researchers found that persons with mental retardation and other developmental disabilities are much less socially integrated than the population without disabilities (Abery & Erickson, 1991; Abery et al., 1990; Hill et al., 1989). Many others have begun to document experiences of individuals and agencies that demonstrate effective methods of promoting and sustaining meaningful social relationships (Green & Schleien, 1991; Lutfiyya, 1991a; Schleien, Fahnestock, Green, & Rynders, 1990; Taylor & Bogdan, 1989; Taylor et al., 1991). Some of the specific areas of focus have been: 1) promoting the continued use of the family social network once a son or daughter has left home; 2) utilizing churches, schools, and civic organizations to establish experiences that initiate mutual social involvements; and 3) involving persons with mental retardation and other developmental disabilities in the activities of organizations that are typical sources of friendship, including recreation centers, social organizations, clubs, and camps (Abery et al., 1989; Abery & Lange, 1990; Schleien, 1990b; Schleien & Ray, 1988; Taylor, 1989).

Valued Cultural Participation

Being part of a society means contributing to it and using its resources. Compared to people in institutions, those living in community settings are much more likely to use community resources, such as movies, restaurants, parks, and stores (Hayden, Lakin, Hill, Bruininks, & Copher, 1992; Lakin, 1989b). In a recent comparison of a random national sample of 336 persons in small community residences and a national random sample of 100 persons in the general population, community resource use was actually slightly higher among people with mental retardation and other developmental disabilities (Hill et al., 1989). However, valued participation means more than drawing on the resources of a society, it also means contributing to those resources in the best way and to the greatest extent that a person can.

Supported Employment In our society, work is the most common, most valued, and most cost-effective way for adults with mental retardation and other developmental disabilities to contribute to their society (Lewis, Johnson, Bruininks, Kallsen, & Guillery, 1991). Supported employment opportunities have been the most visible and rapidly growing method of assisting persons with mental retardation to contribute to society (Amado et al., 1990; Erickson, Johnson, & Nechville, 1989). Unfortunately, such employment opportunities remain scarce. In the United States, the proportion of persons with mental retardation and other developmental disabilities living in community settings who participate in supported employment is estimated to be in the range of 5%–6% (Lakin, Hill, Chen, & Stephens, 1989). Furthermore, persons with severe mental disabilities count for less than 15% of all supported employment recipients (Amado et al., 1990). Increasingly, qualitative research is raising questions concerning the extent to which participation in supported employment programs, per se, is sufficient to provide integrated and valued roles for participants (Hagner, 1989; O'Brien, 1990).

Participating in Household Tasks There are, of course, other culturally valued roles. One such role is participating in the arrangement and maintenance of one's own household. While such participation is considerably higher among persons living in community versus institutional settings, considerable variation does exist within community settings (Hill et al., 1989). Generally, family care settings and persons who are long-time employees of small group homes are less likely to involve people in domestic tasks (Lakin, Bruininks, Hill, Chen, & Anderson, 1993). Domestic involvement is also particularly low among persons with more severe impairments, although research shows that greater participation is associated with higher expectations of participation, more opportunities for partial or assisted participation in tasks, and increased staff training (Hill et al., 1989; Lakin, Bruininks, Hill, Chen, & Anderson, 1993). Orientation and training activities need to better recognize that involvement of persons with mental retardation in the arrangement and maintenance of their own domestic environments not only engages them in a valued role and provides them with skills that are basic to increased capacity for independent living, but is also a fundamental, albeit not always desired, part of making their house their home.

Leisure and Recreation Activities Leisure time is highly valued in our society. Most efforts to develop recreation and leisure for persons with mental retardation and other developmental disabilities have focused on children and youth (Schleien, Baldwin, & Light, 1989; Schleien, Rynders, Mustonen, & Fox, 1990). Increasingly, these opportunities occur in settings that include persons with and without disabilities in integrated recreation and leisure activities (Abery & Lange, 1990; McAvoy et al., 1989; Rynders & Schleien, 1991; Schleien, Fahnestock, Green, & Rynders, 1990). Unfortunately, these efforts have not spread sufficiently to adults, particularly those with severe impairments (Schleien, 1990a, 1991). Exemplary practices of integrating adults with mental retardation and other developmental disabilities into community leisure and recreation activities, however, are being identified and promoted for replication (Dattilo & Schleien, 1991; Schleien et al., 1992).

Personal Self-Determination

Self-determination and empowerment are increasingly recognized as important goals for persons with mental retardation and other developmental disabilities (Abery & Bruininks, 1990; Research and Training Center on Residential Services and Community Living, 1989). These constructs encompass a wide variety of skills and opportunities in the areas of independence, self-expression, choice making, problem solving, self-management, and self-representation (Abery, 1993; Hayden & Shoultz, 1991b). Skills in these areas and the opportunity to use them are fundamental to membership in society.

Developing self-determination is an integral part of enhancing the skills and opportunities that are needed by persons with mental retardation and other developmental disabilities in order to fully benefit from community living. The ability to exert personal control over both daily and periodic aspects of one's life is so basic to living within inclusive communities that it is often taken for granted. Unfortunately, for these persons, denial of personal control in activities, apparel, place of residence, friends, and associates is too often the case (Abery, 1993; Lakin, Bruininks, & Larson, 1991).

Providing opportunities for people to develop their full potential, as well as exercise their full rights of citizenship, requires that much attention be paid to opportunities to make and to act on daily life choices (Abery & Bruininks, 1990; Abery et al., 1992; Hayden & Shoultz, 1990, 1991a). A growing force within the service delivery system is the recent effort of individuals with mental retardation and other developmental disabilities to educate parents, policymakers, professionals, and others about how self-advocacy is an important component in gaining control over their personal lives and in being primary actors in ensuring quality assurance and enhancement within the system (Hayden & Shoultz, 1990, 1991a).

More often, local, state, and national self-advocacy organizations are increasing their opportunities to develop local, state, and national chapters (Hayden & Chelberg, 1992; Hayden & Shoultz, 1991b; Research and Training Center on Residential Services and Community Living, 1989). This type of activity enables self-advocates to create more pervasive general expectations that support the involvement of persons with mental retardation and other developmental disabilities in the making of program and policy decisions that affect their lives (Hayden & Shoultz, 1991a, 1991b; O'Brien & O'Brien, 1990).

CONCLUSION

Progress is being made in providing opportunities for people with mental retardation and other developmental disabilities to live with security in typical neighborhoods with opportunities to grow and develop and to enjoy inclusion and choice in the social and economic lives of their communities. Realistically, however, the struggle for full citizenship of these persons has just begun. For the majority of persons with mental retardation who receive residential services and who remain in institutional settings and within community living arrangements, including nursing home residents, the elements of institutional living are still all too evident. Nationwide, tens of thousands of adults with mental retardation remain at home waiting to obtain access to the community living services that will provide them the opportunity to assume adult roles in society with the kinds of supports they need.

In the system of residential services, specifically those services for persons with mental retardation and other developmental disabilities, there are today more people cohabitating in community living arrangements of 15 or fewer residents than in larger residential settings. The advent of the community majority is shifting focus in many state mental retardation/developmental disabilities services systems—from a general preference of community over institution placements to a more specific preference toward the quality of community living. In the process, persons with mental retardation and other developmental disabilities, their families, and their friends will be more frequently and directly involved in defining a community life-style on their own terms. The effectiveness of service providers, researchers, policymakers, and advocates will increasingly be judged by their abilities to assist these persons to actually live the life-style they envision.

REFERENCES

Abery, B.H., (1993, June). *A descriptive study of the self-determination skills and opportunities of young adults with mental retardation.* Paper presented at the annual meeting of the American Association on Mental Retardation, Washington, DC.

Abery, B.H., & Bruininks, R.H. (1990). *Facilitating the self-determination of youth with disabilities.* Minneapolis, MN: Institute on Community Integration.

Abery, B.H., & Lange, C. (1990, May). *Enhancing the social inclusion of youth with disabilities.* Paper presented at the meeting of The Council for Exceptional Children, Atlanta, GA.

Abery, B.H., McGrew, K., & Bruninks, R.H. (1992). *Research on the self-determination of children and youth with disabilities*. Minneapolis, MN: Institute on Community Integration.

Abery, B.H., Thurlow, M.T., Bruininks, R.H., & Johnson, D.R. (1989, December). *A descriptive study of the social networks of youth and young adults with developmental disabilities*. Paper presented at the meeting of The Association for Persons with Severe Handicaps, San Francisco, CA.

Abery, B.H., Thurlow, M.T., Johnson, D.R., & Bruininks, R.H. (1990, May). *The social networks of adults with developmental disabilities residing in community settings*. Paper presented at the annual meeting of the American Association on Mental Retardation, Washington, DC.

Amado, A.N., Lakin, K.C., & Menke, J.M. (1990). *1990 chartbook on services for persons with developmental disabilities*. Minneapolis: University of Minnesota, Research and Training Center on Residential Services and Community Living, Institute on Community Integration.

Blake, E., Mangan, T., Prouty, R., & Lakin, K.C. (1993). *Reinventing quality: Improving community services for persons with mental retardation and related conditions*. Minneapolis: University of Minnesota, Research and Training Center on Residential Services and Community Living.

Braddock, D., Hemp, R., Fujiura, G.T., Bachelder, L., & Mitchell, D. (1990). *The state of the states in developmental disabilities*. Baltimore: Paul H. Brookes Publishing Co.

Bruininks, R.H., Meyers, C.E., Sigford, B.B., & Lakin, K.C. (Eds.). (1981). *Deinstitutionalization and community adjustment of mentally retarded people*. Washington, DC: American Association on Mental Deficiency.

Dattilo, J., & Schleien, S. (1991). The benefits of therapeutic recreation in developmental disabilities. In C. Coyle, W. Kinney, R. Riley, & J. Shank (Eds.), *Benefits of therapeutic recreation: A consensus view* (pp. 69–150). Philadelphia: Temple University.

Davis, S. (1987). *A national status report on waiting lists of people with mental retardation for community services*. Arlington, TX: Association for Retarded Citizens of the United States.

Erickson, R., Johnson, D.R., & Nechville, T. (Eds.). (1989). Feature issue on supported employment. *IMPACT, 2*(1), 1–16. Minneapolis: University of Minnesota, Institute on Community Integration.

Feuerstein, R., Rand, Y., & Rynders, J. (1989). *Don't accept me as I am: Helping "retarded" people to excel*. New York: Plenum.

Green, F., & Schleien, S. (1991). Understanding friendship and recreation: A theoretical sampling. *Therapeutic Recreation Journal, 25*(4), 29–40.

Hagner, D. (1989). *The social integration of supported employees: A qualitative study*. Syracuse, NY: Syracuse University, Center on Human Policy.

Hayden, M.F. (1992). Adults with mental retardation and other developmental disabilities waiting for community-based services in the U.S. *Policy Research Brief, 4*(3), 1–16.

Hayden, M.F., & Chelberg, G. (1992, March). *Self-advocacy: A guide to self-advocacy organizations, agencies, and projects in Minnesota*. Minneapolis: University of Minnesota, Research and Training Center on Residential Services and Community Living, Institute on Community Integration.

Hayden, M.F., & DePaepe, P.A. (1991). Medical conditions, level of care needs, and health related outcomes of persons with mental retardation: A review. *Journal of The Association of Persons with Severe Handicaps, 16*(4), 188–206.

Hayden, M.F., Lakin, K.C., Hill, B.K., Bruininks, R.H., & Chen, T.H. (1992). Placement practices in specialized foster homes and small group homes for persons with mental retardation. *Mental Retardation, 30*(2), 53–61.

Hayden, M.F., Lakin, K.C., Hill, B.K., Bruininks, R.H., & Copher, J.I. (1992). Social and leisure integration of people with mental retardation who reside in foster homes and small group homes. *Education and Training in Mental Retardation, 27*(3), 187–199.

Hayden, M.F., & Shoultz, B. (Eds.). (1990). *Effective self-advocacy: Empowering people with disabilities to speak for themselves.* Minneapolis: University of Minnesota, Research and Training Center on Residential Services and Community Living, Institute on Community Integration.

Hayden, M.F., & Shoultz, B. (Eds.). (1991a). Feature issue on self-advocacy. *IMPACT, 3*(4), 1–20. Minneapolis: University of Minnesota, Institute on Community Integration.

Hayden, M.F., & Shoultz, B. (1991b). *Self-advocacy by persons with disabilities: Ideas for creating a national organization* (Recommendations of the National Steering Committee of Self-Advocates). Minneapolis: University of Minnesota, Research and Training Center on Residential Services and Community Living, Institute on Community Integration.

Hayden, M.F., Spicer, P., DePaepe, P., & Chelberg, G. (1992). Waiting for community services: Support and service needs of families with adult members with mental retardation and other developmental disabilities. *Policy Research Brief, 4*(4), 1–12. Minneapolis: University of Minnesota Research and Training Center on Residential Services and Community Living, Institute on Community Integration.

Hemp, R. (1992). Financing community services for persons with disabilities: State agency and community provider perspectives. *Policy Research Brief, 4*(1), 1–8. Minneapolis: University of Minnesota, Research and Training Center on Residential Services and Community Living, Institute on Community Integration.

Hill, B.K., Hayden, M.F., Lakin, K.C., Menke, J., & Novak-Amado, A.R. (1990). State-by-state data on children with handicaps in regular foster homes. *Child Welfare, 69*(5), 447–462.

Hill, B.K., Lakin, K.C., Bruininks, R.H., Amado, A.N., Anderson, D.J., & Copher, J.I. (1989). *Living in the community: A comparative study of foster homes and small group homes for people with mental retardation* (Report No. 28). Minneapolis: University of Minnesota, Research and Training Center on Residential Services and Community Living, Institute on Community Integration.

Kennedy, J.F. (1963, February). Message from the President of the United States. *Congressional Record,* 13–14.

Lakin, K.C. (1989a). Strategies for promoting stability of direct-care staff in community-based residential facilities. In M. Janicki, M. Krauss, & M. Seltzer (Eds.), *Here to stay: Operating community residences* (pp. 231–238). Baltimore: Paul H. Brookes Publishing Co.

Lakin, K.C. (1989b). Quality of life in the community. *New Ways, Fall,* 19–24.

Lakin, K.C., Blake, E.M., Prouty, R.W., Mangan, T., & Bruininks, R.H. (1993). *Residential services for persons with developmental disabilities: Status and trends through 1991.* Minneapolis: University of Minnesota, Research and Training Center on Residential Services and Community Living, Institute on Community Integration.

Lakin, K.C., Bruininks, R.H., Hill, B.K., Chen, T.H., & Anderson, D.A. (1993). Personal characteristics and competence of people with mental retardation living in foster homes and small group homes. *American Journal on Mental Retardation, 97*(6), 616–627.

Lakin, K.C., Bruininks, R.H., & Larson, S. (1991). The changing face of residential services. In L. Rowitz (Ed.), *Mental retardation: Year 2000.* New York: Springer-Verlag.

Lakin, K.C., Burwell, B.O., Hayden, M.F., & Jackson, M.E. (1992). *An independent assessment of Minnesota's Medicaid Home and Community-Based Services waiver program* (Report No. 37). Minneapolis: University of Minnesota, Research and Training Center on Residential Services and Community Living, Institute on Community Integration.

Lakin, K.C., Hill, B.K., & Anderson, D.J. (1988). *Persons with mental retardation in nursing homes in 1977 and 1985: A comparison of the findings of the 1977 and 1985*

National Nursing Home Surveys. Minneapolis: University of Minnesota, Research and Training Center on Residential Services and Community Living, Institute on Community Integration.

Lakin, K.C., Hill, B.K., & Anderson, D.J. (1991). Persons with mental retardation in nursing homes in 1977 and 1985: A comparison of findings from the 1977 and 1985 National Nursing Home Surveys. *Mental Retardation, 29*(1), 25–33.

Lakin, K.C., Hill, B.K., & Bruininks, R.H. (1989). Trends and issues in the growth of community residential services. In M. Janicki, M. Krauss, & M. Seltzer (Eds.), *Community residences for persons with developmental disabilities* (pp. 25–42). Baltimore: Paul H. Brookes Publishing Co.

Lakin, K.C., Hill, B.K., Chen, T.H., & Stephens, S.A. (1989). *Persons with mental retardation and related conditions in mental retardation facilities: Selected findings from the 1987 National Medical Expenditure Survey*. Minneapolis: University of Minnesota, Research and Training Center on Residential Services and Community Living, Institute on Community Integration.

Lakin, K.C., Jaskulski, T.M., Hill, B.K., Bruininks, R.H., Menke, J.M., White, C.C., & Wright, E.A. (1989). *Medicaid services for persons with mental retardation and related conditions*. Minneapolis: University of Minnesota, Research and Training Center on Residential Services and Community Living, Institute on Community Integration.

Lakin, K.C., & Jones, R. (Eds.). (1993). Feature issue on the Americans with Disabilities Act and developmental disabilities. *IMPACT, 5*(1), 1–24. Minneapolis: University of Minnesota, Institute on Community Integration.

Lakin, K.C., & Larson, S.A. (1992). Satisfaction and stability of direct-care personnel in community based residential services. In J.W. Jacobson, S. Burchard, & P.C. Carling (Eds.), *Community living for persons with developmental and psychiatric disabilities* (pp. 244–262). Baltimore: Johns Hopkins University Press.

Lakin, K.C., Menke, J., Jaskulski, T., Hill, B.K., & White, C.C. (1993). *Past and projected state utilization of Medicaid options for persons with mental retardation*. Minneapolis: University of Minnesota, Research and Training Center on Residential Services and Community Living, Institute on Community Integration.

Lakin, K.C., Prouty, R.W., White, C.C., Bruininks, R.H., & Hill, B.K. (1990). *Intermediate Care Facilities for Persons with Mental Retardation (ICFs-MR): Program utilization and resident characteristics*. Minneapolis: University of Minnesota, Research and Training Center on Residential Services and Community Living, Institute on Community Integration.

Lakin, K.C., White, C.C., Prouty, R.W., Bruininks, R.H., & Kimm, C. (1991). *Medicaid institutional (ICF-MR) and home and community based services for persons with mental retardation and related conditions*. Minneapolis: University of Minnesota, Research and Training Center on Residential Services and Community Living, Institute on Community Integration.

Larson, S.A., & Lakin, K.C. (1989). Deinstitutionalization of persons with mental retardation: Behavioral outcomes. *Journal of The Association for Persons with Severe Handicaps, 14*(4), 324–332.

Larson, S.A., & Lakin, K.C. (1991). Parent attitudes about residential placement before and after deinstitutionalization: A research synthesis. *Journal of The Association for Persons with Severe Handicaps, 16*(1), 25–38.

Lewis, D.R., Johnson, D.R., Bruininks, R.H., Kallsen, L.A., & Guillery, R.P. (1991). *Costs and benefits of supported employment in Minnesota*. Minneapolis: University of Minnesota, Research Training Center on Residential Services and Community Living, Institute on Community Integration.

Lutfiyya, Z.M. (1990). *A report on Personal Futures Planning: For four people in Washington, D.C.* Syracuse, NY: Syracuse University, Center on Human Policy.

Lutfiyya, Z.M. (1991a). Relationships and community: A resource review. *TASH Newsletter, 15*(8), 3.

Lutfiyya, Z.M. (1991b). The importance of friendships among people with and without learning difficulties. *ARC Facts.* Arlington, TX: Association for Retarded Citizens of the United States.

Lutfiyya, Z.M. (1991c). "A feeling of connected": Friendships between people with and without learning difficulties. *Disability, Handicap and Society, 6*(3), 233–245.

Lutfiyya, Z.M., Hagner, D., O'Connor, S., & Racino, J. (1991). Qualitative research: Its values and role in policymaking. *Policy Research Brief, 3*(1), 1–8. Minneapolis: University of Minnesota, Research and Training Center on Residential Services and Community Living, Institute on Community

McAvoy, L., Schatz, E., Stutz, M., Schleien, S., & Lais, G. (1989). Integrated wilderness adventure: Effects on personal and lifestyle traits of persons with and without disabilities. *Therapeutic Recreation Journal, 23*(3), 50–64.

O'Brien, C., & O'Brien, J. (1990). *Making a move: Advice from People First members about helping people move out of institutions and nursing homes.* Syracuse, NY: Syracuse University, Center on Human Policy.

O'Brien, J. (1989). *Against pain as a tool in professional work on people with severe disabilities.* Minneapolis: University of Minnesota, Research and Training Center on Residential Services and Community Living, Institute on Community Integration.

O'Brien, J. (1990). *Working on . . . A survey of emerging issues in supported employment for people with severe disabilities.* Syracuse, NY: Syracuse University, Center on Human Policy.

O'Brien, J. (1991). *Down stairs that are never your own: Supporting people with developmental disabilities in their own homes.* Syracuse, NY: Syracuse University, Center on Human Policy.

O'Brien, J., & O'Brien C.L. (1991). *More than just a new address: Images of organizations for supported living.* Syracuse, NY: Syracuse University, Center on Human Policy.

O'Brien, J., O'Brien, C.L., & Schwartz, P. (1990, January). *What can we count on to make and keep people safe?* Lithonia, GA: Responsive Systems Associates.

O'Connor, S. (1991, July). *"I'm not Indian anymore." The challenge of providing culturally sensitive services to American Indians.* Syracuse, NY: Syracuse University, Center on Human Policy.

O'Connor, S., & Racino, J.A. (1989). *New direction in housing for people with severe disabilities: A collection of resource materials.* Syracuse, NY: Syracuse University, Center on Human Policy.

Prouty, R.W., & Lakin, K.C. (1991). *A summary of state efforts to positively affect the quality of Medicaid Home and Community-Based Services for persons with mental retardation and related conditions.* Minneapolis: University of Minnesota, Research and Training Center on Residential Services and Community Living, Institute on Community Integration.

Racino, J. (1991a). *Individual agency, community and systems change.* Columbia, MO: Missouri Association of Mental Retardation.

Racino, J. (1991b). *Independent living: Utilization and disseminations of qualitative research and empowerment.* Presentation at the July Symposium on Promising Practices in Human Services, Kitchener, Ontario, Canada.

Racino, J.A., Walker, P., O'Connor, S., & Taylor, S.J. (Eds.). (1993). *Housing, support and community: Choices and strategies for adults with disabilities.* Baltimore: Paul H. Brookes Publishing Co.

Reichle, J., & DePaepe, P. (Eds.). (1991). Feature issue on challenging behavior. *IMPACT, 4*(1), 1–20. Minneapolis: University of Minnesota, Institute on Community Integration.

Reichle, J., & Light, C. (1992). Positive approaches to managing challenging behavior among persons with developmental disabilities living in the community. *Policy Research Brief, 4*(1), 1–12. Minneapolis: University of Minnesota, Research and Training Center on Residential Services and Community Living, Institute on Community Integration.

Reichle, J., Piche-Cragoe, L., Sigafoos, J., & Doss, S. (1989). Optimizing functional communication for persons with severe handicaps. In S.N. Calculator & J.L. Bedrosian (Eds.), *Communication assessment and intervention for adults with mental retardation* (pp. 239–264). San Diego: College Hill Press.

Reichle, J., Sigafoos, J., & Piche, L. (1989). Teaching an adolescent with blindness and severe disabilities: A correspondence between requesting and selecting preferred objects. *Journal of The Association for Persons with Severe Handicaps, 14*(1), 75–80.

Reichle, J., York, J., & Sigafoos, J. (1991). *Implementing augmentative and alternative communication: Strategies for learners with severe disabilities*. Baltimore: Paul H. Brookes Publishing Co.

Research and Training Center on Residential Services and Community Living. (1989, January). *Proceedings of a national conference on self-determination*. Minneapolis: University of Minnesota, Institute on Community Integration.

Research and Training Center on Residential Services and Community Living. (1990). *National working conference on positive approaches to the management of excess behavior: Report and recommendations*. Minneapolis: University of Minnesota, Institute on Community Integration.

Rosenau, N. (Ed.). (1990). *A child's birthright: To live in a family*. Syracuse, NY: Syracuse University, Center on Human Policy.

Rynders, J., & Schleien, S. (Eds). (1991). *Together successfully: Creating recreational and educational programs that integrate people with and without disabilities*. Arlington, TX: Association for Retarded Citizens of the United States.

Rynders, J.E., Schleien, S., & Mustonen, T. (1990). Integrating children with severe disabilities for intensified outdoor education: Focus on feasibility. *Mental Retardation, 28*(1), 7–14.

Schleien, S.J. (1990a). Best professional practices: Programming leisure skills for persons with severe multiple disabilities. In B. Patching (Ed.), *Leisure for people with a disability* (pp. 3–13). Queensland, Australia: Division of Sport and Recreation, Department of Community Services and Health.

Schleien, S.J. (1990b). Community leisure services and persons with mental retardation. In President's Committee on Mental Retardation (Ed.), *A Presidential forum: Citizens with mental retardation and community integration* (pp. 119–123, 243). Washington, DC: U.S. Department of Health and Human Services.

Schleien, S.J. (1991). Severe multiple disabilities. In D. Austin & M. Crawford (Eds.), *Therapeutic recreation: An introduction* (pp. 189–223). Englewood Cliffs, NJ: Prentice Hall.

Schleien, S., Baldwin, C., & Light, C. (1989). Play time: Meeting the needs of your child. *Exceptional Parent, 19*(2), 28–33.

Schleien, S., Cameron, J., Rynders, J., & Slick, C. (1988). Acquisition and generalization of leisure skills from school to the home and community by learners with severe multihandicaps. *Therapeutic Recreation Journal, 22*(3), 53–71.

Schleien, S., Fahnestock, M., Green, R., & Rynders, J. (1990). Building positive social networks through environmental interventions in integrated recreation programs. *Therapeutic Recreation Journal, 24*(4), 42–52.

Schleien, S., Heyne, L., Rynders, J., & McAvoy, L. (1990). Equity and excellence: Serving all children in community recreation. *Journal of Physical Education, Recreation and Dance, 61*(8), 45–48.

Schleien, S., & Larson, A. (1986). Adult leisure education for the independent use of a community recreation center. *Journal of The Association for Persons with Severe Handicaps, 11*(1), 39–44.

Schleien, S.J., & Light, C. (in press). Beyond the 3R's: Integrated recreation for healthy, independent living. In J. Levy, P. Levy, & B. Niven (Eds.), *Ensuring quality of life from infancy through adulthood: Policy and program implications for government, consumers and professionals.* New York: Young Adult Institute.

Schleien, S.J., McAvoy, L., Lais, G., & Rynders, J.E. (Eds.). (1992). Feature issue on integrated outdoor education/adventure, *IMPACT, 4*(4), 1–20. Minneapolis: University of Minnesota, Institute on Community Integration.

Schleien, S., McAvoy, L., Lais, G., & Rynders, J. (in press). *Integrated outdoor education and adventure programs.* Champaign, IL: Sagamore.

Schleien, S., Meyer, L., Heyne, L., & Biel, B. (in press). *Lifelong leisure skills and lifestyles for persons with developmental disabilities.* Baltimore: Paul H. Brookes Publishing Co.

Schleien, S., & Ray, M.T. (1988). *Community recreation and persons with disabilities: Strategies for integration.* Baltimore: Paul H. Brookes Publishing Co.

Schleien, S.J., Ray, M., & Johnson, D. (1989). An architectural accessibility survey of community recreation centers. *Journal of Park and Recreation Administration, 7*(3), 10–22.

Schleien, S., & Rynders, J. (Eds.). (1989). Feature issue on integrated leisure and recreation. *IMPACT, 2*(3), 1–20. Minneapolis: University of Minnesota, Institute on Community Integration.

Schleien, S., Rynders, J.E., & Mustonen, T. (1988). Art and integration: What can we create? *Therapeutic Recreation Journal, 22*(4), 18–29.

Schleien, S., Rynders, J., Mustonen, T., & Fox, M. (1990). Effects of social play activities on the play behavior of children with autism. *Journal of Leisure Research, 22*(4), 317–328.

Shoultz, B. (1990). *Annotated bibliography on community integration, revised.* Syracuse, NY: Syracuse University, Center on Human Policy.

Skarnulis, E., & Lakin, K.C. (Eds.). (1990). Feature issue on consumer controlled housing. *IMPACT, 3*(1), 1–20. Minneapolis: University of Minnesota, Institute on Community Integration.

Taylor, S.J. (1988). Caught in the continuum: A critical analysis of the principle of the least restrictive environment. *Journal of The Association for Persons with Severe Handicaps, 13*(1), 41–53.

Taylor, S.J. (1989). *Best practices in establishing social networks and community relationships for persons with mental retardation: A qualitative study of relationships in the lives of people with mental retardation.* Syracuse, NY: Syracuse University, Center on Human Policy.

Taylor, S.J., & Bogdan, R. (1989). On accepting relationships between people with mental retardation and non-disabled people: Towards an understanding of acceptance. *Disability, Handicap & Society, 4*(1), 21–36.

Taylor, S.J., Bogdan, R., & Racino, J.A. (Eds.). (1991). *Life in the community: Case studies of organizations supporting people with disabilities.* Baltimore: Paul H. Brookes Publishing Co.

Taylor, S.J., Lakin, K.C., & Hill, B.K. (1989). Permanency planning for children and youth: Out of home placement decisions. *Exceptional Children, 55*(6), 541–549.

Taylor, S.J., Lutfiyya, Z., & Musgrave, P. (1989). *The community study: A qualitative study of relationships in the lives of people with mental retardation—Research design and field guide.* Syracuse, NY: Syracuse University, Center on Human Policy.

Taylor, S.J., Racino, J.A., & Walker, P.M. (1990). *Inclusive community living.* Syracuse, NY: Syracuse University, Center on Human Policy.

Traustadottir, R. (1991, August). *Supports for community living: A case study.* Syracuse, NY: Syracuse University, Center on Human Policy.

Wallace, T., Larson, S., & Hewitt, A. (Eds.). (1992). Feature issue on direct service training. *IMPACT, 4*(1), 1–20. Minneapolis: University of Minnesota, Institute on Community Integration.

White, C.C., Prouty, R.W., Lakin, K.C., & Blake, E. (1992). *State-operated residential facilities for persons with mental retardation: Year ending June 30, 1991.* Minneapolis: University of Minnesota, Research and Training Center on Residential Services and Community Living, Institute on Community Integration.

Wieck, C., & McBride, M. (Eds.). (1990). Feature issue on family support. *IMPACT, 3*(2), 1–20. Minneapolis: University of Minnesota, Institute on Community Integration.

— *Chapter 2* _____

Research Perspectives and the Community Living Experience

Glenn T. Fujiura

_____

The community living experiences of persons with mental retardation and other developmental disabilities have been scrutinized by social researchers throughout the twentieth century. Although the character of these experiences has changed over the decades and has modified the substance of research, the importance of science to social inquiry has remained constant. Since Fernald (1917) declared that the "modern scientific study of the dependent and delinquent classes as a whole has demonstrated that a large proportion of our criminals, inebriates, and prostitutes are really congenital defects" (p. 42), research has been used to legitimize different notions of the community living experience.

In studying the community living experience of persons with developmental disabilities, the range of relevant inquiry domains is found to be vast. Indeed, a community living definition could encompass the full range of human experiences in the community. This is not a new idea; it has been promulgated in principle since the early writings of the President's Committee on Mental Retardation (PCMR) (Cherington, 1974). However, in the absence of a clearly delineated domain that strictly defines a body of research, the daunting task of discussing and relating multiple domains of research, each with its own conceptual framework, is confronted. Consider, for example, the many research reviews that are constrained in content and issue to specific areas that may be considered mere subdomains of the larger community living experience. Some of these areas are aging (Janicki & Wisniewski, 1985); behavior management (Meyer & Evans, 1989); costs (Fujiura, 1988; Thorton, 1985); employment (Wehman & Moon, 1988); families (Landesman-Ramey, Krauss, & Simeonsson, 1989); residential placements (Haney, 1988; Heal

Preparation of this chapter was supported by Cooperative Agreement #H33B89948 between the National Institute on Disability and Rehabilitation Research (NIDRR); the Research and Training Center on Residential Services and Community Living in the Institute on Community Integration (UAP) located at the University of Minnesota; and the University Affiliated Program in Developmental Disabilities at the University of Illinois at Chicago.

& Fujiura, 1984; Heal, Sigelman, & Switzky, 1978; Landesman-Dwyer, 1981); skills training (Martin, 1988); and social competence (Siperstein, 1992).

Nevertheless, there are compelling reasons for transcending the distinctions among these varied domains of inquiry. Foremost among these is the reciprocality of the substance and the method of research efforts. The evolution of social policy toward persons with mental retardation and related disabilities suggests the inherent artificiality of discussing a single line of research in isolation. Models of care, shifting from the exclusionary paradigms of institutionalization and deinstitutionalization to the most recent efforts to develop individualized functional supports, require new and more comprehensive perspectives:

> Instead of thinking about how to surround people with services in specially designed and constructed homes, we began to think about moving support to where people lived. Instead of concentrating on how to make the individual adapt to the environment, we began to think about ways of adapting the environment and supports to the individuals. We also began to dig deeper into the concept of normalization and to question whether, by surrounding people with professionals, we may have isolated them from friends and family. We also began to wonder whether the skills we were teaching really had any functional meaning and whether the successful acquisition of abilities had any relationship to increased community participation. (Bradley & Knoll, 1990, p. 6)

Implied in this view of community living are very complex research questions that focus on factors typically treated as random error; for example, individual differences, contextual effects, and philosophical and political issues. In short, this view focuses on the interplay among many different types of variables at different levels of the community experience. These experiences, complex in nuance and varied in type and form, require that a broad perspective of the research enterprise is taken. A single paradigm of research is incapable of addressing all the requisite questions.

THE EMPIRICAL TRADITION

Past reviews of research related to community living have emphasized methods to the exclusion of epistemological considerations (Butterfield, 1985; Haney, 1988; Heal, 1985; Heal & Fujiura, 1984). Exceptions to this rather broad and oversimplistic characterization can be found in discussions of qualitative research (Biklen & Moseley, 1988; Stainback & Stainback, 1984; Taylor & Bogdan, chap. 3, this volume; Taylor & Bogdan, 1981). Research applications based on these traditions are rare in the literature on community living and, perhaps for this reason, its practioners feel compelled to provide a rationale for the approach. Similarly, the character of empirical social research and its rationale serve as the locus of discussion in this section.

Key Concepts

Empiricism is a term burdened with many definitions and gradations of meaning. The original concept—that all knowledge comes from the senses—was formalized by John Locke in *An Essay Concerning Human Understanding* (Locke, 1690). The philosophical basis of this proposition has evolved and been transformed over the centuries. There are now multiple empirical traditions, ranging from the familiar confirmatory experimental methods to the fasificationism of Popper (1959), an approach that excludes the possibility of confirmatory knowledge and views scientific progress as a series of hypothesis disconfirmations. Coexisting with these extremes are what Soltis (1984) called the many voices and logics of empirical inquiry; that is, correlational analyses, naturalistic-qualitative variants that adhere to empirical principles, surveys, and, of course, the experimental tradition. A major purpose of this chapter is to dispel prejudices regarding what is the best approach.

The essential contemporary feature of empiricism is objectivity or, in other words, the emphasis on reliable and valid information and the replicability of methods. Experimentation is not included as an essential feature. The experimental approach, so frequently attacked by critics of traditional methods, is considered here to be a point on a conceptually broader continuum of empirical perspectives.

Objectivity, as the central value of empiricism, is based on the fundamental principle that all information is derived from our senses and is subject to confounding distortions. These subjective dynamics are powerful influences in human affairs—systems of belief, truth, values, meanings, and emotions that serve to modify our perceptions of the external world (Madge, 1965). For the empiricist, an objective reality exists in empirical facts unfettered by these subjective influences. How is this reality obtained? It is obtained by the many methods that were developed to verify the accuracy of measurement and method; for example, elimination of bias, operational definitions, reliability and validity of measurement, replicability of methods, sampling, and standardized data collection (Borg & Gall, 1983; Butterfield, 1985; Campbell & Stanley, 1963; Cook & Campbell, 1979; Heal, 1985; Williamson, Karp, Dalphin, & Gray, 1982).

Despite its importance to social research, objectivity is an elusive ideal. Most contemporary researchers would acknowledge the absence of a pure form of objectivity in social research. Biases affect all phases of the research process, from selection of the research problem through data collection to the manner of analysis (Williamson et al., 1982). However, the obvious futility of pure objectivity does not preclude it being a worthy goal. This characteristic mostly differentiates the empirical perspective from alternative traditions of inquiry.

Experimental Bias

If such a thing as a research pedigree exists, then the conceptual genealogy of a very large part of community living research can be traced to the canons of John Stuart Mill, the 19th century philosopher. In his *System of Logic*, Mill (1879) describes rules of induction that continue to dominate contemporary thought on research methods. His approach shapes the logic of experimental inquiry and how causal inferences are derived; for example, presumed causes will precede effects in time; when causes are present, effects will be present; when causes are absent, effects are absent; and when two phenomenon are observed to covary, they are associated in some manner. Experimentation, especially in the case where the presumed cause was directly manipulated by the investigator, is the only sure path to the truth.

The Logic of the Experiment   In the larger context of the logic of inference-making, the experimental approach is referred to as logic by elimination (Salmon, 1967). The process should be familiar, it is a system of knowledge built upon the elimination of false hypotheses. Mill's rules of induction imply much of the experimental reasoning that has been systematized during the past 100 years (Dewey, 1931; Smith & White, 1929) and that has been codified for educational and psychological research methods (Campbell & Stanley, 1963; Cook & Campbell, 1979). The experimental orientation is represented in the literature on community living in the research reviews and methods of Butterfield (1985), Haney (1988), Heal (1985), and Heal and Fujiura (1984).

In its contemporary manifestation, the essence of experimental logic is comparative, a variable is measured under two or more conditions identical in all respects except one. Differences in the variables are attributed to the differences in the conditions. There are many design variations on this basic theme, most related to the similarity of the two conditions:

> experiments require the manipulation of putative causes and thus are restricted to the subset of all causes that are manipulable. Moreover, experiments are epitomized by control over the independent variable. This permits us to falsify many of the mundane nuisance alternative interpretations that challenge causal inference, nowhere more so than when random assignment occurs. Experiments often involve control groups, and these in their turn contribute to ruling out other alternative interpretations by a process similar to Mill's Method of Concomitant Variation. The experiment is modest, seeking only to elucidate whether a particular cause or a restricted set of causes has an effect. (Cook & Campbell, 1979, p. 32)

While this is a succinct description of the essential logic of the experimental method, those unfamiliar with it should be aware that an extensive treatment is necessary to address even the very basic technical nuances. Furthermore, examination of these details—the language and methods of experimentation—is not the purpose of this chapter. The main point is the importance of the concept of experimentation to the evolution of the social sciences. For many, the experiment was a precondition of scientific status (Dewey, 1931; Lewin, 1947).

The Experiment and Community Living Research   The notion of the experiment being central to our conceptions of research may strike many as a rhetorical overstatement. After all, nonexperimental methods such as surveys, interviews, archival analyses, and naturalistic observation, to name just a few, are standard tools of the social researcher. Furthermore, a careful tally of the community living literature would reveal precious few community living studies involving direct manipulation of an independent variable by the researcher, or use of randomly assigned subjects in treatment and control conditions. The body of experimental literature is modest, and an examination of the literature indicates that even well-designed quasi-experimental efforts (i.e., studies not employing random assignment but capable of controlling most threats to internal validity) are rare (Haney, 1988; Heal & Fujiura, 1984; Landesman & Butterfield, 1987). Nevertheless, experimental concepts affect our ways of thinking about research.

Social researchers are biased toward the tradition; the bias expresses itself in the belief that the experiment is the paragon for inquiry and is evident in the language used in describing research. Not coincidentally, this orientation dominates research training curricula in most subdisciplines of the social sciences (Gage, 1989). Research coursework tends to emphasize experimental design (Lieberson, 1985), and statistical instruction largely focuses on the analysis of data derived from experimental studies.

If the experiment is the paragon, then social research is hierarchical in character. At the summit is the true experiment, the crown jewel towering above the lesser efforts—the observational studies, surveys, interviews, and so forth. Chronbach (1982) noted that less controlled studies are frequently referred to as pre-experimental, a pejorative term that implies a continuum of value ranging from strong to weak. Heal and Fujiura (1984) characterized nonexperimental designs as "compromises" (p. 226), while Borg and Gall (1983) state in their introductory text on educational research methods that "the experiment is the *ultimate* form of research design" (p. 632, italics added for emphasis). The paucity of experimental effort is often attributed to lack of conceptual development within a domain of inquiry (Butterfield, 1985; Fujiura & Johnson, 1986; Haney, 1988). In other words, community living researchers know too little to precisely phrase their research questions into elegant experimental contrasts.

Bias toward an experimental orientation is also subtly manifested in the way in which researchers ask questions about their data. Most community living research is experimental in intent, if not in conduct. The questions are attempts to isolate relationships among variables and establish a probability-based likelihood of a cause-and-effect relationship between them. For example, deinstitutionalization and community integration studies ask how environmental and individual characteristics differ across facility types (i.e., large versus small) and whether these differences affect adaptation and integration or some other community living outcome. Multivariate statistical techniques are routinely applied to nonexperimentally derived data in order to establish explanations from the variance partitions among independent variables. Many other examples are possible. The research questions are merely attempts to sift through large numbers of variables in order to identify likely causal candidates.

Consider the approach to community living inquiry exemplified by integration and adaptation studies, a common research focus of the late 1970s and 1980s. These studies were investigations of the relationship of community living success (or other similar outcomes, such as adaptive behavior and placement status) to individual characteristics (Schalock & Harper, 1978; Thiel, 1981); service provider characteristics (Aninger & Bolinsky, 1977; Eyman, Borthwick, & Miller, 1981); a combination of both (Hull & Thompson, 1980); or other key features of the community environment (Schalock & Lilley, 1986; Willer & Intagliata, 1981).

Contemporary variations include studies of attitudes (Levy, Jessop, Rimmerman, & Levy, 1992); employee turnover (Larson & Lakin, 1992); funding (Braddock & Fujiura, 1991); permanency planning (Heller & Factor, 1991); and residential placement practices (Hayden, Lakin, Hill, Bruininks, & Chen, 1992). Typically, the purpose of these investigations was to identify statistical predictors for the community living outcome or to test a specific relational hypothesis among variables. Studies were usually nonexperimental; that is, variables were not manipulated by the investigators, systematic controls were not applied, and data was extracted from observations in the natural setting (Cook & Campbell, 1979). For example, Braddock and Fujiura (1991) related state mental retardation and developmental disabilities (MR/DD) spending on community services to the political culture. Spending data were derived from archival state sources and related to political indices in the states. Similarly, Larson and Lakin (1992) employed survey data to evaluate the relationship of residential direct care staff turnover to various facility conditions and employee characteristics. In neither study were the independent variables (i.e., political culture and facility conditions, respectively) manipulated by the investigators or by the established control conditions (other than statistical controls). Such investigations, common to the community living research literature, are exploratory in character and intent. These are efforts to impose conceptual order on phenomena not well understood. As such, they serve an extremely important heuristic function.

It is important to note that these types of exploratory investigations represent only one facet of the research process. Although researchers acknowledge the limitations of their nonexperimental inferences, a substantial portion of the community living research literature continues to be built upon such studies as if the phenomena were being explicated through some systematic experimental-like isolation of variables. Thus, Hull and Thompson (1980) correctly ask if normalization is more important than physical safety in predicting adaptive behavior; however, finding a statistically nonsignificant r^2 for the physical setting variables, the investigators draw a conclusion that is unambiguously causal and beyond what should be interpreted from their data. "If one is concerned about improving adaptive functioning, then Quality of the Physical Setting should not be one of the primary variables one attempts to manipulate" (Hull & Thompson, 1980, p. 260). Such an approach is generally endemic to the social sciences and to the empirical literature on community living. As Lieberson (1985) states, "Despite a long-standing awareness of the dangers, social scientists still tend to be uncritically happy when associations are found, and the stronger the better" (p. 92).

The issue is not the adequacy of this type of research, but the role it plays in the larger program of inquiry. Describing these efforts as a search for the most important variable, frequently in the context of regression-based analyses of nonexperimental data and focused on variance partitions, may misrepresent the true value of such research. Identification of the most powerful predictor may not be the most relevant research question. Indeed, such relationships are often illusory (see Pedhazur [1982] for a discussion of the dilemmas of causal interpretations from nonexperimental data). These studies should be acknowledged for what they are—exploratory research efforts—rather than attempting to embellish them with an experimental veneer. The critical point is to pay proper respect to the complexity of the interrelationships that compose the community living experience and to view our research efforts as one facet of a multifaceted research effort.

An Alternative View of the Experiment Is community living research undeveloped? Is the infrequency of experimental research a function of the lack of sophisticated paradigms (Butterfield, 1985; Fujiura & Johnson, 1986; Haney, 1988). The answer to the former question is most certainly "yes." However, whether one can attribute absence of experimentation to lack of development in a field is a matter of substantial debate. In Kuhn's (1970) paradigmatic perspective, paradigms define the problems and methods of a research field. A mature paradigm of community living research would be characterized by commonly accepted theories, measurements, and procedures. Are we, as the experimental critics suggest, preparadigmatic, awaiting some unifying school of thought? From this perspective the lack of well-controlled experimental comparisons is in large part a deficiency of the research community. Either too little is understood for precise translations of research questions into elegant experimental contrasts or researchers lack the initiative to move beyond methods of convenience.

An alternative view of the social sciences, and one that has gained considerable currency in recent years, is that social phenomena are rarely compatible with the experimental tradition (Chronbach, 1982, 1986). Researchers involved in community psychology, for example, have characterized their problems as ill-structured, as opposed to the well-structured, problems that are amenable to the reductionist strategies of experimentalism (Mitroff, 1983). A well-structured problem is one viewed the same from all perspectives (Tolan, Chertok, Keys, & Jason, 1990). Interventions within a behavioral framework also represent well-structured problems. A basic set of principles (e.g., operant conditioning) are applied in the context of structured procedures (e.g., behavioral analysis). However, consider the multiplicity of perspectives and methods encompassed in the broader community living domain: behavioral (Scotti, Evans, Meyer, & Walker, 1991); ecological (Chadsey-Rusch, 1985); econometric (Thorton, 1985), political (Castellani, 1986); psychometric (Hawkins & Cooper, 1990); and public policy (Braddock & Fujiura, 1991). The community living phenomenon is inherently ill-structured by virtue of its breadth and diversity.

The experimental tradition is rigorous, systematic, and potentially definitive. It can also be far too narrow in focus. The descriptors "strong" and "weak," as described earlier, are value-ladened and suggest that the experiment is the sine qua non of research. Many disagree. The well-controlled experiment, while not burdened by threats to internal validity, represents only the outer shell of inquiry. Not all relevant questions are reducible to specific contrasts between narrowly defined conditions. Furthermore, nonexperimental questions are not necessarily inferior questions or representative of inquiry at an undeveloped stage.

Madge (1965) noted that "much ink has been spilt in disputes on the feasibility of experiments in social science" (p. 290). The relevance of the dispute for community living researchers in disability-related fields is contemporary and direct. To conduct programs of research as if the definitive answer awaits the crucial experiment may be counterproductive. It is unlikely that a paradigm will emerge that is capable of unifying the disparate perspectives and methods of inquiry. Arguably, the multiplicity of perspectives is the more authentic representation and unification an undesirable outcome. If the concept of multiplicity is accepted, then multiple perspectives must be explicitly integrated into research programs.

Despite these critiques, the reader should appreciate the intellectual elegance of the experimental tradition, its methods, and the power of its application. The error would be in linking it in some monopolistic fashion with the advancement of theory or in assigning it the special attribution of being more scientific. It is a method derived from a tradition of inquiry that addresses a narrowly prescribed type of problem under a particular set of conditions. What then should the verdict be on the experimental method in community living research? The method should not be held up as a paragon of inquiry, nor should it be rejected as a method of social inquiry, as many critics have suggested. The most important consideration, as Madge (1965) concludes, is that the experiment be the *right* one.

The Functions of Research

Establishing experimental procedures as the sine non qua of research places excessive emphasis on technique. Methods can dictate the substance of inquiry—a caveat that may be applied to all traditions of inquiry. For those involved in community living research, the better question may not be what method best exemplifies the virtues of the empirical tradition, but rather what function research should serve. The functions of community living research can be classified in a very broad three-way taxonomy: 1) fact finding, 2) identifying patterns, and 3) theory testing (Lieberson, 1985). Excluded from Lieberson's (1985) taxonomy is his fourth function—suggesting policy—since relevance to policy in the body of community living research arguably emanates from all research functions.

Fact-Finding A consistent theme throughout the brief history of community living research is the effort to characterize the evolving community service system (Baker, Seltzer, & Seltzer, 1977; Braddock, Hemp, & Howes, 1984; Bruininks, Hauber, & Kudla, 1979; Gollay, Freedman, Wyngaarden, & Kurtz, 1978; O'Connor, 1976; Wehman & Melia, 1990). The reasons for the devotion of such effort to so many descriptive studies over a long period of time are not hard to discern. The character of the developmental disabilities service system has been undergoing rapid and dramatic changes. These changes are largely the result of substantial shifts in public policy. In addition, the provision of research data has played a central role in these shifts. Against the backdrop of dramatic social change, information describing status and trends often highlights essential points of concern and basic priorities. The provision of accurate and current information to policymakers has been an explicit objective of much of this type of research (Braddock, Hemp, & Fujiura, 1987; Bruininks et al., 1979). A classic example in American public policy was the introduction of poverty line statistics (Batchelder, 1966). The simple act of defining poverty and making available raw data upon which the public and policymakers could focus had a galvanizing impact on American politics and government policies in the 1960s. "Information per se cannot change MR/DD policy, but it can dramatically affect the nature of political debate if it is relevant in 'real time' and is conveyed in understandable form to the appropriate leadership in the proper forums" (Braddock et al., 1987, p. 131).

Nonetheless, the descriptive research function is denigrated, often implicitly and frequently, by those who conduct it. Braddock et al. (1987), in summarizing the implications of their national survey of public expenditures, recommended more theoretically oriented public policy research in order to obtain "a deeper and more *scientific* understanding of these forces" (p. 132). Lieberson (1985), reflecting on the bias against the simple gathering of facts, states:

> There are those who look down on this activity, but their disdain is unwarranted. After all, who is better suited to serve this function than social researchers? It is self-destructive for social scientists to denigrate such work on the grounds that it is atheoretical. Fact-finding of this nature can require great elegance and craftsmanship, it is socially useful, and social scientists are uniquely skilled to accomplish it and interpret the results. (p. 153)

Identifying Patterns   A second function of social science research is to facilitate the identification of patterns; that is, associations among variables or regularities that might be invoked as explanatory mechanisms to account for the phenomenon of interest (the word "explanatory" is employed here in its most common denotation). The vast majority of studies reported in the field typify this approach. In addition to the many studies of the community adjustment predictors cited earlier are recent examples of research on family characteristics (Krauss, Seltzer, & Goodman, 1992; Mink & Nihira, 1987).

This second function is best conceptualized as a continuum of research efforts ranging from atheoretical explorations of associations among variables to direct tests of relationships predicted by theory. The end of the continuum represented by the atheoretical explorations was labeled by Heal (1985) as hypothesis discovery analyses, a precise functional description of this type of effort. Whatever the methods employed, the purpose of hypothesis discovery is to identify associations among variables in an area of inquiry relatively unknown and to propose causal hypotheses as a result of this exploratory work (Heal, 1985). The distinction between the gathering of facts and hypothesis discovery is subtle and arguably more conceptual than real, since a subordinate objective of most fact-finding researchers is the identification of themes and the proposal of causal models. Indeed, all of the examples of descriptive research cited in the preceding section could reasonably be employed as examples here. Borthwick-Duffy, Eyman, and White (1987), for example, describe the distribution of persons across a range of alternatives in California's out-of-home residential care system and employ these basic facts to suggest causal linkages between the characteristics of the individual and placement into different facilities.

At the other end of the continuum are studies that are essentially exploratory but within the limits of a theoretical structure. For example, Wynne and Rogers

(1985), employing a discriminant analysis, attempted to identify critical dimensions that distinguished children with severe disabilities who were living at home versus those placed in a residential facility. They used 11 social status and demographic variables, each selected on the basis of "previous empirical research specific to this population as well as broader general educational research" (Wynne & Rogers, 1985, p. 516). A discriminant function was derived and employed to characterize the nature of differences between the two groups. Thus, the researcher brings to bear upon the exploration an *a priori* model, an explanatory template, that is imposed upon the phenomenon. Wynne and Rogers employed past research and theoretical rationale to strategically constrain a variable set. Theory helped to organize the inquiry; however, the adequacy of the theory was of only secondary interest. Thus, Wynne and Rogers felt it unnecessary to comment on the fact that socioeconomic status (SES), a theoretically potent variable and one with a long history in the social sciences, was not retained in the discriminant function.

Theory Testing   The distinction between theory testing this function and the preceding group of studies is again one of degree rather than kind. The distinguishing feature is the centrality of theory to the study's purpose. According to Lieberson (1985), research serving the function of theory testing is centrally focused on evaluating the merits of a given theory. For example, Orr, Cameron, and Day (1991) directly evaluated the Double ABCX model (McCubbin & Patterson, 1983) of family stress and coping. Briefly, the Double ABCX is a mediational model, in which the impact of a stressor event is modifiable by family resources and perceptions of the stressor event. Orr et al. (1991) obtained scores on psychometric assessments stress, perceptions of stress, and family resources for a sample of 86 parents with children classified as having moderate mental retardation. These scores, representing each of the key elements of the Double ABCX, were evaluated in a path analysis. Inconsistencies led the investigators to revise the path model and propose an alternative model. Superficially, there is little to distinguish the research of this and the preceding types, since both seek to establish plausible explanations for observed events. However, theory testing efforts clearly concern themselves first and foremost with evaluating the value of theoretical model.

Although theoretically driven research is not necessarily bound to any specific research methodology, it is most closely associated with the experimental method. Deductive logic begins with testable propositions that are derived from theory and facts and are marshalled in a direct test of theoretical expectations. This is the paradigm of the physical sciences so often held as the exemplar for social inquiry. The relationship between experimental logic and the theory testing functions of research is a close one because both are essentially reductionist and explanatory in character. However, one need not be an experimentalist to engage in theoretically based work. Clearly, this is the case in community living research, which is rarely experimental in method but very often theory-based in concept (e.g., normalization).

The purpose of this too brief discussion is to make explicit what should be apparent from inspection of the literature on community living—that research serves multiple and equally valuable functions. It is probable that a good proportion of community living researchers would agree, yet inspection of commentaries on community living research suggest an abiding faith in the primacy of experimental research. Lamentations over the absence of experimental control over community living research studies are a truism in reviews (Haney, 1988; Heal & Fujiura, 1984; Landesman & Butterfield, 1987; Sigelman, Novak, Heal, & Switzky, 1980).

If the concept of inquiry is accepted as a set of alternatives rather than a hierarchy of methods ranging from weak to strong then a wider range (in the form that our assumptions about the world assume) must be considered. The idea that inquiry has many forms and basic assumptions is not new or radical. While there are programs of community living research that operate within very carefully defined conceptual parameters, there is much that is atheoretical and not devoted to experimental, or even quasi-experimental, tests of logically deduced questions. Thus, while community living researchers may agree that research serves many functions, many appear to regard their efforts as subordinate to higher forms of inquiry. Again, the point of the foregoing discussion is *not* to denigrate or promote one approach over the other. When theory and experiment can move inquiry or when facts serve a need, the approach is good. The point *is* to make clear the implicit and often erroneous values that are employed in judging community living research.

The foregoing discussion and its theme, that the rigid application of experimental research models from the physical sciences has not well served our research agenda, is common among critics of traditional research methods. However, this is not a critique of experimental methods per se. Nor is it a critical evaluation of how these methods are applied. Rather, it is a plea for a broader perspective in research programs.

MULTIPLE PERSPECTIVES

Three thematic elements have been identified in this chapter: 1) the need to appreciate the complexity and expansiveness of the community living experience, 2) the subtle bias toward experimental methods and concepts, and 3) the diversity of research functions. The following sections of the chapter expand upon the theme of multiplicity and alternative perspectives that were previously introduced.

The Meaning of Science

Rarely defined, the words "science" and "research" pervade discussions of community living and are typically employed as if their meanings were universally recognizable and communally accepted. Like some omnipotent adjudicator, our services, care practices, policies, and even philosophies are held before science in judgment. Levine (1986) ascribes this to a fundamental human need for privileged knowledge. During the past two centuries, secular Western societies have met this need via science rather than via the religiosity of traditional cultures. Indeed, references to the importance of a form of knowledge superior to others are ubiquitous in the commentaries of the MR/DD research literature. Writing on behalf of PCMR, Krim asserts that "society has turned to science for the solution of the tragic and baffling problem of faulty brain development" (1969, p. 547). Employing a similar theme, Clarke and Clarke (1977) note the "privileged" position of scientists as asserting the obligation of researchers to "reveal the ways" (p. 532). More recently, Zigler, Hodapp, and Edison (1990), in their discussion of philosophical forces in the field of developmental disabilities, argue on behalf of the primacy of science and research over strict adherence to ideologies. Landesman-Ramey (1990) concurred with Zigler et al. (1990) in her appeal for scientist-advocates, which exemplifies the special value attached to scientific information. "As scientists, we must preserve our special contribution as trained skeptics and reporters, adhering to the highest standards of scientific inquiry in gathering data relevant to the critical issues" (Landesman-Ramey, 1990, p. 29).

But what makes science and research special? In the foregoing commentaries there is heavy emphasis on the process that is perceived to be part of science and research. For example, Krim (1969) describes the "discipline of the scientific method of inquiry" (p. 547) and Bruininks and Lakin (1985) characterize policy research as the "application of scientific (or quasi-scientific) principles" (p. 197). In the introduction to his classic *The Structure of Science*, Nagel (1961) characterizes science and inquiry as the process of objectifying, explaining, generalizing, and confirming. These are the conventional themes, typical of the educational and psychological disciplines (Becker, 1987; Madge, 1965; Williamson et al., 1982) and notions familiar to most readers trained in the social sciences. Beyond these generalities, however, there is considerable disagreement over what constitutes scientific knowledge. The concept of science is found to be less fixed and concrete than current usage suggests. It is often anchored to ideologies and world views far removed from the popular image of an implacably technical and objective endeavor (D'Andrade, 1986). Despite a decade long struggle by philosophers to develop a consensus on the meaningfulness of the term "science," none has emerged (Levine, 1986). For example, D'Andrade (1986) classifies inquiry into the studies of physical, natural, and semiotic sciences. In Meehl's (1986) conceptualization, scientific paradigms vary according to whether they attempt to describe functional-causal relationships (e.g., Newtonian physics, learning theory), to describe and explain how things are constructed (e.g., biochemistry), or whether they emphasize history or development (e.g., psychoanalytic theory). In short, there are different types of sciences since the form of inquiry frequently varies as a function of the phenomenon. Science is a "contested concept" (Gallie, 1964).

To the extent that the scientific attribution holds special privilege in our society, the debate over the scientific value of information can degenerate into substantively meaningless semantic debates. Casual allusions to science or the scientific may not be as conclusive as they appear upon first consideration. What is referred to as science or the scientific most likely conveys substantially different meanings to various audiences. The terms' relevance to the discussion of research concepts, purposes, and methods is direct. Are the different types of sciences parallel forms of inquiry or greater or lesser efforts on a single continuum of value? The more relativistic positions have gained preeminence as the debates over a single standard of science have been judged to be fruitless (Levine, 1986) or pointless (Meehl, 1986).

The Role of Perspective: A Relativistic Approach

During the 1980s, increasing interest in alternative methodologies among social researchers led to what has been referred to as the paradigm wars (Gage, 1989). These were debates focused on the merits of the alternatives, and typically presented the choices in terms of the quantitative and qualitative research traditions (Firestone, 1987; Gage, 1989; Smith & Heshusius, 1986; Soltis, 1984; Tolan et al., 1990). Although the quantitative-qualitative distinction is commonly drawn in our research literature (Lakin, Bruininks, & Sigford, 1981; Lutifiyya, 1991; Stainback & Stainback, 1984, 1989; Taylor & Bogdan, 1981), the dichotomy fails to reflect the diversity and nuances represented in both perspectives. Taylor (see chap. 3, this volume) describes the many different manifestations of the qualitative approach. While the paradigm wars are likely to continue in some limited form (Smith & Heshusius, 1986), a more useful focus would be one emphasizing the complementary qualities of the different traditions. The need for multiple perspectives is one of the central themes emerging from the epistemological literature (Gage, 1989; Miles & Huberman, 1984). Social phenomena are complex and a single perspective cannot adequately serve all our research needs.

These are not new propositions. More than 10 years ago, Lakin et al. (1981) presented the same argument: "The only real obstacle to a wide range of useful approaches to researching the community adjustment process is the unenlightened perspective of more than a few that there is a scientific method for studying psychological or sociological questions" (p. 383). Even Cook and Campbell (1979), vigorous advocates of experimental approaches, decried the use of "specious quantitative studies" and "naive social quantifiers," while encouraging the use of other methods to gather contextual information (p. 93).

What are these perspectives? Like a roster of obscure fourth century monastic religious sects, contemporary epistemological discussions are filled with a bewildering array of perspectives. These perspectives are constructivism, holism, interpretivism, phenomenologicalism, positivism, revisionism, relativism, structural-functionalism, and technocentrism, in addition to the post-, pre-, and pseudo-variations on the -isms. However, at some risk of oversimplification, the central differences across perspectives can be reduced to three variations in emphasis: 1) empiricism with its emphasis on objectivity and verifiable knowledge; 2) interpretive inquiry with its emphasis on meanings and other subjective representations (see Taylor & Bogdan, chap. 3, this volume); and 3) critical inquiry, which attaches central importance to the political, historical, and economic foundations of the phenomenon under study (Soltis, 1984). Indeed, some critical theorists view all research as an explicitly political act (Sjoberg, 1975). These perspectives represent approaches sensitive to different facets of a given social phenomenon. Furthermore, differences among perspectives are often more a matter of degree rather than kind. To emphasize meanings and values in research is not necessarily tantamount to rejecting the importance of objectivity.

The relativistic position advocated here views the process of inquiry in the aggregate (Gage, 1989; Lakin et al., 1981; Miles & Huberman, 1984; Soltis, 1984). All efforts are complementary. From each form of inquiry a different portrait of the phenomenon is revealed; reality is best reconstructed through a combination of different perspectives. The central issue is not what the best method is but rather which method is best suited to answer the research question. Thus, there are no more powerful tools than those available in the empirical tradition for describing social phenomenon with rigor and objectivity. Without these qualities, the practical impact of our research efforts on the lives of persons with disabilities will be severely limited. Conversely, interpretive inquiry provides access to human intersubjective meanings. The centrality of this perspective in the human endeavor of community living research should be obvious. Similarly, the contemporary character of community living in the United States is widely recognized to be inextricably intertwined with history, politics, and economics (Braddock, 1987; Braddock & Fujiura, 1991; Castellani, 1986; Lakin & Bruininks, 1985). The notion of critical inquiry has yet to receive the attention it deserves in community living research applications. These notions are the logical extensions of the themes explored in the preceding section—that we must cast off the biases that suggest a single best avenue for inquiry.

CONCLUSION

Four basic themes have been briefly overviewed. First, a program of research must encompass forms of inquiry capable of representing the sheer breadth and complexity of the community living experience. Although not a new challenge for researchers, it is now especially pressing as service paradigms rapidly evolve toward more individualized functional support models. Second, the conceptual lineage of much of the community living research effort is derived in concept, if not in method, from the logic of experimental inquiry. This orientation leads to a diminution of the value of other forms and functions of research and limits the manner in which the questions of our inquiry are structured. Third, there is no single best form of knowledge. Community living research can and should serve multiple functions and invocations of science should be carefully considered. Finally, the tools of the research trade are limited. Recognition of this fact and of the importance of perspective is crucial for the development of a representative body of knowledge on the community living experience.

Viewed as a whole, what do these thematic threads suggest? They suggest a continuum along which all forms of inquiry lie. The essential basis for a program of research based on diverse perspectives is the view of inquiry as a broadly conceived effort. Our interpretations of the underlying reality of the phenomenon being studied should not be confused with the methods employed in studying it. For example, the study of residential services is more than the identification of the best facility type based on some criterion that is experimentally compared. The empirical evaluation of residential alternatives cannot be disentagled from governmental policies that fund services, or from the family system from whence the resident came, or from the meanings and experiences of the individuals that these service systems are intended to provide for. The human visual system is a nearly perfect metaphor for the research task in community living. Constituted of tens of millions of receptor cells, the human system does not see so much as reconstruct a visual representation of the external world; that is, simple receptors respond to diffuse light, complex cells are sensitive to linear images, higher order hypercomplex cells detect motion, and photoreceptors code color. Each type of receptor cell provides only an incomplete and, therefore, distorted image of reality. Similarly, research programs should be considered an integrative effort. The researcher's task is to appreciate the limitations of a method—the distortions and incomplete images yielded by the different traditions of inquiry—and to focus on the very difficult challenge of using these images to illuminate the reality that is the community living experience.

REFERENCES

Aninger, M., & Bolinsky, K. (1977). Levels of independent functioning of retarded adults in apartments. *Mental Retardation*, *15*, 12–13.

Baker, B., Seltzer, G., & Seltzer, M. (1977). *As close as possible*. Boston: Little, Brown, and Co.

Batchelder, A.B. (1966). *The economics of poverty*. New York: John Wiley & Sons.

Becker, H.J. (1987). The importance of a methodology that maximizes falsifiability: Its application to research about Logo. *Educational Researcher*, *16*, 11–16.

Biklen, S.K., & Moseley, C.R. (1988). "Are you retarded?" "No, I'm Catholic": Qualitative methods in the study of people with severe handicaps. *Journal of The Association for Persons with Severe Handicaps*, *13*, 155–162.

Borg, W.R., & Gall, M.D. (1983). *Educational research* (4th ed.). New York: Longman.

Borthwick-Duffy, S.A., Eyman, R.K., & White, J.F. (1987). Client characteristics and residential placement patterns. *American Journal of Mental Deficiency*, *92*, 24–30.

Braddock, D. (1987). *Federal policy toward mental retardation and developmental disabilities*. Baltimore: Paul H. Brookes Publishing Co.

Braddock, D., & Fujiura, G.T. (1991). Politics, public policy, and the development of community mental retardation services in the United States. *American Journal of Mental Retardation*, *95*, 369–387.

Braddock, D., Hemp, R., & Fujiura, G.T. (1987). National study of public spending for mental retardation and developmental disabilities. *American Journal of Mental Deficiency*, *92*, 121–133.

Braddock, D., Hemp, R., & Howes, R. (1984). *Public expenditures for mental retardation and developmental disabilities in the United States: State profiles*. Chicago: Institute for the Study of Developmental Disabilities, Evaluation and Public Policy Analysis Program.

Bradley, V.J., & Knoll, J. (1990). *Shifting paradigms in services to people with developmental disabilities*. Cambridge, MA: Human Services Research Institute.

Bruininks, R.H., Hauber, F.A., & Kudla, M.J. (1979). *National survey of community residential facilities: A profile of facilities and residents in 1977*. Minneapolis: University of Minnesota, Department of Psychoeducational Studies.

Bruininks, R.H., & Lakin, K.C. (1985). Perspectives on methodology in research and evaluation. In R.H. Bruininks & K.C. Lakin (Eds.), *Living and learning in the least restrictive environment* (pp. 197–198). Baltimore: Paul H. Brookes Publishing Co.

Butterfield, E.C. (1985). The consequences of bias in studies of living arrangements for the mentally retarded. In D. Bricker & J. Filler (Eds.), *The severely mentally retarded: From research to practice* (pp. 245–263). Reston, VA: Council for Exceptional Children.

Campbell, D.T., & Stanley, J.C. (1963). Experimental and quasi-experimental designs for research on teaching. In N.L. Gage (Ed.), *Handbook of research on teaching*. Chicago: Rand McNally.

Castellani, P.J. (1986). *The political economy of developmental disabilities*. Baltimore: Paul H. Brookes Publishing Co.

Chadsey-Rusch, J.G. (1985). Community integration and mental retardation: The ecobehavioral approach to service provision and assessment. In R.H. Bruininks & K.C. Lakin (Eds.), *Living and learning in the least restrictive environment* (pp. 245–260). Baltimore: Paul H. Brookes Publishing Co.

Cherington, C. (1974). Community living and individual needs. In C. Cherington & G. Dybwad (Eds.), *New neighbors: The retarded citizen in quest of a home* (pp. 1–18). Washington, DC: President's Committee on Mental Retardation.

Chronbach, L.J. (1982). *Designing evaluations of educational and social phenomenon*. San Francisco: Jossey-Bass.

Chronbach, L.J. (1986). Social inquiry by and for earthlings. In D.W. Fiske & R.A. Shweder (Eds.), *Metatheory in social science* (pp. 83–107). Chicago: University of Chicago Press.

Clarke, A.D.B., & Clarke, A.M. (1977). Prospects for prevention and amelioration of mental retardation: A guest editorial. *American Journal of Mental Deficiency, 81*, 523–533.

Cook, T.D., & Campbell, D.T. (1979). *Quasi-experimentation: Design and analysis issues for field settings*. Boston: Houghton Mifflin.

D'Andrade, R. (1986). Three scientific world views and the covering law model. In D.W. Fiske & R.A. Shweder (Eds.), *Metatheory in social science* (pp. 19–41). Chicago: University of Chicago Press.

Dewey, J. (1931). Social science and social control. *New Republic, 67*, 276–277.

Eyman, R.K., Borthwick, S.A., & Miller, C. (1981). Trends in maladaptive behavior of mentally retarded persons placed into community and institutional settings. *American Journal of Mental Deficiency, 85*, 473–477.

Fernald, W.E. (1917). The growth of provision for the feeble-minded in the United States. *Mental Hygiene, 1*, 34–59.

Firestone, W.A. (1987). Meaning in method: The rhetoric of quantitative and qualitative research. *Educational Researcher, 16*, 16–21.

Fujiura, G.T. (1988). Cost evaluation of residential alternatives. In L.W. Heal, J.I. Haney, & A.R. Novak-Amado (Eds.), *Integration of developmental disabled individuals into the community* (pp. 227–243). Baltimore: Paul H. Brookes Publishing Co.

Fujiura, G.T., & Johnson, L.J. (1986). Methods of microcomputer research in early childhood special education. *Journal for the Division of Early Childhood, 10*, 264–269.

Gage, N.L. (1989). The paradigm wars and their aftermath. *Educational Research, 18*, 4–10.

Gallie, W.B. (1964). *Philosophy and the historical understanding*. London: Chatto and Windus.

Gollay, E., Freedman, R., Wyngaarden, M., & Kurtz, N.R. (1978). *Coming back*. Cambridge, MA: Abt Books.

Haney, J.I. (1988). Toward successful community residential placements for individuals with mental retardation. In L.W. Heal, J.I. Haney, & A.R. Novak-Amado (Eds.), *Integration of developmentally disabled individuals into the community* (pp. 125–168). Baltimore: Paul H. Brookes Publishing Co.

Hawkins, G.D., & Cooper, D.H. (1990). Adaptive behavior measures in mental retardation research: Subject description in AJMD/AJMR articles (1979–1987). *American Journal of Mental Retardation, 94*, 654–660.

Hayden, M.F., Lakin, K.C., Hill, B.K., Bruininks, R.H., & Chen, T.H. (1992). Placement practices in specialized foster homes and small group homes for persons with mental retardation. *Mental Retardation, 30*(2), 53–61.

Heal, L.W. (1985). Methodology for community integration research. In R.H. Bruininks & K.C. Lakin (Eds.), *Living and learning in the least restrictive environment* (pp. 199–224). Baltimore: Paul H. Brookes Publishing Co.

Heal, L.W., & Fujiura, G.T. (1984). Methodological considerations in research on residential alternatives for developmentally disabled persons. In N.R. Ellis & N.W. Bray (Eds.), *International review of research in mental retardation* (Vol. 12, pp. 205–244). New York: Academic Press.

Heal, L.W., Sigelman, C.K., & Switzky, H.N. (1978). Research on community residential alternatives for the mentally retarded. In N.R. Ellis (Ed.), *International review of research in mental retardation* (Vol. 9, pp. 209–249). New York: Academic Press.

Heller, T., & Factor, A. (1991). Permanency planning for adults with mental retardation living with family caregivers. *American Journal of Mental Retardation, 96*, 163–176.

Hull, J.T., & Thompson, J.C. (1980). Predicting adaptive functioning of mentally retarded persons in community settings. *American Journal of Mental Deficiency, 85*, 253–261.

Janicki, M.P., & Wisniewski, H.M. (Eds.). (1985). *Aging and developmental disabilities: Issues and approaches*. Baltimore: Paul H. Brookes Publishing Co.

Krauss, M.W., Seltzer, M.M., & Goodman, S.J. (1992). Social support networks of adults with mental retardation who live at home. *American Journal of Mental Retardation, 96*, 432–441.

Krim, M. (1969). Scientific research and mental retardation. In J.H. Rothstein (Ed.), *Mental retardation: Readings and resources* (2nd ed.). New York: Holt, Rinehart & Winston.

Kuhn, T.S. (1970). *The structure of scientific revolutions* (2nd ed.). Chicago: University of Chicago Press.

Lakin, K.C., & Bruininks, R.H. (1985). Contemporary services for handicapped children and youths. In R.H. Bruininks & K.C. Lakin (Eds.), *Living and learning in the least restrictive environment* (pp. 3–22). Baltimore: Paul H. Brookes Publishing Co.

Lakin, K.C., Bruininks, R.H., & Sigford, B.B. (1981). Deinstitutionalization and community adjustment: A summary of research and issues. In R.H. Bruininks, C.E. Meyers, B.B. Sigford, & K.C. Lakin (Eds.), *Deinstitutionalization and community adjustment of mentally retarded people* (pp. 382–412). Washington, DC: American Association on Mental Deficiency.

Landesman, S., & Butterfield, E.C. (1987). Normalization and deinstitutionalization of mentally retarded individuals: Controversy and facts. *American Psychologist, 42*, 809–816.

Landesman-Dwyer, S. (1981). Living in the community. *American Journal of Mental Deficiency, 86*, 223–234.

Landesman-Ramey, S. (1990). Staging (and re-staging) the trio of services, evaluation, and research. *American Journal of Mental Retardation, 95*, 26–29.

Landesman-Ramey, S., Krauss, M.W., & Simeonsson, R.J. (1989). Research on families: Current assessment and future opportunities. *American Journal of Mental Retardation, 94*, ii–vi.

Larson, S.A., & Lakin, K.C. (1992). Direct-care staff stability in a national sample of small group homes. *Mental Retardation, 30*, 13–22.

Levine, D.N. (1986). The forms and functions of social knowledge. In D.W. Fiske & R.A.

Shweder (Eds.), *Metatheory in social science* (pp. 271–283). Chicago: University of Chicago Press.

Levy, J.M., Jessop, D.J., Rimmerman, A., & Levy, P.H. (1992). Attitudes of Fortune 500 corporate executives toward the employability of persons with severe disabilities: A national study. *Mental Retardation, 30*, 67–75.

Lewin, K. (1947). Frontiers in group dynamics. *Human Relations, 1*, 5–41.

Lieberson, S. (1985). *Making it count: The improvement of social research and theory.* Berkeley: University of California Press.

Locke, J. (1690). An essay concerning human understanding. In R. Hunter & I. McAlpine (Eds.), *Three-hundred years of psychiatry* (pp. 236–239). Hartsdale, NY: Carlisle Publishing.

Lutifiyya, Z.M. (1991). Qualitative research: Its value and role in policymaking. *Policy Research Brief, 3*(1), 1–8. Minneapolis: University of Minnesota, Center on Residential Services and Community Living.

Madge, J. (1965). *The tools of social science.* Garden City, NY: Anchor Books.

Martin, J. (1988). Providing training in community and domestic skills. In L.W. Heal, J.I. Haney, & A.R. Novak-Amado (Eds.), *Integration of developmentally disabled individuals into the community* (pp. 169–191). Baltimore: Paul H. Brookes Publishing Co.

McCubbin, H.I., & Patterson, J. (1983). Family stress adaptation to crises: A double ABCX model of family behavior. In H. McCubbin, M. Sussman, & J. Patterson (Eds.), *Social stresses and the family: Advances and developments in family stress theory and research* (pp. 7–37). New York: Haworth Press.

Meehl, P.E. (1986). What social scientists don't understand. In D.W. Fiske & R.A. Shweder (Eds.), *Metatheory in social science* (pp. 315–338). Chicago: University of Chicago Press.

Meyer, L.H., & Evans, I.M. (1989). *Nonaversive intervention for behavior problems: A manual for home and community.* Baltimore: Paul H. Brookes Publishing Co.

Miles, M., & Huberman, A. (1984). Drawing valid meaning from qualitative data: Toward a shared craft. *Educational Researcher, 13*, 20–30.

Mill, J.S. (1879). System of logic. Extracts reprinted in E. Nagel (1961), *The structure of science: Problems in the logic of scientific explanation.* New York: Harcourt, Brace & World.

Mink, I.T., & Nihira, K. (1987). Direction of effects: Family life styles and behavior of TMR children. *American Journal of Mental Deficiency, 92*, 57–64.

Mitroff, I. (1983). Beyond experimentation: New methods for a new age. In E. Seidman (Ed.), *Handbook of social interventions* (pp. 163–177). Beverly Hills: Sage.

Nagel, E. (1961). *The structure of science: Problems in the logic of scientific explanation.* New York: Harcourt, Brace & World.

O'Connor, G. (1976). *Home is a place: A national perspective of community residential facilities for developmentally disabled persons.* (Monograph No. 2). Washington, DC: American Association on Mental Deficiency.

Orr, R.R., Cameron, S.J., & Day, D.M. (1991). Coping with stress in families with children who have mental retardation: An evaluation of the double ABCX model. *American Journal on Mental Retardation, 95*, 444–450.

Pedhazur, E.J. (1982). *Multiple regression in behavioral research* (2nd ed.). New York: Holt, Rinehart & Winston.

Popper, K.R. (1959). *The logic of scientific discovery.* New York: Basic Books.

Salmon, W.C. (1967). *The foundations of scientific inference.* Pittsburgh, PA: University of Pittsburgh Press.

Schalock, R.L., & Harper, R.S. (1978). Placement from community-based MR programs: How well do clients do? *American Journal of Mental Deficiency, 83*, 240–247.

Schalock, R.L., & Lilley, M.A. (1986). Placement from community-based mental retardation programs: How well do clients do after 8 to 10 years? *American Journal of Mental Deficiency, 90*, 669–676.

Scotti, J.R., Evans, I.M., Meyer, L.H., & Walker, P. (1991). A meta-analysis of intervention research with problem behavior: Treatment validity and standards of practice. *American Journal of Mental Retardation, 96*, 233–256.

Sigelman, C.K., Novak, A.R., Heal, L.W., & Switzky, H.N. (1980). Factors that affect the success of community placement. In A.R. Novak & L.W. Heal (Eds.), *Integration of developmentally disabled individuals into the community* (pp. 57–74). Baltimore: Paul H. Brookes Publishing Co.

Siperstein, G.N. (1992). Social competence: An important construct in mental retardation. *American Journal of Mental Retardation, 96*, iii–vi.

Sjoberg, G. (1975). Politics, ethics, and evaluation research. In M. Guttentag & E.L. Struening (Eds.), *Handbook of evaluation research* (pp. 29–51). Beverly Hills: Sage.

Smith, J.K., & Heshusius, L. (1986). Closing down the conversation: The end of the quantitative-qualitative debate among educational inquirers. *Educational Researcher, 15*, 4–12.

Smith, T.V., & White, L.D. (1929). *Chicago: An experiment in social science research*. Chicago: University of Chicago Press.

Soltis, J.F. (1984). On the nature of educational research. *Educational Researcher, 13*, 5–10.

Stainback, S., & Stainback, W. (1984). Methodological considerations in qualitative research. *Journal of The Association for Persons with Severe Handicaps, 9*, 296–303.

Stainback, S., & Stainback, W. (1989). Using qualitative data collection procedures to investigate supported education issues. *Journal of The Association for Persons with Severe Handicaps, 14*, 271–277.

Taylor, S.J., & Bogdan, R. (1981). A qualitative approach to the study of community adjustment. In R.H. Bruininks, C.E. Meyers, B.B. Sigford, & K.C. Lakin (Eds.), *Deinstitutionalization and community adjustment of mentally retarded people* (pp. 71–81). Washington, DC: American Association on Mental Deficiency.

Thiel, G.W. (1981). Relationship of IQ, adaptive behavior, age, and environmental demand to community-placement success of mentally retarded adults. *American Journal of Mental Deficiency, 86*, 208–211.

Thorton, C. (1985). Benefit-cost analysis of social programs. In R.H. Bruininks & K.C. Lakin (Eds.), *Living and learning in the least restrictive environment* (pp. 225–244). Baltimore: Paul H. Brookes Publishing Co.

Tolan, P., Chertok, F., Keys, C., & Jason, L. (1990). Conversing about theories, methods, and community research. In P. Tolan, C. Keys, F. Chertok, & L. Jason (Eds.), *Researching community psychology: Issues of theory and methods* (pp. 3–8). Washington, DC: American Psychological Association.

Wehman, P., & Melia, R. (1990). *A national analysis of supported employment growth and implementation*. Richmond: Virginia Commonwealth University, Rehabilitation Research and Training Center on Supported Employment.

Wehman, P., & Moon, M.S. (Eds.). (1988). *Vocational rehabilitation and supported employment*. Baltimore: Paul H. Brookes Publishing Co.

Willer, B., & Intagliata, J. (1981). Social-environmental factors as predictors of adjustment of deinstitutionalized mentally retarded adults. *American Journal of Mental Deficiency, 86*, 252–259.

Williamson, J.B., Karp, D.A., Dalphin, J.R., & Gray, P.S. (1982). *The research craft*. Boston: Little, Brown and Co.

Wynne, M.E., & Rogers, J.J. (1985). Variables discriminating residential placement of severely handicapped children. *American Journal of Mental Deficiency, 89*, 515–523.

Zigler, E., Hodapp, R.M., & Edison, M.R. (1990). From theory to practice in the care and education of mentally retarded individuals. *American Journal of Mental Retardation, 95*, 1–12.

— *Chapter 3* _____

Qualitative Research Methods and Community Living

Steven J. Taylor and Robert Bogdan

_____

The past 12 or so years have witnessed a growing interest in and visibility of qualitative research in mental retardation. Since the early 1980s, there has been a steady stream of books, edited volumes, and articles on the application of qualitative methods to special education, mental retardation, and disability studies (Bogdan & Lutfiyya, 1992; Edgerton, 1984a, 1984b; Edgerton & Gaston, 1991; Ferguson, Ferguson, & Taylor, 1992; Jacob, 1990; Jacobs, 1980; Langness & Levine, 1986; Stainback & Stainback, 1984, 1988, 1989; Taylor, 1988; Taylor & Bogdan, 1981). Similarly, there has been a proliferation of studies based on qualitative methods published in special education and mental retardation journals and by book publishers who are targeting these fields (Bercovici, 1981, 1983; Biklen & Moseley, 1988; Bogdan & Taylor, 1982; Edgerton, 1988; Edgerton, Bollinger, & Herr, 1984; Ferguson, 1987; Ferguson, Ferguson, & Jones, 1988; Foster, 1983; Goode, 1983, 1984; Harry, 1992; Lutfiyya, 1992; Murray-Seegert, 1989; Taylor & Bogdan, 1989). It is no longer necessary to introduce and justify qualitative research methods to researchers in the mental retardation field.

In this chapter, the status of qualitative research methods in the study of mental retardation, and specifically community living, are reviewed. First, the characteristics that define qualitative research methods are presented. Second, the major contributions of qualitative research to our understanding of persons with mental retardation in the community and in society are discussed. Third, in the concluding section of this chapter, the future of qualitative methods in disability-related fields are assessed.

Preparation of this chapter was supported by cooperative agreements #H133B80048 and #H133B00003-90 from the National Institute on Disability and Rehabiltiation Research (NIDRR). The opinions expressed are those of the authors.

The authors would like to thank Rachael Zubal and Debbie Simms for their assistance in the preparation of this chapter.

RECOGNITION OF QUALITATIVE RESEARCH

Qualitative research has become a popular method of inquiry in the fields of mental retardation and special education. The term "qualitative" has been used to refer to anecdotal and impressionistic reports and essays, which are not research-based, and to quasi-quantitative research studies (e.g., open-ended responses on surveys and questionnaires). For some, qualitative is used to characterize any form of reporting that does not build on statistical procedures.

The widespread use of the term qualitative places many qualitative researchers who are trained in sociology or anthropology in an uncomfortable position. On the one hand, qualitative researchers are stubbornly resistant to standardization. Different researchers define and practice qualitative research differently. Social science books and journals are filled with debates on how to conduct and report qualitative research (see, for example, *Street Corner Society Revisited* [Special issue] [1992, April]). On the other hand, if qualitative refers to anything, then it means nothing, and there is no way of judging any piece of work. Therefore, anyone who can tell a good story becomes a qualitative researcher.

While there are no agreed-upon standards in qualitative research, there are traditions and conventions rooted in bodies of anthropological and sociological literature. What distinguishes qualitative research from other endeavors are three characteristics: 1) qualitative research is interpretative, 2) qualitative research is based on descriptive data, and 3) qualitative research is inductive.

Qualitative Research Is Interpretative

In qualitative research, methodology cannot be separated from theoretical perspective; it is not simply a set of research procedures, but a way of approaching reality. Most qualitative researchers identify with what has been termed an interpretative perspective (Denzin, 1989; Ferguson et al., 1992), which includes such theoretical traditions as symbolic interactionism (Blumer, 1969), phenomenology (Psathas, 1973), ethnomethodology (Garfinkel, 1967), and interpretative anthropology or ethnography (Geertz, 1983).

Central to the interpretative perspective is the assumption that reality is socially constructed (Berger & Luckmann, 1967). Reality is not an objective phenomenon that exists externally to people's consciousness, but rather something that is subjectively interpreted by people as they experience the world around them. The qualitative researcher seeks an understanding of how people construct and interpret their reality. This is what Weber (1968) called *verstehen*, personal understanding of other people's perspectives. Since any form of research is itself an interpretation of reality, qualitative researchers can only strive to approximate an understanding of others' perspectives (Ferguson et al., 1992).

As Ferguson et al. (1992) point out, most of the growing acceptance of qualitative research in special education and disability studies has been at the level of method, not theoretical perspective. As a result, qualitative research procedures are sometimes used to address questions for which they are not well-suited, and interpretative studies are sometimes judged by inappropriate standards.

Qualitative Research Is Based on Descriptive Data

A qualitative research report is based on or grounded in some form of descriptive data; for example, people's own written or spoken words, observable behavior, or social products. Although these data are sorted, categorized, or coded, they are not subjected to statistical analysis.

Within qualitative research, data collection procedures vary widely, from participant observation to open-ended interviewing to analysis of documentary materials. Qualitative researchers use different approaches and techniques to collect data. Some advocate a naturalistic approach and attempt to blend into the woodwork (Taylor & Bogdan, 1984), and others adopt a more aggressive posture (Douglas, 1976, 1985). Regardless of the specific data collection procedures, qualitative research is based on one or more of five major types of data, including field notes, transcripts, videotapes, personal documents, and official documents and public records.

Field Notes   Field notes are the researcher's written record of what was seen and heard during an observation or interview, as well as the researcher's own feelings, hunches, and interpretations at the time. Conventions for recording field notes are fairly well established in qualitative research (Bogdan & Biklen, 1982; Taylor & Bogdan, 1984). For example, qualitative researchers usually separate description from interpretation and distinguish between paraphrases and approximate quotations. One common guideline is that if a statement or observation is not recorded in the field notes, it never happened and cannot be used in the analysis.

Most qualitative researchers record their field notes after an observation or interview, rather than taking notes in the field. Of course, recollections recorded after an observation are not as accurate as notes recorded at the time or as audio- and videotapes. Completeness and some degree of accuracy are sacrificed in favor of unobtrusiveness.

In the field of mental retardation, many qualitative studies have focused on everyday life in institutions and in other settings. People say and do different things when they believe that they are being closely watched or recorded. Obtrusive note-taking or mechanical recording can interfere with the flow of everyday life and lead people to act differently than normal. Bogdan, Taylor, deGrandpre, and Haynes (1974) and Taylor (1978, 1987b), for example, studied how institutional attendants undermine programs designed by professionals off of the ward and how they sometimes abuse the residents under their care. The attendants in these studies would have acted differently if the observers had been conspicuously recording their words and deeds.

Transcripts   Transcripts are the verbatim record of a conversation prepared from an audio- or videotape. Many qualitative studies are based on taped recordings. For example, Bogdan and Taylor (1976, 1982) compiled the life histories of a man and woman with mental retardation, presenting their perspectives on their experiences and situations. Edgerton's (1967) *The Cloak of Competence* was based partially on tape-recorded interviews, in addition to field notes recorded after observations. In contrast to participant observation, which is conducted in people's everyday life situations as they go about their normal business, the interview is defined as a research situation, and, therefore, a tape recorder is less likely to have a major effect on what people say.

Distrustful of an observer's selective perception and memory, some qualitative researchers use tape recorders or video cameras for participant observation research (Schwartz & Jacobs, 1979). As previously described, mechanical recording devices offer both an advantage and a disadvantage. Due to their potential effect on the people under study, these devices remain controversial. Douglas (1976) writes, "there is every reason to believe that obtrusive recording devices have fundamental effects in determining what actors think and feel about the researcher (mainly, it makes them terribly suspicious and on guard) and what they do in his presence" (p. 53).

Videotaping   As in other areas of modern life, videotaping is becoming popular in qualitative research circles. In addition to serving as the researcher's eyes and ears in the field, videotaping is used to discover nuances of meaning in people's utterances and gestures that would otherwise escape detection.

Goode (1992) contrasts two radically different views of a man, Bobby, who has Down syndrome: one view, based on clinical information and superficial observations, stresses incompetence; the other, based on videotapes, shows the man as a competent and adaptive adult. Goode (1992) explains how videotapes altered the interpretation of Bobby's competence:

> . . . we had thought that Bobby's utterances were nonsensical and we largely ignored them. When we mechanically altered Bobby's tonal qualities on the tape, many of these formerly senseless utterances became more audible. . . .It had been our common assumption that Bobby did not understand much of what went on around him. But after watching the tape perhaps 30 times, a new definition of the situation emerged: Bobby's behavior seemed more like that of a foreign-speaking person than that of a retarded one. (pp. 204–205)

Videotapes and films can also illuminate social patterns that move too slowly or too fast to be seen (Dabbs, 1982). Whyte (1980) has used time-lapse photography, for example, to examine how people use small urban spaces, such as parks and plazas.

Personal Documents   Personal documents include people's written accounts and reflections as well as their collections and possessions. Qualitative researchers have analyzed such personal documents as letters and diaries (Thomas & Znaniecki, 1927); solicited narratives (Shaw, 1931); and suicide notes (Douglas, 1967).

Bogdan's (1988) *Freak Show* is based largely on photographs, letters, memoirs, and personal documents. As Bogdan argues, many of the people displayed in freak shows as human curiosities would today be defined as persons with mental retardation. Bogdan (1988) examines "the social construction of freaks" and shows how "'Freak' is a frame of mind, a set of practices, a way of thinking about and presenting people" (p. 3).

Official Documents and Public Records   Any form of official document or public record can be a source of qualitative data. Of course, official documents and records are a common source of data in mental retardation research. From a qualitative research perspective, these documents lend insight into the perspectives and assumptions of the people who produce them. As Garfinkel (1967) argues, clinical records tell more about those who prepare them than those on whom they are kept.

Taylor and Bogdan (1980) examine how institutional officials account for the discrepancy between their goals, on the one hand, and actual conditions and practices, on the other. By examining institutional brochures, policy statements, newsletters, and records, they illustrate how these documents are used to manage outsiders' impressions of the institutions and to legitimate their existence symbolically. The popular media also provides a source for understanding cultural images of persons with mental retardation and other disabilities. Newspapers and comics (Bogdan & Biklen, 1977), literature (Kriegel, 1987; Zola, 1992), and television and movies (Longmore, 1985) have been analyzed for their portrayals of persons with disabilities.

A qualitative study is not an off-the-cuff impressionistic report, but an analysis grounded in descriptive data. Qualitative researchers reject traditional notions of validity and reliability, and focus instead on the credibility and trustworthiness of a qualitative research study (Lincoln & Guba, 1985). A study's credibility depends largely on the nature and the amount of descriptive data collected and analyzed by the researcher. By convention in sociology and anthropology, researchers are expected to make data used in publications available for inspection by other researchers. The *Code of Ethics* of the American Sociological Association (1989) explicitly states that researchers must make raw data and pertinent documentation that is collected and prepared at public expense available to other social scientists.

Qualitative Research Is Inductive

Qualitative research is based on inductive reasoning. The qualitative researcher begins a study with only vaguely formulated research interests. In the initial stages of the research, he or she is not even sure of what questions to ask. As data are collected, the researcher starts to look for patterns and makes decisions on future data collection based on the patterns already identified or suspected. Proceeding with the study, the researcher begins to develop theories, concepts, and understandings that fit the patterns in the data. Every additional piece of data collected is used to refine the understandings.

Glaser and Strauss (1967) coined the phrase *grounded theory* to describe the inductive theorizing process commonly used by qualitative researchers. According to these researchers, social scientists have overemphasized testing and verification of theories and neglected the important activity of generating theoretical insights. In generating grounded theories, researchers do not seek to prove their theories, but merely to demonstrate plausible support for them. Glaser and Strauss (1967) further argue that the key criteria in evaluating grounded theories is whether they fit and work: "By 'fit' we mean that the categories must be readily (not forcibly) applicable to and indicated by the data under study; by 'work' we mean that they must be meaningfully relevant to and able to explain the behavior under study" (p. 3).

While qualitative researchers attempt to generate understandings from the data themselves, no theorizing is purely inductive. Researchers do not enter their studies with a tabula rosa, or blank slate. Observations are filtered through the researcher's cultural knowledge and world view. One's theoretical assumptions, as well as social standing, class, gender, race, and cultural background structures, determine how one sees and interprets the data. As Richardson (1990) argues, all knowledge is partial, subjective, and culturally situated (although this knowledge is better than none at all). Thus, qualitative research can only be considered inductive relative to most research that seeks to test specifically formulated theories or hypotheses.

THE CONTRIBUTION OF QUALITATIVE METHODS

While relatively new to the field, qualitative research methods have already made a number of direct and indirect contributions to our understanding of persons with mental retardation in society. These contributions fall into five broad areas: 1) ways of thinking about mental retardation, 2) development of concepts, 3) the subjective experience of persons with mental retardation, 4) behind the scenes, and 5) applied research in mental retardation.

Ways of Thinking About Mental Retardation

Perhaps the major contribution of qualitative methods to the study of mental retardation has been the challenge to the concept of mental retardation itself. Consistent with an interpretivist perspective, mental retardation is a social construct. Mental retardation is not a thing; it is a metaphor (Bogdan & Taylor, 1982). Braginsky and Braginsky (1971) write the following:

> The term mental retardation is simply a metaphor chosen to connote certain assumed qualities of putative, invisible mental processes. More specifically, it is inferred that it appears as if retarded mental processes underlie particular behaviors. Or, we infer that behavior appears as if it were retarded. (p. 15)

As a metaphor, mental retardation exists in the minds of those who apply the label, and not in those to whom the label is applied. The answer to the question, "Who is mentally retarded?", depends on the classification procedures used to define people as such. For example, schooling practices, and not the characteristics of individual children, determine which child is or is not a child with mental retardation (Mehan, 1992).

Since mental retardation is a social construct, different definitions of an individual can coexist. An individual with mental retardation can be incompetent from one perspective, but normal and competent from another (Goode, 1992). Medical and clinical perspectives on persons with mental retardation are not necessarily bad. When, however, these perspectives dominate the definition of people, they become one-sided and distort our view of these persons. The problem with the medical model, which has become increasingly suspect in the field of mental retardation (Gleidman & Roth, 1980; Wolfensberger, 1972), is that it has held an ideological monopoly.

The social constructionist perspective has directed attention to two competing definitions of mental retardation: 1) mental retardation as a form of social deviance and 2) mental retardation and social acceptance.

Mental Retardation as a Form of Social Deviance   Mental retardation is not simply an innocuous social construct; it is a form of social deviance. As Becker (1963) argues, deviance is created by society through the establishment and application of social rules:

> . . . social groups create deviance by making the rules whose infraction constitutes deviance, and by applying those rules to particular people and labeling them as outsiders. From this point of view, deviance is not a quality of the act the person commits, but rather a consequence of the application of others of rules and sanctions to an "offender." The deviant is one to whom that label has been successfully applied; deviant behavior is behavior that people so label. (p. 9)

Once labeled as mentally retarded, a person is likely to be stereotyped, excluded, and treated differently than others. Labeling creates a self-fulfilling prophecy (Merton, 1948). Persons with mental retardation play a social role in which they are rewarded for behavior that conforms to societal expectations and punished for behavior that departs from those expectations. Wolfensberger (1972), who builds on the sociology of deviance in his formulations of normalization and social role valorization, writes as follows:

> When a person is perceived as deviant, he is cast into a role that carries with it powerful expectancies. Strangely enough, these expectancies not only take hold of the mind of the perceiver, but of the perceived person as well. . . .Generally, people will play the roles that have been assigned. This permits those who define social roles to make self-fulfilling prophecies by predicting that someone cast into a certain role will emit behavior consistent with that role. (pp. 15–16)

Mental Retardation and Social Acceptance   The social constructionist perspective on mental retardation as a form of deviance aids in an understanding of social prejudice and discrimination. The fact that persons with mental retardation, and those with other disabilities, are a discriminated-against minority, is widely accepted in the field today. This represents only one side of the story, however. While the social constructionist perspective has been associated with deviance, it is not deterministic by nature and has recently been applied to situations in which people with disabilities are not rejected and excluded.

Recent studies have documented instances in which persons with disabilities, including those with severe mental retardation and multiple disabilities, are accepted and included by persons without disabilities in communities (Bogdan, 1992d; Groce, 1985); groups (Bogdan, 1992a, 1992b, 1992c); and personal relationships (Bogdan & Taylor, 1987, 1989; Lutfiyya, 1992; Taylor & Bogdan, 1989). Groce (1985) conducted a study of how a community in which people with a demonstrable disability—deafness—were not rejected by other community members. In this anthropological and historical account of Martha's Vineyard in Massachusetts, Groce documents how the community unself-consciously accepted people who were deaf as full-fledged, undifferentiated members.

Bogdan and Taylor (1987, 1989) and Taylor and Bogdan (1989) have examined accepting relationships between persons with severe mental retardation and persons without disabilities. Notwithstanding cultural definitions of mental retardation and social discrimination, people without disabilities can and do form accepting relationships with those who have the most severe disabilities, as well as construct positive definitions of them as human beings. Bogdan and Taylor (1989) describe how family members, citizen advocates, and friends can come to see a person with severe disabilities as *someone like me* and attribute to him or her the same characteristics and motives attributed to others.

The interpretivist, or social constructionist, perspective on reality is captured by the phrase, "Beauty is in the eye of the beholder." Like beauty, mental retardation is a matter of social definition. Depending on who is doing the defining, it can lead to rejection or acceptance. It is important to understand the dynamics of exclusion, but it is equally important to recognize the possibility of inclusion.

Development of Concepts

As suggested by Glaser and Strauss's (1967) grounded theory approach, qualitative research methods can be used to develop concepts that aid in understanding social phenomena. In qualitative research, concepts are sensitizing instruments (Blumer, 1969; Bruyn, 1966). According to Blumer (1969), sensitizing concepts provide a "general sense of reference" and suggest "directions along which to look" (p. 148). As he explains, these concepts are communicated by "exposition which yields a meaningful picture, abetted by apt illustrations which enable one to grasp the reference in terms of one's own experience" (Blumer, 1969, p. 148). A good sensitizing concept illuminates things that are only vaguely seen or poorly understood; it serves as a flashlight in the dark.

Qualitative studies have yielded a number of important concepts for understanding persons with mental retardation and their situations. Examples of these include total institution, stigma, subculture, and accepting relationships.

Total Institution In his study, Goffman (1961) develops the concept of total institution to refer to such seemingly disparate settings as prisons, concentration camps, mental hospitals, and facilities for people with mental retardation. Goffman (1961) provides the following definition: "A total institution may be defined as a place of residence and work where a large number of like-situated individuals, cut off from the wider society for an appreciable period of time, together lead an enclosed, formally administered round of life" (p. xiii). As Goffman notes, prisons are one example of total institutions, but what is prison-like about prisons is found in institutions whose members have broken no laws.

Goffman's contribution is to help us understand what institutions are and how they differ from other settings. The concept of total institution stands in contrast to simplistic notions of institutions as publicly operated facilities or settings of an arbitrarily designated size, and distinguishes certain kinds of settings from other types of social institutions. Using Goffman's concept, we can see how some non-institutional or community settings can possess the same characteristics as large state institutions and how institutions differ from families and other forms of social arrangements.

After defining the concept of total institution, Goffman (1961) proceeds to explore the impact of total institutions on a person's self. Based on a study of a mental hospital, he shows how total institutions assault one's definition of the self and how behavior that appears abnormal out of context can be viewed as an adjustment to this assault.

As a sensitizing concept, total institution is imprecise. Goffman does not tell us how large a total institution has to be or how long people have to be cut off from the wider society. Once one understands the concept, however, one can use it to examine the similarities and differences between extreme forms of total institutions and other settings.

Stigma   Like total institution, Goffman (1963) has explored how stigma is experienced by people with disabilities. In the field of mental retardation, Edgerton (1967) has provided the clearest and most in-depth analysis of stigma. As Edgerton argues, mental retardation does carry with it a stigma. A stigma is not merely a difference, but a characteristic that deeply discredits a person's moral character. Edgerton (1967) writes on this theory:

> The label of mental retardation not only serves as a humiliating, frustrating, and discrediting stigma in the conduct of one's life in the community, but it also serves to lower one's self-esteem to such a nadir of worthlessness that the life of a person is scarcely worth living. (p. 145)

Due to the stigma associated with mental retardation, persons with mental retardation, and especially ex-residents of institutions, sometimes devote considerable energy to passing as normal persons. Edgerton shows that for many de-institutionalized persons, almost any other label is better than being identified as a person with mental retardation.

Subculture   In sociology and anthropology, the concept of subculture refers to the distinctive way of life developed by a subgroup within a society. Based on a qualitative study, Bercovici (1981, 1983) concludes that many community settings enmesh people with mental retardation in a subculture with its own set of prescribed behavior. Bercovici (1981) writes, "Many dehospitalized mentally retarded persons are not, and do not perceive themselves to be, living in the normal community, contrary to the assumptions that are generally held" (p. 138).

The concept of subculture directs attention away from the disabilities of persons with mental retardation, and focuses instead on patterns of segregation, separation, and isolation that can lead to the formation of a subculture in community facilities. By virtue of living in a culturally distinct social environment, people with mental retardation can develop different assumptions about the world and different strategies for physical survival and the maintenance of self-esteem (Bercovici, 1981, p. 138).

Accepting Relationship   Taylor and Bogdan have developed the concept of accepting relationship to describe instances of acceptance between persons with mental retardation and persons without disabilities (Bogdan & Taylor, 1989; Taylor & Bogdan, 1989). An accepting relationship is a relationship between a person with a deviant attribute, specifically mental retardation, and a person without a disability, which is long-standing and characterized by closeness and affection and in which the deviant attribute, or disability, does not have a stigmatizing or morally discrediting character in the eyes of the person without a disability (Taylor & Bogdan, 1989, p. 27). Accepting relationships are not necessarily based on a denial of the disability or the difference, but rather on the absence of impugning the person with a disability's moral character based on the disability.

Just as stigma illuminates rejection and exclusion on a societal level, the concept of an accepting relationship highlights positive relations on a personal level. By directing attention to accepting relationships, which might otherwise be overlooked, situations in which rejection does not occur can begin to be understood.

Illuminating Subjective Experience

The life history, or sociological autobiography, has a long tradition in the social sciences and figured prominently in the early development of qualitative research methods (Shaw, 1931, 1966; Sutherland, 1937). Constructed through in-depth interviews or personal documents, the life history presents people's views of themselves and their experiences in their own words. The life history captures the human side of social life. Burgess (quoted in Shaw, 1966) explains, "In the life history is revealed as in no other way the inner life of the person, his moral struggles, his successes and failures in securing his life destiny in a world too often at variance with his hopes and ideals" (p. 4).

A number of qualitative life histories of persons with mental retardation have been published (Bogdan & Taylor, 1976, 1982; Easterday, 1980; Langness & Levine, 1986). In their book *Inside Out*, Bogdan and Taylor (1982) present the extensive life histories of two ex-residents of institutions, Ed Murphy and Pattie Burt. Ed reflects on the meaning of mental retardation:

> I never thought of myself as a retarded individual, but who would want to? I never really had that ugly feeling down deep. You're not knowledgeable about what people are saying behind your back. You get a feeling from people around you—they try to hide it, but their intentions don't work. They say they will do this and that—like they will look out for you. They try to protect you, but you feel sort of guilty. You get the feeling that they love you but that they are looking down on you. You always have that

sense of a barrier between you and the ones that love you. By their own admission of protecting you, you have an umbrella over you that tells you that you and they have an understanding that there is something wrong—that there is a barrier. (Bogdan & Taylor, 1982, p. 86)

This is how Pattie views mental retardation:

You tell people you have been in the state school and they think I am retarded. People go by the school and they see some of the people walking around and they think that everybody is retarded. I would be sitting up on the wall and people would be coming by and say, "Who's up there, are they all retarded? Are you retarded?" "No, I am not retarded." I didn't think about it then. It was really weird looking when they had those old buildings up there. We would tell them that all the people up there weren't stupid acting. It was after I got out of school that the word retarded started bothering me. (Bogdan & Taylor, 1982, p. 200)

While life histories can be subjected to analysis, they stand as a rich source of understanding of the perspectives of persons with mental retardation. A person's own words enable us to look at the world from his or her point of view, unfiltered through a research or professional lens. The life history gives an opportunity for rebuttal to people whom we have put into certain categories and to whom we have attributed certain characteristics, and it provides a touchstone with reality. By reading and taking seriously people's own reflections on their lives, we are forced to focus not on our differences, but on our common humanity.

Getting Behind the Scenes

Public policies, programs, and professional interventions are often designed and implemented without a sufficient understanding of the social context in which they are to be introduced. Policymakers, reformers, and experts may operate under assumptions about the nature of the world that are inaccurate or simplistic. As a result, there is often a poor fit between change efforts and the settings to which they are targeted.

Qualitative research methods provide a first-hand look at how settings actually work and how people experience their day-to-day lives and situations. They can enable people to get behind the scenes of social life; that is, to break through common sense assumptions, superficial appearances, and official versions of reality. People can learn that the world is different than they imagined it to be.

A growing number of qualitative studies are being published on the experiences of persons with mental retardation in residential settings (Bercovici, 1981, 1983; Bogdan et al., 1974; Taylor, 1987a); work settings (Hagner, 1989; Turner, 1983); schools (Ferguson, 1987; Harry, 1992; Murray-Seegert, 1989; Schnorr, 1990); families (Ferguson et al., 1988; Foster, 1983; Goode, 1980; Jacobs, 1980; Traustadottir, 1991); and other environments. The following examples provide glimpses behind the scenes of supported work sites, an integrated classroom, institutions, and families.

Supported Work Sites While social integration is commonly cited as a primary goal of supported work (Wehman & Moon, 1987), relatively little attention has been paid to the nature and quality of relationships between workers with disabilities and workers without disabilities. In a qualitative study of seven supported work sites, Hagner (1989) examines the social interactions between workers with mild and severe disabilities and their coworkers.

Hagner reports that the workers with disabilities in his study were accepted by supervisors and coworkers, but had relatively limited opportunities for social interactions with others. This reflected the nature of the work settings, the types of jobs held by supported employees, and the practices by job coaches that interfered in interactions with others.

The workers with disabilities in Hagner's study held entry-level, low-status jobs. Most of their coworkers were uncommitted to their jobs and resented the low status accorded to them. A typical sentiment was expressed by a coworker at a fast-food restaurant: "This isn't my real job." As a result of the lack of commitment to the jobs, there was a high turnover of coworkers, and supported employees did not have the opportunity to form long-term relationships with others.

According to Hagner, the jobs held by coworkers without disabilities were characterized by overlaps and rough edges. Since their jobs did not have precise boundaries, coworkers interacted with each other formally and informally during the course of the work day. By contrast, workers with disabilities had more isolated positions that required them to work alone. The rough edges had been eliminated through detailed job descriptions, and, hence, workers with disabilities did not interact with others as frequently as their coworkers.

Hagner reports how job coaches assigned to workers with disabilities actually interfere with informal interactions with coworkers. While most workers learn their jobs through on-site mentors, job coaches took over this responsibility for workers with disabilities. In addition, job coaches tended to focus exclusively on job tasks and either ignored or discouraged supported employees from participating in the kinds of informal interactions in which workers without disabilities engaged.

An Integrated Classroom   Schnorr (1990) presents the first graders' perspectives on a part-time mainstream student with severe mental retardation. Based on participant observation in the classroom and interviews with first graders, Schnorr shows the discrepancy between the teacher's efforts to include the student, Peter, in the class and the first graders' definitions of class membership.

Schnorr's study focuses on the meaning of first grade to students. The students defined first grade in terms of three dimensions: "Where you belong" (class assignment, physical space), "What you do" (work, free-time activities, projects, specials), and "With whom you play" (free-time playmates, types).

Although Peter was mainstreamed into this class for a period each day, as well as for "specials," the students did not view him as a classmate. He was seen as a member of "Room 10," and not Mrs. T's first-grade class; he was not seen as doing the same activities as other students (he did art while they "worked"); he did not share free time with other students and was not mentioned by any of the other 23 students as a playmate or friend.

Based on her study, Schnorr examines the implications of part-time participation in regular classes by students with disabilities. She concludes that "part-time" is different, not just less; in other words, a part-time student does not simply spend less time in a classroom, but is not seen as being a full-fledged member of the class. In her conclusion, Schnorr (1990) reflects on the importance of understanding students' perspectives on integration: "Students are the only legitimate source for some of the answers we need for understanding and promoting school inclusion, because it is their world, not ours, that defines it" (p. 240).

Institutions   Based on participant observation at four public institutions for persons with mental retardation, Taylor (1978, 1987b) (see also Bogdan et al., 1974; Taylor & Bogdan, 1980) studied the perspectives and day-to-day practices of direct care staff or attendants. Taylor's research was conducted in the mid-1970s, when institutions were coming under increasing public scrutiny and were adopting new developmental, or therapeutic, goals.

Taylor's study focuses on the discrepancy between institutional goals and policies, on the one hand, and the discrepancy between attendants' practices and perspectives, on the other. Despite the institutions' official goals, attendants' day-to-day practices revolved around custodial tasks and control of the residents under their care. Taylor reports that psychological and physical abuse were commonplace at the institutions. He describes situations in which attendants hit residents, forced them to swallow burning cigarettes, and restrained them in bed.

By observing unobtrusively and interacting with attendants in a nonthreatening manner, Taylor describes how attendants came to act naturally in his presence (for a discussion of the ethical implications of this research, see Taylor, 1987a). According to Taylor, the attendants developed an elaborate series of accounts to rationalize their behavior to themselves and others and employed evasion strategies to hide their actions from supervisors, outsiders, and visitors.

As part of this study, Taylor examines how institutional administrators constructed a world view that denied the reality of poor conditions and abuse. For example, administrators subscribed to a theory of a few rotten apples in every barrel that obscured a pervasive pattern of substandard treatment of institutional residents.

Families   Qualitative studies have contributed to the insider's view of life within families of adults and children with disabilities. Researchers have illuminated gender roles within the family (Traustadottir, 1991); parental perspectives on their children's competence (Goode, 1980); cultural diversity and the family (Harry, 1992); the experiences of families in attempting to receive services (Foster, 1983); and other aspects of family life.

Ferguson et al. (1988) look at how families experience their children's transition from childhood to adulthood. As these researchers point out, professionals have usually defined transition as a single process entailing a shift from special education to adult services. For the families in Ferguson et al.'s study, however, transition is a much more complex process. Families in this study experienced three distinct types of transition associated with their children turning 21 years of age: 1) bureaucratic transitions, or the process whereby agencies and professionals involved with a family change from representatives of the special education system to those of the adult service system; 2) family life transitions, or the internal changes within the family that accompany the child's graduation from school; and 3) status transitions, or the changes in a family's control over the child's fate.

Ferguson et al. (1988) emphasize the importance of understanding families' perspectives and advocate for a redefinition of transition success:

> One implication of this research is that parents and professionals seem to spend at least some of their time in transition planning talking past each other. Professionals need to recognize the different types of transition processes that affect families. Collapsing all of these separate processes into a single transition too often leaves only a rubble of miscommunication. (p. 186)

Applied Research in Mental Retardation

Qualitative methods lend themselves to applied research. As Bogdan and Biklen (1982) note, there are three types of applied qualitative research. The first is qualitative evaluation research (Patton, 1980). In contrast to most evaluation research, qualitative evaluation research is not directed to assessing the effectiveness of a policy or program, but to understanding how policies and programs work. The qualitative evaluation researcher does not ask, "Does the policy or program work?," but rather, "How does the program or policy work?" (Bogdan & Taylor, 1990).

The second type of applied qualitative research is pedagogical research in which a practitioner uses qualitative methods to improve his or her practice. Ferguson (1987) explains how teachers can use qualitative methods to become better observers of what happens in schools and, hence, better teachers. At Options in Community Living in Madison, Wisconsin, staff members record stories that reflect on the meaning and nature of their work, which involves supporting persons with disabilities to live in their own homes. These stories have been edited and compiled in a book titled, *Remembering the Soul of Our Work* (O'Brien & O'Brien, 1992).

The final type of applied qualitative research falls under the category of action research. Action research is distinguished from other types of research in that it is consciously designed to promote social change (Bogdan & Biklen, 1982). Qualitative action research is an example of participatory action research described by Whyte (1989) and recently advocated in mental retardation and disability research (Graves, 1991; Turnbull & Turnbull, 1992).

Qualitative research methods have been used for evaluations of mental retardation programs and policies and the documentation of promising practices for school (Biklen, 1985; Taylor, 1982) and community integration (Taylor, Bogdan, & Racino, 1991; Taylor, Racino, Knoll, & Lutfiyya, 1987). In the following discussion, two examples are presented—an evaluation of the integration of Head Start and an applied study of promising community integration practices.

Integration of Head Start   Bogdan (1984) participated in a national evaluation of the 1972 Congressional mandate to increase the percentage of children with disabilities into Head Start programs to 10% of those served. The evaluation involved site visits using participant observation techniques to 30 Head Start programs. Prior to this evaluation, a survey of Head Start programs had been conducted by the federal Office of Child Development, and based on this survey, it was reported that the number of children with disabilities had approximately doubled to a total of 10.1%.

Bogdan's qualitative evaluation of the integration of Head Start yields a different picture than the national survey on the percentage of children with disabilities. Based on the site visits to programs, Bogdan reports that what changed was not the nature of the population served, but rather, the processes through which children were categorized and labeled. According to Bogdan, Head Start programs labeled and reported children as disabled who were not labeled previously. Many of these children had mild disabilities and would not otherwise be defined as having a disability. Bogdan (1984) writes the following:

> Staff sought professional advice to help clarify the concepts (handicapping conditions). Some threw up their hands in frustration. Others, and this became increasingly true over time, began to think differently about the children they were serving. We were told by one director: "We didn't know we had so many handicapped children until we started counting." Another said: "Now that the staff has an idea of how 'handicapped' is defined, they feel comfortable. They've had them all along—the definition changed them." Although the children might not have changed, staffs changed their definitions and their common sense understandings about children were altered. (p. 217)

Community Integration As part of an applied qualitative study of innovative and promising practices for community integration, the Center on Human Policy in Syracuse University has been conducting site visits to state, regional, and local mental retardation and developmental disability agencies since 1985. The findings from this study are contained in edited volumes (Taylor, Biklen, & Knoll, 1987; Taylor et al., 1991), as well as in reports and newsletter and journal articles.

The center's applied research on community integration is based on a positive, or optimistic, approach (Bogdan & Taylor, 1990; Taylor et al., 1991). The purpose of this study is not to learn about average or representative programs and agencies. Since many community programs are socially isolated, a random sample of them might say very little about integration. Rather than selecting a random sample, agencies and programs are selected based on their reputations for innovative or promising practices.

Consistent with a qualitative approach, this research is open-ended and inductive. Through the analysis of documents and program descriptions, observation of people, settings, and homes, and through interviews with administrators, persons with developmental disabilities, family members, and staff, the researchers attempted to understand how community integration is defined and practiced at the sites.

When the center began this study, it used the terms "model programs" and "best practices" in describing what it was looking for in the research. This terminology was soon abandoned. No agencies are free of problems and dilemmas, and no practices are perfect. What makes some agencies stand out from others is that they seem to be moving in the right direction and are struggling with the right issues.

This applied study has provided two broad sets of findings. The first set of findings relates to community integration practices. Based on the study, the center has documented innovative permanency planning and family support services to enable children to live with families, as well as housing and support approaches to enable adults to live in their own homes. A second set of findings focuses on the characteristics of responsive organizations serving persons with developmental disabilities. As Taylor et al. (1991) argue, the best practices and approaches remain so for only a short period of time. At least as important as specific approaches and practices is the nature of organizations that seek out responsive and respectful ways of supporting persons with mental retardation and their families.

CONCLUSION

This chapter addresses a variety of issues relevant to qualitative research and its usefulness in better understanding the lives of persons with mental retardation. In the future, a greater appreciation of the broad range of qualitative methodologies and discussions of the relative usefulness of these different approaches can be expected in the field. Today, approaches to qualitative research are typically lumped together. Within sociology and anthropology, however, there is a rich diversity of research strategies and theoretical perspectives associated with the qualitative traditions, including interpretivism, postmodern ethnography, ethnomethodology, phenomenology, symbolic interactionism, and feminist methodology.

The 1990s are also likely to be a period during which we witness an expanded use of qualitative methods for applied uses. To date, most of the applied qualitative research in mental retardation has been conducted at Syracuse University, Center on Human Policy. With the current interest in participatory action research in the field, applied qualitative research will become more popular. The focus group technique (Krueger, 1988), which is an applied form of qualitative research, is already widely used in mental retardation. Long before focus groups became popular in the field, some researchers used a participatory group process to identify issues and dilemmas experienced by policymakers, persons with disabilities, and service providers (O'Brien & O'Brien, 1990; O'Brien, O'Brien, & Schwartz, 1990).

Finally, we can look forward to new ways of thinking about and understanding the meaning and experience of being defined as a person with mental retardation in our society. In addition, we will be reminded of the complexity of attempting to support persons with mental retardation to live well in the community.

REFERENCES

American Sociological Association. (1989). *Code of ethics*. Washington, DC: Author.

Becker, H.S. (1963). *Outsiders: Studies in the sociology of deviance*. New York: Free Press.

Bercovici, S. (1981). Qualitative methods and cultural perspectives in the study of de-institutionalization. In R.H. Bruininks, C.E. Meyers, B.B. Sigford, & K.C. Lakin (Eds.), *Deinstitutionalization and community adjustment of mentally retarded people* (pp. 133–144). Washington, DC: American Association on Mental Deficiency.

Bercovici, S. (1983). *Barriers to normalization: The restrictive management of retarded persons.* Baltimore: University Park Press.

Berger, P., & Luckmann, T. (1967). *The social construction of reality.* Garden City, NY: Doubleday.

Biklen, D. (1985). *Achieving the complete school: Strategies for effective mainstreaming.* New York: Teachers College Press.

Biklen, S.K., & Moseley, C.R. (1988). "Are you retarded?" "No, I'm Catholic": Qualitative methods in the study of people with severe handicaps. *Journal of The Association for Persons with Severe Handicaps, 13*(3), 155–163.

Blumer, H. (1969). *Symbolic interactionism.* Englewood Cliffs, NJ: Prentice Hall.

Bogdan, R. (1984). National policy and situated meaning: The case of Head Start and the handicapped. In S.J. Taylor & R. Bogdan, (Eds.), *Introduction to qualitative research methods: The search for meanings* (2nd ed.) (pp. 211–219). New York: John Wiley & Sons.

Bogdan, R. (1988). *Freak show: Presenting human oddities for amusement and profit.* Chicago: University of Chicago Press.

Bogdan, R. (1992a). The Community Choir: Singing for an inclusive society (Part One). *TASH Newsletter, 18*(4), 11–12.

Bogdan, R. (1992b). The Community Choir: Singing for an inclusive society (Part Two). *TASH Newsletter, 18*(5), 14–15.

Bogdan, R. (1992c). The Community Choir: Singing for an inclusive society (Part Three). *TASH Newsletter, 18*(6), 6.

Bogdan, R. (1992d). A "simple" farmer accused of murder: Community acceptance and the meaning of deviance. *Disability, Handicap & Society, 7*(4), 303–320.

Bogdan, R., & Biklen, D. (1977). Handicapism. *Social Policy, 7*(4), 14–19.

Bogdan, R., & Biklen, S. (1982). *Qualitative research for education: An introduction to theory and methods.* Boston: Allyn & Bacon.

Bogdan, R., & Lutfiyya, Z.M. (1992). Standing on its own: Qualitative research in special education. In W. Stainback & S. Stainback (Eds.), *Controversial issues confronting special education: Divergent perspectives* (pp. 243–255). Boston: Allyn & Bacon.

Bogdan, R., & Taylor, S.J. (1976). The judged, not the judges: An insider's view of mental retardation. *American Psychologist, 31*(1), 47–52.

Bogdan, R., & Taylor, S.J. (1982). *Inside out: The social meaning of mental retardation.* Toronto: University of Toronto Press.

Bogdan, R., & Taylor, S.J. (1987). Toward a sociology of acceptance: The other side of the study of deviance. *Social Policy, 18*(2), 34–39.

Bogdan, R., & Taylor, S.J. (1989). Relationships with severely disabled people: The social construction of humanness. *Social Problems, 36*(2), 135–148.

Bogdan, R., & Taylor, S.J. (1990). Looking at the bright side: A positive approach to qualitative research. *Qualitative Sociology, 13*(2), 183–192.

Bogdan, R., Taylor, S.J., deGrandpre, B., & Haynes, S. (1974). Let them eat programs: Attendants' perspectives and programming on wards in state schools. *Journal of Health & Social Behavior, 15*, 142–151.

Braginsky, D.D., & Braginsky, B.M. (1971). *Hansels and Gretels.* New York: Rinehart and Winston.

Bruyn, S.T. (1966). *The human perspective in sociology: The methodology of participant observation.* Englewood Cliffs, NJ: Prentice Hall.

Dabbs, J.M., Jr. (1982). Making this visible. In J. Van Maanen, J.M. Dabbs, Jr., & R.R. Faulkner (Eds.), *Varieties of qualitative research* (pp. 31–64). Beverly Hills: Sage.

Denzin, N.K. (1989). *Interpretive interactionism.* Newbury Park, CA: Sage.

Douglas, J.D. (1967). *The social meaning of suicide*. Princeton, NJ: Princeton University Press.

Douglas, J.D. (1976). *Investigate social research: Individual and team research*. Beverly Hills: Sage.

Douglas, J.D. (1985). *Creative interviewing*. Beverly Hills: Sage.

Easterday, L.M. (1980). War is hell and hell is war: The autobiography of a retarded adult. In J. Jacobs (Ed.), *Mental retardation: A phenomenological approach* (pp. 208–223). Springfield, IL: Charles C Thomas.

Edgerton, R.B. (1967). *The cloak of competence: Stigma in the lives of the mentally retarded*. Berkeley: University of California Press.

Edgerton, R.B. (1984a). Anthropology and mental retardation: Research approaches and opportunities. *Culture, Medicine, and Psychiatry, 8*, 25–48.

Edgerton, R.B. (Ed.). (1984b). *Lives in process: Mildly retarded adults in a large city*. Washington, DC: American Association on Mental Deficiency.

Edgerton, R.B. (1988). Aging in the community—A matter of choice. *American Journal on Mental Retardation, 92*(4), 331–335.

Edgerton, R.B., Bollinger, M., & Herr, B. (1984). The cloak of competence: After two decades. *American Journal of Mental Deficiency, 88*(4), 345–351.

Edgerton, R.B., & Gaston, M.A. (Eds.). (1991). *"I've seen it all!": Lives of older persons with mental retardation in the community*. Baltimore: Paul H. Brookes Publishing Co.

Ferguson, D.L. (1987). *Curriculum decision making for students with severe handicaps: Policy and practice*. New York: Teachers College Press.

Ferguson, P.M., Ferguson, D.L., & Jones, D. (1988). Generations of hope: Parental perspectives on the transitions of their children with severe retardation from school to adult life. *Journal of The Association for Persons with Severe Handicaps, 13*(3), 177–187.

Ferguson, P.M., Ferguson, D.L., & Taylor, S.J. (Eds.). (1992). *Interpreting disability: A qualitative reader*. New York: Teachers College Press.

Foster, S.B. (1983). *Politics of caring*. Unpublished doctoral dissertation, Division of Special Education and Rehabilitation, Syracuse University, Syracuse, New York.

Garfinkel, H. (1967). *Studies in ethnomethodology*. Englewood Cliffs, NJ: Prentice Hall.

Geertz, C. (1983). *Local knowledge: Further essays in interpretive anthropology*. New York: Basic Books.

Glaser, B.G., & Strauss, A.L. (1967). *The discovery of grounded theory: Strategies for qualitative research*. Chicago: Aldine.

Gleidman, J., & Roth, W. (1980). *The unexpected minority: Handicapped children in America*. New York: Harcourt Brace Jovanovich.

Goffman, E. (1961). *Asylums: Essays on the social situation of mental patients and other inmates*. Garden City, NY: Doubleday, Anchor Books.

Goffman, E. (1963). *Stigma: Notes of the management of spoiled identity*. Englewood Cliffs, NJ: Prentice Hall.

Goode, D.A. (1980). The world of the congenitally deaf-blind: Toward the grounds for achieving human understanding. In J. Jacobs (Ed.), *Mental retardation: A phenomenological approach* (pp. 187–207). Springfield, IL: Charles C Thomas.

Goode, D.A. (1983). Who is Bobby? Ideology and method in the discovery of a Down syndrome person's competence. In G. Kielhofner (Ed.), *Health through occupation* (pp. 237–255). Philadelphia: Davis.

Goode, D.A. (1984). Socially produced identities, intimacy and the problem of competence among the retarded. In S. Tomlinson & L. Barton (Eds.), *Special education and social interests* (pp. 228–248). London: Croom-Helm.

Goode, D.A. (1992). Who is Bobby? Ideology and method in the discovery of a Down Syndrome person's competence. In P.M. Ferguson, D.L. Ferguson, & S.J. Taylor (Eds.),

Interpreting disability: A qualitative reader (pp. 197–212). New York: Teachers College Press.

Graves, W.T. (1991). *Participatory action research: A new paradigm for disability and rehabilitation research.* Paper presented at the Annual Conference of the National Association of Rehabilitation Research and Training Centers, Washington, DC.

Groce, N. (1985). *Everyone here spoke sign language: Hereditary deafness on Martha's Vineyard.* Cambridge, MA: Harvard University Press.

Hagner, D. (1989). *The social integration of supported employees: A qualitative study.* Syracuse, NY: Center on Human Policy, Syracuse University.

Harry, B. (1992). *Cultural diversity, families, and the special education system: Communication and empowerment.* New York: Teachers College Press.

Jacob, E. (1990). Alternative approaches for studying naturally occurring human behavior and thought in special education research. *The Journal of Special Education, 24,* 195–211.

Jacobs, J. (Ed.). (1980). *Mental retardation: A phenomenological approach.* Springfield, IL: Charles C Thomas.

Kriegel, L. (1987). The cripple in literature. In A. Gartner & T. Joe (Eds.), *Images of the disabled, disabling images* (pp. 31–46). New York: Praeger.

Krueger, R.A. (1988). *Focus groups: A practical guide for applied research.* Newbury Park, CA: Sage.

Langness, L.L., & Levine, H.G. (Eds.). (1986). *Culture and retardation.* Boston: D. Reidel Publishing Co.

Lincoln, Y.S., & Guba, E.G. (1985). *Naturalistic inquiry.* Beverly Hills: Sage.

Longmore, P.K. (1985). A note on language and social identity of disabled people. *American Behavioral Scientist, 28,* 419–423.

Lutfiyya, Z.M. (1992). "A feeling of being connected": Friendships between people with and without learning difficulties. *Disability, Handicap & Society, 6*(3), 233–245.

Mehan, H. (1992). Understanding inequality in schools: The contribution of interpretive studies. *Sociology of Education, 65*(1), 1–20.

Merton, R.K. (1948). The self-fulfilling prophecy. *The Antioch Review, 7,* 2.

Murray-Seegert, C. (1989). *Nasty girls, thugs, and humans like us: Social relations between severely disabled and nondisabled students in high school.* Baltimore: Paul H. Brookes Publishing Co.

O'Brien, C.L., & O'Brien, J. (1990). *Making a move: Advice from People First members about helping people move out of institutions and nursing homes.* Lithonia, GA: Responsive Systems Associates.

O'Brien, J., & O'Brien, C.L. (1992). *Remembering the soul of our work: Stories by the staff of Options in Community Living, Madison, Wisconsin.* Madison, WI: Options in Community Living.

O'Brien, J., O'Brien, C.L., & Schwartz, D.B. (1990, January). *What can we count on to make and keep people safe? Perspectives on creating effective safeguards for people with developmental disabilities.* Lithonia, GA: Responsive Systems Associates.

Patton, M.Q. (1980). *Qualitative evaluation methods.* Newbury Park, CA: Sage.

Psathas, G. (Ed.). (1973). *Phenomenological society.* New York: John Wiley.

Richardson, L. (1990). *Writing strategies: Reaching diverse audiences.* Beverly Hills: Sage.

Schnorr, R.F. (1990). "Peter? He comes and goes. . .": First graders' perspectives on a part-time mainstream student. *Journal of The Association for Persons with Severe Handicaps, 15*(4), 231–240.

Schwartz, H., & Jacobs, J. (1979). *Qualitative sociology: A method to the madness.* New York: Free Press.

Shaw, C. (1931). *The natural history of a delinquent career*. Chicago: University of Chicago Press.

Shaw, C. (1966). *The jack roller*. Chicago: University of Chicago Press.

Stainback, S., & Stainback, W. (1984). Broadening the research perspective in special education. *Exceptional Children, 50*(5), 400–408.

Stainback, S., & Stainback, W. (1988). *Understanding & conducting qualitative research*. Dubuque, IA: Kendall/Hunt Publishing Co.

Stainback, W., & Stainback, S. (1989). Using qualitative data collection procedures to investigate supported education issues. *Journal of The Association for Persons with Severe Handicaps, 14*(4), 271–277.

Street Corner Society Revisited (Special issue). (1992, April). P. Adler, P.A. Adler, & J.M. Johnson (Eds.). *Journal of Contemporary Ethnography, 21*(1), 3–132.

Sutherland, E. (1937). *The professional thief*. Chicago: University of Chicago Press.

Taylor, S.J. (1978). The custodians: Attendants and their work at state institutions for the mentally retarded (Doctoral dissertation, Syracuse University, 1977). *Dissertation Abstracts International, 39*(1), 1145A–1146A.

Taylor, S.J. (1982). From segregation to integration: Strategies for integrating severely handicapped students in normal school and community settings. *Journal of The Association for Persons with Severe Handicaps, 7*(3), 42–49.

Taylor, S.J. (1987a). Observing abuse: Professional ethics and personal morality in field research. *Qualitative Sociology, 10*(3), 288–302.

Taylor, S.J. (1987b). "They're not like you and me": Institutional attendants' perspectives on residents. *Child and Youth Services: Qualitative Research and Evaluation in Group Care, 8*(3/4), 109–125.

Taylor, S.J. (1988). Preface to *Generations of hope. Journal of The Association for Persons with Severe Handicaps, 13*(3), 175–176.

Taylor, S.J., Biklen, D., & Knoll, J. (Eds.). (1987). *Community integration for people with severe disabilities*. New York: Teachers College Press.

Taylor, S.J., & Bogdan, R. (1980). Defending illusions: The institution's struggle for survival. *Human Organization, 39*(3), 209–218.

Taylor, S.J., & Bogdan, R. (1984). *Introduction to qualitative research methods: The search for meanings* (2nd ed.). New York: John Wiley & Sons.

Taylor, S.J., & Bogdan, R. (1989). On accepting relationships between people with mental retardation and nondisabled people: Towards an understanding of acceptance. *Disability, Handicap & Society, 4*(1), 21–36.

Taylor, S.J., Bogdan, R., & Racino, J.A. (Eds.). (1991). *Life in the community: Case studies of organizations supporting people with disabilities*. Baltimore: Paul H. Brookes Publishing Co.

Taylor, S.J., Racino, J.A., Knoll, J.A., & Lutfiyya, Z. (1987). *The nonrestrictive environment: On community integration for people with the most severe disabilities*. Syracuse, NY: Human Policy Press.

Thomas, W.I., & Znaniecki, F. (1927). *The Polish peasant in Europe and America*. New York: Knopf.

Traustadottir, R. (1991). Mothers who care: Gender, disability and family life. *Journal of Family Issues, 12*(2), 211–228.

Turnbull, H.R., III, & Turnbull, A.P. (1992). *Participatory action research and public policy*. Lawrence, KS: Beach Center on Families and Disability, University of Kansas.

Turner, J.L. (1983). Workshop society: Ethnographic observations in a work setting for retarded adults. In K. Kernan, M. Begab, & R. Edgerton (Eds.), *Environments and behavior: The adaptations of mentally retarded persons* (pp. 147–171). Baltimore: University Park Press.

Weber, M. (1968). *Economy and society*. New York: Bedminster Press.

Wehman, P., & Moon, S. (1987). Critical values in employment programs for persons with developmental disabilities: A position paper. *Journal of Applied Rehabilitation Counseling*, *18*, 12–16.

Whyte, W.F. (1980). *The social life of small urban spaces*. Washington, DC: The Conservation Foundation.

Whyte, W.F. (1989). Advancing scientific knowledge through participatory action research. *Sociological Forum*, *4*(3), 367–385.

Wolfensberger, W. (1972). *Normalization: The principle of normalization in human services*. Toronto: National Institute on Mental Retardation.

Zola, I.K. (1992). "Any distinguishing features?" The portrayal of disability in the crime-mystery genre. In P.M. Ferguson, D.L. Ferguson, & S.J. Taylor (Eds.), *Interpreting disability: A qualitative reader* (pp. 233–250). New York: Teachers College Press.

— *Chapter 4* ——————————————————

A Multidimensional Approach to the Measurement of Community Adjustment

Kevin S. McGrew and Robert H. Bruininks

"Many, probably most, scientific advances have been accomplished by sound observation and measurement and nothing more" (Heal, 1985, p. 210). Social science research is based on a system of methodological assumptions and conventions that are designed to allow the recording of observations that, when organized, lead to empirical laws (Heal, 1985; Heal & Fujiura, 1984). Although the numerous methodological and procedural conventions that regulate this scientific endeavor are admittedly complex (e.g., external and internal validity), Heal and his colleagues have argued for the rigorous application of scientific methods to assess the varied aspects of community adjustment and integration for individuals with disabilities (Heal, 1985; Heal & Fujiura, 1984). Heal (1985) provided the following summary of the research on community adjustment and integration:

> Science and its practitioners are charged with the responsibility of providing society with information that it needs to make decisions about its social progress. With this responsibility comes the obligation to advocate for the best methodology known. There has been a clear failure to meet this obligation. (p. 219)

The reasons for this negative assessment of current research are numerous and intricate. Solutions to these problems are beyond the scope of this chapter; however, the chapter authors are in agreement with Heal in the belief that, in com-

---

Preparation of this chapter was supported in part by a U.S. Department of Education, National Institute on Disability and Rehabilitation Research (NIDRR) grant (#H133B80048-89) to the University of Minnesota and the Rehabilitation Research and Training Center in Community Living (UAP). Points of view or opinions expressed in this chapter do not necessarily represent the official position of the U.S. Department of Education.

Although much of this chapter describes work involving persons with developmental disabilities, the research paradigms are equally applicable to the range of individuals, with and without disabilities, who live in our communities.

munity adjustment research, insufficient attention is often paid to the basic issues of reliability and validity of measurement in data collection protocols that are used to gather information on community adjustment. For example, Heal and Fujiura (1984) suggest that in research focusing on deinstitutionalization of individuals with disabilities, investigators have "usually given only token attention to the validity of the measures used" (p. 215). This inattentiveness is unfortunate since valid measurement is the underlying foundation of scientific research; if treated lightly, the resulting information may be useless, or possibly even misleading. When done properly, the development of reliable and valid measures for use in community adjustment research should contribute to the discovery of important empirical regularities that result in changes in policy and in practice that will ultimately improve the quality of life for individuals with disabilities.

Much of the study of community adaptation for persons with developmental disabilities is also dominated by a focus on relatively narrow aspects of everyday life. However, life in communities is richly varied in terms of experiences, circumstance, and setting. Recent writings on quality of life consistently emphasize the varied aspects of living in communities (Halpern, Nave, Close, & Nelson, 1986; Schalock, Keith, Hoffman, & Karan, 1989). The full description and understanding of adjustment and quality of living will require a broad, multidimensional perspective regarding the adaptation of persons with developmental disabilities in communities.

A MULTIDIMENSIONAL APPROACH TO MEASUREMENT

This chapter emphasizes that the reliability and validity of measures and the perspective used in community adjustment research can be substantially improved if a multidimensional and multivariate approach to measurement is employed. More specifically, the reliability of community adjustment research measures can be improved by developing and using composite scales and multiple indicators to represent important concepts and constructs. It is well-known from psychometric theory that most indicators of a domain or a complex concept contain measurement error, and measurement error can usually be reduced by using multiple indicators. In addition, the comprehensiveness of measurement can be improved by more systematically exploring the construct validity of community adjustment measures through an examination of the interrelationships of the measures through multivariate statistical techniques (e.g., exploratory and confirmatory factor analysis).

Using the developed measures (Heal, 1985), measure development research, and subsequent hypothesis discovery and confirmation research, can be greatly improved if such efforts are driven by theoretical or conceptual models that more fully reflect the varied complexities of community life. Although past efforts at conducting community adjustment research have provided valuable descriptive information regarding the characteristics, adjustment, and integration of individuals with disabilities, this research has often failed to accurately capture the complexity of community adjustment due to an over-reliance on simple and restrictive measures.

There is little evident concern for the concept of referent generality in research on community adjustment. *Referent generality* refers to the notion that the selection of measures should consider the total population of measures (Heal & Fujiura, 1984), and measures should be sampled from the total domain of possible measures (Heal, 1985). Frequently, research on the characteristics and community adjustment of individuals with disabilities is compromised by the use of convenience measures, favorite measures used in prior research, or by only using a few measures in a domain (Heal & Fujiura, 1984). Community adjustment research could be substantially improved if the selection of measures used to describe samples and community adjustment outcomes were driven more by theoretical or conceptual considerations. Not only would the referent generality of research studies improve, but the inclusion of a wider, conceptually based number of measures would increase the ability to systematically study the complex process of community adjustment.

THE MEASUREMENT OF COMMUNITY ADJUSTMENT

Most research on the community adjustment of individuals with disabilities has been limited to descriptive studies that frequently define successful community adjustment in simple dichotomous terms (e.g., employed versus unemployed, or remaining in the community versus being returned to an institutional setting) (Heal, 1985; Zetlin, 1988). The difficulties of interpreting findings on community outcomes are often compounded when more than one measure is presented. Many community adjustment studies ask respondents to indicate whether an individual with a disability had participated in any of a number of activities during a specified period of time. For example, if 20 different recreation and leisure activities are listed, each of which is answered in a dichotomous form (i.e., yes or no), the result is frequently numerous tables of cross-tabulations that indicate the percent of the sample and subgroups within the sample that participated in each of the activities. If similar types of variables in other community adjustment domains (i.e., employment, education, social network) are also included in the study, the result is often research studies dominated by a discussion of single indicator results. The richness of such descriptions often makes it difficult for researchers and the consumers of the research to see the forest for the trees, as extensive and detailed descriptive summaries often overwhelm even the most careful reader.

While single outcome measures have produced valuable descriptive information, they often fail to capture the complexity of community integration and adjustment that is needed to develop and evaluate more comprehensive explanatory models. The use of multiple outcome measures in community adjustment and related research (e.g., quality of life research) has been suggested by a number of authors (Emerson, 1985; Gaylord-Ross & Chadsey-Rusch, 1991; Irvin, Crowell, &

Bellamy, 1979; Ittenbach, Bruininks, Thurlow, & McGrew, in press; McGrew & Bruininks, 1990; McGrew, Bruininks, Thurlow, & Lewis, 1992; Schalock et al., 1989). To date, however, only a limited number of studies have focused on the development of multidimensional community adjustment outcome measures (McGrew, Bruininks, Thurlow, & Lewis, 1992; McGrew, Johnson, & Bruininks, 1992; Zetlin, 1988). Unlike more descriptive research paradigms, recent strategies attempt to assess the complexity of community living and the formulation, based upon empirical relationships, of conceptual multidimensional models of community adjustment. Research that focuses on the validation of measures and the development of conceptual models typically follows three steps: 1) identifying outcome domains, 2) constructing composite outcome measures with multiple indicators of a single construct, and 3) completing exploratory or confirmatory factor analyses with the complete set of outcome measures to derive a conceptual understanding of community adaptation for persons with developmental disabilities.

Identification of Outcome Domains

Addressing the issue of referent generality is an arduous task since it is difficult to identify the full range of possible community adjustment outcomes. We have approached the issue of referent generality in community adjustment research by combining a bottom-up and top-down approach to selecting and developing variables and measures.

The *bottom-up approach* starts with a comprehensive review of outcome areas that are represented in most community adjustment research studies. These domains, which by their repeated presence in the literature imply some form of consensus, are then represented in final data collection instruments. Such a process is an ongoing component of systematic programs on community adjustment and integration. The result of this research has been the development and refinement of instruments that measure common outcome areas (i.e., employment, postsecondary education, engagement in productive activities, residential independence, and quality of life) (DeStefano & Wagner, 1991).

The alternative perspective, the *top-down approach*, starts with the question: "Regardless of what variables are currently included in current research studies, what needs to be included to build a comprehensive ideal conceptual model of community adjustment?" This approach is represented by a number of recent attempts to develop outcome models that focus primarily on community adjustment or transition issues, or more broadly based models that attempt to specify a general outcome model for all individuals with disabilities. One such approach is represented by the *Conceptual Framework of Transition Experiences and Outcomes of Youth with Disabilities* that was used to guide the design, analysis, and interpretation of results from the National Longitudinal Transition Study of Special Education Students (DeStefano & Wagner, 1991; SRI International, 1991). The Young Adult Outcomes component of this model suggests that community adjustment outcome research needs to include measures in the areas of postsecondary education, employment, social activities, independence, and productive engagement.

Another conceptual framework is represented by the recent attempt to develop a conceptual model of outcome indicators for students and youth with disabilities by the National Center on Educational Outcomes (NCEO) for students and youth with disabilities at the University of Minnesota (Ysseldyke et al., 1992). This model is presented in Figure 1. The Enabling Outcome and Educational Outcome components of this broad model suggest a number of areas that are important to assess in outcome research efforts involving persons with disabilities. In its current version, this dynamic model includes the areas of presence and participation; accommodation, adaptation, and compensation skills; physical and mental health; independence and responsibility; contribution and citizenship; social and behavioral skills; literacy; and satisfaction. The value of such conceptual models is that they serve a heuristic purpose in identifying possible areas of assessment and research.

Construction of Composite Outcome Measures

The lack of consensus on what constitutes community adjustment suggests that the most productive approach to investigating the construct must embrace both a bottom-up and a top-down perspective. Once community adjustment outcome domains are identified, data collection protocols designed, and data collected, the next step is the development of composite measures. The strategy used in this form of research can best be demonstrated by building on an example of the 20 dichotomous recreation-leisure outcome measures that are represented by the rectangles in Figure 2.

The first step is to logically or empirically group the individual survey items into composite measures. The objective is to create composite variables at the ordinal or interval level from combinations of items (e.g., counting, aggregating, combining categories). Based on a number of exploratory factor analyses in a variety of samples, in addition to logical content analyses of the items, it was determined that the 20 recreation/leisure items could be combined into three recreation/leisure composite variables. These three composites are represented by the rectangles in Figure 2, and were determined to measure involvement in social recreation/leisure activities, recreation/leisure activities that are either formal or community-based, and recreation/leisure activities that are more informal or home-based. As a result, three recreation/leisure composite scales were developed that were based on 5–10 different individual items. The reduction of 20 individual variables to 3 composite variables represented an 85% reduction in the number of variables in the recreation/leisure domain, a reduction that also created measures with increased reliability and validity. Finally, the circle in Figure 2 represents one additional form of data reduction based on factor analysis of the composite variables. This step is discussed later. The reduction of variables and their organization into broader composites or constructs yields a more understandable interpretation of recreation/leisure activities in the community.

In other cases, logical considerations result in the construction of meaningful measures. For example, researchers used a continuum scale that reflected the

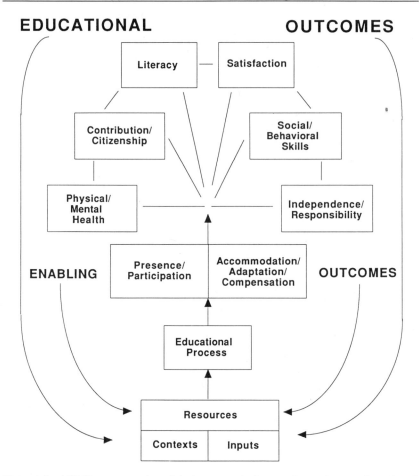

Figure 1. NCEO conceptual model of outcome indicators for students and youth with disabilities.

degree of self-sufficiency and normalization in a person's living arrangements (McGrew, Bruininks, Thurlow, & Lewis, 1992; McGrew, Johnson, & Bruininks, 1992). By combining information from a number of variables from a large data collection protocol, a five-point scale was developed that ranged from a rating of one (living in an institution, hospital, or nursing home) to five (living independently or with friends/spouse). In yet another example of variable construction, the count of the number of names listed in response to two questions about important friendships were tallied in four different types of social network categories (e.g., immediate family member, member of extended family, friend, staff, or professional). This resulted in four different measures that characterized aspects of a person's social network. These three examples illustrate the types of variable construction activities that are a necessary, but often ignored step, in the development of outcome measures for use in community adjustment research. Although

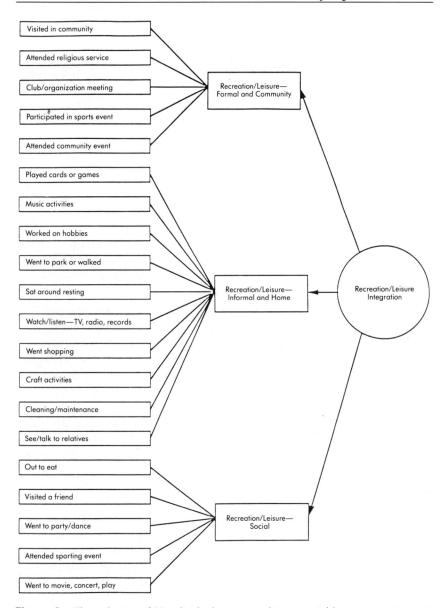

Figure 2. The reduction of 20 individual recreation-leisure variables to composite variables and constructs.

such variable construction can be a time-consuming process that requires a blending of empirical and logical considerations, the result is composite variables that possess stronger reliability and validity characteristics than the individual items. These constructed variables can then serve as the foundation for multivariate statistical studies that seek to identify the major dimensions of community adjustment.

Use of Multivariate Statistical Methods

Recently, there have been a number of studies that have demonstrated the feasibility of developing multidimensional community adjustment outcome measures that may be used to create a conceptual model of community adjustment. These studies have either used exploratory or confirmatory factor analysis methods.

Exploratory factor analysis is a statistical technique that is applied to a set of variables when the investigator is interested in discovering which variables may form coherent and meaningful subsets that are relatively independent of one another. Variables that are correlated with one another, but are mostly independent from other subsets of variables, are combined into factors that are thought to reflect underlying processes that have created the correlations among the variables. The methods are exploratory in the sense that the statistical procedures are used to discover a factor structure with no a priori constraints imposed on the analyses.

In contrast, *confirmatory factor analysis* allows researchers to investigate the factor structure within a collection of variables, but the investigator has significant control in specifying certain constraints. These confirmatory methods call for investigators to specify in advance the number and composition of the factors in their models. The final solution is then evaluated for its goodness-of-fit to the data. The major distinction between the two approaches to data reduction is that one is focused primarily on discovering structure among variables when no a priori structure is hypothesized (exploratory), while the other is best suited to evaluating factor structures when prior research or theory suggests that an a priori model may explain the correlation among the collection of variables (confirmatory).

One of the first multivariate community adjustment outcome studies was by Halpern et al. (1986). In a sample of 257 adults with mild to moderate mental retardation, these investigators used confirmatory factor analyses methods to analyze 12 outcome composite variables that were constructed from a larger number of individual items. Support was found for four multivariate dimensions. An Occupation factor was defined by measures of employment status, income, and degree of integration with individuals who did not have disabilities. The Residential Environment factor was defined by variables that measured the cleanliness and state of repair of the person's residence, the quality of the person's neighborhood (i.e., upkeep and safety), and the person's access to community services. A Social Support/Safety factor was also identified that reflected a person's social network and freedom from minor and major forms of abuse. Finally, a Client Satisfaction factor was defined by a person's overall satisfaction with themselves and their daytime program. The results of this study demonstrated the feasibility of developing multidimensional outcome measures for measuring community adjustment.

More recently, researchers at the Center on Residential Services and Community Living at the University of Minnesota have completed a series of exploratory and confirmatory factor analytic studies that have followed the research strategy outlined above. The first of these studies was an exploratory factor analysis of a pool of both personal competence and community adjustment variables in a sample of 239 individuals with mild to severe mental retardation (Bruininks, Thurlow, McGrew, & Lewis, 1990). This study was then followed by confirmatory factor analysis of 12 community adjustment composite variables (constructed from over 50 individual indicator variables) in separate model development ($n = 119$) and cross-validation samples ($n = 120$), as well as confirmatory factor analysis in separate samples of individuals with mild to moderate ($n = 135$) and severe ($n = 104$) disabilities (McGrew, Bruininks, Thurlow, & Lewis, 1992). The results of these two preliminary studies identified four broad factors or dimensions of community adjustment that were labeled Social/Network Integration, Recreation/Leisure Integration, Community and Economic Integration, and Need for Support Services. Finally, an additional Community Assimilation and Acceptance factor was identified in an exploratory factor analytic investigation of 169 individuals with mental retardation who lived in small group residential facilities (Bruininks, Chen, Lakin, & McGrew, 1992).

Based on these findings, some of which identified weaknesses in the indicator and composite variables, new data protocols were developed to address the problems and to include indicators of additional community adjustment dimensions suggested from the bottom-up and top-down domain selection strategy discussed previously. New data collection efforts in a retrospective study of approximately 173 young adults with mild to severe disabilities were then completed (McGrew, Johnson, & Bruininks, 1992). Exploratory and confirmatory factor analyses of 21 composite variables identified six different factors:

1. Recreation/Leisure Integration—the extent to which individuals are actively involved in formal and informal recreation-leisure activities both in the home setting and in the community
2. Social Network/Integration—the extent to which individuals have developed a social support network
3. Residential Integration—a person's degree of independent living and integration into the community
4. Employment/Economic Integration—the extent to which individuals are economically self-sufficient and involved in stable and integrated daily work or related activities
5. Employment Stability—the extent to which individuals are stable in their employment and satisfied with their daytime activities
6. Personal Satisfaction—the extent to which individuals appear satisfied with their daytime activities, living arrangement, social network, and recreation-leisure activities

These six factors represented most of the factors identified in the preliminary studies (Bruininks, Thurlow, McGrew, & Lewis, 1990; McGrew, Bruininks, Thurlow, & Lewis, 1992), as well as most of the measures used by Halpern et al. (1986). Missing from the McGrew, Johnson, and Bruininks (1992) investigation, and thus precluding their extraction as factors, were measures of the previously identified factors of: 1) Community Assimilation and Acceptance—a reflection of both involvement with and degree of positive response, or acceptance of, a person with a disability by neighbors and others in the community; and 2) Need for Social Support Services—the extent to which a person needs a wide variety of services to function within the community.

Recent studies have resulted in considerable progress in creating measures to describe the community experiences and adaptation of persons with developmental disabilities. This research has generally followed the strategy of developing composite measures that are constructed through exploratory or confirmatory factor analysis of numerous individual variables. Based upon a series of studies, it appears that there are at least eight unique dimensions of community adjustment. As described above, these dimensions include: 1) Recreation/Leisure Integration, 2) Social Network/Integration, 3) Residential Integration, 4) Employment/ Economic Integration, 5) Employment Stability, 6) Personal Satisfaction, 7) Community Assimilation and Acceptance, and 8) Need for Social Support Services. These dimensions and their respective indicators are presented in Figure 3.

These eight dimensions are based on 27 different variables that have been constructed from the reduction of more than 100 individual survey variables. In this figure, the ovals represent the broader validated dimensions or factors that are

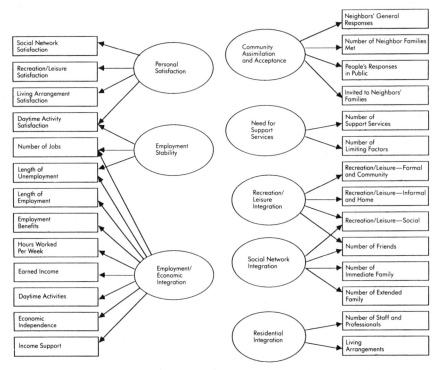

Figure 3. Measures and dimensions of community adjustment identified through research by the Institute on Community Integration (UAP) at the University of Minnesota.

defined by the respective variables that are indicated by the rectangles. The rectangles, in turn, are comprised of several individual variables.

The observation that each factor or dimension is represented by at least two, and most often by four or more measures, illustrates the multidimensionality of the factors, or components, of community adjustment. The complexity and richness of community adjustment is also evident in the low to moderate correlations that have been reported between community adjustment factors (Halpern et al., 1986; McGrew, Bruininks, Thurlow, & Lewis, 1992; McGrew, Johnson, & Bruininks, 1992). These findings indicate that the various areas each represent unique aspects of community adjustment. Not represented in Figure 3 is the finding that certain community adjustment dimensions may vary in composition and importance for persons with different degrees of mental retardation (McGrew, Bruininks, Thurlow, & Lewis, 1992). This finding needs additional investigation prior to including these dimensions in a community adjustment model.

IMPLICATIONS FOR THE
MEASUREMENT OF COMMUNITY ADJUSTMENT

The research in this chapter demonstrates that the ability to reduce hundreds of variables to a smaller number of multidimensional composites or latent factors may facilitate the development and investigation of models of community adjustment. Such developments hold considerable promise for helping to advance measurement, assessment, research, theory, and program planning and evaluation in the field of developmental disabilities.

Measurement and Assessment

The multidimensional and multivariate measurement approach outlined in this chapter has the potential to lead to improvements in our understanding and measurement of important constructs that characterize the experiences and adjustment of persons with developmental disabilities in community settings. At a fundamental level, this measurement approach will increase the reliability, validity, and referent generality of measures used in community adjustment research. The improvement of measurement should increase our understanding of the meaning of community adjustment, as well as increase the chances of discovering important empirical regularities that will result in changes in policy and in practice that will ultimately improve the quality of life of individuals with disabilities.

The investigation of multiple measures of different constructs can further increase our understanding of the nature of commonly used assessment instruments. For example, a review of Figure 3 indicates that the Recreation/Leisure-Social measure is a factorially complex measure of both Recreation/Leisure Integration and Social Network Integration. The interpretation of scores on this measure is facilitated by an awareness of the multiple abilities that it may represent. The simultaneous examination of multiple measures of different constructs increases our ability to select appropriate instruments for assessing specific outcomes, increases our ability to more accurately interpret the results from these measures, and can help guide the development of new assessment instruments (McGrew & Bruininks, 1990) to plan interventions and assess the outcomes of programs and services.

Research Methods

The implications of this approach for community adjustment research are many. Identification of the major dimensions of community adjustment can help with the integration of research studies across different samples and measures. The possibility of different investigators organizing their outcome indicators into similar multidimensional outcome frameworks could result in increased ability to compare and to integrate ideas and findings across studies. Different investigators could still use their favorite measures, but the organization of the measures under a common validated framework could provide a common language to synthesize findings. For example, this program of research led to the development of a minimum indicator data collection protocol (Bruininks, Thurlow, McGrew, Johnson, & Sinclair, 1990), which ensures that various longitudinal studies would include the necessary indicators of most of the community adjustment dimensions presented in Figure 3.

A multidimensional and multivariate approach to research has a greater chance of capturing the complex nature of community adjustment and integration. For example, personal competence and community adjustment models have recently been linked in a meaningful analysis (McGrew, Bruininks, & Thurlow, 1992). Rather than exploring the relationships between numerous indicators of personal competence and community adjustment through many separate regressions, these investigators used the two previously mentioned models to organize an investigation of the relationship between two personal competence dimensions and four community adjustment dimensions via canonical correlation procedures. Significant canonical correlations (ranging from .30 to .74) between a linear combination of practical intelligence and emotional competence indicators, as well as linear composites of community and economic integration, need for support services, social network and integration, and recreation-leisure integration clarified the degree of relationships between these personal competence and community adjustment dimensions. This study illustrated how model-based analysis allows for the exploration of relationships between the broad personal competence and community adjustment constructs, rather than exploring the relationships between hundreds of individual indicators of the constructs.

The use of multidimensional measures will permit investigators to make greater use of multivariate and latent variable procedures (i.e., multivariate analysis of variance, confirmatory factor analysis, and causal modeling), that would allow for the description and comparison of groups on the basis of outcome measures that better capture the complexity of the community adjustment process. It will also make possible the exploration of relationships between variables that more completely represent the range of experience and important theoretical constructs related to the concepts of community adjustment and quality of life.

Theory

Much of the existing community adjustment research has failed to use theory to guide research designs or interpretation of results. The atheoretical nature of much of this work stems from a lack of comprehensive theories and models, as well as the absence of community adjustment outcome measures with solid technical characteristics. The research outlined in this chapter is intended to help facilitate the identification of dimensions of community adjustment that will ultimately lead to the specification and evaluation of theoretical models of the community adjustment process. The eventual development and validation of a model of community adjustment should increase our understanding of the meaning of important constructs and the formulation of theories in the areas of community adjustment and quality of life. Such efforts could also enhance the efficiency and quality of services and supports for persons with developmental disabilities.

Program Planning and Evaluation

The delineation of important constructs in the area of community adjustment can contribute to the development, implementation, and evaluation of services and service systems that are based on sound theory and research. The identification of at least eight dimensions of community adjustment indicates that the evaluation of the success of programs or individual interventions cannot be focused on single outcome domains (e.g., employment). As noted by Schalock et al. (1989), "complex programs require complex outcome measures" (p. 25). The approach to research presented in this chapter facilitates the identification of critical outcomes that can be used to evaluate the status, productivity, quality, and effectiveness of service programs and service delivery systems.

Not only does this approach to research facilitate the delineation of critical outcome dimensions, it can also facilitate the identification and development of reliable and valid individual or composite indicators, or standardized measures that better capture the complexity of the community adjustment process (Halpern et al., 1986). Although based on complex statistical procedures, the end result can be the development of indicators or measures that more accurately and efficiently describe policy analysis, decision making, and program evaluation efforts of the community adjustment process.

Finally, without research that identifies the most critical components of community adjustment and quality of life, it would be difficult to develop reliable and valid accreditation, quality assurance, and accountability standards and systems. For example, accreditation agencies are attempting to develop outcome-based performance measures to assess the appropriateness and quality of supports and services provided to persons with disabilities. These and other standard development activities would benefit by being based on advances in theory and on research of the critical outcomes that define the dimensions of community adjustment, integration and inclusion, and overall quality of life. The research presented in this chapter can help by identifying the domains for standards and by facilitating the development of reliable and valid outcomes measures for measuring adherence to those standards.

CONCLUSION

The search to describe the many and varied aspects of community participation and adaptation is beginning to identify important components that describe quality of life for citizens with disabilities in our communities. Early findings strongly suggest that adaptation and quality of life comprise many broad areas, including personal satisfaction, employment and economic integration, employment stability, community assimilation and acceptance, the need for social support services, recreation-leisure integration, social network integration, and residential integration. The identification of these and other components will hopefully assist in the further exploration of the meaning of community adjustment and quality of life, the refinement of measurement instruments, and the eventual improvement and evaluation of programs that support persons with disabilities.

REFERENCES

Bruininks, R.H., Chen, T.H., Lakin, K.C., & McGrew, K.S. (1992). Components of personal competence and community integration for persons with mental retardation in small residential programs. *Research in Developmental Disabilities, 13*, 463–479.

Bruininks, R.H., Thurlow, M., McGrew, K.S., Johnson, D., & Sinclair, M. (1990). *Minimum community adjustment protocol*. Minneapolis, MN: Institute on Community Integration.

Bruininks, R.H., Thurlow, M., McGrew, K.S., & Lewis, D. (1990). Dimensions of community adjustment among young adults with intellectual disabilities. In W.I. Fraser (Ed.), *Key issues in mental retardation: Proceedings of the Eighth Congress of the International Association for the Scientific Study of Mental Deficiency* (pp. 435–448). New York: Routledge.

DeStefano, L., & Wagner, M. (1991). *Outcome assessment in special education: Lessons learned*. Champaign: University of Illinois at Urbana-Champaign, SRI International.

Emerson, E.B. (1985). Evaluating the impact of deinstitutionalization on the lives of mentally retarded people. *American Journal of Mental Deficiency, 90*, 277–288.

Gaylord-Ross, R., & Chadsey-Rusch, J. (1991). Measurement of work-related outcomes for students with severe disabilities. *Journal of Special Education, 25*, 291–304.

Halpern, A., Nave, G., Close, D., & Nelson, D. (1986). An empirical analysis of the dimensions of community adjustment for adults with mental retardation in semi-independent living programs. *Australia and New Zealand Journal of Developmental Disabilities, 12*, 147–157.

Heal, L. (1985). Methodology for community integration research. In R.H. Bruininks & K.C. Lakin (Eds.), *Living and learning in the least restrictive environment* (pp. 199–224). Baltimore: Paul H. Brookes Publishing Co.

Heal, L., & Fujiura, G. (1984). Methodological considerations in research on residential alternatives for developmentally disabled persons. In N.R. Ellis & N.W. Bray (Eds.),

International review of research in mental retardation (Vol. 12) (pp. 205–244). New York: Academic Press.

Irvin, L., Crowell, F., & Bellamy, G. (1979). Multiple assessment evaluation of programs for severely retarded adults. *Mental Retardation, 17,* 123–128.

Ittenbach, R., Bruininks, R., Thurlow, M., & McGrew, K. (in press). Community integration of young adults with mental retardation: A multivariate analysis of adjustment. *Research in Developmental Disabilities.*

McGrew, K., & Bruininks, R. (1990). Defining adaptive and maladaptive behavior within a model of personal competence. *School Psychology Review, 19,* 53–73.

McGrew, K., Bruininks, R., & Thurlow, M. (1992). Relationship between measures of adaptive functioning and community adjustment for adults with mental retardation. *Exceptional Children, 58,* 517–519.

McGrew, K., Bruininks, R., Thurlow, M., & Lewis, D. (1992). An empirical analysis of multidimensional measures of community adjustment for young adults with retardation. *American Journal of Mental Retardation, 96,* 475–487.

McGrew, K., Johnson, D., & Bruininks, R. (1992). *Factor analysis of community adjustment outcome measures for young adults with mild to severe disabilities.* Unpublished manuscript.

Schalock, R., Keith, K., Hoffman, K., & Karan, O. (1989). Quality of life: Its measurement and use. *Mental Retardation, 27,* 25–31.

SRI International. (1991). *Youth with disabilities: How are they doing? The first comprehensive report from the National Longitudinal Transition Study of Special Education Students.* Menlo Park, CA: Author.

Ysseldyke, J., Thurlow, M., Bruininks, R., Deno, S., McGrew, K., Shriner, J., & Gilman, C. (1992). *A conceptual model of educational outcomes for children and youth with disabilities.* Minneapolis: National Center on Educational Outcomes, University of Minnesota.

Zetlin, A.G. (1988). Adult development of mildly retarded students: Implications for educational programs. In M.C. Wang, M.C. Reynolds, & H.J. Walberg (Eds.), *Handbook of special education: Research and practice* (Vol. 2)(pp. 77–90). New York: Pergamon Press.

PART II

PROMOTING COMMUNITY INTEGRATION AND SOCIAL RELATIONSHIPS

Chapter 5

Enhancing the Social Inclusion of Persons with Developmental Disabilities

Brian H. Abery and Maurice Fahnestock

The importance of regular social contact with valued significant others cannot be underestimated. Human beings are innately social animals; thus, social relationships provide one of the primary foundations for the quality of life that an individual experiences. Associations with significant others have a direct and indirect impact on the manner in which we view ourselves and our world, and by which we meet a myriad of personal needs. A review of the literature suggests that such ties are crucial for the successful community adjustment of persons both with and without disabilities (Edgerton, 1967; Edgerton & Bercovici, 1976; Landesman-Dwyer & Berkson, 1984; Schalock & Lilley, 1986).

The past 20 years have witnessed substantial change in the provision of services to individuals with developmental disabilities. Fewer persons are institutionalized, more children are raised at home by their families, and there have been significant increases in community placements (Krantz, Bruininks, & Clumpner, 1979; Larson & Lakin, 1989). During this time, there have also been changes in the service delivery system that have resulted in the greater inclusion of persons with developmental disabilities in a variety of community settings. Unfortunately, as persons with mental retardation have moved out of state institutions and into community residences, they have often experienced a degree of social isolation that rivals what they encountered within institution placements (Bercovici, 1983). Despite social inclusion being a clearly articulated goal of normalization (Haney,

Preparation of this chapter was supported by a cooperative agreement (#H133B80048) between the National Institute on Disability and Rehabilitation Research (NIDRR) and the Research and Training Center on Residential Services and Community Living at the University of Minnesota (College of Education) located within the Institute on Community Integration. The opinions expressed herein are those of the authors.

1988; Rosen & Burchard, 1990) and evidence suggesting that persons with severe disabilities place great value on their social life and interactions with others (Edgerton, 1967; Edgerton & Bercovici, 1976; Edgerton, Bollinger, & Herr, 1984; Landesman-Dwyer & Berkson, 1984), little has been done to ensure that such individuals have the opportunity to develop close social ties (McKnight, 1989a; Strully & Strully, 1985).

In this chapter, the social relationships of persons with developmental disabilities are examined from a variety of perspectives, and the reader is introduced to a number of tools and/or strategies that have the potential to facilitate social inclusion. First, the nature of social relationships is briefly explored. Second, the reader is introduced to social network theory, a tool that holds great promise for assisting in the development of strategies to enhance social inclusion. Third, the functions of social relationships are discussed. Fourth, research pertaining to the social networks and relationships of persons with mental retardation is reviewed with special attention given to work that has emphasized the development of friendships. Fifth, a number of strategies are explored that, used in the proper context and with appropriate cautions, hold promise in assisting persons with developmental disabilities to build and maintain a network of social relationships that will meet their personal needs.

THE NATURE OF SOCIAL INCLUSION AND SOCIAL RELATIONSHIPS

The term "social inclusion," while appearing quite frequently in the literature during the last few years, has yet to be well-defined. Although attempts have been made to develop operational definitions (e.g., the daily frequency of contact with persons without disabilities who are not service providers), most efforts at defining social inclusion have fallen short primarily because of the highly personal, individualized nature of the construct itself. No guidelines exist for determining the degree, type, and context of social interaction necessary for an individual to feel included in, or a part of, a community. A set of social relationships that is sufficient to allow one individual to feel included may be totally insufficient for another.

While most theorists agree that social relationships form the basis of feelings of inclusion, the construct of social relationship itself is also difficult to define. Social relationships are by their very nature fragile. They are in a constant flux due to changes in the individuals involved (e.g., personal growth, change in interests) and due to transformations in the context in which interaction takes place (e.g., work versus a recreation-leisure environment). There are various types of social relationships that people develop, all of which, while serving similar functions, are in their own right unique. In studying the social relationships of individuals without disabilities, developmental psychologists (e.g., Hartup, 1983; Ladd, 1990) have made a distinction between acquaintanceships, peer relationships, and friendships. All of these forms of relationships are likely to play a role in social inclusion and are worthy of further attention.

The term "acquaintance" has been used in the social relationship literature to refer to a degree of familiarity between individuals (Hartup, 1983). An acquaintance is someone with whom one interacts on a regular basis, but is not especially close in the emotional sense. The relationships we establish with those with whom we work, go to school, or interact with on a professional basis are often of this type. The familiarity characteristic of acquaintance has been found to enhance social interaction, although the exact process, from infancy through adulthood, is not completely understood (Hartup, 1983).

The concept of *peer relations* is most often used to refer to an individual's acceptance, based on both popularity and status, by a group of same-age peers (Hartup, 1983). As early as the preschool years, groups of children have been found to be organized on this basis (Ladd, 1990). Levels of acceptance by peers attain stability in the early elementary school years and remain relatively stable well through adolescence (Hartup, 1983). During the past few years, a number of developmental psychologists (e.g., Asher & Parker, 1989; Parker & Asher, 1987) have postulated that poor peer relations in childhood (e.g., isolation or rejection by peers) may place individuals at risk of adjustment problems during adolescence and adulthood.

When most individuals consider social relationships, they think of *friendships*. Psychologists and sociologists studying this type of relationship have identified a number of qualities that characterize friendships and differentiate them from other types of social relationships. These include high frequency of interaction, stability in interaction over time, reciprocity, exchange of positive behaviors, and well-developed negotiation and conflict resolution strategies (Gersham & Hayes, 1983; Hartup, Lawsen, Stewart, & Eastenson, 1988; Hinde, Titmus, Easton, & Tamplin, 1985; Mannarino, 1980; Masters & Furman, 1981). The nature of friendship changes significantly over time as the individuals involved develop and mature. During the early years, it is characterized by mutual preference, contact seeking, and positive affect (Buysse, 1992; Howes, 1987). In adulthood, as friendships become more stable, reciprocity takes on greater importance and friendship interactions are characterized by mutual support, intimacy, and collaboration as the "I" and "you" of childhood become the "we" of adolescence and the adult years.

In summary, a wide variety of social relationships would appear to be necessary for the development of feelings of inclusion. These relationships vary with respect to frequency of contact, levels of intimacy, and the functions they serve. Social relationships also change dramatically over time as a result of changes in individuals and/or in the context in which interaction takes place. Experiencing a feeling of inclusion, however, is dependent not only on the affiliations one has with other persons, but also on the relationships these individuals have with each other. Understanding these interconnections and the manner in which they have an impact on the individual is the province of social network theory.

THE SOCIAL NETWORK CONSTRUCT

What is a social network? At its most simple level, it consists of that set of individuals with whom one interacts on a regular basis and perceives as important (McCallister & Fischer, 1974). A more in-depth understanding, however, is necessary if one is to understand and facilitate social inclusion. The literature has yet to produce a clear definition of the social network construct (Bott, 1971; Brownell & Shumaker, 1984; Cochran & Brassard, 1979; Lewis, 1982; Lewis & Feiring, 1978; Thoits, 1982). One aspect common to most definitions, however, is reference to the linkages or connections between an individual and the social units with whom the person has regular contact. Direct linkages between the target person and both the individuals and organizations with which he or she has contact, as well as the manner in which these individuals and organizations are interrelated, are represented. The social networks of a typical individual living in the community might include parents, siblings, and members of the extended family (e.g., grandparents, aunts, uncles, cousins); peers from education, work, and recreation-leisure environments; and neighbors and other community members with whom social interaction takes place on a less frequent, but nevertheless regular, basis.

House and his colleagues (House, Umberson, & Landis, 1988) suggest that an increase in clarity can be attained if the terms "social network" and "social inclusion" are used to represent the *structures* of social relationships. Social support, social conflict, and social regulation may then be considered social *processes* through which these structures have their effects. Social structures and processes, in turn, operate through more microscopic biological, psychological, and behavioral processes.

Review of the social network research literature suggests that a wide variety of variables are typically used to describe social networks. These include: network density (who within the network has contact with others in the network); network multistrandedness/multiplexity (the number of functions each individual within the network serves); frequency of contact; and overall size of the network (the number of individuals in the person's social network). These network descriptors tend to describe aspects of social integration and the content of social relations, as well as various aspects of the structure of an individual's network. As House et al. (1988) suggest, considerable confusion can be eliminated if a tripartite model or framework is used to conceptualize aspects of an individual's network of social contacts. In this framework, the term "social inclusion" refers to the existence or *quantity* of social ties or relationships. Attempts can then be made to distinguish the quantity of social relationships based upon the following: 1) type of relationship (e.g., kin versus nonkin, same gender versus opposite gender); 2) frequency of contact (e.g., daily, weekly, monthly); 3) size of network (i.e., the number of people in the network); and 4) recent losses or additions to the network.

Social network structure refers to the structure that characterizes a set of relationships. These structural properties can be either *dyadic* or *network* variables.

Dyadic variables that would appear to be important considerations include reciprocity of relationships, durability of relationships, and the homogeneity of dyads. Network variables of interest include: 1) network density (who within the network has contact with others in the network); 2) network multistrandedness (the number of functions each individual within the network serves); 3) network homogeneity; and 4) context of contact (e.g., school, church, formal versus informal group associations).

Relational content refers to the functional nature or quality of social relationships. Relational content may be distinguished in terms of its source (e.g., parent, friend, professional) and type, including: 1) social support (i.e., the positive aspects of social relationships, such as emotional support, instrumental aid, concern, information); 2) social conflict (i.e., the negative or conflictual aspects of relationships that may be stress-producing in and of themselves); and 3) social regulation (i.e., the controlling or regulating quality of social relationships).

The results of a variety of research efforts suggest that an individual's network of social relationships is influenced by numerous factors. These encompass characteristics of the individual as well as his or her environment. Individual characteristics found to influence social relationships include social skills, levels of extroversion and/or introversion, anxiety level, physical appearance, and locus of control, to name a few (Sarason, Sarason, Hacker, & Basham, 1985; Sarason, Sarason, & Shearin, 1986). Research results indicate that ecological factors, such as family size, residential location, the population and density of neighborhoods, and societal/community perceptions of members of particular groups (e.g., persons of color, individuals with disabilities) also have a significant impact on social relationships and networks (Abery, Thurlow, Johnson, & Bruininks, 1990; Bryant, 1985; Cochran & Brassard, 1979; McCallister & Fischer, 1974).

The Function of Social Relationships and Social Networks

The development of a supportive network of social relationships is important for a variety of reasons. Since the early 1980s, evidence has accumulated linking the quality and quantity of one's social network and social support resources to psychological and physiological outcomes including depression, psychological distress, job dissatisfaction, child abuse, and parenting styles (Broadhead et al., 1983; Caplan, 1974; Cohen & McKay, 1984; Cohen & Syme, 1985; Gottleib, 1985; House, Robbins, & Metzner, 1982; Kessler & McLeod, 1985; Kessler & Wethington, 1986; Pilisuk & Minkler, 1985; Sarason et al., 1986). In addition, such networks have been found to play crucial parts in stress reduction and effective coping (Cassel, 1976; Cobb, 1976; Cohen & McKay, 1984; Cohen & Willis, 1985, 1988; Mitchell, Billings, & Moos, 1982; Taylor, 1983), and to promote enhanced mental well-being (Caplan, 1974; Gottlieb, 1983; Hirsch, 1981; Mitchell & Trickett, 1981).

While an individual's social network serves a myriad of functions, one of the most important is the provision of social support. This concept, originally developed by researchers interested in the part played by psychosocial processes in the epidemiology of physical illness, is currently conceptualized as having a number of dimensions (Barrera, 1986).

Cobb (1976) provided one of the classic general definitions of social support, conceptualizing it as "information leading the subject to believe that he/she is cared for and loved, esteemed and valued, and belongs to a network of communication and social obligation" (p. 300). Pilisuk and Hillier Park (1985) define support as a set of exchanges that provide the individual with material and physical assistance, social comfort and sharing, and the sense that one is the continuing object of concern of others. In recent years, theorists have conceptualized social support as having a variety of distinct aspects and have attempted to specify how each of these might relate to stress, illness, and psychological adjustment (Barrera, 1986; Wheaton, 1985).

Berndt (1989) and others (e.g., Cohen, Mermelstein, Kamarck, & Hoberman, 1985) currently consider the construct of social support to have at least four relatively independent aspects. *Esteem/emotional support* refers to statements or actions that convince people of their own worth and value. Esteem/emotional support reaffirms the individual's sense of worth and assures him or her of a personal and separate identity. This aspect of support has also been referred to as emotional support because its goal is to make people feel better about themselves and assure them that they are loved and valued (Cobb, 1976, 1979; Thoits, 1982).

The concept of *informational support* refers to advice or guidance from others that is perceived as being helpful in solving problems (Berndt, 1989). This cognitively oriented form of support may involve suggestions on how to deal effectively with a personal problem, or it may suggest a referral to another individual within a person's social network who possesses the resources to help the individual effectively (Barrera, 1986; Hirsch, 1980). Depending on the task at hand, a person may solicit this type of support from family members, friends, or professionals (e.g., teachers, psychologists).

Instrumental support refers to the provision of resources or services that are necessary for solving practical problems. Referred to as tangible support by some individuals in the field, this aspect of social support involves the provision of concrete assistance to others (Cohen et al., 1985; Wellman, 1981). This may include financial aid, material resources, and needed services. Instrumental support plays an important role in that it may lead to the direct resolution of instrumental problems or result in increased time for activities that have the potential to facilitate relaxation (Cohen & Willis, 1985).

The fourth aspect of social support is most frequently referred to as *social companionship*. One of the most important forms of support, it involves the opportunity to share activities with another person or to have a companion who is supportive (Berndt, 1989). The individuals with whom one engages in common free-time activities and with whom one plays and recreates provide this aspect of support. Companionship may play an important role in reducing stress through fulfilling a need for affiliation and contact with others, by helping individuals distract themselves (thereby reducing time spent worrying), and through the facilitation of positive mood.

Social support is provided to an individual by way of interactions with members of one's social network. There are differences in the types of support provided by various individuals within a person's network. Furman and Robbins (1985) hypothesized that different types of relationships in one's network result in different social provisions to the individual (see Figure 1). Peer relations have the potential to provide the individual with instrumental aid, companionship, enhancement of worth, and nurturance. Friendships are capable of serving all of the functions of peer relations and, in addition, have the capacity to provide affection, intimacy, and reliable alliances. A sense of inclusion is postulated to be derived from a general set of social relationships developed with both close friends and peers with whom one is less intimate.

Recent research tends to support the notion that different social relationships serve different functions. Furman and Buhrmeister (1985), for example, found that companionship was judged as greater between friends than between parents and children, and that mothers and fathers were turned to for affection and enhancement of worth more frequently than friends. The results of other investigations

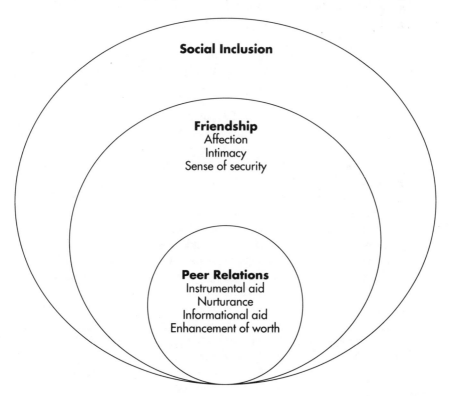

Figure 1. Provisions of social relationships. (Adapted from Furman & Robbins [1985].)

suggest differences with respect to other aspects of social support as well. Abery et al. (1990), for example, found that while support from mothers was noncontingent, social support from fathers, siblings, and friends was contingent upon a minimum degree of reciprocity having been established within the dyad. In addition, changes in both the degree of support provided by different individuals within the network and in who serves particular support functions have been found to be influenced by age (Furman & Bierman, 1984; Hunter & Youniss, 1982).

Social Relationships and Social Networks of Persons with Developmental Disabilities

Until recently, insufficient attention has been devoted to gaining an understanding of the personal and environmental factors that are critical to the development and maintenance of social relationships and social networks of persons with developmental disabilities. At the present time, we know relatively little about the nature of those relationships that are formed by such persons or the ecological factors that influence these interactions. A review of the available literature, however, does allow one to draw some tentative conclusions.

In general, the results of research on the community inclusion of persons with developmental disabilities demonstrate that limited community participation and relatively high degrees of social isolation are common themes in the lives of such individuals (Bogdan & Taylor, 1987; Crapps, Langione, & Swain, 1985; Lakin, Burwell, Hayden, & Jackson, 1992), and that physical integration does not guarantee that persons with developmental disabilities will establish and maintain desired social and interpersonal contacts with members of the community (Abery, Thurlow, Bruininks, & Johnson, 1989; Abery et al., 1990; Bercovici, 1981, 1983; Brunininks, Thurlow, & Lange, 1987; Bruininks, Thurlow, & Steffans, 1988; Hill et al., 1989; Hill, Rotegard, & Bruininks, 1984; Meyer, McQuarter, & Kishi, 1984; Rosen & Burchard, 1990).

The social networks of persons living in community residences typically include parents, siblings, fellow residents, professionals, and members of the community without disabilities (Abery et al., 1990). These networks have been found to be much smaller than those of individuals of similar age without disabilities and to contain significantly fewer reciprocal social relationships. Community-based activities, while relatively frequent, appear to take place primarily in large groups with fellow residents under the supervision of staff (Rosen & Burchard, 1990). Social contact between persons with disabilities and individuals other than staff or fellow residents appears to occur infrequently (Crapps & Stoneman, 1989; Donegan & Potts, 1988; Schalock & Lilley, 1986).

Research results also suggest significant differences in the composition of the social networks of persons with and without developmental disabilities. In a number of recent efforts (Abery et al., 1990; Rosen & Burchard, 1990), it has been found that the proportion of network members who are paid staff/professionals or family members is significantly greater for persons with developmental disabilities than for individuals with no disability label. For the most part, these professionals are residential service staff who, while viewed by residents as members of their networks, are seen as having control functions and are not perceived as providing sufficient social support. Family representation in these networks is significantly more likely than in the networks of persons without disabilities to be limited to parents (Abery et al., 1990).

A general lack of friendships between persons with mental retardation and typical members of the community has been reported in numerous studies. Horner, Dunlap, and Koegel (1988) for example, found that while 67 deinstitutionalized persons with developmental disabilities had an average of 12.3 important social relationships only .45 of these were neighbors. Similar studies (Abery et al., 1990; Hill et al., 1989) found that only 3% and 4% of the close friends of persons living in community settings were community members and that a majority of respondents did not have a single friend without a disability who was a member of the community. Despite a physical presence in the community, persons with developmental disabilities appear to have few close intimate relationships with persons without disabilities (Todd, Evans, & Beyer, 1990). This general lack of friendship with persons other than professionals and family members characterizes the lives of individuals with developmental disabilities whether they are receiving community-based services or are living at home with their families (Lakin et al., 1992). Even more unfortunate are research results that suggest that when persons with mental retardation do establish social relationships with typical members of the community, they often experience a difficult time maintaining those friendships (Kennedy, Horner, & Newton, 1989; Zetlin & Murtaugh, 1988).

For many years, it has been assumed that the lack of community inclusion experienced by persons with developmental disabilities was a direct result of the severity of the disability. It might therefore be assumed that factors such as level of mental retardation or number of disabilities would be powerful predictors of the degree to which a person experienced social inclusion. The results of recent research, however, suggest that this may not necessarily be the case. In a recent study, Parker and Boles (1990) found that for 50 residents living in eight supported community residences operating under the same service model, the specific residential site was a powerful predictor of both levels of community integration and social inclusion. Person-specific variables (i.e., level of mental retardation, number of disabling conditions) did not significantly predict either of these outcomes.

What is the impact of having a limited network of individuals upon whom to rely for support? The absence of an informal support network would likely have an adverse effect on the life of any individual, with or without a disability. The absence of such supportive relationships, however, could be expected to be especially critical to the community inclusion of persons with developmental disabilities. High intensity, reciprocal, multidimensional bonds with others are typically found to be the most reliable sources of social and emotional support (Bott, 1971; Broadhead et al., 1983; Cauce, 1986; Cohen & Willis, 1985; Heller & Swindle, 1983; Tolsdorf, 1976).

In his classic study of deinstitutionalized persons with mental retardation, Edgerton (1967) found that the majority of individuals with a high degree of community inclusion were persons who had a community benefactor. This friend and advocate served as a bridge builder, easing the individual's inclusion into the community by creating opportunities for the development of social networks and removing barriers to integration. Few examples of such relationships have been found in other research efforts involving persons with developmental disabilities (Abery et al., 1990; Malin, 1982; Mest, 1988), with the majority of individuals primarily relying on staff or fellow residents for support. Those affiliations of the benefactor type that do develop appear to be more serendipitous in nature, rather than a result of programming (Bogdan & Taylor, 1987).

The most common friendships established by persons with mental retardation, outside of those with staff and family, are those with other persons with developmental disabilities (Abery et al., 1989; Hill & Bruininks, 1981; Lakin, Anderson, & Hill, 1988; O'Connor, 1976; Willer & Intagliata, 1984). This appears to hold true regardless of the age of the persons involved. Individuals report drawing significant amounts of support from these friendships. Unfortunately, in many cases, these friendships are context-bound, failing to generalize to settings beyond those in which they are initially generated (Abery et al., 1990) and they may not have the capacity to provide the individual with the degree of social support that he or she needs (Burchard & Hutchins-Fuhr, 1990; Rosen & Burchard, 1990; Zetlin & Murtaugh, 1988).

In addition, professionals in disability-related fields have a history of failing to appreciate the importance of these relationships. At a direct service level, this often results in the separation of persons who have well-developed friendships with little forethought and a lack of support for finding ways to maintain these relationships (e.g., providing transportation). A good number of the academic community would also appear to implicitly devalue relationships between persons with disabilities. An examination of recent applied research in the area of social relationships, for example, reveals that the large majority of studies focus almost exclusively on the development of social relationships between persons with and without disabilities.

The results of those studies reviewed emphasize the passive, solitary, family-dependent nature of many persons with mental retardation. They suggest a need to examine the social and interpersonal networks of such individuals and to identify effective interventions that will promote a stronger sense of inclusion and belonging within programs and communities. Before this can be accomplished, however, those factors that contribute to the exclusion of persons with developmental disabilities must be understood so that they might be removed or their influence minimized.

FACTORS INFLUENCING SOCIAL INCLUSION

The social isolation of persons with mental retardation and their associated lack of skills in developing and maintaining supportive social networks have many facets and contributing factors. In the past, the majority of work conducted in this area has concentrated on the skill deficits of persons with disabilities, primarily focusing on adaptive behavior and related social skills (Craig & McCarver, 1984; Hill et al., 1989; Holman & Bruininks, 1985). Hill and his colleagues (Hill et al., 1989), for example, found that higher levels of adaptive behavior and less severe levels of retardation were associated with significantly greater social inclusion. Research results suggest that a variety of other individual characteristics may result in the social isolation of persons with developmental disabilities, including higher levels of shyness and avoidance (Taylor, Asher, & Williams, 1987); a greater incidence of inappropriate social behavior (Gottleib, Semmel, & Veldman, 1978; Siperstein, Bak, & O'Keefe, 1988; Taylor et al., 1987); deficits in social perception (Kronick, 1978); low levels of academic competence (Budoff, Siperstein, & Conant, 1979; Gottlieb et al., 1978); and physical appearance (Siperstein et al., 1988).

Deficits in the social skill area have long been considered to be the primary reason that persons with disabilities lead socially isolated lives and often experience difficulties in employment (Gaylord-Ross & Chadsey-Rusch, 1991) and independent living (Gaylord-Ross & Haring, 1987). When persons with disabilities experience job loss, it is often found to be a result of social rather than production problems (Greenspan & Shoultz, 1981; Hanley-Maxwell, Rusch, Chadsey-Rusch, & Renzaglia, 1986). Additional barriers to social inclusion related to the personal characteristics of persons with developmental disabilities have been found to include the following: insufficient social skills to successfully access environments in the community within which friendships are made (Schloss, Smith, & Kiehl, 1986); a lack of knowledge regarding community programs (Schleien & Ray, 1988); and inadequate transportation skills (Schleien & Ray, 1988). Social inclusion may also be inhibited by the self-perceptions of persons with disabilities. Zetlin and Turner (1985), for example, found that as individuals with developmental disabilities reach adulthood, they became more aware of their limitations and differences, resulting in possible increases in anxiety in social situations.

While past research has focused on the characteristics of persons with disabilities as the primary limiting factor related to social inclusion, recent work highlights the negative impact of societal attitudes and perceptions of persons with developmental disabilities. A rather consistent finding of peer acceptance research is that persons without disabilities have more negative attitudes toward individuals with disabilities than toward peers without disabilities (Goodman, Gottleib, & Harrison, 1972; Gottleib, 1975; Wisley & Moregan, 1981). Persons with mental retardation are perceived by community members as exhibiting less favorable social behaviors and being less physically attractive; therefore, they are more likely to be rejected by peers than other community members (Gibbons, 1985; Sabornie & Kaufman, 1987). Societal attitudes appear especially nonaccepting when social relationships are involved. In a survey focusing on the acceptance of persons with disabilities by the general public, Roth and Smith (1983) found that although 95% of the participants sampled thought that persons with mental retardation could be successfully employed, only 63% believed that they had the right to date, and fewer still (41%) were of the opinion that they had the right to marry. These negative attitudes appear to increase as children mature into adolescents and adults.

Meyer and Putnam (1987) reported that while 40% of a sample of elementary school students indicated that they would voluntarily interact with a peer with a disability, only 15% of a high school sample indicated the same.

It has only been in recent years that researchers have begun to consider the impact that the systems and environments in which persons with mental retardation function have on social inclusion. In work that focused on the nature of the residential setting itself, Willer and Intagliata (1981) found significantly higher rates of social inclusion among persons residing in homes in which practical skills were taught and where fewer residents lived. Other research suggests that the degree to which typical community members are included in the social networks of adults with mental retardation is influenced by the type of community placement, with individuals living in foster homes being more likely to have these types of relationships (Hill et al., 1989). However, this type of placement may be a mixed blessing in that at least two research efforts have found that although persons living in family and foster settings have significantly more relationships with neighbors and members of the community, they are significantly more likely than residents of small community residences to be identified as having no friends (Hill et al., 1989; Lakin et al., 1992).

On a broader systemic level, social inclusion is influenced by the extent to which the service system promotes and provides opportunities for such interactions. Human services agencies have a long record of removing and isolating people who are perceived as different or "deviant" (Wolfensberger, 1975). McCord (1982) persuasively argues that human service agencies pinpoint and label the differences exhibited by individuals with special needs; isolate them (thus, excusing society from responsibility for their care and support); develop programs to control rather than to empower; and teach such individuals acceptance of their status and isolation. This orientation enables programs to maintain the status quo and survive. Available research tends to support this notion. Most support programs are developed and managed in such a fashion as to limit the contact that persons with developmental disabilities have with community organizations (e.g., social clubs, recreation programs). In addition, there have been few efforts by existing community agencies to reduce the social isolation of individuals with severe disabilities (Bruininks & Lakin, 1985; Bruininks et al., 1988; Certo, Schleien, & Hunter, 1983; Halpern, Close, & Nelson, 1986).

If human services personnel, educators, and families are sincerely interested in improving the quality of life of persons with developmental disabilities, opportunities to develop and maintain social relationships must be provided continuously from an early age. In order to fully participate in the community, one must be given opportunities to develop a sense of belonging and connectedness with others or risk feeling as if they are a temporary visitor. Limited community participation and social isolation are the themes common in the lives of far too many adults with developmental disabilities. Recent studies demonstrate increasing social isolation of individuals with disabilities, even with expanded options for living within community settings (Bruininks & Hill, 1981; Bruininks & Lakin, 1985;

Bruininks et al., 1987; Halpern et al., 1986). Unless effective programs to facilitate the development and maintenance of supportive relationships are developed and implemented, the goal of full inclusion in the community will remain unrealized.

INCLUSION: WEAVING THE TAPESTRY OF COMMUNITY

Assisting a person to become a full and accepted member of his or her community is a process that is best described in metaphorical terms. It is the careful weaving of uniquely sized and textured threads into a beautiful and valuable tapestry. Tapestries are treasured for their worth and beauty. The value of the weaving is much more than the sum of the individual threads. In human tapestries, we are weaving an interconnectedness and interdependence among people. A community is quite literally a tapestry of human relationships that capitalizes on each individual's capacities and abilities. In working to facilitate inclusion, one must seek to build a strong community in which all individuals have the opportunity to prosper and in which the inclusion of a single individual is a direct enhancement to the strength of the whole community. The ultimate goal is to weave together the threads—all human beings—to form a new tapestry—a community in which everyone has the opportunity to thrive.

The Service System Dilemma

An understanding of social inclusion and the manner in which it relates to individuals with developmental disabilities requires a comprehension of the difference between living in the community and living within the service system. For those who live in the community, social relationships are based on—*common values and beliefs, trust, and interdependence*. For many persons with disabilities, however, relationships are typically with people who are paid to be in their lives. These relationships are based on authority, control, and dependence. This contrast results in drastic differences in the quality and quantity of social relationships a person establishes and makes it difficult to develop a "common ground" between persons with and without disabilities (McKnight, 1987, 1989a, 1989b). It is only when one is able to move beyond the typical service system mode of thinking, and focus instead on the personal beliefs, values, and visions of *individuals*, that assistance that will allow persons to develop a sense of inclusion and value, and to become interdependent parts of the community, can be provided.

Service systems typically do not, and often cannot, work in this manner. Relationships within the service system context are grounded in lines of authority, to include the making of decisions, the creation and management of policies and procedures, and the dissemination and accounting of a finite amount of resources. To receive services, an individual must fit a predetermined needs description. The system then applies a predetermined service prescription describing how, what, when, where, and by whom the service will be delivered (McKnight, 1989a). This process often becomes rigid, in that services cannot be easily or quickly renegotiated, redesigned, stopped, or started without a lengthy process of professional involvement and/or litigation. Often, service systems provide their product only to those individuals who can politically and/or legally leverage the right to receive services. Today in Minnesota, for example, there are hundreds of people with developmental disabilities on waiting lists because there is no money to serve them.

In conversations with many individuals employed by human services systems, the concept of the least restrictive environment (LRE) is often brought forth as an example of how those systems serving persons with developmental disabilities are actively working toward social inclusion. The LRE principle specifies a continuum of services and environments "specifically designed" to meet the needs of individuals with disabilities of varying types and levels of severity. These environments range from fully segregated to fully inclusive, with a variety of options between. Theoretically, as a person's abilities and/or needs change, he or she is moved to a different level of the service continuum.

Taylor (1988), however, clearly points out that the LRE principle may actually support segregation. First, in containing a presumption in favor of the LRE, the LRE principle implies that there are circumstances under which restrictive environments are in fact appropriate. Second, the principle equates segregation with more intensive services and integration with less intensive services instead of indicating that the intensity of services should be determined by the needs of the individual and the environment in which they are participating. Third, the LRE principle is based on a "readiness model." Implicit in this model is the assumption that people with developmental disabilities must earn the right to move to the LRE. Fourth, the principle supports the primacy of professional decision making. Inclusion, however, is ultimately based upon values rather than the decisions of professionals. Fifth, when applied categorically to persons with developmental disabilities, the LRE principle sanctions infringements on the basic rights to freedom and community participation beyond those imposed on persons without disabilities. Sixth, the principle implies that people must move as they develop and change. Persons with developmental disabilities sometimes move to LREs because new programs open or space is needed to accommodate persons with more severe disabilities. This often destroys any sense of home and permanency that the individual has developed, disrupting relationships with roommates, neighbors, and friends. Seventh, the LRE principle directs attention to physical settings rather to the services and supports people need to be integrated into the community. By its very name, the principle of the LRE emphasizes facilities and environments designed specifically for persons with developmental disabilities.

Each of the identified shortcomings of the LRE principle can lead directly or indirectly to the exclusion of persons with developmental disabilities from their communities and from relationships with friends, neighbors, and others. When service systems are undertaking inclusionary processes or are attempting to support the inclusion of a person, those representing the system need to be acutely aware of these potential issues so that they can be avoided or overcome. In closing his discussion of the LRE principle, Taylor (1988) writes:

The principle of the least restrictive environment was extremely forward-looking for its time. . . . It is now time to find new ideas, concepts, and principles to guide us. . . . Now we must define the challenge in terms of total integration for people with developmental disabilities. As a social policy direction, integration means the elimination of social, cultural, economic, and administrative barriers to community integration and the design of services and supports to encourage, rather than impede, relationships between people with developmental disabilities and nondisabled people. (p. 50)

As it exists today, the system that provides services to persons with developmental disabilities does not supply the support necessary for the building of friendships or the creation of a sense of community inclusion. If the goal of our society is truly one of full inclusion, efforts to facilitate the development and maintenance of the social relationships of persons with developmental disabilities must be based on values and beliefs that promote the development of trusting and interdependent relationships between community members.

Enhancing Social Inclusion: A Person-Centered Process

To understand the process of enhancing social inclusion, it is crucial to first frame the manner in which it is perceived. How, for example, does one know if and when a person is included and supported to the degree necessary to thrive in their community? What frame of reference or paradigm should be used to assess the individual's current degree of inclusion or whether full inclusion has been attained? A useful frame of reference can be drawn from the Latin root or definition of the word *assess*—"to sit beside, assist in the office of a judge" (*Webster's New Collegiate Dictionary*, 1991, p. 67). A careful examination of this definition sets apart three constructs that are useful in framing this issue. First, one's duty, as a professional or advocate, is 'to sit beside' the individual and attempt to see through his or her eyes and to understand his or her world as he or she sees it. This means that the observer must come to know the individual's:

Values and beliefs
Goals and objectives
Power to make decisions
Physical abilities
Resources

Second, one must join the individual in his or her natural environment. Observation and work with the person must take place where he or she typically spends his or her time so that insight can be gained and the who, what, where, why, and when of the person's life put into perspective. Third, professionals must recognize and value the fact that the individual and his or her family have the final authority as to quality of life. Furthermore, we must ensure that, along with the individual, the individual's family, friends, and loved ones are empowered to be major assistants and decision makers. These persons, after all, are directly affected by any change in the person's life.

Inclusion Processes and Strategies

There is no quick fix that can be prescribed to enhance the social inclusion of persons with developmental disabilities. A process, tool, or technique that works with one individual may not be effective with another. This may, at times, lead to frustration on the part of an inclusion facilitator. It is, however, unavoidable—a result of uniqueness of the social needs of each individual. Keeping in mind that all individuals with or without disabilities are unique and that a network of social relationships that meets the needs of one person is unlikely to meet the needs of another, it becomes clear that a successful inclusion facilitator must have available numerous strategies to facilitate an individual realizing his or her own personal vision of social inclusion. Not every individual will need to be the recipient of intensive intervention efforts. A number of persons with disabilities with whom the authors have worked, for example, have been able to create their own means of enhancing social inclusion through setting priorities on building friendships and finding the supports that would allow them to do so. The only facilitation necessary involved stimulating the process of the individual and their circle of significant others, crystallizing the individual's vision of inclusion and beginning discussions of how to make it happen. In one family's case, a parent who spent 2 hours speaking to one of the authors about her daughter's situation. This conversation primarily centered on a mother's desire to see more friends in her daughter's life. The discussion ranged from how family members might reprioritize their personal and family goals to make this dream a reality, to an exchange related to steps the family could take to better utilize resources for social inclusion currently available within their community. This parent returned 2 years later with a story of how she had gone back to her family with a stronger vision, which was sufficient for the family to begin to create a new life for their daughter.

In the remainder of the chapter, several intervention approaches and tools that have proven successful in enhancing the social inclusion of persons with developmental disabilities are examined. The first is referred to as a person-centered planning process. The second strategy is based upon sociometry. Also reviewed are community mapping and the utilization of social inclusion facilitators, two tools and/or strategies that can be of use when either person-centered inclusion planning or sociometric techniques are employed. The difference between the two processes and the value of each are best explored by considering the role a facilitator plays in the environment and the type of environment in which the individual is being included. Person-centered planning is an excellent tool that facilitates a holistic approach to inclusion engaging the friends, family, and community of the focus person to explore and expand new opportunities for inclusion in all areas of the individual's life. This process is utilized most effectively when there is a desire or a need to focus on multiple domains of a person's life. Sociometric processes are likely to be most valuable in cases in which the environment into which the person is being integrated is overseen or structured by a leader or teacher. Classrooms, residences, and recreational programs are examples of the types of environments in which sociometric processes have been successfully used by the authors to empower participants to restructure arrangements to enhance inclusion.

A Person-Centered Approach to Inclusion Planning

During the past 10 years, a number of person-centered planning processes have been developed and successfully used to enhance the inclusion of individuals with developmental disabilities. The McGill Action Planning System (MAPS) (Forest & Lusthaus, 1987; Vandercook, York, & Forest, 1989); Personal Futures Planning (PFP) (Mount, 1987; Mount & Zwernik, 1988); and Life-Style Planning (LSP) (O'Brien, 1987; O'Brien & Lyle, 1987) are variants of group brainstorming and empowerment processes. The MAPS process has been used extensively by Forest and her colleagues to develop and implement inclusive educational programs for children and youth with disabilities. PFP and LSP have been used with adults with developmental disabilities to facilitate the generation of service plans that more adequately meet their needs and foster a higher quality of life through greater inclusion within a variety of community settings.

The MAPS, PFP, and LSP processes all begin with the recruitment and preparation of a small group of family members, friends, and significant professionals to come together and work with the focus person to brainstorm ideas for enhancing their life. Each of the members of this group is viewed as having an intimate and unique knowledge of the individual.

The initial phases of person-centered planning sessions typically require each participant to articulate their special knowledge and understanding of the focus individual. This often occurs as part of a review of the individual's life history through the eyes of each member of the group (Forest & Lusthaus, 1987; O'Brien, Forest, Snow, & Hasbury, 1989). Engaging in this activity allows the group to gather information about the individual's current relationships, where the individual spends time, and his or her likes and dislikes, interests, gifts, and abilities. Participants then concentrate on how the focus person can contribute to others and on the assistance and/or accommodations that they may need to enhance their inclusion.

Creating a *vision* is a necessary step that must be accomplished before one can determine *how* to go about creating opportunities for enhanced inclusion (Amado, Conklin, & Wells, 1990; Forest & Lusthaus, 1987; Mount, 1987). As a result, the second phase of person-centered planning entails the group developing or creating a vision, or dream, for the focus individual. This vision is a highly personalized view of what the individual wants for him- or herself and what the group wants for the individual, with respect to a network of social relationships. At times, these visions are quite large and encompass almost every aspect of the person's life. In other cases, they are quite simple and may consist of nothing more than the individual wanting to establish one close friendship. In a group focusing on social inclusion, the creation of this vision might entail open discussion of the kind of community, quantity, and type of social relationships, as well as the degree of support and intimacy, that would be necessary for the person in question to develop and maintain a sense of inclusion.

During this phase of person-centered planning, some facilitators (e.g., Vandercook et al., 1989) also encourage planning groups to initiate discussion of the *worst nightmare* members have pertaining to outcomes for the focus individual. This serves to validate the anxiety that many participants have regarding the future of those individuals with developmental disabilities to whom they are close and often results in the group being able to better prioritize during the planning stage of the process so that the probability of this worst-case scenario is minimized.

The initial phases of person-centered planning often take a full 3-hour session or longer to complete. Upon completion, the facilitator, the focus person, and members of the planning group should have an in-depth knowledge of the individual, their needs, and their personal vision for life within the community. The task then shifts into an ongoing intervention phase that engages the group in the development of a plan the goal of which is to make the focus person's vision a reality. By carefully directing the discussion, the facilitator guides the group through barriers to inclusion, assisting participants to create solutions that will promote acceptance of the focus person.

Developing an *action plan* is the beginning of the intervention phase of person-centered inclusion planning and involves the group deciding *what* can be done to enhance the focus person's social inclusion and *how* this can be accomplished (Amado et al., 1990; Mount & Zwernik, 1988; O'Connell, 1988, 1990). Based on the vision created for the individual, group members must first decide on the particular environmental contexts the individual frequents or would like to frequent that are most likely to yield social relationships and enhance feelings of inclusion. Some environments are more conducive to the development of social ties than others. Frequenting a local coffee shop that has regular patrons, for example, is probably more likely to lead to the development of friendships than going out to a restaurant that does not have repeat clientele or one where people "eat and run."

The planning group will also need to determine the specific types of ties and connections that will be most likely to enhance the individual's feelings of belonging in the community. Amado et al. (1990) and the Ordinary Life Working Group (1988) have delineated a number of different types of ties and connections that might be useful to think of in this regard (see Table 1). Each type of connection has the potential to uniquely contribute to one's sense of social inclusion. For some individuals, membership in one or more organizations may serve their needs, for others the most appropriate strategy may be to facilitate the development of new relationships. A third individual may maximally benefit from the strengthening of existing friendships. The specific type of connection(s) that best meets the needs of a particular individual must be determined by the person in question in conjunction with other members of the inclusion planning group.

Following identification of the specific type(s) of connections that will be the initial focus of intervention efforts, the group needs to explore a variety of connect-

Table 1. Types of connections

Type	Definition
Friendships	Having strong ties including friends and "best" friends
Acquaintances	Having a network of individuals with whom one associates and has familiarity
Membership	Being a member of organizations and/or associations
Keeping in touch	Belonging to a variety of social worlds by keeping aware of trends and interests
Being part of a family	Active involvement in family life
Having a partner	Having a relationship with an individual to whom a long-term commitment has been made
Being a neighbor	Living next door or close to others with whom one has contact
Recognition	Recognizing and being recognized by others in the community

Adapted from Amado, Conklin, & Wells (1990).

ing strategies or methods that can be used to enhance the social life of the focus individual (Amado et al., 1990; O'Connell, 1990). It must be remembered, however, that there is no set formula for determining the specific types of strategies that will be most effective in enhancing inclusion. This is likely to be different for each individual based upon his or her personal vision of social inclusion.

In most cases, if one of the goals of the focus person is the development of new relationships, ongoing activities that are available in the community can serve as a starting point for increasing levels of inclusion. Community associations such as cultural groups, church organizations, and recreation and leisure clubs can serve as contexts for the development of social relationships. As Amado et al. (1990) caution, however, person-centered inclusion planning groups need to be careful to focus on opportunities for relationship-building rather than on activities.

Throughout the inclusion planning and implementation process, the group facilitator and other participants continue to meet, though not necessarily as a complete group, to ensure that the inclusion plan developed is effectively implemented and that changes are made when necessary. One strategy often used by the authors is to facilitate the formation of subgroups who agree to take responsibility for overseeing the implementation of particular aspects of the more comprehensive intervention plan. These persons communicate with each other on a regular basis to implement their assigned aspects of the intervention plan, as well as to keep the entire group abreast of the activities in which they are engaged. The intervention phase of person-centered planning continues until the focus person and the group decide that the vision created at initial meetings (in this case, the development of a sense of social inclusion) has been achieved.

The process of person-centered planning is by its very nature flexible. The person-centered planning group may vary in size and membership in accordance with current needs and goals. New people are recruited and invited to join as the group or new members express an interest in participation. The goals and needs of the focus person may change as they become more included and as they experience an enhanced sense of empowerment to participate in the community. The group may dissolve after a period of time and reform later to assist the focus person when problems or issues arise. Regardless of its membership, or how often it meets, person-centered planning will only be effective if both participants and the facilitator have a working knowledge of their roles. The facilitator serves in the role of navigator, making sure that the course charted by the individual with a disability and significant others is the course followed. Most important, the vision of participants drives the entire planning process.

The Role of the Inclusion Facilitator   To be or act inclusively is to be grounded in the interaction between one's personal actions and beliefs (see Figure 2). The focus is on one's *actions*, as well as on one's *belief system*. An individual's actions may be viewed as being either active or passive, and the individual's beliefs are viewed as either exclusive and oppressive or inclusive and welcoming. A person who is actively exclusive is bigoted, while an individual who is passively exclusive is conforming. A person who is actively inclusive is an inclusion advocate, while those who are passive in their actions and inclusive in their beliefs are viewed as conformists. From this perspective, to be an advocate for inclusion, one must not only have inclusive beliefs, but must be rigorous and immediate in one's inclusive behavior. If a person's actions are passive, for example, or they respond by advocating inclusion for some and not others, they are exclusionary in their behavior.

What are the characteristics of a successful inclusion facilitator? McKnight (1989a) has identified five specific attributes that seem to contribute to the degree to which such individuals experience success in enhancing inclusion. First, successful inclusion facilitators focus on the gifts and capacities of those who have been excluded and use these positive characteristics to introduce the newcomers to the community. Second, a community guide needs to be well-connected and well-trusted within their community, even though he or she is not a representative of the service system. Third, inclusion facilitators must be able to develop relationships of trust rather than those based on the authority of systems, for it is this trust that will help define the path to inclusion. Fourth, a guide needs to believe that the community is filled with hospitality for strangers. Fifth, a successful inclusion facilitator must learn to leave the person he or she guides so that the community can surround the person and a sense of interdependence can develop.

The role of an inclusion facilitator is multifaceted. The individual must draw on his or her accumulated and organized residue of experience, allow the freedom for relationships to happen, approach the process without a rigid set of theories and processes, and be maximally responsive to authenticity and growth impulses. A facilitator must also recognize that the integrity of the individual and his or her family must be respected at all costs. The individual must write his or her own

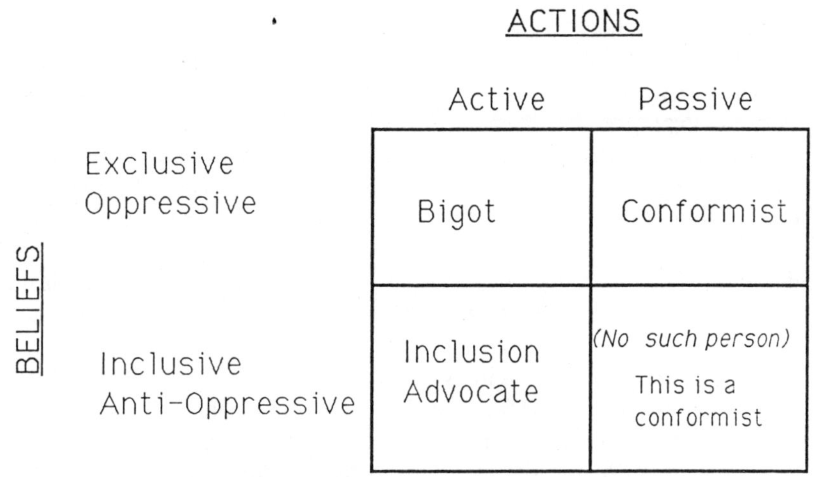

ACTIONS

	Active	Passive
Exclusive Oppressive	Bigot	Conformist
Inclusive Anti-Oppressive	Inclusion Advocate	*(No such person)* This is a conformist

BELIEFS

Figure 2. The beliefs and actions of the inclusion facilitator.

destiny. "The facilitator is a coach, *but* is not playing on the team" (Whitaker, 1976, p. 163). Facilitators must work *with* individuals (and, when appropriate, with their families) *where* they are at, and with processes that *empower* them to choose their own destiny and *how* they will achieve their vision.

The Role of the Participant The participant is the most important part of person-centered planning. The interest, enthusiasm, and commitment of those taking part in the planning process will ultimately determine the success of the plan developed. How can one effectively participate in person-centered planning? Are there prerequisites that one must have, a certain type of knowledge or expertise? Is it appropriate to speak one's mind or to disagree with the focus person or other experts who attend planning sessions?

How can one most effectively contribute to the planning process? Several thoughts summarized by staff from the Study Circles Resource Center (1990) should be kept in mind. First, in order to work effectively together, participants need to develop a relatively high level of comfort with other members of the person-centered inclusion planning group. This will depend on each individual's familiarity with other participants, not just as acquaintances or members of the same organization, but as peers in this particular group with its own special history and fellowship. It is therefore crucial for group members to develop a sense of cohesion. This will only evolve if participants view and treat each other as equals, attend all planning sessions, listen carefully to each other, and give all group members the chance to speak.

Second, the facilitator of a person-centered planning group is responsible for guiding the discussion, summarizing key ideas, and soliciting clarifications of unclear points. However, he or she may need advice on when this is necessary and to what extent. It is likely that when one group member does not understand what someone has said, others have also not understood. Through communicating their needs to the facilitator, participants not only will have the opportunity to clarify points that they themselves do not understand, but will also, in effect, be facilitating a greater degree of understanding for the group as a whole.

Third, while it is the facilitator's role to ensure that the opinions of all group members are taken into consideration, participants themselves can facilitate this process. Through addressing content-oriented remarks to the group rather than to the facilitator and being willing to question others to learn more about their ideas, participants increase the likelihood that all persons will stay involved. This enhances the probability that quieter individuals, who may have special insight, will be heard.

Fourth, when any group of individuals gets together, it is likely that differences in opinion will occur. However, this should not be perceived as a negative occurrence since differences can invigorate the group, especially when it is relatively homogeneous on the surface. By challenging ideas with which they disagree, while at the same time maintaining an open mind and striving to understand why others may have different opinions, group members can create a synergistic environment in which the ultimate product of the group far exceeds that of each individual.

Sociometry

The authors have successfully employed person-centered planning processes to enhance the inclusion of individuals with disabilities who are not members of currently existing social groups. With similar success, when an individual is a member of an existing social group and the goal is one of increasing positive social interaction between participants with and without disabilities, sociometry can be an extremely effective tool to facilitate enhanced inclusion.

Sociometry (Moreno, 1934; Murray, 1953) is a group reconstruction process that identifies qualitative social dimensions within a given group of individuals. These dimensions include group cohesiveness, the existence of subgroups or cliques, interpersonal attractions and rejections among members, and the social ranking of each group member by his or her peers. Beyond the study of group structure, this technique has proven quite valuable as a means to assess and promote the inclusion of individuals both with and without disabilities (Schleien, Fahnestock, Green, & Rynders, 1990).

The sociometric process allows an inclusion facilitator to assess a preexisting group and identify isolated and excluded members. The facilitator can then restructure and integrate these identified individuals through the use of what has been termed an empowerment process. More specifically, in this process, each group member is empowered to restructure the group through the use of a social criterion. Social criteria are carefully constructed questions that request, in a confidential manner, specific information concerning the individual's social relationships (Connolly, 1983; Morrison, 1981). This information is then used to alter subgrouping arrangements (e.g., seating arrangements, partner arrangements, teammates, and workmates) to enhance the social dynamics of the group. Further-more, sociometric measurements are conducted to evaluate the inclusion of the originally isolated and excluded group members. This process can be used throughout the life of the group to continually empower the members to enhance their own social experiences.

Six rules for using the sociometric process have been suggested (Hart, 1976; Moreno, 1934).

1. The limits of the group in which the assessment is given should be indicated (describe who can be chosen).
2. There should be unlimited choices of other people (select as many peers as appropriate).
3. Individuals should be asked to choose or reject other group members with a specific criterion in mind (choose people based on a specific criterion/ question).
4. The results of the sociometric assessment should be used to restructure the group (the group should be reorganized by placing people together who have chosen each other).
5. The opinions (i.e., selections) of group members should be kept confidential.
6. Questions should be phrased in such a way that all members can understand.

An example of a sociogram of a group is illustrated in Figure 3. This socio-gram depicts a group of participants who were planning a 5-day wilderness trip. The group facilitator used the sociometric process in order to more fully under-stand the social dynamics of the group, to empower members to select the camp-site partners, and to enhance the inclusion of participants. The specific social cri-terion questions used by the facilitator in this situation were quite simple and included the following: 1) "With whom would you like to set up a campsite?", and 2) " With whom do you not want to set up camp?" Participants were informed that they could choose from all of the people who were on the trip and requested to nominate as many people as they wished. Each participant filled out a $3'' \times 5''$ card with their answers to the previous questions. These were collected by the facilita-tor. The facilitator then constructed a sociogram using the initials of each partici-pant and arrows to indicate the direction of each choice. If two participants chose each other, the arrowheads were eliminated and a slash was marked across the center of the line. If a participant indicated that he did not want to camp with a particular individual, a dashed line with an arrow recorded the rejection.

Inspection of the sociogram in Figure 3 indicates that: 1) there are two "stars" within the group (SS and MK)—these individuals were most frequently chosen by others; 2) three mutual attractions exist within the group (between KM-MK, SS-RG, and MF-JR); 3) two "isolates" are present (PD and JS) who were not se-lected by the others; and 4) one member of the wilderness group (TS) was rejected and not chosen by any group members.

Provided with this information, an inclusion facilitator can then begin the process of restructuring the group to enhance the inclusion of isolated/rejected

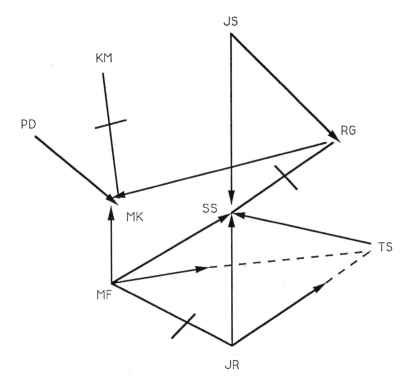

Figure 3. Sociometric measurement of a group's relationships.

members. To restructure the group in question, a facilitator might begin by focusing on the rejected and isolated members (TS, PD, and JS). This was accomplished in the following manner (see Figure 4). The group facilitator first attempted to stimulate interaction between the isolated/rejected members of the group and other group members by pairing together isolates, those persons selected as their first choices of camping partners, and a third individual who was selected by the nonisolate of the pair. At the same time, a concerted effort was made to draw isolates away from contact with those group members who rejected them. Remaining participants were then assigned camping positions based on the sociometric data in a manner such that isolates were located closest to those individuals with whom they expressed the greatest interest in interacting.

Following the initiation of an inclusion-enhancing intervention, a facilitator can check on the success of restructured groupings by conducting informal interviews and by observing interactions among participants. In the case in question, the leader evaluated the impact of group restructuring through observations, personal interviews, and additional sociometric measurements at the midway point of the wilderness trip and at its conclusion. Adaptations can be made at any point in the sociometric assessment process when deemed necessary. For example, pic-

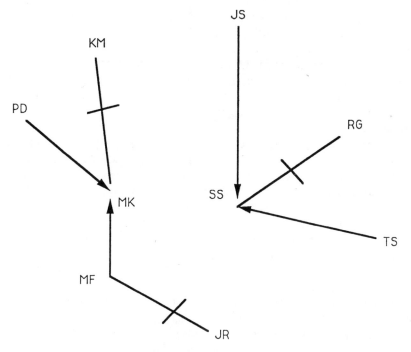

Figure 4. Restructured groups based on member's choices.

tures of participants rather than names can be used when assessing the social networks of individuals with developmental disabilities who have poorly developed expressive language (Hart, 1976).

Social Inclusion Facilitators and Community Mapping

Two additional connecting strategies and/or tools that the authors have utilized quite successfully in recent years are the recruitment, training, and use of social inclusion facilitators and community mapping. Social inclusion facilitators (Abery & Lundeen, 1991), also referred to as "bridgebuilders" (Amado et al., 1990) and "community guides" (McKnight, 1989a) are individuals with an in-depth knowledge of and connections with the community. They recognize and are recognized by other community members and are well-respected by their peers. Social inclusion facilitators may become friends with the persons with whom they work, but their primary responsibility is to facilitate the individual's making connections with other people of his or her choosing in the community. They have the potential to introduce the focus person to community members without disabilities, facilitate the removal or minimization of barriers to inclusion, aid in the problem solving that will inevitably be required to integrate the individual more fully into the community, and serve as an advocate for the person with whom they are working (Abery & Lundeen, 1991; Amado et al., 1990).

Social inclusion facilitators are most effective when they are not service providers, but regular community members. This is due to the fact that, in many instances, the roles of service providers will be directly at odds with the goal of enhanced inclusion (McKnight, 1989a, 1989b). Taking a relatively large group of adults with developmental disabilities into the community, for example, is much more cost-effective than having a staff person accompany one person on a neighborhood experience. The former approach, however, is unlikely to facilitate the development of social relationships.

Where might one recruit inclusion facilitators? At the University of Minnesota's Institute on Community Integration, undergraduate students have been successfully trained to assume this role and have been instrumental in enhancing the social inclusion of more than 60 persons with developmental disabilities during the past 4 years. All participants in the Community Service Training Program commit to a full academic year of instruction and working to facilitate the community inclusion of persons with disabilities. After a period of basic training, students are paired with one or more young adults with developmental disabilities who have similar interests and who reside in their neighborhood. These dyads work together for the remainder of the year to develop and implement strategies designed to enhance inclusion. Participants can take part in the program on a volunteer basis or register for academic credit based on the number of hours they work. A similar program involves training high school juniors and seniors to serve in this role with peers with developmental disabilities (Abery & Schoeller, 1991).

Community mapping is a tool that can be used by inclusion facilitators as well as others in order to gain a better understanding of the people, places, and associations that provide the individual with a sense of belonging. It is a process that allows those working with the focus person to truly understand in what contexts and from whom he or she gains his or her sense of inclusion. A relatively simple procedure, community mapping begins with the focus individual being asked to give their inclusion facilitator a tour of their community. This may be a tour in the literal sense with visits to physical locations that the individual frequents on a regular basis or it can be figurative in nature. An individual's community map may consist of a well-defined geographic region (e.g., the neighborhood) or may be defined by the persons from whom support is available on a regular basis. During a period of time, a visual representation is created of people and environments that have the potential to create a sense of belonging and inclusion for the individual. Facilitators working with the focus person can then concentrate their efforts on promoting the development of relationships with specific persons within these environments and/or may use these contexts as avenues through which to further develop existing relationships.

By developing a community map with a young man with a developmental disability, one of the authors found that a local garage/service station and the individuals who worked there formed the primary community for this young man. The information was then used to recruit an individual from that community to serve as a social inclusion facilitator for the person in question. Once trained, this individual, through his community connections, was able to successfully expand the number of contexts in which the person with whom he was working experienced a sense of belonging. The focus individual joined a local billiards league and was integrated into one of its teams. The socializing that occurred during tournaments served as an excellent context for the building of social relationships and enhanced feelings of inclusion. As multiple connections were made by the focus person, his social inclusion facilitator gradually faded his involvement. This has progressed to the extent that, at the present time, the facilitator and the young man see each other only occasionally when the latter makes visits to the garage.

A Case Study: Enhancing Mark's Social Inclusion

The following example of a person-centered inclusion plan is drawn from a plan that the authors have facilitated. The names, events, and places have been changed to protect the privacy of the individuals involved.

Mark is a 32-year-old man who was living in a suburban community outside of a large mid-western city. As we learned in the planning process, he had lived in 22 different group homes and institutions since moving out of his family's home at the age of 17. The major reason he lived in so many settings was that he was reported to engage in challenging behaviors that were injurious to both himself and others, as well as damaging to property. When staff at his most recent residence decided that they could not handle him anymore, it appeared that he would be transferred to another group home or back to a state institution.

When the authors met Mark, he was taking part in a vocational training program within a segregated work site for persons with disabilities. He was interested in meeting new people, in finding a "real" job in the community, and in getting more involved in "fun things" in the neighborhood. The person-centered process began with the creation of a circle of friends diagram that included all the people who Mark knew and had gotten to know since joining his new service provider and moving into his apartment. The diagram included people to whom he felt very close, people who were acquaintances that he would like to get to know better, and those individuals who were paid to be in his life. From this diagram, Mark chose the persons whom he wanted to be involved in the person-centered plan and get to know better.

Mark and the facilitators then invited these people to come and participate in his planning process. They were given the questions that would be discussed beforehand so that they could think about their answers. The first questions were informational in nature and sought to "paint a picture" of Mark. They included questions such as: Who is Mark? What is Mark's history? What words describe Mark? What are Mark's strengths and abilities? What does he like to do? Where does Mark go in the community? What choices does Mark make and what choices are made by others? These questions allowed all members of the group to get to know Mark from a variety of perspectives since many participants knew him in only a single context. As the discussion progressed, a holistic picture began to emerge of a dynamic person with many capacities.

The person-centered inclusion planning group next focused on developing a vision for Mark. Questions used to gather information that would be helpful to Mark in developing a personal vision of social inclusion included: What is Mark's dream? What is our dream for Mark? What is Mark's nightmare? What do we worry about for Mark? What would an ideal day look like for Mark? These questions allowed Mark and his circle to explore ideas and visions that could later be developed into specific activities in which participants could get involved with Mark. After considerable discussion, Mark was able to clearly articulate his dream to the planning group. It consisted of a social network that included two to three new friends with whom he could engage in his favorite pasttimes of fishing, playing basketball, and listening to music, as well as more frequent contact with an acquaintance he had made while living at another residence.

The vision created for Mark led the group into the third phase of person-centered inclusion planning—the creation and implementation of action plans. Questions used to facilitate brainstorming in this phase of planning focused on "*who* will do *what* and *when?*" Questions used included: What are our long-term, 3, 5, and 10 year goals? Where do we want to be in 1 year? 6 months? 3 months? What is our first step? How can we grow stronger? Whom do we need to enroll to make this a success? These questions sought to identify who might be interested in helping work toward specific goals and to engage them in assisting Mark to pursue them. Mark's father and brother, both of whom enjoyed many of the same leisure activities as he did, expressed interest in facilitating Mark to meet and get acquainted with persons in the community with similar leisure interests. One of the staff members at his new residence indicated that she would attempt to facilitate Mark getting back into contact with his old acquaintance and finding a job that would be both more enjoyable and more likely to lead to the development of social relationships with members of the community.

The process next shifted into the development of short-term tasks for which participants would take responsibility and the scheduling of additional meetings for the facilitators and Mark to get together to report on progress, determine new tasks, and brainstorm new ideas to overcome barriers that have appeared. For Mark's plan, several subgroups were formed to focus on different goals that were developed. These groups worked on such things as finding Mark a new job, finding new recreational and social activities in the neighborhood and community, identifying and trying to build new friendships, strengthening old friendships, and looking for volunteer opportunities in which Mark could participate.

The subgroups set their own schedules to accomplish tasks and reconvened as a whole to celebrate and discuss what was happening. The gatherings were done at Mark's apartment or in comfortable community settings with food and drinks that added to the celebration and sense of friends and community. Mark found a new job, one that he located and applied for on his own. His circle of friends helped him fill out the forms, and prepare for his interview and the first day of work. They stayed with him as he struggled with learning new skills and dealt with unfriendly coworkers. They celebrated his first paycheck and helped him open his own bank account. Other members of the circle asisted him in finding a volunteer job walking dogs and cats for a local veterinarian. Animals were always a great love of his, but his apartment complex did not allow animals. His volunteer activity allowed him to contribute and to share his love of animals.

Mark has now moved into a new apartment that is more centrally located. His circle of friends has changed as old friends moved away and new ones entered his life. The entire person-centered planning group is not currently meeting as the majority of Mark's goals are being realized and as he has many friends who are involved in his life. Mark and the members of his inclusion group know, however, that if the need arises they are still available. Celebrations now occur at holidays, birthdays, and major events, such as weddings. Mark has become a member of the crew, one of the friends, and an important part of the community.

CONCLUSION

Person-centered inclusion planning, sociometry, social inclusion facilitators, and the circle of friends and community mapping strategies are tools that, when used appropriately and in the right circumstances, have the potential to enhance the social inclusion of persons with disabilities. It must be remembered, however, that they will only be successful if used by individuals who view inclusion in the community as a right to which all individuals are entitled and who are committed to seeing this value put into practice. The increased use, in recent years, of the processes and strategies highlighted in this chapter is encouraging because of their environmental focus. The intent of these techniques is to affect changes in the targeted individual's *environment* in order to make that environment more accessible and conducive to learning, socialization, friendship development, and inclusion. This represents a new way of thinking about the social relationships of persons with developmental disabilities and about what needs to take place to enhance inclusion in the community.

It is all too often the case in today's society that persons with developmental disabilities are not afforded the opportunity to establish and maintain friendships. Despite research results revealing that individuals with severe disabilities value friendships, profit from them and, in most cases, have the skills necessary to engage in sustained social interaction, rich social networks are the exception rather than the rule for children, youth, and adults with developmental disabilities.

Why is this case? Some researchers (e.g., McKnight, 1989a, 1989b) place the onus squarely on the shoulders of the service system. The problem may be deeper than this, however, perhaps lying within society as a whole. In a country in which differences more often than not are used to exclude others, it is not surprising that persons with developmental disabilities are often not warmly accepted into the community. The service system, as it currently exists, is merely a reflection of this unaccepting society. Can service providers be expected to make social inclusion a priority if it is not a priority within our society? The strategies highlighted in this chapter, while effective, must be regarded as stop-gap measures that, it is hoped, will at some point in the near future, be unnecessary.

REFERENCES

Abery, B.H., & Lundeen, R. (1991). Promoting social inclusion beyond the school community. *IMPACT*, *4*(3), 16–17.
Abery, B.H., & Schoeller, K. (1991). *The "Yes I Can" Program: Promoting the social inclusion of youth with disabilities*. Minneapolis: University of Minnesota, Institute on Community Integration.
Abery, B.H., Thurlow, M.T., Bruininks, R.H., & Johnson, D.R. (1989, December). *A descriptive study of the social networks of youth and young adults with developmental disabilities*. Paper presented at the meeting of The Association for Persons with Severe Handicaps, San Francisco, California.
Abery, B.H., Thurlow, M.T., Johnson, D.R., & Bruininks, R.H. (1990, May). *The social networks of adults with developmental disabilities residing in community settings*. Paper presented at the annual meeting of the American Association on Mental Retardation, Washington, DC.
Amado, A.N., Conklin, F., & Wells, J. (1990). *Friends*. St. Paul, MN: Human Services Research and Development Center.
Asher, S.R., & Parker, J.G. (1989). Significance of peer relationship problems in childhood. In B.H. Schneider, G. Attil, J. Nadel, & R.P. Weissberg (Eds.), *Social competence in developmental perspective*. Amsterdam: Kluwer Academic Publishing.
Barrera, M. (1986). Distinctions between social support concepts, measures, and models. *American Journal of Community Psychology*, *14*, 413–445.
Bercovici, S.M. (1981). Qualitative methods in cultural perspectives in the study of deinstitutionalization. In R.H. Bruininks, C.E. Meyers, B.B. Sigford, & K.C. Lakin (Eds.), *Deinstitutionalization and community adjustment of mentally retarded people* (Monograph #4, pp. 133–144). Washington, DC: American Association on Mental Deficiency.
Bercovici, S.M. (1983). *Barriers to normalization: The restrictive management of retarded persons*. Baltimore: University Park Press.
Berndt, T.J. (1989). Obtaining support from friends during childhood and adolescence. In D. Belle (Ed.), *Children's social networks and social supports* (pp. 308–311). New York: John Wiley & Sons.
Bogdan, R., & Taylor, S.J. (1987). The next wave. In S.J. Taylor, D. Biklen, & J. Knoll (Eds.), *Community integration for people with severe disabilities*. New York: Teachers College Press.
Bott, E. (1971). *Family and social networks* (2nd ed.). New York: Free Press.
Broadhead, W.E., Berton, B.H., Jeams, S.A., Wagner, E.H., Schoenbach, V.H., Grimson, R., Heyden, S., Tibblin, G., & Gehbach, S.H. (1983). The epidemiologic evidence for a relationship between social support and health. *American Journal of Epidemiology*, *117*(5), 521–537.
Brownell, A., & Shumaker, S.A. (1984). Social support: An introduction to a complex problem. *Journal of Social Issues*, *40*, 1–9.
Bruininks, R.H., & Hill, B.K. (1981). *Family leisure and social activities of mentally retarded people in residential facilities*. Minneapolis: University of Minnesota, Department of Psychoeducational Studies.
Bruininks, R.H., & Lakin, K.C. (Eds.). (1985). *Living and learning in the least restrictive environment*. Baltimore: Paul H. Brookes Publishing Co.
Bruininks, R.H., Thurlow, M.L., & Lange, C. (1987). *Outcomes for students with moderate-

severe handicaps in an urban school district. Minneapolis: University of Minnesota, University Affiliated Program.

Bruininks, R.H., Thurlow, M.L., & Steffans, K. (1988). *Follow-up of students after schooling and suburban special education district: Outcomes for people with moderate to severe handicaps.* Minneapolis: University of Minnesota, Institute on Community Integration.

Bryant, B.K. (1985). The neighborhood walk: Sources of support in middle childhood. *Monographs of the Society for Research in Child Development, 50* (Serial No. 210).

Budoff, M., Siperstein, G.N., & Conant, S. (1979). Children's knowledge of mental retardation. *Education and Training of the Mentally Retarded, 14,* 277–281.

Burchard, S.N., & Hutchins-Fuhr, M. (1990, December). *Comparison of characteristics of social support and personal satisfaction over three years for adults living in community settings.* Paper presented at the annual conference of The Association for Persons with Severe Handicaps, Chicago, Illinois.

Buysse, V. (1992). *Friendships of young children with disabilities in community based child care settings.* University of North Carolina, Chapel Hill. Unpublished doctoral dissertation.

Caplan, G. (1974). *Support systems and community mental health.* New York: Behavioral Publications.

Cassel, J. (1976). The contribution of the social environment host resistance. *American Journal of Epidemiology, 102*(2), 107–123.

Cauce, A. (1986). Social network and social competence: Exploring the effects of early adolescent friendships. *American Journal of Community Psychology, 14,* 607–628.

Certo, N., Schleien, S., & Hunter, D. (1983). An ecological assessment inventory to facilitate community recreation participation by severely disabled individuals. *Therapeutic Recreation Journal, 17,* 29–38.

Cobb, S. (1976). Social support as a moderator of life stress. *Psychosomatic Medicine, 38*(5), 300–314.

Cobb, S. (1979). Social support and health through the life course. In M.W. Riley (Ed.), *Aging from birth to death.* Boulder, CO: Westview Press.

Cochran, M., & Brassard, J.S. (1979). Child development and personal social networks. *Child Development, 50,* 601–616.

Cohen, A., & McKay, G. (1984). Social support, stress and the buffering hypothesis: A theoretical analysis. In A. Baum, J.E. Singer, & S.E. Taylor (Eds.), *Handbook of psychology and health* (Vol. 4) (pp. 253–268). Hillsdale, NJ: Lawrence Erlbaum.

Cohen, S., Mermelstein, R., Kamarck, T., & Hoberman, H.N. (1985). Measuring the functional components of social support. In I. Sarason & B. Sarason (Eds.)., *Social support: Theory, research, and applications* (pp. 73–94). Dordrecht, Netherlands: Martinus Nijhoff.

Cohen, S., & Syme, L.S. (1985). *Social support and health.* New York: Academic Press.

Cohen, S., & Willis, T.A. (1985). Stress, social support, and the buffering hypothesis. *Psychological Bulletin, 97,* 310–357.

Connolly, J.A. (1983). A review of sociometric procedures in the assessment of social competencies in children. *Applied Research in Mental Retardation, 4,* 315–327.

Craig, E.M., & McCarver, R.B. (1984). Community placement and adjustment of deinstitutionalized clients: Issues and findings. In N.R. Ellis & N.W. Bray (Eds.), *International review of research in mental retardation* (pp. 19–31). New York: Academic Press Inc.

Crapps, J., Langione, J., & Swain, S. (1985). Quantity and quality of participation in community environments by mentally retarded adults. *Education and Training of the Mentally Retarded, 20,* 123–129.

Crapps, J.M., & Stoneman, Z. (1989). Friendship patterns and community integration of family care residents. *Research in Developmental Disabilities, 10,* 153–169.

Donegan, C., & Potts, M. (1988). People with mental handicap living alone in the community: A pilot study of their quality of life. *British Journal of Mental Subnormality, 34,* 10–22.

Edgerton, R.B. (1967). *The cloak of competence: Stigmas in the lives of the mentally retarded.* Berkeley: University of California Press.

Edgerton, R., & Bercovici, S. (1976). The cloak of competence: Years later. *American Journal of Mental Deficiency, 80*(5), 485–497.

Edgerton, F., Bollinger, M., & Herr, B. (1984). The cloak of competence after two decades. *American Journal of Mental Deficiency, 88,* 345–351.

Forest, M., & Lusthaus, E. (1987). The kaleidoscope: Challenge to the cascade. In M. Forest (Ed.), *More education/integration* (pp. 1–16). Downsview, Ontario: G. Allan Roeher Institute.

Furman, W. (1982). Children's friendships. In T.M. Field, A. Huston, H.C. Quay, L. Troll, & G.E. Finley (Eds.), *Review of human development* (pp. 327–339). New York: Wiley.

Furman, W., & Bierman, K.L. (1984). Children's conceptions of friendship: A multimethod study of developmental changes. *Developmental Psychology, 20,* 925–931.

Furman, W., & Buhrmeister, D. (1985). Children's perceptions of the qualities of sibling relationships. *Child Development, 56,* 448–461.

Furman, W., & Robbins, P. (1985). What's the point? Issues in the selection of treatment objectives. In B. Schneider, K. Rubin, & J. Ledingham (Eds.), *Children's peer relations: Issues in assessment and intervention* (pp. 41–54). New York: Springer-Verlag.

Gaylord-Ross, R., & Chadsey-Rusch, J. (1991). Measurement of work-related outcomes for students with severe disabilities. *Journal of Special Education, 25,* 291–304.

Gaylord-Ross, R., & Haring, T. (1987). Social interaction research for adolescents with severe handicaps. *Behavioral Disorders, 12,* 264–275.

Gersham, E.S., & Hayes, D.S. (1983). Differential stability of reciprocal friendships and unilateral relationships among preschool children. *Merrill-Palmer Quarterly, 29*(2), 169–177.

Gibbons, F.X. (1985). Stigma perception: Social comparison among mentally retarded persons. *American Journal of Mental Deficiency, 90*(1), 98–106.

Goodman, H., Gottlieb, J., & Harrison, R.H. (1972). Social acceptance of EMRs integrated into a non-graded elementary school. *American Journal of Mental Deficiency, 76,* 412–417.

Gottlieb, B. (1985). Social support and community mental health. In S. Cohen & S.L. Syme (Eds.), *Social support and health* (pp. 303–326). New York: Academic Press.

Gottlieb, B.H. (1983). *Social support strategies: Guidelines for mental health practice.* Beverly Hills, CA: Sage.

Gottlieb, J. (1975). Public, peer and professional attitudes toward mentally retarded persons. In M.J. Begab & S.A. Richardson (Eds.), *The mentally retarded and society: A social science perspective* (pp. 99–125). Baltimore: University Park Press.

Gottlieb, J., Semmel, M.I., & Veldman, D. (1978). Correlates of social status among mainstreamed mentally retarded children. *Journal of Educational Psychology, 70,* 396–405.

Greenspan, S., & Shoultz, G. (1981). Why mentally retarded adults lose their jobs: Social competence as a factor in work adjustment. *Applied Research in Mental Retardation, 2*(1), 23–28.

Halpern, A.S., Close, D.W., & Nelson, D.J. (1986). *On my own: The impact of semi-independent living programs for adults with mental retardation.* Baltimore: Paul H. Brookes Publishing Co.

Haney, J.I. (1988). Toward successful community residential placements for individuals with mental retardation. In L.W. Heal, J.I. Haney, & A.R. Novak-Amado (Eds.), *Integration of developmentally disabled individuals into the community* (2nd ed.) (pp. 126–168). Baltimore: Paul H. Brookes Publishing Co.

Hanley-Maxwell, C., Rusch, F.R., Chadsey-Rusch, J., & Renzaglia, A. (1986). Reported factors contributing to job terminations of individuals with severe disabilities. *Journal of The Association for Persons with Severe Handicaps, 12,* 280–286.

Hart, J.W. (1976). Identifying ways of distinguishing "choice activity" from "closure movements" when administering pictorial sociometric techniques (PST) to the mentally retarded. *Group Psychotherapy, Psychodrama and Sociometry, 29*, 121–126.

Hartup, W. (1983). Peer relations. In E. Hetherington (Ed.) & P. Mussen (Series Ed.), *Handbook of child psychology* (Vol. 4) (pp. 103–196). New York: John Wiley & Sons.

Hartup, W.W., Lawsen, B., Stewart, M.I., & Eastenson, A. (1988). Conflict and the friendship relations of young children. *Child Development, 51*, 1590–1600.

Heller, K., & Swindle, R.W. (1983). Social networks, perceived social support and coping with stress. In R.D. Felner, L.A. Jason, J. Montsugu, & S.S. Farber (Eds.), *Preventive psychology: Theory, research and practice in community intervention* (pp. 67–91). Elmsford, NY: Pergamon Press.

Hill, B.K., & Bruininks, R.H. (1981). *Physical and behavioral characteristics and maladaptive behavior of mentally retarded people in residential facilities.* Minneapolis: University of Minnesota, Department of Psychoeducational Studies.

Hill, B.K., Lakin, K.C., Bruininks, R.H., Amado, A.N., Anderson, D.J., & Copher, J. (1989). *Living in the community: A comparative study of foster homes and small group homes for people with mental retardation* (Report No. 29). Minneapolis: University of Minnesota, Center for Residential and Community Services.

Hill, B.K., Rotegard, L.L., & Bruininks, R.H. (1984). The quality of life of mentally retarded people in residential care. *Social Work, 29*(3), 275–281.

Hinde, R.A., Titmus, G., Easton, D., & Tamplin, A. (1985). Incidence of friendship and behavior toward strong associates versus nonassociates in preschoolers. *Child Development, 56*, 234–245.

Hirsch, B.J. (1980). Natural support systems and coping with major life changes. *American Journal of Community Psychology, 8*(2), 159–172.

Hirsch, B. (1981). Social networks and the coping process. In B. Gottlieb (Ed.), *Social networks and social support.* Beverly Hills, CA: Sage.

Holman, J.E., & Bruininks, R.H. (1985). Assessing and training adaptive behaviors. In K.C. Lakin & R.H. Bruininks (Eds.), *Strategies for achieving community integration of developmentally disabled citizens* (pp. 73–104). Baltimore: Paul H. Brookes Publishing Co.

Horner, R.H., Dunlap, G., & Koegel, R.L. (Eds.). (1988). *Generalization and maintenance: Life-style changes in applied settings.* Baltimore: Paul H. Brookes Publishing Co.

House, J.S., Robbins, C., & Metzner, H.M. (1982). The association of social relationships and activities with mortality: Prospective evidence from the Tecumseh Community Health Study. *American Journal of Epidemiology, 116*, 123–140.

House, J.S., Umberson, D., & Landis, K.R. (1988). Structure and process of social support. *Annual Review of Sociology, 14*, 293–318.

Howes, C. (1987). Social competence with peers in young children: Developmental sequences. *Developmental Review, 7*, 252–272.

Hunter, F.T., & Youniss, J. (1982). Changes in functions of three relations during adolescence. *Developmental Psychology, 18*, 806–811.

Kennedy, C.H., Horner, R.H., & Newton, C. (1989). Social contacts of adults with severe disabilities living in the community: A descriptive analysis of relationship patterns. *Journal of The Association for Persons with Severe Handicaps, 14*(3), 190–196.

Kessler, R.C., & McLeod, J.D. (1985). Social support and mental health in community surveys. In S. Cohen & S.L. Syme (Eds.), *Social support and health* (pp. 219–240). New York: Academic Press.

Kessler, R.C., & Wethington, E. (1986). Perceived support, received support, and adjustment to stressful life events. *Journal of Health and Social Behavior, 27*, 78–89.

Krantz, G.C., Bruininks, R.H., & Clumpner, J.L. (1979). *Mentally retarded people in state-operated residential facilities: Year ending June 20, 1978*, Project Report #4. Minneapolis: University of Minnesota, Department of Psychoeducational Studies.

Kronick, D. (1978). An examination of psychosocial aspects of learning disabled adolescents. *Learning Disabilities Quarterly*, *1*, 86–93.

Ladd, G. (1990). Having friends, keeping friends, making friends, and being liked by peers in the classroom. Predictors of children's early school adjustment. *Child Development*, *61*, 1081–1100.

Lakin, K.C., Anderson, D.J., & Hill, B.K. (1988). *Community integration of older persons with mental retardation*. Minneapolis: University of Minnesota, Research and Training Center on Community Living.

Lakin, K.C., Burwell, B.O., Hayden, M.F., & Jackson, M.E. (1992). *An independent assessment of Minnesota's home and community based services waiver program* (Project Report #37). Minneapolis, MN: Center for Residential Services and Community Living.

Landesman-Dwyer, S., & Berkson, J. (1984). Friendships and social behavior. In J. Wortis (Ed.), *Mental retardation and developmental disabilities: An annual review* (Vol. 13). New York: Plenum Press.

Larson, S.A., & Lakin, K.C. (1989). Deinstitutionalization of persons with mental retardation: The impact on daily living skills. *Journal of The Association for Persons with Severe Handicaps*, *14*(4), 324–332.

Lewis, M. (1982). The social networks system model: Toward a theory of social development. In T.M. Fields, A. Huston, H.C. Quay, L. Trowl, & E. Finely (Eds.), *A review of human development*. New York: Wiley Interscience.

Lewis, M., & Feiring, C. (1978). The child's social world. In R.M. Lerner & G.D. Spanier (Eds.), *Child influences on marital and family interaction: A life-span perspective*. New York: Academic.

Malin, N.A. (1982). Symposium on changes of environment: Personal and social consequences: III. Group homes for mentally handicapped adults: Residents' views on contacts and support. *British Journal of Mental Subnormality*, *28*, 29–34.

Mannarino, A.P. (1980). The development of children's friendships. In H.C. Foot, A.J. Chapman, & J.R. Smith (Eds.), *Friendship and social relations in children*. New York: Wiley.

Masters, J.C., & Furman, W. (1981). Popularity, individual friendship selection, and specific peer interaction among children. *Developmental Psychology*, *17*(3), 131–148.

McCallister, L., & Fischer, C.S. (1974). A procedure for surveying personal networks. *Sociological Methods & Research*, *7*, 131–148.

McCord, W.T. (1982). From theory to reality: Obstacles to the implementation of the normalization principle in human services. *Mental Retardation*, *20*(6), 247–253.

McKnight, J. (1987). Regenerating community. *Social Policy*, *17*, 54–58.

McKnight, J. (1989a). Do no harm: Policy options that meet human needs. *Social Policy*, *20*(1), 5–15.

McKnight, J. (1989b). Regenerating community. *Social Policy*, *20*(1), 54–58.

Merriam-Webster. (1991). *Webster's collegiate dictionary* (9th Edition). Springfield, MA: Merriam-Webster.

Mest, G.M. (1988). With a little help from their friends: Use of social support systems by persons with mental retardation. *Journal of Social Issues*, *44*, 117–125.

Meyer, L., McQuarter, R., & Kishi, G. (1984). Assessing and teaching social interaction skills. In W. Stainback & S. Stainback (Eds.), *Integration of severely handicapped students with their nondisabled peers: A handbook for teachers*. Reston, VA: Council for Exceptional Children.

Meyer, L., & Putnam, J. (1988). Social integration. In V.B. Van Hasselt, P.S. Strain, & M. Hersen (Eds.), *Handbook of developmental and physical disabilities* (pp. 103–133). New York: Pergamon Press.

Mitchell, R.E., Billings, A.G., & Moos, R.H. (1982). Social support and well-being: Implications for prevention programs. *Journal of Primary Prevention, 3*(2), 77–98.

Mitchell, R.E., & Trickett, E. (1980). Social networks as indicators of social support: An analysis of the effects and determinants of social networks. *Community Mental Health Journal, 18*, 27–44.

Moreno, J.L. (1934). *Who shall survive?* Washington DC: Nervous and Mental Disease Publishing.

Morrison, G.M. (1981). Perspectives of social status of learning-handicapped and nonhandicapped students. *American Journal of Mental Deficiency, 86*, 243–251.

Mount, B. (1987). *Personal futures planning: Finding directions for change* (Doctoral dissertation, University of Georgia). Ann Arbor, MI: UMI Dissertation Information Service.

Mount, B., & Zwernik, K. (1988). *It's never too early, it's never too late.* St. Paul, MN: Metropolitan Council, Publication No. 421-88-109.

Murray, H. (1953). The sociometric stability of personal relations among retarded children. *Sociometry, XVI*(2), 113–141.

O'Brien, J. (1987). A guide to life-style planning: Using *The Activities Catalog* to integrate services and natural support systems. In B. Wilcox & G.T. Bellamy, *A comprehensive guide to The Activities Catalog: An alternative curriculum for youth and adults with severe disabilities* (pp. 175–189). Baltimore: Paul H. Brookes Publishing Co.

O'Brien, J., Forest, M., Snow, J., & Hasbury, D. (1989). *Action for inclusion: How to improve schools by welcoming children with special needs into regular classrooms.* Toronto, Ontario, Canada: Centre for Integrated Education.

O'Brien, J., & Lyle, C. (1987). *Framework for accomplishment.* Decatur, GA: Responsive Systems Associates.

O'Connell, M. (1988). *The gift of hospitality: Opening the doors of community life to people with disabilities.* Evanston, IL: The Community Life Project, Center for Urban Affairs and Policy Research, Northwestern University.

O'Connell, M. (1990). *Community building in Logan Square: How a community grew stronger with the contributions of people with disabilities.* Evanston, IL: The Community Life Project, Center for Urban Affairs and Policy Research, Northwestern University.

O'Connor, G.O. (1976). *Home is a good place: A national perspective on community residential facilities for developmentally disabled persons.* Washington, DC: American Association on Mental Deficiency.

Ordinary Life Working Group. (1988). *Ties and connections.* London: King's Fund Centre.

Parker, J.G., & Asher, S.R. (1987). Peer relations and later personal adjustment: Are low-accepted children at risk? *Psychological Bulletin, 102*, 357–389.

Parker, R., & Boles, S. (1990). Integration opportunities for residents with developmental disabilities: Differences among supported living sites and residents. *Education and Training in Mental Retardation, 25*(2), 76–82.

Pilisuk, M., & Hillier Park, S. (1985). Support networks: The measure of caring. *Academic Psychology Bulletin, 7*, 337–360.

Pilisuk, M., & Minkler, M. (1985). Supportive ties: A political economy perspective. *Health Education Quarterly, 12*(1), 93–106.

Rosen, J.W., & Burchard, S.N. (1990). Community activities and social support networks: A social comparison of adults with and without mental retardation. *Education and Training in Mental Retardation, 25*, 193–204.

Roth, R., & Smith, T.E. (1983). A statewide assessment of attitudes toward the handicapped and community living programs. *Education and Training of the Mentally Retarded, 18*(3), 164–168.

Sabornie, E.J., & Kaufman, J.M. (1986). Social acceptance of learning disabled adolescents. *Learning Disabilities Quarterly, 9*, 55–60.

Sarason, B.R., Sarason, I.G., Hacker, T.A., & Basham, R.B. (1985). Concomitants of social support: Social skills, physical attractiveness, and gender. *Journal of Personality and Social Psychology*, *49*(2), 469–480.

Sarason, I.G., Sarason, B.R., & Shearin, E.N. (1986). Social support as an individual difference variable. *Journal of Personality and Social Psychology*, *50*(4), 845–855.

Schalock, R.L., & Lilley, M.A. (1986). Placement from community-based mental retardation programs: How well do clients do after 8 to 10 years? *American Journal of Mental Deficiency*, *90*, 669–676.

Schleien, S.J., Fahnestock, M., Green, R., & Rynders, J.E. (1990, Fourth Quarter). Building positive social networks through environmental interventions in integrated recreation programs. *Therapeutic Recreation Journal*, *24*(4), 42–52.

Schleien, S.J., & Ray, M.T. (1988). *Community recreation and persons with disabilities: Strategies for integration*. Baltimore: Paul H. Brookes Publishing Co.

Schloss, P.J., Smith, M.A., & Kiehl, W. (1986). Rec. club: A community centered approach to recreational development for adults with mild to moderate retardation. *Education and Training of the Mentally Retarded*, *21*(4), 282–288.

Siperstein, G.N., Bak, J.J., & O'Keefe, P. (1988). Relationship between children's attitudes toward and their social acceptance of mentally retarded peers. *American Journal of Mental Retardation*, *93*(1), 24–27.

Strully, J., & Strully, C. (1985). Friendship and our children. *Journal of The Association for Persons with Severe Handicaps*, *10*, 224–227.

Study Circles Resource Center. (1990). *The role of the participant*. Pomfret, CT: Author.

Taylor, A.R., Asher, S.R., & Williams, G.A. (1987). The social adaptation of mainstreamed mildly retarded children. *Child Development*, *58*, 1321–1334.

Taylor, S.E. (1983). Adjustment to threatening events. *American Psychologist*, *38*, 1161–1173.

Taylor, S.J. (1988). Caught in the continuum: A critical analysis of the principle of the least restrictive environment. *Journal of The Association for Persons with Severe Handicaps*, *13*(1), 41–53.

Thoits, P.A. (1982). Conceptual, methodological, and theoretical problems in studying social support as a buffer against life stress. *Journal of Health and Social Behavior*, *23*(2), 145–149.

Todd, S., Evans, G., & Beyer, S. (1990). More recognised than known: The social visibility and attachment of people with developmental disabilities. *Australian and New Zealand Journal of Developmental Disabilities*, *16*(3), 207–218.

Tolsdorf, C.C. (1976). Social networks, support, and coping: An exploratory study. *Family Process*, *15*, 407–417.

Vandercook, T., York, J., & Forest, M. (1989). MAPS: A strategy for building the vision. *Journal of The Association for Persons With Severe Handicaps*, *14*(3), 205–215.

Wellman, B. (1981). Applying network analysis to the study of support. In B.H. Gottlieb (Ed.), *Social networks and social support* (pp. 171–200). Beverly Hills: Sage.

Wheaton, B. (1985). Models for the stress-buffering functions of coping resources. *Journal of Health and Social Behavior*, *26*, 352–364.

Whitaker, C., M.D. (1976). The hindrance of theory in clinical work. In P.J. Guerin, Jr., M.D. (Ed.), *Family therapy theory and practice* (pp. 154–164). New York: Gardner Press, Inc.

Willer, B., & Intagliata, J. (1981). Social environment as predictors of adjustment of deinstitutionalized mentally retarded adults. *American Journal of Mental Deficiency*, *86*, 252–259.

Willer, B., & Intagliata, J. (1984). *Promises and realities for mentally retarded citizens: Life in the community*. Baltimore: University Park Press.

Wisley, D.W., & Moregan, S.B. (1981). Children's ratings of peers presented as mentally retarded and physically handicapped. *American Journal of Mental Deficiency*, *86*, 281–286.

Wolfensberger, W. (1975). *The origin and nature of our institutional models.* Syracuse, NY: Human Policy Press.

Zetlin, A.G., & Murtaugh, M. (1988). Friendship patterns of mildly learning handicapped and nonhandicapped high school students. *American Journal of Mental Retardation, 92*(5), 447–454.

Zetlin, A.G., & Turner, J.L. (1985). Transition from adolescence to adulthood: Perspectives of mentally retarded individuals and their families. *American Journal of Mental Deficiency, 89*(6), 570–579.

Chapter 6

Facilitating Integration in Recreation Environments

Stuart J. Schleien,
John E. Rynders, and Frederick P. Green

Participation in recreation and leisure activities promotes physical health and conditioning, leads to the development and expansion of skill repertoires, provides new outlets for hobbies, expands social networks, and contributes to a higher quality of life. From a socialization standpoint, participation in community recreation offers an individual the opportunity to develop a more positive self-concept through satisfying relationships with peers. Channels for self-expression, creativity, and character development; opportunities to interact with and befriend a variety of peers; and the establishment of a more fulfilling way of life are all attributes of successful participation in integrated community recreation programs (Schleien & Ray, 1988).

Unfortunately, in the past, integrated recreation services have had a relatively low priority in programs for persons with developmental disabilities. Only in the last 15 years have specific recreation-skill instructional techniques been developed (Rynders & Schleien, 1991; Voeltz, Wuerch, & Wilcox, 1982; Wehman & Schleien, 1981) and recreation curricula become available (Bender & Valletutti, 1976; Dattilo & Murphy, 1991; Schleien, Meyer, Heyne, & Biel, in press; Wehman & Schleien, 1981; Wessel, 1976). The relative neglect of recreational programming for people with developmental disabilities is unfortunate because successful participation in such activities plays an important role in community adjustment (Cheseldine & Jeffree, 1981; Eyman & Call, 1977; Gollay, 1981; Hill & Bruininks, 1981; Schleien & Ray, 1988). Furthermore, participation in recreation activities is associated with the development of collateral skills, including skills in the motor

Preparation of this chapter was supported by a cooperative agreement (#H133B80048) from the National Institute on Disability and Rehabilitation Research (NIDRR) and the Research and Training Center on Residential Services and Community Living at the University of Minnesota (College of Education) located within the Institute on Community Integration (UAP).

121

and social domains (Dattilo & Schleien, 1991; Newcomer & Morrison, 1974; Schleien, Kiernan, & Wehman, 1981; Strain, Cooke, & Apolloni, 1976). More important, these services have empowered persons with developmental disabilities to utilize community recreation and leisure programs, assisting them to live more productive and satisfying lives.

Nevertheless, there is considerable room for improvement in the quantity and quality of integrated recreation services for children and adults with developmental disabilities. For a person with a disability to participate maximally in community recreation activities, recreation skill training should begin at home, be continued in supportive school environments throughout his or her childhood and youth, and culminate in specific efforts by community agencies to incorporate the person into recreation activities as an adult (McGrew, Bruininks, Thurlow, & Lewis, 1992; Rynders & Schleien, 1991).

HISTORICAL AND LEGISLATIVE
OVERVIEW OF COMMUNITY RECREATION SERVICES

Purposeful, or functional, recreation did not play a large role in the lives of individuals with developmental disabilities until the early 1900s. In 1906, the Playground Association of America was formed (later to be known as the *Playground and Recreation Association,* and renamed in 1965 as the *National Recreation and Park Association*). From its inception, the association declared its services were for *all* people, including those who had been discriminated against due to developmental disabilities (Schleien, Green, & Heyne, 1993).

During the 1920s and 1930s, public schools began offering a small number of after-school recreation programs for persons with developmental disabilities. Most of these were segregated, a practice that still exists today in many communities (Schleien & Ray, 1988). In the 1940s, the use of outdoor or wilderness areas as therapeutic environments became popular. These programs were designed to improve the emotional, behavioral, and social skills of participants (Gibson, 1979; Schleien, McAvoy, Lais, & Rynders, in press), and to create a sense of renewal and strength in these persons (Sessoms, 1992).

Summer camps for children and adolescents who did not have disabilities first appeared in the United States in 1861. However, it was not until the 1940s that camping became popular as a programmatic activity for children with developmental disabilities. Camping programs attempted to meet the needs of individual campers by exploring alternative methods to meet these needs. Today, many national organizations, such as The Arc (formerly Association for Retarded Citizens of the United States), the National Easter Seal Society, and the United Cerebral Palsy Association provide camping and community recreation experiences for individuals with a wide gamut of abilities. The expansion of recreation opportunities for persons with developmental disabilities has resulted in several benefits for such persons and their families. These include improved diagnostic assessment procedures; positive out-of-home placement policies; remedial programs; techniques for development and maintenance of personal, social, emotional, and physical functions; and respite opportunities for families (Dailey, 1989; Robb, 1980; Shea, 1977).

Paralleling community recreation service development, legislation passed during the past 20 years has had a dramatic impact on the quality of life experienced by persons with developmental disabilities and has championed the principle of normalization (Wolfensberger, 1983). This principle advocates that persons with developmental disabilities experience living routines that approximate those of community members without disabilities. The normalization principle has fostered a greater understanding of how integrated recreation programs might take form.

The Education for All Handicapped Children Act of 1975 (PL 94-142), and its amendments, the Education of the Handicapped Act Amendments of 1990 (PL 101-476), (now known as the Individuals with Disabilities Education Act [IDEA]) address the need to provide integrated recreation programs to persons with developmental disabilities, mandating the consideration of service provisions in least restrictive environments (LREs). The LRE concept acts as a societal imperative, energizing the idea that persons with developmental disabilities are to work, recreate, and be educated to the greatest extent possible, alongside peers without disabilities. In the past, persons segregated on the basis of their disability missed opportunities for learning and developing socially with their peers. Individuals were often characterized by their disabilities, and any opportunities they were given reflected what they were *unable* to do, rather than what they were *able* to do. The LRE principle sought to correct this by enabling individuals with all types and degrees of developmental disabilities to participate in the programs and the activities that are available to members of the community who do not have disabilities.

As organizations attempted to expand recreational programs to serve individuals with developmental disabilities, many program leaders found accessibility to be an issue. Inaccessible buildings and an inability to communicate with people who have sensory impairments segregate the walking, hearing, and seeing population from persons with developmental disabilities. The Architectural Barriers Act of 1968 (PL 90-480) requires that buildings and facilities constructed, altered, or leased through the use of federal funds be accessible and usable by individuals with disabilities—this legislation excludes buildings constructed entirely through private capital. The Architectural and Transportation Barriers Compliance Board (ATBCB), under Section 502 of the Rehabilitation Act of 1973 (PL 93-112), was created by Congress to enforce the Architectural Barriers Act. This act enabled individuals with disabilities to participate in programs that were available to the general public. Section 504 of the Rehabilitation Act prohibited exclusion of persons with disabilities from any program or activity receiving federal assistance. The regulation required states to avoid unnecessary segregation of services and to modify existing services in order to offer people with disabilities quality services equal to those of the general public (Lakin & Bruininks, 1985).

In 1990, the Americans with Disabilities Act (PL 101-336) was enacted to eliminate discrimination against persons with disabilities in the areas of employment, transportation, public accommodations, public services, and telecommunications. Of great importance to providers of recreation services, Section 302 of the Act prohibits discrimination (denying full and equal access and enjoyment of any public facilities or services) against an individual on the basis of disability. The mandate defines separate, albeit equal, programs and services as discriminatory practices. In addition, under this law, services must be offered to persons with disabilities in the most integrated setting appropriate to the needs of the individual. The intent of the law is to allow consumers, not service providers, to determine the extent of integration deemed appropriate.

APPROACHES TO INTEGRATED COMMUNITY RECREATION SERVICES

Segregated recreation programs are certainly more beneficial than the complete absence of such services. There are alternatives, however, whereby people with developmental disabilities can become involved in integrated recreation and leisure activities. The selection of one of these alternatives depends on the needs of the individual and the availability of programs, and should not be dictated by the preferences of service providers or the agency itself. Each approach possesses advantages and disadvantages that should be considered prior to program selection. The following paragraphs describe and contrast three integration approaches.

Integration of Generic Recreation Programs

The integration of a generic program approach can be defined as the inclusion of individuals with developmental disabilities into existing programs that serve individuals who do not have disabilities. This approach is implemented by supporting the individual with a disability in the selection of such an existing age-appropriate community recreation program. In selecting this approach, a support person works in cooperation with a generic recreation program leader to identify and to ameliorate the discrepancy between program skill requirements and the individual's capabilities. A review of best practices for socially integrating persons with developmental disabilities into generic community recreation programs reveals that the following sequential, seven-step strategy could be highly useful (Moon & Bunker, 1987; Schleien & Green 1992; Schleien, Light, McAvoy, & Baldwin, 1989):

1. *Assessment of individual recreation preferences and needs* (Moon & Bunker, 1987)
2. *Selection of an age-appropriate, community recreation activity* (Browder & King, 1987; Wehman & Schleien, 1981; Wuerch & Voeltz, 1982)
3. *Conduct an environmental analysis to determine the constraints and demands of the activity* (Certo, Schleien, & Hunter, 1983; Peterson & Gunn, 1984; Schleien & Ray, 1988)

4. *Conduct an assessment of individual skill levels and personal skill deficits relative to the identified demands of the activity (i.e., discrepancy analysis)* (Certo et al., 1983; Moon & Bunker, 1987; Peterson & Gunn, 1984; Schleien & Ray, 1988; Snell, 1983; Snell & Grigg, 1987; Wehman, Renzaglia, & Bates, 1985)

5. *Develop strategies to facilitate the social inclusion of the individual with a disability by overcoming individual deficits and environmental barriers* (Amado, 1988; Ellis, Forsyth, & Voight, 1983; Green & Schleien, 1991; Johnson & Johnson, 1987; O'Brien, Forest, Snow, & Hasbury, 1989; Rynders, Johnson, Johnson, & Schmidt, 1980; Rynders & Schleien, 1988; Schleien, Fahnestock, Green, & Rynders, 1990; Schleien et al., 1989; Wehman & Schleien, 1981)

6. *Implementation of program by integration specialists who work in collaboration with generic services providers when implementing integration strategies* (Center on Human Policy, 1991; Green & Schleien, 1991; Schleien & Green, 1992; Schleien & Ray, 1988; Walker & Edinger, 1988; Walker, Edinger, Willis, & Kenney, 1988)

7. *Conduct ongoing evaluation of integrated programs* (Patton, 1987; Peterson & Gunn, 1984; Snell, 1987)

Advantages of a Generic Programs Approach   The successful implementation of a generic programs approach ensures that persons with developmental disabilities will participate in activities alongside a natural proportion of peers without disabilities. During actual programming, it is essential to promote collaboration between program leaders and integration facilitators to ensure that programs maintain an appropriate ratio of participants with and without severe disabilities (Brown, Branston, Hamre-Nietupski, Wilcox, & Gruenewald, 1979). Participation in existing, age-appropriate recreation programs has the potential to assist persons with developmental disabilities to acquire skills required for contemporary, appropriate, high-interest activities within the community. It is rare for this potential to be realized in segregated programs where the participatory limitations of group members with disabilities may lead programmers to offer little to challenge participant growth (Bedini, 1990; Certo et al., 1983). Another significant advantage offered by the integration into an existing generic services approach is the potential that participants with and without disabilities may develop social relationships. While generic programs serve the majority of the community culture, segregated programs often exist in relative isolation, outside the usual community network (Brown et al., 1991).

Disadvantages of a Generic Programs Approach   The success of generic integration efforts relies heavily on the acceptance of the individual who is disabled by people without disabilities in the program, including regular staff members. Inclusionary efforts can be hampered by unnecessary attention being focused on the individual, emphasizing the perception of difference (Bedini, 1991; Green & Schleien, 1991). A result of unnecessary attention is that persons with developmental disabilities experience social isolation while attempting to blend into community recreation programs (Gollay, Freedman, Wyngaarden, & Kurtz, 1978; Gottlieb, Semmel, & Veldman, 1978). Often, these persons feel stigmatized by the undue attention, as they are aware of, and may prefer to deny, their disability (Szivos & Griffiths, 1990). This dilemma often leaves the individual with a difficult decision to make. He or she can either withdraw from the social setting or demonstrate competence equal to that of peers without disabilities (often not immediately achievable or perhaps not achievable at all in some cases), or play the role of "helpee" and accept the lower end of a vertical relationship with peers (Bullock, 1988).

Generic recreation programs are usually coordinated by professionals who often lack training in therapeutic recreation or special education. Staff may also lack the specific programming skills necessary to include the person with a disability into the program successfully. This may foster passive or even negative attitudes toward the individual with a disability. Although an integration facilitator often shoulders the responsibility for integration efforts, it is the generic service provider who typically creates and maintains the general social environment (Schleien & Ray, 1988). Ill-prepared generic service providers can often inadvertently create less-than-friendly environments for individuals with disabilities (Schleien, Olson, Rogers, & McLafferty, 1985). Finally, given the limited resources available, the time and effort necessary for genuine integration of persons with disabilities may result in only a small percentage of these individuals being served (Schleien & Ray, 1988).

Reverse Mainstreaming Approach

A second approach to facilitating the integration of people with and without developmental disabilities in community recreation programs is referred to as *reverse mainstreaming* (Block & Krebs, 1992; Reynolds, 1981; Schleien & Green, 1992). In reverse mainstreaming, programs exclusively for people with developmental disabilities (i.e., segregated programs) are modified to attract peers without disabilities. The success of reverse mainstreaming in promoting interactions between people with and without developmental disabilities appears to be linked with the use of the following five-step process:

1. Identification of a currently segregated program that has the potential to attract and to maintain the interest of participants without disabilities
2. Assessment of the needs, interests, and capabilities of all potential participants
3. Comparison and prioritization of the needs of participants with and without disabilities
4. Retraining of program leaders (who have experienced only segregated programs) to meet the needs of participants without disabilities, as well as individuals with disabilities
5. Modifying a program to attract and sustain the interest of all participants (Schleien & Green, 1992)

This approach to recreation integration, currently practiced by Special Olympics International through their Unified Sports Program, has successfully accelerated interactions between people with and without mental retardation. Unified Sports combines, on the same team, approximately equal numbers of athletes with mental retardation and athletes without disabilities, similar in age and ability. Unified Sports leagues have been developed throughout the country in basketball, bowling, soccer, softball, and volleyball. The benefits of these programs have predominantly been based on personal observations of coaches, family members, and program advisers (Shriver, 1990).

Advantages of a Reverse Mainstreaming Approach   The large amount of time and effort necessary to facilitate inclusion on an individual basis is not required when a reverse mainstreaming approach is utilized. This service delivery approach opens segregated programs to community members without disabilities. The success of reverse mainstreaming is often dependent on the restructuring of a program to make it highly attractive to all participants. Once the participants without disabilities are in the door, participating alongside their peers with disabilities, efforts can be made to facilitate social interactions and friendship.

Through reverse mainstreaming, a large number of persons with developmental disabilities can continue to participate in recreation activities to which they are accustomed, while receiving exposure (and one would hope, positive interactions) to peers without disabilities. For many persons with disabilities, interactions with peers who do not have disabilities—in familiar surroundings and among friends with disabilities—become manageable. Hence, meeting the recreation and leisure needs of people with developmental disabilities can be ensured, assuming that these needs were already being met prior to integration efforts.

Program leaders, having had substantial experience working with individuals with disabilities, should be adequately trained to meet their needs. However, these leaders will require additional training on how to include people without disabilities into the program. If accomplished successfully, participants without disabilities, recruited into a traditionally segregated program, are made to feel welcome by their peers with disabilities.

Disadvantages of the Reverse Mainstreaming Approach   In a reverse mainstreaming approach, the ratio of people with developmental disabilities to individuals without disabilities will remain disproportionate to the normalized ratio existing in the community in general, perhaps perpetuating a distorted view of community for participants with disabilities. Experience with reverse mainstreaming reveals that efforts toward social integration are often episodic in nature—temporarily opening the doors for a few brave souls to venture in, briefly experience people with developmental disabilities, and quickly venture out (Kennedy, Horner, & Newton, 1989).

It may be a discrepancy in needed social skills, or the perception of a discrepancy, that results in episodic social relationships. In reverse mainstreaming settings, peers without disabilities often adopt an ambivalent attitude, simultaneously expressing admiration for and aversion to their peers with developmental disabilities (Gibbons, 1985). Peers without disabilities often assume that their peers with developmental disabilities are less capable of understanding and contributing to social interaction (Bullock, 1988). Sneegas (1989) proposed that deficits in social skills prevent persons with developmental disabilities from gaining social acceptance from peers without disabilities, perpetuating these ambivalent attitudes. This ambivalence often results in the development of vertical social relationships (Bullock, 1988).

Another disadvantage of the reverse mainstreaming approach is that, although participants with developmental disabilities are exposed to peers without disabilities, they continue to participate in and identify with "programs for the disabled." Therefore, reverse mainstreaming may perpetuate the use of nonfunctional recreation and social behaviors, limit the generalization of skills to other people and environments, and inhibit friendships from developing. A skilled programmer can avoid these pitfalls by structuring reverse mainstream programs to ensure high quality and by making them attractive enough to capture and maintain the interests of participants of widely varying abilities.

The Zero Exclusion Team Approach

The need to meet broad consumer demand is the basis for a third approach to integration: the zero exclusion team approach. In this approach, therapeutic recreation specialists and generic recreation program leaders do not plan programs in isolation. Rather, collaborative efforts occur prior to program implementation. The success of this approach appears to be dependent on the use of the following program components (Schleien & Green, 1992):

1. Demand for new programs to meet the changing needs of persons with and without disabilities
2. Productive, collaborative relationships based on mutual respect between professionals in therapeutic recreation and generic community recreation
3. Aggressive recruitment of participants with and without disabilities through user-friendly, nondiscriminatory advertisements
4. Accurate assessment of the needs, skills, and interests of all members of the community
5. Commitment of agencies to make inclusive programs the rule rather than the exception, so that people with and without disabilities are given a variety of options for recreation participation
6. Commitment to the social inclusion of all community members by the community recreation agency

As new programs are created, it is assumed, from the onset, that they will include participants with and without developmental disabilities. Because programs are not targeted for a particular group, agencies can practice the art of full inclusion. People of widely varying abilities are recruited aggressively, expected to participate, and prepared to do so skillfully.

Advantages of the Zero Exclusion Approach The creation of new programming requires the investment of an agency. Although initial costs may be higher, the eventual elimination of separate or redundant programs can eventually lead to significant cost reductions. Creating new programming will foster cooperation between therapeutic recreation specialists and generic community recreation providers. This collaboration has the potential to promote program creativity and, eventually, foster a commitment to zero exclusion in which no interested participant is denied access. Unlike the integration of generic programs and reverse mainstreaming approaches, the zero exclusion approach promotes equal status among community members. Rather than creating programs for one group or the other, and making concessions at a later time to accommodate a special individual, zero exclusion programs are designed for the full inclusion of all members.

Disadvantages of the Zero Exclusion Approach The *initial* cost of developing recreational programs based upon the zero exclusion approach may result in program leaders resisting a shift to this paradigm. Participants without disabilities who are accustomed to separate but equal programs for people with disabilities may believe their programs will become watered down due to the inclusion of special populations. When structured appropriately from the beginning, however, it is not necessary that a program's quality suffer. Participants are offered community recreation programs that meet and maintain a high level of quality and interest. The significant difference created by the zero exclusion approach is that persons with developmental disabilities are free to choose to participate in any scheduled activity. Finally, persons with developmental disabilities and their supporters may perceive a commitment to zero exclusion programming as a step toward eliminating all segregated programs.

The total segregation of individuals, with or without disabilities is, in most instances, inappropriate. There are times and places, however, where separation is advantageous because of highly specialized individual needs. As Brown et al. (1991) point out, for example, the (total) mainstreaming of young adults with disabilities into regular high school classrooms—during the time that individuals with disabilities need to have a community-referenced program—denies them crucial learning opportunities. In other words, under rare circumstances, a particular integrated environment can become a most restrictive, rather than a least restrictive, environment.

In the future, the majority of recreation professionals' efforts will not be spent on programming for predetermined groups (e.g., children with autism), but on creating a community in which all members are included. Promising intervention strategies have been developed and field-tested in recent years that give generic recreation providers, integration facilitators, and families and consumers the strategies and methods they will need to make the full inclusion of all members of a community a reality.

PROMISING INTERVENTION STRATEGIES

Although all of the strategies necessary to develop, implement, and sustain a strong integrated recreation program have yet to be identified, success in this area of intervention rests primarily on adults (e.g., program leaders, parents, program directors) who take an active and skillful interest in the effort. Working together in direct and supportive roles, adults—more than any other factor—determine the quality and staying power of inclusive programs. In this section, the focus will be on the role of the recreation program leader. Other adults, however, such as parents, community volunteers, and agency directors, can contribute as much, and sometimes more than can the leader him- or herself, to integration efforts.

The Crucial Contribution of the Adult Leader

The manner in which an adult leader of an integrated recreation activity selects and uses resources will be a major determiner of the success or failure of an inclusionary program. Every program leader can draw upon at least four of the resources as follows: 1) directions for participation (structuring), 2) recreation activities or materials, 3) interaction preparation for participants with and without disabilities, and 4) the facilitation role assumed in promoting peer interactions.

Cooperatively Structuring Directions for Participation In the early days of the integration movement it was common for program leaders to believe that simply putting children with and without disabilities together in the same recreation center would cause them to interact positively, and perhaps even become close friends. It soon became evident, however, that physical proximity alone did not, in and of itself, ensure positive results. In fact, in the 1970s, it was evidenced that without proper structuring by an adult (e.g., wording activity directions to promote enjoyable interdependent interaction) children without disabilities might view their peers with disabilities in negative ways (Novak, 1975) and feel discomfort and uncertainty in interacting with them (Jones, 1970). Thus, it became clear that the seeds of positive attitudes and behaviors in children without disabilities could not be assumed to sprout on their own, but had to be carefully planted and actively cultivated. Cooperative structuring techniques, based on the work of Johnson and Johnson (1981, 1984) and activated through selected recreation programs and activities, appear to hold special promise.

Following a recreational bowling study in which a comparison was made between the effects of structuring an activity for either cooperative, competitive, or independent participation, cooperative structuring work was extended to determine the extent to which cooperative behavior could be enhanced further by encouraging social interactions within the context of the creative art classes. The results of this study showed clear advantages for cooperative structuring in terms of promoting positive heterogeneous interactions (Rynders et al., 1980). In the first of these studies (Schleien, Rynders, & Mustonen, 1988), elementary-age students with autism and students without disabilities, all of whom attended a regular suburban school, were brought together in an art education program called Kidspace, an interactive studio and gallery program housed within the Minnesota Museum of Art in downtown St. Paul, Minnesota.

In the Kidspace study (Schleien et al., 1988), the cooperative goal structure employed was a modified version of the approach developed by Johnson and Johnson (1981, 1984). The study included the following components. First, directions focused on an interdependent outcome. Second, a task was adapted to be conducive for a cooperative (interdependent) outcome approach, with considerable attention being placed on task adaptation, depending on the nature of the participants' disabilities. Third, participants without disabilities received portions of the Special Friends curriculum (Voeltz et al., 1983), learning a variety of behaviors, including turn-taking and the use of prosthetic devices. They also received both simulated practice in and instruction on how to assist, as a friend, interactions when they occurred, without cuing or prompting them. Fourth, adult facilitators also redirected participants who exhibited off-task behavior or appeared to be performing an unsafe activity. Fifth, participants with disabilities sometimes received individual instruction from an adult in a particular skill area. Although cooperatively structured environmental context often provided the instruction, individual attention was deemed crucial for enabling positive peer-to-peer participation.

Following this training, cooperatively structured studio and gallery activities were introduced (e.g., members of small integrated groups worked together on decorating and then assembling the pieces of a giant puzzle). During these activities, adults reinforced cooperative puzzle-making interactions between children of differing abilities, but did not cue or prompt them since the goal was to allow the children, rather than the adults, to call the shots. Data were collected via a partial interval time-sampling procedure, which employed a behavior target checklist.

Whereas participants had exhibited low levels of social interaction during the baseline phase, participants without disabilities significantly increased the number of social interactions initiated toward participants with disabilities during the intervention phase. This was replicated in the performance of the second group. In both groups, however, social bids by peers without disabilities were seldom reciprocated by participants with autism. Moreover, there was a slight decrease in the percentage of appropriate behavior in one group of children with autism. Although functional analyses of the challenging behaviors exhibited by the students with autism were not conducted, decreased levels of appropriate behavior may have been motivated by students' desires to escape from or avoid socialization-oriented activities (Durand & Carr, 1985).

In a second study that examined whether cooperative behavior could be enhanced by encouraging social interactions within the context of the creative art classes, Miller, Rynders, and Schleien (in press) focused on improving peer interactions through cooperatively structured sociodramatic play. Results showed that children with disabilities were approached significantly more often by children without disabilities when in the cooperative sociodrama group than when in the cooperative games group. Similarly, children with disabilities in the drama group approached their peers without disabilities more often than did their counterparts with disabilities in the cooperative games group, but this difference was not statistically significant.

In summary, research findings show that a cooperative goal structure generally produces a much higher rate of positive social interactions between persons with and without disabilities than either an independent or competitive goal structure. Furthermore, a variety of recreation contexts (e.g., art and sociodrama) have proven to be conducive for promoting positive social interactions, with encouragement to practice their social and cooperative play skills adding an enhancing dimension. However, structuring a task for cooperation does not guarantee that participants with disabilities will reciprocate, much less initiate, prosocial bids.

With regard to modifying infrequent social bid reciprocity on the part of recreation participants with disabilities, we do not have a satisfactory solution for this dilemma. One possible solution is to accept it as a problem inherent in persons with severe disabilities—a permanent lack in the social repertoire of the individual due to the disability itself. An alternative explanation is that the problem is attributable to our lack of attention to strengthening the reciprocity repertoire of persons with severe disabilities. It is believed that the lack of social interaction between persons with and without disabilities is due to this inability of certain individuals to verbally express themselves in some instances. In the future, professionals in the field will need to take fuller advantage of the work of Reichle and his colleagues (Reichle, Rogers, & Barrett, 1984; Reichle, Sigafoos, & Piché, 1989), who have taught persons with severe disabilities to request preferred items and socially interact more effectively using a manual sign or graphic symbols. These strategies have the potential to play a key role in facilitating the development of satisfying friendships.

Recreation Activities and Materials To Promote Socialization When adults set out to promote cooperative social interactions between children with diverse abilities, the specific interaction-promoting games, toys, or activities that are used are of great importance. Obviously, social toys (e.g., board and table games) are likely to have a more powerful influence on socialization outcomes among young children than isolate toys (e.g., coloring books) (Odom, Hoyson, Jamieson, & Strain, 1985; Quilitch & Risley, 1973).

Schleien, Heyne, and Berken (1988) examined the type and level of motor skills exhibited across a variety of tasks by children with autism (ages 4–12) who participated in an integrated physical education-leisure education program. While their results did not indicate improvement in motor skills as a function of task type, they did find significant improvement in socially appropriate play in the more advanced activities (i.e., cooperative and group team play). The researchers suggested that exhibiting higher levels of play may go hand-in-hand with improved behavioral appropriateness in children with autism. This implies that a hierarchical view of play intervention emphasizing isolate play mastery as a prerequisite to dyadic play, and mastery of dyadic play as a prerequisite to group play, might be unnecessary and even counterproductive in certain socialization settings when working with children with autism.

Following up on the implications of their findings, Schleien, Rynders, Mustonen, and Fox (1990) set up a study in which activities representing four different levels of social play were presented to children with and without autism in an integrated leisure education program. Employing a multi-element design, children without disabilities received training in how to interact cooperatively, and then participated with peers who had autism in activities representing isolate (e.g., hula hoop), dyadic (e.g., indoor horseshoes), group (e.g., *Twister*), and team (e.g., rope tug-of-war) play activities.

Results indicated that the largest percentage of inappropriate behavior in children with autism occurred in isolate activities, with the highest level of appropriate play behaviors occurring in activities involving peers without disabilities on a coparticipation basis, such as dyadic, group, and team activities. Parenthetically, social interactions were very infrequent in this study regardless of type of activity.

In summary, the findings of several investigations demonstrate that the social components of a play activity—for example, turn-taking in playing horseshoes versus the solitary use of a hula hoop—have an important influence on behavioral appropriateness of children with autism. Moreover, size of play group, ratio of participants with and without disabilities, and the opportunity for choice making are important factors in facilitating social play richness in integrated recreation settings.

Preparation of Participants for Cooperation Recreation leaders often choose to promote either tutorial or socialization roles for participants without disabilities, depending on their desire to promote recreation skill acquisition (e.g., increased ability to toss a bocce ball) or socialization (e.g., increased social interaction). Both roles can be productive in promoting cooperative behavior in an integrated recreation program. According to Meyer and Putnam (1988), however, the peer socialization role appears to carry less risk of inducing an authoritarian attitude in peers without disabilities and any long-term negative results from these attitudes.

In peer tutoring programs, the student without disabilities typically receives systematic instruction on how to provide tutoring to a student with a disability, serving a parallel role to that of a teacher. Peer tutors are usually expected to interact with their peers in a top-down, or vertical, relationship, often using applied behavior analysis techniques. In contrast, a peer socialization program aims to encourage peers to develop relationships as friends do, usually with initial direction from the adult leader. Peer socializers interact in a side-by-side, or horizontal, manner, with an emphasis on behaviors such as turn-taking (Sailor & Guess, 1983).

In an effort to compare the social dynamics of a peer socialization (friend) approach and a peer teaching (tutoring) approach, Cole, Vandercook, and Rynders (1987) conducted a large-scale study involving 10 classrooms in six different schools (60 child dyads). Peer socialization training focused on assisting peers without disabilities to understand disabling conditions, learning new communication and interactive play skills, and discussing what it is that creates and maintains friendship. Peer tutor training sessions also addressed learning how to apply basic teaching principles (e.g., prompting, contingent reinforcement), communication techniques to promote achievement, and problem solving.

Social reciprocity of appropriate play, cooperative play, and positive affect outcomes significantly favored the peer friend program over the peer tutoring program. Children without disabilities who were peer tutors reported having substantially less fun and being less interested in the integrated interactions than did children who were peer friends. However, it is important to note that in this study a peer tutor structure was introduced in a situation where playfulness was the likely expectation. Thus, it is conceivable that the tutorial structure did not fit the expectations of peers without disabilities who probably did not anticipate making play into work. This study highlights the need to monitor tutorial structures carefully to ensure that the interaction does not become unenjoyable for peers without disabilities.

Others compared the efficacy of peer tutoring and peer socialization approaches in fostering social interaction, such as the Special Friends approach (Voeltz et al., 1983). These approaches have also been compared among adolescents with and without autism (Haring, Breen, Pitts-Conway, Lee, & Gaylord-Ross, 1987). In terms of similarities, the two interaction modes did not result in significant differences in attitude. Behavior probes (with familiar and unfamiliar students with autism) showed that the two groups interacted for nearly the same amount of time and that the pattern of interaction was identical. One difference, however, was found. The Special Friends approach produced significantly more social exchange responses toward an unfamiliar person with autism. It is important to note that Voeltz and colleagues' (1983) results were obtained with elementary-age children in most cases, while the Haring et al. (1987) findings involved adolescents.

Sufficient research comparing the effect of vertical (tutoring) versus horizontal (socialization) peer relationships has not been conducted. Making authoritative recommendations as to their best use is, therefore, not warranted at this time. Nonetheless, the two techniques (socialization versus tutoring) raise interesting issues for recreation professionals. The selection of one approach over the other, if a choice needs to be made, would, at first, appear to be quite simple. If the primary objective is the acquisition of specific task skills, employ a peer tutoring approach. Use a peer friendship program if social interaction is the main objective. Rather than making a choice between the two approaches, a more productive option might be to concentrate on the facilitation of friendliness in the recreation program. Later, it may become natural for one partner to teach another to play a new game or learn a new skill, in a friendly manner, and with adult leaders promoting cooperative structuring.

Although the literature is replete with research focusing on social skills training (McConnell, 1987; Sisson, Van Hasselt, Hersen, & Strain, 1985) and leisure skills training (Horst, Wehman, Hill, & Bailey, 1981; Schleien, Certo, & Muccino, 1985; Schleien, Tuckner, & Heyne, 1985) for persons with severe disabilities, studies addressing the acquisition of both social skills and leisure activity skills by individuals with severe disabilities are scarce. Gaylord-Ross, Haring, Breen, and Pitts-Conway (1984) conducted a study that was designed to increase the frequency of initiations and the duration of social interactions between students with autism and those without disabilities. Two students with autism were taught how to use three leisure objects; a radio, gum, and a video game. Object skill training alone had little impact on the social aspects of peer interaction during break time in the high school courtyard. However, the addition of social skills instruction did produce a significant increase in social initiations and the duration of interaction between the students with autism and their high school peers without disabilities.

Haring and Lovinger (1989) examined the effects of social initiation training and the effects of play skill training on the level of initiation exhibited by students with severe disabilities toward peers without disabilities and on the level of responsivity demonstrated by the peers without disabilities to those initiations. Two studies were conducted in free-play settings (the first in a preschool and the second in a kindergarten classroom). The combination of social initiation training and play skill training resulted in increased initiations by the children with severe disabilities and increased responsivity by their peers without disabilities in both studies.

Vandercook (1991) examined the degree to which two skills (bowling and playing pinball) were acquired by students with severe mental and physical disabilities and then generalized to other settings and people when provided the opportunity (with no additional intervention) to bowl and play pinball with high school peers who did not have disabilities. She also investigated the impact of skill demonstration by students with severe disabilities on the social interactions between peers with and without disabilities during the bowling and pinball activities. Results indicated that the skills taught to the students with disabilities by an adult instructor were again demonstrated when these students engaged in the same activities with peers. To examine the impact of skill demonstration on social interactions, correlations were calculated between leisure skill demonstration and specified social behaviors. Only the social skill labeled *cooperative participation* showed a strong correlation coefficient for more than one dyad and for both members of the dyad.

These examples of studies, which attend to both social and recreation skills development, attest to the importance of addressing both in interventions. In this regard, McCord (1983), echoing Wolfensberger's (1983) stance, emphasizes that the strengthening of bonds between people with and without disabilities will depend on interventions that bring about both skill development and image enhancement.

In summary, preparing peers without disabilities to function in a socialization role appears to have more positive results than placing these peers in a tutorial role. These results appear to be due, in part, to the fact that a socialization role appears to carry less risk of becoming authoritarian or of appearing awkward. Equally important, a socialization role is compatible with the cooperative goal structuring that has occurred in integrated recreation situations; that is, desired recreation outcomes have been primarily oriented toward social interaction, not skill acquisition. Nonetheless, a peer tutor role can be very useful in some integrated situations, particularly when the acquisition of a particular recreation skill might serve as a powerful enabling mechanism for socialization success.

Cooperative goal structuring, as it has been applied to date, has been limited in its scope to the use of a similar-age, peer friendship configuration. Too strong a line between a tutorial and a socialization (friendship) integration model may be somewhat artificial because many cooperative recreation programs do employ friendly teaching, as well as friendly socialization. Actually, the two conceptual models (socialization versus tutorial roles) may have relatively untapped complementary possibilities. A community recreation program for young children, for example, might begin with a cooperatively structured, same-age, peer socialization emphasis, and then be judiciously supplemented with cooperatively structured, cross-age, peer tutoring that features recreation task instruction. An integrated horseback riding project located in Minnesota provides an excellent example of how such a program can work. Sponsored by the 4-H club, children with severe disabilities interact with children without disabilities of the same age.

Promotion of Cooperative Peer Interaction   Throughout this chapter, it has been noted that cooperative, collaborative activities have great potential to facilitate social interaction between persons with and without disabilities. Therefore, the specific means through which cooperation is elicited are an important factor that one must consider in program development.

Putnam, Rynders, Johnson, and Johnson (1989) examined the issue of adult leader direction, comparing the effects of instructing peers without disabilities in specific cooperative play behaviors versus the effects of merely describing a cooperative task. The instructed group of peers without disabilities initiated significantly more cooperative play behaviors and verbal interactions than the description-only group. However, the study would be incomplete without looking at the long-term effects of teacher instruction.

In a systematic replication series of studies, the Special Friends program (Voeltz, 1980; Voeltz et al., 1983) was employed to examine the effects of different intensities, frequencies, and durations of teacher directions on children's social and play behaviors. The first study of the series contrasted the high-intrusion condition that the teachers displayed during baseline with a low-intrusion condition that restricted the level of teacher intervention (Meyer et al., 1987). Subsequently, the effects of different types of verbal messages on the children's interactions during play activities were investigated (Cole, 1986; Cole, Meyer, Vandercook, & McQuarter, 1986). The findings of this research can be summarized as follows: 1) initial teacher directions carried out for no more than 2 weeks will provide positive support for children's cooperative play exchanges; 2) if such teacher directions continue over time rather than fading them after an initial, time-limited teacher direction phase, they will eventually be associated with decreases in cooperative play exchanges between the children; and 3) teachers' scripts in the form of friendly comments (comments about the weather, the weekend, and so forth) are more readily tolerated by children than continued social instruction scripts (telling children how to behave). Implied is that friendship is an intimate act, and adults who fail to allow children the necessary intimacy will prevent the very outcomes they are intending to foster.

Findings from research efforts designed to promote cooperative peer interaction indicate that when an adult leader is providing goal structuring in the form of peer interaction directions, he or she needs to avoid being unnecessarily intrusive in direction giving. Moreover, the leader will need to monitor sensitively the impact of directions being given throughout the interaction period in order to adjust the type and frequency of directions as dictated by success, or lack of success, of those interactions. As described by Walker and her colleagues (in press), for successful facilitation to occur, facilitators must be prepared to provide long-term support; must be as invisible as possible (Walker & Edinger, 1988); and should be seen as regular participants in the setting, interacting with everyone present, rather than just the individual with a disability (Walker et al., 1988).

As researchers improve integrated programming for children and adults with and without disabilities through cooperatively structured recreation activities, they help to advance the development of community life itself. No longer shunted off to self-contained environments, individuals with developmental disabilities, living and playing in the community, can teach their peers without disabilities new lessons in personal growth and how to enjoy life more deeply. In doing so, *both* groups benefit.

An Agenda for Future Research

As the body of research on the benefits of recreation participation in inclusive community environments continues to grow, the responsibility for serving people with developmental disabilities will need to shift from the exclusive domain of therapeutic recreation to a collaborative effort between therapeutic recreation specialists, generic providers of community recreation, school teachers, family members, and persons with disabilities themselves. Yet, many issues and questions remain to be answered. Most interventions and modifications that need to be made to accommodate people with developmental disabilities in community recreation programs come with a cost. This cost is justified, however, and there is evidence that it is cost-effective (Schleien, Olson, et al., 1985).

Physical proximity alone does not, in and of itself, ensure social inclusion (Hayden, Lakin, Hill, Bruininks, & Copher, 1992). In fact, research suggests that without proper structuring by a professional, parent, or some type of integration specialist, participants without disabilities will view their peers with disabilities negatively (Novak, 1975). Thus, promising interventions, employed without proper activities and goal structuring, may not diminish the discomfort and uncertainty experienced by the general population when they interact with persons with disabilities (Jones, 1970). Indeed, unstructured interactions may not alter feelings of outright rejection (Goodman, Gottlieb, & Harrison, 1971; Iano, Ayers, Heller, McGettigan, & Walker, 1974), if such feelings have been experienced.

Positive attitudes toward persons with disabilities will not develop on their own but must be actively seeded and cultivated. Cooperative structuring techniques, combined with the other integration strategies discussed in this chapter, appear to hold considerable promise in this regard (Rynders et al., 1993). Advocates for accessibility, however, realize that the goal of full inclusion in community recreation will not be reached immediately or without considerable effort. Indeed, improved and more innovative models and strategies to promote integration need to be developed. Schleien and Ray (1988), for example, have suggested that functional social skills instruction needs to be included, along with recreation skills instruction, during community recreation programming. In this way, individuals with disabilities will be far more likely to gain access to the community from the outset.

In addition, new inclusion models must be applied. A promising approach is that of Taylor (1988); in his model, recreation and social skill needs of the individual are addressed while, at the same time, the receiving environment is carefully prepared so as to ensure a smooth transition. People with developmental disabilities are often more disabled by the receiving environment than by their disabilities themselves. The most dramatic shift in thinking about models is the recognition that social and physical environments are often a greater issue than abilities and disabilities (Certo et al., 1983; Kappel, Nagel, & Wieck, 1990; Schleien, Fahnestock, et al., 1990).

Many issues and questions must be addressed when formulating a comprehensive and long-term plan to facilitate the social inclusion of individuals with developmental disabilities. How will key players such as parents, consumers, teachers, recreation leaders, and agency administrators, for example, figure out how to combine and to embed strategies to accommodate all participants with and without disabilities? Ideas that address both the facilitation of inclusive community recreation and social skills and friendship development are presented next in an attempt to promote a future research agenda.

At the present, there is an immediate need to develop programs to assist children and adults with developmental disabilities to move beyond mere physical presence in the community and into an array of social opportunities as active and equal participants. A number of innovative strategies will need to be applied to ensure that this goal is achieved. These include: 1) assessing individuals' preferences in order to increase the use of recreation opportunities (Dattilo & Mirenda, 1987; Dattilo & Schleien, 1991); 2) approaches such as sociometry, Circle of Friends, and cooperative learning for including people with developmental disabilities in existing recreation programs (Schleien, Fahnestock, et al., 1990); 3) strategies to maximize cooperation and coordination among consumers, families, teachers, generic community recreation professionals, and therapeutic recreation specialists (Schleien & Ray, 1988; Schleien, Rynders, & Mustonen, 1988); and 4) identification of barriers that impede progress toward achieving the goal of inclusive community integration and the introduction of programmatic strategies designed to overcome them (Dattilo & Schleien, 1991; Kennedy, Smith, & Austin, 1991; Schleien & Ray, 1988).

Promoting Friendship

Research on the community adjustment of persons with developmental disabilities clearly indicates that living in community settings does not ensure meaningful participation in recreation activities (Green, 1991; Hayden et al., 1992). Individuals with disabilities often spend the majority of their lives in passive, meaningless activities regardless of where they live. Numerous factors influence the quality of recreation activity participation, including availability of transportation, service provider involvement, and availability and interest of friends or escorts to accompany and to participate in activities with individuals. The relative influence of each of these variables needs to be determined.

A number of investigators have reviewed research on the generally positive effects of cooperative goal structures on heterogeneous group task performance and social interaction behaviors (Johnson, Johnson, & Maruyama, 1983; Rynders et al., 1980). However, more information is needed to determine whether cooperative group structures are effective in the promotion of long-term social interactions and in friendship development between individuals of widely varying abilities and across various types of tasks and settings.

As individuals acquire age-appropriate recreation skills, the likelihood that they will become socially connected in their communities increases. However, there is a paucity of research on the relationship between recreation skills acquisition and social behavior and friendship development among peers with and without developmental disabilities. It is widely believed that as individuals acquire age-appropriate recreation skills, the likelihood that they will become socially connected with same-age peers in their communities will be increased. Yet, preliminary results of recent studies contradict this belief (Green, 1991). Instead, an age-appropriate recreation skill appears to serve as the medium in which one's social connection skills can be developed and used. Environmental deficits in social skills appear to neutralize the social integration power of recreation skill acquisition. Future research is needed to assist practitioners and parents in identifying the best combination of recreation, social, and friendship skills that will maximize the individual's chances of making friends.

Research on skill acquisition and social interactions among individuals with and without developmental disabilities reveals that people with developmental disabilities are more likely to interact with peers without disabilities when participating in activities in which they are adept (Green & Schleien, 1991; Rynders & Schleien, 1991). Studies have also demonstrated that peers without disabilities often adopt a service-type role (i.e., teacher, service provider), rather than a friendship role, when interacting with peers with developmental disabilities. Further research is necessary to develop strategies that promote authentic, lasting *friendships* between people of varying abilities.

If therapeutic recreation specialists and other service providers are to develop programs that can be used in a variety of environments, integration strategies will need to be evaluated in naturalistic settings with the most natural strategy used initially. If this fails, more supportive techniques can be undertaken. Ultimately, procedures that are identified as being effective must be replicable across settings and be able to promote maintenance and generalization.

Researchers must also systematically identify additional recreational materials and activities that promote cooperative social interactions among peers with and without developmental disabilities. In particular, stimulating and attractive recreational materials and activities that are associated with positively reinforcing events that facilitate communication need to be developed and systematically studied.

CONCLUSION

The facilitation of social networks and friendships are among the most significant outcomes of integrated community recreation participation. A combination of program elements, including teaching appropriate recreation, social, and friendship skills, and preparing participants without disabilities for integrated activities makes it possible for persons with developmental disabilities and their peers without disabilities to share recreation experiences in a mutually gratifying way. The time has come to adapt a new way of thinking, one founded on the premise that the community belongs to everyone, and that everyone, regardless of level and type of ability, belongs to the community. Inclusive community recreation programming can be a powerful vehicle for promoting this ideal.

REFERENCES

Amado, R. (1988). Behavioral principles in community recreation. In S. Schleien & M.T. Ray (Eds.), *Community recreation and persons with disabilities: Strategies for integration* (pp. 79–90). Baltimore: Paul H. Brookes Publishing Co.

Bedini, L. (1990). Separate but equal? Segregated programming for people with disabilities. *Leisure Today, 16*, 16–20.

Bedini, L. (1991). Modern day "freaks?" The exploitation of people with disabilities. *Therapeutic Recreation Journal, 25*(4), 61–70.

Bender, M., & Valletutti, P. (1976). *Teaching the moderately and severely handicapped: Curriculum, objectives, strategies, and activities* (Vol. 2). Baltimore: University Park Press.

Block, M., & Krebs, P. (1992). An alternative to least restrictive environments: A continuum of support to regular physical education. *Adapted Physical Activity Quarterly, 9*(2), 97–113.

Browder, D., & King, D. (1987). Comprehensive assessment for longitudinal curriculum development. In D.M. Browder (Ed.), *Assessment of individuals with severe handicaps: An applied behavior approach to life skills assessment* (pp. 25–54). Baltimore: Paul H. Brookes Publishing Co.

Brown, L., Branston, M., Hamre-Nietupski, S., Wilcox, B., & Gruenewald, L. (1979). A rationale for comprehensive longitudinal interactions between severely handicapped and nonhandicapped students and other citizens. *AAESPH Review, 4*(1), 3–14.

Brown, L., Schwarz, P., Udvari-Solner, A., Kampschroer, E., Johnson, F., Jorgenson, J., & Gruenewald, L. (1991). How much time should students with severe intellectual disabilities spend in regular education classrooms and elsewhere? *Journal of The Association for Persons with Severe Handicaps, 16*(1), 39–47.

Bullock, C. (1988). Interpretive lines of action of mentally retarded children in mainstreamed play settings. *Studies in Symbolic Interaction, 9*, 145–172.

Center on Human Policy. (1991). *Principles for integrated recreation: Research and Training Center on Community Integration.* Syracuse, NY: Author.

Certo, N., Schleien, S., & Hunter, D. (1983). An ecological assessment inventory to facilitate community recreation participation by severely disabled individuals. *Therapeutic Recreation Journal, 17*(3), 29–38.

Cheseldine, S., & Jeffree, D. (1981). Mentally handicapped adolescents: Their use of leisure. *Journal of Mental Deficiency Research, 25*(1), 49–59.

Cole, D. (1986). Facilitating play in children's peer relationships: Are we having fun yet? *American Educational Research Journal, 23*(2), 201–215.

Cole, D., Meyer, L., Vandercook, T., & McQuarter, R. (1986). Interactions between peers with and without severe handicaps: Dynamics of teacher intervention. *American Journal of Mental Deficiency, 91*(2), 160–169.

Cole, D., Vandercook, T., & Rynders, J. (1987). Dyadic interactions between children with and without mental retardation: Effects of age discrepancy. *American Journal of Mental Deficiency, 92*(2), 194–202.

Dailey, M. (1989). *The search for competencies for counselors of campers with developmental disabilities.* Unpublished master's thesis, University of Minnesota, Minneapolis.

Dattilo, J., & Mirenda, P. (1987). An application of a leisure preference assessment protocol for persons with severe handicaps. *Journal of The Association for Persons with Severe Handicaps, 12*(4), 306–311.

Dattilo, J., & Murphy, W. (1991). *Leisure education program planning: A systematic approach.* State College, PA: Venture.

Dattilo, J., & Schleien, S. (1991). The benefits of therapeutic recreation in developmental disabilities. In C. Coyle, W. Kinney, B. Riley, & J. Shank (Eds.), *Benefits of therapeutic recreation: A consensus view* (pp. 69–150). Philadelphia: Temple University

Durand, V., & Carr, E. (1985). Self-injurious behavior: Motivating conditions and guidelines for treatment. *School Psychology Review, 14*(2), 171–176.

Ellis, G., Forsyth, P., & Voight, A. (1983). Leadership awareness of groups through sociometry. *Parks and Recreation, 18*(9), 54–57.

Eyman, R., & Call, J. (1977). Maladaptive behavior and community placement of mentally retarded persons. *American Journal of Mental Deficiency, 82*(2), 137–144.

Gaylord-Ross, R., Haring, T., Breen, C., & Pitts-Conway, V. (1984). The training and generalization of social interaction skills with autistic youth. *Journal of Applied Behavior Analysis, 17*(2), 229–247.

Gibbons, F. (1985). A social-psychological perspective on developmental disabilities. *Journal of Social and Clinical Psychology, 3*, 391–404.

Gibson, P. (1979). Therapeutic aspects of wilderness programs: A comprehensive literature review. *Therapeutic Recreation Journal, 13*(2), 21–23.

Gollay, E. (1981). Some conceptual and methodological issues in studying the community adjustment of deinstitutionalized mentally retarded people. In R. Bruininks, C. Meyers, B. Sigford, & K. Lakin (Eds.), *Deinstitutionalization and community adjustment of mentally retarded people* (pp. 89–106). Washington, DC: American Association on Mental Deficiency.

Gollay, E., Freedman, R., Wyngaarden, M., & Kurtz, N. (1978). *Coming back: The community experiences of deinstitutionalized mentally retarded people.* Cambridge, MA: Abt.

Goodman, H., Gottlieb, J., & Harrison, R. (1971). Social acceptance of EMR's integrated into a nongraded elementary school. *American Journal of Mental Deficiency, 76*(4), 412–417.

Gottlieb, J., Semmel, M., & Veldman, D. (1978). Correlates of social status among mainstreamed mentally retarded children. *Journal of Educational Psychology, 70*(3), 396–405.

Green, F. (1991). *A study of the impact of community recreation skill acquisition on the social lives of adults with mental retardation.* Unpublished doctoral dissertation, University of Minnesota, Minneapolis.

Green, F., & Schleien, S. (1991). Understanding friendship and recreation: A theoretical sampling. *Therapeutic Recreation Journal, 25*(4), 29–40.

Haring, T., Breen, C., Pitts-Conway, V., Lee, M., & Gaylord-Ross, R. (1987). Adolescent peer tutoring and special friend experiences. *Journal of The Association for Persons with Severe Handicaps, 12*(4), 280–286.

Haring, T., & Lovinger, L. (1989). Promoting social interaction through teaching generalized play initiation responses to preschool children with autism. *Journal of The Association for Persons with Severe Handicaps, 14*(1), 58–67.

Hayden, M., Lakin, K., Hill, B., Bruininks, R., & Copher, J. (1992). Social and leisure integration of people with mental retardation in foster homes and small group homes. *Education and Training in Mental Retardation, 30*(2), 53–62.

Hill, B., & Bruininks, R. (1981). *Family, leisure, and social activities of mentally retarded people in residential facilities*. Minneapolis: Developmental Disabilities Project on Residential Services and Community Adjustment, University of Minnesota.

Horst, G., Wehman, P., Hill, J., & Bailey, C. (1981). Developing age-appropriate leisure skills in severely handicapped adolescents. *Teaching Exceptional Children, 4*(1), 11–15.

Iano, R., Ayers, D., Heller, H., McGettigan, J., & Walker, V. (1974). Sociometric status of retarded children in an integrated program. *Exceptional Children, 40*(4), 267–271.

Johnson, D., & Johnson, R. (1984). *Cooperation in the classroom*. Edina, MN: Interaction Book Company.

Johnson, D., & Johnson, R.(1987). *Joining together: Group theory and group skills*. Englewood Cliffs, NJ: Prentice Hall.

Johnson, D., Johnson, R., & Maruyama, G. (1983). Interdependence and interpersonal attraction among heterogeneous and homogeneous individuals: A theoretical formulation and a meta-analysis of the research. *Review of Educational Research, 53*(1), 5–54.

Johnson, R., & Johnson, D. (1981). Building friendships between handicapped and nonhandicapped students: Effects of cooperative and individualistic instruction. *American Educational Research Journal, 18*(4), 415–423.

Jones, O. (1970). Mother-child communication with pre-linguistic Down's syndrome and normal infants. In H.R. Schaffer (Ed.), *Studies in mother–infant interaction* (pp. 379–401). New York: Academic Press.

Kappel, B., Nagel, S., & Wieck, C. (1990). *The heart of the community is inclusion*. St. Paul: Minnesota Governor's Planning Council on Developmental Disabilities.

Kennedy, C., Horner, R., & Newton, J. (1989). Social contacts of adults with severe disabilities living in the community: A descriptive analysis of relationship patterns. *Journal of The Association for Persons with Severe Handicaps, 14*(3), 190–196.

Kennedy, D., Smith, R., & Austin, D. (1991). *Special recreation: Opportunities for persons with disabilities*. Dubuque, IA: Wm. C. Brown.

Lakin, K., & Bruininks, R. (1985). Contemporary services for handicapped children and youth. In R. Bruininks & K. Lakin (Eds.), *Living and learning in the least restrictive environment* (pp. 3–22). Baltimore: Paul H. Brookes Publishing Co.

McConnell, S.R. (1987). Entrapment effects and the generalization and maintenance of social skills training for elementary school students with behavioral disorders. *Behavioral Disorders, 12*(4), 252–263.

McCord, W. (1983). The outcome of normalization: Strengthened bonds between handicapped persons and their communities. *Education and Training of the Mentally Retarded, 18*(3), 153–157.

McGrew, K., Bruininks, R., Thurlow, M., & Lewis, D. (1992). Empirical analysis of multidimensional measures of community adjustment for young adults with mental retardation. *American Journal of Mental Retardation, 96*(1), 475–487.

Meyer, L., Fox, A., Schermer, A., Ketelson, D., Montan, N., Maley, K., & Cole, D. (1987). The effects of teacher intrusion on social play interactions between autistic and nonhandicapped peers. *Journal of Autism and Developmental Disorders, 17*(3), 315–332.

Meyer, L., & Putnam, J. (1988). Social integration. In V. Van Hasselt, P. Strain, &

M. Hersen (Eds.), *Handbook of developmental and physical disabilities* (pp. 107–133). New York: Pergamon.

Miller, H., Rynders, J., & Schleien, S. (in press). Drama: A medium to enhance the social interaction of students with and without mental retardation. *Mental Retardation*.

Moon, M., & Bunker, L. (1987). Recreation and motor skills programming. In M. Snell (Ed.), *Systematic instruction of persons with severe handicaps* (3rd ed.) (pp. 214–244). Columbus, OH: Merrill.

Newcomer, B., & Morrison, T. (1974). Play therapy with institutionalized mentally retarded children. *American Journal of Mental Deficiency, 78*(6), 727–733.

Novak, D. (1975). Children's responses to imaginary peers labeled as emotionally disturbed. *Psychology Schools, 12*(1), 103–106.

O'Brien, J., Forest, M., Snow, J., & Hasbury, D. (1989). *Action for inclusion: How improve schools by welcoming children with special needs into regular classroo* Toronto, Ontario, Canada: Frontier College.

Odom, S., Hoyson, M., Jamieson, B., & Strain, P. (1985). Increasing handicappe schoolers' social interaction: Cross-setting and component analysis. *Journal of / Behavior Analysis, 18*(1), 3–16.

Patton, M. (1987). *Utilization-focused evalution* (2nd ed.). Beverly Hills, CA: S

Peterson, C., & Gunn, S. (1984). *Therapeutic recreation program design: Prir procedures* (2nd ed.). Englewood Cliffs, NJ: Prentice Hall.

Putnam, J., Rynders, J., Johnson, R., & Johnson, D. (1989). Effects of colla' instruction on promoting positive interpersonal interactions betweer severely mentally handicapped and nonhandicapped children. *Excepti 55*(6), 550–557.

Quilitch, R., & Risley, T. (1973). The effects of play materials on socia *Applied Behavior Analysis, 6*, 573–578.

Reichle, J., Rogers, N., & Barrett, C. (1984). Establishing pragm' among the communicative functions of requesting, rejecting, and cc lescent. *Journal of The Association for Persons With Severe Han*

Reichle, J., Sigafoos, J., & Piché, L. (1989). Teaching an adolesc severe disabilities: A correspondence between requesting and jects. *Journal of The Association for Persons With Severe Han*

Reynolds, R. (1981). A guideline to leisure skills programmin; uals. In P. Wehman & S. Schleien (Eds.), *Leisure program Adaptations, techniques, and curriculum* (pp. 1–13). Aust'

Robb, G. (1980). Developing model camps responsive to th children. *The Bradford papers* (Vol. 1). Bradford: Indiar

Rynders, J., Johnson, R., Johnson, D., & Schmidt, B. (19 tion among Down syndrome and handicapped teenager turing. *American Journal of Mental Deficiency, 85*(3'

Rynders, J., & Schleien, S. (1988). Recreation: A prom' munity integration of young adults with Down sy *syndrome: A resource handbook* (pp. 181–198). F

Rynders, J., & Schleien, S. (1991). *Together success tional programs that integrate people with and* sociation for Retarded Citizens-United States, munity Integration, University of Minnesota

Rynders, J., Schleien, S., Meyer, L., Vandercc K. (1993). Improving integration outcomes ties through cooperatively structured recre tion, 26*(4), 386–407.

Sailor, W., & Guess, D. (1983). *Severely Boston: Houghton Mifflin.

Schleien, S., Certo, N., & Muccino, A

handicapped adolescent: A data based instructional program. *Education and Training of the Mentally Retarded, 19*(4), 297–305.

Schleien, S., Fahnestock, M., Green, R., & Rynders, J. (1990). Building positive social networks through environmental interventions in integrated recreation programs. *Therapeutic Recreation Journal, 24*(4), 42–52.

Schleien, S., & Green, F. (1992). Three approaches for integrating persons with disabilities into community recreation. *Journal of Park and Recreation Administration, 10*(2), 51–66.

Schleien, S., Green, F., & Heyne, L. (1993). Integrated community recreation. In M. Snell (Ed.), *Instruction of students with severe disabilities* (4th ed.). Columbus, OH: Macmillan.

Schleien, S., Heyne, L., & Berken, S. (1988). Integrating physical education to teach appropriate play skills to learners with autism: A pilot study. *Adapted-Physical Activity Quarterly, 5*, 182–192.

Schleien, S., Kiernan, J., & Wehman, P. (1981). Evaluation of an age-appropriate leisure skills program for moderately retarded adults. *Education and Training of the Mentally Retarded, 16*(1), 13–19.

Schleien, S., Light, C., McAvoy, L., & Baldwin, C. (1989). Best professional practices: Serving persons with severe multiple disabilities. *Therapeutic Recreation Journal, 23*(3), 27–40.

Schleien, S., McAvoy, L., Lais, G., & Rynders, J. (in press). *Integrated outdoor education and adventure programs.* Champaign, IL: Sagamore.

Schleien, S., Meyer, L., Heyne, L., & Biel, B. (in press). *Lifelong leisure skills and lifestyles for persons with developmental disabilities.* Baltimore: Paul H. Brookes Publishing Co.

Schleien, S., Olson, K., Rogers, N., & McLafferty, M. (1985). Integrating children with severe handicaps into recreation and physical education programs. *Journal of Park and Recreation Administration, 3*(1), 74–78.

Schleien, S., & Ray, M. (1988). *Community recreation and persons with disabilities: Strategies for integration.* Baltimore: Paul H. Brookes Publishing Co.

Schleien, S., Rynders, J., & Mustonen, T. (1988). Art and integration: What can we create? *Therapeutic Recreation Journal, 22*(4), 18–29.

Schleien, S., Rynders, J., Mustonen, T., & Fox, A. (1990). Effects of social play activities the play behavior of children with autism. *Journal of Leisure Research, 22*(4), 317–328.

Schleien, S., Tuckner, B., & Heyne, L. (1985). Leisure education programs for the severely abled student. *Parks and Recreation, 20*(1), 74–78.

Smith, H. (1992). Lessons from the past. *Parks and Recreation, 27*(2), 46–53.

(1977). *Camping for special children.* St. Louis: C.V. Mosby.

E. (1990). Special Olympics—The Unified Sports program. *OSERS News in 3*(1), 10–11.

, Van Hasselt, V., Hersen, M., & Strain, P. (1985). Peer interventions: Increasing behaviors in multihandicapped children. *Behavior Modification, 9*(3), 293–321.

(1989). Social skills: An integral component of leisure participation and therarecreation services. *Therapeutic Recreation Journal, 23*(2), 30–40.

983). Implementing the IEP. In M. Snell (Ed.), *Systematic instruction of the and severely handicapped* (pp. 113–145). Columbus, OH: Merrill.

87). What does an "appropriate" education mean? In M. Snell (Ed.), *Systemtion of persons with severe handicaps* (3rd ed.) (pp. 1–6). Columbus, OH:

Grigg, N. (1987). Instructional assessment and curriculum development. In d.), *Systematic instruction of persons with severe handicaps* (3rd ed.) . Columbus, OH: Merrill.

e, T., & Apolloni, T. (1976). The role of peers in modifying classmates' r: A review. *Journal of Special Education, 10*(4), 351–356.

Szivos, S., & Griffiths, E. (1990). Group processes involved in coming to terms with a mentally retarded identity. *Mental Retardation, 28*(6), 333–341.

Taylor, S. (1988). Caught in the continuum: A critical analysis of the principle of the least restrictive environment. *Journal of The Association for Persons with Severe Handicaps, 13*(1), 41–53.

Vandercook, T. (1991). Leisure instruction outcomes: Criterion performance, positive interactions, and acceptance by typical high school peers. *The Journal of Special Education, 25*(3), 320–339.

Voeltz, L. (1980). Children's attitudes toward handicapped peers. *American Journal of Mental Deficiency, 84*(5), 455–464.

Voeltz, L., Hemphill, N.J., Brown, S., Kishi, G., Klein, R., Furehling, R., Collie, J., Levy, G., & Kube, C. (1983). *The special friends program: A trainer's manual for integrated school settings* (Rev. Ed.). Honolulu: University of Hawaii, Department of Special Education.

Voeltz, L., Wuerch, B., & Wilcox, B. (1982). Leisure and recreation: Preparation for independence, integration, and self-fulfillment. In B. Wilcox & B.T. Bellamy (Eds.), *Design of high school programs for severely handicapped students* (pp. 175–209). Baltimore: Paul H. Brookes Publishing Co.

Walker, P., & Edinger, B. (1988). The kid from Cabin 17. *Camping Magazine, 60*(7), 18–21.

Walker, P., Edinger, B., Willis, C., & Kenney, M. (1988). *Beyond the classroom: Involving students with disabilities in extracurricular activities at Levy School.* Syracuse, NY: Center on Human Policy.

Wehman, P., Renzaglia, A., & Bates, P. (1985). Leisure skill instruction. In P. Wehman, A. Renzaglia, & P. Bates (Eds.), *Functional living skills for moderately and severely handicapped individuals* (pp. 123–154). Austin, TX: PRO-ED.

Wehman, P., & Schleien, S. (1981). *Leisure programs for handicapped persons: Adaptations, techniques, and curriculum.* Austin, TX: PRO-ED.

Wessel, J. (1976). *I CAN program.* Northbrook, IL: Hubbard Scientific.

Wolfensberger, W. (1983). Social role valorization: A proposed new term for the principle of normalization. *Mental Retardation, 21*(6), 234–239.

Wuerch, B., & Voeltz, L. (1982). *Longitudinal leisure skills for severely handicapped learners: The Ho'onanea curriculum component.* Baltimore: Paul H. Brookes Publishing Co.

_ Chapter 7

Distinguishing Between Socially and Nonsocially Motivated Challenging Behavior

Implications for the Selection of Intervention Strategies

Jeff Sigafoos,
Joe Reichle, and Cheryl Light-Shriner

Challenging behavior usually refers to actions that result in injury to the individual (i.e., self-injury) or to others in the environment, cause damage to the physical environment, interfere with the acquisition of new skills, or socially isolate an individual. In addition to creating a barrier to initial community placement (Hill, Lakin, & Bruininks, 1984; Hill et al., 1989; Pagel & Whitling, 1978), challenging behavior is a major cause of admission and readmission to state institutions (Hill & Bruininks, 1982; Nihira & Nihira, 1975; Pagel & Whitling, 1978).

During the past 20 years, a tremendous number of people with developmental disabilities have moved from large congregate institutions (16 or more residents) to more normalized community living environments (Hill et al., 1984). Between

Preparation of this chapter was supported in part by Grant #DCSH-30 from the Australian Commonwealth, Department of Community Services and Health and by a cooperative agreement (#H133B80048) between the National Institute on Disability and Rehabilitation Research (NIDRR) and the Research and Training Center on Residential Services and Community Living at the University of Minnesota (College of Education) located within the Institute on Community Integration (UAP). The opinions expressed herein are those of the authors and do not necessarily reflect the position or policy of the Australian Commonwealth, Department of Community Services and Health, NIDRR, the Research and Training Center on Residential Services and Community Living, University of Minnesota (College of Education), or the Institute on Community Integration (UAP).

1967 and 1989, the populations of large public institutions were reduced by more than 50%, from about 195,000 to 88,000 (Lakin, 1979; Scheerenberger, 1988). Most of the individuals discharged from public institutions during that period were placed in community residential facilities, which today house about 135,000 persons with developmental disabilities (Lakin, Prouty, White, Bruininks, & Hill, 1989). States are virtually unanimous in their conviction that these trends will continue (Lakin, Jaskulski, et al., 1989).

Evidence also suggests that a large proportion of those individuals who remain in large, state-operated facilities engage in serious patterns of challenging behavior. For example, a 1989 survey of all state institutions indicated that 46% of current residents have behavior disorders (Scheerenberger, 1988). While longitudinal studies of people moving from public institutions to community settings show that positive gains in basic skills of daily living are consistently associated with community placement, this same research indicates no predictable pattern of reduction or increase in behavior problems associated with the change (Larson & Lakin, 1989). The provision of community programs that can meet the behavioral challenges of persons yet to be discharged from institutional settings will require significant advances in access to and in application of behavior management technology in community settings.

Although addressing challenging behavior must be a major part of planning for continued deinstitutionalization, many community programs are already called on to meet the needs of persons who present serious behavior problems and have been integrated into the community. For example, the 1987 National Medical Expenditure Survey found that 23% of residents of private community facilities of 3–15 persons were reported to engage in physically aggressive behavior directed at other people, and 18% were reported to engage in self-injurious behavior (Lakin, Hill, Chen, & Stephens, 1989). Another 1987 national sample of 336 people living in foster homes and small group homes of six or fewer residents obtained the same estimates for physically aggressive and self-injurious behavior (Hill et al., 1989).

If effective programs are to be developed that will support persons with developmental disabilities, including those who engage in challenging behavior within community environments, it is important to understand the specific variables that maintain this behavior. During the past two decades, various theories have been advanced to explain the origin of challenging behaviors (see Carr, 1977, for a review). Regardless of theory, it is clear that challenging behaviors are often maintained by their consequences. These maintaining consequences are referred to when the function, motivation, or purpose of the challenging behavior is inferred (Day, Johnson, & Schussler, 1986; Evans & Meyer, 1985; Smith, 1990). Other challenging behaviors appear to be less directly influenced by environmentally based antecedents or consequences. Biological conditions, such as earaches, headaches, allergies, and a host of other pain-creating conditions, may precipitate challenging behavior that is neither more or less apt to occur in the presence of another individual. The purpose of this chapter is to differentiate between socially and nonsocially motivated challenging behavior and to discuss a range of intervention strategies that have been demonstrated to be effective decelerating behaviors associated with each of these motivations.

DISTINGUISHING AMONG
MOTIVATIONS FOR CHALLENGING BEHAVIOR

A number of investigators (Parrott, 1986; Skinner, 1953; Vargas, 1988) assert that some behaviors are maintained primarily by the consequences that, in the past, followed as a direct or indirect result of the act itself. A thirsty person, for example, reaches for and grasps a cup because this action has previously enabled him or her to drink the beverage, thus quenching his or her thirst. Turning away from a bright light is similarly reinforced in that it enables a person to escape from an otherwise annoying stimulus.

Other behaviors are maintained primarily by the consequences that indirectly follow through the mediation of others. Asking another person to "pass the cup " is only likely to be effective in the presence of a listener predisposed to pass objects upon request. Telling another to "turn out the light" is also indirectly effective. In these two instances, asking and telling have no direct effect on the location of the cup or the brightness of the light, respectively. Instead, these behaviors produce reinforcing consequences by changing the actions of others. Whether challenging behaviors are maintained primarily by the consequences that directly or indirectly follow them, these behaviors can also be either socially or nonsocially motivated.

Although some investigators have emphasized the social motivations for challenging behavior, others have maintained a distinction between social and nonsocial motivations (Carr & Durand, 1985b). In discussing types of self-injurious acts among persons with mental retardation who reside in a state-operated institution, researchers found that various forms of self-injury can be categorized into either socially motivated and nonsocially motivated behaviors (Schroeder, Schroeder, Smith, & Dalldorf, 1978). Some self-injurious behaviors, for example, appear to produce obvious and direct sensory consequences, presumably of a sufficiently reinforcing nature to maintain the behavior (e.g., pica, mouthing objects). Other types of self-injurious acts are maintained by socially mediated consequences, such as staff attention or the withdrawal of task demands (e.g., head banging, self-biting).

Within each class of behavior, it is important to differentiate between the motivation of a behavior and the form of a behavior. The *motivation* of a behavior refers to the reason a person engages in a behavior; in other words, for what purpose or outcome does the person engage in the action. Many individuals, for example, engage in challenging behavior to: 1) receive attention; 2) obtain the opportunity to escape or avoid unpleasant, undesirable situations; and 3) to obtain desired objects or activities. *Form* refers to the specific actions that a person demonstrates. For example, some individuals with developmental disabilities engage in *head banging*, which is a person's actions while banging his or her head.

The relationship between form and function is complex; that is, one form of challenging behavior can be used across several different motivational classes. In addition, one functional class may accommodate a number of different forms of challenging behaviors. For example, head banging for one person may serve many functions (e.g., to escape or avoid, to gain attention, to obtain desired objects or food). For another individual many forms of behavior (e.g., head banging, hitting others, running away) could serve a single purpose (e.g., to gain attention).

Socially Motivated Challenging Behavior

A behavior is *socially motivated* when it functions to mediate actions from others. This type of behavior functions indirectly to achieve consequences that will maintain the behavior. Defined in this manner, a socially motivated behavior may function communicatively and include graphic (e.g., communication boards, wallets, books) as well as gestural (e.g., natural gestures, signing) modes and does not exclusively refer to *speech*.

Actions may become communicative because, in the past, others have responded in ways that have reinforced the behaviors. An adult with whom one of the authors worked, for example, had no formal means of communicating, but would frequently slap his right thigh. Some of the staff at his work program responded to this gesture as if the person were requesting more of whatever object was appropriate to the context (e.g., more cheese and crackers during lunch, more materials for work). Since this behavior would cease when the appropriate materials were supplied and reappear as the supply was depleted, it seemed likely that thigh slapping represented an idiosyncratic form of communication. It is possible that because staff responded consistently to this behavior by giving this individual the desired object, thigh slapping had become an effective means of requesting objects.

In some instances, a chain of actions may have been effective in achieving a desired outcome without the mediation of another individual. Upon seeing a person move in the direction of a desired item, for example, another person may hand it to the individual. If this history continues, over time, the action of moving toward a desired item may come to represent an informal means of gaining access to items through the mediation of another. As the individual's action serves as an effective indirect method to obtain items, the behavior may be used less as a direct means.

Several general classes of socially motivated challenging behavior have been reported—attention-motivated behaviors, avoidance- or escape-motivated behaviors, and object-motivated behaviors.

Attention-Motivated Behaviors   Attention has long been recognized as an effective type of social reinforcement for the behavior of a substantial number of persons with or without disabilities (Skinner, 1953). For some individuals, attention provided as a consequence of challenging behavior does, in fact, maintain or increase rates of challenging behavior. Lovaas, Freitag, Gold, and Kassorla (1965) demonstrated that when warm, caring statements (e.g., "Wow! That was great.")

were delivered to a child following instances of self-injurious behavior, rates of self-injury increased. When these warm, caring statements were withdrawn, rates of self-injury decreased.

Similarly, O'Neill, Horner, Albin, Storey, and Sprague (1990) described a young woman who engaged in a variety of disruptive and aggressive behaviors (e.g., pounding a work table, pinching staff members) at a community vocational program. They found that during work periods when lower than usual amounts of attention were given to this woman, she engaged in high rates of disruptive and aggressive behavior. In contrast, during work periods when she received higher amounts of attention (e.g., every 30 seconds), she engaged in much lower rates of disruptive and aggressive behavior. O'Neill et al. (1990) concluded that this young woman's disruptive and aggressive behavior was maintained or positively reinforced by attention. Durand (1990) stated that "social attention can have negative effects if it becomes a regular consequence for . . . troubling behaviors" (p. 12). He added that this is especially true when attention is seldom delivered to the person at times when he or she is not engaging in the troubling behaviors.

Avoidance- or Escape-Motivated Behaviors   Escape from nonpreferred events has been demonstrated to reinforce and to maintain challenging behavior (Carr & Durand, 1985a; Iwata, Pace, Kalsher, Cowdery, & Cataldo, 1990; Mace, Page, Ivancic, & O'Brien, 1986). The most commonly studied nonpreferred event is the task demand. An individual might engage in self-injurious or aggressive behaviors when a particular demand is made (e.g., "Time to work."). In the past, such behaviors may have been successful in getting others to withdraw that demand.

Object-Motivated Behaviors   The use of tangibles to reinforce behavior has been a commonly used strategy when teaching new behavior. These same tangible or object consequences can sometimes maintain or increase challenging behavior. *Tangible* refers to both events that are considered permanent products (e.g., objects, food, leisure materials) and those events that do not have permanent products (e.g., activities such as going for a walk, going outside to play). If tangibles identified as reinforcers are delivered immediately following challenging behavior, the likelihood of the challenging behavior occurring in the future increases (Durand, 1990). One of the authors knew of an adult with severe developmental disabilities who was often observed to engage in aggressive behavior toward a peer. This individual's aggressive behavior was interrupted briefly and then the person was led outdoors to calm down during a walk. After numerous instances of aggression, this individual was observed walking toward the door following the interruption procedure. For this individual, it appeared that engaging in aggressive behavior predictably resulted in going for a walk, and at least in this case, this consequence positively reinforced the challenging behavior.

Nonsocially Motivated Challenging Behavior

Research has demonstrated that sensory, perceptual, and tactile stimulation are effective types of reinforcement for some persons with developmental disabilities (Ferrari & Harris, 1981; Green et al., 1988; Pace, Ivancic, Edwards, Iwata, &

Page, 1985; Rehagen & Thelen, 1972; Rincover & Newsome, 1985). Sensory or perceptual feedback produced as a direct result of a behavior may serve to reinforce certain forms of challenging behaviors. In particular, such direct stimulation or feedback is indicated frequently as *the* maintaining consequence for some individuals who engage in challenging behavior (Durand & Carr, 1987; Hung, 1978; Sturmey, Carlsen, Crisp, & Newton, 1988; Wieseler, Hanson, Chamberlain, & Thompson, 1985). Body-rocking, gazing at lights, or finger-flicking are common forms of stereotypic movements that may, for some individuals, be maintained by the vestibular, visual, or tactile stimulation that follows as a direct result of each respective act.

Injurious forms of challenging behavior may also produce direct sensory or perceptual consequences that function to maintain these actions. Eye-poking is a form of self-injury that is sometimes observed among persons with severe intellectual delay and, in particular, among individuals with visual impairments (Schroeder, Mulick, & Rojahn, 1980). In these cases, the behavior may provide a source of visual stimulation not otherwise available to the person and, hence, may occur because of this effect. Other types of challenging behavior, such as head banging, if intense, may prolong and frequently trigger the release of opium-like chemicals in the brain. Cataldo and Harris (1982) speculated that for some individuals, the reinforcing effects of these chemicals may be sufficient to maintain the behavior. Pain associated with these acts may be endured because persistence in the past brought feelings of pleasure.

Perhaps injuries resulting from direct attempts to reduce pain, rather than bring pleasure, are more common (Michael, 1975). Pain from an ear infection can be relieved by hitting or banging one's head, as some children seem to discover (De Lissovoy, 1963). This type of behavior produces temporary escape from aversive stimulation and works in a very direct manner. In addition, there may be a linear relationship between the intensity of the act and the magnitude of the reinforcing effect. The more frequently a person head bangs, the longer may be the interval before the pain in his or her ear again becomes unbearable. However, due to this direct relationship, the behavior may escalate rapidly to the point where injury occurs.

Interrelatedness of Socially and Nonsocially Motivated Behavior

Control by both social and nonsocial effects, as well as the possibility that the consequences maintaining a given behavior could change over time, may be contributing to some of the discrepancies in the current literature regarding the classification of challenging behavior. Often, it appears that socially and nonsocially motivated challenging behaviors are two mutually exclusive categories. There is a growing base of support, however, that views these behaviors as interdependent.

Researchers have indicated that most, if not all, challenging behavior serves a communicative function which, in turn, implies a social motivation (Donnellan, Mirenda, Mesaros, & Fassbender, 1984; Neel & Billingsley, 1989). Challenging behaviors that occur when the individual is alone, for example, could be communicating something equivalent to the statement of "I'm bored" (Donnellan et al.,

1984). Others have speculated that challenging behaviors that occur when an individual is alone indicate a nonsocial motivation in the form of direct sensory or automatic reinforcement (Day, Rea, Schussler, Larsen, & Johnson, 1988; Iwata, Dorsey, Slifer, Bauman, & Richman, 1982). It is possible that, in the past, being alone was a condition in which challenging behaviors resulted in the appearance of others—others who then, at least occasionally, mediated some important consequence (Lovaas, 1982). In fact, in the latter instance, the challenging behavior might have originated as a nonsocially motivated consequence. However, as time passed, the challenging behavior may have come to be associated with the delivery of social attention. If this occurs, it is reasonable to hypothesize that the challenging behavior may serve both a social and nonsocial function depending on whether automatic reinforcement or attention is more salient.

In addition, the consequences that maintain a behavior may not remain stable. Over time, consequences can change from having direct effects to having more indirect effects and vice versa. For example, a person may scratch to relieve themselves of an itch caused by an insect bite and find that scratching always results in attention from another person. The itch caused by the insect bite (nonsocial motivation for scratching) will eventually cease, but the person may continue to scratch to obtain the attention (social motivation). Conversely, in other cases, the process may work in reverse. Some individuals may learn that hitting themselves in the head is an effective means of gaining attention from others. Yet, others may not always attend to the behavior, and when attention is not forthcoming, the individual may engage in a display of more frequent, intense, and prolonged head banging. Perhaps during one of these extinction bursts, endogenous opiates, which have their own reinforcing effects on the behavior, are released. At some stage, the behavior may be maintained by both social and nonsocial consequences, or perhaps if the narcotic-like effects prove more powerful, the behavior may shift from the social to the nonsocial end of the continuum.

Obviously, challenging behaviors do not always lend themselves readily to classification as either socially or nonsocially motivated. This could be due to the possibility that some contingencies into which challenging behaviors enter may include characteristics of both. In other instances, the variables maintaining a given challenging behavior may change from primarily social to primarily nonsocial and vice versa. Distinctions among classes of challenging behavior, in terms of maintaining consequences, will need to account for any such discrepancies. The determination of what maintains and motivates behavior, either socially or nonsocially, has been found to have important implications for the selection of intervention strategies to address challenging behaviors among persons with developmental disabilities.

TYPES OF INTERVENTION STRATEGIES

The goal of intervention strategies that address challenging behavior is to reduce the frequency, duration, or intensity of the challenging behavior, while at the same time improving the individual's quality of life. Researchers have discussed five categories of intervention strategies to reduce challenging behavior. These categories are: 1) ecological manipulations, 2) immediate antecedent manipulations, 3) replacement-based intervention strategies, 4) consequence manipulations, and 5) emergency procedures.

Ecological Manipulations

Ecological manipulations are interventions designed to explore a variety of variables that may be contributing to a problem behavior, such as the establishment or alteration of schedules and routines, the treatment of physical and medical conditions, and the rearrangement or modification of the physical environment. In many situations, establishing predictable schedules and routines and including opportunities for a person to make choices regarding daily activities and tasks is effective in reducing the likelihood that challenging behavior will occur. If a challenging behavior is the result of some type of physical ailment (e.g., allergies, menstrual cramps, sinus infections), the treatment of that ailment will decrease the probability of that behavior occurring again.

Ecological variables are environmental aspects of specific settings, such as a classroom, group home, or vocational placement setting. These environmental aspects are different from "immediate antecedents or consequences of behavior, such as prompts and reinforcers . . ." (Nordquist & Twardosz, 1990, p. 276). Many ecological variables can be considered setting events that may increase the likelihood, or set the stage, for a range of behavior to be emitted (Brown, 1991; Gardner, Cole, Davidson, & Karan, 1986; Leigland, 1984; Nordquist & Twardosz, 1990). More specifically, setting events refer to either internal situations (e.g., hunger, menstrual cramps, headaches) or external situations (e.g., interactions with other people) that influence interactions and behaviors at times and places that are temporarily removed from their original provoking stimuli or situations.

Brown (1991), for example, described an individual who became upset when he wasn't allowed to finish a specific task (i.e., rolling up his car window) in the morning. Later in the day, this individual was more likely to become emotional and engage in self-injurious and destructive behavior. Similarly, Gardner et al. (1986) described an individual who engaged in uncooperative and aggressive behavior when specific immediate antecedent events were delivered. These researchers examined more distant events (e.g., weekend family visits, difficulty rising in the morning, arguments with peers earlier in the day) and found that the setting events identified increased the likelihood that uncooperative and aggressive behavior would occur.

Recently, interventions that involve manipulations of ecological or environmental variables (e.g., setting events) have been developed to decrease challenging behaviors. These manipulations often include modification or rearrangement of the environment, changing the social aspects of the environment, and/or altering programmatic aspects of the environment (Nordquist & Twardosz, 1990). For instance, if having too few activity materials usually causes disruptive behavior because individuals are waiting too long or do not yet have sufficient sharing and turn-taking skills, then more materials could be provided or groups could partake in a variety of activities that require different materials.

Occasionally, inattentive and disruptive behavior emerges in crowded situations. Researchers have found that minimizing crowded conditions by providing groups with a larger area in which to work and interact often prevents such disruptive behavior (Krantz & Risley, 1977). Other investigators have found that developing predictable activity schedules or routines can be effective in reducing the likelihood that challenging behavior will occur (Brown, 1991; Nordquist & Twardosz, 1990).

Ecological variables can be manipulated in many different ways in order to reduce the occurrence of challenging behavior. These manipulations range from establishing predictable routines in a person's life to permanently modifying or altering the physical environment (e.g., carpeting hard surfaces). An examination of potential setting events, and not just immediate antecedent variables, is extremely helpful in developing effective interventions. In some situations, however, it is necessary to identify the immediate antecedents in order to decrease the likelihood that challenging behavior will occur.

Immediate Antecedent Manipulations

Immediate antecedent manipulations are interventions that reduce environmental conditions that may be provoking challenging behavior, such as limiting stimuli for problem behaviors or mixing easy and more difficult requests. In other situations, the environment can be temporarily arranged to decrease the frequency of the problem. If loud noise predictably evokes challenging behavior, for example, the reduction of the noise level would be an appropriate intervention. Similarly, if particular tasks are perceived by the person as nonpreferred and the task is nonfunctional or nonessential, it can be eliminated from the person's schedule and replaced with a more preferred and functional task. It is important to point out that it may be difficult to permanently eliminate some provoking conditions in a person's environment. In other situations, it may be desirable to eliminate these conditions temporarily (e.g., nonpreferred but functional tasks) and then gradually reintroduce these stimuli in small doses to teach the person to tolerate some provoking stimuli.

A list of common antecedent factors that tend to evoke and maintain behaviors are fairly easy to generate. For example, the young child who throws a tantrum at the toy store could be given a single toy or a specific preferred item as a distraction before a tantrum could begin. For the person who hits or kicks to escape task demands, the interventionist could choose one of several intervention options. One option might be to refrain from placing tasks demands on this person. This, however, might conflict with attempts to provide functional treatment. A second option would be to give the person a choice of tasks he or she would like to complete. This option may pose problems, however, if the person never chooses specific, important, functional tasks (e.g., taking a shower, brushing teeth). A third option would be to make a nonpreferred task more enjoyable by presenting the person with a preferred event concurrently with the task demand (e.g., allow a person to listen to a favorite cassette tape while showering). A fourth option would be to implement a behavioral momentum strategy.

Behavior momentum refers to the effect gained from an intervention that is designed to establish a brief history of compliance to easy task demands (i.e., task demands that the individual has a high probability of completing) just prior to placing a more difficult or nonpreferred task demand on the person. This strategy has been effective across a variety of age groups and among individuals with severe disabilities (Davis, Brady, Williams, & Hamilton, 1992; Harchik & Putzier, 1990; Mace & Belfiore, 1990; Singer, Singer, & Horner, 1987).

Assessment of some challenging behavior may demonstrate dysfunctional interactions between a person and others with whom he or she interacts. Coercive interactions may come to dominate, with the individual only being approached when there is a need to give a directive or to correct a problem. Examination of the controlling variables may highlight the dysfunctional nature of the typical interaction patterns that have emerged. Once identified, many of these coercive interactions can be eliminated. For example, an interventionist and others could begin to approach the person with reinforcing objects or events. If a person enjoys music, he or she could be approached with a radio or tape player that is playing a favorite tune. This will help to change or alter the dysfunctional interaction history and begin to build a more functional and reinforcing history of interactions. When used skillfully and under the right conditions, strategies designed to eliminate controlling variables represent an appropriate and potentially effective option for both socially and nonsocially motivated challenging behavior.

Replacement-Based Intervention Strategies

Replacement-based intervention strategies include interventions designed to replace challenging behavior with a new skill. With replacement-based strategies, the person is taught appropriate alternatives to problem behaviors and is provided with personalized reinforcers. For example, if a person engages in self-injurious behavior (e.g., face slapping) because he or she enjoys the attention this behavior recruits, it would be logical that a socially appropriate communicative response could be taught to recruit attention using less effort (e.g., activate a switch to a tape player that plays a message such as, "I want to talk to you."). After a while, this strategy should result in the reduction of challenging behavior because the person now has a better way to obtain the same reinforcer.

There is a growing recognition that an effective approach to the management of challenging behaviors involves teaching socially acceptable alternatives to individuals in order to replace problematic responses (Durand, 1987; Evans & Meyer, 1985; Meyer & Evans, 1989). A critical component of this approach is to teach an alternative that is functionally equivalent to the challenging behavior (Carr, 1988). This means that replacement behavior must provide the individual with an equally, or preferably, more effective means of obtaining the same reinforcement responsible for maintaining the challenging behavior. Selecting a functionally equivalent and maximally effective option to challenging behavior requires a careful and comprehensive functional assessment (Carr & Durand, 1985a; Durand & Crimmins, 1988; Iwata et al., 1982, 1990; Mace et al., 1986; Steege, Wacker, Berg, Cigrand, & Cooper, 1989).

The selection of a functionally equivalent and maximally efficient alternative to an existing challenging behavior is perhaps most obvious as an intervention option if the challenging behavior is socially motivated. Since socially motivated challenging behavior can be viewed as a rather unconventional form of communicative behavior, a logical strategy would be to replace these unconventional forms with more conventional communicative forms, such as speech, manual signs or gestures, or perhaps the use of a picture-based communication board (Baumgart, Johnson, & Helmstetter, 1990; Reichle, York, & Sigafoos, 1991). For example, an individual might attempt to hit or kick others when certain types of demands are made (e.g., "Time to work."). In the past, hitting or kicking under these conditions may have been negatively reinforced in the sense that others would, at least occasionally, withdraw prior demands contingent on such incidents of aggression. Thus, aggressive acts could be interpreted—again with a minimal degree of inference—as a rather unconventional type of demand or more specifically, as a form of rejecting behavior. As the behavior is maintained by consequences mediated by others, it is, by definition, verbal or communicative and socially motivated.

A logical intervention strategy would be to replace hitting and kicking by teaching a more acceptable means of expressing rejection (Reichle, Rogers, & Barrett, 1984). Alternatively, if the challenging behaviors were more likely in the presence of a difficult task, intervention might focus on teaching the individual to request assistance with that activity (Carr & Durand, 1985b). Both of the above examples are consistent with the rationale of replacing socially motivated challenging behavior with more acceptable and conventional forms of verbal or communicative behavior. This particular type of replacement-based intervention strategy has come to be called functional communication training (Bird, Dores, Moniz, & Robinson, 1989; Carr & Durand, 1985a, 1985b).

Not all strategies within the class of replacement-based interventions, however, need necessarily involve functional communication training. For example, consider a person whose repertoire of challenging behavior is maintained by the occasional receipt of preferred objects supplied by others. One obvious intervention strategy would be to teach the individual a more acceptable means of requesting preferred objects (Horner & Budd, 1985). An alternative approach that might also prove effective would be to teach the person to gain access to preferred objects independently, such as to select preferred food items from a refrigerator and then prepare a meal. In this example, a more socially motivated challenging behavior is replaced by teaching an alternative that is directly effective in producing the same consequences previously mediated by others.

Both of the preceding skills may be desirable and useful as part of a comprehensive intervention package to replace challenging behavior. Sometimes it may be necessary or expected for a person to make a request, while at other times it may be more efficient and indeed expected that a person would help themselves. Requesting versus helping oneself often depends on other factors. Due to these types of conditional discriminations (i.e., knowing when to engage in a behavior and when *not* to engage in a behavior), a number of related skills may need to be taught if a given challenging behavior is to be replaced. A certain type of communicative behavior (e.g., requesting) might be taught to replace the challenging behavior under some conditions (i.e., when the mediation of another is expected or required), whereas another cluster of skills (e.g., independently accessing objects) would be taught to replace the challenging behavior under other conditions (i.e., when it is expected or possible to help oneself).

A number of studies have demonstrated that socially motivated challenging behaviors can be reduced by teaching functionally equivalent communicative alternatives (Carr & Durand, 1985a; Durand & Carr, 1991; Wacker et al., 1990). Replacement-based strategies have also been effective in reducing challenging behaviors when other types of approaches were ineffective; for example, approaches based on overriding existing contingencies and the establishment of new and different reinforcement histories (Bird et al., 1989). Such approaches may be effective in part because they are designed to provide the person with an alternative means of accessing the same consequences that were identified to maintain the challenging behavior. Since such consequences were shown to be functional in maintaining the challenging behavior, these same consequences are perhaps likely to represent effective types of reinforcement for more appropriate behaviors as well (Durand, Crimmins, Caulfield, & Taylor, 1989).

Durand and Crimmins (1991) have identified several other potential advantages of strategies designed to replace challenging behaviors with functionally equivalent, yet socially acceptable, alternatives. With a favorable reinforcement schedule ensuring that the functionally equivalent alternative is more efficient (i.e., reinforced more frequently) than the challenging behavior, replacement-based strategies can often work to reduce challenging behaviors very quickly. In addition, because people are taught alternative ways to obtain the same type of reinforcement that maintained the challenging behavior, the effects associated with extinction of the challenging behavior (e.g., initial increase in the challenging behavior, emotional outbursts) should be less likely. This assumes that the alternative behavior is taught using errorless procedures, so that a high rate of reinforcement is available, even during the early stages of intervention when the behavior is being taught.

Improved generalization and maintenance are other potential advantages of replacement-based strategies. A functional communicative skill is likely to be appropriately reinforced by others, providing that the mode of communication is easily interpreted. When such an easy-to-interpret alternative is taught to replace challenging behavior, it may provide the individual with a skill that others will know how to reinforce, and this natural reinforcement should improve generalization and maintenance (Durand & Crimmins, 1991).

Implementation of replacement-based strategies need not necessarily be restricted to instances of socially motivated challenging behavior. Consider the person who is likely to throw a dinner plate containing a nonpreferred food item. To this person, throwing may be an effective and direct means of removing the nonpreferred item. If so, throwing would perhaps be more appropriately classified as a nonsocially motivated challenging behavior. In this case, a replacement-based intervention strategy may be applicable. Specifically, the person might be taught to reject nonpreferred food items more appropriately, perhaps by saying "no," or gesturing. Removal of the nonpreferred item, previously accomplished directly by throwing, would now be mediated by others, contingent upon an acceptable form of expressing rejection. As this example illustrates, the strategy of choice for some nonsocially motivated challenging behavior may also involve teaching an alternative communicative behavior.

Replacement-based intervention strategies reflect a positive and proactive approach to challenging behavior. In addition, the teaching of functionally equivalent and socially acceptable alternatives to replace challenging behavior is an educative approach that promotes development of the individual's skills (Evans & Meyer, 1985; Horner et al., 1990). Consequently, replacement-based intervention strategies are consistent with the general mission of public schools, community residential settings, and other service agencies (Gardner & Chapman, 1990).

Consequence Manipulations

Consequence manipulations are interventions designed to deliver powerful reinforcers contingent upon appropriate behavior. These types of interventions reduce or eliminate reinforcers for problem behaviors, while providing personalized reinforcers for adaptive behaviors. For example, if a person engages in screaming behavior and throws a tantrum because such behavior usually promotes other people delivering food and social contact, the interventionist could instead deliver preferred food and positive social contact at times when the individual is not engaging in the challenging behavior or when the person engages in appropriate behavior. These new contingencies can override consequences that are currently maintaining the challenging behavior. Correspondingly, one may take steps to ensure that the outcome associated with emission of the challenging behavior is not forthcoming.

One strategy to reduce challenging behavior is to identify and deliver an effective type of reinforcement contingent upon the absence of the challenging behavior. Typically, a predetermined and increasing period of time without display of the identified problem behavior would be followed by the reinforcer. If access to this identified reinforcer is of sufficient power, more and more time would be presumably allocated to other behavior, thus reducing the amount of time the person spent engaged in challenging behavior. This technique is known as *differential reinforcement of other behavior* (DRO) and has been used often and effectively to reduce challenging behaviors among people with developmental disabilities (Jones, 1991; Luiselli, 1988; Repp, Barton, & Brulle, 1983; Repp & Deitz, 1974).

Two variations on the DRO technique include the *differential reinforcement of alternative behavior* (DRA) and the *differential reinforcement of incompatible behavior* (DRI). As with DRO, both of these approaches are designed to override variables that are currently maintaining the challenging behavior by introducing a more powerful reinforcement contingency for some alternative or incompatible behavior. With DRA, reinforcement is arranged for a specified behavior that is considered to represent a socially acceptable alternative to the challenging behavior. By contrast, in a DRI procedure, the reinforced behavior is both socially acceptable and incompatible with the challenging behavior. Differential reinforcement schedules have been used successfully to reduce challenging behaviors among persons with developmental disabilities (Jones, 1991). Provided the strengthened other, alternative, or incompatible behaviors are acceptable and valued, these three strategies represent a potentially educative approach as well. Although they do not typically involve direct instruction to establish new skills, increases in more acceptable behaviors are anticipated benefits when the techniques are applied effectively.

Another strategy consistent with an intervention strategy of contingency override is the use of punishment procedures. In these procedures, a stimulus that is undesirable to the person emitting the socially unacceptable behavior is delivered contingent upon challenging behavior emission. If application of this stimulus proves, in fact, to be an effective type of punishment, then the challenging behavior is likely to be suppressed, even though the former maintaining variables may still be operative (Dorsey, Iwata, Ong, & McSween, 1980; Lovaas & Simmons, 1969; Tanner & Zeiler, 1975).

Unlike differential positive reinforcement strategies, punishment procedures are less educative. The punishment of challenging behavior does not necessarily result in the strengthening of more acceptable behaviors. While in some cases few negative side effects and even some positive side effects from the suppression of challenging behaviors through punishment have been reported (Lichstein & Schreibman, 1976), there are a host of potential problems associated with the application of aversive stimuli as part of a punishment contingency (Sidman, 1989). The application of punishment may generate escape and avoidance behaviors that may interfere with the provision of other educational or habilitative services. In addition, a person who has been punished may often retaliate with other problematic behaviors, such as attacking the person who delivers the punishment. Finally, the application of aversive stimuli as part of a punishment contingency has been questioned on ethical principles (Evans & Meyer, 1990; Guess, Helmstetter, Turnbull, & Knowlton, 1987).

Consequence manipulations have been found effective in addressing some challenging behavior. Reinforcement schedules can be effective in reducing challenging behavior by differentially reinforcing other, alternative, or incompatible behaviors and by providing another positive and proactive approach to challenging behavior. In addition, some punishment strategies, although less educative and sometimes problem-provoking, have been found to be effective in suppressing some challenging behaviors. Both types of consequence manipulations address challenging behavior by overriding maintaining variables and contingencies and introducing different and more powerful variables and contingencies. These strategies should be considered in combination with other strategies (e.g., replacement-based strategies).

Emergency Procedures

Emergency procedures, employed to protect, consist of very restrictive measures designed to interrupt serious injurious or destructive behavior. Some of these procedures are manual restraint, mechanical restraint, time out from reinforcement, and temporary deprivation from goods or services. *Manual restraint* refers to physically holding some part of a person to prevent injurious or destructive behavior, either to self or others. *Mechanical restraint* refers to applying a device (e.g., straps) to hold a person immobile, again to prevent injurious or destructive behavior. *Time out from reinforcement* involves removing the person from the current reinforcing environment for a short period of time until the person is calm. *Deprivational procedures* often refer to strategies that limit a person's access to objects or activities that the person has used in an inappropriate or dangerous manner.

Historically, these intrusive procedures have been commonly and frequently used to manage challenging behavior. Although it is sometimes necessary to protect individuals from themselves and others, these procedures are considered outside the range of educative options. Since emergency procedures are not educative, they will not be further elaborated on in this chapter. At best, these procedures should be viewed as last-resort strategies to interrupt those challenging behaviors that are life threatening or represent a significant physical threat to others.

SELECTION OF INTERVENTION STRATEGIES

Comprehensive intervention packages meant to address challenging behavior will often involve the combined implementation of the strategies outlined in this chapter. Selecting the most appropriate intervention to address a given class of challenging behavior will often require further consideration of the characteristics of each type of intervention. After the variables controlling a challenging behavior are identified, there may be several potentially applicable intervention options. For instance, consider a situation in which a self-injurious behavior (i.e., self-biting) appears to be maintained by attention. A logical intervention might be to teach the individual a more appropriate means of gaining attention. Another example involves a person who exhibits aggressive acts when confronted with a particular task demand. Suppose these acts represented are a means of avoiding the task. Logical intervention options here might include teaching the individual more appropriate means to refuse task participation (i.e., a replacement-based strategy); shaping increasing levels of participation through reinforcement (i.e., overriding strategy); or simply removing the task demand from the person's routine (i.e., eliminating the controlling variables). What is the intervention of choice in this latter situation? Ideally, it would be of tremendous benefit to base the selection of an intervention option, not only on a functional analysis of the controlling variables, but also on solid empirical evidence on the comparative effectiveness of various intervention options in terms of their rapidity, generalization, and maintenance of effects, as well as on their potential for having any negative side effects. Efficacy of intervention may be an important determinant when two or more potentially effective interventions are indicated. At present, there have been few studies comparing the relative efficacy of various educative approaches to challenging behavior. Instead, the literature is replete with examples of single intervention strategies being implemented successfully.

Proactively addressing repertoires of challenging behavior will almost always require a comprehensive and coordinated intervention package (Smith, 1990). At a minimum, such packages will need to address any medical or psychiatric concerns (Gunsett, Mulick, Fernald, & Martin, 1989); ensure that the required educational and habilitative services are provided; and create, support, and maintain a valued and integrated lifestyle for the individual (Evans & Meyer, 1990; Wolfensberger, 1983). Selecting and systematically implementing a specific package of secondary preventative measures is one aspect of meeting the educational needs of individuals with severe disabilities who display challenging behavior. For this component of a comprehensive package, certain ecological factors may influence the selection of an appropriate intervention option.

Reinforcer-Related Considerations

An important consideration in the selection of a replacement-based strategy is whether the individual can have access to the reinforcer that currently maintains the challenging behavior. In some circumstances, it may not be appropriate to implement a replacement-based strategy because access to the reinforcers that currently maintain the challenging behavior could not be granted even if more socially acceptable behavior was emitted in an attempt to recruit them. For example, the individual who throws a tantrum to obtain preferred foods would not be taught to request such foods more appropriately if medical concerns required these foods to be restricted.

Additional reinforcement issues become important when considering other types of intervention strategies. Implementing a strategy designed to override the controlling variables, for example, may depend on identifying a reinforcer more effective than whatever consequence maintains the challenging behavior. If a more effective and acceptable reinforcer cannot be identified or cannot feasibly be delivered contingent upon some other, alternative, incompatible behavior, then perhaps this type of strategy is less ecologically tenable.

Task-Related Considerations

Whether it is necessary for the individual to participate in tasks that currently evoke aggressive or self-injurious acts is an important factor to consider when selecting an intervention option to address such escape-motivated challenging behavior. If the task is critical and must be completed (e.g., dressing, bathing, taking medication to control seizures), then perhaps a strategy to override the tendency for escape may be a better option than either eliminating these demands or teaching the person another more appropriate means to escape and avoid. In addition, if participation is likely to promote skill development and integration (e.g., teaching a competitive vocational skill), strategies to override rather than replace or eliminate may be more future-oriented as well. In contrast, if the task is purely optional, the fastest solution may be to simply eliminate it from the individual's routine. Finally, if participation in a task is desirable, but it is also legitimate for the individual to request a break or occasionally refuse the task, then teaching conditional rejection or leave-taking skills are the more appropriate and ecological options.

Characteristics of the Individual's Actions

Certain characteristics of the individual's behavioral repertoire may impact the effectiveness of a particular option and, therefore, the selection of one option over another. For example, if the person has few other acceptable behaviors to reinforce, it may be necessary to consider options other than a DRO procedure. Implementation of a replacement-based strategy that involves the teaching of functional communication skills may require an initial assessment to determine the most appropriate mode of communication (e.g., vocal, gestural, graphic) for any given individual.

Characteristics of the Service Providers

Systematic intervention of some strategies may require expertise that not all caregivers possess. Ensuring that caregivers differentially reinforce other behaviors, for example, may prove difficult. Most caregivers without explicit training, however, would probably be able to effectively reinforce an individual's request to stop (Durand & Crimmins, 1991). Although both examples may represent logical options for addressing certain types of challenging behavior (e.g., escape-motivated behavior), responding to the person's request to stop, which was taught as part of a replacement-based strategy, may be easier and more natural for caregivers to maintain. Actually teaching functional equivalent replacement behaviors may require personnel with expertise in communication intervention. The level of sophistication required to teach new behaviors to persons with severe disabilities could prove greater than that required to implement a viable alternative procedure. Of course, the selection of a particular intervention strategy should be based on the needs of the individual, not on the availability of services or on the level of expertise found among existing staff. Perhaps the most general ecological factor to consider then is how to ensure that all of the resources needed to develop a comprehensive and coordinated intervention program will be obtained and delivered.

CONCLUSION

During the past several years, remarkable advances in our ability to proactively address repertoires of socially motivated challenging behavior have been made. Increasingly, service providers are carefully scrutinizing both the functions as well as the forms of behavior used to obtain socially motivated consequences. Once the functions of a class of challenging behaviors have been identified, the team of individuals responsible for making programmatic decisions can consider the degree to which the client's social motivation can be accommodated. If it can be contingent upon a more socially acceptable overture, the interventionist can design an intervention program that will establish a functionally equivalent and maximally efficient replacement behavior.

In other instances, it may not be possible to honor the desired consequence motivating the individual's challenging behavior. These instances result in the implementation of intervention strategies that alter the environment to make the consequence sought by the individual less necessary. In some instances, it may be possible to increase the salience of the reinforcers that are delivered based on the presence or absence of acceptable social behavior—in order to compete with some challenging behavior.

All of the individualized packages of intervention procedures described in this chapter are alike in that their implementation supports respect for the client's right to personal choice and communication. Strategies advocated do not rely on coercive interactions, which seek to exert tremendous control over the client's actions. Instead, the described proactive intervention procedures seek to establish a set of conditions that minimizes the need for the client to engage in challenging behavior. Once these behaviors are occurring less often, the team who serves the individual can focus on establishing a replacement for the challenging behavior. Alternatively, modifications to the environment that have been removed can be gradually and systematically reintroduced if absolutely necessary. At the same time, a host of other issues can be addressed that might make the client's environment more acceptable without significantly sacrificing productivity or infringing on the rights of others who are operating in the same environment.

In spite of rapid progress in the validation of proactive intervention strategies that address challenging behavior, there are a number of areas that still require significant attention from practitioners and researchers. Virtually all of the procedures that we have described in this chapter have some base of empirical support. Often, however, packages of these strategies are implemented concurrently. There is a critical need to carefully evaluate the cumulative effects versus the individual effects of these intervention strategies. Furthermore, there is a need to determine whether the sequence in which strategies are implemented has differential influence on the emission of challenging behavior. In the area of communicative alternatives to challenging behavior, there is a need to carefully examine the conditions under which an interventionist chooses one communicative alternative over another. In other words, it is important to delineate assessment information that leads to the selection of a request for an assistance as a communicative alternative over a request for a break with an individual who engages in escape-motivated challenging behavior while on the job. For an individual who is attention- and escape-motivated and who has difficulty with a particular component of a job, requesting assistance may be a far more salient communicative option than requesting a break. Analysis of this situation, however, requires that the service provider identify the attention motivation, as well as the problem component, of the individual's work. Although we appear to have the assessment technology needed to make the decisions, there have been limited empirical demonstrations completed in natural environments.

Great strides in efforts to proactively address repertoires of challenging behavior emitted by individuals with developmental disabilities have been made during the last decade. It is encouraging that the bulk of contemporary assessment and intervention strategies addresses social validity with a vigor that is more prominent than in the past. If professionals within disability-related fields can continue to carefully evaluate and disseminate socially valid strategies, persons who engage in challenging behavior can look forward to an increasingly better quality of life.

REFERENCES

Baumgart, D., Johnson, J., & Helmstetter, E. (1990). *Augmentative and alternative communication systems for persons with moderate and severe disabilities*. Baltimore: Paul H. Brookes Publishing Co.

Bird, F., Dores, P.A., Moniz, D., & Robinson, J. (1989). Reducing severe aggressive behaviors with functional communication training. *American Journal on Mental Retardation, 95*, 37–48.

Brown, F. (1991). Creative daily scheduling: A non-intrusive approach to challenging behaviors in community residences. *Journal of The Association for Persons with Severe Handicaps, 16*(2), 75–84.

Carr, E.G. (1977). The motivation of self-injurious behavior: A review of some hypotheses. *Psychological Bulletin, 84*, 800–816.

Carr, E.G. (1988). Functional equivalence as a mechanism of response generalization. In R.H. Horner, G. Dunlap, & R.L. Koegel (Eds.), *Generalization and maintenance: Lifestyle changes in applied settings* (pp. 221–241). Baltimore: Paul H. Brookes Publishing Co.

Carr, E.G., & Durand, V.M. (1985a). Reducing behavior problems through functional communication training. *Journal of Applied Behavior Analysis, 18*, 111–126.

Carr, E.G., & Durand, V.M. (1985b). The social-communicative basis of severe behavior problems in children. In S. Reiss & R. Bootzin (Eds.), *Theoretical issues in behavior therapy* (pp. 219–254). New York: Academic Press.

Cataldo, M.F., & Harris, J. (1982). The biological basis for self-injury in the mentally retarded. *Analysis and Intervention in Developmental Disabilities, 2*, 21–39.

Davis, C., Brady, M., Williams, R., & Hamilton, R. (1992). Effects of high-probability requests on the acquisition and generalization of responses to requests in young children with behavior disorders. *Journal of Applied Behavior Analysis, 25*(4), 905–916.

Day, R.M., Johnson, W.L., & Schussler, N.G. (1986). Determining the communicative properties of self-injury: Research, assessment, and treatment implications. In K.D. Gadow (Ed.), *Advances in learning and behavioral disabilities* (Vol. 5) (pp. 117–139). Greenwich, CT: JAI Press.

Day, R.M., Rea, J.A., Schussler, N.G., Larsen, S.E., & Johnson, W.L. (1988). A functionally based approach to the treatment of self-injurious behavior. *Behavior Modification, 12*, 565–589.

De Lissovoy, V. (1963). Head banging in early childhood: A suggested cause. *Journal of Genetic Psychology, 102*, 109–114.

Donnellan, A.M., Mirenda, P.L., Mesaros, R.A., & Fassbender, L.L. (1984). Analyzing the communicative functions of aberrant behavior. *Journal of The Association for Persons with Severe Handicaps, 9*, 201–212.

Dorsey, M.F., Iwata, B.A., Ong, P., & McSween, T.E. (1980). Treatment of self-injurious behavior using a water mist: Initial response suppression and generalization. *Journal of Applied Behavior Analysis, 13*, 343–353.

Durand, V.M. (1987). "Look Homeward Angel": A call to return to our (functional) roots. *Behavior Analyst, 10*, 299–302.

Durand, V.M. (1990). *Severe behavior problems: A functional communication training approach*. New York: Guilford Press.

Durand, V.M., & Carr, E.G. (1987). Social influences on "self-stimulatory" behavior: Analysis and treatment application. *Journal of Applied Behavior Analysis, 20*, 119–132.

Durand, V.M., & Carr, E.G. (1991). Functional communication training to reduce challenging behavior: Maintenance and application in new settings. *Journal of Applied Behavior Analysis, 24*, 251–264.

Durand, V.M., & Crimmins, D.B. (1988). Identifying the variables maintaining self-injurious behavior. *Journal of Autism and Developmental Disorders, 18*, 99–117.

Durand, V.M., & Crimmins, D.B. (1991). Teaching functionally equivalent responses as an intervention for challenging behavior. In B. Remington (Ed.), *The challenge of severe mental handicap: A behavior analytic approach* (pp. 71–95). Manchester: John Wiley & Sons.

Durand, V.M., Crimmins, D.B., Caulfield, M., & Taylor, J. (1989). Reinforcer assessment I: Using problem behavior to select reinforcers. *Journal of The Association for Persons with Severe Handicaps, 14*, 113–126.

Evans, I.M., & Meyer, L. (1985). *An educative approach to problem behaviors: A practical decision model for interventions with severely handicapped learners*. Baltimore: Paul H. Brookes Publishing Co.

Evans, I.M., & Meyer, L.H. (1990). Toward a science of meaningful outcomes: A response to Horner et al. *Journal of The Association for Persons with Severe Handicaps, 15*, 133–135.

Ferrari, M., & Harris, S.L. (1981). The limits and motivating potential of sensory stimuli as reinforcers for autistic children. *Journal of Applied Behavior Analysis, 14*, 339–343.

Gardner, J.F., & Chapman, M.S. (1990). *Program issues in developmental disabilities: A guide to effective habilitation and active treatment* (2nd ed.). Baltimore: Paul H. Brookes Publishing Co.

Gardner, W.I., Cole, C.L., Davidson, D.P., & Karan, O.C. (1986). Reducing aggression in individuals with developmental disabilities: An expanded stimulus control assessment and intervention model. *Education and Training of the Mentally Retarded, 21*(2), 3–12.

Green, C.W., Reid, D.H., White, L.K., Halford, R.C., Brittain, D.P., & Gardner, S.M. (1988). Identifying reinforcers for persons with profound handicaps: Staff opinion versus systematic assessment of preferences. *Journal of Applied Behavior Analysis, 21*, 31–43.

Guess, D., Helmstetter, E., Turnbull, H.R., & Knowlton, S. (1987). *Use of aversive procedures with persons who are disabled: An historical review and critical analysis*. Seattle: The Association for Persons with Severe Handicaps.

Gunsett, R.P., Mulick, J.A., Fernald, W.B., & Martin, J.L. (1989). Brief report: Indications for medical screening prior to behavioral programming for severely and profoundly mentally retarded clients. *Journal of Autism and Developmental Disorders*, *19*, 167–172.

Harchik, A., & Putzier, V. (1990). The use of high-probability requests to increase compliance with instructions to take medications. *Journal of The Association for Persons With Severe Handicaps*, *15*, 40–43.

Hill, B.K., & Bruininks, R.H. (1982). *Maladaptive behavior of mentally retarded people in residential facilities*. (Brief #9). Minneapolis: University of Minnesota, Research and Training Center on Residential Services and Community Living.

Hill, B.K., Lakin, K.C., & Bruininks, R.H. (1984). Trends in residential services for mentally retarded people, 1977–1982. *Journal of The Association for Persons with Severe Handicaps*, *9*(4), 243–250.

Hill, B.K., Lakin, K.C., Bruininks, R.H., Amado, A.N., Anderson, D.J., & Copher, J.I. (1989). *Living in the community: A comparison study of foster homes and small group homes for people with mental retardation* (Report No. 28). Minneapolis: University of Minnesota, Research and Training Center on Residential and Community Services.

Horner, R.H., & Budd, C.M. (1985). Acquisition of manual sign use: Collateral reduction of maladaptive behavior and factors limiting generalization. *Education and Training of the Mentally Retarded*, *20*, 39–47.

Horner, R.H., Dunlap, G., Koegel, R.L., Carr, E.G., Sailor, W., Anderson, J., Albin, R.W., & O'Neill, R.E. (1990). Toward a technology of "nonaversive" behavioral support. *Journal of The Association for Persons with Severe Handicaps*, *15*, 125–132.

Hung, D.W. (1978). Using self-stimulation as reinforcement for autistic children. *Journal of Autism and Developmental Disabilities*, *8*, 355–366.

Iwata, B.A., Dorsey, M.F., Slifer, K.J., Bauman, K.E., & Richman, G.S. (1982). Toward a functional analysis of self-injury. *Analysis and Intervention in Developmental Disabilities*, *2*, 3–20.

Iwata, B.A., Pace, G.M., Kalsher, M.J., Cowdery, G.E., & Cataldo, M.F. (1990). Experimental analysis and extinction of self-injurious escape behavior. *Journal of Applied Behavior Analysis*, *23*, 11–27.

Jones, R.S.P. (1991). Reducing inappropriate behavior using non-aversive procedures: Evaluating differential reinforcement schedules. In B. Remington (Ed.), *The challenge of severe mental handicap: A behavior analytic approach* (pp. 47–69). Manchester: John Wiley & Sons.

Krantz, D.J., & Risley, T.R. (1977). Behavioral ecology in the classroom. In K.D. O'Leary & S.G. O'Leary (Eds.), *Classroom management: The successful use of behavior modification* (2nd ed.) (pp. 349–366). New York: Pergamon Press.

Lakin, K.C. (1979). *Demographic studies of residential facilities for the mentally retarded: An historical review of methodologies and findings*. Minneapolis: University of Minnesota, Research and Training Center on Residential Services and Community Living.

Lakin, K.C., Hill, B.K., Chen, T.H., & Stephens, S.A. (1989). *Persons with mental retardation and related conditions in mental retardation facilities: Selected findings from the 1987 National Medical Expenditure Survey*. Minneapolis: University of Minnesota, Research and Training Center on Residential Services and Community Living.

Lakin, K.C., Jaskulski, T.M., Hill, B.K., Bruininks, R.H., Menke, J.M., White, C.C., & Wright, E.A. (1989). *Medical services for persons with mental retardation and related conditions*. Minneapolis: University of Minnesota, Research and Training Center on Residential Services and Community Living.

Lakin, K.D., Prouty, R.W., White, C.C., Bruininks, R.H., & Hill, B.K. (1989). *Intermediate care facilities for persons with mental retardation and related conditions*. Minneapolis: University of Minnesota, Research and Training Center on Residential Services and Community Living.

Larson, S.A., & Lakin, K.C. (1989). Deinstitutionalization of persons with mental retarda-
tion: Behavioral outcomes. *Journal of The Association for Persons with Severe Handi-
caps*, *14*(4), 324–332.
Leigland, S. (1984). On "setting events" and related concepts. *The Behavior Analyst, 7*(1),
41–45.
Lichstein, K.L., & Schreibman, L. (1976). Employing electric shock with autistic children:
A review of the side effects. *Journal of Autism and Childhood Schizophrenia, 6*, 163–173.
Lovaas, O.I. (1982). Comments on self-destructive behaviors. *Analysis and Intervention in
Developmental Disabilities, 2*, 115–124.
Lovaas, O.I., Freitag, G., Gold, V.J., & Kassorla, I.C. (1965). Experimental studies in
childhood schizophrenia: Analysis of self-destructive behavior. *Journal of Experimental
Child Psychology, 2*, 67–84.
Lovaas, O.I., & Simmons, T.Q. (1969). Manipulation of self-destruction in three retarded
children. *Journal of Applied Behavior Analysis, 2*, 143–157.
Luiselli, J.K. (1988). Comparative effects of a time-out contingency when combined with
alternate methods of reinforcement. *Journal of the Multihandicapped Person, 1*, 121–127.
Mace, F.C., & Belfiore, P. (1990). Behavioral momentum in the treatment of escape-
motivated stereotype. *Journal of Applied Behavior Analysis, 23*(4), 507–514.
Mace, F.C., Page, T.J., Ivancic, M.T., & O'Brien, S. (1986). Analysis of environmental
determinants of aggression and disruption in mentally retarded children. *Applied Research in Mental Retardation, 7*, 203–221.
Meyer, L.H., & Evans, I.M. (1989). *Nonaversive intervention for behavior problems: A
manual for home and community*. Baltimore: Paul H. Brookes Publishing Co.
Michael, J. (1975). Positive and negative reinforcement: A distinction that is no longer nec-
essary: Or a better way to talk about bad things. *Behaviorism, 3*, 33–44.
Neel, R.S., & Billingsley, F.F. (1989). *Impact: A functional curriculum handbook for stu-
dents with moderate to severe difficulties*. Baltimore: Paul H. Brookes Publishing Co.
Nihira, L., & Nihira, K. (1975). Jeopardy in community placement. *American Journal of
Mental Deficiency, 79*(5), 538–544.
Nordquist, V.M., & Twardosz, S. (1990). Preventing behavior problems in early childhood
special education classrooms through environmental organization. *Education and Treat-
ment of Children, 13*(4), 274–287.
O'Neill, R.E., Horner, R.H., Albin, R.A., Storey, K.S., & Sprague, J.R. (1990). *Func-
tional analysis: A practical assessment guide*. Sycamore, IL: Sycamore Press.
Pace, G.M., Ivancic, MT., Edwards, G.L., Iwata, B.A., & Page, T.J. (1985). Assessment
of stimulus preference and reinforcer value with profoundly retarded individuals. *Journal of Applied Behavior Analysis, 18*, 249–255.
Pagel, S.E., & Whitling, C.A. (1978). Readmissions to a state hospital for mentally re-
tarded persons: Reasons for community placement failure. *Mental Retardation,16*, 164–166.
Parrott, L. (1986). On the differences between verbal and social behavior. In P.N. Chase &
L.J. Parrott (Eds.), *Psychological aspects of language: The West Virginia lectures*
(pp. 91–117). Springfield, IL: Charles C Thomas.
Rehagen, N.J., & Thelen, M.H. (1972). Vibration as positive reinforcement for retarded
children. *Journal of Abnormal Psychology, 77*, 162–167.
Reichle, J., Rogers, N., & Barrett, C. (1984). Establishing pragmatic discriminations
among the communicative functions of requesting, rejecting, and commenting in an adolescent. *Journal of The Association for Persons with Severe Handicaps, 9*, 31–36.
Reichle, J., York, J., & Sigafoos, J. (1991). *Implementing augmentative and alternative
communication: Strategies for people with severe disabilities*. Baltimore: Paul H.
Brookes Publishing Co.
Repp, A.C., Barton, L.E., & Brulle, A.R. (1983). A comparison of two procedures for
programming the differential reinforcement of other behaviors. *Journal of Applied Behavior Analysis, 16*, 435–445.

Repp, A.C., & Deitz, S.M. (1974). Reducing aggressive and self-injurious behavior of institutionalized retarded children through reinforcement of other behaviors. *Journal of Applied Behavior Analysis, 7,* 313–325.

Rincover, A., & Newsome, C.D. (1985). The relative motivational properties of sensory and edible reinforcers in teaching autistic children. *Journal of Applied Behavior Analysis, 18,* 237–248.

Scheerenberger, R.C. (1988). *Public residential services for the mentally retarded, 1987.* Madison, WI: National Association of Superintendents of Public Residential Facilities for the Mentally Retarded.

Schroeder, S.R., Mulick, J.A., & Rojahn, J. (1980). The definition, taxonomy, epidemiology, and ecology of self-injurious behavior. *Journal of Autism and Developmental Disorders, 10,* 417–432.

Schroeder, S.R., Schroeder, C.S., Smith, B., & Dalldorf, J. (1978). Prevalence of self-injurious behaviors in a large state facility for the retarded: A three year follow-up study. *Journal of Autism and Childhood Schizophrenia, 8,* 261–269.

Sidman, M. (1989). *Coercion and its fallout.* Boston: Authors Cooperative.

Singer, G.H.S., Singer, J., & Horner, R.H. (1987). Using pretask requests to increase the probability of compliance for students with severe disabilities. *Journal of The Association for Persons with Severe Handicaps, 12*(4), 287–291.

Skinner, B.F. (1953). *Science and human behavior.* New York: Macmillan.

Smith, M.D. (1990). *Autism and life in the community: Successful interventions for behavioral challenges.* Baltimore: Paul H. Brookes Publishing Co.

Steege, M., Wacker, D., Berg, W., Cigrand, K., & Cooper, L. (1989). The use of behavioral assessment to prescribe and evaluate treatments for severely handicapped children. *Journal of Applied Behavior Analysis, 22,* 23–33.

Sturmey, P., Carlsen, A., Crisp, A.G., & Newton, J.T. (1988). A functional analysis of multiple aberrant responses: A refinement and extension of Iwata et al.'s (1982) methodology. *Journal of Mental Deficiency Research, 32,* 31–46.

Tanner, B., & Zeiler, J. (1975). Punishment of self-injurious behavior using aromatic ammonia as the aversive stimulus. *Journal of Applied Behavior Analysis, 8,* 53–57.

Vargas, E.A. (1988). Verbally-governed and event-governed behavior. *Analysis of Verbal Behavior, 6,* 11–22.

Wacker, D.P., Steege, M.W., Northup, J., Sasso, G., Berg, W., Reimers, T., Cooper, L., Cigrand, K., & Donn, L. (1990). A component analysis of functional communication training across three topographies of severe behavior problems. *Journal of Applied Behavior Analysis, 23,* 417–429.

Wieseler, N.A., Hanson, R.H., Chamberlain, T.P., & Thompson, T. (1985). Functional taxonomy of stereotypic and self-injurious behavior. *Mental Retardation, 23,* 230–234.

Wolfensberger, W. (1983). Social role valorization: A proposed new term for the principle of normalization. *Mental Retardation, 21,* 234–239.

PART III

COMMUNITY SERVICES AND SUPPORT ISSUES

— *Chapter 8* ─────────────────────────

Waiting for Community Services
The Impact on Persons with Mental Retardation and Other Developmental Disabilities

Mary F. Hayden and Paris DePaepe

───

Adults with mental retardation and other developmental disabilities have a higher likelihood of experiencing limitations in major life activities than persons with any other chronic mental, physical, or health condition (LaPlante, 1991). They are also more apt to need ongoing, lifelong assistance in basic daily living activities throughout their lives. Consequently, access to long-term care and related supports for adults with mental retardation and other developmental disabilities has been a long-standing concern among persons with disabilities, family members, advocates, professionals, and policymakers.

Historically, long-term care and related services were primarily provided in large, segregated congregate care facilities. Based on the principles of deinstitutionalization and least restrictive alternative, the service delivery system for persons with mental retardation and other developmental disabilities (MR/DD) attempted to move from institutional to community-based care. As a result of actions following these principles, there has been a dramatic decline in the number of persons living in large public institutions and an increase in the number of persons living in community-based housing. About 80,000 fewer persons with mental retardation and other developmental disabilities were residing in these institutional settings in 1991 than in 1977 (Lakin, Prouty, Blake, Mangan, & White, 1993).

───────────────

Preparation of this chapter was supported by Cooperative Agreements #H133G20207 and #H33B89948 between the National Institute on Disability and Rehabilitation Research (NIDRR) and the Research and Training Center on Residential Services and Community Living, Institute on Community Integration (UAP) located at the University of Minnesota (College of Education). Additional support was provided by a grant from the Administration on Developmental Disabilities (#90DD145102). The opinions expressed herein are those of the authors.

Between 1977 and 1990, the number of individuals living in facilities with 15 or fewer residents increased from 40,400 to 149,700, while the number of people in facilities with 6 or fewer residents grew from 20,400 to 98,900 (Lakin, White, Prouty, Bruininks, & Kimm, 1991).

Despite the major success of states in striving to achieve the almost universally held goals of deinstitutionalization and the accompanying development of a community-based service delivery system, a crisis threatens the movement to insure that all individuals with mental retardation and other developmental disabilities live in the community. As Smull (1989) points out:

> Demands and expectations have risen faster than funding. The "slack" in the system that was used to cope with unanticipated problems is gone. Institutions are operating programs at capacity with plans to reduce their census. Many communities have few vacancies and no plans to expand. For those waiting, the practice of offering no support and only serving the truly desperate is maintaining a backlog of people in crisis. As the community service system, the institutions, and the "waiting list" all move into more acute crisis they create a set of mutually reinforcing pressures. (p. 2)

Recent studies not only support Smull's assertion that there is a growing demand for community-based services, but also that waiting lists have become a common reality for state agencies. In a 1984 national survey, 22 states reported that they had an average of 335 persons waiting for MR/DD day programs or employment services (McDonnell, Wilcox, & Boles, 1986). In a more recent national survey of day programs and employment services, 27 agencies reported that they maintain state-level information on the number of individuals who currently need these services (McGaughey, Lynch, Morganstern, Kiernan, & Schalock, 1991). However, only 22 states were able to supply these data. For these states, an average of 1,177 people per state were waiting for day or employment services.

A national survey of state directors of The Arc (formerly Association for Retarded Citizens of the United States) estimated that more than 63,000 people were identified as waiting for community-based residential services, while more than 76,000 were waiting for daytime programs (Davis, 1987). As of June 30, 1991, an estimated 51,424 persons with mental retardation and related conditions were waiting for residential services in the United States (Lakin et al., 1993). Although limitations to these studies included the use of varying methods of data source identification and data collection across states, few state respondents believed that all people in need of residential services and day programs had been identified. The researchers concluded that the total number of people reported to be waiting for services substantially underestimates the unmet service needs of individuals with mental retardation and other developmental disabilities.

The reduction of waiting lists, like any problem, must begin first by examining the factors that led to and contribute to the problem, determining the scope of the problem, identifying the needs of persons who are affected by the problem, and then identifying solutions to the problem. This process is reflective of the following statement, made by Abraham Lincoln in *A House Divided* (Lincoln, 1858), "If we could first know where we are, and whither we are tending, we could better judge what to do, and how to do it." The purpose of this chapter is to employ this process in order to examine the problem of waiting lists and, as a result of this examination, offer suggestions to resolve the problem.

The chapter initially summarizes current information and statistics related to: 1) the type of agencies that maintain waiting lists, 2) the number of people with mental retardation and other developmental disabilities waiting for community services, 3) the characteristics of the waiting lists, and 4) the characteristics of people waiting for community services. Second, the chapter discusses, at length, the status of people with mental retardation and other developmental disabilities who live either in residential facilities or with their families. These discussions are centered around their needs, barriers that hinder them from receiving community services and supports, and possible solutions to combat these barriers. Finally, the chapter provides suggestions to begin to resolve the waiting list problem.

The information presented in the chapter was derived from three sources of information. The first source is the results of a study conducted to identify and summarize current information and statistics available in the United States in order to document the number and needs of persons with mental retardation and other developmental disabilities currently waiting for community services (Hayden, 1992). The second source is a review of data that are related to people who are waiting for community services while living at home and in a variety of residential settings such as state-operated institutions, nursing homes, large privately operated institutions, and intermediate care facilities for persons with mental retardation (ICFs/MR). The third source is a pilot study conducted to obtain more firsthand knowledge about adults with mental retardation and other developmental disabilities who live at home (Hayden, Spicer, DePaepe, & Chelberg, 1992).

CURRENT INFORMATION AND STATISTICS

The process of identifying, obtaining, screening, and verifying states' data on persons waiting for services took place between March 1, 1990 and June 1, 1992 (Hayden, 1992). Information was gathered from directors of state MR/DD programs, state developmental disabilities councils, state protection and advocacy agencies, University Affiliated Programs (UAPs), and other agencies and individuals potentially having access to or knowledge of statistics on persons with mental retardation and other developmental disabilities who were waiting for services. To ensure that information was obtained from each state, there were six follow-up mailings to people who did not respond to the previous mailings or to people who were nominated as potentially useful referrals. After six mailings, information was obtained from all but four states (Connecticut, Delaware, Indiana, and Maine) and the District of Columbia. Follow-up telephone calls were then made to each of their MR/DD agencies. At least one response was obtained from each of these states and the District of Columbia.

The nature and quality of data varied considerably from state to state. Some states clearly indicated the type of services that individuals were waiting for, other states could not. To provide some type of uniformity and consistency, the following classifications were developed: 1) residential services—people who requested community-based residential placements; 2) day programs—people who requested placement in day activity centers, adult day care, or adult life skills programs; 3) vocational services—people who requested placement in vocational programs, work activity centers, work adjustment programs, sheltered workshops, supported employment programs, or vocational evaluations or job placements; 4) residential and vocational services—people who requested both residential and vocational services; 5) support services—people who requested individual or family support services, adaptive or therapeutic equipment, respite care, or personal assistance services; and 6) other services—people who requested any one of the following services: behavioral intervention, case management, counseling, daily living skills training, dental care, early intervention services, family subsidy, infant and toddler programs, intake assessment, patient services, recreation and leisure activities, and transportation.

As the screening process proceeded, the level of detail within the documents provided proved to be typically inadequate and, as a result, the initial criterion for inclusion was expanded to assure data were derived from the most current and reliable sources. Once the synthesis of information was completed, letters were mailed to respondents to request verification of the data and to obtain clarification if needed. Respondents were told that if they did not respond to the letter within 6 weeks, it would be assumed the information originally provided was correct. Thirty-two states responded to this final request. The following data were concluded.

Types of Agencies that Maintain Waiting Lists

Thirty-six states maintain waiting lists, nine states do not maintain lists (California, Idaho, Illinois, Iowa, Kentucky, Michigan, North Dakota, West Virginia, and Wyoming), and five states, plus the District of Columbia, reported the number of people waiting but did not clearly indicate whether or not they maintain lists (Alaska, Georgia, Oregon, Rhode Island, and Vermont). Of the 36 states that maintain lists, 8 have more than one agency collecting information (Alabama, Louisiana, New Jersey, Ohio, Tennessee, Utah, Vermont, and Washington), 15 have a single-state agency (Arizona, Delaware, Florida, Hawaii, Kansas, Maine, Maryland, Massachusetts, Montana, Nebraska, New Mexico, New York, Oklahoma, South Dakota, and Texas), 6 have a regional or district agency (Colorado, Connecticut, Indiana, Missouri, Nevada, and New Hampshire), 4 have a county agency (Minnesota, Pennsylvania, South Carolina, and Wisconsin), and 3 have service providers (Arkansas, Mississippi, and North Carolina) maintaining this information.

Number of People Waiting for Services

As shown in Table 1, 60,876 people were reported to be waiting for residential services in 36 states and the District of Columbia. Another 35,095 persons in 31 states and the District of Columbia were reported to be waiting for day habilitation or vocational services. Four states reported that 6,320 people were waiting for both residential and vocational services. There were 32,902 people reported to be waiting for some type of support services in 18 states, and 14,273 individuals were reported to be waiting for some other type of services in 20 states. With 45 states reporting, people with mental retardation and other developmental disabilities were identified as waiting for 186,272 separate community-based services.

Six states did not provide any information (California, Idaho, Michigan, North Dakota, Rhode Island, and West Virginia) and, as a result, it was necessary to estimate missing data for these states. A proportional adjustment, based on the total number of people living in nonreporting states and the total number of people living in reporting states, yielded an estimated additional 39,480 separate community-based services. In other words, approximately 225,752 separate community-based services are being waited for in the United States.

To try to estimate the actual number of persons who are waiting for services, states were asked if reported numbers were a duplicate count and, if yes, what percentage of the total count they attribute to duplicated counting. Of 32 states that responded to this query, 26 states provided information regarding whether all of or parts of their reported statistics included duplicate counts. Based on these reports, it was estamted that 19.5% of the reported number of persons waiting for services could be attributed to duplicate counting. As a result, the total number of services being waited for by people with mental retardation and other developmental disabilities in the United States was adjusted to 181,835.

Characteristics of the Waiting Lists

Waiting List Tracking Systems During the final mailing, states were asked if they had a computerized system to maintain data related to people who are waiting for services. Of the 26 states that responded to the question, 46.2% said they had a fully operational computerized system, 30.8% indicated that they were in the process of developing a computerized system, and the remaining 23.1% said their system was not computerized.

When asked what type of information is contained in their waiting lists, 26 states responded. These states indicated that 20.8% of the respondents said they collect demographic characteristics of each individual; 19.8% include the date of entering the system; 18.8% list the types of programs and funding sources for which each individual is eligible; 16.6% provide information related to an individual's personal characteristics; 10.9% collect assessment information related to an individual's needs, strengths, and limitations; 10.9% indicate if the individual is receiving complete and appropriate services; and 2.0% provided other information.

When asked what type of services are requested by individuals, 25 states responded. These states reported that 15.6% needed residential services, 14.9% needed adult day training and habilitation, 12.3% needed supported employment, 11.7% needed supportive living or semi-independent living services, 11.7% needed family support services, 11.0% needed respite care, 9.7% needed competitive employment, 7.1% needed case management, and 5.8% needed specialized

Table 1. Type of services people are waiting for by state

State (reference number[a])	Date data were collected	Residential[b]	Day habilitation/vocational services[c]	Residential/vocational[d]	Support[e]	Other[f]	Total
AL (6)	6/9/90	1,086	1,325	—	776	—	4,018
AK (20)	5/1/90	—	—	—	517	601[g]	1,118
AZ (21)	12/11/90	145	416	—	—	701	1,262
AR (37)	1990	271	272	—	7	338	888
CA (28)[h]	3/9/92	1,616	1,202	—	—	15	2,833
CO (41)	11/30/90	937	453	—	—	—	1,390
CT (24)	1/1/92	179	24	—	—	—	203
DE (27)	4/1/91	210	52	—	—	—	262
DC (48)	10/2/91	—	—	—	—	—	4,673
FL (32)	1/14/91	1,179	—	—	—	—	1,179
GA (51)	11/29/89	201	277	—	—	—	478
HI (53)	9/30/90	—	—	—	—	—	—
ID (n/a)[h]	—	—	—	—	—	—	—
IL (9) (29)	1986	10,000	1,989	—	—	—	11,989
IN (42)	4/31/91	2,048	1,096	—	—	—	3,144
IA (9)	1986	2,000	1,700	—	—	—	3,700
KS (39)	1/15/91	932	672	—	156	48	1,808
KY (31)	11/15/91	4,503	3,087	—	—	807[i]	8,397
LA (45)	4/18/90	0	550	—	1,400	1,750	3,700
ME (2)	1/91	732	872	—	—	1	1,605
MD (46)	7/1/91	2,392	2,968	—	3,917	—	9,277
MA (25)	2/18/92	1,749	513	265	2,000	—	4,527
MI (n/a)[h]	—	—	—	—	—	—	—
MN (15)	1991	—	—	—	340	—	—
(16)	1991	560	1,272[i]	—	340	963[i]	3,135

State	Date						Total
MS (36)	5/31/91	240	—	—	—	—	240
MO (3)	1/1/92	1,617	—	—	—	1,925	3,542
MT (7)	1/27/92	719	852	—	561	—	2,132
NE (33)	4/20/90	—	—	—	—	—	539
NV (4, 13, 18, 22)	11/13/91	116	381	—	104	171	287
NH (34)	12/91	494	360	—	—	—	979
NJ (14)	2/92	3,023	274	—	172	442	4,472
NM (8)	12/18/91	127	5,251	—	—	1,089[k]	1,015
NY (19)	2/15/92	9,674	1,727[l]	—	16,007	300	30,932
NC (38)	1989–1990	—	—	—	—	—	2,027
ND (30)[h]	1/15/91	2,719	1,242	—	535	227	—
OH (49)	10/91	391	—	—	486	306[m]	4,723
OK (17)	5/20/91	—	—	—	—	—	2,158
OR (23)	1987[n]	—	—	2,000	4,600	—	6,600
PA (44)	1990–1991	3,995	—	—	—	—	3,995
RI (12)[h]		847	441	—	—	—	1,288
SC (1)	7/17/90	—	—	—	—	—	174[o]
SD (5)	7/91	544	869	—	—	—	1,413
TN (35)	12/31/91	370	205	207	43	1,262	25,313
TX (43)	1989	140	160	—	72	194	2,087[p]
UT (52)	12/2/91	2,100	1,130	—	—	—	566
VT (50)	12/91	—	2,208	—	—	1,249	4,479
VA (11)	1991	1,640	—	3,848	—	—	7,696
(19)	1989	—	1,255	—	1,209	—	—
WA (47)	7/90	—	—	—	—	1,884	5,728
WV (n/a)[h]		1,380	—	—	—	—	4,301
WI (40)	9/1/90	—	—	—	—	—	—
WY (26)	1989	—	—	—	—	—	—
Total reported		60,876	35,095	6,320	32,902	14,273	186,272

(continued)

Table 1. *(continued)*

Reprinted with permission from Hayden (1992). Adults with mental retardation and other developmental disabilities waiting for community-based services in the United States. *Policy Research Brief, 4*(4), 1–12. Minneapolis: University of Minnesota, Research and Training Center for Residential Services and Community Living, Institute on Community Integration (UAP).

a Reference number is the number preceding each entry in the *Sources of Information for Table 1* section (at end of chapter).

b Residential services include people who requested community-based residential placement.

c Day programs include people who requested placement in day activity centers, adult day care, and/or adult life skills programs. Vocational services include people who requested placement in competitive employment, sheltered workshops, supported employment programs, vocational evaluations or job placements, vocational programs, work activity centers, and/or work adjustment programs.

d Residential and vocational services include people who requested both residential and vocational services.

e Support services include people who requested individual or family support services, adaptive/therapeutic equipment, respite care, and/or personal assistance services.

f Other services include people who requested any one of the following services: behavioral intervention, case management, cash subsidies, counseling, daily living skills training, dental care, early intervention services, family subsidy, infant and toddler programs, intake assessment, patient services, recreation and leisure activities, and transportation.

g Alaska indicated that, at a minimum, 250 people in rural areas are not identified or receiving services and 351 people requested services and were on the state's waiting list for services.

h Data are unavailable or not collected.

i Data were obtained from Davis (1987).

j Number of people waiting to receive Title XIX Home and Community-Based Services (HCBS).

k Number of people for whom services are presently being sought. They are individuals who are known to the service delivery system but are not actively seeking services.

l North Carolina indicated that there were 990 people currently unserved and/or unfunded, 305 people inappropriately served and needing vocational activation services, and 432 people who cannot be served in supported employment because no transportation is available.

m Oklahoma reported 875 people currently receive Title XIX Home and Community-Based Services (HCBS), and 35% of this group require additional or more complete services.

n Only 29 counties responded to state survey.

o South Dakota indicated that 94 people are "truly waiting" for services where 80 people are on the planning list. The planning list includes people whose needs (e.g., medical conditions or behavioral problems) are such that the community services system cannot serve them. They will wait until the state expands the system.

p Utah indicated that 1,456 people were provided with case management.

transportation services. Only 7.1% of the 25 states stated that they determine if individuals do not receive complete and appropriate services.

Prioritization for Service Delivery States were also asked if they had written or informal policies for choosing the order in which persons with mental retardation and other developmental disabilities will receive services. Of the 32 states who responded, 40.6% indicated that they had written procedures, 15.6% said they had informal policies, 40.6% said they had no formal or informal policies, and 3.1% said they did not know of any policies. When asked to characterize these policies, 18 states responded. Specifically, 36.2% indicated that they serve people based on the urgency of their situation or their level of need. Approximately 15% said they consider the timeline for placement. Others (10.6%) indicated they determine their responsibility to a particular individual. Only 10.6% consider the reason for the service request. About 6% consider the location of the service provider, and 6.4% assess the potential for the recipient to become more independent. Finally, others consider the cost of the program or services (4.3%).

States were also asked to rank order six groups of adults with mental retardation and other developmental disabilities by the priority by which they would receive services within their state. Of those responding, 22 states ranked adults living at home and who were in a state of crisis as their first priority. Seventeen states ranked persons living in state-operated facilities as second. Eighteen states ranked young adults graduating from special education programs needing residential and/ or day habilitation or vocational services as third. Eighteen states ranked adults living at home with elderly parents who were not in a state of crisis, but who were waiting for out-of-home placement or day habilitation as fourth priority. Those living in nursing homes were ranked as fifth by 18 states. Finally, 13 states ranked adults living in large private institutions as sixth, and last, priority.

Documents that were reviewed identified 10 states with specific guidelines used to prioritize requests for community-based services (Colorado, Connecticut, Delaware, Georgia, Maryland, Nebraska, New Hampshire, South Dakota, Texas, and Washington). Since this information was not specifically asked for during the initial requests, it should not be inferred that only these states have such guidelines. In fact, there often appeared to be an almost implicit understanding that people living in state-operated facilities, nursing homes, or benefiting from a court order or a legislative mandate would receive preferential treatment. For example, a report from Oklahoma observed that "new clients are out in the cold because funds are allocated to implement community-based programs to comply with the court order" (D. Goodell, personal communication, May 20, 1991). In addition, an Oregon report stated that people who reside in state hospitals get preferential treatment in the allocation of resources (Human Services Research Institute, 1990).

Characteristics of People Waiting for Services

Information received on the characteristics of persons waiting for services varied across states. Few states reported much detail on the characteristics of people who were waiting for services. No state had statistics describing the level of mental retardation, functional limitations, and adaptive or maladaptive behaviors of persons waiting for services. However, many states reported the number of people living at home, the number of elderly parents maintaining an adult child at home, and the number of older adults with mental retardation and other developmental disabilities. These data were not requested initially and, therefore, it cannot be assumed that nonreporting states did not have this information.

During the final mailing, states were asked to indicate what groups of people were included in the reported numbers. Of the 31 states who responded, 30.9% of persons reported were living with their family or in their own homes; 25.5% were living in non–state-operated facilities other than nursing homes; 20.2% were living in state-operated facilities other than nursing homes; 19.1% were living in nursing homes; and 4.3% were living independently, in other states, in noncertified residences, or in community-based facilities and waiting to be transferred to another residence. States did not provide additional information for persons living outside their biological home. However, states provided additional information related to persons living with their families. The following section will describe this information.

Number of People Living at Home Seven states provided information related to the number of people waiting for services who are living with their families (California, Colorado, Georgia, Indiana, Maryland, New Hampshire, and Ohio). California expects an increasing demand for community-based living options from people who are living at home and who are aging. A report by California's Department of Developmental Disabilities (1990) indicated that, between 1983 and 1989, the number of people 22 years of age and older who live in the community increased by 61%, as compared to a 23% increase of their counterparts under 22 years of age. As these people age, they are less likely to be cared for in their families' homes. Consequently, although only a small portion of children live out-of-home, a large proportion of adults do. Put another way, 87% of persons living in the community under the age of 19 now live with their families, but only 51% of their counterparts, ages 19 to 49, live with family members. Among community members ages 50 or older, only 23% live with their families (R.A. Marlowe, personal communication, April 1, 1991).

Other states provided similar information, such as Ohio, which reported that of 6,035 people waiting for services, 41% currently live with their family (D. Wood, personal communication, May 28, 1992). Georgia noted that 44.5% of 1,179 people waiting for services currently live with their family or a relative (G.M. Wrenson, personal communication, 1991, February 18). Of all individuals needing a residential program in Colorado ($N = 2,442$), 56.5% currently live at home (L. Struxness, personal communication, 1991, January 3). For adults and children with MR/DD who live in Indiana and are waiting for services ($N = 2,290$), 67.3% are currently living with family members (N. Swaim, personal communication, 1991, April 30).

In addition, as of July 1, 1989, 3,506 adults in Maryland were waiting for one or more community services (Gold, Bowen, & Smull, 1990). Of this number,

56.8% lived with parents or other relatives (W.T. Wacker, personal communication, 1992, March 18). Of 1,028 surveyed caregivers of adults over the age of 21, 53% reported that caring for a family member was a moderate to severe problem. Of caregivers who reported their own health status ($N = 2,195$), about 42% indicated their health was a moderate to severe problem. New Hampshire (B. Reed, personal communication, 1992, March 25) conveyed the difficulty that many of these families face:

> Persons of this waiting list (adults living at home with families) can change priority need at a moment's notice, with the death of a parent, or an increase in the health or behavior needs of the disabled family member, or a stroke or heart attack afflicting one of the parents can require an immediate need for alternative residential services for the person with a developmental disability. The waiting list should therefore, be seen as dynamic, with the needs of the individuals and families changing at any time. Over time, some of these individuals will become number 1 priority clients in their need for residential services.

Adults Living with Elderly Parents   Four states provided information related to people with mental retardation and other developmental disabilities who are living with elderly parents (Maryland, New Hampshire, Ohio, and Washington). Washington stated that "there are 353 clients . . . who are 40 years of age or older and are living with parents or relatives. These people will likely need residential support in the future" (State of Washington Developmental Disabilities Planning Council, 1991, p. 36). New Hampshire reported:

> . . . the daily demands for supervision placed by developmentally disabled persons on their families take a tremendous toll on their parents and siblings. Many of these families have been on these waiting lists for several years, including families who felt that they would get immediate relief as a result of (a court order) in the early 1980's. Typically, these parents are in their 50's and 60's and still have their son or daughter living with them, with many of the family members in their 30's or 40's, well past the time when "non-disabled children would have left the family home." (B. Reed, personal communication, 1992, March 25)

For the 3,506 adults over the age of 21 and in need of services, Maryland found 37% of the caregivers were over 60 years of age, 12% were over 70 years of age, and 1% were over 80 years of age. Moreover, 23% of the aging caregivers were single, and 44% were employed outside the home (W.T. Wacker, personal communication, 1992, March 18). Oregon indicated that for a sample of 200 people residing in the community and waiting for either vocational or residential services or both, almost 25% of the persons identified as primary caregivers were 61 years of age or older.

Older Adults   Five states provided information on the number of elderly people with mental retardation and other developmental disabilities who were waiting for services (Colorado, Ohio, Oregon, New York, and Washington). Colorado reported that of 843 adults over 21 years of age who were requesting day services, 87.9% were between the ages of 21–55 years, and 12.1% were 55 years old or older. Of 1,677 adults over 21 years old who were in need of residential services, 91.2% were 21–55 years old and 8.8% were 55 years old or older.

Ohio reported that of 6,035 adults over the age of 40 waiting for services, 22.9% were 40–55 years old, 10.5% were 56–69 years old, and 2.9% were 70 years old or older. In a similar analysis, New York indicated that of 5,673 people waiting for services, 62.9% were 22–40 years old, 8.8% were 45–59 years old, and 2.7% were 60 years old or older. Similarly, in an Oregon sample of 238 people living in the community who were waiting for services, 16% were 31–40 years old, 10% were 41–50 years old, 3% were 51–60 years old, and 1% were 61-70 years old.

In the state of Washington, 76.6% of the 3,033 unserved people were 22–59 years old, and 4.5% were 60 years old or older (State of Washington Developmental Disabilities Planning Council, 1991). A report conducted by the State of Washington Developmental Disabilities Planning Council (1991) noted the following:

> Increasing life expectancy, efforts to reduce nursing home placement of people with developmental disabilities, and the increasing number of clients 55 to 64 years old, are all factors which suggest that the population of people with developmental disabilities 65 years and older is likely to increase substantially by the end of the decade. (p. 36)

Young Adult Graduates Approximately 35,000–40,000 students with developmental disabilities leave special education programs each year (Wright, King, & National Conference of State Legislatures, 1991). Research indicates that high levels of unemployment, economic instability and dependency, and social isolation among these graduates are common (Johnson, Bruininks, & Wallace, 1992). Frequently, there is insufficient coordination among schools and community service agencies, and attempts by graduates and their families to access the community service delivery system are met with long waiting lists. Data provided by respondents of this study support current research in this area.

Information related to the number of people graduating from special education programs was provided by eight states (Colorado, Maryland, Massachusetts, Ohio, Oregon, New York, Texas, and Vermont). Persons leaving special education services are a special concern for Oregon. Similar to their counterparts in other states, they have no guarantee of gaining entry into the adult services system. A recent planning document reported the following:

> The number of persons with unmet needs grows every year by at least the number of high school special education graduates for whom no adult services are available. According to Division staff, this number totals as many as 200 individuals per year. Recent development of supported employment opportunities tied specifically to graduating high school students has dented this problem, but there are more graduating students in need than there are committed resources. In light of the state's considerable investment in educating students with developmental disabilities, it is troubling that the support they need to maintain their goals and continue as productive citizens is in many cases lacking. (Human Services Research Institute, 1990, p. 34)

A report from Massachusetts indicated that it has a program named "Turning 22" for recent special education graduates. In 1989, there were 1,200 people in this program. In 1990, Colorado reported that 367 of the persons enrolled in public school needed day services, and 66.2% were between the ages of 18 and 20.9

years. Moreover, 344 needed residential services, with 58.7% of these individuals being between the ages of 18 and 20.9 years.

Reports from Vermont and New York noted the current problems in providing access to community-based services to students "aging out" of educational services. Of the 5,673 individuals reported in need of residential services in New York, 15.5% were between the ages of 18 and 21 years, and 62.8% were between the ages of 22-44 years (A. Hanley, personal communication, 1992, February). From 1988 to 1989, Texas indicated that 29,372 persons with mental retardation and 1,091 persons with autism attended public school. Of this group, 1,721 left the public school system from 1988 to 1989. A recent Texas state strategic plan noted that "On graduation there are often few—if any—services that help students leaving the public school to continue their individual development and that help their integration in the community" (Texas Department of Mental Health and Mental Retardation, 1990, p. 28). The Texas Department of Mental Health and Mental Retardation (1990) estimated that 632 of these ex-students will be part of the state's priority population. The state intends to seek special funding for 258 people who require intensive services. Another 374 people will require less intensive services, such as prevocational and vocational services. The report further indicated that, at the same time, transition planning for persons who will leave the public school system will take place for 2,814 persons.

Although data provided by states indicate that people who live in every type of residence are waiting for community services, detailed information was limited to those living at home. To compensate for this lack of information, a literature review was conducted. The following section presents findings from this review, describing how people who live in either residential facilities or with their families continue to place pressure on the service system to expand its community component. It also addresses the barriers that hinder these persons from moving into the community and the strategies that can be implemented to overcome these barriers.

STATUS OF PERSONS PLACING PRESSURE ON THE SERVICE SYSTEM

People Living in State-Operated Institutions

During the early years of the deinstitutionalization movement, "creaming" became commonplace; that is, individuals with mild disabilities were moved into community placement before other individuals with more severe impairments. As a result of this practice, people who currently live in public institutions and nursing homes are primarily people with more severe intellectual or medical disabilities, and people who display more severe challenging behavior (Lakin et al., 1993; Scheerenberger, 1990). However, research shows that the number of persons with severe disabilities in the community is rapidly growing. Data indicate that: 1) persons with severe disabilities successfully live in the community (Larson & Lakin, 1989), and 2) persons with significant medical conditions and challenging behavior can be placed and maintained in more normalized community settings (Hayden & DePaepe, 1991; Hill & Bruininks, 1981; Hill et al., 1989; Lakin, Hill, Chen, & Stephens, 1989).

Nonetheless, the availability of and access to current community-based services may be more limited for people who currently live in institutions. For example, persons with mental retardation and medical conditions may face four types of barriers to the provision of community medical care and services (Hayden & DePaepe, 1991). First, initial disincentives may exist toward the support of this population in community residences. Primary disincentives include inadequate per diem rates and budgets to cover the level of care or service required for some individuals and an inadequate number of foster and small group homes equipped to care for this population. Problems related to the funding and actual payment of medical care and services create the second category of barriers, including limited availability of funding for in-home medical and support services and the Medicaid fee structure, inefficient payment mechanisms, and delays in Medicaid reimbursements.

The third group of barriers are related to inadequate community medical care and services. Many physicians lack formal training related to persons with mental retardation and other developmental disabilities. Furthermore, some medical service providers may be hesitant to provide health care because of a lack of experience with this population. In addition, there can be an inadequate dissemination of information among developmental disabilities professionals, health care professionals, and direct care providers. The final category of barriers includes unavailability or inaccessibility of medical care and services as a result of geographic location (e.g., rural areas) or poor coordination of community health care (e.g., an individual who receives Medicaid but has difficulty in obtaining routine health services).

Persons who display challenging behavior are also often excluded from integrated community settings or are served in more restrictive environments. The reluctance to serve this population is often due to the lack of information and the lack of staff adequately trained in positive approaches to the management of challenging behavior (Reichle & Light, 1992). Increased resources to train service providers and to develop systems and resources that allow intervention to be implemented in the context of normalized integrated settings are critical to enable people with challenging behavior to live in the community. The recession and the federal and state budget deficits, however, may continue to hinder the service delivery system's ability to provide the necessary supports and services to persons with challenging behavior. In addition, high turnover rates in the service delivery system hinder its ability to retain qualified and informed direct care staff.

Planning for continued deinstitutionalization will require significant advances in access to and application of behavior management technology (Reichle & Light, 1992), the removal of barriers that hinder access to community-based medical services (Hayden & DePaepe, 1991), and the development of strategies and assurances that enable the system to become more responsive to the needs of people with severe intellectual disabilities. Additional training and education is necessary for medical and nonmedical professionals and direct care service providers who work with people with severe disabilities, challenging behavior, and significant medical conditions. Improved interdisciplinary and interagency coordination and ongoing monitoring of the quality of services provided will also be needed to allow for the provision of quality community-based services to all persons with mental retardation and other developmental disabilities.

People Living in Nursing Homes

Early supporters of the deinstitutionalization movement were eager to reduce the number of individuals living in large public institutions. Initial efforts moved a large number of people with mental retardation and other developmental disabilities into nursing homes. Nursing homes were also used to avoid placement in large public institutions. Unfortunately, people neglected to see that most intermediate care facilities (ICFs) or skilled nursing facilities (SNFs) had medical orientations, and most were not specifically designed to meet the needs of people with developmental disabilities. Consequently, for many people, the change in residence did not result in significant changes in their quality of life.

Findings from the 1977 and 1985 National Nursing Home Surveys indicate that residents with mental retardation were much younger than the nursing home population in general (Lakin, Hill, & Anderson, 1991). Moreover, there was a relatively low prevalence of substantial physical and sensory limitations in residents with mental retardation. Additionally, they had extremely limited involvement in therapeutic services. In 1988, there were approximately 50,606 persons with mental retardation living in nursing homes and most of them did not present specialized geriatric or medical needs (Braddock, Hemp, Fujiura, Bachelder, & Mitchell, 1990).

As the result of growing concerns over individuals with mental retardation living in nursing homes, a provision of the Consolidated Omnibus Budget Reconciliation Act (COBRA) of 1987 (PL 100-203) attempted to discourage further admissions to nursing homes and to move people out of these facilities. Since its enactment, only a few people have been released from nursing homes. As of June 30, 1991, an estimated 37,817 persons with mental retardation lived in nursing homes (Lakin et al., 1993). There were only 3,653 fewer people living in nursing homes between 1989 and 1991 and only 1,209 individuals were released between 1990 and 1991. These data suggest that continual pressure has to be placed on states to follow through the intent of PL 100-203.

In addition to the question of the appropriateness of nursing homes for persons with mental retardation, policymakers need to address the cost effectiveness of this type of residential service. In 1988, nearly $900 million was expended on nursing home care for approximately 50,606 people with mental retardation (Braddock et al., 1990). As stated earlier, the majority of persons with mental retardation who currently live in nursing homes do not present specialized physical and sensory limitations. Consequently, the service delivery system could provide many people who live in nursing homes with the necessary services they need to live in the community, while providing a more normalized and less costly housing option.

People Living in Large Private Institutions

Despite the progress that the service delivery system has made in deinstitutionalization, there is a continuing bias toward large (16 or more people) congregate residences. As of June 30, 1991, the number of individuals living in large private institutions was 46,524 (Lakin et al., 1993). Large privately operated facilities have been and continue to be utilized extensively across the country. In fact, there has been little reduction in their population. From June 30, 1982 to June 30, 1991, the number of people living in large private institutions that were licensed as ICFs/MR increased by 9,311, while there were 31,830 fewer people living in large state-operated ICFs/MR (Lakin et al., 1993). Not only have these facilities avoided deinstitutionalization, but they also continue to serve people who are higher functioning than their counterparts who live in state-operated institutions and who could easily live in, and benefit from living in, the community.

In 1987, large private institutions served 62,156 people, whereas state-operated facilities served 91,541 individuals (Lakin, Jaskulski, et al., 1989). The large private institutions served approximately 46% more people with "borderline" mental retardation, 43% more individuals with mild mental retardation, and 68% more persons with moderate mental retardation (Lakin, Jaskulski, et al., 1989). Furthermore, these institutions typically serve people who are less likely to exhibit challenging behavior than those living in state institutions (Lakin, Hill et al., 1989).

For persons who advocate to deinstitutionalize these large private facilities, three barriers will need to be confronted. First, there is, at best, limited information about the quality of life residents of these facilities experience and how their experiences compare with their counterparts who live in the community. Second, large private facilities cost less than most other residences and, as a result, may be viewed as the most optimal alternative for placement. For example, large private facilities that receive ICF/MR funding are considerably cheaper ($19,690 per year) than large state-operated ICFs/MR ($42,812 per year). Furthermore, they are cheaper than small (15 or fewer people) state-operated ICFs/MR ($35,473 per year) and small private ICFs/MR ($32,683 per year) (Congressional Research Services, 1988). Yet, the quality and quantity of care and services across these four settings are unknown. Third, some parents of currently institutionalized family members with mental retardation reported high levels of general satisfaction with placements and with more than 50% opposed to moving family members to a small community residence (Larson & Lakin, 1991). Consequently, supporters of Medicaid reform will need to find ways to facilitate parental satisfaction with deinstitutionalization. Furthermore, similar legislation to PL 100-203 may need to be in place before a substantial number of people living in large privately operated institutions are moved into the community. Consequently, if the service delivery system makes a concerted effort to deinstitutionalize these large private facilities, there will be additional pressure for the community to expand the types of supports and services it offers to this population.

People Living in Intermediate Care
Facilities for Persons with Mental Retardation

The ICF/MR program, created in 1971 as an optional Medicaid service, is a federal financial participation program that funds long-term congregate care. This program was established by Congress to respond to the steadily increasing costs of institutional care incurred by states and the substandard living conditions that persons with mental retardation had to bear while living in public institutions. The supporters of the ICF/MR program envisioned that persons with mental retardation and other disabilities would receive health and rehabilitation services and "active treatment." Critics of the program, however, charge that it has fallen short of its protective and custodial obligations and active treatment requirements (Wisconsin Coalition for Advocacy, 1986, 1989).

Research has shown that ICFs/MR provide a relatively poor quality of life for persons with mental retardation (Holburn, 1992), and they benefit only a small fraction of the population with mental retardation and developmental disabilities (Helms, 1988). Yet, ICFs/MR are the largest source of funds for the population (Braddock et al., 1990; Fernald, 1986). In 1986, approximately 145,000 people lived in ICFs/MR at an average annual cost of approximately $35,000 per person (Helms, 1988). As of June 30, 1991, an estimated 146,727 individuals lived in ICFs/MR at an average annual cost of $55,609 (Lakin et al., 1993).

Another criticism of the program is that it primarily supports large congregate residential facilities. In the 1986 National Study of Public Expenditures, researchers found that 87% of ICF/MR funding ($3.38 billion) was used to underwrite care in public institutions (Braddock et al., 1990). As of June 30, 1991, total federal and state ICF/MR budgets were approximately $8.16 billion, serving 146,727 people (Lakin et al., 1993). The majority of these people (73.8%) lived in ICFs/MR that had 16 or more people residing in them.

A final criticism of the ICF/MR program is that it is heavily influenced by the medical service delivery model. As a result, people are placed in residences regardless of their needs, desires, and the nature and degree of their disabilities. Consequently, people are expected to adapt to the residence rather than the residence's environment and staff adapting to the individual. Many persons with mental retardation and other developmental disabilities frequently find themselves receiving a level of supervision or a level of nursing care that does not meet their needs. The day-to-day operations of ICFs/MR are not always conducive to the typical day-to-day rhythms that most people would like to experience and they do not provide an environment for self-expression. Researchers noted, for example, many service agencies, such as the ICFs/MR, are required to implement hour-by-hour schedules and opportunities for choice are limited (Bannerman, Sheldon, Sherman, & Harchik, 1990). They asserted the following:

Inflexible scheduling often precludes opportunities for choice. For instance, clients may not be allowed to choose the order or timing of activities. They may be discouraged from taking breaks or from choosing activities that are not scheduled. Staff may pick out clients' clothes. A dietitian may plan clients' meals. Leisure materials may be locked in a cabinet until scheduled leisure times. (Bannerman et al., 1990, p. 81)

Similar to nursing homes and large private institutions, creative financial strategies need to be developed in order for states to be able to shift their ICF/MR funding from primarily institutional care to supporting and assisting people with mental retardation and other developmental disabilities to live in the community. Rearranging federal spending levels to favor living in the community is one possible strategy. Even though certain individuals with mental retardation and other developmental disabilities may necessitate high per diem rates, many people currently living in ICFs/MR could benefit from living in more normalized community options and, as a result of the change in residence, could be offered a less costly housing option that could, in turn, compensate for those persons who have greater and more expensive service needs.

For many people living in the residential facilities described in this section, involvement in the MR/DD service system is meaningless because they do not have access to community living. Yet, their counterparts who do live in the community with their families often receive little, if any, support from the system. In fact, the vast majority of people with mental retardation and other developmental disabilities live in noninstitutional settings, receiving the least amount of financial support from the service delivery system. The following section will summarize the most current information from the literature that is related to individuals with mental retardation and other developmental disabilities who live with their families. The text will present more detailed information from these persons, their parents, advocates, case managers, and other stakeholders who have first-hand knowledge about waiting for services while living at home.

People Living in the Community and Waiting for Services and Supports

According to the National Health Interview Survey (LaPlante, 1988), there are an estimated 2 million people with developmental disabilities living in the United States. Only 15.6% of these individuals live in institutional settings. Of those living in noninstitutional settings, the vast majority live at home with their families. Consequently, families play a significant role in the service delivery system (Smull, 1989). In fact, families provide more support and services to people with developmental disabilities than all of the formal components of the service system, but many are doing so without any type of formal assistance from the system (Lakin & Bruininks, 1985). Many of these families have difficulties in gaining access to the MR/DD service system. Hayden (1992) estimated that nearly 31% (57,558) of the reported number of persons waiting for some type of community services lived with their families or in their own homes.

The most serious obstacles in gaining access to the MR/DD service delivery system appear to be present for the following groups of people: 1) families with young adults who have graduated from special education programs and who are waiting for vocational, habilitation, and community residential services; 2) parents of adult family members with mental retardation and other developmental disabilities who want them to remain at home, but are seeking respite care and other support services; and 3) elderly parents of adult children who are seeking out-of-home placement, as well as vocational and habilitation services, for the first time. There are several reasons why family members are waiting for services while living at home. They include the following: 1) the rising service costs in a time of tight state and local budgets; 2) disjointed and uncoordinated services; 3) inadequate planning and policy development to meet the needs of families who currently sustain the system while waiting for services; 4) ineffective attention to the growing concerns of families with members who present particularly high demands, such as persons with intensive medical or physical disabilities or those who exhibit challenging behavior; and 5) the fact that more and more states target higher proportions of new community service development for persons being discharged from institutional settings (Hayden, 1992).

Although these families are waiting for various services and supports, their requests are typically modest. In one study, families often wanted day habilitation services and at least one type of social support (Black, Molaison, & Smull, 1990). The main reason for seeking assistance was to obtain normalizing activities that would promote the adult family member's independence. Although the service requests are reasonable, the service delivery system often neglects families who choose to have adult family members with mental retardation and other developmental disabilities remain at home.

A report to the Ohio Joint Legislative Study Committee on Community MR/DD Services (1990) stated that "For each disabled family member kept at home, these families save the Ohio taxpayers a total of $376,486,700 per year" (p. 4). Voluntary contributions of families choosing to have their members with mental retardation and other developmental disabilities stay at home result in additional savings. However, the cumulative personal, social, and economic costs associated with families waiting for services present a substantial counterbalance to the service dollar savings. These costs often include long-term financial instability, family dependence, and isolation from other community members.

Historically, service programs for families with adult members who have mental retardation and other developmental disabilities have supplanted, rather than supported the family (Knoll, 1990). In other words, services became available to these persons only after leaving their family. This orientation has changed. Today, it is recognized that family living offers much to family members with mental retardation and other developmental disabilities. Families often provide a vehicle to community integration, employment, social relationships, and other opportunities that are not easily replicated in the service system. Although family support programs are steadily growing, they remain tentative and far fewer than the demand for them. As Knoll (1990) pointed out:

> Each new fiscal year brings substantial change to the depth and breadth of family support programs around the country. Though much of the change is positive and reflects expansion, many programs no longer exist because they were pilot (short-term, trial) projects that did not become permanent. Further, many family support initiatives are not firmly established by legislative mandate and, therefore, while they may continue, they are susceptible to the state budgetary process. (p. 28)

ADULTS LIVING AT HOME

A pilot study was conducted to obtain first-hand knowledge about how waiting for services affects individuals with mental retardation and other developmental disabilities who live at home (Hayden et al., 1992). Methods employed to obtain initial information were qualitative in nature and included focus groups, interviews with several families, and semistructured interviews with adults with mental retardation. These methods are described in the following paragraphs.

Focus Groups Four focus groups were formed. The first group included nine parents of adult family members with mental retardation and other developmental disabilities who were waiting for services and representatives from parent advocacy organizations who either had similar experiences or worked with families that had these experiences. Seven county case managers made up the second group. The third group included four service providers, one county case manager, and one state employee from the state department of human services (division for people with developmental disabilities). Finally, three professional advocates met with three self-advocates who have mental retardation and other developmental disabilities.

Semistructured Interviews Self-advocates were included in the focus group process, however, their involvement during the group was limited. As a result, semistructured interviews were added in an attempt to better gain the perspective of persons with mental retardation and other developmental disabilities. Four people were identified through county case managers.

Family Interviews Two families were chosen by a parent advocacy organization to participate in a family interview related to waiting for services. To maintain confidentiality, the names of family members who participated were changed. The parents in each family were single mothers of adult children with autism. The two mothers were from very different backgrounds and had different experiences with the service delivery system; however, each had experienced ongoing difficulties in gaining adequate supports and services. The following descriptions of each family are provided to serve as background for the quotes from each parent that are discussed.

Donna lives with her son, Mike, who is 26 years old and has autism, and another adult sibling who has no disabilities. Another sibling frequently visits the household. To make ends meet, Donna currently holds both a full-time day job and a part-time evening job. Mike attends a sheltered workshop each weekday and does a variety of paid vocational tasks. Donna is attempting to find a good personal care attendant (PCA) to assist in daily caregiving for Mike. Eventually, she would also like to find a good family-like group home in a nearby area so Mike can continue a familiar routine.

Jan and Sue live in a house where they have lived for 15 years. Jan, Sue's mother, is in her 60s and Sue is 22 years old. Other extended family members live in the home. Sue graduated from high school more than a year ago. She has not received day program services since graduation and, as a result, she stays home each weekday with her mother and Marie, a PCA. Marie has worked with Sue for about 1 year.

For purposes of this chapter, data related to the services and supports needed by adults with mental retardation and other developmental disabilities and their families, the needs of these adults during the transition from living at home to living elsewhere in the community, and barriers to gaining access to community services are discussed. Readers who are interested in the specific scope of the study, methodology employed, and all of the results of the study should see Hayden et al. (1992).

Services and Supports Needed by Adults and Their Families

All participants from the focus groups agreed that family members with mental retardation and other developmental disabilities needed recreation and leisure services, as well as training in independent living skills. Parents, case managers, and advocates expressed a need for improved medical services, while parents and service providers agreed on a need for crisis services and effective advocacy. Both parents and case managers identified a need for improved assessment, and case managers and service providers believed there was a great need for support groups and counseling, while case managers and advocates concurred that adequate transportation was needed.

Different focus group participants identified different needs of families and adult family members with mental retardation and other developmental disabilities. Parents talked about specific problems they had in gaining access to community services, whereas case managers identified specific types of services. The service providers emphasized needs similar to those expressed by the case managers. Advocates concurred with the case managers and service providers, but added concerns that were specific to policy issues, such as the need for employment and employment assistance, community education, and residential options. The need for day habilitation was forcefully articulated by Jan, Sue's mother, and Marie. As Jan said:

> I think the longer she (her daughter) stays here, her mental thing will . . . lessen . . . She doesn't want to go out no more. She's gonna want to be stuck in there [her bedroom] for the rest of her life. You can't do that. A child like that can't be like that. They have to be out . . . (Hayden et al., 1992, p. 6)

During a previous visit, Marie said that she had seen a decline in Sue's skills during the year that she had been out of school:

> The more she's out—she gets used to it and she wants to do it more. The more she's in that room, then that's where she's rotting away. She's getting slower, her sign language is fallen. . . . But if we're in the community . . . she's great. . . . But once she's in here, her attitude can swing. . . . So the more she's out, the better off she is. (Hayden et al., 1992, p. 6)

Focus group participants identified services and supports needed by families that are frequently not received. In both cases, parents and case managers emphasized a need for crisis care and respite services, while the service providers agreed that crisis mental health services were needed. Donna, Mike's mother, stated the need for crisis services in unequivocal terms:

> So Mike threw this whopping, big temper tantrum, and I called 911. Usually what happens when 911 comes is that they don't know what to do, and they just kind of stand around . . . . And most of them are not familiar with autism. They don't know of any services for me, 'cause I probably at that time need crisis intervention. But I don't need somebody to talk to me on the telephone. I need somebody here, *right now*, who can take charge and do something with this kid who is over six feet tall, and who is hitting, breaking, screaming, yelling, throwing. (Hayden et al., 1992, p. 6)

Funding flexibility dominated the concerns expressed by the case managers, though both they and the service providers also stressed the need for central sources of information and referral. Advocates, in turn, spoke about the need for basic services, such as independent living skills training, recreation and leisure, housing, and client advocacy. Participants talked at length about the needs of individuals who are in transition—from living with their families to living elsewhere in the community. The following section summarizes their perspectives about the issues surrounding transition.

Needs During the Transition from Family Living to Community Living

Case managers, service providers, and advocates stated that independent living skills training was essential, whereas parents and case managers agreed that a mentor program and a slower transition, facilitated by a defined planning process, would be helpful. The service providers also recommended more widespread use of the Medicaid Home and Community Based Services (HCBS) program and allowing the adult family member with mental retardation and other developmental disabilities to earn money while keeping their Supplemental Security Income (SSI) benefits. The advocates emphasized the need for coordinated services, integrated community education, transportation, and housing.

Donna, Mike's mother, spoke of the way she was almost forced to take the first residential option offered to her when she had finally succeeded in having her son determined eligible for medical assistance (MA):

> So now that he is on MA, he can qualify for things. We began to look at group homes. As a matter of fact, now I think everybody is real pushy about it. Y'know you have to be quick, do all this. (Hayden et al., 1992, p. 8)

Later in the visit, she talked about her reluctance to be hasty in placing Mike:

> This isn't about me, this is about Mike . . . . I can't do something for Mike that isn't fair for him either . . . . It's like when we looked at this hundred bed residential facility . . . and I said, 'I can't. It's not fair. Mike's lived at home all his life. Why would I want to put him in a hospital. I'm not gonna do that.' (Hayden et al., 1992, p. 8)

Indeed, some adults with mental retardation and other developmental disabilities are equally aware of the need to plan transitions. Peter, one of the individuals we interviewed, discussed his plans to move out of the home when he turned 26. The interviewer asked, "Do you look forward to living alone?" Peter responded, "Well, I feel kind of sad, but actually I don't have no choice. In the near future, Mom and Dad won't be around." Peter was equally aware that there were areas in life with which he would need help. When asked if he would want to keep his service provider after he left the home, Peter said, "Yeah . . . . Somebody to check up on me once in a while, to see how I do."

Barriers to the Access of Community Services and Supports

There was more agreement on barriers to the access of community services than on perhaps any other area that was discussed, primarily as these barriers related to funding. Parents pointed out many issues related to funding, including priorities on deinstitutionalization, the level of funding for community services, and the service delivery system's lack of capacity to expand the number of family support services. The case managers agreed that funding was a major obstacle. One of their primary concerns was related to how the service delivery system is based on open slots or available beds, rather than on the needs of each individual who is seeking services.

Other concerns expressed by the case managers were that the overall funding level is low and that there is a lack of capacity to expand the number of services to people. The service providers believed that funding rules that gave a priority to people being deinstitutionalized were a barrier and, again, the advocates saw the level of funding issue and the priority on deinstitutionalization as significant obstacles.

Parents also identified other barriers including a conflict of interest for the case manager as a gatekeeper, a lack of available information, and a generally uncoordinated system both within and between counties. Case managers agreed with parents in so far as they conceded that there was a significant lack of information and that the service delivery system was antagonistic. They cited their heavy caseloads as a major problem for them in providing adequate services. Service providers agreed with both the parents and the case managers that the service delivery system does not provide adequate outreach to inform people of available services, such as MA, SSI, and Social Security disability income (SSDI). Similar to the parents, they viewed the system as uncoordinated both within and across counties, and like the case managers, they believed large caseloads were a major problem. They went further, however, arguing that regulations governing eligibility, assessment, and authorization were also obstacles to the provision of needed services.

When it came to alleviating these barriers, all agreed that funding needed to be increased and allocated for individuals rather than services. Both service providers and advocates agreed that funding for families with adult family members should gain some of the emphasis that deinstitutionalization has received. Changes in case management were mentioned by both advocates and parents. Parents suggested privatizing the system, while advocates saw a need for increasing the service.

The parents we visited had much experience with overburdened case managers and an antagonistic service system. Jan reported initiating Sue's transition plans to obtain day habilitation services 2 years prior to her graduation. At that time, Jan was told that her case manager would have to pursue the matter.

> Actually, he (the case manager) didn't start until the last year before she was gonna be out of school, and then he had to talk to his teachers there, and everything, and, well . . . it just seemed like it was impossible . . . . No matter how many times I'd call him up to talk to him, he just kept saying, 'Oh yeah. Things are going just fine. Things are going just fine.' But it never turned out that way. So now all we have to do is wait. (Hayden et al., 1992, p. 7)

At our second visit, Jan was even more irate, complaining that her case manager went along with whatever the provider told him. Jan stated that she was becoming increasingly frustrated with being unable to obtain day habilitation services for her daughter.

> He (the case manager) doesn't argue the matter, . . . If I tell him, 'Well, they told me (next month).' He'll say, 'Well, that's fine.' I mean not to me it isn't fine, 'cause it shouldn't take that long. (Hayden et al., 1992, p. 7)

Donna's frustrations in the past centered around having Mike determined eligible for MA, which took her nearly 8 years to obtain. Donna related some of the following problems:

> I could never get Mike on MA. Those people told me that if Mike lived at home, he lived on my income, and that he couldn't get MA . . . . All my other friends, their handicapped kids were on MA, and I could never get Mike on MA. The guy would hang up on me. I'd call him and I'd say . . . . 'Oh. You must be mistaken, because my friends have handicapped kids, and their kids are on MA.' (The) guy said, 'You're wrong lady . . . . You can't get MA.' And he would just hang up on me . . . . These people were just rude . . . . They are indifferent. They are obnoxious. They have a lot of control, and they issue it all. I mean they can do whatever. I complained once to my social worker about that, and she's almost as bad because she never did anything either. She would listen to me and she would do nothing. (Hayden et al., 1992, p. 7)

Information provided in this section indicates that persons with mental retardation and other developmental disabilities who live with their families are in need of a variety of community services and supports. The ways in which states find the means to provide these services remains a challenge. For persons who attempt to find equity through legal action, they may find minimal, if any, support from the federal government. For example, the Philadelphia Police and Fire Association for Handicapped Children brought a class action against the City of Philadelphia on behalf of persons with mental retardation living at home to challenge the constitutionality of cuts in services (874 F.2d 156 [3rd cir. 1989]). The Appellate Court found the reduction or elimination of benefits for the class did not violate equal protection or due process. The court stated:

> Philadelphia could have believed that residents who lost habilitative services and therefore regressed would be more likely to be institutionalized than their counterparts who live with their families. The families, which already have demonstrated their devotion to their retarded children by caring for them at home, might be willing to keep them at home after they have regressed. In contrast, the residences might not be able to continue to care for such residents who, because of their regression, place greater demands on the residential staff. The district court characterized the situation as follows: '[I]t is as if [Philadelphia and the Commonwealth] seek to capitalize upon the love and dedication of the families of the class members.' Dist.Ct.Op. at 10, App. 844. Whatever our individual beliefs about the desirability of such a policy may be, such reliance on family dedication is not irrational because it may serve to minimize institutionalization. (Philadelphia Police and Fire Association for Handicapped Children, 1989)

CONCLUSION

The problem of waiting for services is of great concern for persons with mental retardation and other developmental disabilities and their families, service providers, professionals, and advocates. Reliably estimating the number and characteristics of people on waiting lists for services, however, is problematic at best. Problems related to identifying adults with mental retardation and other developmental disabilities who are waiting for community services are numerous. Less than half of the states have formal data collection systems; the remaining states are either in the process of developing a state-wide data collection system, do not have a data collection system, or have an informal system. In addition, states that do have some type of data collection system collect data in a variety of ways and, typically, do not collect statistics related to demographic or personal characteristics. Few states believe they can accurately identify all of the people with service needs. Finally, eligibility for services is dependent on whether the state uses the federal definition of developmental disability or other functional definitions. This factor also complicates attempts to identify all those persons who are waiting for services.

Additional problems are created by the fact that some state agencies only report numbers of people with particular developmental disabilities who are waiting for services, but do not provide information on persons with other types of disabilities who also need services. Furthermore, the waiting lists include only people who contacted the local or state authorities and, as a result, the numbers do not reflect people who for one reason or another did not request, but may still need, services.

Despite these problems, several conclusions from the Hayden (1992) study can be drawn. First, there are a large number of states that maintain waiting lists.

Second, there are a large number of people waiting for every type of MR/DD service in virtually every state; however, few states gather information that can be useful for planning and for finding the means or methods to serve people who are unserved or underserved. Third, few states track who needs services and what type of services are being sought. Fourth, many states have written procedures to prioritize service requests, but these procedures are typically centered around crisis situations. Finally, most people who are on waiting lists live at home with their families and, specifically, include young adults who recently graduated from high school, older adults who live with elderly parents, and elderly persons with mental retardation and other developmental disabilities.

Waiting lists can become permanent indicators of our society's inability or unwillingness to respond to the needs of individuals. At their worst, waiting lists are indicators of system crisis and failure, but we can use waiting lists for community-based services as meaningful tools for planning and policy development. These lists can provide information regarding individuals' ages, levels of mental retardation, functional limitations, adaptive behaviors, presence of challenging behaviors, and other demographic and personal characteristics that can assist policy-makers in developing the amounts and types of services actually needed. Waiting lists can also serve as a safety valve to take pressure off the system to respond to individuals who are in immediate need of assistance.

The data summarized in this chapter present waiting lists as a reflection of a service delivery system that is currently driven by crisis—underrepresenting those who are in need of services and supports, and unable to distinguish what services are needed and which individuals need the services and supports. In addition, the waiting lists can be viewed as a symptom of the larger problem, which is the manner in which we deliver services to people with mental retardation and other developmental disabilities.

The recent goal of the service delivery system has been deinstitutionalization. With this goal came the lack of foresight to see the potential pitfall of early practices employed in the deinstitutionalization movement (e.g., "creaming," moving individuals from state-operated institutions to nursing homes, overutilization of ICFs/MR, and not deinstitutionalizing large private institutions). Furthermore, earlier supporters failed to conceptualize the service delivery system as a more comprehensive and inclusive system that serves not only persons who live in public institutions, but also those who live with their families and who live in nursing homes and private institutions. Consequently, the federal government continues to support institutions that serve a dwindling population at a great expense to taxpayers. Braddock et al. (1990) predicted that although the United States institutional census will drop below 60,000 in the year 2000, more than $6 billion will be associated with the financing of institutional care that year.

Lack of foresight resulted in the state officials and service provider agencies needing to "re-deinstitutionalize" individuals living in nursing homes, to deinstitutionalize those living in private institutions, and to move people out of restrictive ICFs/MR. Furthermore, we have been remiss in our responsibilities to persons with mental retardation and other developmental disabilities who live with their families and to those who currently live in public institutions whose additional conditions or disabilities pose increased challenges to us. Both groups challenge the service system to find the means to strengthen and expand our communities.

Resolution of waiting lists will occur when stakeholders examine the entire service delivery system. We need to conceptualize our goal as the conversion of a service system (Schalock, 1985). Furthermore, we need to understand that changes in one part of the service delivery system will affect other parts of the system. In other words, if we shift our energies toward individuals currently living at home, we will risk the possibility of neglecting those who live in other settings. Any adjustments made to the system need to be made in the spirit of equal access to services.

Criteria for altering our current service delivery system to one that is more comprehensive should include, at a minimum, a shift of services and resources from institutions to the community and to equal access to services (Fernald, 1986). In addition, Schalock (1985) proposed that the following principles should guide a more comprehensive community service delivery system: 1) services are provided as a right, rather than a privilege, on a noncategorical basis, and under the least restrictive, most normalized circumstances possible; 2) services are available in sufficient quantity, flexibility, and variety to ensure that a person's needs are met in the most appropriate manner possible; 3) agencies providing services are accountable to persons with mental retardation and other developmental disabilities; and 4) service providers utilize the most up-to-date techniques and meet at least minimum performance standards regarding the provision and outcome of services and supports.

In addition to these criteria, an examination of constraints against community-based service development must occur, and strategies to overcome these constraints need to be identified. State MR/DD directors identified a number of private sector and federal, state, and local government constraints against community-based services and supports (Hemp, Braddock, Bachelder, & Hassen, 1990). For example, federal constraints include restrictions, adverse interpretations, and institutional incentives inherent in the federal Medicaid program. In addition, state constraints include insufficient funding, inappropriate or low reimbursement systems, and funding restrictions and interpretations.

We need to better understand creative finance strategies that will enable governments and the private sector to provide services and supports to all citizens with mental retardation and other developmental disabilities. A number of strategies that states can employ include flexible and individualized funding approaches, increased family support services, and improved state government collaboration with communities, local governments, and community-based service providers (Hemp, 1992). We also need to examine the methods and procedures for service delivery employed by the community-based system.

The service delivery system for persons with mental retardation and other developmental disabilities is at a crossroad. People in the late 1960s had the foresight to promote the development of community-based services. Now, we must decide whether we will strive to make the necessary adjustments to the current system that will enable us to include and support those persons in need of services. We can either continue to avoid confronting the issues raised, or we can begin to take action. We can continue to serve primarily people who are currently in the MR/DD service delivery system, or we can develop a more inclusive model for service delivery. We can also continue to fiscally pit people who live in institutional settings against those who live in the community. However, if we fail to respond, the current problems in the system will take hold and continue to grow until the MR/DD system becomes completely unresponsive to the people it serves. If we choose to take action, we will need to reconceptualize how the MR/DD system will develop and deliver community-based programs. As a result, we will be more likely to attain the service delivery system that was first envisioned.

REFERENCES

Anderson, D.J., Lakin, K.C., Bruininks, R.H., & Hill, B.K. (1987). *A national study of residential and support services for elderly persons with mental retardation*. Minneapolis: University of Minnesota, Center for Residential Services and Community Living.

Bannerman, D., Sheldon, J., Sherman, J., & Harchik, A. (1990). Balancing the right to habilitation with the right to personal liberties: The rights of people with developmental disabilities to eat too many doughnuts and take a nap. *Journal of Applied Behavior Analysis, 23*, 79–89.

Black, M., Molaison, V., & Smull, M. (1990). Families caring for a young adult with mental retardation: Service needs and urgency of community living requests. *American Journal of Mental Deficiency, 95*(1), 32–39.

Braddock, D., Hemp, R., Fujiura, G., Bachelder, L., & Mitchell, D. (1990). *The state of the states in developmental disabilities*. Baltimore: Paul H. Brookes Publishing Co.

Congressional Research Services. (1988, November). *Medicaid source book: Background data and analysis*. Washington, DC: U.S. House of Representatives, Subcommittee on Health and the Environment, Committee on Energy and Commerce.

Davis, S. (1987). *A national status report on waiting lists of people with mental retardation for community services*. Arlington, TX: Association for Retarded Citizens of the United States.

Department of Developmental Disabilities (California). (August, 1990). *Long range plan: 1990–95*. Sacramento, CA: Office of Planning and Policy Development.

Fernald, C.D. (1986). Changing Medicaid and Intermediate Care Facilities for the Mentally Retarded (ICFs/MR): Evaluation of alternatives. *Mental Retardation, 24*(1), 36–42.

Gold, L.C., Bowen, G.E., & Smull, M.W. (1990). *1990 source book: Individuals on the waiting list for services funded by the developmental disabilities administration*. Baltimore: University of Maryland School of Medicine, Department of Pediatrics (Developmental Disabilities Program: Applied Research and Evaluation Unit).

Hayden, M.F. (1992). Adults with mental retardation and other developmental disabilities waiting for community-based services in the U.S. *Policy Research Brief, 4*(3), 1–16. Minneapolis: University of Minnesota, Research and Training Center on Residential Services and Community Living, Institute on Community Integration.

Hayden, M.F., & DePaepe, P.A. (1991). Medical conditions, level of care needs, and health-related outcomes of persons with mental retardation: A review. *Journal of The Association for Persons with Severe Handicaps, 16*(4), 188–206.

Hayden, M.F., Spicer, P., DePaepe, P., & Chelberg, G. (1992). Waiting for community services: Support and service needs of families with adults who have mental retardation and other developmental disabilities. *Policy Research Brief, 4*(4), 1–12. Minneapolis: University of Minnesota, Research and Training Center for Residential Services and Community Living, Institute on Community Integration.

Helms, R.B. (1988, March). *Report to the Secretary: The working group on policies affecting mentally retarded and developmentally disabled persons.* Washington, DC: Author.

Hemp, R. (1992). State agency and community provider perspectives on financing community services. *Policy Research Brief, 4*(1), 1–8. Minneapolis: University of Minnesota, Research and Training Center on Residential Services and Community Living, Institute on Community Integration.

Hemp, R., Braddock, D., Bachelder, L., & Haasen, K. (1990, April). *Creative financing of community services: The state agency perspective—A working paper (Monograph No. 51).* Chicago: Illinois University Affiliated Program in Developmental Disabilities, Institute for the Study of Developmental Disabilities and the School of Public Health.

Hill, B.K., & Bruininks, R.H. (1981). *Physical and behavioral characteristics and maladaptive behavior of mentally retarded people in residential facilities.* Minneapolis: University of Minnesota, Department of Psychoeducational Studies.

Hill, B.K., Lakin, K.C., Bruininks, R.H., Amado, A.N., Anderson, D.J., & Copher, J.I. (1989). *Living in the community: A comparative study of foster homes and small group homes for people with mental retardation.* Minneapolis: University of Minnesota, Center for Residential Living and Community Services.

Holburn, C.S. (1992). Rhetoric and realities in today's ICF/MR: Control out of control. *Mental Retardation, 30*(3), 133–141.

Human Services Research Institute. (1990, August). *Oregon long range plan for developmental disability services: Commitment to community.* Monmouth, OR: Author.

Johnson, D.R., Bruininks, R.H., & Wallace, T. (1922, Fall). Transition: The next five years. *IMPACT, 5*(3), 1. Minneapolis: University of Minnesota, Institute on Community Integration.

Knoll, J.A. (1990). Family Support: A challenge for the 1990's. *Exceptional Parent, 20*(4), 28–34.

Lakin, K.C., & Bruininks, R.H. (1985). Challenges to advocates of social integration. *Strategies for achieving community integration of developmentally disabled citizens.* Baltimore: Paul H. Brookes Publishing Co.

Lakin, K.C., Hill, B.K., & Anderson, D.J. (1991). Persons with mental retardation in nursing homes in 1977 and 1985: A comparison of findings from the 1977 and 1985 national nursing home surveys. *Mental Retardation, 29*(1), 25–33.

Lakin, K.C., Hill, B.K., Chen, T.H., & Stephens, S.A. (1989). *Persons with mental retardation and related conditions in mental retardation facilities: Selected findings from the 1987 National Medical Expenditure Survey* (Report No. 29). Minneapolis: University of Minnesota, Research and Training Center on Residential Services and Community Living.

Lakin, K.C., Jaskulski, T.M., Hill, B.K., Bruininks, R.H., Menke, J.M., White, C.C., & Wright, E.A. (1989). *Medicaid services for persons with mental retardation and related conditions.* Minneapolis: University of Minnesota, Research and Training Center on Residential Services and Community Living, Institute on Community Integration.

Lakin, K.C., Prouty, R.W., Blake, E.M., Mangan, T., & White, C.C. (1993). *Residential services for persons with mental retardation and related conditions: Year ending June 30, 1991.* Minneapolis: University of Minnesota, Research and Training Center on Residential Services and Community Living, Institute on Community Integration.

Lakin, K.C., Prouty, R.W., White, C.C., Bruininks, R.H., & Hill, B.K. (1990). *Intermediate Care Facilities for Persons with Mental Retardation (ICFs-MR): Program utilization and resident characteristics.* Minneapolis: University of Minnesota, Research and

Training Center for Residential Services and Community Living, Institute on Community Integration.

Lakin, K.C., White, C.C., Prouty, R.W., Bruininks, R.H., & Kimm, C. (1991). *Medicaid institutional and home and community based services for persons with mental retardation and related conditions.* Minneapolis: University of Minnesota, Research and Training Center on Residential Services and Community Living, Institute on Community Integration.

LaPlante, M.P. (1988). *Data on disability from the National Health Interview Survey, 1983–1985.* An InfoUse Report. Washington, DC: U.S. National Institute on Disability and Rehabilitation Research.

LaPlante, M.P. (1991). Medical conditions associated with disability. In I. Fitzgerald & S. Thompson-Hoffman (Eds.), *Disability in the United States* (pp. 34–72). New York: Springer Publishing Co.

Larson, S.A., & Lakin, K.C. (1989). Deinstitutionalization of persons with mental retardation: Behavioral outcomes. *Journal of The Association for Persons with Severe Handicaps, 14*(4), 324–332.

Larson, S.A., & Lakin, K.C. (1991). Parent attitude about residential placement before and after deinstitutionalization: A research synthesis. *Journal of The Association for Persons with Severe Handicaps, 16*(1), 25–38.

Lincoln, A. (1858, June 16). *A house divided.* Speech given at the Illinois Republican state convention, Springfield.

McDonnell, J., Wilcox, B., & Boles, S.M. (1986). Do we know enough to plan for transition? A national survey of state agencies responsible for services to persons with severe handicaps. *Journal of The Association for Persons with Severe Handicaps, 11*(1), 53–60.

McGaughey, M.J., Lynch, S.A., Morganstern, D.R., Kiernan, W.E., & Schalock, R.L. (1991, April). *A national survey of day and employment programs for persons with developmental disabilities: Results from state MR/DD agencies.* Boston: Training Research Institute for People with Disabilities, Developmental Evaluation Center (UAP) and Children's Hospital.

Ohio Joint Legislative Study Committee on Community MR/DD Services. (1990, March). *Issues and funding requirements for community MR/DD residential services, support.* Columbus: Author.

Philadelphia Police and Fire Association for Handicapped Children, Inc. v. City of Philadelphia, 874 F.2d 156 (3rd cir. 1989).

Reichle, J., & Light, C. (1992). Positive approaches to managing challenging behavior among persons with developmental disabilities in the community. *Policy Research Brief, 4*(1), 1–12. Minneapolis: University of Minnesota, Research and Training Center on Residential Services and Community Living, Institute on Community Integration.

Schalock, R.L. (1985). Comprehensive community services: A plea for interagency collaboration. In R.H. Bruininks & K.C. Lakin (Eds.), *Living and learning in the least restrictive environment* (pp. 37–63). Baltimore: Paul H. Brookes Publishing Co.

Scheerenberger, R.C. (1990). *Public residential services for the mentally retarded, FY 1988–1989.* Madison, WI: National Association of Superintendents of Public Residential Facilities for the Mentally Retarded.

Smull, M.W. (1989). *Crisis in the community.* Baltimore: University of Maryland, Department of Pediatrics, School of Medicine (Applied Research and Evaluation Unit).

State of Washington Developmental Disabilities Planning Council. (1991, January 25). *Analysis of selected agencies' proposed budgets for the 1991–1993 biennium.* Olympia: Author.

Texas Department of Mental Health and Mental Retardation. (February, 1990). *Draft: Strategic plan—1992–1997.* Unpublished manuscript.

Wisconsin Coalition for Advocacy. (1986, May). *Out of sight, out of mind. A report on the human and civil rights of residents of Wisconsin's three state centers for the developmentally disabled, 1982 to date.* Madison, WI: Author.

Wisconsin Coalition for Advocacy. (1989, May). *The "active treatment" myth: People with developmental disabilities trapped in Wisconsin institutions.* Madison, WI: Author.

Wright, B., King, M.P., & National Conference of State Legislatures' Task Force on Developmental Disabilities. (1991, February). *Americans with developmental disabilities: Policy directions for the states.* Washington, DC: National Conference of State Legislatures.

SOURCES OF INFORMATION FOR TABLE 1

(1) Anderson, D.A. (personal communication, correspondence, February 28, 1992). Department of Mental Retardation (Data Management and Research). Columbia, SC.

(2) Braddick, J. (personal communication, correspondence, April 22, 1991). Planning and Advisory Council on Developmental Disabilities (data was from the Bureau of Mental Retardation). Augusta, ME.

(3) Bright, J. (personal communication correspondence, February 1992). Department of Mental Health (Division of Mental Retardation and Developmental Disabilities). Jefferson City, MO.

(4) Bynum, D. (personal communication, correspondence, January 24, 1991). Department of Human Services (Division of Mental Hygiene and Mental Retardation, Northern Nevada Mental Retardation Services). Sparks, NV.

(5) Campbell, E. (personal communication, telephone conversation, November 13, 1991). Department of Human Services (Division of Developmental Disabilities). Pierre, SD. *Data confirmed by response to 2/14/92 mailing.*

(6) Campbell, V.A. (personal communication, correspondence, April 17, 1992). Department of Mental Health and Mental Retardation (Applied Research Bureau), University of Alabama. Tuscaloosa, AL. *Data confirmed by 2/14/92 mailing.*

(7) Crosbie, D. (personal communication, correspondence, February 28, 1992). Department of Social and Rehabilitation Services (Developmental Disabilities Division). Helena, MT.

(8) Dalessandri, T. (personal communication, telephone conversation, December 2, 1991). Department of Health and Environment (Division of Developmental Disabilities). Santa Fe, NM.

(9) Davis, S. (1987). *A national report on waiting lists of people with mental retardation for community services.* Arlington, TX: Association for Retarded Citizens. *Data confirmed by response to 2/14/92 mailing.*

(10) Department of Mental Health, Mental Retardation, and Substance Abuse Services. (September 1989). *Virginia comprehensive state plan: 1990–1996.* Richmond, VA: Author.

(11) Department of Mental Health, Mental Retardation, and Substance Abuse Services. (1991). *Mental retardation system review: Directions for the year 2000.* Richmond, VA: Author.

(12) DiMaio, F. (personal communication, telephone conversation, December 3, 1991). Department of Mental Health, Mental Retardation, and Hospitals (Division of Retardation and Developmental Disabilities). Cranston, RI. *Data are not available.*

(13) Dodd, S. (personal communication, telephone conversation, November 12, 1991). Department of Human Services (Division of Mental Hygiene and Mental Retardation, Southern Nevada Mental Retardation Services). Las Vegas, NV.

(14) Fettweis, P. (personal communication, correspondence, March 30, 1992). Depart-

ment of Human Services (Division of Developmental Disabilities, Program Support Unit-Community Services). Trenton, NJ.

(15) Fields, T. (personal communication, telephone conversation, October 1991). Department of Human Services. Minneapolis, MN. *Data confirmed by response to 2/14/92 mailing.*

(16) Franczyk, J. (personal communication, telephone conversation, November 14, 1991). Department of Human Services. St. Paul, MN. *Data confirmed by response to 2/14/92 mailing.*

(17) Goodell, D. (personal communication, telephone conversation, May 20, 1991). Department of Human Services (Division of Developmental Disabilities, Community Services Programs). Oklahoma City, OK.

(18) Guidera, S. (personal communication, telephone conversation, November 12, 1991). Department of Human Services (Division of Mental Hygiene and Mental Retardation). Carson City, NV.

(19) Hanley, A. (personal communication, correspondence, February 1992). State Office of Mental Retardation and Developmental Disabilities (Program Research Unit). Albany, NY.

(20) Hoke, T. (personal communication, correspondence, May 1, 1990). Department of Health and Social Services (Division of Mental Health and Developmental Disabilities). Anchorage, AK.

(21) Holmes, D. (personal communication, correspondence, December 11, 1990). Department of Economic Security (Division of Developmental Disabilities). Phoenix, AZ.

(22) Hosselkus, D. (personal communication, telephone conversation, November 12, 1991). Department of Human Services (Division of Mental Hygiene and Mental Retardation, Rural Nevada Mental Retardation Services). Carson City, NV.

(23) Human Services Research Institute. (August 1990). *Oregon long range plan for developmental disability services: Commitment to community.* Monmouth, OR: Author.

(24) Johnson, L. (personal communication, telephone conversation, March 1992). Department of Mental Retardation (Strategic Planning). East Hartford, CT. *Data confirmed by response to 2/14/92 mailing.*

(25) Keilson, J. (personal communication, correspondence, March 1992). Department of Mental Retardation (Community Programs and Operations). Boston, MA. *Data confirmed by response to 2/14/92 mailing.*

(26) Kor, R. (1990). *Wyoming: Developmental disabilities two-year transitional plan: 1990–91.* Governors' Planning Council on Developmental Disabilities. Cheyenne, WY. *Data confirmed by response to 2/14/92 mailing.*

(27) Love, W.E. (personal communication, correspondence, April 1, 1991). Department of Health and Social Services (Division of Mental Retardation). Dover, DE. *Data confirmed by response to 2/14/92 mailing.*

(28) Marlowe, R.A. (personal communication, correspondence, March 9, 1992). Department of Developmental Services (Information Systems). Sacramento, CA. *Data confirmed by response to 2/14/92 mailing.*

(29) McIntosh-Wilson, E. (personal communication, correspondence, March 4, 1992). Department of Mental Health and Developmental Disabilities. Springfield, IL. *Data confirmed by response to 2/14/92 mailing.*

(30) Noble, S. (personal communication, telephone conversation, November 12, 1991). Department of Human Services (Division of Developmental Disabilities). Bismarck, ND.

(31) O'Connell, G. (personal communication, telephone conversation, November 15, 1991). Department of Mental Health and Mental Retardation (Division of Mental Retardation). Frankfort, KY.

(32) Putnam, C. (personal communication, correspondence, March 4, 1992). Department of Health and Rehabilitation Services (Developmental Services). Tallahassee, FL.

(33) Randall, V. (personal communication, correspondence, January 10, 1991). Depart-

ment of Public Institution (Office of Mental Retardation). Lincoln, NE. *Data confirmed by response to 2/14/92 mailing.*

(34) Reed, B. (personal communication, correspondence, March 25, 1992). Department of Health and Human Services (Division of Mental Health and Developmental Services). Concord, NH.

(35) Riggall, G. (personal communication, correspondence, February 1992). Department of Mental Health and Mental Retardation (Division of Mental Retardation). Nashville, TN.

(36) Romine, L. (personal communication, correspondence, July 12, 1991). Department of Mental Health (Bureau of Mental Retardation, Community Mental Retardation Services). Jackson, MS. *Data confirmed by response to 2/14/92 mailing.*

(37) Routon, J. (personal communication, correspondence, 1990). Department of Social Services (Developmental Disabilities Services). Little Rock: AR. *Data confirmed by response to 2/14/92 mailing.*

(38) Sabula, M. (personal communication, memorandum to Regional Directors, July 12, 1990, regarding 1989–90 ADAP Program Survey and Cost Findings). Department of Human Resources (Division of Mental Health, Developmental Disabilities and Substance Abuse Services). Raleigh, NC. *Data confirmed by response to 2/14/92 mailing.*

(39) Sherraden, L.D. (personal communication, correspondence, January 15, 1991). Department of Social and Rehabilitation Services (Mental Health and Retardation Services). Topeka, KS.

(40) Stanek, S.J. (personal communication, correspondence, February 1991). Council on Developmental Disabilities. Madison, WI. *Data confirmed by response to 2/14/92 mailing.*

(41) Struxness, L. (personal communication, correspondence, January 3, 1991). Department of Institutions (Division for Developmental Disabilities). Denver, CO. *Data confirmed by response to 2/14/92 mailing.*

(42) Swaim, N. (personal communication, correspondence, April 30, 1991). Department of Mental Health (Integrated Field Services). Indianapolis, IN.

(43) Texas Department of Mental Health and Mental Retardation. (February 1990). *Draft: Strategic Plan—FY 1992–1997.* Unpublished manuscript.

(44) Toth, M. (personal communication, telephone conversation, December 3, 1991). Department of Public Welfare (Office of Mental Retardation). Harrisburg, PA. *Data confirmed by response to 2/14/92 mailing.*

(45) Vincent, J.J. (personal communication, correspondence, February 17, 1992). Department of Health and Hospitals (Office of Human Services, Division of Mental Retardation). Baton Rouge, LA. *Data confirmed by response to 2/14/92 mailing.*

(46) Wacker, W.T. (personal communication, correspondence, March 18, 1992). Department of Health and Mental Hygiene (Developmental Disabilities Administration, Planning and Statistics). Baltimore, MD. *Data confirmed by response to 2/14/92 mailing.*

(47) Washington Developmental Disabilities Planning Council. (January 25, 1991). *Analysis of Selected Agencies Proposed Budgets for the 1991–1993 Biennium.* Olympia: Author. *Data confirmed by response to 2/14/92 mailing.*

(48) Wells, R.F. (personal communication, correspondence, October 2, 1991). Department of Human Services (Mental Retardation and Developmental Disabilities Administration). District of Columbia.

(49) Wood, D. (personal communication, correspondence, May 28, 1992). Department of Mental Retardation and Developmental Disabilities (Office of Information System). Columbus, OH.

(50) Wood, T. (personal communication, correspondence, April 1992). Department of Mental Health and Mental Retardation (Division of Mental Retardation). Waterbury, VT.

(51) Wrensen, G.M. (personal communication, correspondence, February 18, 1991). Department of Human Resources (Division of Mental Health, Mental Retardation, & Substance Abuse). Atlanta, GA.
(52) Wynkoop-Green, D. (personal communication, correspondence, February 26, 1992). Department of Human Services (Division for Services for People with Disabilities, Planning and Program Development). Salt Lake City, UT.
(53) Yamane, E. (personal communication, correspondence, December 3, 1990). Department of Health (Division of Developmental Disabilities). Honolulu, HI. *Data confirmed by response to 2/14/92 mailing.*

— *Chapter 9* _____

Assessment and Enhancement of Quality Services for Persons with Mental Retardation and Other Developmental Disabilities

K. Charlie Lakin,
Sheryl A. Larson, and Robert Prouty

People can not only be degraded when other people care for them, but they can also be degraded if others do not care for them. Much of the challenge in developing appropriate quality assurance service practices for persons with developmental disabilities involves attending to this delicate distinction. Quality assurance for persons with developmental disabilities must protect against too little care, as was so shockingly demonstrated in the institution scandals of the 1960s and 1970s, and too much care, as is often said to be the case today. During the 1900s, the widely accepted societal response has been for the state—acting in the role of the good parent (*in loco parentis*)—to step in to meet the needs, protect the interests, and promote the well-being of persons viewed as dependent on public support. While such efforts reflect our instinct to respond to the needs of fellow society members (even if only by proxy), much of the attention given to needs and well-being is at substantial cost to individual rights, much less wants.

Rothman (1971) referred to the idea of the government acting as the wise and beneficent parent as progressivism. The era of progressive doctrine and reform in

Preparation of this chapter was supported by a cooperative agreement (#H133B80048) from the National Institute on Disability and Rehabilitation Research (NIDRR), the Research and Training Center on Residential Services and Community Living, Institute on Community Integration at the University of Minnesota (College of Education). The opinions expressed herein are those of the authors.

207

America grew, crested, and began to wane in the first three-quarters of the twentieth century. This era was characterized by the exercise of governmental control over how people with disabilities should live and be treated and by a broad faith, at least outside the communities of people being controlled, that this could be done wisely and to the benefit of these persons. Such faith has diminished considerably in the last 25 years. However, belief in the benefits of government control has decreased considerably more rapidly than the control itself.

Looking back on this progressive era, it is apparent that the government's efforts to address society's shortcomings by responding to the needs of certain members were often successful in achieving their intended goals. Unfortunately, these perceived successes seem considerably weakened by unanticipated negative consequences. Government efforts, for example, successfully created public housing for poor people; however, these same efforts often created congregated misery, danger, and a sense of powerlessness. At the cost of billions of dollars, government efforts also improved public institutions by reducing crowding, improving health care, and expanding therapeutic services; yet, according to dozens of court cases, the government failed to protect even the most basic constitutional rights of institution residents (Laski, 1985), fell short of their protective and custodial obligations (Wisconsin Coalition for Advocacy [WCA], 1986), and failed to meet active treatment requirements (WCA, 1989).

For the most part, the progressive faith that government could define what would be good for all people or all people of some governmentally defined group and then cause that good to occur has virtually died. This faith is not dying because the government failed to identify real social problems (e.g., squalid conditions in institutions), but because the solutions were undesirable and inadequate for the people. The legacy of this era of progressive reform includes increased understanding that: 1) whatever the cosmetic changes, real reforms produce perceptible improvements in the lives of the people; 2) there is no one perfect definition of what will meet the needs of all people who share externally imposed distinctions (e.g., being impoverished or homeless, or having mental retardation); and 3) the use of discretionary authority by the government on behalf of another person without that person's involvement will usually be abusive, or at least perceived that way.

Unfortunately, some persons who are responsible for caring for persons with mental retardation and other developmental disabilities neglect, abuse, exploit, or irresponsibly endanger them (Hurst, 1989; Mitchell, 1988). Others do what they are required to do as a minimum, but lack the concern, commitment, knowledge, or experience that is needed to positively contribute to the quality of life of such people. These shortcomings and the effects they have on persons with developmental disabilities have promoted government action. Rules have been developed to preclude or substantially reduce the potential for neglect, abuse, and exploitation, and to motivate service providers to do more to benefit persons with developmental disabilities.

The first initiatives designed to address these problems focused on requiring adequate physical, safety, and health conditions and the provision of habilitation, or active treatment, for persons living in institutions. During the 1960s and 1970s, organizations such as the Accreditation Council on Services for People with Developmental Disabilities (ACDD), the Commission on Accreditation of Rehabilitation Facilities (CARF), and the National Institute on Mental Retardation developed standards for the provision of care to persons with developmental disabilities in institutions (Gardner & Parsons, 1990; Pearce, 1990). These private initiatives were important. However, it was the creation of the federal Medicaid Intermediate Care Facility for persons with mental retardation (ICF/MR) program in 1971 and the promulgation of the final rule in 1974 that caused nearly every state to undertake significant action and spend billions of dollars (between 1972 and 1982) to bring their institutions into compliance with the prevailing standards for institutional care (Boggs, Lakin, & Clauser, 1985; Gettings & Mitchell, 1980).

The ICF/MR program was created by Congress to improve institutional care by providing Medicaid federal financial participation. The federal government paid 50% to 83% of program costs, depending on a state's per capita income, for residential settings that met a comprehensive and detailed set of program standards taken almost verbatim from the 1971 ACDD standards (Boggs et. al., 1985). The 1974 ICF/MR final regulations focused on instructional activities through the provision of active treatment (Sparr & Smith, 1990). About half of the 400 standards in the final rule were directly related to active treatment (Kuhlberg, 1977). Demonstration of compliance to those standards required detailed inspection of settings and records, and extensive documentation of active treatment procedures (Kuhlberg, 1977). The ICF/MR program was widely and rapidly adopted by states. In fact, by June 1989, 147,148 people lived in ICF/MR certified facilities (Lakin, White, Prouty, Bruininks, & Kimm, 1991).

Unfortunately, the activities and documentation that are required to demonstrate compliance with ICF/MR conditions of participation have been increasingly viewed as unnecessarily burdensome and even counterproductive, particularly as the locus of most residential services has moved from institutional to community settings (Bradley, 1990a, 1990b; Chaflee, 1990; Holburn, 1992; Meinhold & Mulick, 1990; Shea, 1992). The growing consensus on ICF/MR standards is that, despite the intention to create positive outcomes, as monitored and implemented they require above all else, "good paperwork, a tidy environment and safety in a rather absolute sense" (Shea, 1990, p. 11). The establishment of contemporary regulations and the required documentation of efforts to adhere to them grew out of typically noble, positivistic efforts to compel desirable outcomes for persons with developmental disabilities. However, due to the rule makers' folly as to what rules can accomplish, the inherent power of rules to supercede and eventually supplant moral commitment, the inflexibility or ignorance of inspectors, and an inability to create meaningful rules about truly important aspects of life, adherence to these rules has generally become the end-product, rather than the means, to assure quality in services for persons with developmental disabilities.

The by-products of these protections have included: 1) frustrating and counterproductive paperwork demands for service providers, 2) the development of adversarial relationships between service providers and the government, 3) inhibition of innovation and rational risk-taking in favor of playing it safe by following the rules, 4) loss of self-determination for the people being protected, 5) loss of involvement by government agencies in enhancing the well-being of persons with developmental disabilities through means other than rules, and 6) promotion of a perspective that all persons with developmental disabilities can be well-served and best protected in the same way (Chaflee, 1990; Holburn, 1990a; Repp & Barton, 1980; Shea, 1992). There is growing conviction that these concerns must be addressed, but this will not be accomplished without careful attention being given to the improvement or redesign of quality assurance.

MAJOR CHALLENGES IN THE
REDESIGN OF QUALITY ASSURANCE

Several major trends in residential services for persons with developmental disabilities are challenging the adequacy and value of old approaches to defining and monitoring quality. These trends have contributed to the crisis in confidence in the predominant, existing methods of quality assurance. Even the traditional term *quality assurance* is challenged by these trends because quality is not assured, and according to critics of the current system, is not even adequately monitored. The term "quality assessment" is preferred for a number of reasons. First, it suggests a likely break from the traditional focus on structural and process variables. Second, it implies that the information gathered should have both summative and formative value. Finally, it suggests that approaches to information gathering should include multiple informants, vary according to the issue at hand, and focus on identifying the variables of greatest importance. The trends highlighted here represent significant challenges to future quality assessment practices.

1. *The challenge of the vastness and rapid growth of community services.* Residential care systems have become extremely dispersed and, as a result, they challenge government quality assurance monitoring efforts. In 1977, there were 11,025 separate households in which persons with developmental disabilities received out-of-family residential services. By 1990, that number had exploded to 41,000 separate settings (Lakin, unpublished raw data). This growth will continue and, in light of budgetary problems facing most states, can be expected to continue growing more rapidly than the number of persons available to monitor community services. Even case management services, which have traditionally been viewed as a supplement to traditional monitoring agencies, are facing unprecedented demands. A 1991 study of Medicaid Home and Community-Based Services (HCBS), in which the federal government shared the costs of case management, reported the average number of Medicaid HCBS recipients per case manager was nearly 50 (Prouty & Lakin, 1991). To meet the challenge of rapid growth, quality assessment and enhancement systems must become more efficient. They must reduce standards to the essential, eliminate redundancy, and effectively use resources beyond those available in traditional monitoring agencies.

2. *The challenge to improve the reliability and validity of traditional quality assurance approaches.* Currently, quality assurance approaches are not producing the promised results. Present approaches to quality assurance are clearly inadequate in terms of efficacy, reliability, and validity. For example, more than half of the federal court rulings and settlements related to institutional care in the past 15 years have involved facilities with ICF/MR certifications. Moreover, different monitors who survey the same residence cite different deficiencies (Reid, Parsons, Green, & Schepis, 1991). In addition, evidence indicates that there are no significant differences between quality life measures in residences that are ICF/MR certified and those that are not (Hill et al., 1989; Lakin, Amado, Bruininks, Hayden, & Li, 1992; Reid et al., 1991; Repp & Barton, 1980).

3. *The challenge to ensure that quality assurance and monitoring will contribute to improved services.* A recent report of the U.S. General Accounting Office (1990), focusing on quality assurance in health care, contained an observation that is highly relevant to services for persons with developmental disabilities:

> Quality assurance systems typically concentrate on quality assessment and the identification of the relatively small number of providers whose care is obviously unacceptable. They do comparatively little in attempting to directly improve the overall levels of quality provided by the majority of health professionals. . . . If we think of performance of health care providers in terms of the bell-shaped curve of a normal distribution, the challenge is to devise a quality assurance strategy that not only deals appropriately with the outliers but also assists in moving the entire distribution to a higher level of quality. (p.8)

Service delivery enhancement activities are those activities provided to improve the quality of service delivery received by persons with mental retardation and other developmental disabilities beyond the minimum levels assured by current regulatory practices. It is important for quality assessment systems and the enhancement systems linked to them to be focused on the variables and resources that can actually improve quality. In essence, then, quality assessment and enhancement have both a formative, as well as a summative, value to contribute to the quality of services.

4. *The challenge to protect persons with mental retardation and other developmental disabilities from abuse and neglect in the community.* Clearly, there is a growing tendency toward equating individualization or personalization of services and supports with quality of services. There is also substantial challenge in recognizing that with personalization comes the challenge of personalizing quality assessment and enhancement activities. Replacing current approaches to quality assurance must not be done flippantly. Persons with developmental disabilities are vulnerable to neglect, exploitation, and abuse.

The documented record of actual abuse and neglect is clear; it happens within the current quality assurance efforts and it can happen, or even increase, under alternative approaches (Hurst, 1989; Mitchell, 1988). Therefore, when improving approaches to quality assessment and enhancement, basic health and safety standards must be established to assure that, when the individual is not independently self-sufficient, appropriate steps have been taken to protect the individual and to guarantee actual delivery of needed supports, services, training, and opportunities.

5. *The challenge to measure quality in terms of outcomes, not structures or processes.* There is a growing commitment to developing an outcome-based service system for persons with mental retardation and other developmental disabilities. The new draft standards of the Accreditation Council on Services for Persons with Disabilities (The Accreditation Council, 1992) are perhaps the furthest along in their development and in their field-testing of the outcome assessments. However, outcome systems are very complex when compared with systems focused on relatively concrete structural or process factors (Donabedian, 1966). It is much easier to assure that a person has a bedroom of a specified square footage, or that there is documentation that staff have the proper hours of training (structure), or that service recipients have been assessed and that, based on that assessment, certain individual programs have been developed and implemented (process), than it is to determine whether people have improved functionally, increased their social network, or become more satisfied with their lives (outcomes). Despite this complexity, there is too little satisfaction with quality definitions, assessments, and monitoring practices that rely exclusively or even heavily on structure and process measures. The challenge and the opportunity to develop and test systems of quality definition, assessment, and improvement that are focused primarily on improving outcomes in the lives of persons with developmental disabilities must be taken seriously.

DEFINING EFFECTIVE QUALITY
ASSESSMENT AND QUALITY ENHANCEMENT

The primary question in any discussion of assurance and quality enhancement activities is, "What is quality?" Once this question is answered, one can ask, "How do we get it?" The view of quality as a universal, readily observable characteristic of a service program or setting has been challenged in recent years (Bradley, 1990a; Crutcher, 1990). As appreciation of the diverse needs, desires, and circumstances of persons with developmental disabilities has grown, quality in services has increasingly become defined as a congruence between those individual factors and the services that the individual receives rather than as an inherent quality of the services per se (Kennedy, 1990).

Good services fill or help others fill gaps between a desired lifestyle and the lifestyle one would lead in the absence of services. In that sense, there can be no single standard of quality except in meeting the needs, recognizing the rights, and fulfilling the desires of the individual. The critical challenge of such judgments is their strength. They require sensitivity, knowledge of and participation by the person afflicted, and may not presume a single definition of quality. The multiple dimensions and individual differences in people's lives make defining and measuring quality largely idiosyncratic and definable in only the broadest terms.

Quality of services must be viewed in broad terms: preventing abuse and neglect; protecting the individual's right to maximum personal freedom; meeting the individual's basic needs; supporting the individual in the life-style he or she chooses; and teaching the individual skills that increase his or her ability to participate and contribute to the home, neighborhood, and society. These must be done according to the individual's own terms. Providing quality assessment and enhancement systems that contribute to this broad view of quality and its manifestations for each individual is a hugely challenging proposition. It completely rearranges the roles and expectations that have governed service systems and their standards and mechanisms for defining and determining the quality of the services. Depending on the individual, minor to radical departures in the definition of quality can be expected. For example, if personal freedom is one dimension in the definition of quality, a lower staff ratio may be preferable to a higher one.

Quality, as it must be approached in systems of quality assurance and quality enhancement, is both metatheoretical and arbitrary. It cannot be witnessed or measured directly, but is dependent on a series of observable indicators. The presence of folders full of individual habilitation plans, charts, and graphs does not mean that people have been taught anything useful, but to program monitors such information is taken as evidence of such. Even broad social goals held in highest regard, such as independence, productivity, and community integration, are subject to the limitations of generalized imposition. Quality in services will not always and should not always be reflected by movement in the same direction and rate among all indicators (e.g., personal empowerment will permit one to choose not to be involved in his or her community). However, a society that provides and pays for services for persons with developmental disabilities has a right and a responsibility to articulate its expectations for those services.

In order to define, assess, and enhance quality in services for persons with developmental disabilities, the services must have a purpose. The single most commonly articulated purpose of services today is to enhance quality of life (Lakin, Bruininks, & Larson, 1992; Landesman, 1986; Schalock et al., 1990). People with developmental disabilities have, want, and deserve a certain quality of life defined around experiences common to cultural membership, but on their own terms (Goode, 1988; Taylor & Bogdan, 1990). Such goals and purposes for service delivery are articulated not only by persons with developmental disabilities (Kennedy, 1990; Martinez, 1990) and their family members and advocates (Crutcher, 1990), but increasingly by service providers (Dufresne, 1990) and state and federal officials (Chafee, 1990; Gant, 1990).

The concept of quality of services, as contributing to quality of life, is largely personal. It defies specification. Yet, any effort to observe or to instill it in services requires some agreement on its components. The broad areas described in Chapter 1 are important to the definition of quality services for persons with developmental disabilities. These areas include physical presence in the community; health, safety, and comfort; personal growth and development; social relationships; participation in valued roles of the society; and independence, individuality, and choice. Of course, others have outlined different but, generally, similar components to what quality services should contribute to quality of life of persons with developmental disabilities (Blunden, 1988; Goode, 1990; Knoll, 1990; Schalock, 1990; Schalock et al., 1990). Comprehensive profiles of quality clearly show that most of the energy currently exerted to assure or enhance the quality of services for persons with developmental disabilities focuses on the areas of health, safety, and development. These profiles also reveal how little attention is given to assuring and enhancing the involvement of services in areas that are most important to fulfilling the potential and promise of community living (e.g., relationships, valued social roles, personal freedom).

Quality in human services is not a status to be assessed and certified, but a process in which a service recipient, a service provider, family, friends, and others articulate goals, establish a plan for reaching those goals, and work effectively toward those goals (American Association on Mental Retardation [AAMR], 1990; Bradley, 1990a, 1990b; Kennedy, 1990). Quality is thereby manifested in the achievement of desired outcomes. The desired outcomes may, and inevitably do, vary from individual to individual.

There should be great diversity in the standards applied to services in different settings and even to different people within the same setting. Indeed, the move to Medicaid HCBS and other supported community living services is based on the presumption that the nature and amount of services received by individuals should not be fixed as in the ICF/MR programs, but should vary according to the individual's needs and life circumstances. In providing services for persons with developmental disabilities that reflect individual differences, efforts to assess and enhance the quality of those services must be sensitive and attentive to individual differences and to the ways services are being used to respond to those differences.

COMPONENTS OF A COMPREHENSIVE
APPROACH TO QUALITY OF COMMUNITY SERVICES

A system of quality assessment and quality enhancement that is responsive to individual differences in service needs must be flexible in its approach, efficient in its use of resources, and comprehensive in the activities available that will affect service quality. A comprehensive approach to quality assessment and quality enhancement that is able to meet the needs of a person-centered, individualized service delivery program would minimally contain four areas of emphasis: 1) individualized assessment and service planning, 2) individualized outcome monitoring, 3) promotion of individual choice, and 4) service delivery enhancement activities. As shown in Table 1, there are several activities related to each area. The remainder of this chapter describes the components of each area and provides examples of how some of these approaches are currently being used. Additional examples may be found in *Reinventing Quality: A Sourcebook of Innovative Programs for Quality Assurance and Service Improvement in Community Settings* (Blake, Mangan, Prouty, & Lakin, 1992).

Table 1. Components of a comprehensive approach to quality of community service

Individualized assessment and service planning
- Person-centered planning
- Involvement of family, friends, and others
- Effective service coordination

Individualized outcome monitoring
- Defining outcomes to be monitored
- Benefits of outcome measures

Promotion of individual choice
- Increasing opportunities to choose services and vendors
- Providing information about the quality of services from different vendors
- Consumer control over home and resources

Service delivery enhancement activities
- Organizational development for quality enhancement
- Staff development activities
- Technical assistance, program support, and crisis response activities

Individual Assessment and Service Planning

Person-Centered Planning Assessment and program planning have long been part of the concept of service quality. The ICF/MR program that began in 1971 established a requirement for active treatment assessment and program planning that became a federally required part of the lives of the 144,509 people receiving ICF/MR services by 1988 (White, Lakin, & Bruininks, 1989). This requirement has spread in one fashion or another to almost all provisions for authorizing and offering community services. While assessment and service planning activities can be valuable, as implemented by the authorizing agencies and the service providers, these activities have focused on the deficiencies of the individual.

Person-centered assessment and planning is a radical departure from traditional methods of service and program planning because it focuses primarily on individuals' abilities, preferences, current circumstances, and desired life-style outcomes. Whereas traditional medical models focused on identifying deficits and planning interventions to remove them, person-centered assessment and planning views service planning and delivery as support to enable an individual, capable of enjoying and contributing to a community, to enjoy social relationships and to express and carry out choices. Individual assessment and service delivery are means by which to communicate with individuals, on their own terms, how these or other preferred outcomes will be realized. In a person-centered assessment and planning model, quality assessment and quality enhancement focus on the relative success and needed supports in realizing these outcomes.

Fundamental to the person-centered assessment and planning approach is the replacement of psychologists and other professionals as the primary source of relevant expertise. Instead, the individual service recipients, their families, their friends, service providers, service coordinators/case managers, and others who know and care about these recipients, with support from professionals, work with a facilitator to define the life-style to be supported and the services needed to make it work. Such an approach identifies an individual's personal sense of quality of life as the primary goal and standard for defining, assuring, and improving the quality of services. Finally, person-centered assessment and planning requires commitments from all involved to support the broad personalized life-style plan. These commitments are far broader than agreement from the service provider to adhere to an individual habilitation plan with 6–10 narrow treatment objectives and comply with government regulations. In a subsequent section, brief examples are given of actual person-centered program approaches currently being implemented.

Involvement of Family, Friends, and Others It is increasingly acknowledged in law and in general practice that family members and others with ongoing, committed relationships with individuals should have important roles in determining the services that the individual needs. The roles of persons with disabilities, their family members, and committed significant others, however, are often considered ancillary to the roles of a professional. In reality, given the demands and large number of individuals whose services are typically monitored by case managers, not only are family, members and significant others better able than case managers to know the individual's needs and the effectiveness of services in meeting them, but they are also often the only people able to do so adequately. In the United States, case managers have an average caseload of 50 and are required to make only two face-to-face visits annually (Prouty & Lakin, 1991). Under these conditions, case managers simply cannot effectively monitor and respond to the changing situations and services needs of persons with developmental disabilities with sufficient continuity.

Effective Service Coordination Just as it is important to assure that individual service plans are based on individual needs, preferences, and circumstances, it is also important that those same variables are attended to on an ongoing basis. People and their circumstances are constantly changing. Even the most sensitive person-centered assessment and service planning procedures will not always project people's needs and interests for the typical services planning period. The benefits of personalized services planning can only be sustained when people who attend to the needs and interests of individuals and the services that have been planned for them have maximum involvement in the lives of the person with developmental disabilities.

Ideally, effective service coordination efforts are built around service coordinators: 1) with a small number of people to serve; 2) who can interact with the individual frequently; 3) who are committed to responding to changing individual needs; 4) who have the authority and resources to respond to people's needs, including changing services, with relative speed when needed in the eyes of the individual, family, or service providers; 5) who present themselves as being on call to meet the needs of individuals as they arise both from a sense of personal concern and professional responsibility; and 6) who actively seek information from others in the individual's environment about what the individual needs to improve his or her daily life. Moreover, these efforts build off person-centered planning and are responsive to individual needs, especially in times of transition to less restrictive settings or during periods of personal change. They are built around service providers who plan and implement services that meet people's specific individual needs. Effective service coordinators demand respect for persons with developmental disabilities. Further, in this era of limited resources, they demand value and performance in the services they authorize. Clearly, these efforts would move away from facility placement and toward individual services responding to specific individual needs. This movement will require more sensitive, knowledgeable, empowered, sophisticated, creative, and intensified case management than we have known in the past. Recruiting, developing, and enabling people who can fill such roles effectively is one of the major challenges in assuring and enhancing the quality of human services.

Individualized Outcome Monitoring

Defining Outcomes To Be Monitored   As noted throughout this chapter, there is a high degree of dissatisfaction with traditional monitoring of specific program standards because they do not successfully control service quality. A primary source of dissatisfaction with these models is their attention to structural and process standards as measures of quality, and their required efforts to comply with standards that make little contribution to the quality of life of persons with mental retardation and other developmental disabilities (Bellamy, Newton, LeBarron, & Horner, 1990; Blunden, 1988; Bradley, 1990a; Conroy & Feinstein, 1990; Dufresne, 1990; Holburn, 1990b; Landesman, 1986; Moore & Moore, 1988; Skarnulis & Skarnulis, 1990). Current structure and process standards have also been criticized because they perpetuate mediocrity by presenting minimum compliance thresholds (Bradley, 1990b).

As a result of the perceived lack of congruence between the focus of monitoring and the individual's desired life-style, there is a growing commitment to developing outcome-based approaches to the monitoring of services for persons with mental retardation and other developmental disabilities. Movement toward outcome-based monitoring of services seems inevitable for a number of reasons. First, the call for outcome-based monitoring is occurring throughout American society. Second, persons with mental retardation and other developmental disabilities and their families and advocates are asserting their own definitions of how services should be provided. These definitions inevitably view services as a means to an outcome rather than as an outcome in themselves. Third, the cost of services to persons with mental retardation and other developmental disabilities varies tremendously from person to person. A means to account for the products of those costs that is more satisfying and more conducive to gross program comparisons than simple process documentation must be developed.

Benefits of Outcome Measures   Outcome-based monitoring of service quality has a number of benefits. First, the intent of outcome-based monitoring is to ascertain and assure the well-being and growth of every person. Resources for persons with mental retardation and other developmental disabilities should be devoted to individuals, not to programs. Structural and process variables are largely attendant on facilities and programs. As such, facilities and programs can be judged as doing adequately (i.e., meeting all structural and process standards), although individuals may not be having their individual needs met well at all. Since program outcomes are no more than the aggregate of individual outcomes, it is possible to attend to the products of whole programs while also monitoring individual outcomes. As a result, individuals should be less likely to fall through the cracks in outcome-based monitoring.

Second, outcome-based systems are better able to measure the changing status of individuals and to identify potential negative or crisis situations through emphasis on direct and multiple observations of the individual. Consequently, situations that might be harmful to an individual can be changed before they become highly detrimental. Third, outcome-based monitoring can be tailored to the individual and can be driven by their personal goals and interests, taking into account change over time in areas of individual need and preference. Consequently, they can focus on the effectiveness of activities to accomplish objectives such as increased community participation, not just the presence and duration of such activities. Fourth, outcome-based measures can be used to identify areas in which providers may be providing relatively weak or excellent services within a range of acceptable criteria. Structural and process monitoring tends to identify only passing or failing.

Effective outcome-based service monitoring requires use of an appropriate range of respondents and information to establish expected levels and types of service delivery and expected outcomes of those services, and to determine by whom and how those services will be evaluated. Respondents and information should include whomever and whatever sources best indicate achievement of a desired outcome. Typically, in structural and process monitoring, people who have no knowledge of the individual are trained to identify deviations from requirements on numerous narrowly defined criteria. The people who know the individual best often have little to contribute to structural and process assessment and, in fact, are sometimes specifically rejected as useful informants in the monitoring process (Shea, 1990).

Outcome-based monitoring does not preclude examination of structural and process variables. Few would argue that certain minimum standards for the protection of individuals' basic health, safety, and rights should not be monitored. Minimum standards, however, are not sufficient in assuring that the products of compliance are outcomes of value to the individual. They are also not sufficient in assuring that compliance on paper produces the health, safety, and recognition of basic rights that were promised. In areas of basic health, safety, and rights, outcome approaches look for demonstrations of needed outcomes in daily life. Key sources of outcome data include families, friends, consumer and voluntary monitoring groups, case managers, and the individual service recipients. Furthermore, those individuals may be able to actually carry out some of the monitoring and quality assurance activities needed (Provencal & Taylor, 1983).

The implementation of outcome-based, individualized program monitoring efforts must not occur in a vacuum. Quality enhancement efforts must continually be reevaluated to adapt, modify, or change practices or standards that are unsound, inefficient, or that no longer match state-of-the-art practices (Baer, 1990; Bradley, 1990b; Holburn, 1990a; Landesman, 1988; Moore & Moore, 1988). This process can be facilitated by making rules less specific and more flexible when possible (Holburn, 1990a). When the rules do not lead to the enhancement of quality of life, changes are clearly needed. In addition, outcome-based monitoring should keep assessments separate from technical assistance efforts (Conroy & Feinstein, 1990). It should use criteria for evaluating quality assurance standards that are consistent, flexible, clear, and measurable; use monitoring efforts that are cost-effective, reliable, valid, timely, and that provide feedback; and establish response mechanisms that are reasonable, credible, constructive, certain, and useful (Bradley, 1990a). Finally, research should be conducted on the effect of the monitoring standards used on persons with mental retardation and other developmental disabilities (Hemp & Braddock, 1988). Monitoring practices that do not meet these standards may be invalid or unreliable, and may create more problems than solutions for quality of life issues.

Promotion of Individual Choice

In the market economy of the United States, choice operates as the single most effective influence on quality. Companies whose products are chosen by consumers succeed, while those who fail to meet the current, ever-changing needs and desires of consumers fail. Conversely, the primary factor in the lower quality products of controlled economies is the lack of choice. That is, if government limits consumer choice to deciding only whether or not to have an item, such as a refrigerator, rather than allowing the consumer to purchase the desired item from any one of several distinct manufacturers, little, if any, choice exists. Unfortunately, the market for community services operates much like a controlled economy, with the makers of the product highly standardized and the market largely controlled. Similar to the products of controlled economies, human services products tend to meet some minimal standards. However, marketplace opportunities, incentives, and sources of requisite knowledge to make informed choices that elevate the general level of quality are far too rare in human services marketplaces. In this context, three approaches to elevating quality through choice seem especially fruitful. These approaches are: 1) increasing opportunities for persons with developmental disabilities to choose services and vendors, 2) providing information on the quality of services provided by different vendors, and 3) providing people with developmental disabilities with control over their own homes and furnishings so that they are free to fully exercise choice and control over their individual services.

Increasing Opportunities To Choose Services and Vendors   There are assurances in federal Medicaid regulations and in the regulations for many state programs that people will have choices of services and vendors. Congress and legislatures have established such rules to keep people from being assigned to a provider and then becoming a vassal of that provider unless and until the provider is found grossly deficient in the services it provides. In services for persons with developmental disabilities, however, these protections generally work poorly. For example, in the case of ICF/MR services, federal efforts to contain costs have led to severe limits on expansion of ICF/MR services. Consumers entering the ICF/MR market today have a choice of vendors only if more than one vendor has an appropriate vacancy. Since the demand for residential service vacancies exceeds the supply by tens of thousands (Hayden, 1992), consumer choice is virtually nonexistent. Strategies to increase opportunities to choose services and vendors will, by necessity, have to address supply and demand issues.

Providing Information about the Quality of Services from Different Vendors Choices without information are at best haphazard. Even if people are able to make a true choice among services and vendors, unless they have information about the relative strengths and weaknesses of available providers, as experienced by persons who have tested those services, their choices will not be informed ones. On the most superficial level, knowing that a provider is licensed or certified can be helpful, but no more so than knowing that a car has passed federal safety standards when making a purchase.

Using further the analogy of purchasing a car, seeing and test-driving a car is also valuable. However, most people making a major investment, such as the purchase of a car, turn to the opinion of experts and previous buyers to guide their decisions. Such information is readily available to people who want to make purchases as important as a car; yet, it is seldom available to people needing to make choices as to whom to entrust with the care and support of persons with developmental disabilities. In our present service delivery system, with its long waiting lists for services, information about the good providers is closely guarded by case managers who want to reserve the meager supply for their own clients. Such an environment does little to enhance the information available to persons with developmental disabilities and their family members who wish to make informed decisions. Furthermore, individuals with developmental disabilities and their families are typically offered an opening within a particular program, rather than a variety of options. Typically, it is unclear when their next opportunity to secure services will occur. Under these circumstances, what people know about a program may be put to the side in order for the individual to have services that meet some of his or her needs. Although increasing information about the quality of services provided by available vendors is important, systemic changes need to occur within the service delivery system to increase the number of available services and to allow more competition to occur among vendors.

Consumer Control Over Home and Resources Once an individual moves into the house of a service provider he or she relinquishes much of his or her control over services. If a person lives in a provider's home he or she will almost always receive that provider's services. Choosing a new provider must then be balanced against leaving home. Not only is there no opportunity to seek another service provider without giving up one's home and often primary relationships with roommates, there is often little opportunity to seek other specific services from other vendors (e.g., to enroll in an evening recreation program). The recommendation of the recent evaluation of Minnesota's Home and Community-Based Services waiver program (HCBS) spoke to this issue:

> A second reasonable step in improving the individualization and efficiency of HCBS would be to limit service providers' vested financial interest in the housing, furnishings, food purchases and other basic components of the room and board charge. It does not serve the personal interest of the HCBS recipient (nor probably the economic interest of the State) to have service providers with a primary economic interest in where people receiving HCBS live. Making HCBS a more personalized service program, which was viewed as desirable by most of the state and county officials, case managers and direct care staff interviewed, requires that each individual's housing be as much of a personal option as is feasible, with choices dictated primarily by personal interests, not the economic interests of another individual. (Lakin, Burwell, Hayden, & Jackson, 1992, p. 105)

Service Delivery Enhancement Activities

Service delivery enhancement activities are designed to improve the quality of services beyond the minimum levels assured by current regulatory practices, which focus intervention only on the low-end outliers. Ideally, in an open choice-driven system, government would have a relatively limited role in service delivery enhancement. Service consumers, their families, and their consultants would have access to information about, and the power to select among, an ample supply of service providers so that services of relatively poor quality would either improve or wither and die because of market forces.

There is much need to move toward having more consumer influence on the nature and quality of services provided to individuals with developmental disabilities. Current services systems, however, have many intractable and expectably long-term impediments to realization of choice as a sole insurer of quality. These drawbacks include a much greater current demand for services than the available supply, with numerous regulatory and financial restrictions to creating new small businesses to increase the supply of service providers. These restrictions create enormous limitations on the choices that individuals can make for themselves. Of course, many consumers have limited capacities to analyze options, and most governments still consider locating, selecting, and making financial arrangements with providers from their traditional pools as their legitimate, if not primary, responsibility.

For all these reasons, the power to choose among providers that meet minimum standards is not likely soon, if ever, to be in itself sufficient to assure appropriate quality and skillful response from service providers. Therefore, government commitments to quality in service must include a commitment to improving the capacity of existing organizational structures and resources to deliver services. Quality enhancement activities include three types of efforts: 1) organizational development for quality enhancement; 2) staff development activities; and 3) technical assistance, program support, and crisis assistance activities.

Organizational Development for Quality Enhancement   Most community services are provided under the auspices of organizations whose culture is made up of a mission, an orientation toward its clients, and a definition of and commitment to providing effective services. The organization's culture has a major effect on how and how well the needs and desires of the individual service recipients are met. One of the most effective mechanisms for improving the experiences of those served by an organization is to assist agencies in improving their organizational culture. Such efforts permit organization leaders and staff to reflect on their purpose as service providers, to set goals, to take stock of their effectiveness, to solve problems, and to improve organizational, team, and interpersonal relationships. It permits people the opportunity to reflect on their services as experienced by the people who receive them. It allows people to learn of and assess themselves according to new perspectives in an evolving field. A few programs, most notably *Framework for Accomplishment* (O'Brien & Lyle, 1988), have been designed specifically for person-centered organization development in human services agencies.

Another effort that agencies can use to enhance the quality of services is to develop internal quality monitoring mechanisms. These systems need to be based on a provider's mission statement and should identify operating principles that the provider will implement throughout all the services in the agency (Dufresne, 1990). Internal mechanisms include both self-analysis and evaluation efforts (Bradley, 1990b; Jacobson, 1990; Landesman, 1988), and peer review processes among provider groups (AAMR, 1990). These efforts provide opportunities for agencies to identify and to correct weaknesses in their service delivery efforts before major deficiencies are noted by external monitoring agencies.

Staff Development Activities   Although direct service staff members are the primary implementers of services to persons with mental retardation and developmental disabilities in community service settings, they are often the least well-trained and least experienced staff in those settings (Wallace & Johnson, 1992). Further, with national turnover rates of 70.7% in community residential settings in 1989 (Braddock & Mitchell, 1992), this direct service staff contingent is constantly changing and new staff members are continually in need of training. As personnel issues, direct service staff recruitment, retention, and training are challenging, but the real issue is the impact of these personnel challenges on the quality of services provided to persons with mental retardation and developmental disabilities. As a 1992 report on the outcome of 12 town meetings in Minnesota pointed out, "the issues for people with developmental disabilities are quality of support, continuity of relationships with staff, and fundamental issues of safety" (Governor's Planning Council on Developmental Disabilities, 1992, p. 22).

Staff development activities refer to organizational efforts to recruit and to retain the best possible staff members to provide initial and ongoing training of those individuals to assure effective skills and attitudes. Recognizing the need for such activities, beginning in 1987, Congress appropriated funds for the Administration on Developmental Disabilities to provide University Affiliated Programs (UAPs) with money to sponsor training initiatives for direct service staff members. Such efforts are but one way to address the challenges to quality posed by personnel issues. Discussions of other strategies such as the initiation of statewide training efforts and local interagency training projects, as well as of other issues and recommendations for addressing personnel problems, are addressed in Chapter 13.

Technical Assistance, Program Support, and Crisis Response Activities Most community services agencies are small in terms of total budget and employees. Being small keeps community service agencies focused on individual service recipients. However, although staff are fewer and more dispersed, most community service agencies have the same basic functions to fulfill in support of their consumers as do institutions. This necessitates considerably less division of labor than found in institutions. It also means that agencies are less able to have staff with expertise to meet every client need. Community agencies, for example, are less likely to have full-time physical, occupational, and language therapists, behavior analysts, crisis management team members, or even business managers on site in each home. Yet, many will be called on to perform the skills of such specialists. Recognizing and supporting the realities of community service providers requires ample provisions to support the technical and crisis needs of such agencies as they arise. As one provider suggested, "true quality of life for consumers is enhanced when the provider's opportunities for technical assistance and training explore new methodologies, ways of thinking, and various 'cutting edge' approaches to service delivery" (Dufresne, 1990, p. 141).

Effective change in services will only occur when high quality is rewarded (Conroy & Feinstein, 1990), and when training and technical assistance supports the development of needed skills among providers (Bradley, 1990b). Failing to provide needed training and technical assistance will contribute to: 1) fewer community service agencies coming into operation and, consequently, less choice and competition; 2) a generalized growth in existing organizations beyond a size many consider most effective; 3) less willingness by small community agencies to accept individuals with complex needs; 4) continuing demissions of persons with developmental disabilities from their own homes; and 5) the failure of many community agencies that have skills in providing services, but need support in the business skills of agency operation and other related problems. While the quality assessment and quality enhancement system described in this chapter does not currently exist, efforts to improve the quality of community services for persons with developmental disabilities do exist. The remainder of this chapter is devoted to sharing examples of efforts to address components of this quality assurance model.

PROMISING PRACTICES IN QUALITY ASSESSMENT AND ENHANCEMENT EFFORTS

Parents as Casemanagers: Minnesota

The *Parents as Casemanagers* program is based on the conviction that individuals with disabilities and their families are the most informed and, therefore, important members of any assessment and planning team. The program seeks to challenge and enable parents to accept the responsibility of that role. Participants in the program receive training, support, and consultation on individual rights and privacy, on the state-of-the-art ideas in service planning and delivery, on indicators of quality in services, on planning for transitions and change, on fostering community participation, and on the use of technology and case management rules, regulations, procedures, and strategies. In addition, participants are also trained in the skills of service coordination, including effective use of resources, maintaining appropriate records, leading and participating in meetings, and identifying goals, service needs, and resources. The program also trains parents and interested persons to serve as trainers and facilitators for other parents.

Evaluations of the program have indicated that participants feel better able to assess their own and/or their family member's abilities, needs, and progress and better able to identify and plan services based on that assessment. Participants report having a more active role in service decision and also an improved working relationship with official case managers. Participants also report an improved sense of empowerment, improved networks with other people, and better knowledge of services and the service system (Blake et al., 1992).

Improved Compliance and Outcome Monitoring: Utah

In recent years, the state of Utah has developed a program that combines best practice outcome measures with active encouragement of flexible and innovative quality assurance efforts by providerd (Blake et al., 1992). The goal was to develop a quality assurance approach that depended more on observations and interviews with involved people than on document reviews.

This new approach to quality assurance began with a Quality Assurance Academy. The academy brought together consumers, families, and staff, and in 2-day meetings, provided the opportunity to share ideas, plan, make recommendations, and evaluate quality assurance on an annual basis. It was determined that the quality assurance system should be based on the principles of informed choice, community membership, individualization, and system attributes that will further these principles, including collaboration, staff competency, flexibility, creativity, and staff commitment.

A new model for quality assurance was developed based on a set of state standards broad enough to be variable among regions, yet specific enough to assure a common base of minimum quality criteria. Under this system, providers develop their own quality assurance plans within certain guidelines. Regional and state monitoring of state and provider standards and plans is maintained.

The primary goal is to motivate providers to achieve and to maintain the highest standards through internal quality assurance plans. These plans place decision-making responsibility at the level closest to the individual being served and incorporate quality assurance activities into the routine practices of all agencies involved in service delivery. In all areas, the system focuses on the individual, with an emphasis on outcomes, proactive measures that can improve outcomes, and provider strengths. Some of the specific activities of the Utah system include:

1) provider self-survey, 2) case manager training, 3) volunteer monitoring, 4) formation of a human rights committee, 5) a variety of enhancements for excellence, and 6) a consumer satisfaction survey.

Data Collection Systems: Oregon's Outcomes and Lifestyle Information Systems

The state of Oregon has recently developed a multifaceted system to assure service quality for persons with developmental disabilities. This system includes, in addition to licensing or certification of providers, self-monitoring and reporting by providers, monitoring by case managers, and evaluation by an advocacy group of recipient's quality of life (Blake et al., 1992). A personal computer (PC) data base, separate from the statewide management information system, is used by Oregon to monitor certain valued outcomes of residential services for HCBS recipients. Direct care staff participate in semi-annual planning meetings in which a new goal for integrated community activity is defined for each HCBS recipient. Using one of two participant life-style outcomes reporting systems—the Valued Outcomes Information Systems (VOIS) or Oregon Residential Lifestyles Information System (ORLIS)—direct service staff monitor and record individual recipients' activities involving physical and social integration in the community. The variety of activities and the number of activities engaged in by recipients without staff support are reported. These observations are reported to the state agency where they are entered in the state quality assurance data base and used to create a statewide average score. This average score is available to service providers for self-assessment of success in achieving outcomes consistent with best practice standards.

Although some state-generated provider averages are less meaningful for some service providers than others, the process, which causes direct service staff to attend to integration of persons with developmental disabilities within the communities in which they live, is considered beneficial in itself. The state agency also reports benefit from its ability to maintain an overall perspective on providers' reported achievements in community integration. The state computerized data base also monitors the status of provider licensing and certification to provide licensing staff with information from the various systems that measures independence, integration, and productivity of persons with developmental disabilities. This data base contains county information, provider corporation information, provider site information, and individual consumer information. In addition, recording licensing and certification activities, the system will assist state staff in determining training and technical assistance needs and in giving feedback to providers that will assist in improving services.

Voluntary Citizen and Consumer Monitoring: The Arc-Ohio

Many local and state advocacy agencies have recently begun to sponsor programs of voluntary citizen and consumer monitoring. One long-standing program was developed by The Arc of Ohio. In this program, monitors are provided with a basic orientation and the guidelines to structure the observations they make while visiting a site (Bersani, 1984a, 1984b). In this program, six areas are the focus of moni-tors: recognition of rights, quality of the living environment, use of community resources, opportunities for personal growth, attitudes, competence and sufficiency of the staff, and opportunities for personal relationships. Guidelines provide monitors with a general description of the kinds of information and assessment they should be making in each area. They are provided with sample questions to assist them in gathering the needed information. Volunteers receive a full day of training before making their first site visit. Visits typically take about half a day, with volunteers subsequently writing a report.

CONCLUSION

Redesigning quality assessment and quality enhancement systems to make service providers more accountable for outcomes that improve the quality of life for persons with developmental disabilities will not be easily accomplished. Although the movement from institutional to small community settings as the predominant model of residential service was accomplished with an intent to substantially change the nature and quality of the lives of persons with developmental disabilities, the mechanisms, expected outcomes, and formal standards for community services changed little. As a result, it is a common and undoubtedly true perception that quality assurance, as currently practiced, has a detrimental effect on quality of life as experienced by persons with developmental disabilities who reside in both institutional and community settings. The incongruity between the purposes of community services and the formal expectations for them has reached an irreconcilable point. Quality assurance must be reinvented, based on the expectations that services of quality are directly linked to the quality of life of persons with developmental disabilities. Quality assessment must become a formative process focused on assessment of person-centered outcomes of value to the individual in order to be effective. To achieve such a change, quality assessment and quality enhancement systems must become an interwoven aspect of total quality approach.

The purpose of quality assessment and quality enhancement systems must shift from searching for the programs that are regulatorily deficient to becoming capable partners with service providers, persons with disabilities, families, friends, advocacy organizations, community groups, and others in order to identify ways to assist persons with developmental disabilities to live lives of higher quality, as defined by the individual. It is this focus on quality, as defined by the individual, that accepts persons with developmental disabilities on their own terms and most distinguishes the future of quality assessment and quality enhancement from the vestiges of positivism that continue to govern quality assurance. These changes and the entirely new ways of thinking and behaving they will require will not come easily, but they will come. Quality assessment and quality enhancement systems will become based on the premise that quality of life should be the prevailing goal of service provision (Bellamy et al., 1990; Blunden, 1988).

REFERENCES

Accreditation Council, The. (1992). *Proposed outcome based performance measures.* Boston: Author.

American Association on Mental Retardation (AAMR). (1990). *AAMR 1990 legislative and social goals.* Washington, DC: Author.

Baer, D.M. (1990). Good rules, bad rules, the rulers, and the ruled. *Mental Retardation, 28,* 101–103.

Bellamy, G.T., Newton, J.S., LeBarron, N.M., & Horner, R.H. (1990). Quality of life and lifestyle outcomes: A challenge for residential programs. In R. L. Schalock (Ed.), *Quality of life: Perspectives and issues* (pp. 127–137). Washington, DC: American Association on Mental Retardation.

Bersani, H. (1984a). *Monitoring community residences: Guidelines.* Columbus, OH: The Arc-Ohio.

Bersani, H. (1984b). *Monitoring community residences: Handbook.* Columbus, OH: The Arc-Ohio.

Blake, E., Mangan, T., Prouty, B., & Lakin, K.C. (1992). *Reinventing quality: A sourcebook of innovative programs for quality assurance and service improvement in community settings.* Minneapolis: University of Minnesota, Research and Training Center on Residential Services and Community Living, Institute on Community Integration.

Blunden, R. (1988). Programmatic features of quality services. In M.P. Janicki, M.W. Krauss, & M.M. Seltzer (Eds.), *Community residences for persons with developmental disabilities: Here to stay* (pp. 117–121). Baltimore: Paul H. Brookes Publishing Co.

Boggs, E.M., Lakin, K.C., & Clauser, S. (1985). Medicaid coverage of residential services. In K.C. Lakin, B.K. Hill, & R.H. Bruininks (Eds.), *An analysis of Medicaid's Intermediate Care Facility for the Mentally Retarded (ICF-MR) program.* Minneapolis: University of Minnesota, Research and Training Center on Residential Services and Community Living.

Braddock, D., & Mitchell, D. (1992). *Residential services and developmental disabilities in the United States: A national survey of staff compensation, turnover, and related issues.* Washington, DC: American Association on Mental Retardation.

Bradley, V. (1990a). Conceptual issues in quality assurance. In V.J. Bradley & H.A. Bersani (Eds.), *Quality assurance for individuals with developmental disabilities: It's everybody's business* (pp. 2–15). Baltimore: Paul H. Brookes Publishing Co.

Bradley, V. (1990b). Quality assurance: Challenges in a decentralized system. In R.L. Schalock (Ed.), *Quality of life: Perspectives and issues* (pp. 215–225). Washington, DC: American Association on Mental Retardation.

Chafee, J.H. (1990). Balancing quality of care and quality of life. In V.J. Bradley & H.A. Bersani (Eds.), *Quality assurance for individuals with developmental disabilities: It's everybody's business* (pp. 95–101). Baltimore: Paul H. Brookes Publishing Co.

Conroy, J.W., & Feinstein, C.S. (1990). Measuring quality of life: Where have we been? Where are we going? In R.L. Schalock (Ed.), *Quality of life: Perspectives and issues* (pp. 227–233). Washington, DC: American Association on Mental Retardation.

Crutcher, D.M. (1990). Quality of life versus quality of life judgements: A parent's perspective. In R.L Schalock (Ed.), *Quality of life: Perspectives and issues* (pp. 17–22). Washington, DC: American Association on Mental Retardation.

Donabedian, A. (1966). Evaluating the quality of medical care. *Milbank Memorial Fund Quarterly, 44,* 166–206.

Dufresne, D.F. (1990). The role of service providers in quality assurance. In V.J. Bradley & H.A. Bersani (Eds.), *Quality assurance for individuals with developmental disabilities: It's everybody's business* (pp. 137–146). Baltimore: Paul H. Brookes Publishing Co.

Gant, S.A. (1990). The Connecticut model. In V.J. Bradley & H.A. Bersani (Eds.), *Quality assurance for individuals with developmental disabilities: It's everybody's business* (pp. 301–341). Baltimore: Paul H. Brookes Publishing Co.

Gardner, J.F., & Parsons, C.E. (1990). Accreditation as synthesis. In V.J. Bradley & H.A. Bersani (Eds.), *Quality assurance for individuals with developmental disabilities: It's everybody's business* (pp. 207–220). Baltimore: Paul H. Brookes Publishing Co.

Gettings, R.M., & Mitchell, D. (1980). *Trends in capital expenditures for mental retardation facilities: A state-by-state survey.* Washington, DC: National Association of State Mental Retardation Program Directors.

Goode, D.A. (1988). *The proceedings of the national conference on quality of life for persons with disabilities.* Valhalla, NY: Mental Retardation Institute (UAP), Westchester County Medical Center in affiliation with New York Medical College.

Goode, D.A. (1990). Thinking about and discussing quality of life. In R.L. Schalock (Ed.), *Quality of life: Perspectives and issues* (pp. 41–57). Washington, DC: American Association on Mental Retardation.

Governor's Planning Council on Developmental Disabilities. (1992). *Minnesotans speak-out: A summary of town meetings held throughout Minnesota on developmental disabilities issues.* St. Paul: Author.

Hayden, M.F. (1992). Adults with mental retardation and developmental disabilities waiting for community-based services in the U.S. *Policy Research Brief, 4*(3). Minneapolis: University of Minnesota, Research and Training Center on Residential Services and Community Living, Institute on Community Integration.

Hemp, R., & Braddock, D. (1988). Accreditation of developmental disabilities programs. *Mental Retardation, 26*, 257–267.

Hill, B.K., Lakin, K.C., Bruininks, R.H., Amado, A.N., Anderson, D.J., & Copher, J.I. (1989). *Living in the community: A comparative study of foster homes and small group homes for people with mental retardation.* Minneapolis: University of Minnesota, Research and Training Center on Residential Services and Community Living, Institute on Community Integration.

Holburn, C. S. (1990a). Rules: The new institutions. *Mental Retardation, 28*, 89–94.

Holburn, C.S. (1990b). Symposium overview: Our residential rules—Have we gone too far? *Mental Retardation, 28*, 65–66.

Holburn, C.S. (1992). Rhetoric and realities in today's ICF/MR: Control out of control. *Mental Retardation, 30*, 133–141.

Hurst, J. (1989, January 8). Private care for the retarded—A gamble. *Los Angeles Times*, 22–26.

Jacobson, J.W. (1990). Regulations: Can they control staff compliance in human services systems? *Mental Retardation, 28*, 77–82.

Kennedy, M.J. (1990). What quality assurance means to me. In V.J. Bradley & H.A. Bersani (Eds.), *Quality assurance for individuals with developmental disabilities: It's everybody's business* (pp. 35–45). Baltimore: Paul H. Brookes Publishing Co.

Knoll, J.A. (1990). Defining quality in residential services. In V.J. Bradley & H.A. Bersani (Eds.), *Quality assurance for individuals with developmental disabilities: It's everybody's business* (pp. 235–261). Baltimore: Paul H. Brookes Publishing Co.

Kuhlberg, K.T. (1977). Assessing active treatment in ICFs/MR. In Pacific Consultants (Eds.), *Assessment of residential care in Intermediate Care Facilities for the Mentally Retarded: Conference summary* (pp. 103–121). Washington, DC: U.S. Department of Health, Education, and Welfare, Medicaid Bureau.

Lakin, K.C., Amado, A.N., Bruininks, R.H., Hayden, M.F., & Li, X. (1992). Programs and services received by persons with mental retardation in three models of small community residences. *Journal of Disability Policy Studies, 3*(1), 17–44.

Lakin, K.C., Bruininks, R.H., & Larson, S.A. (1992). The changing face of residential services. In L. Rowitz (Ed.), *Mental retardation in the year 2000* (pp. 197–247). New York: Springer-Verlag.

Lakin, K.C., Burwell, B.O., Hayden, M.F., & Jackson, M.E. (1992). *An independent assessment of Minnesota's Medicaid Home and Community Based Services program.* Minneapolis: University of Minnesota, Research and Training Center for Residential Services and Community Living.

Lakin, K.C., White, C.C., Prouty, R.W., Bruininks, R.H., & Kimm, C. (1991). *Medicaid Institutional (ICF-MR) and Home and Community Based Services for persons with mental retardation and related conditions.* Minneapolis: University of Minnesota, Research and Training Center for Residential Services and Community Living.

Landesman, S. (1986). Quality of life and personal life satisfaction: Definition and measurement issues. *Mental Retardation, 24,* 141–143.

Landesman, S. (1988). Preventing "institutionalization" in the community. In M.P. Janicki, M.W. Krauss, & M.M. Seltzer (Eds.). *Community residences for persons with developmental disabilities: Here to stay* (pp. 105–116). Baltimore: Paul H. Brookes Publishing Co.

Laski, F.J. (1985). Right to habilitation and right to education: The legal foundation. In R.H. Bruininks & K.C. Lakin (Eds.), *Living and learning in the least restrictive environment* (pp. 67–79). Baltimore: Paul H. Brookes Publishing Co.

Martinez, C. (1990). A dream for myself. In R.L. Schalock (Ed.), *Quality of life: Perspectives and issues* (pp. 3–7). Washington, DC: American Association on Mental Retardation.

Meinhold, P.M., & Mulick, J.A. (1990). Counter-habilitative contingencies in institutions for people with mental retardation: Ecological and regulatory influences. *Mental Retardation, 28,* 67–75.

Mitchell, G. (1988). *Hearing before the U.S. Senate Subcommittee on Health on the Medicaid Home and Community Quality Services Act of 1987.* Washington, DC: U.S. Government Printing Office.

Moore, C., & Moore, R. (1988, November). Quote. In Research and Training Center on Community Integration (Ed.), *From being in the community to being part of the community: Summary of the proceedings of a Leadership Institute on Community Integration for People with Developmental Disabilities.* Syracuse, NY: Syracuse University, Research and Training Center on Community Integration, Center on Human Policy.

O'Brien, J., & Lyle, C. (1988). *Framework for accomplishment.* Atlanta: Responsive Systems.

Pearce, C.K. (1990). Building values into accreditation practices. In V.J. Bradley & H.A. Bersani (Eds.), *Quality assurance for individuals with developmental disabilities: It's everybody's business* (pp. 221–232). Baltimore: Paul H. Brookes Publishing Co.

Prouty, R., & Lakin, K.C. (1991). *A summary of states' efforts to positively affect the quality of Medicaid Home and Community Based Services for persons with mental retardation and related conditions.* Minneapolis: University of Minnesota, Center for Residential Services and Community Living.

Provencal, G., & Taylor, R. (1983). Security for parents: Monitoring of group homes by consumers. *The Exceptional Parent, 13,* 39–44.

Reid, D.H., Parsons, M.B., Green, C.S., & Schepis, M.M. (1991). Evaluation of components of residential treatment by Medicaid ICF-MR surveys: A validity assessment. *Journal of Applied Behavior Analysis, 24,* 293–304.

Repp, A.C., & Barton, L.E. (1980). Naturalistic observations of institutionalized retarded persons: A comparison of licensure decisions and behavioral observations. *Journal of Applied Behavior Analysis, 13,* 333–341.

Rothman, D.J. (1971). *The discovery of the asylum: Social order and disorder in the new republic.* Boston: Little, Brown.

Schalock, R.L. (1990). Where do we go from here? In R.L. Schalock (Ed.), *Quality of life: Perspectives and issues* (pp. 235–240). Washington, DC: American Association on Mental Retardation.

Schalock, R.L., Bartnik, E., Wu, F., Konig, A., Lee, C.S., & Reiter, S. (1990, May). *An international perspective on quality of life: Measurement and use.* Paper presented at the 104th Annual Convention of the American Association on Mental Retardation, Atlanta, Georgia.

Shea, J.R. (1990). *Where's the Jello? The continuing saga of one home's experience with the ICF-MR program.* Napa, CA: Allen, Shea and Associates.

Shea, J.R. (1992). From standards to compliance, to good services, to quality lives: Is this how it works? *Mental Retardation, 30,* 143–149.

Skarnulis, D., & Skarnulis, E. (1990). In-home support from a user's point of view. *Impact, 3*(2), 12, 17. Minneapolis: University of Minnesota, Institute on Community Integration.

Sparr, M.P., & Smith, W. (1990). Regulating professional services in ICFs/MR: Remembering the past and looking to the future. *Mental Retardation, 28,* 95–99.

Taylor, S.J., & Bogdan, R. (1990). Quality of life and the individual's perspective. In R.L. Schalock (Ed.). *Quality of life: Perspectives and issues* (pp. 27–40). Washington, DC: American Association on Mental Retardation.

U.S. General Accounting Office. (1990, February). *Quality assurance: A comprehensive, national strategy for health care is needed* (GAO/PEMD-90-14BR). Gaithersburg, MD: Author.

Wallace, T., & Johnson, D.R. (1992). Training challenges for the 1990s. In T. Wallace, S.A. Larson, & A. Hewitt (Eds.), *IMPACT: Feature issue on training for direct service staff* (pp. 1, 22–23). Minneapolis: University of Minnesota, Institute on Community Integration.

White, C.C., Lakin, K.C., & Bruininks, R.H. (1989). *Persons with mental retardation and related conditions in state-operated residential facilities: Year ending June 30, 1988 with longitudinal trends from 1950 to 1988* (Report No. 30). Minneapolis: University of Minnesota, Department of Educational Psychology.

Wisconsin Coalition for Advocacy (WCA). (1986, May). *Out of sight, out of mind: A report on the human and civil rights of residents of Wisconsin's three state centers for the developmentally disabled. 1982 to date.* Madison, WI: Author.

Wisconsin Coalition for Advocacy (WCA). (1989, May). *The "active treatment" myth: People with developmental disabilities in Wisconsin institutions.* Madison, WI: Author.

— Chapter 10

Costs of Community-Based Residential and Related Services to Individuals with Mental Retardation and Other Developmental Disabilities

Darrell R. Lewis and Robert H. Bruininks

During the 1980s and early 1990s, there have been significant societal changes in the manner in which services have been provided to individuals with mental retardation and other developmental disabilities (Lakin, Bruininks, & Larson, 1992). The most dramatic of these changes has been the deinstitutionalization of individuals from large state-operated facilities to smaller, community-based residences. Although an increasingly diverse array of community-based services has become available, the number and type of services needed by people with mental retardation and other developmental disabilities far exceeds the current and planned expansion of community-based programs (Davis, 1987; Hayden, 1992; Lakin, Bruininks, et al., 1992).

In society, public policies are directed toward addressing important human needs. Two of the most important areas of recent public investment have been

Preparation of this chapter was supported by a cooperative agreement (#H133B80048) between the National Institute on Disability and Rehabilitation Research (NIDRR) and the Research and Training Center on Residential Services and Community Living at the University of Minnesota (College of Education) located within the Institute on Community Integration (UAP). The opinions expressed herein are those of the authors.

directed at the residential and related service needs of adults with mental retardation and other developmental disabilities who live outside natural or adopted family settings and of adults who continue to reside at home with their families. Understanding the allocation of public expenditures is an important aspect of the evaluation of the direction of current policies and programs, the use of available resources, the efficiency of current allocations, and the relationship of resource usage to public priorities in providing appropriate and effective services to persons with mental retardation and other developmental disabilities.

This chapter, which reviews general costs and expenditures for persons with mental retardation and other developmental disabilities, focuses primarily on the service costs of persons who live in supervised residential care programs. These services serve approximately 270,000 persons with mental retardation and other developmental disabilities in state-operated and privately operated residential care programs (White, Prouty, Lakin, & Blake, 1992). They require nearly $15 billion in state and federal expenditures (Braddock, Hemp, Fujiura, Bachelder, & Mitchell, 1990), with most of this supporting residential programs. While trends in expenditures obviously reflect a public commitment to increased deinstitutionalization and community integration, substantial public investment still supports large congregate care settings.

The analysis of costs and expenditures is an important aspect of evaluating and managing public policies that affect citizens with developmental disabilities and their families. In an era of declining resources such analyses provide an opportunity to evaluate the use of resources in relationship to policy objectives and to assist policymakers and others in identifying directions to improve the quality and productivity of current services. Unfortunately, much of the current literature on the services costs is inadequate for policy development, management, and decision making (Fujiura, 1988). The study of the costs of community-based residential and related services to individuals with developmental disabilities requires knowledge of several critical dimensions. These dimensions include an understanding of: 1) the methodological problems inherent in most past studies, 2) the reported cost findings from these studies, and 3) the factors that might cause variations in these costs. This chapter examines current studies on these three dimensions and, in addition, discusses the implications from available knowledge for policy, research, and practice.

METHODOLOGICAL PROBLEMS

During the past two decades of deinstitutionalization, a frequent argument supporting this social policy has been the belief that it costs less to support people with developmental disabilities in community-based residential facilities than in large public institutions. As a result, an increasing number of researchers have attempted to examine the likely cost consequences of moving individuals with developmental disabilities into community settings. These studies are identified in Table 1. All of these empirical studies, however, have had methodological prob-

Table 1. Cost studies of residential and community services for individuals with developmental disabilities

Cost study	Sample and design	Data sources	Cost components collected	Control for client characteristics	Analysis
Ashbaugh and Allard (1984)	Cost comparisons of residential and other programs in Pennhurst State School with 102 community-based programs in area	Institutional and county offices	Direct care, day programs, habilitative, behavior mgt., case mgt., medical, administrative operations, repair and maintenance	Age, adaptive behavior, and medical need	Costs were analyzed by type of facility, program size, years in operation, staffing patterns, wage scales, hours of service per client
Ashbaugh and Nerney (1990)	Cost comparisons of residential per diem for 160 group homes, 130 family homes, and 41 apartments in Michigan and Nebraska	Expenditure records in funding agencies	Residential, medical, and transportation	Level of service need	Costs were compared in per diem terms between types of facilities, level of client need, staffing patterns, wage rates
Bensberg and Smith (1984)	Cost comparisons of 12 public institutions (PRFs) with 16 group homes (CRFs) in Texas	Agency and facility records	Administration, medical, support services, food, rent, operations, salaries, and other	Not reported	Costs were compared in per diem terms between types of facilities and size
Campbell and Smith (1989)	Cost comparisons of all large public institutions with matched pairs in community facilities in South Dakota	Facility records and follow-along data from sample of individuals	Residential, day programs, case mgt., administration, medical, all other services attributed to individuals through follow-along sample	Levels of service need	Costs were compared for 40 matched pairs at different levels of service need in institutions and community settings

(continued)

Table 1. (continued)

Cost study	Sample and design	Data sources	Cost components collected	Control for client characteristics	Analysis
Greenberg, Lakin, Hill, Bruininks, and Hauper (1985)	Cost comparison of 325 state facilities certified as ICFs/MR	National survey of facility records	Per diem rates	Age and adaptive behavior of sample population	Costs were functionally related to size, and various resident and institutional characteristics
Heal, Copher, Wieck, and Bruininks (1989)	Cost comparisons of 80 public and 150 privately owned residential facilities drawn from random sample of national survey data	Facility records	Direct residential services	Maladaptive and adaptive behavior	Costs were functionally related to environmental, facility, and client characteristics
Intagliata, Willer, and Cooley (1979)	Cost comparisons of a state institution with group, foster, and natural family homes in Buffalo, New York	Agency and state budget records	Direct care and professional services	Not reported	Costs were compared across residential settings
Jones, Conroy, Feinstein, and Lemanowicz (1984)	Cost comparisons of 70 clients deinstitutionalized from Pennhurst State School with 70 matched pairs in institution	Institutional and client records	Per diem rates for residential and day programs, medical, entitlements, and others	Matched by age, IQ, gender, level of MR, self-sufficiency, years institutionalized	Costs of alternative settings were compared with outcome of developmental growth

Knoll and Bersani (1989)	Cost comparison of 29 children and youth with severe disabilities deinstitutionalized from congregate facility to family care setting	Facility, agency, and client records matched to individual	Direct care, medical, professional services, respite, and other	Pre- and post–follow-up	Costs were compared between residential settings
Lakin, Kimm, and Li (in press)	Cost comparisons across 288 state institutions	National survey of facility records	Per diem rates	Adaptive behavior	Costs were functionally related to resident, facility, and several contextual characteristics
Mayeda and Wai (1975)	Cost comparisons of care and services for 4,284 clients in institutional and community settings in California, Florida, and Washington	Institutional expenditure and billing records	Direct care and operations, special programs, professional services, indirect costs of support and administrative services	Age, level of MR, adaptive behavior	Costs of alternative settings were compared between institution and community settings
Minnesota Department of Welfare (1979)	Cost comparison of public and private ICFs/MR in Minnesota	Facility records	Per diem in public, components of residential, day programs, transportation, medical, and social services in private	Not reported	Costs were compared between public and private institutions, and community settings
Murphy and Datel (1976)	Cost comparisons of institutions and community care through follow-up with 52 former institutional residents in Virginia	Facility records	Direct care, community support services, project costs	Level of service support, prognosis of employability	Costs were compared between institutional and community settings

(continued)

Table 1. (continued)

Cost study	Sample and design	Data sources	Cost components collected	Control for client characteristics	Analysis
Nerney, Conley, and Nisbet (1991)	Cost comparisons of 375 model group and community-based homes across three regions of Michigan, Nebraska, and New Hampshire	Facility and home expenditure records	Direct care, family fringe payments, operations, administration, transportation, medical, case mgt., day/vocational program	Level of service support, age, severity of DD	Costs were examined by type of facility/ownership, effect of regulations, size, level of client need, groupings, staffing patterns
Nihira, Mayeda, and Eyman (1979)	Cost comparisons of institutions with community group and natural homes through matched groups consisting of 51 in institutions, 54 in group homes, and 54 in natural homes in California	Facility records	Direct care	Level of functioning	Costs of direct care were compared across the three groups
Richard (1983)	Follow-up of 8 individuals from institution to community living in Maine	Not reported	Not reported	Not reported	Costs were compared between state institution and several community settings in the eight cases
Templeman, Gage, and Fredericks (1982)	Follow-up of 21 children moved from institution through group homes to family residences in Oregon	Facility records	Not reported	Not reported	Costs were compared between state institution, group homes, foster homes, and natural homes

Study	Description	Data source	Cost components	Matching variable	Findings
Touche Ross and Co. (1980)	Cost comparisons of state institution (Beatrice) with state supported group homes in Nebraska	Institutional, state, and regional agency records	Residential, day activity, support, social services, administration, medical	Level of severity	Costs were compared between state institution and community placement
Wieck and Bruininks (1980)	Cost comparisons of 78 public institutions with 180 community-based facilities randomly selected from national survey	National survey sample of facility records	Per diem rates, direct care, operations, capitalization	Age, level of MR	Costs were functionally related to client's age and level of MR, facility location, size, ownership, and staffing patterns

Comparisons within community settings

Study	Description	Data source	Cost components	Matching variable	Findings
Arkana and Mueller (1978)	Cost comparisons of 43 matched pairs of foster families with and without children with disabilities in Idaho	Family interviews	Estimated expenditures	Families matched by SES	Costs were compared by levels of disabling conditions within control groups
Dunaway, Granfield, Norton, and Greenspan (1992)	Cost comparisons of 66 individuals randomly selected from private agency settings of community living, supported living, and community training homes in Connecticut	State and agency records	Residential services converted to per diem rates	Level of service need	Costs were compared in per diem across the three residential options for groups with similar needs

(continued)

Table 1. (continued)

Cost study	Sample and design	Data sources	Cost components collected	Control for client characteristics	Analysis
Heal and Daniels (1986)	Cost comparisons of 29 individuals with disabilities living in independent apartments, natural family homes, and foster family homes in Wisconsin	Household records and family estimates	Direct labor care, capitalization, equipment and furnishings related to residential care	Not reported	Costs were compared across the three options for client, family, and society
Nerney, Conley, and Nisbet (1991)	Cost comparisons of 375 group and foster family homes across Michigan, Nebraska, and New Hampshire	Facility records	Direct care, fringe, operations, administration, transportation, some medical and therapy, case mgt., and day/vocational programs	Not reported	Costs were compared across the group and family homes

PRFs = public residential facilities; CRFs/MR = community residential facilities; ICFs/MR = intermediate care facilities for persons with mental retardation; MR = mental retardation; DD = developmental disabilities; SES = socioeconomic status.

lems. Consequently, the true cost effects of community-based care are still largely unknown and ambiguous at best. Several earlier reviews of cost studies on institutional and community care for individuals with developmental disabilities have been conducted by others, and they similarly concluded that all extant studies were methodologically suspect (Benz & Agosta, 1982; Bersani, Caruso, & Knoll, 1987; Conroy & Bradley, 1985; Fujiura, 1988; Greenberg, Lakin, Hill, Bruininks, & Hauber, 1985; Kotler, Wright, Jaskulski, & Kreisberg, 1985; Nerney, Conley, & Nisbet, 1991).

Several common characteristics can be seen in a majority of the studies reported in Table 1. Evident in most of these investigations are methodological problems of selection bias in the characteristics and abilities of clients in alternative residential settings, in cost accounting for comparable services being delivered in different settings, and in linking costs with outcomes for estimating true efficiency effects. These research efforts have tended to: 1) focus on residential facility types within single states and on public institutions, 2) employ measurement procedures focused on rates of reimbursed per diem for expenditure estimates, 3) estimate cost comparisons independent of the scope and intensity of services to individuals, 4) use widely varying accounting procedures for estimating common cost components, 5) employ accidental versus planned design procedures in the seleciton of sample populations, 6) ignore the costs of many community-based services, 7) have limited controls for explanatory factors built into their evaluation design, and 8) ignore differential outcomes for individuals in service programs.

Problems of Selection Bias

A potential problem of selection bias arises when different sample populations are compared in alternative settings without appropriate controls for differing characteristics of the population under study. Controlling for client characteristics through careful sample selection procedures has been almost nonexistent in the literature. Only four studies employed matched groups of individuals (Arkana & Mueller, 1978; Campbell & Smith, 1989; Jones, Conroy, Feinstein, & Lemanowicz, 1984; Nihira, Mayeda, & Eyman, 1979); one study randomly selected individuals (Dunaway, Granfield, Norton, & Greenspan, 1992), and three studies used a pre- and post-design in their follow-up studies (Knoll & Bersani, 1989; Murphy & Dantel, 1976; Templeman, Gage, & Fredericks, 1982). Most studies comparing residential settings focused on broad facility characteristics (e.g., public institutions versus small community facilities) and took their populations as given, although several attempted to control for client characteristics through statistical controls (Ashbaugh & Allard, 1984; Ashbaugh & Nerney, 1990; Greenberg et al., 1985; Heal, Copher, Wieck, & Bruininks, 1989; Lakin, Kimm, & Li, in press; Nerney et al., 1991; Touche Ross & Co., 1980; Wieck & Bruininks, 1980). As noted by Fujiura (1988), "one of the most profound methodological weaknesses of residential cost comparison studies has been the selection bias that has resulted from the confounding of facility type and resident characteristics. Types and levels of disabilities vary systematically across facility alternatives" (p. 228). As Fujiura correctly observes, if the differences in costs result primarily from the nature of the population, then such comparisons tell us little about the relative efficacy or efficiency of the facilities or programs.

Problems of Cost Accounting

There is a persistent problem in the identification and measurement of the cost components of both residential and other community-based services. The most notable accounting problems have been those relating to the capitalization of facilities in public ownership and the neglect of many services provided in community settings outside the residential facility. With a few exceptions, most studies underestimate the capital costs of public facilities. Although several investigators attempted to collect cost information on some community services provided to individuals living in community-based residences, no comprehensive taxonomy of such services and their related costs has been developed or used to date (Ashbaugh & Allard, 1984; Ashbaugh & Nerney, 1990; Bensberg & Smith, 1984; Campbell & Smith, 1989; Jones et al., 1984; Minnesota Department of Welfare, 1979; Nerney et al., 1991; Touche Ross & Co., 1980). Although several taxonomies of residential alternatives have been developed for use in the United States (e.g., Hauber et al., 1984; Hill & Lakin, 1986) and a taxonomy of services available to individuals with developmental disabilities has been outlined for identifying community services in the United Kingdom (Shiell & Wright, 1988), no systematic cost profile of such services has been reported.

Surprisingly, none of the studies reviewed for this chapter focused on a comprehensive list of services being delivered to residents. Rather, most concentrated on residential care costs. Additional service costs were only added as they were evident through expenditure records of the facility or program. Many community-based service costs outside of readily available budget records were simply ignored. This was particularly true for those studies that included group homes and foster and natural family settings.

The cost studies reviewed also included several important identification and measurement errors that often contribute to confounding our understanding of factors relating to cost differences among residential alternatives. Almost all of the studies used budgeted expenditures to estimate costs and did not focus on the total resources employed in the delivery of services. The most frequent problem was the use and comparison of per diem rates.

Often, per diem rates were assumed to represent all social services to individuals. Many of the services provided to individuals within community settings, however, are outside reimbursed per diem rates of service agencies. Day programs, medical services, therapeutic services, case management, and other services were often ignored in community settings, yet they are routinely included in the per diem and budgeted responsibilities of almost all larger public institutions and many larger private institutions. In addition, most studies ignored state and regional administrative costs for all types of facilities as well as long-term capital costs (Heal & Daniels, 1986; Heal et al., 1989; O'Connor & Morris, 1978; Wieck

& Bruininks, 1980). Similarly, many nonmarket and voluntary contributions of services and their respective shadow prices and opportunity costs were ignored or overlooked. This problem becomes especially important when examining costs within foster and family home alternatives (Boggs, 1979).

When the costs of certain components are approximately equal among alternatives, ignoring or not measuring such costs may not be problematic. When such costs are different across various alternatives, however, important measurement errors and misleading results often arise. A useful framework for identifying and measuring the costs of all community-based services for individuals with disabilities is through a comprehensive set of taxonomies that identify each of the functional service areas and their related alternative types of services. An outline of six functional service areas for adults with developmental disabilities is illustrated in Table 2. This simplified classification is compatible with most existing data sets and consistent with the principal recommendations of others who have thought extensively about the issue (Hill & Lakin, 1986).

Surprisingly little attention has been given to the full range of these services in the literature. Most studies have tended to focus on only one or two service areas and, most often, only on domiciliary care. The following paragraphs summarize the literature for each area.

Residential Services   The importance of establishing a consistent and generally accepted taxonomy for residential facilities is especially problematic when comparing data among states. States not only exhibit substantial variety in the characteristics of their residential care systems, but they have also developed unique nomenclatures for types of facilities that mask similarities among facilities (Hill, Lakin, & Bruininks, 1984). Licensing categories, for example, are of little use when comparing or discussing cost or outcome data from residential care systems due to interstate differences. In response to this problem, several taxonomies for classifying residential facilities have been developed in the literature.

During the past decade, a number of taxonomies have been developed in an effort to better conceptualize the commonalities and differences between residential facilities (Baker, Seltzer, & Seltzer, 1977; Bruininks, Hill, Weatherman, & Woodcock, 1986; Hauber et al., 1984; Hill & Lakin, 1986; Scheerenberger, 1983; Wieck & Bruininks, 1980). Each of the classification systems implicitly assume that each alternative is mutually exclusive and a reasonably discrete category. Although all of the taxonomies attempt to account for type of program and size, most are different in description, resulting in particular difficulties in accounting for and interpreting evidence across different studies. Useful additional discussion on these problematic issues can be found in Fujiura (1988), Heal and Fujiura (1984), Hill and Lakin (1986), and Landesman (1986). The most important distinguishing characteristic of all these classification systems is that they implicitly assume a continuum relating to community integration, generally from large public institutions to independent living. In the middle of this continuum are a variety of settings, including nursing homes, ICFs/MR, group homes, foster care homes, family home care, and semi-independent living arrangements.

Table 2. Taxonomy of services to community-based adults with developmental disabilities

Residential services
- Regional state institution
- Nursing home
- Nonmedical group home with more than 15 clients
- Nonmedical group home with 14 or less clients
- Family home with foster family
- Family home with parents or relatives
- Room and board with staff support in building but no personal care
- Semi-independent living with supervisory staff in building
- Independent living with regular home-based services or monitoring
- Independent living in owner occupied home or rental

Vocational and training services
- Competitive employment
- Supported employment
- Sheltered workshop
- Day activities and habilitation training
- Other education or training
- Transportation to work, school, or training

Medical services
- Physician services
- Dental services
- Visiting nurse services
- Therapeutic services (e.g., physical, occupational, speech)
- Mental health/behavior services (e.g., evaluation/consultation)
- Hospitalization
- Drugs and medical supplies/equipment (e.g., wheelchairs, glasses)
- Other medical services (e.g., ambulance, medical tests, dietary)

Other social services
- Personal and attendant care
- Provision of meals including food banks, shelters, stamps
- Legal services
- Social workers and case managers
- Volunteer assistance

Family services
- Transportation by family
- In-home family support services (e.g., respite care)
- Telephone and other

Other personal services
- Meals independent of residential provisions
- Transportation separate from vocational training
- Recreation, entertainment, hobby-related services
- Clothing (purchase, cleaning, mending) services
- Personal requisites

Note: Some training, medical, and other support services may be delivered by and through residential facilities and must be appropriately measured as separate dimensions.

Although many states have designed their service systems for persons with developmental disabilities according to a continuum that includes institutions as well as community living arrangements (Lakin, Hill, Street, & Bruininks, 1986), most state service systems are currently targeted to promoting the principle of least restrictive environment (LRE). This principle has been interpreted in most states in terms of a continuum of residential environments ranging from large to small settings, from more to less structured living, from segregation to community presence and integration, and from dependent to independent living. A continuum of service options that embraces the LRE principle is implicit in the design of most state service programs and has been described by several researchers (Lakin et al., 1986; Schalock, 1983; Taylor, 1988).

Training and Other Services Through close examination of cost studies relating to community-based services, it is possible to construct other useful taxonomies relating to vocational and training services (Kerachsky, Thornton, Bloomenthal, Maynard, & Stephens, 1985; Lewis, Johnson, Bruininks, Kallsen, & Guillery, 1992); medical services (Jacobs & McDermott, 1989); and other social and family services (Castellani, Downey, Tausig, & Bird, 1986). Each of these other service areas has been identified and framed together to construct the overall taxonomy recommended in Table 2.

These areas are mutually exclusive, except when they might be included in particular residential service programs. Within each of the functional areas, all of the available services are identified in measurable dimensions.

Problems of Linking Costs with Outcomes

The assessment literature relative to residential services and community integration indicates two lines of evaluation. One has focused on the average costs of alternative residential facilities. A second line has tended to focus on the effectiveness of deinstitutionalization independent of any relationship to cost. Surprisingly, few attempts have been made to examine both of these issues together and address the related public policy issue of cost-effectiveness and efficiency.

Efficiency in its simplest form can be measured by the comparison of any set of ratios that relate inputs to outputs in a service program or service delivery system. The resulting ratios can be expressed in monetary terms as cost-benefit ratios and net benefits or, if outcomes are measured in standardized nonmonetary terms, in cost-effectiveness and cost-utility ratios. These ratios of cost-effectiveness are often used for policy purposes in determining the most efficient alternative from among two or more options.

There is consistent evidence from previous cost studies that variability in levels and amounts of services largely determines variability in average costs. For example, there is strong evidence that significant changes take place in the quality of the lives of individuals as a result of deinstitutionalization and community-based services (Heal, Sigelman, & Switzky, 1980; Lakin et al., 1989; Larson & Lakin, 1991). However, there is only one study in the literature that has effectively linked these services and cost inputs with output measures of effectiveness (Conroy & Bradley, 1985; Jones et al., 1984). Although many cost comparison investigations purport to be cost-benefit or cost-effectiveness studies, they have measured benefits solely in terms of perceived cost savings of moving from one type of residence to another.

In a recent survey of the deinstitutionalization follow-up literature, researchers found that studies that met minimum research standards provided a remarkably consistent body of evidence on the benefits of deinstitutionalization (Lakin et al., 1989; Larson & Lakin, 1991). After reviewing this work, the researchers concluded that *all* investigations reported consistent findings that gains in personal development accrue more rapidly to people living in community settings than those who lived in institutions. Thirteen out of 17 studies reported significantly greater achievement in either overall adaptive behavior or in basic self-care/domestic skills for those who moved to community living arrangements relative to those who remained in state-operated institutions. In the four remaining studies, community samples all showed greater achievement, but differences did not reach a level of, or were not estimated for, significance.

The most carefully designed cost-effectiveness study in the literature was reported by Jones et al. (1984) in their evaluation of community placements resulting from deinstitutionalization. Seventy people with mental retardation who had moved from a large state-operated institution (i.e., Pennhurst in Pennsylvania) to small community living arrangements were matched with 70 people who remained at the same institution. Results indicated that the individuals living within the community demonstrated significantly more growth in measures of adaptive behavior and basic self-care skills, while their costs of services were, on average, less than comparable with the state institution. Assuming that these average cost differences were due largely to differing wage rates between the two settings (Ashbaugh & Allard, 1984), the results still indicated that the community-based settings of this study were more cost-effective (e.g., efficient per unit of gain in adaptive behavior scores) than those at the state facility.

It is instructive to note that many other related studies have found that community placement may be *both* more costly and more cost-effective (i.e., more efficient per levels of outcomes). Cost-effectiveness does not necessarily result from lower costs, but rather from the relationship of costs to a common measure of outcomes. Cost-effectiveness and benefit-cost evaluation techniques also have been applied in the examination of alternatives for special education in the schools (Lewis, Bruininks, Thurlow, & McGrew, 1988); post-school employment training of young adults with developmental disabilities (Kerachsky et al., 1985); and supported employment programs (Lewis, Johnson, Bruininks, et al., 1992). Two excellent reviews of these latter efforts are provided by Noble and Conley (1987) and Rhodes, Ramsing, and Hill (1987). Many of these sources provide excellent discussions of the conceptual and technical features of cost-benefit and cost-effectiveness analyses. The weight of evidence in these cases also suggests that integrated service models in community settings generally produce greater favorable results per unit of costs than more restricted alternatives. Since cost studies that do not relate to some measure of outcome tell us little about the relative efficiency of the alternatives being examined, it is important to add these important dimensions in future studies.

REPORTED COST FINDINGS

Costs of Care and Related Services: Institutions Versus Community Settings

When comparable, comprehensive services and employee compensation rates are included in the total computed program costs for residents of large public institutions and community-based facilities, average costs are fairly similar (Lakin, Burwell, Hayden, & Jackson, 1992). Several studies, however, have found slightly lower costs among some community-based facilities (Amado, Lakin, & Menke, 1990). A previous review of many of these same studies "obtained relatively consistent findings that comprehensive 'community' programs had costs that were from 75% to 92% of total public institution program costs" (Greenberg et al., 1985, p. 14). The investigators properly caution readers that when only aggregated average costs and per diem rates are used for comparisons between different types and sizes of residential facilities, the results may be highly misleading. Indeed, costs have been reported to be the same (Mayeda & Wai, 1975) or even lower (Bensberg & Smith, 1984; Greenberg et al., 1985) in state-operated large institutions than in smaller community-based facilities.

In making such cost comparisons, it is important to remember that: 1) most large publicly operated institutions provide services to individuals with more serious disabilities than do community-based residences (Hayden & DePaepe, 1991; Krauss & Seltzer, 1986); 2) per diem rates are essentially reimbursement funds for all services provided and, in most cases, almost all services are provided directly by large state-operated institutions, unlike the more decentralized service delivery system for most community-based facilities; and 3) capital costs are invariably underestimated in larger publicly operated programs. In many smaller community-based facilities, many services are provided outside of the stated per diem and often go unmeasured. When using such revenue and per diem rates in comparing costs, especially for estimating cost savings in various residential options, the results are often misleading at best.

Costs of Care and Related Services: In Community Settings

The study of smaller programs in community settings often provides more useful information on the use of public resources than comparisons of public and community congregate care arrangements. The study of family care is a particularly interesting and important area of study. Although several investigations have focused on the costs of maintaining a family member with disabilities in a natural family setting (Baldwin, 1985; Chetwynd, 1985; Gunn & Berry, 1987; Hyman, 1977; Rees & Emerson, 1983), none of these studies compared estimated costs with alternative residential programs.

Several other research efforts have examined the costs of foster care. One important difference, however, must be noted when comparing costs of care between natural family and foster family settings. All of the family studies focused on the *extra* costs resulting from a family member's disability. These studies routinely assumed that the family would have had to bear the costs of child-rearing for their children without disabilities in any case and, thus, excluded these costs from their cost and expenditure calculations. Yet, estimates on the costs of care in foster families almost always assumed that the full costs of residential and related habilitation services must be accounted for in some way. Consequently, comparing the estimated costs of natural family care with foster family care is almost always problematic because of differences in accounting for costs and expenditures. Only four of the reviewed studies employed an expenditures accounting approach in their collection of data for individuals with disabilities living in foster homes and compared their findings with alternative community-based settings (Arkana & Mueller, 1978; Heal & Daniels, 1986; Nerney et al., 1991; Wieck & Bruininks, 1980).

In a small-scale study of 29 residents with developmental disabilities in northern Wisconsin (Heal & Daniels, 1986), an effort was made to comprehensively determine residential costs across the three options of independent apartment living, natural family home care, and foster family care. In this study, the residential costs found in the natural family home setting were accounted for. The total cost of residential service considered the dollar value of both residents' and supervisors' (including parents') labor; anticipated investment return on household capitalization, including household furnishings; and all other costs that were seen to be residential. Both average and marginal costs were estimated for all three options and for the differing perspectives of the client, family, and society. The authors estimated the average annual social costs of independent apartments, natural homes, and group homes to be $1,834, $4,602, and $5,361, respectively.

A recent study examined costs in 375 group and foster family-types of homes across three regional areas in Michigan, Nebraska, and New Hampshire (Nerney et al., 1991). The examination areas included cost categories for wages of direct care and supervisory staff, fringe benefits of staff, operational expenses that included depreciation along with food and supplies, administrative costs that included area and regional administration, transportation costs, some medical and therapy costs, case management costs, and costs relating to day and vocational programs. As expected, most group homes were from two to three times more costly per resident than were the extended family and foster homes. However, the study did not account for some Medicaid services or for extra expenses and any indirect costs that foster homes may have incurred beyond the stipulated per diem payments made to them from the public sector. While the study does illustrate relative cost advantages favoring foster homes, these accounting problems undoubtedly underestimated actual program costs and magnified the differences.

An important conclusion of this study was the explanation that many of these cost differences arose primarily from the fundamental conceptual difference between what costs that the public sector reimbursement is meant to cover in specialized foster care in group home placements. The budget of a group home has to include nearly all costs associated with operating the home. Consequently, on one hand, the cost per person represents the *average* cost of the expenses required to maintain and operate the group home. On the other hand, when a person is placed in a specialized foster home, many of these budget items (i.e., rent or a mortgage payments, utilities) are already being met by the family unit. Public payment in this case "need only be equal to the amount required to induce him/her to assume the responsibility of caring for a person with a disability" (Nerney et al., 1991, p. 10). These additional payments (i.e., costs) are roughly equivalent to the *marginal*, or added, costs of providing residential and other supportive services in the foster home. The public costs involved in foster care usually are not based on actual expenditure items as they are in the case of group homes, but on an amount that the state independently sets and allocates to families that provide foster care.

A recent study in Minnesota (Minnesota Department of Administration, 1991) conducted an analysis of nearly $600 million in annual services provided to persons with developmental disabilities. More than half of every dollar was spent in support of residential services. Despite variation in personal needs, it appeared that the most substantial costs were associated with state-operated regional centers and newly developed state-operated group homes (about $85,000 per individual per year). Services provided to persons in their own homes cost considerably less (about $7,000–$25,000 per individual per year). As with other states, the report highlighted the perverse incentives for local units of government to opt for higher cost service alternatives, funded mostly by Medicaid resources that reduce the fiscal impact on local budgets. Data from national surveys of per diem reimbursements indicate that costs of larger state operated ICFs/MR are most costly, with lower costs existing in small privately operated programs. These higher costs are associated with several factors, including service to persons with more severe disabilities, higher staffing ratios, and differential pay rates (White et al., 1992).

Several other studies have compared the per diem rates for children (Hill et al., 1989; Intagliata, Willer, & Cooley, 1979; Lakin, Hill, & Bruininks, 1985; Templeman et al., 1982; Willer & Intagliata, 1984) or older persons with disabilities in foster homes as compared to alternative residential settings (Anderson, Lakin, Bruininks, & Hill, 1987; Braun & Rose, 1987).

Based on their findings, Willer and Intagliata (1984) subsequently estimated that the cost of group home care for individuals with mental retardation could be expected to be at least two to three times higher than the cost of family care. Similar findings were estimated from a small-scale Oregon study (Templeman et al., 1982). A national sample of facilities, with one or more persons age 63 or older with mental retardation, also found dramatic differences in per diem reimbursements among family foster care and other residential options (Anderson et al., 1987). Average resident per diem collected in 1985–1986 were $14.30 for foster care, $31.70 for group homes of up to 15 persons, and $35.10 for large private facilities with 16 or more residents. Another study that examined Medicaid per diem rates for the residential placements of elderly patients found similar differences among facilities (Braun & Rose, 1987).

In a recent study based on a national sample of small foster homes and staffed group homes in the United States, researchers reported very large differences among facility types in average monthly reimbursements for residential services (Hill et al., 1989). Foster care was by far the lowest reimbursed residential option. On average, in 1986, foster care homes received $21.61 per day, compared with approximately $53 per day for small group homes and $86 per day for ICFs/MR certified group homes of comparable size. The study attempted to roughly estimate the impact of costs outside of normal public reimbursements. Only 25% of all facilities in the study indicated that they had received any supplemental funding in addition to their base rate for facility residents in the previous 12 months and then they averaged less than 1%–2% of base reimbursements. This assessment obviously ignores variations in the use of family resources to cover basic costs of care. Cost variations within facility types were substantial, with small group homes having the greatest relative variability.

As Hill and his colleagues (1989) note in their study of foster families and small group care, two factors stand out in the universally observed lower costs of family foster care. The first factor is the cost of staffing. It is simply "less expensive to offer a fee for a qualified foster care provider than to pay wages to the usual number of persons who are needed to staff a small group home" (Hill et al., 1989, p. 48). The second factor is that capital costs are virtually eliminated from the estimated costs of foster family care in most studies and in rate setting. Family care is assumed to be provided in the facility that serves as the provider's primary domicile, and the use of furniture, transportation, and so forth is assumed to be already used by the household at no extra cost. Capital costs, however, are typically included in the approved rates for group homes.

Using an individually focused design, Dunaway and her colleagues (1992) focused on 66 randomly selected individuals with mental retardation who were receiving residential services through private agencies from three different community-based settings in Connecticut, which they characterized as community living arrangements, supported living, and community training homes. While attempting to control for the level of service need, they estimated that per diem costs ranged from $20 to a high of more than $300. Their study was essentially a series of 66 case studies wherein they examined the relationships between residential services and consumer needs and satisfaction.

Although the use of per diem rates in estimating costs of community care is almost always problematic, it is important to remember that per diem rates and other rates of reimbursement play important roles in the delivery of foster family care. Recent research has confirmed that such rates and economic incentives do indeed influence the amount of foster care services that foster parents provide (Campbell & Downs, 1987). If the rates of reimbursement for foster family care underestimate the actual costs of care, then the level and quality of services are likely to be similarly reduced. Equally important, this failure to address the true added costs of care for foster or natural families provides a powerful financial incentive to reduce such options and to increase pressures to utilize more costly and less normative alternatives.

FACTORS ACCOUNTING FOR COST DIFFERENCES

Research on the cost of residential alternatives for people with developmental disabilities is at about the same point of development that cost analysis of nursing homes was almost two decades ago (Greenberg et al., 1985). Since the early 1970s, many carefully constructed studies have been developed to investigate the factors that cause variations in the cost of long-term care for older persons in different residential arrangements and facilities (Bishop, 1980). In contrast, within the area of developmental disabilities, only a few studies have employed adequate research designs (Jones et al., 1984) or appropriate multivariate statistical techniques, with estimated cost functions to explain variations in costs for persons with varying levels of disabilities in different types of facilities (Ashbaugh & Allard, 1984; Ashbaugh & Nerney, 1990; Greenberg et al., 1985; Heal et al., 1989; Lakin et al., in press; Nerney et al., 1991; Wieck & Bruininks, 1980). There appear to be two different types of factors that account for most differences in costs between residential alternatives for individuals with developmental disabilities. These are: 1) variations in facility and resident characteristics, and 2) the likely underutilization of needed services in community settings.

Variations in Facility and Resident Characteristics

Variations in facility and resident characteristics in residential facilities account for most of the difference in average costs and resource usage among such facilities. Characteristics with positive relationships to the costs of services include: 1) the type of facility, 2) the needs and disabilities of residents, 3) wage rate differences between facility types and programs, 4) the size of the residential facility, 5) requirements for governmental certification, 6) quality of care, 7) private ownership and provision of services, and 8) regional variations in resource prices and associated costs. When cost functions relating to residential facilities for individuals with developmental disabilities were properly specified with these variable dimensions, it was possible to estimate and explain 74% (Greenberg et al., 1985) to 76% (Johnes & Haycox, 1986) of the average variation in the costs of residential care.

Type of Residential Facility Almost all of the reviewed cost studies focused on and attempted to estimate cost differences between types of residential facilities for individuals with mental retardation and developmental disabilities. Although most of these comparisons were between state-operated facilities and smaller community-based group homes, several investigators focused exclusively on community residences. Some researchers have argued that there is "incontrovertible evidence that institutions are inherently more expensive than community services" (Heal & Daniels, 1986, p. 137). Others have concluded that "since firm generalizations on relative cost may be impossible in the face of a multiplicity of community types and program parameters, the most significant result of the research to date may be the identification of factors which determine program costs" (Kotler et al., 1985, p. II–10). Several studies in public health have similarly concluded that expanding publicly financed community-based care, as compared to nursing home care, does not necessarily result in cost savings and, in many cases, it is likely to result in increased costs (Yeatts, Capitman, & Steinhardt, 1987). As Fujiura (1988) has correctly pointed out, "it is not clear whether the cost differences reflect greater economy in the community based facilities or fundamental differences in service type due to selection factors in the placement of residents" (p. 229).

The literature clearly documents differences in service costs by type of facility, from a high level of resources expended for larger publicly operated programs to substantially lower levels of resources in support of foster care and family support models. These trends are militated, however, by a number of factors that contribute to service costs that are covariant with facility types, including the needs and disabilities of residents, differential compensation rates for employees, widely varying service provision and usage patterns, certification requirements, and other factors.

Needs and Disabilities of Residents On the basis of cost information collected from a national survey of public and private residential facilities, researchers concluded that, while costs for nonpersonnel items were similar among differing types of facilities, there were major differences in personnel costs between residential settings (Wieck & Bruininks, 1980). The researchers reported that most of these differences in personnel costs were due to substantial differences in the number and types of labor intensive services, which, in turn, were related to the levels of disability in the populations being served. In a related study employing the same data set, others estimated that less than 2% of the variance in costs for residential care can be attributed to facility type when other facility and resident characteristics are appropriately controlled (Heal et al., 1989). In a national survey on residential facilities, researchers reported similar conclusions from their estimated cost functions (Greenberg et al., 1985). One of their most important findings was that variations in costs did not necessarily result from facility types, but rather from the levels of services provided and levels of disability of the residents served in various programs.

A recent cost function study examined factors related to the cost of several types of residential services in South Dakota (Campbell & Heal, 1992). This study used detailed data from nearly 1,700 persons with developmental disabilities. Using a series of regression analyses, a variety of predictors (e.g., service location, agency characteristics, client behavioral characteristics, and service funding classification) were used to assess relationships to total public reimbursement of services. The best single predictor of reimbursement rate was a combined measure of the client's adaptive and maladaptive behaviors that was derived using a service score from the *Inventory for Client and Agency Planning* (Bruininks et al., 1986). Significant statistical relationships were also found between costs and facility type, public versus private ownership, total numbers served, and size and unemployment rate of the community. These relationships were found for small ICFs/MR and home and community-based services, but not for state-funded community training services.

Wage Rate Differences It is important to note that the largest cost component of most residential and related services is the cost of the personnel providing these services, generally about 57%–85% of operating costs. Cost differentials related to the use of such personnel can come about in several ways. They may result from: 1) different intensities of staffing (e.g., employment of live-in staff as compared with shift staff, or different ratios of different care staff to numbers of clients); 2) different ways of delivering the service (e.g., employment of paraprofessionals versus professionals, or use of community-based medical clinics as opposed to having medical personnel on staff); or 3) different rates of pay for the same role or skill requirements. In all studies that focused on large publicly owned institutions, average staff pay and direct care staff ratios were found to account for some of the largest variations in costs in such institutions (Greenberg et al., 1985; Lakin et al., in press; Wieck & Bruininks, 1980).

Several studies have questioned whether the general perception that community-based programs have lower average costs when compared to institutional programs might be misleading because a large component in the lower reported costs is frequently a lower wage structure in private settings. Although Ashbaugh and Allard (1984) reported that community-based programs serving people who formerly lived at a state-operated institution were less costly on average than the programs at the institution in terms of most typical cost measures, they also noted that between 80% and 90% of the cost differential could be traced almost entirely to differences in salaries and fringe benefits between state employees and the private employees. Other studies similarly concluded that the perceived cost advantage of community-based care appeared to be due in large measure to lower effective wage rates (Ashbaugh & Nerney, 1990; Kotler et al., 1985; Walsh, 1982). Unfortunately, no consideration was given in these other studies as to whether some of these lower wage rates might have resulted from the greater use of differentiated staffing models in community settings.

It also has been suggested that lower wage rates in community facilities have contributed directly to a high turnover of direct care staff and contributed to a lower quality of care in such facilities. Findings on staff turnover are especially evident in private facilities, where the rate of turnover is almost three times higher than in public institutions (Larson & Lakin, 1992; see also Mitchell & Braddock, chap. 12, this volume). These rates of turnover are frequently linked to lower wage rates or the attraction of jobs with higher compensation.

Size of Facility Although issues of scale and economies of size are frequently addressed in the generic cost evaluation literature, surprisingly few studies have directly examined these dimensions with respect to the cost of services for persons with developmental disabilities. Both the theoretical and empirical literature in other institutional settings would suggest that there is likely to be a

U-shaped cost curve relative to size or scale of residential facilities (Bishop, 1980; Dor, 1989). It is believed that as size increases, certain fixed costs can be spread over a larger population, resulting in a decline in average costs to a certain point. Beyond this point (or size range), average costs are likely to increase. It is not known whether this frequently documented relationship in health care facilities applies to the cost and organization of service programs for persons with developmental disabilities, where the central issue is habilitation and support versus only health care.

When Greenberg and his colleagues (1985) examined this issue with national data, they found that there were economies of scale to a certain point in size, with the smallest and largest facilities being most costly. It is important to note, however, that both family and foster care homes were excluded from their analyses. When examining the literature on this issue, others have given mixed reviews to the possible existence of such economies of scale in residential care facilities. One study, for example, found smaller group homes serving 6–10 residents to be twice as expensive as larger group homes serving 21–40 residents (Baker et al., 1977). Others found a natural U-shaped average cost schedule when examining the size of hospital wards for persons with mental retardation (Johnes & Haycox, 1986). In addition, size was found to be significant and inversely correlated with average daily costs in a recent national survey of large state-operated institutions (Lakin et al., in press). Some researchers who examined this issue, however, found that larger facilities showed consistent diseconomies of scale in both the private and public sectors (Heal et al., 1989). Still other researchers report a slight cost advantage to smaller settings for populations with developmental disabilities wherein staff might be expected to perform many different labor functions as contrasted to larger settings where the employment of specialists is standard and labor time may be underutilized (Conroy & Bradley, 1985).

In summary, it appears that the literature produces confusing results on the issue of cost, size, and economies of scale. Conventional wisdom would suggest that larger units, whether physical or organizational, would consume less per capita revenues. Extant studies, however, have not directly examined this issue with the full range of possible options (e.g., family-scale independent living to larger scale congregate living), alternative organizational support strategies, or comparable populations.

Requirements for Governmental Certification of Facility The resource requirements to meet standards for governmental certification and funding of ICFs/MR facilities undoubtedly influence costs as they have in nursing homes for elderly citizens (Bishop, 1980; Jarrett, 1982; Palmer & Cotterill, 1983). The medical orientation of the regulations and standards for physical facilities have been noted as especially problematic for community settings in several studies (Conroy & Bradley, 1985; O'Neill et al., 1990; Taylor, McCord, & Searl, 1981). In two studies where variations in client services were at least statistically controlled, it was clearly noted that, on the average, certified ICF/MR programs cost more per client day than non–ICF/MR programs (Ashbaugh & Allard, 1984; Greenberg et al., 1985). Nevertheless, this still could be accounted for by *quality* of care differences among programs, or relevant *intensity of services*. Few of the studies attempted to measure or control for these very important dimensions. In terms of quality of care, there is growing sentiment and evidence that relatively smaller, often higher cost, facilities tend to be associated with better habilitative outcomes (Lakin et al., 1989). In the Pennhurst follow-up cost study, it was reported that very substantial differences can exist in quality of care even when costs are similar (Ashbaugh & Allard, 1984). In their final report on the Pennhurst study, Conroy and Bradley (1985) make several strong recommendations for relaxing ICF/MR regulations for purposes of both cost savings and improved program quality within community-based residential alternatives.

Quality of Care   Although often expressed as a concern in the developmental disabilities literature, no cost studies have directly addressed quality of care as a measured and controlled dimension of costs. Several cost studies have measured dimensions of effectiveness, but none of these directly examined the issue of qualitative differences in service components (Dunaway et al., 1992; Heal & Daniels, 1986; Jones et al., 1984; Murphy & Datel, 1976). Heal and Daniels (1986) came close to examining this issue when they related residents' satisfaction to measures of cost in several different community settings. Their results indicated that higher domiciliary costs were associated with lower satisfaction with residential arrangements and care. Dunaway and her colleagues (1992) indirectly examined the relationship between costs and satisfaction by noting that those individuals in their study who were overserved were more likely to report dissatisfaction than those who were underserved.

Private Ownership   Cost studies in other fields have revealed that the cost of residential care varies significantly by type of ownership (Birnbaum, Bishop, Lee, & Jensen, 1981; Bishop, 1980). Only two studies that focused on residential facilities for persons with developmental disabilities have directly examined the cost effects of public facilities as compared to private ownership (Greenberg et al., 1985; Heal et al., 1989). While statistically controlling for the proportion of residents with selected characteristics, both studies found that governmentally certified facilities, particularly those with an ICF/MR designation, were significantly more expensive than any other form of ownership.

Although it is possible that the profit incentive has encouraged for-profit operators to be more efficient so that they deliver similar services with fewer or lower priced resources, it is also possible that private facilities serve different clients or provide different services. It is important not to draw firm conclusions from these results because the variable descriptors may be confounded by differences in wage rates, location, and quality of services, and by selection bias and types and levels of disabilities in residents. Even though it is clearly beneficial to use statistical controls for these factors, it is highly likely that the joint operation of these factors still differentially influences costs of service beyond what can be controlled through such adjustments.

Regional Variations   Cost studies in other fields have routinely found that the average cost of residential care varies significantly across the nation and among regions within states. Most of these studies have concluded that such regional variations are accounted for by variations in resource prices (most notably wage rates and construction costs). This was also found to be true in national surveys of nursing home costs (Bishop, 1980). Four comparative cost studies on residential facilities and services for persons with developmental disabilities were directly attentive to this issue of regional variations in resource prices, and all found that regional differences were a significant factor in the variation of service costs (Greenberg et al., 1985; Heal et al., 1989; Lakin et al., in press; Weick & Bruininks, 1980).

Underutilization of Community Services

The possibility that many needed services in community settings are often underutilized may also account for differences in costs when comparing across residential settings. Several controlled studies (Conroy & Bradley, 1985; Nihira et al., 1979) have indicated that the costs of services to persons with developmental disabilities in state institutions do not differ significantly from the adjusted (i.e., generically supplemented or privately funded) costs of services in community settings, *if* the community-based clients receive a full array of comparable and needed services. Mayeda and Wai (1975) similarly argued that if clients in both community and institutional settings were provided comprehensive services, "the costs of services to developmentally disabled persons in state hospitals would not differ significantly from the adjusted, true costs of services in community settings" (p. 4). Equally important, another cost study has shown that the "service utilization patterns in community settings are lower than utilization patterns of services in state institutions" for individuals with similar disabilities (Nihira et al., 1979, p. 7).

Although largely unexamined in the cost literature, research by others indicates that these lower utilization patterns may be due to: 1) the lack of information concerning the availability of services on the part of residents or providers in the community (Shoultz & Racino, 1988); 2) diffused responsibility in the community that is reflected in weak coordination of community-based services to the client (Woodsmall, 1987); 3) differences in eligibility and repayment criteria and policies of funding agencies (Burwell, 1988); or 4) barriers within the medical service delivery system itself (Buehler, Menolascino, & Stark, 1986; Hayden & DePaepe, 1991).

There is evidence that shows that individuals in institutions receive more medical services than their counterparts who live in the community (Nihira et al., 1979). One study that examined Medicaid costs for acute care for individuals with developmental disabilities reported that community-based recipients averaged more per day in costs than recipients in ICFs/MR (Lakin, Burwell, et al., 1992). These researchers, however, noted that part of this difference was attributable to ICF/MR residents, particularly those in larger facilities, having access to acute care services as part of their basic ICF/MR reimbursement rate.

It is unclear as to whether the medical conditions of persons who reside in institutions are more serious and, thus, require more frequent medical care and monitoring, than are those of their peers who live in the community (Hayden &

DePaepe, 1991). Differences can be attributed to "administrative procedures" (Silverman et al., 1984), regulatory practices, or to the organizational differences in the service delivery models utilized in those facilities (Lakin, Anderson, Hill, Bruininks, & Wright, 1991). The higher service intensity in larger institutional settings may derive from the same regimentation and routinization of services as is alleged in the treatment of individuals. Everybody within the institution receives the same full set of services of pre-established frequency, whether they need them or not, from an institutionalized service delivery system that is designed primarily around discipline-based service delivery staffing patterns and ratios.

CONCLUSION

As noted in the beginning of this chapter, the recent deinstitutionalization of individuals with developmental disabilities from large state institutions to community living alternatives has given rise to the need for reliable cost information relative to new patterns of public services and expenditures. Unfortunately, the current literature on service costs is largely inadequate for rational policy development and decision making. Almost all of the extant studies exhibit methodological problems of either selection bias or cost accounting and do not address the central policy issue of efficiency through linking costs with outcomes.

A review of the literature indicates that future cost studies in the field need to more carefully control for possible selection bias in their sample selections, examine community-based services through a comprehensive set of taxonomies that identify all functional service areas and their measurable service dimensions, and do a more effective job of linking costs with outcome effects to examine the central policy issue of cost-effectiveness of preferred service alternatives. In spite of the recent spate of cost and outcome studies, we still have little empirical data that directly tells us which alternatives might be most efficient and provide the best results for people with developmental disabilities in the use of society's resources.

Our review of these studies and the related cost literature indicates that two major factors account for most perceived cost differences between residential alternatives for individuals with mental retardation: 1) variations in facility and resident characteristics, and 2) the differential use of services in community settings. Evidence in several studies indicates, for example, that when cost functions have been properly specified, with appropriately measured variations in their facility and resident characteristics, it is possible to estimate and explain more than three-fourths of the average variance in costs. Accordingly, it is still possible to draw some tentative conclusions about the costs of community-based residential care and other services that have relevance to policymakers.

The extant literature, for example, indicates that gains in personal development accrue more rapidly for individuals with developmental disabilities when they live in community settings rather than in institutions. We also know that the average costs of residential care in institutions are at least as expensive as those in community settings. From these findings, it can be inferred with some confidence that deinstitutionalization and placement of individuals with developmental disabilities in community settings is a rational economic and social policy that leads to greater efficiency in the use of society's resources. Although only one study in the entire literature we reviewed adequately addressed this issue of cost-effectiveness (Jones et al., 1984), a composite of all other cost and outcome studies does permit us to draw this conclusion.

The existing research also suggests several other findings that have importance to policymakers. The requirements of governmental certification and public ownership of residential facilities appear to adversely affect costs, perhaps in ways that are not entirely consistent with the needs of persons served by such programs. Both of these issues, however, are so confounded by their unknown effects on service quality that firm conclusions cannot be made at this time. In spite of the problematic nature of most of the cost studies, we do know that most family home settings, including both natural and foster families, are being underserved with services and materially underreimbursed for the full costs of those services being rendered. We also know that the most important explanations for variations in the costs of residential care result not so much from facility type, but rather from levels of services provided and levels of disability in the residents served, and from the public policies of states with respect to rates of pay for public employees. An examination of unnecessary regulatory requirements, particularly in community programs, would aid in the development of strategies to increase efficiency and quality of service. The lowering of overhead costs is obviously an area of some priority for the restructuring of public services in this decade (Osborne & Gaebler, 1992).

The normal progression of studies in evaluating the implementation of public policies is generally from that of normative-descriptive to an explanation of relationships and, finally, to assessment of outcomes in relationship to strategies and models of innovation. The literature on the costs and outcomes of residential and related services appears to be following a similar developmental course. The future of research investment in this area, therefore, would benefit from the application of strategies that combine the methodologies of good cost analysis with evaluation of outcomes that reflect achievement of policy goals to improve the efficiency, appropriateness, and quality of life for persons with developmental disabilities. Over the next decade, the current policy environment and policy needs will require combined attention to the economics of services, to the decentralization and normalization of services, and to the achievement of results (Osborne & Gaebler, 1992).

As these combined efforts are undertaken, researchers will need to be more attentive to estimating costs through a more refined resource components approach. This accounting framework focuses on the type and amount of resources that are employed in the delivery of programs, rather than exclusively on the budget categories, expenditure records, or per diem rates of an agency or target population. Only by focusing on the actual use of resources in program and service areas is it possible to get an accurate accounting of the costs of each program or of services to individuals. This approach requires the listing of a comprehensive set of the functional activities and services provided through programs or to individuals and the identification, measurement, and valuation of the specific resources employed in each functional area and service area in order to determine costs to either programs or individuals. Details on this cost methodology, along with procedures for using the cost accounting framework, are presented and illustrated in several recent sources (Lewis, Bruininks, & Thurlow, 1989; Lewis, Johnson, Bruininks, et al., 1992).

Multiattribute evaluation techniques, along with cost estimates, have been employed in the management sciences for a number of years as a means of structuring evaluation decisions for selecting alternatives with multiple outcomes (Carroll & Johnson, 1990; Edwards & Newman, 1982; Keeney & Raiffa, 1976; Poole & DeSanctis, 1990). This approach has been used extensively in the private sector, in assessing social programs, and especially in the fields of public health (Kaplan, Atkins, & Wilson, 1988); criminal justice (Edwards, 1980); education (Lewis, 1989); and special education (Lewis, Johnson, Erickson, & Bruininks, 1992). The multidimensional nature of goals and the multiple number of stakeholders who are serving individuals with developmental disabilities in communities requires the unique methods and procedures of multiattribute evaluation techniques.

In simplest terms, a multiattribute evaluation process structures the decision process for a group of stakeholders to make judgments about identifying outcomes that measure effectiveness, weight the importance of these indicators, and rank the alternatives. It requires a comparison of two or more alternatives against two or more criteria. These criteria also may have several different dimensions (i.e., measurable attributes) that need to be identified. After importance weights are attached to each of the criteria and attributes, measured dimensions of each attribute are then assigned utility values for varying degrees of performance. Based on the measured performance of each attribute (either through actual measured performance or judgments about performance) within each alternative, utility scores are then computed and attached to each of the attributes. These attribute values are then multiplied by their importance weights and summed to derive a composite score for each alternative. If cost data are available and cost is not one of the criteria or attributes in the evaluation model, cost per unit of utility can be estimated for determining the relative cost-effectiveness or cost-utility of each alternative. Such modeling and policy analysis is a logical and needed next step in the evaluation of community services so that resource usage patterns can be more directly linked to assessment of policy goals and service alternatives to ensure quality of services for persons with developmental disabilities and their families.

The study of resource use is relatively recent in the evaluation of educational and social services. It is even less evident in the disability studies literature. With increasing public concern about the investment of limited public resources, pressures will invariably increase to assess the extent to which tax dollars and private contributions produce intended policy results and benefits for individuals. Even with its limitations, the literature on the costs of residential services supports the directions of decentralization, small family-scale service models, and integration into community settings. The measurement of costs, however, is only one aspect of evaluating the direction, progress, and impact of public policies. The quest for improved quality of life depends *both* on the prudent use of resources and on the achievement of outcomes deserved by citizens with developmental disabilities and their families. It is time to direct future analyses on the use of public and private resources to the consideration and achievement of both efficiency and results.

REFERENCES

Amado, A.N., Lakin, K.C., & Menke, J.M. (1990). *1990 chartbook on services for people with developmental disabilities*. Minneapolis: University of Minnesota, Center for Residential Living and Community Services.

Anderson, D.J., Lakin, K.C., Bruininks, R.H., & Hill, B.K. (1987). *A national study of residential and support services for elderly persons with mental retardation*. Minneapolis: University of Minnesota, Center for Residential Living and Community Services.

Arkana, M.L., & Mueller, D.N. (1978). Components of foster care for handicapped children. *Child Welfare, 57*(6), 339–345.

Ashbaugh, J., & Allard, M.A. (1984). *Comparative analyses of the cost of residential, day and other programs within institutional and community settings*. Boston: Human Services Research Institute.

Ashbaugh, J., & Nerney, T. (1990). Costs of providing residential and related support services to individuals with mental retardation. *Mental Retardation, 28*, 269–273.

Baker, B., Seltzer, G., & Seltzer, M. (1977). *As close as possible: Community residences for retarded adults*. Boston: Little, Brown.

Baldwin, S. (1985). *The costs of caring: Families with disabled children*. Boston: Routledge and Kegan Paul.

Bensberg, G.J., & Smith, J.J. (1984). Comparative costs of public residential and community residential facilities for the mentally retarded. *Education and Training of the Mentally Retarded, 19*.

Benz, M., & Agosta, J. (1982). An examination of research on cost-effectiveness. In J. Agosta, M. Benz, M. Bullis, J. Carter, A. Neulicht, & E. Thorin (Eds.), *Deinstitutionalization of persons with mental retardation: An analysis of the research literature (1965–1981)*. Eugene: University of Oregon, Rehabilitation Research and Training Center on Mental Retardation.

Bersani, H.A., Jr., Caruso, G., & Knoll, J.A. (1987). *Research on the economics of residential services in mental retardation and related fields: An annotated bibliography*. Syracuse, NY: Syracuse University, Research and Training Center on Community Integration, Center on Human Policy.

Birnbaum, H., Bishop, C., Lee, A., & Jensen, G. (1981). Why do nursing home costs vary? The determinants of nursing home costs. *Medical Care, 19*(11), 1095–1107.

Bishop, C. (1980). Nursing home cost studies and reimbursement issues. *Health Care Financing Review*, Spring, 47–64.

Boggs, E.M. (1979). Economic factors in family care. In R.H. Bruininks & G. Krantz (Eds.), *Family care of developmentally disabled members* (pp. 47–60). Minneapolis: University of Minnesota.

Braddock, D., Hemp, R., Fujiura, G., Bachelder, L., & Mitchell, D. (1990). *The state of the states in developmental disabilities*. Baltimore: Paul H. Brookes Publishing Co.

Braun, K.L., & Rose, C.L. (1987). Geriatric patient outcomes and costs in three settings: Nursing home, foster family and own home. *Journal of American Geriatric Society, 35*(5), 387–397.

Bruininks, R.H., Hill, B.K., Weatherman, R.F., & Woodcock, R.W. (1986). *ICAP: Inventory for client and agency planning*. Allen, Texas: DLM Teaching Resources.

Buehler, B.A., Menolascino, F.J., & Stark, J.A. (1986). Medical care of individuals with developmental disabilities. In W.E. Kiernan & J.A. Stark (Eds.), *Pathways to employment for adults with developmental disabilities* (pp. 241–249). Baltimore: Paul H. Brookes Publishing Co.

Burwell, B.O. (1988). *The Maryland Medicaid waiver program for persons with disabilities: A case study* (Working paper I.13). Lexington, MA: Health Care Financing Administration.

Campbell, C., & Downs, S.W. (1987). The impact of economic incentives on foster parents. *Social Service Review, 8*, 599–609.

Campbell, E.M., & Heal, L.W. (1992). *The effects of client and provider characteristics on the cost to state and federal governments of providing services for developmentally disabled people*. Pierre: South Dakota Division of Developmental Disabilities.

Campbell, E.M., & Smith, G.A. (1989). *Predictors of service costs for people with developmental disabilities*. Paper presented at the Pacific Rim Conference on Quality of Life for Persons with Disabilities, Honolulu, Hawaii.

Carroll, J., & Johnson, E. (1990). *Decision research: A field guide*. London: Sage.

Castellani, P.J., Downey, N.A., Tausig, M.B., & Bird, W.A. (1986). Availability and accessibility of family support services. *Mental Retardation, 24*(1), 71–79.

Chetwynd, J. (1985). Some costs of caring at home for an intellectually handicapped child. *Australia and New Zealand Journal of Developmental Disabilities, 11*(1), 35–40.

Conroy, J., & Bradley, V. (1985). *The Pennhurst longitudinal study: A study of five years of research and analysis*. Philadelphia: Temple University Developmental Disabilities Center.

Davis, S. (1987). *National status report on waiting lists of people with mental retardation for community based services*. Arlington, TX: Association for Retarded Citizens-United States.

Dor, A. (1989). The costs of Medicare patients in nursing homes in the United States. *Journal of Health Economics, 8*, 253–270.

Dunaway, J., Granfield, J., Norton, K., & Greenspan, S. (1992). *Costs and benefits of privately-operated residential services for persons with mental retardation in Connecticut*. Storrs, CT: Pappanikou Center (UAP), University of Connecticut.

Edwards, W. (1980). Multiattribute utility for evaluation: Structures, uses and problems. In M. Klein & K. Teilmann (Eds.), *Handbook of criminal justice evaluation*. Beverly Hills, CA: Sage.

Edwards, W., & Newman, J. (1982). *Multiattribute evaluation*. Beverly Hills, CA: Sage.

Fujiura, G.T. (1988). Cost evaluation of residential alternatives. In L.W. Heal, J.I. Haney, & A.R. Novak Amado, (Eds.), *Integration of developmentally disabled individuals into the community* (pp. 227–243). Baltimore: Paul H. Brookes Publishing Co.

Greenberg, J.N., Lakin, K.C., Hill, B.K., Bruininks, R.H., & Hauber, F.A. (1985). Costs of residential care in the United States. In K.C. Lakin, B.K. Hill, & R.H. Bruininks (Eds.), *An analysis of Medicaid intermediate care facility for the mentally retarded (ICF-MR) program* (pp. 7:1–7:82). Minneapolis: University of Minnesota, Department of Educational Psychology.

Gunn, P., & Berry, P. (1987). Some financial costs of caring for children with Down syndrome at home. *Australia and New Zealand Journal of Developmental Disabilities, 13*(4), 187–193.

Hauber, F.A., Bruininks, R.H., Hill, B.K., Lakin, K.C., Scheerenberger, R.C., & White, C.C. (1984). National census of residential facilities: A 1982 profile of facilities and residents. *American Journal of Mental Deficiency, 89*, 236–245.

Hayden, M.F. (1992). Adults with mental retardation and other developmental disabilities waiting for community-based services in the U.S. *Policy Research Brief, 4*(3), 1–16.

Hayden, M.F., & DePaepe, P.A. (1991). Medical conditions, level of care needs, and health-related outcomes of persons with mental retardation: A review. *Journal of The Association of Persons with Severe Handicaps, 16*, 188–206.

Heal, L.W., Copher, J.I., Wieck, C.A., & Bruininks, R.H. (1989, May). *Predictors of home care cost for public and private residential facilities in the United States.* Paper presented at the annual meeting of the American Association on Mental Retardation, Chicago, Illinois.

Heal, L.W., & Daniels, B.S. (1986). A cost effectiveness analysis of residential alternatives. *Mental Retardation Systems, 3*, 35–49.

Heal, L.W., & Fujiura, G. (1984). Methodological considerations in research on residential alternatives for developmentally disabled persons. *International Review of Research in Mental Retardation, 12*, 205–244.

Heal, L.W., Sigelman, C.K., & Switzky, H.N. (1980). Research on community residential alternatives for the mentally retarded. In R.J. Flynn & K.E. Nitsch (Eds.), *Normalization, social integration, and community services* (pp. 215–258). Baltimore: University Park Press.

Hill, B.K., & Lakin, K.C. (1986). Classification of residential facilities for individuals with mental retardation. *Mental Retardation, 24*(2), 107–115.

Hill, B.K., Lakin, K.C., & Bruininks, R.H. (1984). Trends in residential services for people who are mentally retarded. *Journal of The Association for the Severely Handicapped 9*(4), 243–250.

Hill, B.K., Lakin, K.C., Bruininks, R.H., Amado, A.N., Anderson, D.J., & Copher, J.I. (1989). *Living in the community: A comparative study of foster homes and small group homes for people with mental retardation* (Report No. 28). Minneapolis: University of Minnesota, Center for Residential and Community Services.

Hyman, M. (1977). *The extra costs of disabled living.* London: National Fund for Research into Crippling Diseases and Disablement Income Group.

Intagliata, J.C., Willer, B.S., & Cooley, F.B. (1979). Cost comparison of institutional and community based alternatives for mentally retarded persons. *Mental Retardation, 17*, 154–156.

Jacobs, P., & McDermott, S. (1989). Family caregiver costs of chronically ill and handicapped children: Method and literature review. *Public Health Reports, 104*(2), 158–163.

Jarrett, J.E. (1982). The relationship of cost variation, prospective rate setting and quality of care in nursing homes: A hedonic examination. *Review of Business and Economic Research, 17*(2), 67–77.

Johnes, G., & Haycox, A. (1986). Cost structures in a large hospital for the mentally handicapped. *Social Science and Medicine, 22*(6), 605–610.

Jones, P.A., Conroy, J.W., Feinstein, C.W., & Lemanowicz, J.F. (1984). A matched comparison study of cost-effectiveness: Institutionalized and deinstitutionalized people. *Journal of The Association for Persons with Severe Handicaps, 9*, 304–313.

Kaplan, R., Atkins, C., & Wilson, D. (1988). The cost utility of diet and exercise interventions in non–insulin-dependent diabetes mellitus. *Health Promotion, 2*, 331–340.

Keeney, R., & Raiffa, H. (1976). *Decisions with multiple objectives: Preferences and value tradeoffs.* New York: Wiley.

Kerachsky, S., Thornton, C., Bloomenthal, A., Maynard, R., & Stephens, S. (1985). *Impacts of transitional employment on mentally retarded young adults: Results of the STETS demonstration.* Princeton: Mathematica Policy Research, Inc.

Knoll, J., & Bersani, H. (1989). *A comparison of the costs of supporting children with severe disabilities in family and group care settings.* Syracuse, NY: Syracuse University, Research and Training Center on Community Integration.

Kotler, M., Wright, G., Jaskulski, T., & Kreisberg, I. (1985). *Synthesis of cost studies on the long term care of health impaired elderly and other disabled persons.* Washington, DC: Macrosystems, Inc.

Krauss, M.C., & Seltzer, M.M. (1986). Comparison of elderly and adult mentally retarded persons in community and institutional settings. *American Journal of Mental Deficiency*, *91*, 237–243.

Lakin, K.C., Anderson, D.J., Hill, B.K., Bruininks, R.H., & Wright, E.A. (1991). Programs and services received by older persons with mental retardation. *Mental Retardation*, *29*(2), 65–74.

Lakin, K.C., Bruininks, R.H., & Larson, S.A. (1992). The changing face of residential services. In L. Rowitz (Ed.), *Mental retardation in the year 2000*. New York: Springer-Verlag.

Lakin, K.C., Burwell, B.O., Hayden, M.F., & Jackson, M.R. (1992). *An independent assessment of Minnesota's Medicaid home and community based services waiver program* (Project Report No. 37). Minneapolis: University of Minnesota, Institute on Community Integration.

Lakin, K.C., Hill, B.K., & Bruininks, R.H. (Eds.). (1985). *An analysis of Medicaid's intermediate care facility for the mentally retarded (ICF/MR) program*. Minneapolis: University of Minnesota, Center for Residential and Community Services.

Lakin, K.C., Hill, B.K., Street, H., & Bruininks, R.H. (1986). *Persons with mental retardation in state-operated residential facilities*. Minneapolis: University of Minnesota, Center for Residential and Community Services.

Lakin, K.C., Jaskulski, T.M., Hill, B.K., Bruininks, R.H., Menke, J.M., White, C.C., & Wright, E.A. (1989). *Medical services for persons with mental retardation and related conditions*. Minneapolis: University of Minnesota, Institute on Community Integration.

Lakin, K.C., Kimm, C., & Li, X. (in press). The costs of state institutions in the United States and factors associated with variability. *Journal of Disability Studies*.

Landesman, S. (1986). Toward a taxonomy of home environments. *International Review of Research in Mental Retardation*, *14*, 259–289.

Larson, S.A., & Lakin, K.C. (1991). Deinstitutionalization of persons with mental retardation: Behavioral outcomes. *Journal of The Association for Persons with Severe Handicaps*, *14*, 324–332.

Larson, S.A., & Lakin, K.C. (1992). Direct-care staff stability in a national sample of small group homes. *Mental Retardation*, *30*, 13–22.

Lewis, D. (1989). Use of cost-utility decision models in business education. *Journal of Education in Business*, *64*, 275–278.

Lewis, D., Bruininks, R., & Thurlow, M. (1989). Cost analysis for district level special education planning, budgeting, and administrating. *Journal of Education Finance*, *14*(4), 466–483.

Lewis, D., Bruininks, R., Thurlow, M., & McGrew, K. (1988). Using benefit-cost analysis in special education. *Exceptional Children*, *55*, 203–214.

Lewis, D., Johnson, D., Bruininks, R., Kallsen, L., & Guillery, R. (1992). Is supported employment cost-effective in Minnesota? *Journal of Disability Policy Studies*, *3*(1), 67–92.

Lewis, D., Johnson, D., Erickson, R., & Bruininks, R. (1992). *Linking costs to multiattribute outcomes in special education*. Minneapolis: University of Minnesota, Institute on Community Integration.

Mayeda, T., & Wai, F. (1975). *The cost of long term developmental disabilities care*. Los Angeles: University of California-Los Angeles, Neuropsychiatric Institute.

Minnesota Department of Administration. (1991). *Public expenditures for services to persons with developmental disabilities in Minnesota*. St. Paul, MN: Author.

Minnesota Department of Welfare. (1979). *Residential care study*. St. Paul, MN: Author.

Murphy, J.G., & Datel, W.E. (1976). A cost-benefit analysis of community versus institutional living. *Hospital and Community Psychiatry*, *27*, 163–176.

Nerney, T., Conley, R., & Nisbet, J. (1991). *A cost analysis of residential systems serving persons with severe disabilities: New directions in economic and policy research*. Cambridge, MA: Human Services Research Institute.

Nihira, L., Mayeda, T., & Eyman, R. (1979). *Costs for care of matched developmentally disabled clients in three settings.* Los Angeles: University of California-Los Angeles, Neuropsychiatric Institute, Research Group at Lanterman State Hospital.

Noble, J.H., & Conley, R. (1987). Accumulating evidence on the benefits and costs of supported and transitional employment for persons with severe disabilities. *Journal of The Association for Persons with Severe Handicaps, 12*, 163–174.

O'Connor, G., & Morris, L. (1978). *A research approach to cost analysis and program budgeting of community residential facilities.* Eugene: University of Oregon, Rehabilitation Research and Training Center on Mental Retardation.

O'Neill, J., Brown, M., Gordon, W., Orazem, J., Hoffman, C., & Schonhorn, R. (1990). Medicaid versus state funding of community residences: Impact on daily life of people with mental retardation. *Mental Retardation, 28*(3), 183–188.

Osborne, D., & Gaebler, T. (1992). *Reinventing government.* Reading, MA: Addison-Wesley.

Palmer, H.C., & Cotterill, P. (1983). Studies of nursing home costs. In R. Vogel & H. Palmer (Eds.), *Long-term care* (pp. 665–722). Washington, DC: Health Care Financing Administration.

Poole, M., & DeSanctis, G. (1990). Understanding the use of group decision support systems. In C. Steinfield & J. Fulk (Eds.), *Theoretical approaches to information technologies in organizations.* Beverly Hills, CA: Sage.

Rees, S., & Emerson, A. (1983). The costs of caring for disabled children at home. *Australian Rehabilitation Review, 7*, 26–31.

Rhodes, L., Ramsing, K., & Hill, M. (1987). Economic evaluation of employment services: A review of applications. *Journal of The Association for Persons with Severe Handicaps, 12*, 175–181.

Richard, D. (1983). Independent living: Cost-effective in Maine. *American Rehabilitation, 9*, 18–22.

Schalock, R.L. (1983). *Services for developmentally disabled adults.* Baltimore: University Park Press.

Scheerenberger, R.C. (1983). *Public residential services for the mentally retarded: 1982.* Madison, WI: National Association of Superintendents of Public Residential Facilities for the Mentally Retarded.

Shiell, A., & Wright, K. (1988). *Counting the costs of community care.* York, UK: University of York, Centre for Health Economics.

Schoultz, B., & Racino, J.A. (1988). *Supporting people with medical and physical needs in the community.* Syracuse, NY: Syracuse University, Center on Human Policy, Research and Training Center on Community Integration.

Silverman, W.P., Silver, E.J., Lubin, R.A., Zigman, W.B., Janicki, M.P., & Jacobson, J.W. (1984). Health status and community placement of people who are profoundly retarded and multiply disabled. In R. Antonek & J. Mulik (Eds.), *Transitions in mental retardation* (Vol. 3, pp. 108–124). Norwood, NJ: Ablex Publishing.

Taylor, S. (1988). Caught in the continuum: A critical analysis of the principle of the least restrictive environment. *Journal of The Association of Persons with Severe Handicaps, 13*(1), 41–53.

Taylor, S.J., McCord, W., & Searl, S.J. (1981). Medicaid dollars and community homes: The community ICF/MR controversy. *Journal of The Association for the Severely Handicapped, 6*, 59–64.

Templeman, D., Gage, M., & Fredericks, H. (1982). Cost effectiveness of the group home. *Journal of The Association for the Severely Handicapped, 6*, 11–16.

Touche Ross & Co. (1980). *Cost study of the community based mental retardation regions and the Beatrice State Development Center* (Report to the Nebraska Department of Public Institutions and Department of Public Welfare). Kansas City, MO: Author.

Walsh, T. (1979). Patient-related reimbursement for long-term care. In V. LaPorte & J. Rubin (Eds.), *Reform and regulation in long-term care* (pp. 153–167). New York: Praeger.

Walsh, T. (1982). The development of residential services in the 80s and beyond: The private sector perspective. *Training Quarterly on Developmental Disabilities*. Philadelphia: Temple University, Woodhaven Center and Developmental Disabilities Center.

White, C.C., Prouty, R.W., Lakin, K.C., & Blake, E.M. (1992). *Persons with mental retardation and related conditions in state-operated residential facilities: Year ending June 30, 1990 with longitudinal trends from 1950 to 1990.* Minneapolis: University of Minnesota, Center on Residential Services and Community Living, Institute on Community Integration.

Wieck, C.A., & Bruininks, R.H. (1980). *The cost of public and community residential care for mentally retarded people in the United States.* Minneapolis: University of Minnesota, Department of Educational Psychology.

Willer, B., & Intagliata, J. (1984). *Promises and realities for mentally retarded citizens: Life in the community.* Baltimore: University Park Press.

Woodsmall, E. (1987). *A study of medically involved developmental services clients in Florida.* Tallahassee, FL: Developmental Services Program Office, Department of Health and Rehabilitative Services.

Yeatts, D., Capitman, J., & Steinhardt, B. (1987). Evaluation of Connecticut's Medicaid community care waiver program. *The Gerontologist, 27*(5), 652–659.

Chapter 11

State Agency and Community Provider Perspectives on Financing Community Services

Richard Hemp

Together, community provider organizations and state governments plan for, establish, and maintain community services for persons with mental retardation and other developmental disabilities in local communities. This shared responsibility must be carried out in the context of multiple government and private sector funding sources and other resources, each with special requirements and limitations. In order to carry out this responsibility, a better understanding of creative ways to finance community services must be developed. This chapter attempts to document the financing approaches taken by states in an effort to move toward the ultimate goal of full community inclusion for all persons with disabilities. A wide variety of strategies and models for financing community living are explored at both the state and local levels, keeping in mind current and future

Preparation of this chapter was supported by a cooperative agreement (#H133B80048) between the National Institute on Disability and Rehabilitation Research (NIDRR); the Research and Training Center on Residential Services and Community Living, Institute on Community Integration (UAP), University of Minnesota (College of Education); and the University Affiliated Program in Developmental Disabilities at the University of Illinois at Chicago. The opinions expressed herein are those of the author.

Dr. Lynn Bachelder and Karen Haasen assisted in the surveys of state mental retardation/developmental disabilities agencies and community-based provider organizations. Dr. David Braddock provided overall guidance for the study. We gratefully acknowledge state agency and community organization leadership staff in the 20 states that shared valuable information for this report.

Community respondents were guaranteed confidentiality. Therefore, the quoted statements from community providers are referenced only in terms of the states in which they were located and their service or support classifications (e.g., a group home respondent in Iowa; a family support respondent in Maine). To parallel the references to community respondents, state agency respondents also were identified by the names of the states that they represented.

service priorities of state and community providers. In addition, the start-up and maintenance costs of the strategies and models employed are examined, along with recommendations for future programs.

The United States has experienced more than two decades of deinstitutionalization and increases in spending aimed at fostering the community inclusion of persons with mental retardation and other developmental disabilities. During this time, there has been great variation across the states in rates of institutional depopulation, total resource commitments to community alternatives, and relative contributions by various levels of government to the funding of community services (Braddock, Hemp, Fujiura, Bachelder, & Mitchell, 1990). The United States' overall institutional population declined between 1977 and 1988 by 39%. For example, Michigan's population alone declined 79%, while Arkansas and Tennessee saw declines of less than 5%, and Nevada experienced an increase of 51%.

Braddock and Fujiura (1987) note that "some states are addressing a given political objective such as mental retardation more vigorously than others" (p. 450). Bahl (1982) defined the measurement of fiscal performance, or fiscal effort, in state and local governments as an index predicated on relative, rather than absolute, values. Braddock et al. (1990) developed a fiscal effort ratio, expressed as developmental disabilities spending divided by state-wide personal income, for each state and for the United States as a whole. Fiscal effort, expressed in terms of 1988 community spending as a share of statewide personal income, consisted of an expenditure of $1.46 per $1,000 of personal income in the nation as a whole. Community fiscal effort levels, however, ranged from $4.08 in North Dakota to $.40 in Mississippi.

In addition to state variations in rates of deinstitutionalization and in fiscal effort devoted to community services, the levels of support that states obtained from federal, state or local governments and from individual federal programs varied greatly. In the United States, federal funding constituted 25% of the $5.637 billion spent on community services. However, state-by-state federal percentages ranged from 75% in South Dakota to 7% in Arizona. Local county and municipality funding contributed 12% of total national spending, with 6.2% in the form of required matches to Medicaid and other federal programs, and the remaining 5.8% consisting of local government overmatch funding. In the 22 states that employ match and overmatch dollars, Iowa received 48% from these local government sources compared to only 1% in North Carolina and North Dakota.

The efforts of states and service providers to develop and maintain community services have been impeded by several factors including limited funding (Gettings, 1977; National Association for Retarded Citizens, 1976; President's Committee on Mental Retardation, 1976); inferior wages and benefits and the resultant high turnover rates for community workers (Mitchell & Braddock, 1991); and governmental restrictions and disincentives (Boggs, Hanley-Maxwell, Lakin, & Bradley, 1988; General Accounting Office, 1977). There is also an institutional bias in federal reimbursements concerning intermediate care facilities for persons with mental retardation (ICFs/MR) (Braddock, 1987). Furthermore, as Lakin et al. (1989) reported, 38 out of 51 state mental retardation and developmental disabilities agencies supported Medicaid reform even though such legislation would cap the federal institutional ICF/MR reimbursements on which most states relied heavily. State institutions are "closed enterprises" benefiting from incremental federal, state, and local funding, while community-based "open systems" must utilize generic services and a number of public agencies (Smith & Aderman, 1987). Community service providers must therefore frequently employ creative strategies in order to maintain adequate funding (Allard, 1988; Copeland & Iversen, 1981).

Individualized, supported approaches to community living and employment for persons with disabilities are being developed in a growing number of states (Wright & King, 1991). These developments reflect a growing concern about established methods of service delivery and the models on which they are based. Smull (1989) has warned about a community crisis, which may result from state agencies' and community provider organizations' preoccupation with funding services when a support paradigm involving relatives, neighbors, and friends would be more appropriate. "A new social policy: disability services and supported community life" (Ferguson, Hibbard, Leinen, & Schaff, 1990, p. 16) has recently been proposed. This policy includes supported employment, community living, education, recreation, and services to families.

PURPOSE AND METHOD OF THE STUDY

In 1991, the University Affiliated Program (UAP) in Developmental Disabilities at the University of Illinois at Chicago conducted a survey of state mental retardation and developmental disabilities agencies and community-based provider organizations. The purpose of the study was to acquire a better understanding of the perspectives and experiences of these organizations in developing and financing community services. The following questions guided the development of the two survey instruments that provided the data that formed the basis of the study:

- Which models or strategies for financing community services have been most effective?
- What are the current and future community service priorities of states and providers?
- How have particular actions or policies of federal, state, or local governments affected the efforts of states and providers to develop and finance community services?

The Definition and Selection of Survey Respondents

State mental retardation and developmental disabilities agencies are the state government departments or divisions accountable for community service general fund appropriations. These state agencies are also responsible (sometimes jointly with other state agencies) for managing federal, state, and local government community service funds directed at meeting the needs of persons with mental retardation and other developmental disabilities, and their families. Community service providers contract with state mental retardation and developmental disabilities agencies through grants-in-aid or purchase-of-service arrangements and are directly responsible for the establishment and operation of community programs, services, and supports (Braddock et al., 1990).

The first step in the selection of survey respondents involved the development of a purposive sample of 20 states. States were identified on the basis of 1988 community fiscal effort rankings and the recommendations of a panel of experts in community service development. The panel recommended four states (Arizona, California, Georgia, and Illinois) because of their community living, employment, family support, or other community initiatives (Hemp, Braddock, Bachelder, & Haasen, 1990). The other 16 states (Colorado, Connecticut, Iowa, Maine, Massachusetts, Michigan, Minnesota, Nebraska, New Hampshire, New York, North Dakota, Ohio, Pennsylvania, Rhode Island, Vermont, and Wisconsin) ranked among the nation's top 20 states on the community fiscal effort index (Braddock et al., 1990).

As a second step, developmental disabilities councils, state mental retardation and developmental disabilities agencies, and the state Arc (Associations for Retarded Citizens) nominated a number of community providers to participate. Two of the three state-wide groups combined to nominate an additional 29 community providers and, in one state, all three combined to nominate a consumer-owned housing project. In all, there were 157 nominations for community provider participation in the study.

Survey Instruments,
Survey Administration, and Method of Analysis

One of the two survey instruments consisted of an outline for telephone interviews conducted with state mental retardation and developmental disabilities agency directors. The state directors were first asked to identify constraints against community programs inherent in the fiscal or other practices of the federal, state, or local governments, or of the private sector. The respondents were then asked to provide recommendations for the financing of community services at each of these levels of government and for the private sector. Finally, state directors were asked to outline successful strategies for community service development and list their two or three priorities for future development (Hemp et al., 1990). Project staff administered telephone interviews to the 20 state directors from October to December 1989.

The second survey instrument was mailed to the 157 nominated community provider organizations. Providers were first asked to identify sources of assistance for or constraints against program start-up. A second set of questions addressed assistance or constraints affecting the maintenance and operation of services and supports. In addressing these start-up and operations issues, the respondents were encouraged to focus on a specific service or support that they had recently developed, or that they intend to develop in the future. The third part of the survey for community providers sought examples of assistance or constraints associated with other factors in program development. The final portion sought their recommendations about developing and financing community services for persons with developmental disabilities.

Community respondents returned 33 mailed survey instruments between November 1989, and January 1991. In addition, project staff completed 60 telephone interviews. The 93 completed surveys represented a 59% rate of response. In addition to private nonprofit provider organizations, community respondents included state agencies operating community services or supports, larger organizations operating distinct mental retardation and developmental disabilities programs or supports, and for profit business ventures employing persons with disabilities.

Community organizations were classified according to 11 types of services or supports. These types included: 1) case management and life planning, 2) family support, 3) early intervention and integrated preschool, 4) group home, 5) affordable housing, 6) supported and individualized housing, 7) personal care assistant (PCA), 8) consumer-owned housing, 9) employment, 10) conversion from center-based services, and 11) self-advocacy.

The accounts of community providers were content analyzed and summarized. Project staff also classified providers' recommendations as most relevant to start-up, to ongoing maintenance of services, and to the missions and values of community provider organizations.

STATE MENTAL RETARDATION
AND DEVELOPMENTAL DISABILITIES
AGENCIES: EXPERIENCES AND RECOMMENDATIONS

Data from surveys returned by state agencies were first analyzed with respect to perceived constraints against community programs. The principal *federal* constraints reported were the restrictions, adverse interpretations, and institutional incentives inherent in the federal Medicaid program. Difficulties identified at the *state government* level consisted of insufficient funding, inappropriate or low reimbursement systems, and funding restrictions and interpretations. The primary constraints reported to exist at the *local government* level were insufficient funding, lack of community acceptance, and neighborhood zoning restrictions. Finally, in addressing the *private sector,* state agency respondents identified community provider opposition to integrated services and lack of provider participation as major factors having an impact on the provision of services. The responses of state directors regarding constraints, successful strategies, and priorities for future community service development were consolidated into 10 major recommendations (Hemp et al., 1990). These recommendations are summarized as follows in order of priority.

Funding Flexibility The director in the one state without a history of Medicaid programs (Arizona) stressed the importance of funding flexibility in the establishment of community services and supports for individuals with developmental disabilities. "The primary reason for innovation and individualized services in Arizona is that state general fund dollars are flexible, with a family and individual focus." The directors of agencies in all 20 states recommended Medicaid reform in one form or another. Six specifically recommended adoption of the Medicaid Home and Community Quality Services Act of 1989 (S. 384).

Increased Family Support Services State agency respondents were unanimous in recommending more services for families and in emphasizing the importance of recognizing families' competence in determining their own needs. In addition, it was stressed that government funding should more effectively complement natural supports from extended families, friends, and neighbors.

Increased Opportunities for Employment Respondents suggested that state agencies and community providers expand supported employment programs and better market the abilities of these workers to the private sector. In particular, state directors recognized the opportunity for government agencies to move beyond the role of provider and funding agent, and to more aggressively promote to business the benefits that can be realized from employing individuals with disabilities.

Improved Collaboration with Local Governments State directors identified the need for state government to provide more training and technical assistance to community providers. The need for officials at the local level to keep in touch with state and federal initiatives and innovative practices was also stressed. In states with strong county systems, respondents identified the need for all counties to understand and to support the state agency's philosophy and mission for community services.

Creative Use of Traditional Models A need for community residences for individuals with special behavior or physical needs, individuals involved with the criminal justice system, and persons with dual psychiatric and developmental disabilities diagnoses was viewed as an important priority. In addition, directors saw the need for more innovative approaches to staffing, such as the use of intermittent supervision and support.

Legislative Mandates for Community Services Directors from five states described the importance of mandated community funding. In other states, their counterparts described community mandates that, while not specifying community financing, nevertheless enhanced community service development.

Improved Collaboration with Community Service Providers The opposition of providers to integrated services, and lack of participation were identified by state agency heads as major private sector constraints. However, the state leaders were nearly unanimous in recognizing government's responsibility for improved funding and technical assistance to promote greater inclusion. Government support was viewed as especially important when community organizations underwent change from center-based models of service to more individualized supports for work and community living.

Development of Independent Case Management Services   At least one respondent recommended improvement in his state's case management system. It was recommended that case managers independently create individualized program plans by going outside the agency boundaries and, thereby, encouraging the development of necessary services and supports. Several states were identified as using Medicaid targeted case management to provide more individually focused service coordination.

Advocacy and Self-Advocacy   State agency directors recommended actively involving persons with disabilities and their families in the development of services and supports. Directors in two states commended coalitions of providers, state agencies, and advocacy groups. These collaborative state-wide efforts were seen as agents in improving and expanding community services and supports.

Federal/State Collaboration with Businesses and Local Communities   Respondents commended the efforts and positive responses of businesses, industries, and neighborhoods to increased community inclusion. State directors often reflected on the limitations that government programs place on developing and maintaining community services, and emphasized involving the private sector as a partner in community service development.

COMMUNITY PROVIDERS—EXPERIENCES

Community providers' survey responses were, to a large degree, consistent with the experiences and recommendations of the state directors who were surveyed. Concerns included federal program restrictions, problems with community acceptance, and inadequate funding. Providers also expanded on other issues introduced by state directors, especially the need for improved government technical assistance, problems with government regulations, and excessive paperwork. In addition, community providers discussed inadequate public and private interagency collaboration and the importance of employing better management techniques within their organizations.

Characteristics of the Respondent Organizations

The 93 responding organizations had annual budgets totalling more than $300 million. They served more than 30,000 individuals in nearly 2,000 different services or supports. Respondents' combined budgets consisted of state (58%), federal (24%), and local government (10%) funds as well as other funds, including donations, federal income maintenance, and fees (8%). Community respondents classified 44% of those served as having a severe disability. The age groups of those served were as follows: birth to 4 years (14%); 5–14 years (18%); 15–21 years (12%); 22–54 years (49%); and 55 years and older (7%).

Profiles of the Services and Supports Being Developed

Eleven categories of recently developed services and supports are listed in the following sections. Six respondents did not identify one specific service or support.

The five remaining respondents were: 1) one of the nation's first Centers for Independent Living, 2) a comprehensive community mental health center involved in its state's aggressive deinstitutionalization efforts, 3) a senior companion program matching elderly citizens and persons with disabilities, 4) a dental program established in a rural area, and 5) a state-wide private residential association. The following detailed profiles within these categories are summarized to illustrate how these respondent organizations dealt with a wide variety of community development issues. These more detailed profiles are outlined in terms of: 1) start-up issues, 2) issues in the maintenance of services and supports, and 3) the provider's recommendations for more effectively developing and maintaining community services and supports.

Case Management Two multicounty organizations and one respondent serving a single county emphasized the importance of public and private interagency collaboration in the coordination of services and supports for individuals with disabilities and their families.

The *county life service planning organization* was one of four such pilot services in Michigan, coordinating the efforts of all human services agencies in one county. The respondent attributed the organization's success to the participating agency director's commitment to the system and to the respondent's voluntary participation on the boards of directors of many of these participating agencies. Effective life service planning meant not competing for the individual, but rather learning to appreciate that much work had been done by others.

Start-Up Costs The organization broke down its planning process to look at individuals' needs, at the existing service system, and at issues related to individuals' rights. The state developmental disabilities (DD) council provided funding for the first 3 years. In 1984 and 1985, the organization developed a computerized taxonomy addressing education, employment, health, mental health, and social-recreational issues.

Maintenance of Services and Supports To avoid competing with participating county and state agencies, the organization did not approach United Way or other private sources for funding. The state DD council extended its initial 3-year pilot funding to 4 years, and the state department of education provided vocational education funding. A county Medicaid agency contract financed a prevention plan for all age groups. This contract also helped the organization identify gaps between the state mental health department and local community mental health (CMH) centers. The intermediate school district, coordinating 11 local school districts and the state special education agency, provided additional funding including a contract for planning related to the federal mandates of Part H, the Handicapped Infants and Toddlers section, of the Education of the Handicapped Act Amendments of 1986 (PL 99-457). The respondent organization extended its work on the individualized service plan (ISP) with teens and developed the individualized family service plan (IFSP). Staff focused on parents' vocational needs and on their feeling good about themselves.

Recommendations The director of the county life service planning organization indicated that human service agencies need to integrate budgets and planning at the local level in order to minimize overlapping services. Part H planning, if done effectively, could lead to nonthreatening coordination and facilitation of a system that currently exists. The director further recommended that:

An individual should be hired to work across agencies in serving the most difficult individuals referred. Reports back to participating agencies at the board of directors' meetings would offer valuable information on how agencies worked or did not work.

Family Support The four respondents providing family support included a small organization working with local hotels, restaurants, and theaters in order to provide *respitality* support for families. Two larger multiprogram respondents offered family supports and a state agency provided cash subsidies to 3,500 families.

Developing Respite Care and Respitality The respite care and respitality programs were originally a pilot project of the local United Cerebral Palsy affiliate. The Bureau of Children with Special Needs assumed responsibility in October 1985. Respitality consisted of the recruitment of hotels, meals, and entertainment opportunities that could be donated to families. Parents often received a night or a weekend away from home, with meal coupons and reimbursement for mileage and baby-sitting.

Start-Up Costs A 3-year federal Administration on Developmental Disabilities (ADD) grant to the respondent organization established respitality and other family supports. This federal demonstration grant addressed training and certification for respite care providers. A toll-free telephone line provided information, referral, and coordination of respite resources. A state-wide computerized directory provided information on participating agencies, service eligibility information, the fee for services structure, and a listing of certified respite care workers. The bureau contracted with 90 private community organizations state-wide.

Maintenance of Services and Supports By the spring of 1987, the organization needed additional respite service dollars. Families and the state DD council educated state legislators about the many families who had to forego respite due to other expenses. The legislature's next appropriations bill added $75,000 for services and for training of respite care workers. The state, however, was projecting a $200 million deficit in 1989 that made it necessary to hold over an additional $600,000, which would have been appropriated.

Training, information, and referral had to be the first priority. However, family referrals continued at 30–40 per month and the holdover of the 1989 legislative session's bill started a debate about options such as tightening eligibility requirements or establishing waiting lists. Both the bureau and parents promoted to legislators the cost-effective nature of family support in contrast with the expenses incurred at the state's mental retardation institution. The same number of staff working with 60 families in 1985 were serving 750 families in 1990. The bureau developed a pilot program to contract with a private agency and initiated training contracts with some of the state's American Red Cross chapters. One chapter served as the fiscal agent and provided a regular payroll for respite workers. The state's delayed payments had been a major factor in the lack of retention of workers.

Recommendations One respondent emphasized that "parents must know that respite is a service they have long deserved." The respondent had learned to encourage other family members to provide respite only when the family was uncomfortable with a nonrelative, or when there was no qualified provider nearby. It was viewed as very important to provide clear written policies on provider certification, pay scale, and family eligibility. A continuous review to assure that policies remain flexible was also suggested.

Early Intervention and Integrated Preschool Programs Two respondents provided county-wide early intervention services. A state agency was responsible for implementation of the mandates of PL 99-457. A Hispanic community organization developed a bilingual integrated preschool serving 22 at-risk children and eight children with severe mental retardation.

One of the respondents developed a *county-wide early childhood resource network.* The network was responsible for information and referral, service coordination, developmental screening, and coordination of 30 local early childhood providers in Ohio. The network worked in an urban community and served as a single referral center for parents and professionals. Each of 30 participating agencies donated professional staff four times a year to a neutral site. The resulting free developmental screening, which was established in September 1987, covered hearing, vision, language, and fine or gross motor skills.

Start-Up Costs In 1985, a state DD council grant provided the network with $61,000 during a 3-year period. In addition, 2 years of foundation start-up dollars allowed the director to work full-time and to continue collaborative screening. In April 1988, the network convinced the county's child welfare board to support developmental screening through June 1991.

Maintenance of Services and Supports The fiscal agent for the resource network was the county board of mental retardation and other developmental disabilities. The annual budget at the time of the survey consisted of federal Part H funding authorized by PL 99-457 (30%), United Way (30%), county community services funding (30%), and in-kind and financial donations (5% to 10%). The network applied successfully for the urban model component of a request for proposal of Part H, Infant and toddler funding, distributed by the state-wide interagency coordinating council (ICC). This additional funding in 1988 to 1989 enabled the network to work with professionals in the development of an early identification prescreening tool. The prescreening tool was shared with people who were routinely seeing children in day care centers or in Women, Infants, and Children (WIC) clinics, with community groups, and with the state's ICC.

The network also received a small grant to help parents find child care for their children with disabilities and worked with integrated day care centers to gather data on 30 parent/provider dyads. They found that many providers who were experienced in working with children with developmental disabilities were likely to continue working with children with developmental needs, but that technical assistance to these providers was very important.

Recommendations The respondent noted that it was important to employ a director who was not tied to any participating provider, and described one of her first initiatives as a network leader:

> The network provided an information form which parents could use for referral to any of the thirty participating organizations. I laid all the providers' forms out on a table, pulled some items out and refined other items.

The network was one of the state's initial collaborating groups, and the development by the state of additional early intervention collaborative efforts, was encouraged. Although federal money was viewed as an effective incentive, it was important that state legislators understand how such networks for early intervention were worthy of state expenditures.

Group Homes The 15 respondents in this area included those serving individuals with autism, mental illness, and dual psychiatric and mental retardation diagnoses. Respondents used a variety of strategies in program start-up and operation. These included combined private banking and state low-interest loan programs for capital financing, state waivers of institution-like standards, and individualized rate setting.

Medicaid Home and Community Based Services (HCBS) Waiver One respondent organization in Maine operated Medicaid HCBS waiver group homes for individuals who were difficult to serve. Many had recently resided in a state institution. Thirty-two individuals were served under the HCBS waiver.

Start-Up Costs The organization could not bill for waiver reimbursement until prior authorization was received, which was usually 6 weeks after start-up. In addition, the organization could not charge pre-operating costs, such as training or first-month deposit, to the waiver. The organization therefore needed 45 days of cash flow reserve. Due to the state's requirement that a physical plant be on display at the time of license application, the new home had to sit vacant, yet fully equipped.

Maintenance of Services and Supports A major maintenance issue was the state's decision to cap the level of waiver reimbursements based on the state's average ICF/MR cost. Since all individuals served by the organization were at the top of the state's four-level reimbursement system, there were forced choices about whether to shortchange physical plant expenses or staffing levels. In each of the last 2 years, the organization had received waiver per diem increases of 2%, compared to a 20.5% salary increase for state employees 2.5 years previously. Community providers as a group had fought recently for community ICF/MR wage parity, assuming that there would be a resulting benefit to all nonprofit services. However, the disparity within a community organization was harder to cope with than the disparity between the community provider and the state. As noted by the respondent, "Community providers might start a new staff person in foster care which was the type of work they preferred, but to get paid more the individual had to work in an ICF/MR."

Recommendations   The respondent indicated that the agency for which she worked budgeted on an individualized basis. As a result, a case mix of $80 per day on average could in fact range from $65 to $95 per day. In addition, she noted that her state's recent HCBS Waiver assessment typified the problems within Medicaid:

> Until we revamp it, the Waiver will not meet the needs of people in the community. It is easier to get people into ICFs/MR. Because our state has done a good job with deinstitutionalization, we cannot increase the cap. We need funding, such as the Medicaid reform proposed by Senator Chafee, to buy pieces of services as needed by the individual.

The respondent also stressed the importance of community providers working together to learn about fiscal management and cost-effectiveness techniques. State agencies were viewed as having the responsibility to provide technical assistance in this area.

Affordable Housing   Three responding organizations utilized low interest tax-exempt bonds, state housing department loans, U.S. Department of Housing and Urban Development (HUD) loans and rent subsidies, and other strategies to help individuals with disabilities benefit from lower monthly housing expenses. Another respondent advocated on behalf of persons with disabilities and assisted them with housing issues.

A Housing Cooperative with Four Accessible Units   This 16-unit housing cooperative in Connecticut was scheduled to begin operation in January 1992. The cooperative set March 1991 as the date for ground-breaking. Four families with members who have disabilities, some of them having severe physical disabilities, would receive housing. Annual operating costs were projected at $53,000.

Start-Up Costs   The state's department of housing offered grants and 0% interest loans to support housing cooperatives with very affordable units. The cooperative also received three grants totalling $84,500 from private foundations. A cooperative initiative organization provided additional grants to cover operating expenses. The funds from the department of housing, however, came with many regulations. The resulting bureaucratic requirements may add 1–1.5 years to the development process.

Maintenance of Services and Supports   Although the initially substantial state subsidies made housing costs affordable for the cooperative members, the state has restrictive funding for personal care assistant (PCA) services for persons with severe disabilities. One potential cooperative member, for example, received $7,300 annually to pay for her personal care assistants instead of the required $20,000. She intended to supplement the $7,300 by offering free rooming to one or two live-in assistants. The cooperative argued on her behalf that the live-in assistants should be considered contractual employees and not part of the family as defined by the state department of housing. Their income, therefore, should not be included in determining the monthly charge for the unit. Second, the cooperative maintained that the three-bedroom unit used by the woman and her assistants should be defined in terms of a family with children, a type of living situation for persons with disabilities that had been implemented in parts of Canada and California.

Recommendations The cooperative worked to develop and design housing in which people with disabilities and other families committed to being part of the community could be fully involved in the planning. In other states (e.g., Massachusetts) and in Canada, this participation in planning apparently did not conflict with fair housing laws. In the future, the cooperative hoped to offer pre-marketing of the various options prior to design and site selection. Residents would be fully involved in the planning.

Supported and Individualized Living Sixteen respondents developed options including foster homes with natural supports, supported apartments, and supported living in family-scale houses.

Foster Parents Providing Supported Living The respondent in Illinois served 23 individuals in foster homes with natural home supports. The organization allocated nearly one-quarter of its $4.3 million budget for supported and individualized living. This multiprogram provider organization recently converted its sheltered workshop program to integrated community employment. The organization was also converting shift-staff group homes to more individualized housing options.

Start-Up Costs The state mental health and developmental disabilities department provided funding for furnishings, equipment, and building rehabilitation. Capital financing for home acquisition was available through a state-wide loan program administered by the state health facilities authority. The authority sold tax-exempt bonds to private investors in order to enable financing 100% of acquisition costs and to provide all loan fees at an 8.5% rate of interest on the loan principle.

Maintenance of Services and Supports The organization's foster family rental contracts, along with residents' social security funds, covered the debt service for the health facility authority's loan. The social security funds also covered the balance of mortgage payments, property taxes, and the maintenance costs of the home. The foster care model costs less compared to a shift-staff arrangement, and recruitment of the organization's employees as foster parents reduced initial training and staff development costs. An Internal Revenue Service (IRS) classification for "difficulty of care" foster family payments provided exclusions from gross income for payments for up to four adults with mental disabilities who were living together. The organization could recruit its best employees and pay them more as contractual foster parents than if they were to remain regular employees.

Neighbors preferred the foster care model because it operated more like a regular home; shift staff did not periodically come and go. As noted by the organization's executive director, "neighbors of the shift-staffed homes actually contacted us requesting that we convert to foster care." Zoning restrictions were nonexistent for the foster homes and shift-staff problems such as call-ins, no-shows, and inadequate communication from shift to shift, were eliminated. Finally, the foster parents used their contractual per diem payments to pay all operating costs, such as food, utilities, transportation, and supplies. The organization could therefore budget more accurately for these expenses.

Recommendations The executive director of the Illinois foster parent/supportive employment program indicated that the state should develop administrative rules for serving adults in foster care. These rules should specifically meet the IRS foster care regulations and, thus, assure the future stability of the program. The state department of rehabilitation services should refocus its grant system to fund supported employment rather than sheltered workshops. Medicaid reform is essential to permit funding for family supports, foster care, supported employment and other, nonfacility based and nonmedical services.

Personal Care Assistant (PCA) Organizations in three states utilized funding through the HCBS waiver or through Medicaid's PCA reimbursement system. The PCA funding option provided a mechanism for separating housing from support.

A New Personal Care Assistant (PCA) Funding Mechanism An organization in New York developed a community residence in March 1987, serving 10 individuals at an annual cost of $500,000. The organization worked with the state Medicaid agency to institute PCA funding to support the individuals in their new residence.

Start-Up Costs Start-up costs for the program included two grants from the state mental retardation and developmental disabilities agency. First, a state-aid capital construction grant of $125,000 helped pay for construction and land costs. Second, a program development grant of $150,000 paid for furniture, equipment, and pre-opening expenses associated with staff, staff training, and construction costs. The only major start-up constraint was the square footage cost containment guidelines developed by the state mental retardation and developmental disabilities agency. Although the house was fully accessible, there was inadequate space for individuals in wheelchairs.

Maintenance of Services and Supports Residents used their Supplemental Security Income (SSI) payments to pay room and board. Additional dollars were available through a contract with the state mental retardation and developmental disabilities agency. The organization billed directly through the state's Medicaid Management Information System (MMIS) for reimbursements to the PCAs. The organization negotiated the PCA rate for more than a year with the state Medicaid agency; this placed serious fiscal constraints on the organization. The PCA-funded program required a higher staff-to-resident ratio than a typically staffed community residence. The agency had to spend the extra money each year and then submit a rate appeal to the state mental retardation and developmental disabilities agency to receive adequate reimbursement.

The state's mental retardation and developmental disabilities agencies and Medicaid agencies worked together to develop a memorandum of understanding enabling the organization to develop the first PCA vendor unit in the state. This

PCA vendor unit provided the same services and adhered to the same regulations as a licensed home health agency, except for "level one" for more intensive medical services. The PCA model enabled individuals who had lived in an institution to live in a less costly and less restrictive residential setting. The individuals served had the option of retiring from work. Six of the current residents could participate in meaningful activities at home instead of attending day programs.

Recommendation The director of the New York State PCA program suggested that states should suspend or waive the rate-setting methodologies used for traditional program models. This would encourage providers to develop cost-effective, innovative programs.

Consumer-Owned Housing Six respondents combined sources, including state mental health and developmental disabilities department funding, federal SSI monies, and HUD Section 8 rent subsidies, to create opportunities for apartment leases or home ownership for individuals with disabilities or their families.

Tim's House This respondent, the director of a local Arc in Michigan, stressed that the consumer-directed housing option was not a form of independent living or other typical model. "Models get in the way of an individual's options in the community. Parents and advocates should look for outcomes rather than models."

Start-Up Costs The project's success was attributed to a process involving the local Arc, another nonprofit organization, and state agencies. The Arc and cooperating state and private organizations proposed a consumer-centered concept, but the families involved could not initially agree on any approach.

During an open meeting, several families drew the following conclusions in working together to plan for one family's son, Tim. First, they concluded that Tim should remain in the neighborhood. Second, he should leave the family home. Third, he should not live with other persons with disabilities, since in school and other programs his friendships were with persons who did not have disabilities. Finally, he needed the permanency that a house would provide. Tim's parents approached the Arc's executive director and started the process of securing housing for their son. The real estate agent and the executive director found an appropriate house and indicated to the seller that the family had limited credit. To their amazement, the sellers offered a rent-with-option-to-buy contract and, thus, became members of the team of parents and professionals planning for Tim's housing.

Maintenance of Services and Supports Tim moved into the house a few months before the survey was conducted. The lease for the home was in his parents' name. The team advertised in the paper for roommates and 16 applicants responded. The roommates selected were a physical therapist from the local hospital and a chemist. The team's recent mission statement affirmed the importance of providing affordable housing for persons with developmental disabilities. Any persons with a reasonable life plan could submit it to the team for discussion. The state had recently approved a $5 million fund for consumer-owned housing.

This housing program soon received the attention of the state department of mental health. The program started somewhat questionably, since it was unlicensed and represented a rejection of the department of mental health's semi-independent living model. If the team had been stopped early, they would have lost the house. The Arc director responding to the survey recalled that, "Not only were we spared reprimands. We have won awards."

Recommendations The director of The Arc indicated that it was necessary to reduce paperwork, and that the organization was moving to computerize its record system. He also suggested that there were too many bureaucratic obstacles to participation in community living through the ICF/MR program, and complained that:

> If it is so much pain for me as an executive director to deal with the ICF-MR program, I can imagine how bad it is for residents. Next year our Arc will start to close down ICFs/MR. Virtually everyone can live in supported living.

Employment There were seven respondents who focused on employment: two industry-based training programs, a computer training program, contract work with the U.S. Department of Defense, two organizations obtaining private sector employment underwritten by foundation grants, and state vocational rehabilitation agency funding for mobile work crews. Six for-profit business ventures included a lumber mill, a kiln-dried lumber operation, a bicycle shop, a typewriter and VCR repair shop, a greenhouse business, and a lawn care company. Three respondents focused on services for persons with traumatic head injury.

The Industry-Integrated Training Program This program in Pennsylvania started in 1977 and had one central administrative office and nine field offices throughout the states of Pennsylvania and Delaware. Individuals received industry-integrated training directly within the private sector. The respondent described a volunteer interview network of employers (VINE). Through simulated interviews offered by members of VINE, individuals could improve their interviewing and job procurement skills. The employer was not obligated to hire the individual, but was only asked to help the person in developing their interviewing skills and in filling out a form that provides feedback to the individual who was interviewed.

Start-Up Costs The organization sold the idea for an industry-integrated training program to the Mellon Foundation, and the state DD council provided a 3-year seed grant. The agency presented an analysis of needs and solutions in employment services. The fact that the organization was ahead of its time affected maintenance of services and supports and ongoing funding. Sheltered workshops and rehabilitation facilities became the organization's biggest opponents. The agency's primary program goals for the first phase of the program were as follows: 1) showing that the program worked, 2) helping others develop similar models, 3) approaching the business sector, and 4) developing management information systems (MIS).

The respondent believed the second phase of the program was to train the private sector to provide such services on their own for individuals with mental retardation and other developmental disabilities. In addition, the respondent saw the agency's role in the future as that of a consultant rather than a service provider:

In the future, we'll be consultants, not direct providers. Already we are losing people to the private sector, which may be good. However, we still need people in human services to help the private sector during this transition stage.

Recommendations   Interview results indicated that the respondent believed that organizations should provide services in a normalized environment in the private sector. It was his opinion that "business is evolving to look more like human services, and human services are evolving to be more like the private sector." He recommended that the state human resources department build a bridge to the private sector. Tasks such as seeking employment opportunities, recruiting businesses, and training employers were worthwhile approaches, but the business sector was also viewed as having needs. Current labor shortages in many areas require the private sector to reach out to persons with disabilities. As the director of the industry-integrated training program pointed out:

> Other options include retaining aged workers, extending retirement, hiring minorities, and implementing literacy programs. The Americans with Disabilities Act (ADA) is a symbolic gesture, and provides a glimpse of the future. We are now in the transition stage, and the rehabilitation system must evolve.

Conversion from Center-Based Services   Seven respondents were redirecting resources from sheltered workshops, day training, or day habilitation programs into support for integrated employment. One respondent was closing a five-person group home, and another was using the equity from a campus with 46 closed ICF/MR beds as collateral in the purchase of community housing.

Planning and Implementing Community Employment   This industry training organization in Michigan had a 20-year history of providing work services for persons with mental disabilities. For the first 15 years, work adjustment centers and sheltered workshops were the organization's only vocational alternatives.

Start-Up Costs   The respondent noted that 5 years ago the industry training organization and the local Good Will organization, respectively, received traditional funding in the form of community mental health/mental retardation (MH/MR) and vocational rehabilitation dollars. Both developed proposals seeking community mental health (CMH) center funds to develop a new sheltered workshop. The CMH director talked to the local Arc about its reluctance to fund the sheltered workshop. A task force was formed with representatives from United Way, from Job Training Partnership Act (JTPA), from the state's rehabilitation services agency, and from the CMH center. As described by the respondent:

> The task force reviewed the assumptions and the model and asked for data from programs. The task force found that only two or three people had ever been successful in the sheltered workshop system. It was clear that 'train and place' did not work and that people needed support on the job after placement.

A supported employment conference that was held by the Arc director included persons from Georgia, Washington, and Oregon. This conference reinforced the proposed supported employment model. The CMH center provided a small grant for planning and program development and, within 6 weeks, the project supported six people in employment. Shortly after this, the state received funds from the Office of Special Education and Rehabilitative Services (OSERS), and the respondent organization became a funded supported employment site. The state DD council and the CMH also provided money.

Maintenance of Services and Supports The OSERS grant ended the year before the survey, and the state DD council money ended 6 months later in February 1990. Although state vocational rehabilitation funding had increased, it was difficult to budget for the services that each individual needed. The organization projected a $60,000 deficit for the coming year, and the respondent declared, "We are in the transition stage and are trying to figure out the costs, but we are committed to do it."

Recommendations The organization learned of the need to place people more than once; this was costly. The most stable jobs meet needs for the employer. The respondent believed it was useless to try to sell employment opportunities on the basis of charity or altruism, and concluded that:

> Success exists where the employer wants the person to succeed and is interested in all employees as people. The least successful placement is when the motivation is strictly economic. The key players must buy in to planning at the local level. Interagency collaboration is crucial.

Self-Advocacy One respondent was an individual with a disability who was self-employed with state DD council support. The other respondent was a director of a community agency that had developed a self-advocacy initiative. Funding was from the state's University Affiliated Program (UAP) and from state agency and private foundation resources.

Start-Up Planning Issues Planning began when a board member of the respondent organization attended an Arc meeting at which the director of the Minnesota Developmental Disabilities Council presented "Partners in Policy-Making," an innovative self-advocacy training program. The board responded positively to this concept of preparing parents and persons with disabilities to become effective advocates in public policy issues. Motivation to support self-advocacy included better communication with families about issues facing the organization and a stronger understanding by the organization of families' concerns.

Meetings with the state DD council, the state Arc, and the UAP focused on the development of self-advocacy programs. A UAP graduate fellow interned at the community organization, conducted a national survey of advocacy programs, and attended training sessions on "Partners in Policy-Making." Next, the respondent organization formed a professional advisory board of parents, professionals, and persons with disabilities. In meetings and in a retreat, each of the three groups identified and ranked concerns. A priority for all groups was education empowering people to act in an informed way. Subcommittees to the professional advisory board addressed curriculum and training, marketing, and funding.

Maintenance of Services and Supports The community education and advocacy project had been operating for 2.5 years at the time of the survey. Funding from the state department of mental health and developmental disabilities supported a full-time, on site person. In the third year of operation, the organization worked for additional support from the state's rehabilitation agency and from private sources.

Recommendations The director of the community agency indicated that university and state supports were crucial to the program. The idea of having funding be granted to a university and having graduate students work in the community benefited both students and the community agency. According to the executive director:

> If the state mental health/developmental disabilities director weren't such a client and family advocate, it would have been more difficult. Fortunately, we did not have to try to sell this to a stifled bureaucrat.

Other Services and Supports There were five respondents not classified according to the 11 types of services and supports. Some of these were: 1) one of the nation's first Centers for Independent Living, 2) a comprehensive community mental health center involved for several years in its state's aggressive deinstitutionalization efforts, and 3) a senior companion program matching elderly citizens and people with disabilities. The fourth, a dental program, was set up in a rural area and a state-wide private residential association responded in terms of its advocacy and policy efforts in support of community development.

A Center for Independent Living (CIL) As defined by the Rehabilitation Act of 1973 (PL 93-112), Centers for Independent Living are consumer-controlled, community-based, cross-disability, nonresidential private nonprofit agencies that are designed and operated within a local community by individuals with disabilities. These centers provide an array of independent living services. In 1976, the nation had three Centers for Independent Living located in Berkeley, Boston, and Houston.

Start-Up Costs In 1976, Michigan's Governor's Planning Council on Developmental Disabilities provided start-up costs for a Center for Independent Living in the state. Funded under PL 93-112 as amended, the responding organization also received support from the state Medicaid agency and the state vocational rehabilitation agency. However, funding did not grow during the 1980–1991 period despite increased expenses, and it became a challenge to raise other funds.

Maintenance of Services and Supports Many other Centers for Independent Living were dependent on federal funds. Yet, the center in question diversified funding to include United Way, fee for service, city monies, donations, and other private funds. Together, these other sources had come to exceed the federal money.

Centers for Independent Living have traditionally been active in system advocacy, but it was quite difficult to obtain funding to encourage empowerment, integration, and independence. The center often had to change funding sources, and the responding director complained that "the federal government provides perverse incentives such as SSI, Social Security Disability Insurance (SSDI), and Medicaid and the state can't wean itself from them." The respondent also reported spending too much time obtaining adequate funding and not enough time on direct service. This is emphasized in the following:

> The paperwork is enormous, since all people ask for information in a different format: private agency, state agency, United Way, the state rehab services agency, the city. Some people ask for hours, some ask for the number of individuals served, some look for the number of contacts.

Recommendations   The director of the Center on Independent Living suggested that the government, when asking increased accountability on the part of funded projects, should provide structured feedback to community organizations. The director noted that the state and federal governments should address the problem of the large number of people with developmental disabilities waiting for community services and supports.

COMMUNITY PROVIDERS—RECOMMENDATIONS

The Start-Up of Services and Supports

State developmental disabilities councils, the United Way, private foundations, and other private resources have been instrumental in the initiation of services and supports outside the mold of established funding. Community respondents commended state mental retardation and developmental disabilities program development grants and changeover grants from the OSERS for integrated employment. The ADD provided family support start-up grants, and the National Institute on Disability and Rehabilitation Research (NIDRR) awarded grants for small business development. Without public or private funding dedicated to start-up, community organizations had to conduct general fund-raising or re-allocate start-up funds from within their total budgets.

Specific *capital funding* strategies included investment tax credits, no-interest or low-interest loan funds, and formation of a pool of nonprofits to allow access to the bond market. The capital funding and rent subsidies afforded by HUD received major complaints ("HUD would rather build a new building, and serve only people with mental retardation"—An independent skills teaching center in Maine). In contrast, HUD was commended by specialized housing agencies. They noted that the McKinney Homeless Act amendments offered a more user-friendly housing development application process. They also cited as exemplary a HUD and U.S. Department of Health and Human Services memorandum of understanding on the problems of persons who are homeless.

Organizations addressing *community acceptance* described maintaining a low profile before opening a community residence as recommended by Seltzer (1984) and Sigelman (1976). They underscored the right of persons with disabilities to live in regular community housing. Community living options, however, must be compatible with neighborhood housing patterns. One community respondent developing staffed apartments in Massachusetts, for example, expressed concern that four-person group homes would have adverse effects on the surrounding communities by having four unrelated adults living together with their staff as well. Respondents saw improved relationships within communities, resulting from education and from provider involvement in community activities.

The Maintenance of Services and Supports

The first set of community provider recommendations addressed organizations' *management expertise* and their use of *creative personnel practices*. Program success required having experts on organizations' boards of directors and keeping the experts in close touch with the objectives and needs of the organization. A supported and individualized living organization in Michigan, for example, used a real estate attorney, a housing development expert, and a property management expert on its board.

Community organizations' experiences with the best use of limited personnel resources were revealed in their recommendations about improved selection, orientation, training, and scheduling of staff. They emphasized the need for a clear mission and goals, the need to build strong internal systems, and the importance of developing leadership at all levels of the organization including line staff who are, in fact, "ambassadors to the business community" (an employment respondent in Massachusetts).

In the second set of recommendations concerning the operation of services and supports, providers addressed *overregulation* and the need for *improved interagency collaboration*. Respondents saw regulatory redundancies and the burden of paperwork as symptoms of poor coordination and collaboration between providers and government agencies. Family support, case management, and early intervention respondents stressed breaking down public and private agency turf issues. Specific problems included cumbersome licensing, certification, and oversight regulations. Duplicated effort, contradictions, and excess paperwork resulting from numerous fiscal and program audits and other reviews were viewed as common occurrences. Several respondents also saw the need for more effective quality assurance systems.

A third series of recommendations focused on the areas of *federal Medicaid reform, funding flexibility,* and better *government incentives*. Respondents indicated that there were major problems in using the Medicaid waiver to do what it was intended to do. There was concern that the waiver, unless revamped, could not effectively meet the needs of people in the community. The ICF/MR active treatment requirements prohibited integrated community living and employment. Four respondents specifically recommended Medicaid reform as outlined in the Chafee Bill (S. 384). Seven others recommended reform that would allow more flexible community financing. Several organizations discussed the need for a stronger message of incentive from the federal government.

Fourth, there was concern about the related issues of *wage parity* and the need for *adequate funding*. "There must be parity between community and institutional salaries. In our state, the community staff turnover rate is 45%" (a group home respondent in Iowa). To address inadequate community funding, many organizations, especially for-profit business ventures, were looking beyond traditional government programs.

Fifth, *government leadership* and *technical assistance* were seen as affecting both the start-up and operation of services and supports. Community respondents frequently commended state agency management and funding flexibility. State government leadership was implicit in the more complicated housing finance programs involving the coordination of state mental retardation and developmental disabilities agencies' policies and procedures with those of other public and private organizations.

The Missions and Values of Community Organizations

A dominant theme in the missions of respondent agencies was achieving independence and productivity for persons with disabilities through *employment* and *regular work*. Respondents recommended improved collaboration with and more integrated employment funding from state vocational rehabilitation agencies. Businesses, through Employee Assistance Programs (EAPs), were becoming similar to human service agencies. There were also recommendations about blending human services and best business practices.

The other major theme entailed recommendations regarding shifting the focus from service system programs to *individualized services* and *support for families*. Family support was viewed as benefiting from the use of volunteers, improved funding, and the redirection of funding. Several respondents called for tax incentives to families and to individuals with disabilities. "It is important to let families know that family support is a service which they have long deserved" (a family support respondent in Maine).

CONCLUSION

Many of the state agency and community provider respondents described how to build systems of *individual support* for community living and employment, and for families. In response to a survey question about models in community services, state agency respondents discussed abandoning past program models. As expressed by the state director in Arizona, "the best programs are those support systems that are the most invisible."

Survey results also suggested important principles for developing and financing community services and supports. First, besides the acquisition of funding, the initiation and maintenance of community services were viewed as requiring improved collaboration and coordination among governmental agencies and private providers. State agencies and providers will need to learn to work together within the larger system of neighborhoods, private businesses, and county and local services, such as the public schools. Community service financing should come to mean *community development* in which state agencies and providers carefully assess local needs and resources. Business and other local community leaders should participate in planning and developing opportunities for employ-ment and community living.

Second, financing community services and supports can be understood through innovative examples. PCA services in Colorado, New York, and Wiscon-sin represented individualized adaptations to Medicaid. Case management organi-zations working across agency boundaries were seen as more effectively directing resources and energy toward the individual and the family. Early intervention and case management respondents outlined both promise and current problems inher-ent in Part H of the 1986 amendments (PL 99-457) to the Education of the Handi-capped Act. They saw these amendments as a model for interagency collabora-tion. They also indicated, however, that there needed to be more funding and more incentives for states striving for a true family focus.

Community employment respondents provided an overview of major changes in the vocational services system. Businesses were seen as needing to maintain a stable work force. This, along with the spirit of the Americans with Disabilities Act (ADA) of 1990, was thought to create an opportunity for human service organizations to become consultants to the private business sector. Em-ployment respondents reported adopting more business-like techniques, working to become members of local industry or business associations, and not competing unfairly with community businesses. These respondents converting from center-based programs noted the importance of public and private bridge financing dur-ing the transition. However, it was believed that in order to benefit from such tran-sitional funding, providers and their boards of directors must commit to planned organizational change. This included carefully assessing the needs of local busi-nesses and the surrounding community.

Community organizations consistently faced bureaucratic inefficiencies, in-stitutional bias inherent in major government funding programs, and other govern-ment policies that frustrated individuals' efforts to live and work in the commu-nity. Nevertheless, community survey respondents frequently commended federal and state government leadership, policy direction, and technical assistance. They also consistently commended financing designed to complement the strengths and abilities of individuals and their families. The two groups of respondents illus-trated how they could be effective partners. This was evident in the development of individualized funding approaches, family supports, consumer ownership of housing, and self-advocacy initiatives.

A community respondent in Minnesota whose organization closed its ICFs/MR and developed individualized living alternatives explained perhaps the most important principle for community financing: "We receive dollars for indi-viduals. It is their money. Consumers must drive the system."

REFERENCES

Allard, M.A. (1988). Public and private financing options for community residences. In M.P. Janicki, M.W. Krauss, & M.M. Seltzer (Eds.), *Community residences for persons with developmental disabilities: Here to stay* (pp. 69–84). Baltimore: Paul H. Brookes Publishing Co.

Bahl, R. (1982). Fiscal health of state and local governments: 1982 and beyond. *Public Budgeting and Finance, 2,* 5–21.

Boggs, E.M., Hanley-Maxwell, C., Lakin, K.C., & Bradley, V.J. (1988). Federal policy and legislation: Fiscal or programmatic factors that have constrained and facilitated community integration. In L.W. Heal, J.I. Haney, & A.R. Novak Amado (Eds.), *Integration of developmentally disabled individuals into the community* (pp. 245–272). Baltimore: Paul H. Brookes Publishing Co.

Braddock, D. (1987). *Federal policy toward mental retardation and developmental disabilities.* Baltimore: Paul H. Brookes Publishing Co.

Braddock, D., & Fujiura, G.T. (1987). State government financial effort in mental retardation. *American Journal of Mental Deficiency, 91,* 450–459.

Braddock, D., Hemp, R., Fujiura, G.T., Bachelder, L., & Mitchell, D. (Eds.). (1990). *The state of the states in developmental disabilities.* Baltimore: Paul H. Brookes Publishing Co.

Copeland, W.C., & Iversen, I.A. (1981, January). Not just the aged, not just health care and not just nursing homes: Some proposals for policy and legislative changes in long-term care. In J.J. Bevilacqua (Ed.), *Changing government policies for the mentally disabled* (pp. 159–162). Cambridge, MA: Ballinger.

Ferguson, P.M., Hibbard, M., Leinen, J., & Schaff, S. (1990). Supported community life: Disability policy and the renewal of mediating structures. *Journal of Disability Policy Studies, 1,* 9–35.

General Accounting Office. (1977). *Returning the mentally disabled to the community: Government needs to do more.* Washington, DC: U.S. Government Printing Office.

Gettings, R.M. (1977, Autumn). Hidden impediments to de-institutionalization. *State Government, 50,* 214–219. (Council of State Governments, Lexington, Kentucky.)

Hemp, R., Braddock, D., Bachelder, L., & Haasen, K. (1990, April). *Creative financing of community services: The state agency perspective.* Chicago: The University of Illinois at Chicago, University Affiliated Program in Developmental Disabilities.

Lakin, K.C., Jaskulski, T.M., Hill, B.K., Bruininks, R.H., Menke, J.M., White, C.C., & Wright, E.A. (1989, May). *Medicaid services for mental retardation and related conditions.* Minneapolis: University of Minnesota, Institute on Community Integration.

Mitchell, D., & Braddock, D. (1991, April 19). *Compensation and turnover of direct care staff in developmental disabilities residential facilities: A summary of results* (Monograph #54). Chicago: University of Illinois at Chicago, University Affiliated Program in Developmental Disabilities.

National Association for Retarded Citizens. (1976). *Report on the task force on funding and standards for community residential services.* Arlington, TX: NARC Research and Demonstration Institute.

President's Committee on Mental Retardation. (1976). *Mental retardation: The known and the unknown.* Washington, DC: Author.

Seltzer, M.M. (1984). Correlates of community opposition to community residences for mentally retarded persons. *American Journal of Mental Deficiency, 89,* 1–8.

Sigelman, C.K. (1976). A Machiavelli for planners: Community attitudes and selection of a group home site. *Mental Retardation, 14,* 26–29.

Smith, G.A., & Aderman, S. (1987, July). *Paying for services.* Alexandria, VA: National Association of State Mental Retardation Program Directors, Inc., Community Management Initiative Series.

Smull, M. (1989, February). *Crisis in the community.* Baltimore: University of Maryland, Applied Research and Evaluation Unit, Department of Pediatrics, School of Medicine.

Wright, B., & King, M.P. (1991, February). *Americans with developmental disabilities: Policy directions for the states.* Denver, CO: National Conference of State Legislatures, Task Force on Developmental Disabilities.

— *Chapter 12* ————————————————

Compensation and Turnover of Direct Care Staff
A National Survey
Dale Mitchell and David Braddock

The changes that have occurred during the past decade in the residential service system are well documented. The number of individuals with developmental disabilities living in public institutions has decreased from 149,169 in 1977 to 91,440 in 1988 (Braddock, Hemp, Fujiura, Bachelder, & Mitchell, 1990). Twenty-nine public institutions closed during that 12-year period. In the years from 1977 to 1988, institutional spending adjusted for inflation remained essentially constant, while spending for community services increased by 226% (Braddock & Fujiura, 1991). Along with this growth in community services, several problems have been identified in the literature. Two of the most significant are low wages and high turnover among direct care workers (Bruininks, Kudla, Wieck, & Hauber, 1980; O'Connor & Sitkei, 1973). Failure to successfully solve these two problems will affect the growth and quality of community services in the future. The following sections summarize the existing research on compensation and turnover of direct care workers in residential facilities serving individuals with developmental disabilities.

COMPENSATION OF DIRECT CARE WORKERS

Low pay of direct care workers has long been a problem in the developmental disabilities field. For example, Kirkbride (1912) cited "notoriously insufficient pay" as a major factor contributing to an annual turnover rate of more than 70% among direct care employees working in New York public institutions. Although it

Preparation of this chapter was supported by Cooperative Agreement #H33B89948 between the National Institute on Disability and Rehabilitation Research (NIDRR); the Research and Training Center on Residential Services and Community Living in the Institute on Community Integration (UAP) located at the University of Minnesota; and the University Affiliated Program in Developmental Disabilities at the University of Illinois at Chicago. The opinions expressed herein are those of the authors.

had generally been recognized that wage levels of direct care workers were very low, national and state studies documenting this fact were few until the past decade. In a national study of more than 200 public and private residential facilities, Lakin and Bruininks (1981) found that direct care workers in private community facilities earned $3.49 per hour. Seven studies in individual states conducted between 1986 and 1989 also reported very low wages for direct care workers in private community facilities, ranging from $4.49 to $6.35 (Al Fisher Associates, Inc., 1988; Arthur Young's Human Resources Consulting Group, 1988; Colorado Developmental Disabilities Funding Coalition, 1988; Minnesota Department of Employee Relations, 1989; Pennsylvania Legislative Budget and Finance Committee, 1989; Pivirotto & Bothamley Consulting, 1986; Wisconsin Community Direct Service Worker Task Force, 1989). These findings are consistent with studies that examined wage levels for direct care workers in other human service occupations. For example, a national study of nursing facilities in 1988 found that the average hourly wage for nursing aides was only $4.32 (Older Womens' League, 1988), while another study in the same year reported the average hourly wage for child care workers to be only $4.67 (Child Care Employee Project, 1989).

In comparing the findings of the above studies with wages earned in other occupations, it is clear that the wages of direct care workers in human service organizations are significantly lower than what the typical worker in the private sector earned. For example, the national average hourly wage for private workers in nonagricultural occupations was $9.96 in 1989, ranging from $6.54 per hour in retail trade occupations to $13.54 per hour for construction occupations (Bureau of Labor Statistics, 1990).

At least three major factors appear to contribute to the low wage level of direct care workers in human service organizations. First, a significant *wage differential* between male and female workers in the United States has long been documented. In 1890, the average pay for women in the United States was 46% of the average pay for men (Goldin, 1984). By 1983, while this differential had decreased, the average pay for women was still only 66% of the average pay for men (O'Neill, 1984). The historical differences in pay between male and female workers in this country has particular relevance since direct care occupations are filled primarily by women. Two studies already cited in the chapter indicate a high proportion of women in these jobs: 88% of nursing home aides (Older Women's League, 1988) and 79% of direct care staff in DD facilities (Lakin & Bruininks, 1981).

A second contributing factor to low wages is a *low esteem* given to most service provider occupations. In their review of the United States's labor history, Marshall and Paulin (1984) observed that "because home work was (and is) considered less valuable than man's market work, jobs that are seen as an extension of home work, women's jobs, are undervalued also" (p. 207). Similarly, a study in the long-term care field concluded that:

> Nursing aides and home health aides are oppressed by the acute medical model that still dominates long-term care services. . . since 'anyone can do it' is the general perception and those who do are nearly all women, the work is not truly valued. In

contemporary American society, that means it is not valued economically; low compensation is the norm. (Older Women's League, 1988, p. 22)

Society needs to accept the fact that women who remain at home and provide care to their families hold an important job. This may eventually lead to increased importance being given to caregiving professions in general.

A third factor contributing to low wages of direct care workers are factors associated with the *history* of many community agencies. Most of the earliest community agencies were charitable organizations that depended primarily on a casual labor pool. Efforts of volunteers and parents often subsidized the actual cost of providing care in these organizations. During the 1960s and 1970s, many of the early reimbursement systems developed by state agencies utilized methodologies that locked in these low compensation levels. Smith and Aderman (1987) observed that:

in MR/DD community services, like many other areas of human services, pure 'market prices' do not exist . . . the state [MR/DD] agency 'makes' the market by virtue of its funding dominance. . . loosely, this means that a service 'costs' whatever the [state] agency decides to pay. (pp. 92–93)

In classical economic theory, the free market determines prices for goods and, to a large extent, employee wages. However, in the mental retardation/developmental disabilities (MR/DD) service system, prices for services (and, thus, employee wages) may not be competitive with other industries in the surrounding area unless state government concedes the effect that its near monopoly has in the marketplace and adjusts its funding strategies accordingly. Such recognition has rarely happened, and the impact on employee wages has been substantial.

TURNOVER OF DIRECT CARE WORKERS

The recruitment and retention of direct care workers has been a long-standing problem. O'Connor and Sitkei (1973) conducted a national survey of 474 community mental retardation residential facilities and reported that 37% of the responding facilities listed "difficulty of finding qualified staff" as one of the three most serious problems facing their facilities. Less than 10 years later, Bruininks et al., (1980) conducted a similar survey of more than 2,000 community facilities asking administrators to list the most serious problem they faced in operating their programs. The most frequently reported concern was the recruitment, retention, and development of staff (85%). This was reported as an even more serious problem than obtaining adequate funding (65%). Today, the retention of staff is still a major problem, as is recruitment and training of staff since they are so closely related to retention. Low wages in the field are definitely, in part, responsible for turnover.

During the past 5 years, numerous studies of individual states have documented average turnover rates for direct care workers in community facilities ranging from 31% to 71% (Colorado Developmental Disabilities Funding Coalition, 1988; Jacobson & Ackerman, 1989; Minnesota Department of Employee Relations, 1989; Pennsylvania Legislative Budget and Finance Committee, 1989; Pivirotto & Bothamley Consulting, 1986; South Dakota Association of Community-based Services, 1989; Wisconsin Community Direct Service Worker Task Force, 1989). As with studies of wages, these findings are consistent with research studying turnover in other human services organizations. For example, two studies examining turnover in hospitals reported average rates of 70% (Levine, 1957) and 52% (Tuchi & Carr, 1971) among direct care workers. Three studies examining direct care turnover in nursing homes reported average rates between 70% and 150% (Kasteler, Ford, White, & Carruth, 1979; Stryker-Gordon, 1982; Wagnild, 1988; Weisfeld, 1984).

The rate of direct care turnover in human services occupations appears to be generally higher than the rates reported for many other occupations. In a review of 53 different organizations, Price (1977) reported turnover rates ranging from 13% to 68% per year with a median rate of 29%. A recent study of more than 300 companies reported an average rate of employee turnover of 12.4% (Bureau of National Affairs, 1989), with the highest rate reported for health care companies (18.7%). For a summary of the existing research on the correlates of turnover, see Braddock and Mitchell (1992).

LIMITATIONS OF EXISTING RESEARCH

Despite the growing number of studies on the subject, there are several methodological limitations that limit the utility of findings from these studies. For example, the majority of community studies have been limited to a single state sample only (Al Fisher Associates, Inc., 1988; Arthur Young Human Resources Consulting Group, 1988; Ganju, 1979; George & Baumeister, 1981; Jacobson & Ackerman, 1989; Minnesota Department of Employee Relations, 1989; Pennsylvania Legislative Budget and Finance Committee, 1989; Pivirotto & Bothemley Consulting, 1986; Wisconsin Community Direct Service Worker Task Force, 1989; Zaharia & Baumeister, 1979). A nation-wide study, utilizing relatively large samples from each of the 50 states, would allow useful comparisons to be drawn among and between the states.

Another inconsistency in sampling is that some studies have examined employee wages and turnover at the agency level rather than at the individual facility level (George & Baumeister, 1981; Pivirotto & Bothamley Consulting, 1986). Sampling at the agency level does not disaggregate results according to type of community facility; therefore, comparisons across studies are very difficult. In addition, none of the studies have included publicly operated community facilities in their sample. Since the number of such facilities has increased during the past decade, it is important to document the level of direct care compensation and turnover in these facilities.

Other methodological problems stem from the type of wage and turnover data reported by most of these studies. Most studies have collected information on either starting or average wages. Collection of starting, average, and maximum wages for direct care workers would provide a more complete picture of direct care compensation. Equally important, most studies have failed to adjust wages for geographical cost of living differences. Such an adjustment would provide for a more accurate comparison of the purchasing power of wages among direct care workers in different geographic areas of the country. In addition, most studies have collected turnover data for less than 1 year, typically, for 1 month. Data collected for a full year would be less likely to be influenced by seasonal fluctuations in employee turnover. For example, at the beginning or end of a fiscal year, there could be either an increase or decrease of funding, which would affect the number of persons who are hired, laid off, and so forth. Temporary holiday or summer help would also account for such fluctuations.

SUMMARY OF EXISTING RESEARCH

Wages of direct care workers in private community facilities are low, typically ranging between $4.00 and $6.00 per hour. These rates are significantly lower than wages of most other occupations, but are similar to wage levels reported for direct care workers in other human service organizations. The rate of turnover of direct care workers in private community facilities is high, often exceeding 50% annually. These rates are also considerably higher than those in other occupations.

Despite the growing interest in the subject of direct care compensation and turnover, there are several factors that limit the ability to generalize findings from existing research to the United States as a whole. These include samples restricted to a single state, wage and turnover data often reported at the agency (instead of facility) level, and utilization of different measures of wages and turnover. As a result, several key questions remain unanswered:

1. Have real wages for direct care workers in private community facilities kept pace with inflation during the last decade?
2. Are wages for direct care workers in public institutions significantly higher than wages for direct care workers in private community facilities across all states?
3. How do wage levels for direct care workers in publicly operated community facilities compare to wage levels found in privately operated community facilities?
4. What effect do cost of living differences among the states have on direct care wages?
5. How do employee benefits in private community facilities compare to benefits in public institutions?
6. Is direct care turnover significantly higher in private community facilities than in public institutions across all states?
7. Have any states implemented policies to minimize turnover among direct care workers?

A NATIONAL SURVEY

The following section summarizes the study's methodology including sample selection, development of the survey instrument, and collection of data. Results are reported for direct care wages, benefits, and turnover. Study findings are presented for public institutions, privately operated community facilities, and publicly operated community facilities.

Methodology

To address questions not answered by previous research, a nationwide study on compensation and turnover of direct care staff was conducted at the University of Illinois at Chicago. The study used a state-by-state sample of more than 1,600 public and private facilities and had six main objectives: 1) to obtain information related to starting and average wages for direct care workers in all 50 states and the District of Columbia, 2) to determine the effect that cost of living differences across the states have on direct care wages, 3) to compare wages for direct care workers in public institutions and private community facilities, 4) to collect information on benefits for direct care workers, 5) to collect information regarding state policy initiatives to improve the compensation of direct care workers, and 6) to compare the turnover rates for direct care workers in public institutions and private community facilities for the 50 states and the District of Columbia.

Sample Selection A definition of eligible facilities was employed that would enhance comparability of results for the present study to previous turnover research (George & Baumeister, 1981; Lakin & Bruininks, 1981; Minnesota Department of Employee Relations, 1989; Pivirotto & Bothamley Consulting, 1986). A community facility was defined as follows:

> . . . any community-based residential setting licensed or contracted to provide residential services to persons with developmental disabilities. The setting must primarily rely on shift (versus live-in or drop-in) staff who are responsible for direct supervision of residents during waking hours. This definition would typically exclude foster care, nursing homes, boarding homes, semi-independent living, and apartment settings.

State MR/DD agencies, state licensing agencies, and provider groups were contacted and asked to supply their most current registry of residential facilities. This effort resulted in the identification of approximately 11,000 institutional and community facilities meeting the study definition. To obtain samples of sufficient size to ensure adequate precision, a modified 10% random sample selection process was used (for a further discussion of the sample selection process, see Braddock and Mitchell, 1992). Table 1 lists the number of eligible facilities, number of facilities selected for the sample, and the number of returned surveys.

Survey Instrument An extensive literature review identified eight similar survey instruments. Upon review of these instruments, an initial draft of the instrument was developed, which then underwent an external review by a technical advisory committee. The committee was composed of seven state and national experts having experience in developing and administering the previously mentioned surveys. The committee provided recommendations that were incorporated into a second draft. The survey instrument was then field-tested in 15 community facilities in two states. A final version of the survey was developed and sent to the 1,612 facilities in the study sample in December 1989.

Table 1. Study sample

Item	Pub inst[a]	Priv com[b]	Pub com[c]	Total facs[d]
No. of eligibile facilities	248	9,413	1,172	10,833
No. of facilities in sample	248	1,167	197	1,612
No. of surveys returned	186	700	126	1,012

[a]Public institutions.
[b]Private community facilities.
[c]Public community facilities.
[d]Total facilities.

Wage data collected by the survey included starting, average, and maximum wages. Data on *employee benefits* included paid days off and health and other benefits offered to both the direct care worker and his or her dependents. Paid days were summarized for direct care workers with both 1 and 5 years of experience. The other benefits consisted of health insurance, dental, retirement, child care, and tuition.

The survey also collected data on three measures of turnover. The first of these measures, the *crude separation* rate indicated all movement out of an organization and was calculated as the proportion of staff leaving in the entire work force. The second turnover measure, the *average length of service* (leavers), indicated the mean number of months that separated staff had been on the job. The third measure, the *instability* rate, indicated the size of the work force actually experiencing turnover.

Data Collection and Analysis To increase the reliability of the study results, three follow-up mailings and two telephone contacts were made to each nonrespondent. More than 1,000 of 1,612 surveys were returned, resulting in the establishment of a substantial national data base. Potential errors were identified, and project staff contacted individual facilities for clarification. Approximately 90% of the returned surveys required additional telephone follow-up to clarify information provided by the respondents.

To increase the utility of the study's results, the wage information was adjusted for cost of living differences across the states. A procedure developed by McMahon and Chang (1991) was utilized to calculate cost of living indices for the 50 states and the District of Columbia. The procedure involved the construction of a predictive model that employed variables demonstrated to have a logical relationship to the cost of living for different geographic areas. These variables included the cost of living index for metropolitan and nonmetropolitan areas for each state, per capita personal income, value of single family housing, and the percent change in population during the previous 5 years. Individual state indexes were weighted according to the state's distribution of population between metropolitan and nonmetropolitan areas.

Results

Description of Sample   General descriptive information was collected for each responding facility regarding number of facilities, size of facility, number of years the facility has been open, per diem information, and general information about the types of clients served (see Table 2). In general, public institutions were larger in size, had been open longer, had higher daily costs, and served a larger proportion of individuals with more severe disabilities than either privately or publicly operated community facilities. These differences are not surprising given the trend in most states during the last decade to place more individuals with disabilities into smaller, more home-like settings.

Compensation of Direct Care Staff   The mean *starting* hourly wage for public institutions in the national sample was $6.85, compared to $5.22 for private community facilities (see Figure 1). The mean *starting* wage for publicly operated community facilities was $7.00, slightly higher than the rate for public institutions. However, there was a large difference between the mean *starting* wage for county government-operated community facilities ($5.58) and the wage for community facilities operated by state governments ($7.67).

The difference between the mean *starting* wage for public institutions and private community facilities varied across the states. Table 3 ranks each state according to the differential between the mean *starting* wages for public institutions and private community facilities in each state. Seven states reported that the starting wage for institutions was 50% more or higher than the rate for privately operated community facilities. At the other extreme, 11 states reported a wage differential of less than 10% (four of these states actually reported a higher *starting* wage for their private community facilities than for their public institutions).

Examination of Table 3 indicates that the magnitude of the wage differential in most states between public institutions and private community facilities may be related more to the institutional wage rate rather than the community rate. For example, the mean wage differential for the first 10 states listed in Table 3 (those

Table 2. Description of sample

Characteristic	Pub inst[a]	Priv com[b]	Pub com[c] County	State
No. of facilities	186	618	40	86
Average size	345.6	14.8	10.9	9.2
Years open	44.4	7.9	8.5	5.0
Per diem	$186.60	$85.29	$80.33	$141.60
Clients Sev/prof	82.1%	42.4%	48.7%	57.5%
Clients Nonamb	28.6%	9.9%	6.4%	11.3%

[a]Public institutions.
[b]Private community facilities.
[c]Public community facilities.

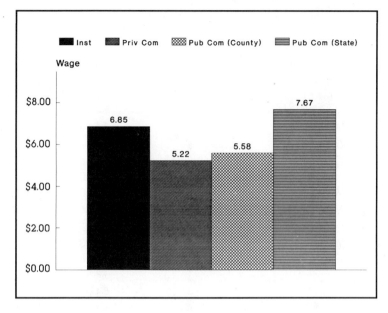

Figure 1. Starting wages for direct care workers.

states with the greatest differential) was 59% (see Figure 2). For these 10 states, the mean institutional *starting* wage rate was $7.83 and the mean rate for private community facilities was $4.93. At the other extreme, the mean wage differential for the bottom 10 states in Table 3 (those states with the smallest differential) was zero (0%). For the last 10 states, the mean institutional wage rate ($5.47) was more than $2.00 lower than the mean institutional rate for the first 10 states ($7.83). However, the mean community rate for the bottom 10 states ($5.47) was only about $.50 higher than the community rate for the first 10 states ($4.93). This suggests that those states with a small wage differential between institutional and community facilities were characterized by abnormally low institutional wage rates rather than by high community rates.

As noted previously, cost of living varies across the states. The mean *starting* wages listed in Table 3 are nominal wages and have not been adjusted for geographic cost of living. Table 4 lists the mean *starting* wage for the private community facilities in each state, both before and after adjustment for cost of living differences (states are ranked according to mean wages after adjustment for cost of living). Seventeen states decreased in rankings after this adjustment, six retained the same ranking, and 28 states increased in their ranking. The effect of cost of living ranged from an increase of $.55 in New Mexico's adjusted mean *starting* wage to a decrease of $1.67 in Connecticut's adjusted mean *starting* wage.

The mean *average* wage for direct care workers in public institutions was $8.72, compared to $5.97 in privately operated facilities and $8.41 in publicly operated community facilities ($6.46 for county-operated and $9.40 for state-

Table 3. Starting wage differential between institutions and community

Rank	State	Institutions	Community	% Diff
1	Michigan	$9.53	$5.18	84.1%
2	Iowa	$8.18	$4.64	76.3%
3	Ohio	$8.22	$4.80	71.1%
4	Illinois	$6.89	$4.45	54.9%
5	Wisconsin	$7.21	$4.66	54.8%
6	California	$7.99	$5.16	54.8%
7	Oregon	$7.19	$4.66	54.4%
8	Hawaii	$7.45	$5.00	49.0%
9	Washington	$7.72	$5.28	46.2%
10	Minnesota	$7.95	$5.46	45.8%
11	District of Columbia	$7.66	$5.27	45.3%
12	Wyoming	$5.61	$3.93	42.9%
13	Georgia	$5.93	$4.18	41.9%
14	Florida	$6.13	$4.33	41.4%
15	Kansas	$6.39	$4.56	40.3%
16	North Carolina	$6.61	$4.77	38.5%
17	Connecticut	$10.94	$8.13	34.5%
18	Alaska	$9.93	$7.41	33.9%
19	New York	$8.01	$5.99	33.9%
20	Alabama	$5.49	$4.16	31.9%
21	Arizona	$6.23	$4.75	31.2%
22	South Carolina	$5.75	$4.39	31.0%
23	Idaho	$5.94	$4.58	29.6%
24	Utah	$5.51	$4.27	29.0%
25	Texas	$5.64	$4.40	28.1%
26	Arkansas	$5.51	$4.34	26.9%
27	Nevada	$7.59	$6.09	24.7%
28	North Dakota	$5.37	$4.40	22.0%
29	Nebraska	$5.78	$4.79	20.6%
30	Rhode Island	$8.84	$7.42	19.2%
31	Missouri	$5.49	$4.64	18.3%
32	Maine	$6.70	$5.74	16.6%
33	South Dakota	$5.23	$4.49	16.4%
34	Indiana	$5.45	$4.75	14.7%
35	Montana	$5.89	$5.15	14.3%
36	Maryland	$6.46	$5.66	14.2%
37	Pennsylvania	$6.23	$5.46	14.2%
38	Louisiana	$4.86	$4.27	13.8%
39	Vermont	$6.76	$5.94	13.7%

(continued)

Table 3. *(continued)*

Rank	State	Institutions	Community	% Diff
40	Oklahoma	$5.09	$4.49	13.3%
41	Mississippi	$4.07	$3.73	9.1%
42	Kentucky	$4.38	$4.05	8.1%
43	New Hampshire	$6.68	$6.19	7.9%
44	West Virginia	$4.26	$4.03	5.5%
45	Colorado	$5.23	$4.96	5.5%
46	Tennessee	$4.31	$4.20	2.7%
47	Massachusetts	$7.63	$7.60	0.3%
48	Delaware	$5.47	$5.57	−1.8%
49	New Jersey	$6.36	$6.59	−3.5%
50	New Mexico	$4.59	$4.96	−7.5%
51	Virginia	$5.75	$6.57	−12.4%
	Nation	$6.85	$5.22	31.2%

operated facilities). Study participants were also requested to report the *maximum* wage paid to a direct care worker in their facility. The state-wide mean *maximum* wage for the public institutions in the national sample was $10.54 compared to $7.05 in privately operated community facilities. The mean maximum wage for publicly operated community facilities was $9.94 ($7.69 for county-operated and

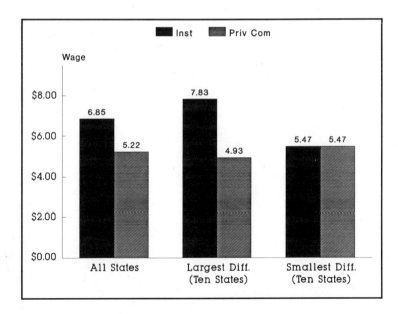

Figure 2. Starting wage differential between institutions and private community facilities.

Table 4. Starting wages adjusted for cost of living (private community facilities)

State	Adjusted rank	Adjusted wage	Nominal rank	Nominal wage
Rhode Island	1	$6.90	3	$7.42
Connecticut	2	$6.46	1	$8.13
Nevada	3	$6.40	8	$6.09
Massachusetts	4	$6.34	2	$7.60
Virginia	5	$5.99	6	$6.57
Alaska	6	$5.91	4	$7.41
New Hampshire	7	$5.84	7	$6.19
Vermont	8	$5.79	10	$5.94
Montana	9	$5.62	20	$5.15
Maine	10	$5.57	11	$5.74
New Mexico	11	$5.51	22	$4.96
New Jersey	12	$5.45	5	$6.59
Minnesota	13	$5.44	15	$5.46
Washington	14	$5.42	16	$5.28
Pennsylvania	15	$5.42	14	$5.46
New York	16	$5.37	9	$5.99
Maryland	17	$5.33	12	$5.66
Michigan	18	$5.29	18	$5.18
Arizona	19	$5.28	27	$4.75
Delaware	20	$5.15	13	$5.57
Nebraska	21	$5.09	25	$4.79
South Dakota	22	$4.99	35	$4.49
Indiana	23	$4.96	28	$4.75
Ohio	24	$4.96	24	$4.80
Colorado	25	$4.96	23	$4.96
Oregon	26	$4.94	29	$4.66
North Carolina	27	$4.91	26	$4.77
South Carolina	28	$4.90	40	$4.39
Arkansas	29	$4.89	41	$4.34
Iowa	30	$4.88	32	$4.64
Oklahoma	31	$4.83	36	$4.49
Utah	32	$4.81	43	$4.27
Idaho	33	$4.79	33	$4.58
Missouri	34	$4.79	31	$4.64
North Dakota	35	$4.77	38	$4.40
Wisconsin	36	$4.76	30	$4.66
Kansas	37	$4.75	34	$4.56

(continued)

Table 4. (continued)

State	Adjusted rank	Adjusted wage	Nominal rank	Nominal wage
Louisiana	38	$4.69	44	$4.27
Texas	39	$4.69	39	$4.40
Alabama	40	$4.60	47	$4.16
Florida	41	$4.58	42	$4.33
Tennessee	42	$4.52	45	$4.20
Georgia	43	$4.44	46	$4.18
West Virginia	44	$4.40	49	$4.03
Kentucky	45	$4.39	48	$4.05
California	46	$4.37	19	$5.16
Illinois	47	$4.34	37	$4.45
District of Columbia	48	$4.28	17	$5.27
Mississippi	49	$4.27	51	$3.73
Wyoming	50	$4.14	50	$3.93
Hawaii	51	$3.92	21	$5.00
Nation		$5.22		$5.22

$10.98 for state-operated facilities). Figure 3 illustrates the mean *average* and *maximum* wages for the four groups of facilities.

Direct Care Benefits Information was collected on six different types of benefits. These included health, dental, retirement, child care, tuition assistance, and paid days off. Respondents were asked if a particular benefit was offered and if the facility paid for all, some, or none of the cost. In terms of paid days, facilities were asked for the number of paid holiday and vacation days off earned each year by employees (after 1 and 5 years of employment).

Almost all public and private facilities offered a health plan to direct care workers, but a smaller proportion of facilities offered a dental plan (see Table 5). Nearly all public institutions (99%) and state-operated community facilities (98%) in the sample offered a retirement plan to their direct care workers, while a lower but still large proportion of the county-operated community facilities (83%) provided this benefit. However, only slightly more than half (57%) of the privately operated community facilities offered a retirement plan to their direct care workers.

A larger proportion of public institutions (23%) and state-operated community facilities (19%) provided a child care benefit than did either county-operated (7%) or privately operated community facilities (3%). Similarly, a greater number of both public institutions and state-operated community facilities provided some type of tuition assistance (63% and 61%, respectively), than privately or county-operated community facilities (38% and 30%, respectively).

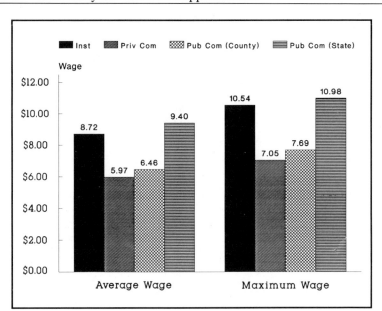

Figure 3. Average and maximum wages for direct care workers.

In terms of paid days off, there was a differential in favor of direct care workers in the public institutions and state-operated community facilities that was similar to the differential found for wages. After 1 year on the job, direct care workers in private facilities earned from 4 to 5 less paid days off than their counterparts in the other three facility groups. After 5 years on the job, this differential still existed but had decreased somewhat.

Turnover of Direct Care Staff The mean *crude separation* rate for all three groups of facilities in each state is summarized in Table 6. The mean *crude separation* rate for public institutions in the national sample was 25%, compared to 71% for privately operated community facilities and 34% among publicly operated community facilities (50% for county and 26% for state). Thirty-nine states reported a mean *crude separation* rate at or above 50% for their privately operated community facilities, while only five states had mean rates above 50% for their public institutions.

The turnover rates listed in Table 6 reflect rates for both full- and part-time workers. Data was collected separately for both types of workers. It was found that the *crude separation* rate among part-time workers was considerably higher than the rate for full-time workers for all four groups of facilities (see Figure 4). The annual mean *separation* rate for part-time workers in privately operated community facilities approached 100%.

To minimize the limitations of utilizing a single measure of turnover, information was also collected that would allow the *instability* rate to be calculated for each facility. The *instability rate* is the proportion of direct care positions that have

Table 5. Direct care benefits[a]

Benefit		Pub inst[b]	Priv com[c]	Public com[d] County	State
Health	Worker	100.0	96.8	100.0	100.0
	Dependent	99.4	92.1	93.3	98.3
Dental	Worker	93.7	63.8	70.0	84.7
	Dependent	93.2	59.4	56.7	84.7
Retirement	Worker	99.4	56.8	83.3	98.3
Child care	Worker	23.3	2.6	6.7	18.6
Tuition	Worker	63.1	38.1	30.0	61.0
Paid days	After 1 year	23.4	18.2	22.1	22.9
	After 5 years	26.7	23.4	24.9	26.3

[a]All benefits except "paid days" expressed as percent of facilities offering benefit.
[b]Public institutions.
[c]Private community facilities.
[d]Public community facilities.

experienced turnover during the last year. The *instability* rate for private community facilities (43%) was 2.7 times the *instability* rate for public institutions (16%). In other words, turnover affects nearly three times the number of workers in privately operated community facilities, as compared to public institutions. The *instability* rates among both state- and county-operated community facilities (21% and 29%) were slightly higher than the public institution *instability* rate.

The third and final measure of turnover reported in the study was the tenure of separating staff. The national mean *length of service (leavers)* for full-time staff in responding public institutions was 50.3 months, compared to 14.7 months in privately operated community facilities. More than half (56%) of the direct care staff who separated in privately operated community facilities did so before completing 1 year on the job, compared to less than one-third (31%) of the workers in public institutions.

Analysis and Conclusions of National Survey Findings

Wage Differential   Real wages for direct care workers have declined during the past decade. In fact, increases in starting wages have failed to keep pace with inflation. The mean starting wage for direct care workers in privately operated community facilities ($5.22 per hour) was only about 3% above the poverty level for a family of three in 1989. The number of direct care workers who were actually living in poverty could not be determined since the number of family members and the amount of other family income would have to be considered. However, more than one-half of privately operated community facilities in the study sample reported *starting* wages for full-time workers that were below the poverty level for a family of three.

Table 6. Crude separation

State	Pub institutions	Priv community	Pub community
Alabama	31.1%	82.7%	
Alaska	62.0%	42.2%	
Arizona	26.9%	178.6%	21.7%
Arkansas	23.3%	34.2%	
California	20.8%	106.5%	
Colorado	31.6%	53.1%	0.0%
Connecticut	41.8%	53.8%	23.7%
Delaware	39.0%	25.0%	
District of Columbia	13.3%	48.5%	
Florida	12.1%	125.7%	
Georgia	14.2%	53.3%	59.0%
Hawaii	19.2%	35.7%	
Idaho	28.8%	88.9%	
Illinois	13.7%	87.2%	
Indiana	31.2%	75.6%	
Iowa	12.3%	71.7%	6.3%
Kansas	30.6%	66.8%	
Kentucky	13.7%	68.5%	
Louisiana	32.5%	29.7%	35.0%
Maine	11.4%	53.8%	25.0%
Maryland	15.9%	77.9%	
Massachusetts	38.9%	44.9%	66.7%
Michigan	21.3%	59.2%	
Minnesota	14.3%	66.8%	18.0%
Mississippi	69.3%	50.0%	0.0%
Missouri	23.0%	61.1%	50.8%
Montana	30.1%	56.3%	
Nebraska	37.4%	146.3%	66.3%
Nevada	36.2%	—	62.5%
New Hampshire	30.5%	82.7%	
New Jersey	20.3%	67.8%	
New Mexico	50.7%	46.2%	
New York	27.1%	58.5%	17.3%
North Carolina	25.5%	72.0%	72.2%
North Dakota	21.6%	66.9%	
Ohio	13.5%	63.6%	26.1%
Oklahoma	16.2%	55.7%	
Oregon	25.4%	108.0%	
Pennsylvania	14.5%	87.3%	

(continued)

Table 6. (continued)

State	Pub institutions	Priv community	Pub community
Rhode Island	17.1%	32.1%	26.8%
South Carolina	17.2%	40.7%	41.5%
South Dakota	51.4%	71.9%	
Tennessee	37.8%	31.9%	
Texas	22.9%	64.4%	52.7%
Utah	52.0%	115.0%	
Vermont	41.7%	54.5%	
Virginia	36.5%	51.3%	24.9%
Washington	18.0%	83.1%	
West Virginia	26.1%	64.2%	
Wisconsin	15.2%	57.4%	
Wyoming	31.8%	157.4%	
Nation	24.8%	70.7%	34.2%

Compounding the low wage level of most direct care workers is the fact that wages have failed to keep pace with inflation. Lakin and Bruininks (1981) determined that the mean *starting* wage for direct care workers in private community facilities was $3.49 in 1979. Using the results from the present study, the mean *starting* wage for community facility staff, in real economic terms, has declined 15% from 1979 to 1989.

Furthermore, the wage differential between direct care workers in private community facilities and public institutions has grown larger during the past decade. The present study indicated that direct care workers in public institutions were paid, on the average, 46% more than direct care workers in privately operated community facilities ($8.72 versus $5.97). Job tenure accounts for part of this disparity. However, there was still a significant difference (31%) between the two groups of workers in terms of *starting* wages ($6.85 versus $5.22). Lakin and Bruininks (1981) reported a 15% difference between *starting* wages for direct care workers in private community facilities and comparable workers in public institutions. The pay differential between direct care workers in public and in private facilities has tripled during the last 10 years.

The goal of pay equity itself, however, should be re-evaluated in some states. This study has demonstrated that those states with a small wage differential between the institutional and community sector were more often characterized by abnormally low institutional wage rates rather than by relatively high community wages. This illustrates the importance of paying an adequate wage to direct care staff working in community programs instead of merely achieving pay equity with institutional wages, especially when considering the high staff turnover rates.

It has also been determined that wage rates for direct care workers in privately operated community facilities are significantly lower than wage rates for compar-

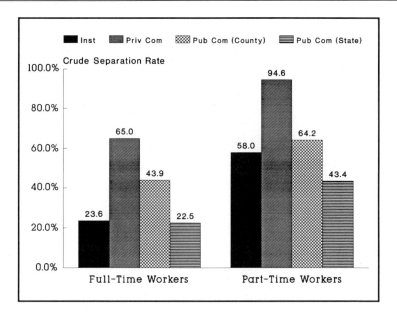

Figure 4. Separation of full-time and part-time direct care workers.

able workers in publicly operated community. The mean starting wage for publicly operated community facilities ($7.00) was almost $2.00 higher than the mean *starting* wage for privately operated community facilities ($5.22). However, publicly operated community facilities are not a homogeneous group; the state-operated facilities reported a *starting* wage ($7.67) almost $2.00 higher than the wage reported for county-operated facilities ($5.58). Therefore, future studies should examine state- and county-operated community facilities as two separate facility groups.

Cost of Living Adjustment for cost of living has also had a major impact on the wage-level data in several states, especially those reporting high community wages. In terms of *starting* wages for private community facilities, four states dropped more than 10 rankings after wages were adjusted for cost of living. The most dramatic example of this occurred in the District of Columbia, which dropped from a ranking of 17th to 48th after the cost of living adjustment. These differences should be considered when policies are developed that affect different geographical areas within a state. Employing a cost of living adjustment more accurately reflects the purchasing power of employee wages.

Benefits The level of benefits for direct care workers in privately operated community facilities compared unfavorably with those of direct care workers in public institutions. In fact, direct care staff in public institutions, on the average, earned 29% more holiday and vacation days after the first year of employment than their counterparts in privately operated community facilities. Although the present study did not assess the comprehensiveness of other benefits, the proportion of privately operated community facilities that offered other benefits (health, dental, retirement, child care, and tuition assistance) was smaller for each benefit than the proportion of public institutions that offered these benefits. In most other occupations, fringe benefits have assumed an increasingly important role in employee compensation. In fact, during the 1960s and 1970s, the cost of benefits to employers increased faster than the cost of wages.

The solution to improving benefits for direct care workers in privately operated community facilities may not be just a matter of playing catch-up. Stelluto and Klein (1990) cautioned that "traditional approaches to employee pay and benefits (targeted to the 'traditional' worker of the mid-20th century) may well become impractical" (p. 42). Future efforts should consider the development of cafeteria-style benefit plans and portable retirement plans. State MR/DD agencies might also assist community agencies in setting up benefit packages in certain geographical areas prone to high turnover. For example, public officials in New York are studying a proposal that would enroll employees in private community agencies in the same health insurance plan held by state employees. Portable retirement benefits for community employees would also be established.

Turnover Turnover among direct care workers in privately operated community facilities is significantly higher than the turnover for direct care workers in public institutions. The mean rate in private community facilities (71%) was almost three times the turnover of direct care workers in public institutions (25%). During the past decade, the rate of turnover among direct care workers has apparently increased. Lakin and Bruininks (1981) reported a mean turnover rate of 55%, compared to a rate of 71% in the present study.

The large difference between institutional and community wages raises legitimate concerns regarding the stability of community residential services in many states. Community integration efforts in some states have encountered resistance from parents because of the perceived instability and high employee turnover in community facilities (Frohboese & Sales, 1980; Heller, Bond, & Braddock, 1986; Meyer, 1980; Payne, 1976; Spreat, Telles, Conroy, Feinstein, & Colombatto, 1987). Confidence in community programs will be compromised as long as turnover rates in community facilities compare so unfavorably to rates in public institutions.

In addition, some of the states have instituted policies to minimize the turnover of direct care workers. To obtain the most current information regarding state-wide initiatives to improve direct care compensation, resource groups in each state were identified. These groups included the primary state MR/DD agency, the DD Planning Council, the Arc (Association for Retarded Citizens), and the primary community residential provider association(s) in each state. During the summer of 1990, a letter was sent to each group requesting information about legislative or other policy initiatives to improve the wages of direct care workers in community facilities. One year later, in June 1991, a follow-up letter was sent asking for an update on the prior information that had been submitted.

Twenty-two states reported no policy initiatives to improve direct care compensation (see Table 7). Among the remaining states, only three reported legislation that had specifically focused on direct care wages. For example, in Maine, the law applied only to community facilities certified as intermediate care facilities for persons with mental retardation (ICFs/MR), while the Connecticut law did not speak to the pay disparity directly but instead specified that the state must consider the costs mandated by collective bargaining in setting provider rates. In Nebraska, legislation mandates a uniform system of compensation for direct care workers. Fifteen states identified explicit budgetary actions through the appropriations process that increased the pay of direct care workers in community facilities, and 24 states identified commissions set up to study the problem of low wages for direct care workers.

It is clear that the wages paid to direct care workers in most private community facilities must be increased substantially if the work force is to be stabilized. Both previous research and the present study have found a significant correlation between wages and employee turnover. Given the current seriousness of the problem and the likelihood that it will increase in severity in the future, state-wide initiatives to improve compensation of direct care staff have been quite limited. While the current recession may be an important short-term factor contributing to the lack of state activity to improve direct care wages, the pay inequity between public and private direct care workers predate the current recession. Significant improvement in the compensation of direct care workers is needed now as a first step to minimize turnover.

The negative effects of turnover are likely to increase in severity in the future if effective policies are not implemented soon. Despite high rates of turnover during the past decade, aggressive recruitment efforts and a surplus of new young workers entering the work force have permitted many community agencies to maintain an adequate level of manpower. However, several projected national demographic trends over the next decade are likely to make the recruitment of applicants to replace separated workers more difficult, increasing the need to decrease

Table 7. Number of states with policy initiatives to improve direct care wages[a]

Initiative	Number of states
Substantive legislations	3
Appropriations activity	15[b]
Task force creation	24
Litigation filed	3
Other activity	2
Total states with initiatives	29[c]

[a]51 states responded to the survey; 22 states reported no policy initiatives.

[b]Restricted to funding in excess of cost of living adjustments.

[c]This is a nonduplicated count of states with initiatives; some states were involved in multiple initiatives.

the rate of direct care turnover. First, the number of new workers entering the labor force each year is decreasing significantly. The number of young workers is projected to decrease from 24% of the total labor force in 1976 to only 16% of the labor force by the end of the 1990s (Fullerton, 1989).

A second demographic trend, the shift from manufacturing to a service-dominated national economy, will also have a major impact on the recruitment of direct care workers. Service jobs are projected to increase from 25 million to 33.7 million by the year 2000, while manufacturing jobs are projected to decrease slightly (Fullerton, 1989). In fact, service jobs alone will account for almost 50% of the new jobs that will be created during the next decade. As a result, human service agencies are likely to face more competition in recruiting job applicants who have the abilities to successfully complete agency inservice training programs.

A third demographic trend that is likely to magnify the negative effects of direct care turnover is the need for continued expansion of the community service system. Several factors will likely contribute to this need for expansion during the next decade, leading to an even greater need for manpower. These factors include: 1) continuing phase-downs of public institutions (Braddock et al., 1990); 2) current long waiting lists for out-of-home placements (Davis, 1987; Hayden, 1991); 3) a substantial number of persons with developmental disabilities living in nursing homes needing alternative placements (Mitchell & Braddock, 1990); 4) a significant number of people living at home with elderly parents (Fujiura & Braddock, 1992; Heller & Factor, 1988); and 5) a large number of young people graduating from special education programs each year (U.S. Department of Education, 1988).

CONCLUSION

Ten years ago, Lakin, Bruininks, Hill, and Hauber (1982) reported that the mean starting pay for direct care workers in private community facilities was near the minimum wage and that more than half of the direct care workers in these facilities left their jobs each year. These findings led them to conclude that:

> direct-care staff turnover is one of the major problems in the residential services system today. Present rates of employee compensation and related factors are the factors most highly related to the problem . . . clearly, the present service structure will be hard pressed to respond to this challenge. (Lakin et al., 1982, p. 71)

Unfortunately, it appears that the situation that Lakin and his colleagues described has not improved during the last decade. Wages for direct care staff have eroded, and the rate of direct care staff turnover has increased. A significant increase in wages of persons working in privately operated community facilities is necessary if a stable system of community services is to be realized and maintained.

REFERENCES

Al Fisher Associates, Inc. (1988). *1988 salary and benefits survey of Maryland agencies serving individuals with developmental disabilities*. Baltimore: The Maryland Coalition of Agencies Serving Individuals with Developmental Disabilities.

Arthur Young's Human Resources Consulting Group. (1988). *Salary and benefits survey: Montana Association of Independent Disabilities Services.* Helena: Montana Department of Social and Rehabilitative Services.

Braddock, D., & Fujiura, G. (1991). Politics, public policy, and the development of community mental retardation services in the United States. *American Journal of Mental Retardation, 95*(4), 369–387.

Braddock, D., Hemp, R., Fujiura, G., Bachelder, L., & Mitchell, D. (1990). *The state of the states in developmental disabilities.* Baltimore: Paul H. Brookes Publishing Co.

Braddock, D., & Mitchell, D. (1992). *Residential services and developmental disabilities in the United States: A national survey of staff compensation, turnover, and related issues.* Washington, DC: American Association on Mental Retardation.

Bruininks, R., Kudla, M., Wieck, C., & Hauber, F. (1980). Management problems in community residential facilities. *Mental Retardation, 18,* 125–130.

Bureau of Labor Statistics. (1990). Establishment data: Historical hours and earnings. *Employment and Earnings, 37*(5), 7–111.

Bureau of National Affairs. (1989). Turnover report. *Bulletin to Management,* March 9 (pp. 77–78), June 8 (pp. 181–182), September 14 (pp. 293–294), December 14 (pp. 397–398).

Child Care Employee Project. (1989). *The national child care staffing study.* Oakland, CA: Author.

Colorado Developmental Disabilities Funding Coalition. (1988). *Colorado community challenge: Investing in our future.* Denver: Author.

Davis, S. (1987). *National status report on waiting lists of people with mental retardation for community-based services.* Arlington, TX: Association for Retarded Citizens-United States.

Frohboese, R., & Sales, B. (1980). Parental opposition to deinstitutionalization: A challenge in need of attention and resolution. *Law and Human Behavior, 4,* 1–87.

Fujiura, G., & Braddock, D. (1992). Fiscal and demographic trends in mental retardation services: The emergence of the family. In Lou Rowitz (Ed.), *Mental retardation in the year 2000* (pp. 316–338). New York: Springer–Verlag.

Fullerton, H. (1989, November). New labor force projections, spanning 1988 to 2000. *Monthly Labor Review,* 3–12.

Ganju, V. (1979). *Turnover trends among MHMR series employees in Texas state schools.* Austin: Texas Department of Mental Health and Mental Retardation.

George, M., & Baumeister, A. (1981). Employee withdrawal and job satisfaction in community residential facilities for mentally retarded persons. *American Journal of Mental Deficiency, 85*(6), 639–664.

Goldin, C. (1984). The earnings gap in historical perspective. In Office of Civil Rights, *Comparable worth: Issue for the 80s–A consultation of the U.S. Commission on Civil Rights, Vol. 1.* Washington, DC: U.S. Government Printing Office.

Hayden, M. (1991). *Waiting: Status of adults waiting for community-based services in the U.S.* Minneapolis: University of Minnesota, Research and Training Center on Residential Services and Community Living, Institute on Community Integration (UAP).

Heller, T., Bond, M., & Braddock, D. (1986). *Family reactions to institutional closures.* Chicago: University of Illinois at Chicago, Institute for the Study of Developmental Disabilities.

Heller, T., & Factor, A. (1988). Development of a transition plan for older adults with developmental disabilities residing in the natural home. *Public Policy Monograph Series, #37.* Chicago: Illinois University Affiliated Program on Developmental Disabilities.

Jacobson, J., & Ackerman, L. (1989). *Factors associated with staff tenure in group homes* (Technical report #89-5). Albany: New York State Office of Mental Retardation and Developmental Disabilities.

Kasteler, J., Ford, M., White, M., & Carruth, M. (1979). Personnel turnover: A major problem for nursing homes. *Nursing Homes, 28*, 20–25.

Kirkbride, F. (1912). The institution as a factor in race conservation. In T. Mulry (Ed.), *Third New York City conference on charities and corrections*. Albany, NY: J.B. Lyon.

Lakin, K., & Bruininks, R. (1981). *Occupational stability of direct-care staff of residential facilities for mentally retarded people*. Minneapolis: University of Minnesota, Department of Psycho-Educational Studies.

Lakin, K., Bruininks, R., Hill, B., & Hauber, F. (1982). Turnover of direct-care staff in a national sample of residential facilities for mentally retarded people. *American Journal of Mental Deficiency, 87*, 64–72.

Levine, E. (1957). Turnover among nursing personnel in general hospitals. *Hospitals, 31*, 50–53.

Marshall, R., & Paulin, B. (1984). The employment and earnings of women: The comparable worth debate. In Office of Civil Rights, *Comparable worth: Issue for the 80s–A consultation of the U.S. Commission on Civil Rights, Vol. 1*. Washington, DC: U.S. Government Printing Office.

McMahon, W., & Chang, S. (1991). *Geographical cost of living differences: Interstate and intrastate, update 1991*. Normal, IL: MacArthur/Spencer Foundation Special Series (#20), Center for the Study of Educational Finance, College of Education and the Graduate School, Illinois State University.

Meyer, R. (1980). Attitudes of parents of institutionalized mentally retarded individuals toward deinstitutionalization. *American Journal of Mental Deficiency, 85*, 184–187.

Minnesota Department of Employee Relations. (1989). *Study of employee wages, benefits, and turnover in Minnesota direct care facilities serving persons with developmental disabilities*. St. Paul, MN: Author.

Mitchell, D., & Braddock, D. (1990). Historical and contemporary issues in nursing home reform (PL 100-203). *Mental Retardation, 28*, 201–210.

O'Connor, G., & Sitkei, E. (1973). *The study of a new frontier in community services: Residential facilities for developmentally disabled persons*. Eugene: University of Oregon, Rehabilitation Research and Training Center in Mental Retardation.

Older Women's League. (1988). *Chronic care workers: Crisis among paid caregivers of the elderly*. Washington, DC: Author.

O'Neill, J. (1984). An argument against comparable worth. In Office of Civil Rights, *Comparable worth: Issue for the 80s–A consultation of the U.S. Commission on Civil Rights, Vol. 1*. Washington, DC: U.S. Government Printing Office.

Payne, J. (1976). The deinstitutionalization backlash. *Mental Retardation, 3*, 43–45.

Pennsylvania Legislative Budget and Finance Committee of the General Assembly. (1989). *Report on salary levels and their impact on quality of care for client contact workers in community-based MH/MR and child day care programs*. Harrisburg: Legislative Budget and Finance Committee of the Pennsylvania General Assembly.

Pivirotto & Bothamley Consulting. (1986). *Examination of factors associated with compensation and turnover for direct service staff employed by private sector community residential providers for citizens with mental retardation*. Hartford: State of Connecticut, Department of Mental Retardation.

Price, J. (1977). *The study of turnover*. Ames: The Iowa State University Press.

Smith, G., & Aderman, S. (1987). *Paying for services: Community management initiative series*. Alexandria, VA: National Association of State Mental Retardation Program Directors.

South Dakota Association of Community-Based Services. (1989). *Salary survey*. Pierre, SD: Author.

Spreat, S., Telles, J., Conroy, J., Feinstein, C., & Colombatto, J. (1987). Attitudes toward deinstitutionalization: National survey of families of institutionalized persons with mental retardation. *Mental Retardation, 25,* 267–274.

Stelluto, G.L., & Klein, D.P. (1990). Compensation trends into the 21st century. *Monthly Labor Review,* February, 38–45.

Stryker-Gordon, R. (1982). The effect of managerial intervention on high personnel turnover in nursing homes. *Journal of Long-Term Care Administration, 10*(2), 21–33.

Tuchi, B., & Carr, B. (1971). Labor turnover. *Hospitals, 45,* 88–92.

U.S. Department of Education. (1988). *Tenth annual report to Congress on the implementation of the Education of the Handicapped Act.* Washington, DC: Author.

Wagnild, G. (1988). A descriptive study of nurse's aide turnover in long-term care facilities. *Journal of Long-Term Care Administration, 16,* 19–23.

Weisfeld, N. (1984). *Accreditation, certification and licensure of nursing home personnel: A discussion of issues and trends.* Background paper prepared for Committee on Nursing Home Regulation, Institute of Medicine, National Academy of Sciences, Washington, DC.

Wisconsin Community Direct Service Worker Task Force. (1989). *A summary of findings of the 1987 community direct service worker survey.* Madison: State of Wisconsin, Council of Developmental Disabilities.

Zaharia, E., & Baumeister, A. (1979). Technician losses in public residential facilities. *American Journal of Mental Deficiency, 84*(1), 36–39.

_ **Chapter 13** _____

Residential Services Personnel

Recruitment, Training, and Retention

Sheryl A. Larson,
Amy Hewitt, and K. Charlie Lakin

Increasing numbers of persons with developmental disabilities live in small community homes rather than in institutions. Although improvements in specific quality of life outcomes are associated with moving to community homes (Conroy & Bradley, 1985; Horner, Stoner, & Ferguson, 1988; Larson & Lakin, 1989, 1991; Malony & Taplin, 1988), such improvements are not automatic (Hill et al., 1989; Larson & Lakin, 1992a). Quality of life depends not only on where a person lives, but also on the nature of the experiences and opportunities available in both home and community environments (Bellamy, Newton, LeBaron, & Horner, 1990; Schalock, 1991). Residential direct care providers (e.g., group home staff members, foster family members, roommates in supported living arrangements) are the primary providers of support, training, supervision, and personal assistance to persons with developmental disabilities in home and community settings. As a result, they play an important role in influencing the experiences, opportunities, and quality of life outcomes experienced by persons with developmental disabilities.

Nationwide, approximately 100,000 full-time equivalent staff members worked in direct service positions in community residential facilities in 1989 (Lakin, Hill, Chen, & Stephens, 1989; White, Lakin, Bruininks, & Li, 1991). The attitudes and actions of those staff members clearly influence the quality of life of

Preparation of this chapter was supported by a subcontract (#H133B0003-90) between the National Institute on Disability and Rehabilitation Research (NIDRR); the Research and Training Center on Residential Services and Community Living, Institute on Community Integration (UAP) and the University of Minnesota (College of Education); and the Research and Training Center on Community Integration, Center on Human Policy at Syracuse University. Additional support was provided by a grant from NIDRR (#H133B80048). The opinions expressed herein are those of the authors.

persons with developmental disabilities who are living in community homes. Unfortunately, recruiting, training, and retaining qualified direct service staff members are serious personnel challenges for residential service agencies. Characteristics of the residential service system, the direct service role, and the staff members themselves influence these challenges. This chapter examines each of these factors. Following this examination, the research related to recruitment, training, and retention is summarized and innovative personnel practices and recommendations for personnel research, policy, and practice are forwarded.

FACTORS INFLUENCING
RECRUITMENT, TRAINING, AND RETENTION

Characteristics of the Residential Service System

Two major characteristics of the service delivery system influence the recruitment, training, and retention of people who provide residential support to persons with developmental disabilities. First, the movement of thousands of people with developmental disabilities from institutions to community residential settings in the last 20 years has resulted in the decentralization of residential services. This movement has led to a dramatic increase in the number and types of residential service agencies. While decentralization of services has produced important benefits for persons with developmental disabilities, the results for staff have been mixed. On one hand, increased opportunities for autonomy and responsibility for direct service personnel may have positive effects on worker commitment and job satisfaction (Price & Mueller, 1986). On the other hand, recruitment, training, and retention have become more difficult.

Decentralization has enabled a wide range of community residential service models to be employed. Models such as in-home services, semi-independent living arrangements, supported living arrangements, and group homes demand a variety of skills. This may make it difficult for new recruits to identify and select job openings that match their skills and interests. Consequently, high turnover rates among those whose expectations do not match the job requirements may occur. Scheduling and arranging for training has also become more difficult because individual staff are spread out over larger geographic areas (Langer, Choisser, & Agosta, 1987). Furthermore, decentralization has reduced access to professional staff within the home setting and increased reliance on direct service staff for the provision of training and supervision of other direct service staff. Finally, retention has become more difficult because small work units have fewer backup staff readily available to cover shortages due to staff illness, vacation, or training. These factors have the potential to increase stress and reduce job satisfaction, both of which may contribute to turnover of personnel.

The second characteristic influencing recruitment, training, and retention is the size of the human services industry. The number of human services jobs in America is large and continually growing. As the number of persons with developmental disabilities who receive services in community settings increases, so also does the need for more workers in those settings. Competition for recruits comes from at least three sources: 1) other service industries, such as the tourism industry (Orcutt, 1989); 2) other types of services provided to persons with developmental disabilities, such as schools and vocational settings that often offer full-time day positions; and 3) other growing care provision industries, such as nursing homes, community services for persons with psychiatric disabilities, and personal care attendant services.

Characteristics of the Direct Service Role

The most prominent negative characteristic of direct service employment is the rate of pay. Direct service workers in private community settings earn an average of $5.97 per hour nation-wide (Braddock & Mitchell, 1992). This compares to average hourly wages of $6.53 in retail trade, $9.39 across all service trades, and the national average hourly wage, which was $9.66 in 1989 (U.S. Bureau of the Census, 1991). In a recent national study, salaries in community settings were found to be 31.2% lower than similar positions in institutions (Braddock & Mitchell, 1992). Administrators in Massachusetts identified the lack of competitive salaries as the primary obstacle in recruiting qualified staff (Coleman & Craig, 1981). The impact of low wages on recruitment and retention was also confirmed in a Wisconsin study in which residential staff ranked low salaries as one of their top five job stressors (Knight & Hayden, 1989).

Other job characteristics that create recruitment and retention challenges include the frequent requirement for early morning, evening, and/or overnight shifts (Coleman & Craig, 1981), and the necessity for staff to work weekends and holidays. In addition, not all positions are full-time. National figures indicate that 32.3% of direct service staff who work in private community facilities are part-time employees (D. Mitchell, personal communication, January 1992). For recruitment purposes, the proportion of part-time positions that need to be filled may be much higher than this because full-time positions are more stable (Braddock & Mitchell, 1992).

Direct service positions may be viewed negatively because they lack professional status, and are not held in particularly high regard by society (Baumeister & Zaharia, 1987). This lack of respect relates to both low wages and to negative societal perceptions of persons with developmental disabilities (Braddock & Mitchell, 1992). These are stressful jobs that demand much from workers. Staff are frequently asked to fill multiple roles such as receptionist, chauffeur, teacher, counselor, friend, accountant, advocate, medication manager, custodian, and cook (Turner, 1992). Training requirements for these roles extend far beyond how to fill the teacher and counselor roles that are most often considered part of direct service positions. Staff are also burdened with heavy paperwork requirements, while simultaneously being pushed to spend increased time facilitating activities in a broad range of community settings. The number of people attracted to work under such conditions is understandably limited.

Characteristics of Direct Service Staff

The characteristics of people who work in residential direct service positions are important because they influence the probability that such individuals will remain on the job and be responsive to training. Staff characteristics reported in three national reports and six state reports are summarized in Table 1. Examination of the table reveals that the majority of staff are female and white; most are under 35 years old, and about half are married. Educational attainments vary. In the two national studies that sampled only experienced staff, a large proportion had completed at least some college courses. In the other national study and in four of the six statewide studies, the largest proportion of staff members have a high school education or less. In the statewide study that included only full-time live-in staff, most have college degrees (Dellinger & Shope, 1978). Average tenure varies across studies. Studies examining only experienced staff found average tenure to be between 4.6 and 6.5 years, while studies examining all staff members found average tenure to be between 0.5 years and 2.7 years. In summary, the characteristics of the staff varies depending on when and where the study was conducted, and on the type of sample drawn.

Based on the characteristics in Table 1, recruitment strategies to replace current staff with those of similar demographic characteristics would target young people with limited post-secondary education. However, the number of people in those age groups are diminishing. Between 1990 and 2000, the U.S. Census Bureau (1991) projects that the proportion of the U.S. population ages 18–34 will drop by 19%. This trend creates a major problem for agencies wishing to recruit young staff. Yet, although older workers (over 35 years of age) are not currently well-represented among staff, they often are more stable employees (Cotton & Tuttle, 1986; Lakin, 1988). Increased recruitment among their ranks could address both recruitment and retention problems.

RESEARCH RELATED TO RECRUITMENT

In a recent compilation of surveys conducted in each of the 50 states, many states identified recruitment as a major human resource barrier to providing adequate community services to persons with developmental disabilities (Jaskulski & Metzler, 1990). Pennsylvania reported vacancy rates for staff ranging from 6% to 13% (Legislative Budget and Finance Committee, 1989). Further, open direct service positions in Pennsylvania were vacant for an average of 3.4 months before being filled (Task Force on Human Resources Development, 1989). In Massachusetts, direct service positions were routinely vacant for a month (Coleman & Craig, 1981). Problems recruiting staff are exacerbated by high rates of turnover experienced by residential facilities (Braddock & Mitchell, 1992; Larson & Lakin, 1992b).

Many factors can affect recruitment efforts, and only a few studies have examined recruitment of staff in detail. Initially, information about recruitment came from researchers in institutional settings. For example, one study noted that, of the many recruitment sources available, employee referrals and newspaper advertisements accounted for most of the people who were hired, but a higher proportion of rehires stayed for at least 16 weeks (Schiers, Giffort, & Furtkamp, 1980). Such findings support assertions that knowledge about job content, particularly if it is first-hand knowledge from a referral source, is associated with greater stability among new hires.

Research about recruitment in small community settings has been limited to the past decade. In one study, researchers estimated that replacement costs were $446 for workers in small community homes (serving an average of eight people) and $581 for workers in large community homes (serving an average of 24 people) (George & Baumeister, 1981). A recent national study of small foster homes and group homes found that most staff were recruited by other service providers (38%), by self-initiated contact with the agency (20%), or through media advertisements (19%) (Hill et al., 1989). Further analysis revealed that 64.9% of staff in group home settings reported having difficulties recruiting new colleagues (Larson & Lakin, 1992b). Staff perceptions of the severity of turnover problems were more strongly related to their perceptions of problems with recruitment than with the actual turnover rate. Apparently, perceptions of the difficulty caused by staff turnover were heavily influenced by whether recruitment of replacement workers was a problem in those agencies.

Innovative Solutions

One creative solution to recruitment problems, which may provide multiple benefits for service agencies, was developed in Oregon (Orcutt, 1989). In Multnomah County, a grant was used to set up a "relief pool." The agency managing the pool recruited, screened, and provided orientation to workers who were then used by residential agencies that had staffing needs due to illness, vacation, or vacancy. This strategy became a recruitment tool in that these personnel were often later hired by individual agencies. Long-term funding for this pool has not yet been finalized, but it may come either from the state or from a fee for service from agencies. The development of professional personnel service centers throughout the state was recommended to attract, screen, train, and support new employees. Both relief pools and personnel service centers would allow service agencies to pool resources to improve access to qualified applicants for open positions.

Recommendations

Recommendations for Research   To date, research on recruitment practices has been limited to demonstrating that the recruitment of direct service personnel is a problem (Jaskulski & Metzler, 1990), that it costs a considerable amount of money (George & Baumeister, 1981), and that current providers use certain recruitment strategies more than others (Schiers et al., 1980). In a time of decreasing human resources, increased attention must be given to the development of effective recruitment practices. In addition, research is needed to examine whether spe-

Table 1. Characteristics of direct service staff members in community residential settings

Study	1	2	2	3	3	4
Date collected	1978	1986	1986	1986	1986	1978
State	National	National	National	National	National	PA
Setting type	Comm	Group	ICF/MR	Private	Private	Comm
Setting size	All	1 to 6 bed	1 to 6 bed	1 to 15 bed	16+ bed	1 to 8 bed
N	174	67	34	89	52	76
Data limitations		1	1	1,2	1,2	3
Age						
% 18 to 25	36					
% 18 to 26						
% 18 to 29	33.9	31	41			
Mean/median age				39	34	26.5
Sex						
% Female	82	71	81	77	83	53
Race						
% White		85	73			
% Black		10	21			
% Other		5	6			
Marital status						
% Married/ married like	48		52			56
% Divorced/ widowed	13		18			
% Never married	39		30			44
Education						
% High school or less	46	19	18	20	29	24
% Some college	21	43	50	38	25	28
% College grad +	33	36	32	42	47	48
Tenure in agency						
% Less than 1 year						
% 1 to 2 years						
Mean/median tenure	48	4.6	5.4	5	6.5	0.5
Experience						
% Experience in MR				65	47	38
% Coursework in MR	54			47	46	

Notes: Comm = Community residential settings (does not include public institutions)
Source: Study 1—Hauber & Bruininks (1986); 2—Hill, Lakin, Bruininks, Hauber, & Copher (1989); 3—Anderson, Lakin, Bruininks, & Hill (1987); 4—Dellinger & Shope (1978); 5—Janicki, Jacobson, Zigmond, & Gordon (1984); 6—Developmental Disabilities Program (1983); 7—Jacobson & Ackerman (1990); 8—Knight & Hayden (1989); 9—Task Force on Human Resources Development (1989); 10—Legislative Budget and Finance Committee (1989).

5 1980 NY Comm 1 to 14 bed 2,035	6 1981 MN Comm All 243	7 1986 NY Private 3 to 15 bed 181	7 1986 NY Public 3 to 15 bed 114	8 1987 WI Comm All 217	9 1988 PA County All 252 4	9 1988 PA Private All 8,544	10 1988 PA Comm All 4,479
					17	26	
63				46			
26.8		35	38				
68		72	75	79	69	74	
					93	77	
					6	22	
					1	1	
43	36			65	83	79	69
23	26			6			6
34	38			26	17	20	25
	21			12	47	43	
	25				26	21	
1.5		2.7	2.6				

Data Limitations: 1—Staff who knew specific clients "best" were sampled; 2—These facilities served at least one person age 63 or older; 3—These represent only full-time, live-in staff members; 4—These include state-funded personal care workers in both the MI and MR system.

cific recruitment practices improve the number and quality of people who are hired, and to examine the link between recruitment practices, training, and retention success. Such research will enable agencies to focus their available resources on recruitment strategies that will most likely meet agency personnel needs.

Recommendations for Policy A primary policy recommendation is to improve the pay and benefits available to direct service workers, particularly those in community residential agencies (Alpha Group, 1990; Braddock & Mitchell, 1992; Knight & Hayden, 1989; Orcutt, 1989; Task Force on Human Resources Development, 1989). Broad strategic approaches to increasing money available for wages and benefits for direct service workers include: 1) raising per person service rates; 2) lowering government, agency, physical plant, or other nondirect service costs; and 3) increasing staff productivity by using flexible staffing, volunteers, or accessing existing generic community programs, and increasing resident-to-staff ratios (Lakin, 1988). Another potential strategy is to identify alternative forms of compensation for some staff members (e.g., free room and board for people recruited to work in supported living programs). Policy changes that provide equitable funding to staff in community agencies would make direct service positions more attractive to potential recruits.

Improvements in wages and benefits would likely have multiple effects on recruitment. For example, such improvements would make residential service positions more attractive to those who want to work in human services, making it possible for qualified individuals who could not otherwise afford to work in such positions to do so. Further, a specific link between wage enhancements and training could increase the willingness of potential staff to participate in preservice instruction and master the content of that training.

Recommendations for Practice There are four recommendations pertinent to practitioners. First, there is a need to expand the notion of what recruitment means and what it involves. Since recruitment is a chronic problem for many agencies, recruitment efforts should not take place only when a specific opening occurs. Instead, short-term, medium-term, and long-term recruitment efforts are required (Levy, Levy, Freeman, Feiman, & Samowitz, 1988). Short-term recruitment strategies, such as the posting of help-wanted advertisements to fill a specific opening, are the type most often employed. Medium-term strategies, such as cultivating relationships with career and placement offices and agencies through mailings of job listings, and long-term strategies, such as networking with area high school guidance counselors, university department chairpersons, and specific professors, are key to finding high-quality job candidates over the long term (Levy et al., 1988). Marketing entry-level career options to employment agencies, vocational rehabilitation agencies, and high school students would also increase the visibility of direct service jobs.

Second, there is a need to carefully consider the changing nature of direct service positions. Historically, most staff were hired to work in a facility. Today, with the expansion of supported living options, some recruitment efforts must focus on working with individuals to find compatible and caring roommates who may be compensated through free room and board rather than finding paid staff to work with several people in a facility (O'Brien & O'Brien, 1992).

Third, there is a need to increase recruitment efforts among those who have not traditionally been hired for direct service work (Lakin, 1988; Scheerenberger, 1981). The base of recruits may be broadened through targeting groups such as parents whose children have left home, elderly persons who want to work part-time during retirement, and people from groups that have traditionally experienced high unemployment rates. Efforts to increase recruitment among these persons must be accompanied by a commitment to ensure that recruits are able to develop the skills needed to perform the essential functions of the direct service role.

Finally, there is a need to enhance the image of the direct service role. This includes both agency actions to communicate to staff that they are valuable and valued (Lakin, 1988), and enhancement of the public perception of direct service work. Public awareness activities should be implemented to educate both the public and policymakers on the importance of direct service workers, and to enhance the image of community workers and the individuals with developmental disabilities they assist (Knight & Hayden, 1989). The status of direct service workers must be enhanced if they are to be viewed as an integral part of the developmental disabilities service delivery team (Knight & Hayden, 1989). Actions that strengthen the psychological benefits, as well as the economic benefits, of direct service work may also contribute to both the retention of employees and to increasing the number of persons who will initially consider entering this type of employment. This is particularly important since approximately two out of five people entering direct service work do so on the suggestion of a current, presumably satisfied, direct service worker (Hill et al., 1989).

RESEARCH RELATED TO TRAINING

The training of direct service employees is critically important for residential service agencies for several reasons. First, these organizations have a direct regulatory mandate to provide training on specific topics or for a designated number of hours. Second, staff training and competence have been identified as key elements in achieving quality services (Alpha Group 1990; Fiorelli, Margolis, Heverly, Rothchild, & Krasting, 1982). Third, training enables staff to develop the attitudes, knowledge, and skills needed to perform their jobs. Effective training provides the opportunity for individual employees to learn critical job functions, develop new skills, and cope with their job roles while also furthering the goals of the organization (Camp, Blanchard, & Huszczo, 1986). Finally, training represents an important avenue for promoting positive changes in employees, which in turn may influence the overall social ecology of residential environments and the quality of life of individuals with developmental disabilities (Jones, Blunden, Coles, Evens, & Porterfield, 1981).

A recent national study of public institutions and private and public community service agencies found that 89%–99% require classroom inservice training for direct service workers (Braddock & Mitchell, 1992). Between 80% and 90% provide on-the-job-training experiences for their staff. Furthermore, most state developmental disabilities agencies participate in training activities for residential service agencies. A recent study reported that 33 of 36 states fund, provide, or arrange training to improve the quality of services for recipients of Medicaid Home and Community-Based Services (HCBS) (Prouty & Lakin, 1991). Among those 33 states, 22 develop or disseminate training materials, 20 purchase contracts with nonstate trainers, 17 employ state staff for training, and 12 enhance HCBS rates to support agency-based training (Prouty & Lakin, 1991).

What Do Direct Service Personnel Need To Know? Two strategies were used to determine the training needs of direct service personnel working in community residential agencies. Training needs were identified through interviews with direct service personnel, Qualified Mental Retardation Professionals (QMRPs), and program directors; a review of federal and Minnesota state training regulations; and an analysis of accreditation standards and other materials that discuss competencies and training needs for direct service personnel in residential, educational, and vocational settings. Second, a review of 165 articles addressing staff training issues was undertaken. This review yielded 17 empirical studies that identified training needs (contact the authors for a complete list of these studies). Altogether, 268 training needs were identified. Those needs were condensed into a set of initial core competencies needed by staff working in all types of residential settings serving people of any age or with any level of disability (see Table 2). Other skills may also be important depending on the characteristics of the persons served.

While Table 2 provides an overview of staff training needs, it is not intended to define the exact skills within each area that must be mastered. An agency-specific training needs analysis, which includes consideration of organizational goals, a task analysis of the attitudes, knowledge, and skills needed on the job, and an analysis of the people to be trained, is necessary to guide the selection of specific instructional objectives and training criteria (Tannenbaum & Yukl, 1992).

How Should Staff Be Trained? Once the skills are identified, a training plan should be developed that considers learning objectives, trainee characteristics, current knowledge about adult learning, and constraints and costs (Tannenbaum & Yukl, 1992). The training plan also should: 1) specify what staff will be able to do at the conclusion of training, 2) define exemplary performance standards, 3) identify current skill levels prior to training, 4) assess training outcomes directly, and 5) result in changes in staff performance leading to increased independence or improved quality of life for persons with developmental disabilities served by the agency (Bernstein & Ziarnik, 1982). Finally, staff should have opportunities to be involved in the design, implementation, and evaluation of training activities (Salisbury, 1984; Tannenbaum & Yukl, 1992).

Many large agencies employ a staff trainer. Smaller agencies may have supervisors or managers who provide training in addition to their other responsibilities. Other times, outside consultants are retained to provide training.

Table 2.   Core training competencies for residential staff

Rights of Individuals with Disabilities
• Resident bill of rights
• Vulnerable adults and maltreatment of children acts
• Use of aversive and deprivation behavioral procedures
• Legal status/guardianship
• Human sexuality
• Major legislation (e.g., IDEA, ADA)

Confidentiality
• Release of information issues
• Copying or providing information to people
• Right to privacy

Legal Documentation Procedures
• When/what should be documented
• Objective versus subjective documentation
• How to document in a legal manner

Incident/Accident Reporting
• When to complete a report
• Procedures for reporting
• How to complete a report

Introduction to Program Planning
• Teaching techniques
• How to conduct a program
• Assessment
• Functional activities and instruction
• How to develop and write goals and objectives
• Basic behavior management principles

Appropriate Responses to Seizures
• Description of types of seizures
• What to do if someone has a seizure
• Treatment issues for seizure disorders

Infection Control/Safe Practices
• Hepatitis B
• AIDS
• Universal precautions
• Critical job functions related to risk of transmission

Introduction to Developmental Disabilities
• History of MR/DD services
• Causes/syndromes
• Acronyms, terminology, and jargon
• Levels of mental retardation

(continued)

Table 2. (continued)

- Least restrictive environments (LREs)
- Child/human development
- Interdisciplinary program planning and service coordination

Value-Based Services
- People-first language/labeling
- Social role valorization
- Myths and value clarification
- Age appropriateness
- Self-determination/empowerment
- Normalization
- Inclusive recreation/leisure
- Community integration
- Facilitating friendships/socialization with peers
- Staff as role models for persons with developmental disabilities
- Working with families

Dietary Issues
- Family-style dining
- Special diets
- Meal substitution
- Use of menus
- Nutrition pyramid

Training for staff should lead to the development of critical generalizable job skills that can be used often, with many persons who have developmental disabilities, and within a variety of environments (Christian & Hannah, 1983), and should foster permanent, positive changes in job performance (Jones et al., 1981). Specific instructional strategies vary in effectiveness in producing skills that meet these goals. Didactic training strategies using lectures, audiovisual aides, self-paced learning texts, and other written information with or without discussion are commonly employed in human services organizations (Christian & Hannah, 1983). While such strategies may increase awareness of topics and build initial skills, their isolated use does not lead to the development of enduring generalized skills (Feldman & Dalrymple, 1984). A preferred training strategy for developing generalized skills is to provide opportunities to practice learned skills in multiple settings (including the actual work setting) (Buckley, Albin, & Mank, 1988). Accurate, credible, timely, and constructive feedback is another critical component of effective training strategies (Neef, Trachtenberg, Loeb, & Sterner, 1991; Tannenbaum & Yukl, 1992).

Several reviews of training research confirm that multimodal techniques that incorporate practice and feedback are more effective than techniques that focus solely on didactic instruction (Anderson & Kratochwill, 1988; Feldman & Dalrymple, 1984; Kazdin, 1984; Ziarnik & Bernstein, 1984). The effectiveness of training must be evaluated using strategies such as written exams, direct observation of trainee performance, and assessments of satisfaction with service performance by employers and persons with developmental disabilities (Renzaglia, 1986). Once generalized skills have been developed, ongoing support from supervisors and managers should be provided to facilitate maintenance of those skills (Bernstein & Ziarnik, 1982).

When Should Training Be Provided? Training may be provided either preservice, during orientation, or as inservice instruction. Each of these formats provides specific types of information and benefits. Most employees will receive a combination of these types of training. The selection of a training format should depend on the type of information needed, the level of understanding required, and when the information is needed on the job.

Preservice training includes training on issues related to developmental disabilities at various levels of understanding. It is usually provided in academic settings such as community colleges, vocational/technical schools, and universities. Employees come to their new positions with knowledge and skills developed through this training. Preservice training can produce staff who have at least some basic knowledge about disabilities prior to starting work, develop a pool of trained workers, and foster job-esteem and a sense of professionalism among prospective direct service workers (Karan & Mettel, 1989; Langer, Agosta, & Choisser, 1988).

Orientation is training that orients the new employee to the agency and its policies and procedures, or that teaches basic knowledge and skills required to begin to perform direct care tasks. It is typically provided by the agency within the first few months of employment. This type of training can provide information particular to an agency that must be acquired by new staff within a short period of time (Langer et al., 1988).

Inservice training includes technical information provided to enhance attitudes, knowledge, and skills related to job performance. It is usually provided on an ongoing basis after orientation. Inservice training can also provide detailed information about specific job skills (Langer et al., 1988).

Innovative Solutions

In the past, staff have received training on a variety of topics, in a variety of formats, and at different times during their employment experience. While some training focuses on developing state-of-the-art skills in supporting people with developmental disabilities, more commonly training topics are regulation driven rather than needs-based. Instructional formats are often geared toward increasing awareness and initial skills rather than toward building generalized skills. Further, training is frequently timed to meet regulatory standards rather than to meet specific needs of staff in a particular agency. Fortunately, several models for staff training have been highlighted in the writings of professionals who are in disability-related fields (Knight, Karan, Timmerman, Griffeth, & Dufresne, 1986; Langer et al., 1987; Wallace, Larson, & Hewitt, 1992). Selected examples of such programs are included in the following paragraphs.

North Dakota Career Ladder System In July 1983, the North Dakota Department of Human Services, Division of Developmental Disabilities, working with Minot State University, developed and implemented a statewide training program to enhance the skills and knowledge of staff (Vassiliou, 1992). The North Dakota program utilizes a "train-the-trainer" approach to make instruction available to all direct service personnel. The program incorporates a variety of training approaches including: on-the-job training, self-instruction, workshop, lectures, on-site instruction, and small-group discussion. The seven-step career ladder includes orientation, position-based competency, certificate of completion, advanced certification, an Associate of Arts (AA) degree in mental retardation, a Bachelor of Arts degree in developmental disabilities, and a Master of Science degree in special education (Vassiliou, 1992). This program has been implemented statewide and is supported by agencies providing residential services in North Dakota (Haring & Johnson, 1992).

St. Louis County Community College Program The Productive Living Board for St. Louis County Citizens with Developmental Disabilities and the St. Louis Community College created a program that offers noncredit 3-hour workshops to increase the number of skilled paraprofessionals entering the field of developmental disabilities, and to respond to the continuing training needs of currently employed paraprofessionals (Bassin & Hanks, 1992). The program also offers noncredit workshops that provide training in areas such as developing personal and professional values as a direct service worker, advanced behavior modification, and anger management training for persons with MR/DD (Bassin & Hanks, 1992). In 1991, credit courses leading to an AA degree were added to the curriculum.

Recommendations

Recommendations for Research While previous research has provided some direction for training in residential settings, a great deal of information is still needed. In community residential settings, there have been few attempts to study the effects of orientation and inservice training programs on important outcomes for persons with developmental disabilities and direct service personnel (see Burchard & Thousand, 1988, and Smith, Parker, Taubman, & Lovaas, 1992 for notable exceptions). Future research efforts should address this issue and identify specific factors that influence whether training will produce its intended effect. Future investigations also should systematically examine the immediate outcomes of training, and the long-term costs and benefits of specific training strategies. Finally, researchers should develop guidelines regarding the most efficient timing for training to achieve intended outcomes. If training is to be mandated and service agencies are to invest large amounts of money on staff instruction, then an improved knowledge base on the selection of training topics and delivering effective training is needed.

Recommendations for Policy Policymakers can take several steps to improve access to high-quality training for staff. The first step is to support systematic preservice training programs that include practicum experiences. This would give students opportunities to discuss and learn from practical situations before being hired by individual agencies. Preservice training could ensure that new staff have a common core of information. Service agencies could then focus on providing agency specific information during orientation. Preservice core competency training could also facilitate recruitment efforts. For example, agencies offering training could recruit students into their programs. Once students completed their education, those agencies could assist them in job placement.

The second step is to increase access to inservice training opportunities. One strategy to accomplish this is to support the development of in-house training capacities. Policymakers in Minnesota, for example, recently funded a pilot project in which an agency was granted a one-time rate adjustment to hire an in-house trainer and to provide wage increases to staff who completed competency-based skill training (Houston County Group Homes, Inc., 1990). The project allowed the agency to develop a training curriculum, supply in-depth training to staff, provide incentives to staff members to complete training, and identify and monitor training outcomes for the agency, staff members, and persons receiving services. For agencies that are too small to support an in-house trainer, provider networks and consortiums should be supported for training purposes.

The third step to improve access to training is to support appropriate and inexpensive inservice training opportunities sponsored by developmental disabilities councils, University Affiliated Programs (UAP), community and technical colleges, private advocacy organizations, and employee unions (Langer et al., 1987). These external training opportunities can address the need for cost-effective training for staff. They can also provide information to agency trainers and managers about effective training techniques and available training tools.

Finally, policymakers must support the identification and development of cost-effective training materials for staff. Many available training materials, written in train-the-trainer formats, are targeted toward training/management-level personnel, or include concepts, language, or reading levels that are inappropriate for direct service staff. Training materials for direct service personnel must be specifically designed, taking into account that a large majority of these persons do not have college degrees. The materials must be written in nontechnical language at a basic reading level. Ideally, such materials would be accompanied by posttests, skill demonstration at program sites, or other demonstrations of learning to ensure that what was taught was learned.

Recommendations for Practice   Several steps can be taken by practitioners to improve the quality of training available to staff. The first is to include persons with developmental disabilities, parents, and direct service personnel in the identification of staff training needs and the evaluation of training outcomes. The self-advocacy movement demonstrated the importance of involvement by persons with developmental disabilities in the design and provision of services (Jensen, 1992). Clearly, this should extend to involvement in identifying what they want staff to know about meeting their needs and expectations.

Second, service agencies could focus on competency-based training efforts to improve skill generalization. Previous descriptions of training efforts and needs rarely identified competency-based training needs. Of 17 empirical studies reviewed in the preparation of this chapter, only three identified competencies related to training needs (Gage, Fredericks, Johnson-Dorn, Lindley-Southard, 1982; Intagliata & Willer, 1981; Thousand, Burchard, & Hasazi, 1986). Most identified needs were described in one- and two-word phrases and, in addition, the content to be taught and desired staff performance/competence following the training session was not specified. Training should draw on participant experiences and be designed to develop specific skills that are useful and can be evaluated at the actual work site.

Third, agencies should develop multimodal training approaches. Training modes include didactic instruction, discussion, practice sessions, and generalized practice. Retention and application of knowledge jumps from 5% for training based on lectures alone to 75% for training in which presentations of information are followed by specific skills practice (Templeman & Peters, 1992). Multiple modes of instruction followed by repeated practice should be used to ensure that staff will actually be able to apply the information they receive.

Finally, agencies should increase attention to training for supervisors and managers. Only a few studies discuss the importance of training staff in supervision and management skills (Forrest, 1982; Gage et al., 1982; Langer et al., 1987). This is problematic because supervisory staff are often responsible for carrying out training programs and for supervising the implementation of newly developed skills. The generic training literature suggests that the attitudes of supervisors toward training activities, as well as their supervision and follow-up after instruction, has had an important impact on employee attitudes about training (Tannenbaum & Yukl, 1992). As the service delivery system becomes more decentralized, making supervision more difficult, efforts should be made to identify and meet supervisory training needs.

RESEARCH RELATED TO RETENTION

Finding and training staff are critical personnel problems; however, even more critical is retaining them over time. In fact, an inability to retain staff only exacerbates recruitment challenges. The retention of residential staff has long been an important concern of administrators (Bruininks, Kudla, Wieck, & Hauber, 1980); researchers (Braddock & Mitchell, 1992; Butterfield & Warren, 1963; George, 1980; Jacobson & Ackerman, 1989; Lakin & Bruininks, 1981; Zaharia & Baumeister, 1978b); policymakers (Department of Employee Relations, 1989; Pivirotto & Bothamley Consulting, 1987); and service providers (Ganju, 1979). A primary reason for this interest has been the extraordinarily high rates of turnover reported for residential service staff.

During the past 11 years, three national studies have estimated the extent of turnover in residential settings. The first found an annual turnover rate of 29.5% in public institutions and 54.2% for both large and small nonpublic residential facilities during 1978 (Lakin & Bruininks, 1981). The second examined small (one to six person) community residential settings and found an annual turnover rate of 57% during 1986 (Larson & Lakin, 1992b). The third found a turnover rate of 24.8% among institutions, 34.2% among public community settings (serving an average of 10 people), and 70.7% among private community settings (serving an average of 14 people) in 1989 (Braddock & Mitchell, 1992).

These turnover estimates suggest that for every 100 positions in private community residential settings, between 50 and 70 persons leave their positions every year. Considering that 159,866 people with mental retardation or related conditions lived in nonpublic residential facilities in 1988 (Amado, Lakin, & Menke, 1990) and that, on average, .84 individual staff members were employed per resident in community facilities (Braddock & Mitchell, 1992), somewhere between 67,000 and 95,000 staff leave private community residential settings in the United States per year. This is a staggering number of people to replace annually and train.

Staff turnover has a significant impact on agencies, remaining staff members, and persons with developmental disabilities living in residential facilities. Among the potential positive consequences of turnover are the displacement of poor performers, the infusion of new people with innovative ideas, reduction in conflict between workers if combatants leave, reduction in retention costs (salaries increase as tenure increases), and increased opportunities for innovation, flexibility, and adaptability (Baysinger & Mobley, 1983; Bluedorn, 1982; Dalton & Todor, 1979; Mobley, 1982; Mowday, Porter, & Steers, 1982). However, while the potential positive outcomes of a certain level of turnover must be acknowledged, few if any of those who note the possibility of positive outcomes suggest that turnover rates of more than 50% are healthy for any organization.

Unfortunately, turnover can produce several negative outcomes as well. High turnover rates increase costs of residential services, decrease the quality of communication among staff, decrease continuity of treatment and care, increase administrative costs and job stress, reduce productivity and job satisfaction, and lead to staff shortages (Bersani & Heifetz, 1985; Bluedorn, 1982; Kasarda, 1973; Lakin, 1988; Mobley, 1982; Price, 1977; Zaharia & Baumeister, 1978a). Since low staff retention rates lead to frequent changes in the people having day-to-day contact with and knowledge of individuals with developmental disabilities, turnover may also have a negative impact on quality of services. Finally, the expense of recruiting, orienting, training, and supervising new staff members is immense. Adjusting figures supplied by others (George & Baumeister, 1981), by adjusting for inflation and applying national estimates of the numbers of staff replaced, the estimated cost of recruiting, orienting, training, and supervising replacement staff in residential settings is 80–100 million dollars annually.

During the last 20 years, the research literature from industrial-organizational psychology and sociology has provided a vast amount of important information regarding the correlates of turnover. In 1973, a seminal literature review was published that examined organizational, work environment, job content, and personal factors that contribute to turnover (Porter & Steers, 1973). The authors concluded that the degree to which expectations about the job are met plays a critical role in turnover. They recommended that future research emphasize the interactive influence of variables on the turnover process rather than continuing to isolate a multitude of individual variables that have an impact on turnover. That advice was heeded by many researchers, setting the stage for the next era in turnover research.

Between 1977 and 1982, several groups of researchers developed models to demonstrate how different types of variables worked together to influence staff turnover (Arnold & Feldman, 1982; Mobley, Griffeth, Hand, & Meglino, 1979; Muchinsky & Morrow, 1980; Price, 1977; Steers & Mowday, 1981). These models varied in content and focus but several common themes emerged. For example, three models suggested that intention to stay or leave the organization was the immediate precursor of actual turnover behavior (Arnold & Feldman, 1982; Mobley et al., 1979; Steers & Mowday, 1981). Other variables that appeared in most or all models were personal characteristics (e.g., age and tenure); job satisfaction; organizational commitment (i.e., identification with and involvement in the organization) (Mobley, 1982); and labor market conditions. When the models were tested, the importance of these variables was confirmed (Bluedorn, 1982; Carston & Spector, 1987; Michaels & Spector, 1982; Price & Mueller, 1986).

Although researchers continue to work on models of staff turnover using increasingly sophisticated methods (Gerhart, 1990; Williams & Hazer, 1986), the use of quantitative methods, such as meta-analyses, to combine research findings across studies has become the focus of turnover studies during the latter part of the 1980s and early 1990s. The results of several meta-analyses support the presence of a significant relationship between staff turnover and behavioral intentions (e.g., to leave or stay), job satisfaction, and organizational commitment (Cotton & Tuttle, 1986; Randall, 1990; Steel, Hendrix, & Balogh, 1990; Steel & Ovalle, 1984); perceived employment options (Cotton & Tuttle, 1986; Steel & Griffeth, 1989); job performance (Cotton & Tuttle, 1986; McEvoy & Cascio, 1987); and met expectations (Cotton & Tuttle, 1986; Wanous, Poland, Premack, & Davis, 1992). One meta-analytical study supports the presence of a significant relationship between turnover and union presence, pay, age, tenure, gender, education, number of dependents, biographical information, unemployment rate, and role clarity (Cotton & Tuttle, 1986). Thus, the importance of key variables from staff turnover models developed in the 1970s, especially intent to stay or leave, job satisfaction, and organizational commitment, was supported by the meta-analytic research of the 1980s and 1990s. It is important to note that the correlations between staff turnover and these variables rarely exceed .40 in the meta-analyses, leaving much variability unexplained. Researchers are currently exploring methodological reasons for this inability to explain more of the variability (Abelson, 1987; Kemery, Dunlap, & Bedeian, 1989; Peters & Sheridan, 1988; Steel & Griffeth, 1989).

While industrial-organizational psychology researchers were developing staff turnover models and testing for relationships among the correlates of turnover, researchers interested in turnover in residential settings that serve persons with developmental disabilities were primarily pursuing information about the correlates of turnover. Early research primarily focused on correlates of turnover among staff working in institutions (Ganju, 1979; Zaharia & Baumeister, 1979). Beginning in the early 1980s, researchers began to investigate turnover among staff members working in community settings. This research was sometimes conducted in combination with research on institutions (Department of Employee Relations, 1989; Lakin & Bruininks, 1981), and sometimes it focused solely on community settings (George & Baumeister, 1981; Jacobson & Ackerman, 1989, 1990; Larson & Lakin, 1992b). Recent literature reviews and annotated bibliographies have detailed the findings of these and other studies (Baumeister & Zaharia, 1987; Braddock & Mitchell, 1992; Lakin, 1988; Lakin & Larson, 1992; Mitchell, Bachman, Longhurst, & Braddock, 1990).

Rather than repeating those reviews, the following section summarizes six recent studies that used multivariate analyses to examine the joint impact of several variables on turnover. These studies provide information about the overall influence of a set of variables on turnover. Moreover, they provide information about which variables are most influential in predicting turnover. Together, these studies provide a complex picture of which variables most influence turnover among staff in community residential settings.

In the early 1980s, the first national study of staff turnover in private community facilities investigated turnover among 73 community residential settings, ranging in size from 1 to 64 people (Lakin & Bruininks, 1981). These investigators found that 9% of the variability in turnover rates was accounted for by starting salary indexed by average per capita income and by the number of staff employed by the facility. In another study, researchers examined turnover among 38 staff members. They found that 34% of the variability in turnover rates was accounted for by length of unit operation, age of residents, number of residents with severe behavior problems, and community skills of the residents (George & Baumeister, 1981).

During the late 1980s and early 1990s, four additional multivariate studies of turnover in community settings were published. In one, researchers found that 16% of the variability in turnover was explained by average hourly pay, by whether the facility was certified as an intermediate care facility for persons with mental retardation (ICF/MR), and by region of the state (Department of Employee Relations, 1989). A second study investigated turnover in 38 small, community residential settings. Researchers found that only public versus private operation and resident disability level provided unique contributions to predicting tenure of staff. Furthermore, these two variables, along with six others, accounted for only 22% of the variability in turnover rates (Jacobson & Ackerman, 1989).

In a recent national study, investigators examined 85 small community facilities (Larson & Lakin, 1992b). They found that 7% of the variability in turnover was accounted for by number of staff and the use of shift versus live-in staff members. In the final national study, researchers examined 618 private community facilities that served an average of 15 people each. Eight percent of the variability in turnover rates was accounted for by a group of intra-organizational variables, including average wage, starting wage, health benefits, direct care ratio, per diem, severity of mental retardation, unionization, facility size, facility age, ICF/MR certification, and hours of inservice training (Braddock & Mitchell, 1992).

While researchers have begun to identify factors associated with staff turnover rates in small community settings, much work in this area remains to be done. The variables studied so far account for only a small proportion of the variation in staff turnover rates. The studies have analyzed dissimilar sets of variables, making comparisons of important variables across studies difficult. In addition, few efforts have examined turnover from the perspective of the individual employee. As a result, variables such as commitment, job satisfaction, and intent to leave or stay, which have been very important in explaining variability in turnover in other work environments, have been included in only a few of these investigations.

Innovative Solutions

Although a vast amount of research has been conducted to identify the determinants of staff turnover, little has been done to evaluate the success of interventions to reduce turnover rates. The major exception has been a line of research examining what are called realistic job previews (RJPs) (Wanous, 1989, 1992). RJPs involve providing written, spoken, or audiovisual information about a specific position to job candidates. The information provides a realistic picture of the work. This picture balances positive features of the job with negative information about the job and the work environment. RJPs are designed to reduce recruits' unrealistic expectations about the job for which they have applied (Wanous, 1992).

RJPs are based upon the theory that, if expectations held by recruits actually match the nature of the job experience, they will be less likely to quit their jobs. In residential service settings, where up to 50% of the new hires quit within 6 months (Ganju, 1979), the implementation of RJPs has the potential to reduce orientation and training costs. Unfortunately, the only study examining the effectiveness of RJPs for staff working with persons with developmental disabilities was conducted in an institution. Findings from that study did suggest that the use of a written RJP was associated with increases in the mean length of service for newly hired staff members (Zaharia & Baumeister, 1981).

Meta-analyses of the effects of RJPs across several studies with many subjects provide a clearer picture of the potential usefulness of this technique (Breaugh, 1983; McEvoy & Cascio, 1985; Premack & Wanous, 1985). In one meta-analysis, RJPs improved retention rates (the rate at which new hires remain on the job for a specific length of time) by 9%–17% (McEvoy & Cascio, 1985). In another meta-analysis, RJPs increased retention by 12% for agencies with annual retention rates of 50%, and by 24% for agencies with retention rates of 20% (Premack and Wanous, 1985). In short, RJPs make a difference, one that is larger for agencies that have higher turnover rates.

Recommendations

Recommendations for Research   Future research on staff turnover in community residential settings must consider recent findings from the generic industrial-organizational psychology literature. This literature has identified several variables that are related to turnover, such as satisfaction, commitment, intent to stay or leave, wages, and personal characteristics. Many of these variables have not been included in studies of staff turnover in residential settings. Research that ignores these variables is, at best, incomplete and, at worst, misleading. In examining these factors, researchers must go beyond simple correlational or descriptive studies. Instead, designs that simultaneously consider a range of variables associated with retention should be used.

Future research must also examine the impact of specific job demands and stressors such as injuries or working under extreme staff shortages on turnover. The relationship of such factors to staff turnover is currently supported only by anecdotal evidence. Finally, no retention study is complete without considering the actual or perceived effect of turnover and the strategies used to reduce turnover on the quality of life and skills of persons receiving services (Lakin & Larson, 1992). Residential staff play an important role in influencing the experiences and opportunities of persons with developmental disabilities. The effect of staff, and policies and interventions that are designed to influence personnel problems, on the quality of life of persons with developmental disabilities is a key issue in any future research on personnel.

Recommendations for Policy A frequently mentioned strategy to reduce personnel problems is to increase wages and benefits (Alpha Group, 1990; American Federation of State, County, and Municipal Employees, 1991). Improved starting wages combined with regular wage increases would reduce the number of people who leave community residential positions for related work in schools, day training settings, vocational programs, and institutions. Furthermore, improved starting wages combined with regular wage increases would reduce the likelihood of people leaving their positions solely because they cannot afford to remain in them. Low wages are clearly related to high turnover rates among staff (Braddock & Mitchell, 1992). Several studies found increased pay as one of the primary strategies to improve working conditions for staff. Residential staff who work in community settings should receive wages that minimally allow them to meet their own living expenses and, ideally, would be comparable to wages paid to people performing functionally equivalent tasks in institutional settings. Policymakers should also invest in research that examines the relationship between staff retention and outcomes for persons with developmental disabilities and in research on the results of various interventions to address retention and other personnel problems (Lakin & Larson, 1992).

Recommendations for Practice In addition to using realistic job previews, several other strategies may be useful for providers who wish to reduce problems with turnover. Recruitment efforts, for example, could be directed at people who have been demonstrated to be stable employees such as older, less formally educated people who are long-term area residents (Lakin, 1988). Providers might also examine factors that affect staff satisfaction, organizational commitment, and quality of work life within their agency. Ongoing assessment of staff satisfaction and turnover should be used to determine the need for personnel interventions, to define personnel intervention strategies and goals, and to monitor the results of those interventions (Lakin & Larson, 1992).

CONCLUSION

Recruitment, training, and retention issues affect all agencies that provide residential services to persons with developmental disabilities. Individually, each of these issues presents a challenge to those attempting to provide quality services to persons with developmental disabilities, while together the challenge is even greater since recruitment, training, and retention problems are interrelated. Problems with recruitment, for example, can exacerbate the negative effects of turnover by delaying the restoration of full-staffing to agencies. Likewise, problems with retention can exacerbate recruitment challenges by increasing the number of recruits needed and decreasing the level of selectivity agencies can use when screening recruits. Personnel interventions, such as wage and benefit improvements, professionalizing direct service positions, or instituting RJPs, are likely to affect recruitment, training, and retention efforts. The extent of these interrelationships and their effects on overall personnel practices should be explored more carefully in future research.

The recruitment, training, and retention of direct service staff pose serious challenges to residential service agencies. These challenges have many implications, the most important of which is their impact on the quality of services for citizens with developmental disabilities. If left uncorrected, these problems may result in needlessly high public expenditures and, even more damaging, losses of opportunity for employees, agencies, and the people they serve. These challenges can only be addressed through concerted efforts by researchers, service and funding agencies, and federal, state, and local policymakers. Efforts to address these problems should identify, fund, and implement interventions that will result in overall improvements in the quality of life for persons with developmental disabilities who receive residential support services and live in our communities.

REFERENCES

Abelson, M.A. (1987). Examination of avoidable and unavoidable turnover. *Journal of Applied Psychology, 72*, 382–386.

Alpha Group. (1990). *Report to the commissioner of the Minnesota Department of Human Services by the task force on the compensation and training of direct care employees.* St Paul: Minnesota Department of Human Services Task Force on Compensation and Training of Direct Care Staff.

Amado, A.N., Lakin, K.C., & Menke, J.M. (1990). *1990 chartbook on services for people with developmental disabilities.* Minneapolis: Research and Training Center on Residential Services and Community Living, Institute on Community Integration (UAP), University of Minnesota (College of Education).

American Federation of State, County, and Municipal Employees (1991). *Workers at risk: A profile of Michigan group home workers.*

Anderson, D., Lakin, K.C., Bruininks, R.H., & Hill, B.K. (1987). *A national study of residential and support services for elderly persons with mental retardation* (Report No. 22). Minneapolis: Research and Training Center on Residential Services and Community Living, Institute on Community Integration (UAP), University of Minnesota (College of Education).

Anderson, T.K., & Kratochwill, T.R. (1988). Dissemination of behavioral procedures in the schools: Issues in training. In J.C. Witt, S.N. Elliot, & F.M. Gresham (Eds.), *Handbook of behavior therapy in education.* New York: Plenum Press.

Arnold, H.J., & Feldman, D.C. (1982). A multivariate analysis of the determinants of job turnover. *Journal of Applied Psychology, 67,* 350-360.

Bassin, J.J., & Hanks, M. (1992). Cooperative training efforts: A county board and a community college. In T. Wallace, S. Larson, & A. Hewitt (Eds.), *IMPACT: Feature issue on training of direct service staff, 5*(1), 18. Minneapolis: Institute on Community Integration (UAP), University of Minnesota (College of Education).

Baumeister, A.A., & Zaharia, E.S. (1987). Withdrawal and commitment of basic-care staff in residential programs. In S. Landesman & P. Vietz (Eds.). *Living environments and mental retardation* (pp. 229-267). Washington, DC: American Association on Mental Retardation.

Baysinger, B.D., & Mobley, W.M. (1983). Employee turnover: Individual and organizational analysis. *Research in Personnel and Human Resources Management, 1,* 269-319.

Bellamy, G.T., Newton, J.S., LeBaron, N.M., & Horner, R.H. (1990). Quality of life and lifestyle outcomes: A challenge for residential programs. In R.L. Schalock (Ed.), *Quality of life: Perspectives and issues* (pp. 127-140). Washington, DC: American Association on Mental Retardation.

Bernstein, G.S., & Ziarnik, J.P. (1982). Proactive identification of staff development needs: A model and methodology. *Journal of The Association for Persons with Severe Handicaps, 8,* 97-103.

Bersani, H.A., Jr., & Heifetz, L.J. (1985). Perceived stress and satisfaction of direct-care staff members in community residences for mentally retarded adults. *American Journal of Mental Deficiency, 90,* 289-295.

Bluedorn, A.C. (1982). The theories of turnover: Causes, effects, and meaning. *Research in the Sociology of Organizations, 1,* 75-128.

Braddock, D., & Mitchell, D. (1992). *Residential services for persons with developmental disabilities in the United States: A national survey of staff compensation, turnover and related issues.* Washington, DC: American Association on Mental Retardation.

Breaugh, J.A. (1983). Realistic job previews: A critical appraisal and future research directions. *Academy of Management Review, 8,* 612-619.

Bruininks, R.H., Kudla, M.J., Wieck, C.A., & Hauber, F.A. (1980). Management problems in community residential facilities. *Mental Retardation, 18,* 125-130.

Buckley, J., Albin, J.M., & Mank, D.M. (1988). Competency-based staff training for supported employment. In G.T. Bellamy, L.E. Rhodes, D.M. Mank, & J.M. Albin (Eds.), *Supported employment: A community implementation guide* (pp. 229-245). Baltimore: Paul H. Brookes Publishing Co.

Burchard, S.N., & Thousand, J. (1988). Staff and manager competencies. In M.P. Janicki & M.M. Seltzer (Eds.), *Community residences for persons with developmental disabilities* (pp. 251-266). Baltimore: Paul H. Brookes Publishing Co.

Butterfield, E.C., & Warren, S.A. (1963). Prediction of attendant tenure. *Journal of Applied Psychology, 47,* 101-103.

Camp, R.R., Blanchard, N.P., & Huszczo, G.E. (1986). *Toward a more organizationally effective training strategy and practice.* Engelwood Cliffs, NJ: Prentice Hall.

Carston, J.M., & Spector, P.E. (1987). Unemployment, job satisfaction, and employee turnover: A meta-analytic test of the Muchinsky model. *Journal of Applied Psychology, 72,* 374-381.

Christian, W.P., & Hannah, G.T. (1983). Getting staff on-task. *Effective management in human services* (pp. 58-93). Engelwood Cliffs, NJ: Prentice Hall.

Coleman, T.E., & Craig, C. (1981). *The community personnel study: Turnover issues in mental retardation community programs.* Boston: Massachusetts Department of Mental Health, Division of Mental Retardation.

Conroy, J.W., & Bradley, V.J. (1985). *The Pennhurst longitudinal study: A report of five years of research and analysis*. Philadelphia: Temple University Developmental Disabilities Center.

Cotton, J.L., & Tuttle, J.M. (1986). Employee turnover: A meta-analysis and review with implications for research. *Academy of Management Review, 11*, 55–70.

Dalton, D.R., & Todor, W.D. (1979). Turnover turned over: An expanded and positive perspective. *Academy of Management Review, 4*, 225–235.

Dellinger, J.K., & Shope, L.J. (1978). Selected characteristics and working conditions of staff in Pennsylvania CLA's. *Mental Retardation, 16*(1), 19–21.

Department of Employee Relations for the Department of Human Service (Minnesota). (1989). *Study of employee wages, benefits and turnover in Minnesota direct care facilities serving persons with developmental disabilities*. St. Paul: Author.

Developmental Disabilities Program. (1983). *Analysis of nonformal training for personnel working in the field of developmental disabilities in Minnesota: 1981–1982* (Policy analysis series: Issues related to Welsch v. Levine/No. 12). St. Paul: Developmental Disabilities Program, Department of Energy Planning and Development.

Feldman, M.A., & Dalrymple, A.J. (1984). Staff training using instructional and management strategies: A review of the literature. In J.M. Berg (Ed.), *Perspectives and Progress in Mental Retardation, 1*, 331–341.

Fiorelli, J.S., Margolis, H., Heverly, M.A., Rothchild, E., & Krasting, D.J., III (1982). Training resident advisors to provide community residential services: A university-based program. *Journal of The Association for Persons with Severe Handicaps, 7*, 13–19.

Forrest, C.R. (1982). *Final report: Defining staff training needs for those who work with developmentally disabled persons with behavioral or emotional problems*. Madison: University of Wisconsin-Extension, Continuing Education in Administration, Health, and Human Services Area.

Gage, M.A., Fredericks, H.O.B., Johnson-Dorn, N., & Lindley-Southard, B. (1982). Inservice training for staff of group homes and work activity centers serving developmentally disabled adults. *Journal of The Association for Persons with Severe Handicaps, 7*, 60–70.

Ganju, V. (1979). *Employee turnover in the state schools for the mentally retarded: A new approach to the problem*. Austin, TX: Texas Department of Mental Health and Mental Retardation, Office of Program Analysis and Statistical Research.

George, M.J. (1980). *A state-wide study of employee turnover in community residential facilities for developmentally disabled persons*. Unpublished doctoral dissertation, George Peabody College for Teachers, Vanderbilt University, Nashville, Tennessee.

George, M.J., & Baumeister, A.A. (1981). Employee withdrawal and job satisfaction in community residential facilities for mentally retarded persons. *American Journal of Mental Deficiency, 85*, 639–647.

Gerhart, B. (1990). Voluntary turnover and alternative job opportunities. *Journal of Applied Psychology, 75*, 467–476.

Haring, M., & Johnson, D. (1992). Impact of North Dakota's statewide training: A provider's critique. In T. Wallace, S. Larson, & A. Hewitt (Eds.), *IMPACT: Feature issue on direct service staff* (pp. 17, 21). Minneapolis: University of Minnesota, Institute on Community Integration (UAP), University of Minnesota (College of Education).

Hauber, F.A., & Bruininks, R.H. (1986). Intrinsic and extrinsic job satisfaction among direct care staff in residential facilities for mentally retarded people. *Education and Psychological Measurement, 46*, 95–105.

Hill, B.K., Lakin, K.C., Bruininks, R.H., Amado, A.N., Anderson, D.J., & Copher, J.I. (1989). *Living in the community: A comparative study of foster homes and small group homes for people with mental retardation* (Report No. 28). Minneapolis: Research and Training Center on Residential Services and Community Living, Institute on Community Integration (UAP), University of Minnesota (College of Education).

Hill, B.K., Lakin, K.C., Bruininks, R.H., Hauber, F.A., & Copher, J.I. (1989). *Living in the community: A comparative study of foster homes and small group homes for people with mental retardation* (Report No. 28). Minneapolis: Research and Training Center on Residential Services and Community Living, Institute on Community Integration (UAP), University of Minnesota College of Education.

Horner, R.H., Stoner, S.K., & Ferguson, D.L. (1988). *An activity-based analysis of deinstitutionalization: The effects of community re-entry on the lives of residents leaving Oregon's Fairview Training Center*. Salem: University of Oregon, Specialized Training Program of the Center on Human Development.

Houston County Group Homes, Inc. (1990, October). *Competency based staff training project: Annual progress report*. La Crescent, MN: Author. (Contact: Dennis Theede, 1700 Lancer Blvd., La Crescent, MN 55947)

Intagliata, J., & Willer, B. (1981). A review of training programs for providers of foster family care to mentally retarded persons. In R.H. Bruininks, C.E. Meyers, B.B. Sigford, & K.C. Lakin (Eds.), *Deinstitutionalization and community adjustment of mentally retarded people* (AAMR Monograph No. 4, pp. 282–315). Washington DC: American Association on Mental Deficiency.

Jacobson, J.W., & Ackerman, L.J. (1989). *Factors associated with staff tenure in group homes* (Report #89-5). Albany: State of New York, Planning Unit, Office of Mental Retardation and Developmental Disabilities.

Jacobson, J.W., & Ackerman, L.J. (1990). *The precursors and impact of staff turnover on group homes* (A report from the Best Practices Research Project, Report #90-2). Albany: State of New York, Planning Unit, Office of Mental Retardation and Developmental Disabilities.

Janicki, M.P., Jacobson, J.W., Zigman, W.B., & Gordon, N.H. (1984). Characteristics of employees of community residences for retarded persons. *Education and Training of the Mentally Retarded, 19*, 35–44.

Jaskulski, T., & Metzler, C. (1990). *Forging a new era: The 1990 reports on people with developmental disabilities, Appendix*. Washington, DC: National Association of Developmental Disabilities Councils.

Jensen, M.A. (1992). Respect: What consumers want from direct care staff. In T. Wallace, S.A. Larson, & A. Hewitt (Eds.), *Impact: Feature issue on training of direct service staff 5*(1), 7. Minneapolis: Institute on Community Integration (UAP), University of Minnesota (College of Education)

Jones, A.A., Blunden, R., Coles, E., Evens, G., & Porterfield, J. (1981). Evaluating the impact of training, supervision, feedback, self-monitoring, and collaborative goal setting on staff and client behavior. In J. Hogg & P. Mittler (Eds.), *Staff training in mental handicap* (pp. 213–299). Cambridge, MA: The MIT Press.

Karan, O.C., & Mettel, L. (1989). Training needs in integrated settings. In W.E. Kiernan & R.L. Schalock (Eds.), *Economics, industry, and disability: A look ahead*. Baltimore: Paul H. Brookes Publishing Co.

Kasarda, J.D. (1973). Effects of personnel turnover, employee qualifications, and professional staff ratios on administrative intensity and overhead. *Sociological Quarterly, 14*, 350–358.

Kazdin, A.E. (1984). Staff training and technique variations to enhance client performance. *Behavior modification in applied settings*, 3rd ed. (pp. 169–192). Homewood, IL: The Dorsey Press.

Kemery, E.R., Dunlap, W.P., & Bedeian, A.G. (1989). Criterion specification in employee separation research: Tenure or turnover? *Best papers proceedings* (pp. 387–391). Columbia, SC: Academy of Management.

Knight, C.B., & Hayden, M.F. (1989). *Workforce 2000: Will our communities be able to meet the needs of Wisconsin's citizens with developmental disabilities*. Madison, WI: Wisconsin Council on Developmental Disabilities, Community Direct Service Worker Taskforce.

Knight, C.B., Karan, O.L., Timmerman, M., Griffeth, S.C., & Dufresne, D. (1986).

Training community developmental disabilities associates: A collaborative model. *Applied Research in Mental Retardation*, 7, 229–239.

Lakin, K.C. (1988). Strategies for promoting the stability of direct care staff. In M.P. Janicki, M.W. Krauss, & M.M. Seltzer (Eds.), *Community residences for persons with developmental disabilities* (pp. 231–238). Baltimore: Paul H. Brookes Publishing Co.

Lakin, K.C., & Bruininks, R.H. (1981). *Occupational stability of direct-care staff of residential facilities for mentally retarded people*. Minneapolis: Research and Training Center on Residential Services and Community Living, Institute on Community Integration (UAP), University of Minnesota (College of Education).

Lakin, K., & Bruininks, R. (1981). Personnel management and quality of residential services for developmentally disabled people. In T.C. Muzzio, J.J. Koshel, & V. Bradley (Eds.), *Alternative community living arrangements and nonvocational social services for developmentally disabled people* (pp. 125–171). Washington, DC: The Urban Institute.

Lakin, K.C., Hill, B.K., Chen, T.H., & Stephens, S.A. (1989). *Persons with mental retardation and related conditions in mental retardation facilities: Selected findings from the 1987 National Medical Expenditure Survey* (Report No. 29). Minneapolis: Research and Training Center on Residential Services and Community Living, Institute on Community Integration (UAP), University of Minnesota.

Lakin, K.C., & Larson, S.A. (1992). Satisfaction and stability of direct-care personnel in community-based residential services. In J.W. Jacobson, S.N. Burchard, & P.J. Carling (Eds.), *Clinical services, social adjustment, and work life in community living* (pp. 244–262). Baltimore: Johns Hopkins University Press.

Langer, M., Agosta, J., & Choisser, L. (1988). *Proposed model for a state-sponsored direct care staff training system in Iowa: Final report*. Cambridge, MA: Human Services Research Institute.

Langer, M., Choisser, L., & Agosta, J. (1987). *Direct care staff training in facilities serving people with developmental disabilities: A comparative report of training practices in Iowa and in model states*. Cambridge, MA: Human Services Research Institute.

Larson, S.A., & Lakin, K.C. (1989). Deinstitutionalization of persons with mental retardation: Behavioral outcomes. *Journal of The Association for Persons with Severe Handicaps*, 14, 324–332.

Larson, S.A., & Lakin, K.C. (1991). Parent attitudes about residential placement before and after deinstitutionalization: A research synthesis. *Journal of The Association for Persons with Severe Handicaps*, 16, 25–38.

Larson, S.A., & Lakin, K.C. (1992a, May). *Quality of life for people with challenging behavior living in community settings*. Poster presented at the annual meeting of the American Association on Mental Retardation, New Orleans, Louisianna.

Larson, S.A., & Lakin, K.C. (1992b). Direct-care staff stability in a national sample of small group homes. *Mental Retardation*, 30, 13–22.

Legislative Budget and Finance Committee. (1989). *Report on salary levels and their impact on quality of care for client contact workers in community-based MH/MR and child care programs*. Harrisburg: Pennsylvania General Assembly.

Levy, P.H., Levy, J.M., Freeman, S., Feiman, J., & Samowitz, P. (1988). Training and managing residences for persons with developmental disabilities. In M.P. Janicki, M.W. Krauss, & M.M. Seltzer (Eds.), *Community residences for persons with developmental disabilities* (pp. 239–249). Baltimore: Paul H. Brookes Publishing Co.

Malony, H., & Taplin, J. (1988). Deinstitutionalization of people with developmental disability. *Australia and New Zealand Journal of Developmental Disabilities*, 14, 109–122.

McEvoy, G.M., & Cascio, W.F. (1985). Strategies for reducing employee turnover: A meta-analysis. *Journal of Applied Psychology*, 70, 342–353.

McEvoy, G.M., & Cascio, W.F. (1987). Do good or poor performers leave? A meta-analysis of the relationship between performance and turnover. *Academy of Management Journal, 30,* 744–762.

Michaels, C.E., & Spector, P.E. (1982). Causes of employee turnover: A test of the Mobley, Griffeth, Hand, and Meglino model. *Journal of Applied Psychology, 67,* 53–59.

Mitchell, D., Bachman, K., Longhurst, N., & Braddock, D. (1990). *Research on wages and turnover of direct care staff in residential facilities for people with developmental disabilities: An annotated bibliography.* Chicago: University of Illinois at Chicago, University Affiliated Program in Developmental Disabilities.

Mobley, W.H. (1982). *Employee turnover: Causes, consequences, and control.* Reading, MA: Addison-Wesley.

Mobley, W.H., Griffeth, R.W., Hand, H.H., & Meglino, B.M. (1979). Review and conceptual analysis of the employee turnover process. *Psychological Bulletin, 86,* 493–522.

Mowday, R.T., Porter, L.W., & Steers, R.M. (1982). *Employee-organization linkages: The psychology of commitment, absenteeism, and turnover.* New York: Academic Press.

Muchinsky, P.M., & Morrow, P.C. (1980). A multidisciplinary model of voluntary employee turnover. *Journal of Vocational Behavior, 17,* 263–290.

Neef, N.A., Trachtenberg, S., Loeb, J., & Sterner, K. (1991). Video-based training of respite care providers: An interactional analysis of presentation format. *Journal of Applied Behavior Analysis, 24,* 473–486.

O'Brien, J., & O'Brien, C.L. (1992). *Remembering the soul of our work: Stories by the staff of options in community living.* Madison, WI: Options in Community Living.

Orcutt, C. (1989). *A review of the staffing situation of the direct care workers in the developmental disabilities field.* Salem: State of Oregon, Executive Department, Budget and Management Division.

Peters, L.H., & Sheridan, J.E. (1988). Turnover research methodology: A critique of traditional designs and a suggested survival model alternative. In K.M. Rowland & G.R. Ferris (Eds.), *Research in personnel and human resources management,* Vol. 6 (pp. 231–262). Greenwich, CT: JAI Press.

Pivirotto & Bothamley Consulting. (1987). *Examination of factors associated with compensation and turnover for staff employed by private sector community residential providers for citizens with mental retardation.* Hartford: State of Connecticut, Department of Mental Retardation.

Porter, L.W., & Steers, R.M. (1973). Organizational, work, and personal factors in employee turnover and absenteeism. *Psychological Bulletin, 80,* 151–176.

Premack, S.L., & Wanous, J.P. (1985). A meta-analysis of realistic job preview experiments. *Journal of Applied Psychology, 70,* 706–719.

Price, J.L. (1977). *The study of turnover.* Ames: Iowa State University Press.

Price, J.L., & Mueller, C.W. (1986). *Absenteeism and turnover of hospital employees.* Greenwich, CT: JAI Press.

Prouty, R.W., & Lakin, K.C. (1991). *Summary of states' efforts to positively affect the quality of Medicaid Home and Community Based Services for persons with mental retardation and related conditions* (Report No. 34). Minneapolis: Research and Training Center on Residential Services and Community Living, Institute on Community Integration (UAP), University of Minnesota (College of Education).

Randall, D.M. (1990). The consequences of organizational commitment: Methodological investigation. *Journal of Organizational Behavior, 11,* 361-378.

Renzaglia, A. (1986). Preparing personnel to support and guide emerging service alternatives. In F.R. Rusch (Ed.), *Competitive employment issues and strategies* (pp. 303–316). Baltimore: Paul H. Brookes Publishing Co.

Salisbury, C.L. (1984). Respite care provider training: Current practices and directions for research. *Education and Training of the Mentally Retarded, 19,* 210–215.

Schalock, R.L. (1991, May). *The concept of quality of life in the lives of persons with men-*

tal retardation. Paper presented at the Annual Meeting of the American Association on Mental Retardation, Washington, DC.

Scheerenberger, R. (1981). Human services person power for developmentally disabled persons. In T.C. Muzzio, J.J. Kostel, & V. Bradley (Eds.), *Alternative community living arrangements and nonvocational social services for developmentally disabled people* (pp. 172–204). Washington, DC: The Urban Institute.

Schiers, W. Giffort, D., & Furtkamp, S. (1980). Recruitment source and job survival for direct care staff. *Mental Retardation, 18*, 285–287.

Smith, T., Parker, T., Taubman, M., & Lovaas, O.I. (1992). Transfer of staff training from workshops to group homes: A failure to generalize across settings. *Research in Developmental Disabilities, 13*, 57–71.

Steel, R.P., & Griffeth, R.W. (1989). The elusive relationship between perceived employment opportunity and turnover behavior: A methodological or conceptual artifact? *Journal of Applied Psychology, 74*, 846–854.

Steel, R.P., Hendrix, W.H., & Balogh, S.P. (1990). Confounding effects of the turnover base rate on relations between time lag and turnover study outcomes: An extension of meta-analysis findings and conclusions. *Journal of Organizational Behavior, 11*, 237–242.

Steel, R.P., & Ovalle, N.K., II. (1984). A review and meta-analysis of research on the relationship between behavioral intentions and employee turnover. *Journal of Applied Psychology, 69*, 673–686.

Steers, R.M., & Mowday, R.T. (1981). Employee turnover and post-decision accommodation processes. *Research in Organizational Behavior, 3*, 235–281.

Tannenbaum, S.I., & Yukl, G. (1992). Training and development in work organizations. *Annual Review of Psychology, 43*, 399–441.

Task Force on Human Resources Development. (1989). *Human resources in community human service programs: Report to the Secretaries of Aging, Health, and Public Welfare*. Harrisburg, PA: Author.

Templeman, T.P., & Peters, J.M. (1992). Training for impact. In T. Wallace, S. Larson, & A. Hewitt (Eds.), *IMPACT: Feature issue on training of direct service staff 5*(1), 8–9. Minneapolis: Institute on Community Integration (UAP), University of Minnesota (College of Education).

Thousand, J.S., Burchard, S.N., & Hasazi, J.E. (1986). Field-based generation and social validation managers and staff competencies for small community residences. *Applied Research in Mental Retardation, 7*, 263–283.

Turner, K. (1992). Options. In J. O'Brien & C.L. O'Brien (Eds.), *Remembering the soul of our work: Stories by the staff of Options in Community Living*. Madison, WI: Options in Community Living.

U.S. Bureau of the Census. (1991). *Statistical abstract of the United States: 1991* (111th ed.). Washington, DC: U.S. Government Printing Office.

Vassiliou, D. (1992). The North Dakota Statewide MR/DD staff training program. In T. Wallace, S. Larson, & A. Hewitt (Eds.), *IMPACT: Feature issue on training of direct service staff 5*(1), 17. Minneapolis: Institute on Community Integration (UAP), University of Minnesota (College of Education).

Wallace, T., Larson, S.A., & Hewitt, A. (Eds.). (1992). *IMPACT: Feature issue on training of direct service staff, 5*(1). Minneapolis: Institute on Community Integration (UAP), University of Minnesota (College of Education).

Wanous, J.P. (1989). Installing a realistic job preview: Ten tough choices. *Personnel Psychology, 42*, 117–134.

Wanous, J.P. (1992). *Organizational entry: Recruitment, selection, orientation, and socialization of newcomers* (2nd ed.). New York: Addison-Wesley.

Wanous, J.P., Poland, T.D., Premack, S.L., & Davis, K.S. (1992). The effects of met expectations on newcomer attitudes and behaviors: A review and meta-analysis. *Journal of Applied Psychology, 77*, 288–297.

White, C.C., Lakin, K.C., Bruininks, R.H., & Li, X. (1991). *Persons with mental retardation and related conditions in state-operated residential facilities: Year ending June 30, 1989 with longitudinal trends from 1950 to 1989.* Minneapolis: Research and Training Center on Residential Services and Community Living, Institute on Community Integration (UAP), University of Minnesota (College of Education).

Williams, L.J., & Hazer, J.T. (1986). Antecedents and consequences of satisfaction and commitment in turnover models: A reanalysis using latent variable structural equation methods. *Journal of Applied Psychology, 71,* 219–231.

Zaharia, E.S., & Baumeister, A.A. (1978a). Estimated position replacement costs for technical personnel in a state's public facilities. *Mental Retardation, 16,* 131–134.

Zaharia, E.S., & Baumeister, A.A. (1978b). Technician turnover and absenteeism in public residential facilities. *American Journal of Mental Deficiency, 82,* 580–593.

Zaharia, E.S., & Baumeister, A.A. (1979). Technician losses in public residential facilities. *American Journal of Mental Deficiency, 84,* 36–69.

Zaharia, E.S., & Baumeister, A.A. (1981). Job preview effects during the critical initial employment period. *Journal of Applied Psychology, 66,* 19–22.

Ziarnik, J.P., & Bernstein, G.S. (1984). Effecting change in community-based facilities: Putting staff training in perspective. *The Behavior Therapist, 7,* 39–41.

PART IV

ENHANCING INDEPENDENCE AND AUTONOMY

_ **Chapter 14** _____

A Conceptual
Framework for
Enhancing
Self-Determination

Brian H. Abery

A conceptualization of man as having an inherent need to exert control over his environment has existed since the time of Aristotle. A sense of self-determination is necessary for the development of individual identity (O'Brien, 1987), and it is a crucial catalyst of independence and autonomy (Guess, Benson, & Seigel-Causey, 1985; Zeph, 1984). The ability of a person to make his or her own decisions has a significant impact on that person's self-esteem and sense of self-efficacy, and is closely linked to a person's quality of life. As one self-advocate states:

> What it all comes down to is power, choice, and the right to chase our dreams. What I mean is this—the chance to direct our lives the way we want to, not the way others expect us to; the ability to use the power we have as citizens to vote, to choose where and with whom we want to live, to decide where and when we want to work; and to make decisions that are right for us as people. Most importantly, self-determination means respecting our right to pursue our own goals and dreams. I don't think that's asking too much, do you? (I.M., 1992)

Striving to attain a sense of personal autonomy is a life-long process that begins at birth and is never complete. From the 2-year-old who responds to every parental request by saying "no" to the adolescent who chooses to engage only in those activities that are least preferred by parents, the struggle for independence

Preparation of this chapter was supported by a cooperative agreement (#H133B80048) between the National Institute on Disability and Rehabilitation Research (NIDRR) and the Research and Training Center on Residential Services and Community Living at the University of Minnesota (College of Education) located within the Institute on Community Integration, and two research and demonstration projects (#H158K00034; #H023J2001) funded through the U.S. Department of Education, Office of Special Education and Rehabilitative Services (OSERS). The opinions expressed herein are those of the author.

shapes our personality and has an enormous impact on our lives. A sense of self-determination is equally important to persons with and without disabilities. It has a tremendous influence not only on how an individual views himself, but also on how he or she is perceived by others in society. For a variety of reasons, persons with developmental disabilities often fail to acquire, or to effectively use, those skills necessary to exert control over their lives. As a result, they remain dependent on others to make both long-term and day-to-day decisions for them.

Self-determination, or the attitudes and abilities that lead people to define goals for themselves and to take the initiative to reach these goals (Ward, 1988), is a highly valued personal characteristic in our society. Achieving self-determination cannot be accomplished without the development and exercise of social and interpersonal skills, including the ability to establish preferences, make informed decisions, communicate clearly with others, and exert personal control. Failure to acquire these skills, a frequent experience for individuals with disabilities, can lead to a life of isolation and passivity (Lakin, 1988). Despite the fact that most professionals agree that the exercise of self-determination is critical to the autonomy of persons with disabilities (Abery & Bruininks, 1990; Guess & Helmstetter, 1986; Guess & Seigel-Causey, 1985; Holvoet et al., 1983), it has only been in recent years that practitioners, researchers, and family members have given attention to the area.

The purpose of this chapter is five-fold. First, a brief introduction to the construct of self-determination is provided, and its importance in the lives of adults with developmental disabilities is explored. Second, current perspectives on self-determination are discussed, and an attempt is made to arrive at a working definition of the construct. Third, an ecological perspective is presented that takes into consideration the many factors that need to be contemplated to adequately understand the concept. Fourth, a working process model of self-determination is provided, taking into consideration the person and the environmental context in which the person lives. Fifth, programs to enhance outcomes in this area are discussed.

THE IMPORTANCE OF SELF-DETERMINATION

Implementing the principles and policies of normalization, least restrictive environment (LRE), deinstitutionalization, and community-based services in the last two decades has created a situation in which professionals must reassess and restructure services for persons with mental retardation and other developmental disabilities. In the past, the adjustment of individuals with developmental disabilities was often measured by the degree of their compliance. Parents, teachers, residential staff, and others often equated the term "adaptive behavior" with conformity. Most professionals have now come to understand that if individuals with developmental disabilities are to become fully integrated into the community, socially as well as physically, strategies must be developed that focus on ways to foster autonomy, self-reliance, and self-sufficiency (Kishi, Teelucksingh, Zollers, Seunghee, & Meyer, 1988; Lakin, 1988; Wehman & McLaughlin, 1981).

Although the exercise of self-determination is important for persons both with and without disabilities, it would appear to be especially crucial for individuals with developmental disabilities. As a society, we have come to recognize the rights of these individuals to have the opportunity to be an integral of the community. In order to make this possible, they must have the opportunity to develop those skills necessary to exert control over their lives. At the current time, however, this does not appear to be the case. The results of postschool follow-up studies suggest that students with disabilities have a very difficult time adjusting to life after graduation from high school. During their final years in school, these youth remain dependent on others to make decisions, assess performance, and make linkages with service agencies (Chadsey-Rusch, Rusch, & O'Reilly, 1991). Rarely are they taught or required to advocate for their own interests (Mithaug, Martin, Agran, & Rusch, 1988). The unemployment, underemployment, continued dependence on parents, social isolation, and lack of involvement in community-oriented activities characteristic of many individuals with disabilities (Hasazi, Gordon, & Roe, 1985; Mithaug, Horiuchi, & Fanning, 1985; Weatherman, Stevens, & Krantz, 1986) are factors that foster continued dependence.

During the past several years, professionals in the field of developmental disabilities have begun to take greater interest in ensuring that the persons they serve develop the requisite autonomy and independence needed to live within the community. The Department of Education's Office of Special Education and Rehabilitative Services (OSERS), for example, has funded a number of research and demonstration projects, hoping to acquire greater knowledge on the self-determination of persons with disabilities and how to facilitate the development and use of skills in this area. At the present time, however, relatively little is known about the capabilities of individuals with developmental disabilities to exercise self-determination, how they acquire these skills, or the opportunities that they have to engage in such activity. In assessing the current situation, participants in the National Conference on Self-Determination in 1989 developed a list of 29 recommendations for OSERS and other government agencies that will need to be implemented if all individuals with disabilities are to acquire and exercise self-determination skills. These recommendations reflect the belief that, given the appropriate opportunities, persons with even the most severe disabilities have the capacity to become more autonomous and better able to contribute to society.

DEFINING THE CONSTRUCT OF SELF-DETERMINATION

What is self-determination? To date, it has been a fairly elusive construct for researchers, practitioners, and persons with disabilities to operationally define and agree upon. The current research literature is far from complete and provides only a portion of the total picture necessary to develop and implement effective programs in this area.

While there is currently no generally accepted definition of self-determination, considerable time has been spent during the past several years attempting to clarify the construct. Most researchers and practitioners currently view self-determination as including the attitudes, abilities, and skills that lead people to define goals for themselves and to take the initiative to reach these goals (Ward, 1988). More specifically, persons who are self-determined are aware of their personal preferences and set goals for themselves accordingly (Deci & Ryan, 1985; Martin, Mithaug, Maxson, & Riley, 1992; Mithaug, 1991). They are assertive—mindful of opportunities to exert personal control.

Knowing what he or she desires, the self-determined person uses the skills within his or her behavioral repertoire to achieve desired ends. This is accomplished through making one's needs known to others through self-advocacy, informed decision making and choice making, and the self-regulation of behavior, including the development and implementation of creative action plans to achieve personal goals. Conducting ongoing effectiveness evaluations to monitor progress, the self-determined individual is able to adjust initial action plans when necessary (Abery & Bruininks, 1990; Allen, 1989; Miller, LaFollette, & Green, 1990). When success is attained, self-reinforcement is provided; the individual self-critiques when desired goals are not attained. Whether or not success is initially encountered, the person with a sense of self-determination seeks to learn from his or her behavior and is both capable and willing to engage in self-reflection, analyzing what went right and what went wrong in specific situations to avoid repeated mistakes in the future.

There would appear to be general consensus in the field that there are numerous characteristics and skills underlying self-determination. The skill clusters most frequently cited include choice-making and problem-solving abilities, self-advocacy skills, and the ability to regulate one's own behavior. There is no question that the acquisition and use of such skills is related to the personal characteristics of the individual. A person's level of cognitive functioning, communication skills, and social skills influences his or her ability to ascertain preferences and exercise choice. Self-determination, however, is more than the sum of its parts (Ward, 1988). The learning and effective application of these skills is directly linked to the environmental contexts of the family, school, and community in which development takes place. Environments in which the individual is provided with few choices, preferences are not recognized, or behavior is regulated primarily through external means inhibit the exercise of personal choice and self-determination. Not only must persons with severe disabilities develop the abilities and skills to take control over their lives, but the community and society at large must acknowledge and provide opportunities to exercise this basic right.

THE DEVELOPMENT OF SELF-DETERMINATION SKILLS

Most persons acquire the capacity for self-determination in the absence of any formal programming. This has led many professionals to take the development of these skills for granted. It would be quite unusual to find educational programs that focus on the development and use of such skills in a population without disabilities. The majority of individuals acquire the skills necessary for self-determination as a result of interactions with parents, siblings, peers, and others. The manner in which these skills are learned, as a result of direct instruction from parents and observational learning involving peers and siblings, is well documented in the child development literature (Baumrind, 1976, 1977; Berndt, 1979; Brody & Stoneman, 1981; Bronfenbrenner, Devereaux, Suci, & Rogers, 1965; Grusec & Abramovitch, 1982). Interactions with members of one's peer/friendship group, with which there is "developmental equivalence," have been found to be especially important in the acquisition of these skills (Hartup, 1983).

In contrast, as Shevin and Klein (1984) have pointed out, it is quite difficult to predict whether self-determination skills will be developed by individuals with developmental disabilities. Cognitive or physical limitations and language and communication deficits may hinder the spontaneous acquisition of these skills. It should not be assumed, however, that the primary problem lies within the individual, for environmental factors usually play a more important role. Persons with developmental disabilities are typically provided with few opportunities to set personal goals, make choices, creatively solve problems, or develop personal advocacy skills in either home or school environments (Abery & Eggebeen, 1992). Recent research suggests that many young adults, especially those with disabilities, are given little opportunity to practice and refine the skills necessary for self-determination. Rather, compliance is reinforced by parents and teachers alike (Abery & Eggebeen, 1993). In addition, the limited opportunities available for most persons with severe disabilities to interact socially with same-age peers without disabilities may hinder the acquisition of self-determination skills through processes of observational learning (Abery, Bruininks, Johnson, & Thurlow, 1989).

Many professionals in the field (e.g., Goode & Gaddy, 1976; Kishi et al., 1988; Ward, 1991) have emphasized the importance of incorporating instruction with respect to decision making and other aspects of self-determination into educational and rehabilitation programs due to the restricted social contacts of individuals with disabilities. The implementation of programs specific to the development of self-determination, however, appears to be the exception rather then the rule for students with or without disabilities. Despite evidence that learning is enhanced when opportunities for instructional choice are available, our educational and social services systems continue to vest almost all decision-making power in persons (i.e., administrators, teachers, parents) without disabilities.

PREVIOUS APPROACHES TO
THE STUDY OF SELF-DETERMINATION

Researchers who have examined self-determination among persons with developmental disabilities have typically concentrated their efforts on the characteristics or skills of the learner. Whether observed inhibitions (Mithaug & Hanawalt, 1978), contextual variables, or a variety of other factors in this area are the result of insufficiently developed communication skills remains unknown. Unfortunately, many professionals have interpreted these data as suggesting that persons with severe disabilities are incapable of self-determination.

One by-product of this focus on the lack of skills of persons with disabilities has been a lack of appreciation of the important role that a person's ecological contexts (e.g., school, home, community) play in the development and use of skills relevant to self-determination. In order to develop and refine competencies in these areas, an individual needs the opportunity (i.e., practice) to exert control over his or her life. Unfortunately, in many instances, these opportunities are not provided even when basic skills are present. Because of the belief that self-determination is beyond the capacity of most persons with development disabilities, parents, siblings, residential staff, employment supervisors, teachers, and other professionals with whom persons with severe disabilities work on a regular basis often provide limited opportunities for the exercise of personal choice and self-regulation (Mithaug & Hanawalt, 1978; Pace, Ivancic, Edwards, Iwata, & Page, 1985). Without opportunities to practice such skills, individuals with severe disabilities are unlikely to develop the degree of self-determination needed for independent living in the community.

AN ALTERNATIVE PERSPECTIVE: AN ECOSYSTEMS FRAMEWORK

Facilitating the development of self-determination and encouraging its exercise in multiple settings is a complex task. This task can be affected by the personal characteristics of the individual (e.g., cognitive competencies, communication skills, assertiveness), and the environments in which the person functions, including the family and work/school contexts, as well as the community in which the individual resides. Therefore, in order to fully understand the self-determination construct, it is necessary that the contributions of both the individual and the environment are acknowledged (Sameroff & Seifer, 1983).

Bronfenbrenner (1977) and Garbarino (1982) have proposed models of environmental organization that begin to capture the complexity of the social structure in which self-determination develops (see Figure 1). In these ecological perspectives, the individual and the environment are viewed as mutually shaping nested systems or structures, each changing over time. The context in which skills are learned and practiced is referred to as the individual's ecosystem and can be viewed as consisting of a number of levels that can be arranged on a scale from the smallest to the largest or from microsystem to macrosystem.

The immediate settings in which most persons function are the family, school/work, and the peer group. They are therefore the first context or *microsystems* in which self-determination is learned and refined. The family mediates between the person and society and supports the individual in his or her interactions with the outside world (Lerner & Spanier, 1978). As individuals with developmental disabilities reach adulthood and leave their families for independent liv-

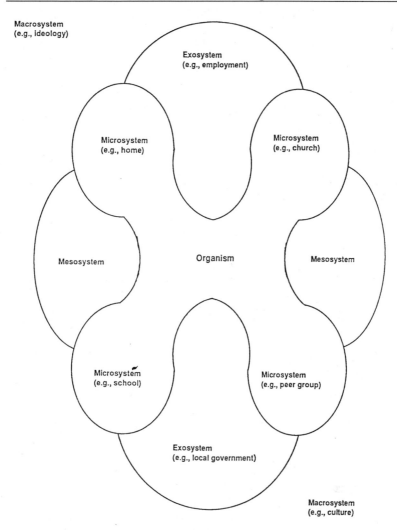

Figure 1. An ecosystem's model of development. (From Garbarino, J. [1982]. *Children and families in the social environment.* New York: Aldine Press; reprinted with permission.)

ing situations or other types of community residential placements, roommates, staff, and fellow residents assume at least part of the role previously played by the family.

Self-determination also develops and is practiced in the school, an environment that is replaced during adulthood by the work setting. The person's school and eventual place of employment contribute to cognitive as well as social development. By providing a setting in which the individual can be challenged and can engage in interaction with nonrelated adults and peers, these environments facilitate skill development initiated at home. In a similar manner, family interaction has an impact on the individual's behavior and performance in both school and work settings (Abery, 1988).

Interactions with peers also serve as a context for learning and practicing self-determination. Through observational learning and direct instruction, these interactions enhance the acquisition of skills that are necessary for the individual to exert control over his or her life. One of the most influential aspects of social interaction is the equality that exists among peers. As Hartup (1983) suggests, there are some aspects of social competence that may only be learned when participants are on equal footing. This unique characteristic of the peer group is likely to make it a fertile ground for the development of self-determination.

An individual's interactions with family members, service providers, and roommates in the home; teachers; employment supervisors and fellow employees; and the peer group does not occur in isolation. What occurs in one environment has an effect on what happens in others. This bidirectional process, in which phenomenon in one setting have the potential to have a direct and an indirect impact on events in other settings, constitutes the second level of analysis in an ecological framework. It is at this level, referred to as the *mesosystem* (Bronfenbrenner, 1977; Garbarino, 1982), that behaviors and skills learned in one environment are practiced in others, allowing generalization and stimulus discrimination to occur. Self-determination skills will be of little value if they are only exercised in the home, and not in the community or workplace. Little generalization will occur if opportunities for personal control are supplied in one setting but not in others.

At the third analysis level, a person must consider the impact on more immediate settings of the external contexts in which a person is imbedded (Bronfenbrenner, 1979). Events occurring at this level, referred to as the *exosystem*, may be both formal and informal and include: characteristics of the neighborhood; the relationship between the family or community residence and community; the quality and type of training to which teachers, work supervisors, and residential staff have been exposed; and a host of other factors. To date, there have been few attempts to explore the impact of exosystem level variables on personal growth, including the development of skills that will facilitate self-determination. This does not imply, however, that less importance should be attributed to these variables. The training a work supervisor receives is likely to have a significant impact on the frequency with which opportunities for choice are allowed in the employment setting and the support provided to enhance decision making, problem solving, and other skills crucial to the exercise of self-determination.

One needs to go beyond immediate settings and examine larger contexts that affect events at lower levels of the individual's ecosystem in order to fully understand development. This fourth level of analysis of the individual's ecosystem is referred to as the *macrosystem*. Bronfenbrenner (1979) and Garbarino (1982) both stress the importance of investigating these aspects—the overarching institutional and ideological patterns of the culture as they affect human development—of the ecosystem. Stereotypes of persons with developmental disabilities and the resulting discrimination against such individuals, for example, are based on the manner in which members of western society perceive persons who are different from themselves and who do not meet the preconceived expectations of the community. The common belief that persons with developmental disabilities are unable to know what they want out of life and, therefore, must have others make decisions for them is rooted in the way that society perceives and devalues such individuals and the resulting system of services that has been developed to provide support (i.e., control).

AN ECOSYSTEMS MODEL OF SELF-DETERMINATION

Viewed from an ecosystems perspective, self-determination can be conceived as a by-product of an ongoing interaction between the individual and the multiple environments in which he or she functions (see Figure 2). In this section, a working model of self-determination is presented. The contributions of the individual's personal characteristics (e.g., skills, attitudes) are first discussed. The impact of the family or home environment is next explored. The characteristics of employment and school contexts that hinder or facilitate self-determination are addressed in the third part of this section. The impact of the linkages between the many behavioral contexts in which the individual functions is then considered. Finally, the influence of the larger community is contemplated.

Individual Characteristics

There are a multitude of factors at the individual level that have an impact on self-determination. The majority of these entail specific social skills that enhance an individual's ability to exert personal control. These include:

Personal choice and decision-making skills
Self-management/regulation skills
Personal advocacy skills
Problem-solving skills

In addition, additional personal factors, including the individual's knowledge base, social and communication skills, sense of self-efficacy, and attributions for success and failure, must also be considered. The first of these factors is based on the person's experiential history as well as his or her understanding of his or her rights and responsibilities as a citizen. The latter two factors relate closely to the individual's personal perceptions as to whether he or she has the capacity to exert control over events in his or her life.

Personal Choice and Decision Making During the past two decades, behavioral scientists have gained increased understanding of the manner in which humans make decisions. Extensive literature currently exists regarding the manner or sequence of steps through which an individual progresses in arriving at a decision. The work of a majority of theorists (e.g., Beatty, 1988; Hurst, Kinney, &

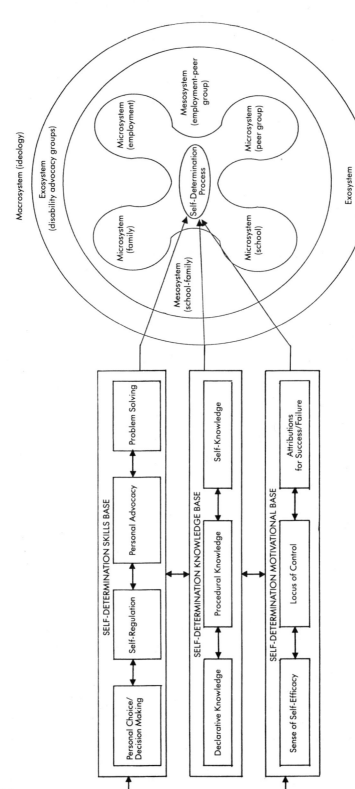

Figure 2. A process model of self-determination.

354

Weiss, 1983; Janis & Mann, 1977; Moody, 1983; Smith, Hamrick, & Anspaugh, 1981; Tymchuk, 1985) conceptualizes the choice-making process as consisting of a number of distinct steps as illustrated in Figure 2. These include: 1) an awareness of preferences, 2) an appreciation that choices among preferences are possible, 3) recognition of decision-making opportunities, 4) definition of the choice or decision at hand, 5) setting of personal outcome standards or goals, 6) generation of alternative choices, 7) evaluation of alternatives, and 8) selection of the alternative that most closely meets the individual's goals.

An awareness of preferences—that certain stimuli are liked, enjoyed, or appreciated more than others—is a basic human capacity. Unfortunately, some individuals, especially those with developmental disabilities, have for many years been considered to be too disabled to have such likes and dislikes. As a result of the expressive language and communication difficulties they experience, it has often been assumed that members of this group have no preferences simply because they are not able to effectively communicate them verbally.

The ability to make decisions is also dependent on the individual's recognition of the fact that choices among preferences are possible. While all individuals have personal preferences, it is likely that many persons with developmental disabilities do not appreciate that they have the right to exercise choice among available options. While this may be due to a variety of factors, it is often because the individual has rarely been given the opportunity to engage in choice making. In order to make informed decisions, a person also needs to have been exposed to a variety of alternatives to such an extent that differences among the stimuli have been noticed. Choosing to attend a baseball game rather than an art gallery, for example, is not an informed choice if the individual has never had the opportunity to experience the latter option or has never had that option explained.

As conceptualized by Tymchuk (1985) and other researchers (Beatty, 1988; MacPhail-Wilcox & Bryant, 1988; Moody, 1983) (see Figure 2), the third step in making a decision involves an awareness of situations in which choices need to be, or can be, made. If a person is not aware of the necessity of choice, no decision will be forthcoming. In some cases, there are several decisions that need to be made, each one leading to the next. If the individual fails to recognize one or more of these subdecisions, a less than satisfactory outcome may be the result. Finally, children and youth are typically allowed by parents and other significant adults in their lives (e.g., teachers) to make choices in some areas (e.g., the clothes that will be worn to school), but not in others (e.g., whether to attend school). A knowledge and understanding of discriminative stimuli that indicate a high probability of choice-making opportunities can help the individual avoid conflict in those situations in which it is evident that choices will not be allowed.

As a fourth step in the choice-making process, the choice or decision at hand needs to be clearly defined. If an individual views a person who is using a wheelchair having difficulty entering a building, for example, it might be considerate to ask the individual if he or she desires assistance. If the response is "yes," it would have to be ascertained exactly what type of assistance the individual wanted. It would be wise to ask the individual to provide such information. If the situation is one that the individual has previously experienced, it would be likely that he or she could provide a bystander with information detailing the specific type and form of assistance they desired. If the situation is unique or one that the person using the wheelchair has never experienced, the problem would have to be further defined. Aid to this person can be offered in a variety of ways including holding the door open or helping the person maneuver their chair. Defining the nature of the decision to be made allows parameters to be specified, standards to be set, and possible outcomes to be conceptualized.

Adequate choice definition is also necessary in order for the individual to identify who should be involved in making the choice in question. As Tymchuk (1985) points out, although many decisions appear to be made by individuals independently, most choices, either directly or indirectly, involve or affect others. This would appear to be especially salient for persons with severe disabilities since, when some choices are made, someone else will need to provide support to the person in following through on the choice. For example, an individual with a severe physical disability might be able to select a dinner menu effectively, yet need support in the preparation of the food. Communicating with others about a choice to be made may also serve the function of providing the individual with alternative points of view and additional information that will allow the decision to be a more informed choice.

A fifth step in effective choice making involves setting standards with respect to the outcomes that are expected from the choices that are made. These standards or expectations will provide the individual with information necessary to evaluate the effectiveness of the decision after it is made. They are also an important source of information with respect to the effort needed in making and carrying out the choice. If an individual has low expectancies regarding the outcomes of a decision that will be made, then little effort may be expended. If standards are set higher, then it is likely that the person will more carefully search for alternatives and carefully evaluate them.

The identification of alternative solutions or choices is the sixth step in making informed decisions (Beatty, 1988; Moody, 1983). The exploration of a number of alternative choices during this phase allows the individual to maximize positive outcomes, while minimizing negative consequences. If alternatives are unavailable because of the situation, the individual's experiences are so limited that available options are not recognized, or the declarative and procedural knowledge the person has regarding his or her environment is severely limited, the opportunity for informed choice may not exist (Rose, 1987). Next to understanding the consequences of one's choices, this is the most critical step in the choice-making process.

Following the generation of alternative choices in response to a decision-making opportunity, an analysis or evaluation of the alternatives that have been identified needs to be conducted, including the possible positive and negative consequences, and whether the alternatives are feasible and appropriate. This seventh step in the choice-making process involves several subcomponents. The first entails the identification of ongoing, short-term, and long-term consequences of the various alternative responses to a situation that have been generated. This analysis, along with the available alternatives, and the standards that the individual has set for himself or herself will guide choice selection. If the outcomes expected from available alternatives do not appear to facilitate the individual reaching or approaching his or her goal, he or she may elect to attempt to generate further alternatives before making a choice.

A second subcomponent of the evaluation process entails a feasibility analysis of each of the alternatives generated. This includes a self-assessment of whether the individual in question possesses the skills necessary to carry out the decision and an evaluation of whether they have available the resources to successfully implement possible alternatives.

A third subcomponent in the evaluation of alternatives involves the identification of the possible chain of events related to a particular decision (Tymchuk, 1985). Specifying the chain of events related to a specific choice-making opportunity allows the individual to more easily recognize relationships between events and conceptualize the possible outcomes of various behaviors.

The eighth stage of the choice-making process involves the selection by the individual of a choice based on the best alternatives available at the time, their predicted consequences, and their feasibility. If the person has explored a number of alternative decisions, is aware of their consequences, and has identified the behavioral outcomes that he or she wishes to experience as a result of his or her choice, a decision can be made that will have a high probability of meeting the person's needs.

The Self-Regulation of Behavior   While making informed choices is a skill necessary for the exercise of self-determination, the process of choice making alone is only one of the abilities that an individual must possess in order to achieve independence. Autonomy is enhanced very little if a person, despite his or her ability to make a choice from among several alternatives, does not have the skills to carry out that choice in either a direct or indirect manner. In order for this to occur, the individual must be able to regulate his or her own behavior or solicit support or assistance if they are unable to carry out a decision on their own.

As Whitman (1990b) and others (Jackson & Boag, 1981; Kendall, 1990; Meichenbaum, 1990; Shapiro, 1986) have suggested, self-regulation is an extremely complex response system that requires a number of skills to be effectively integrated. If self-regulatory capacities are to develop, an individual must first learn when and how to employ specific cognitive strategies to control his or her behavior. As a repertoire of cognitive strategies are developed, the person must learn which of these are most useful in specific situations. If no strategies are available that would appear useful, skills must be developed that will allow already existing strategies to be modified to the point at which they will be of use. Finally, there must be a recognition of the advantages of applying these cognitive strategies to situations in which opportunities for choice are available.

Whitman (1990a) has summarized the commonalities among current models of self-regulation, viewing the process as consisting of consecutive stages during which the individual must: 1) attend to his or her behavior (self-monitor); 2) make judgments about the acceptability of this behavior through comparing it to previously set standards and goals (self-evaluation); 3) self-reinforce or self-criticize based upon the results of this self-evaluation; and 4) make a decision, or series of decisions, regarding whether to modify a limited number of aspects, or many aspects, of one's behavior.

Self-regulation procedures can be activated either prior to a behavior occurrence (antecedent approach) or following the occurrence of a behavior (consequence approach). Two antecedent approaches to enhancing self-regulation have been developed during the past several years. In the first type, referred to as environmental planning (Whitman, 1990a), individuals are taught to develop plans that will aid them in achieving their goals. The second approach to antecedent self-regulation relies on self-instructions. In this paradigm, individuals are taught to use self-talk to gain greater control over their behavior (Meichenbaum, 1977).

Conceptualizations of self-regulation offered by other theorists (Gardner & Cole, 1989) may be best referred to as consequence models of self-regulation. The first component of this model involves the specification of the standards that will be used by the individual to judge the effectiveness of outcomes and behavior. These standards may specify short- or long-term goals and may either be self-specified or adapted from standards held by others. The second component involves the process of self-monitoring. This describes a covert process in which the individual agrees to observe his own behavior and compare it against some specified performance standard. The overt process of self-recording is the third component of the model. This activity involves the recording of information yielded by the individual's observations. The individual next engages in self-evaluation, which serves as the fourth component of this conceptual framework. This refers to a covert process in which the person compares his or her behavior against previously set standards. Self-evaluative decisions are overtly recorded during self-assessment, the fifth component of this framework. Based upon this assessment, the sixth component of the model involves the self-determination of the consequences that will result from the behavior in which the person has engaged. The seventh and final component of the model specifies the self-administration of consequences.

Persons with severe mental retardation have been found to be capable of self-monitoring (Litrownik et al., 1978c; Matson, 1978, 1979), evaluating their performance according to set standards (Litrownik et al., 1978a), and engaging in both self-assessment and self-reinforcement (Litrownik et al., 1978b, 1978d; Litrownik & Steinfield, 1981). While Litrownik and his colleagues found that children and adolescents with mental retardation often did not initially exhibit any self-management skills, the results from their research program do indicate that such behaviors can quickly be acquired with a minimum of effort on the part of interventionists.

During the 1970s and 1980s an impressive number of research and demonstration projects have been conducted in an attempt to investigate the usefulness of self-regulatory procedures in facilitating the development and maintenance of a wide variety of types of adaptive behaviors in populations with mental retardation. In general, research findings give support to the idea that self-regulation procedures can be effectively used to help persons with severe disabilities gain greater control over their own behavior. Self-management and self-instructional strategies have been successfully used to increase on-task behaviors and reduce disruptiveness (Horner & Brigham, 1979; Robertson, Simon, Pachman, & Drabman, 1980; Shapiro & Klein, 1980); reduce off-task behavior (Long & Williams, 1976); increase task performance and accuracy (Johnston, Whitman, & Johnson, 1980; Keogh, Whitman, & Maxwell, 1987; Shapiro & Klein, 1980; Whitman & Johnston, 1983; Whitman, Spence, & Maxwell, 1986); increase work output (Wehman, Schutz, Bates, Renzaglia, & Karan, 1978); facilitate the development and exercise of appropriate social behaviors (Matson, Ollendick, & Adkins, 1980); decrease impulsivity (Peters & Davies, 1981); and facilitate the development and exercise of a wide variety of other adaptive behaviors (Bauman & Iwata, 1977; Fisher, 1986; Franzini, Litrownik, & Magy, 1980; Guralnick, 1976; Jackson & Patterson, 1979, 1980; Litrownik, Franzini, Geller, & Geller, 1977; Ross & Ross, 1973).

Personal Advocacy   What is personal advocacy? It is a term that is often misunderstood and frequently used synonymously with self-determination. In the current context, its definition is narrower and refers to speaking out or acting on behalf of oneself or others, or on behalf of a particular issue (Williams & Shoultz, 1982). It involves being aware of one's rights as a citizen and taking responsibility for ensuring that infringements of those rights are addressed. Personal advocacy may be manifested individually or in group settings (e.g., self-advocacy organizations). Traditionally, important decisions regarding the lives of persons with disabilities and advocacy on their behalf have been undertaken by family members, friends, and a variety of professionals (Mitchell, 1988). The assumption has often been made that the cognitive or physical limitations inherent in disabilities make it impossible for these individuals to function as effective self-advocates. The growing self-advocacy movement in this country, however, has dispelled the belief that a disability necessarily impairs the capacity of an individual to advocate on his or her own behalf (Hayden & Shoultz, 1991; Ward, 1989; Williams, 1989).

Gaining its initial momentum in 1974 with the establishment of the People First organization, the self-advocacy movement has experienced phenomenal growth in the past 15 years in both the United States and Canada (Browning, Rhoades, & Thorin, 1986; Browning, Thorin, & Rhoades, 1984). A recent directory of self-advocacy groups prepared by Arc-U.S. (now The Arc) identified 380 active groups in the United States with 45 local chapters of People First in the state of Washington alone (Shoultz, 1991). The effect of self-advocacy groups on the delivery of services to persons with disabilities and the manner in which they have stimulated change have not been well documented in the research literature. This is not to imply, however, that the impact of such groups on systems change has been minimal. In fact, quite the opposite would appear to be true. Recent research suggests that one of the most powerful predictors of a state's financial commitment to services for persons with developmental disabilities is the strength and activity level of consumer advocacy groups (Braddock & Bachelder, 1990). Documentation of systems change associated with the efforts of self-advocacy groups is also readily available in the nonresearch literature. People First of Nebraska, for example, effectively worked with the Nebraska Legislature to eliminate outdated terminology concerning disabilities from state statutes (Shoultz, 1991). People First of Washington, working with the King County Board for Developmental Disabilities, developed and implemented a program that has employed persons with developmental disabilities to enhance transportation accessibility for persons with disabilities within the Seattle area (People First of Washington, 1991). In Minnesota, the presence of lobbyists trained by Advocating Change Together, Inc. (ACT) and Partners in Policymaking, a program run by the Governor's Council on Developmental Disabilities, has shown that the voices of persons with developmental disabilities can be a powerful force in stimulating legislature action on a variety of issues crucial to quality of life (Rupp, 1991).

While there is strong evidence to suggest that self-advocacy organizations have had a significant impact on the delivery of services to persons with disabilities, much less is known about the content and degree to which the self-advocacy training programs used by such groups lead to the development and generalization (i.e., use within the community) of personal-advocacy skills. A recent qualitative review of 25 self-advocacy instructional programs developed by local and state self-advocacy organizations (e.g., People First), advocacy groups (e.g., Arc) and universities revealed that despite common goals and objectives: 1) the manner in which self-advocacy skills are currently being taught is quite idiosyncratic, with each group tending to use its own methodology; 2) few organizations have conducted outcome evaluations of their instructional programs; 3) the content of the material would appear most appropriate for persons with mild disabilities; and 4) little attention has been given to the *process* through which persons move as they become empowered (Abery, manuscript in preparation).

Other than the work of a few investigators (e.g., Browning et al., 1986; Sievert, Cuvo, & Davis, 1988), there is currently little research data available concerning the general impact of self-advocacy training programs on individuals, including their effectiveness in facilitating the development and generalization of self-determination skills. While most self-advocacy programs have common goals and possess face validity, without research data, it is impossible to determine which of the many methods currently used to facilitate empowerment are most effective with which individuals. This makes it quite difficult for consumer organizations to make informed choices when selecting programs for self-advocacy instruction.

An additional problem with many personal-advocacy training programs is their primary focus on persons with mild disabilities. This is evidenced by the large numbers of abstract concepts covered in training sessions, the relatively high level of reading skills necessary to comprehend program printed material, a general lack of use of alternative methods of presentation (e.g., videotape), and what appears to be an assumption that persons completing such instructional programs will have sufficient expressive communication skills to successfully engage in a large number of verbally oriented role play and simulation exercises (Abery, manuscript in preparation). This focus on individuals with mild disabilities is evidenced not only in the training programs developed and used by advocacy and self-advocacy organizations, but is also reflected in the population of persons with disabilities targeted by the majority of research and demonstration projects in self-determination funded during the past 3 years by the U.S. Department of Education.

One possible explanation for the wide variety of self-advocacy instructional programs currently available is that, until recently, little information has been available regarding the process through which individuals progress as they become empowered. In a recent study, however, just this phenomenon has been examined. Based on their experience in assisting in the development of two self-advocacy programs in the state of Illinois, Keys and Foster-Fishman (1991) posited a six-phase cycle for the process of advocacy and self-advocacy development including: 1) low initial power, 2) opportunity to participate, 3) voice own reality and experience, 4) affirmation of voice, 5) positive outcome, and 6) enhanced dignity and self-respect. For the individuals involved in these groups, their self-advocacy experiences provided them with opportunities for empowerment and self-affirmation in a process perceived to be quite similar to other patterns of personal development.

Closely related to the concept of personal advocacy is assertiveness, or the ability to stand up for one's self and exercise one's rights. In western culture, such attributes are considered to be highly desirable skills that are necessary for success in the community. Although there is conflicting evidence, the research literature does suggest that persons with disabilities are less assertive than their counterparts without disabilities and often acquiesce to others (Mishel, 1978; Percell, Berwick, & Beigel, 1974). A considerable body of research indicates that nonassertive persons can be successfully trained to assert themselves, and that this skill often leads to greatly enriched lives (Bornstein, Bellack, & Werson, 1977; Joanning, 1975; Onoda & Bassert, 1978; Pearlman & Mayo, 1977). Much less is known about the impact of such training on the social skills and quality of life experienced by individuals with disabilities. Available data docs, however, suggest that persons with developmental disabilities can benefit substantially from such training (Bregman, 1984; Gentile & Jenkins, 1980; Mishel, 1978; Sengstock & Kaufman, 1982). Whether the effects of such interventions generalize to contexts outside of those in which training occurred or have a significant impact on self-determination, remains an unanswered question.

Interpersonal Problem Solving There appears to be little question that among the general population, effective interpersonal problem solving is related to emotional adjustment (Platt & Spivack, 1972; Shure & Spivack, 1972; Spivack & Shure, 1974). The ability to attain personal goals in interpersonal relationships has long been considered a central component of social competence (Foster & Ritchie, 1979; Krasnor & Rubin, 1983). There is an important distinction, however, between problem solving and emitting an effective response in a situation that is problematic. As it is typically defined, problem solving refers to the process through which one attempts to arrive at a solution to a problem. It is a cognitive-behavioral process in that it deals with cognitive processes and their relationship to behavioral adjustment (Urbain & Kendall, 1980). The problem-solving task is conceptualized as one of learning to combine previously acquired responses in a novel way so as to produce a new response. This outcome is related not only to the process of problem solving, but also to the individual's learning history (D'Zurilla & Goldfried, 1971). Among the abilities that bear a relationship to successful problem solving are alternative thinking, consequential thinking, and means-ends thinking (Shure & Spivack, 1972, 1982).

Although many conceptualizations of interpersonal problem solving have been offered in recent years, the majority are variants of the model first presented by D'Zurilla and Goldfried (1971) more than 20 years ago. Setting aside variations in terminology, most theorists view the problem-solving process as consisting of five general phases. The first of these, which might be best labeled as "problem orientation," includes the acceptance of the fact that problematic situations are part of everyday life, the recognition that a problem exists, and the inhibition of the tendency to respond to the problematic situation in an impulsive (i.e., automatic) manner (Nezu, Nezu, & Arean, 1991). While this step may appear simple, it should be recognized that it may not always be an easy task to identify problematic situations as they occur and control one's tendency to respond to them in an immediate fashion.

A second phase in the problem-solving process described by most theorists involves *problem formulation and definition*. This entails defining all aspects of the situation in operational terms and separating relevant from irrelevant information (D'Zurilla & Goldfried, 1971). By specifying problems in meaningful, concrete terms, the individual will be more likely to consider all available facts and seek additional information when necessary.

The *generation of possible solutions* to the problem at hand is the third stage of the problem-solving process. Much of the activity engaged in during this portion of the problem solving can be termed "brainstorming." In this process, criticism is ruled out, freewheeling (i.e., the generation of what may appear to be wild ideas) is encouraged, quantity is desired, and combination and improvement are sought (Osborn, 1963).

The fourth stage of the problem-solving process involves the *selection of the alternative* that best fits the problem. This involves the evaluation of the probable consequences of each alternative, assessment as to whether the individual has the specific means to implement alternatives, and, finally, selection of the best alternative (Castles & Glass, 1986). This process corresponds to decision making as discussed earlier.

The fifth and final stage of the problem-solving process involves *verification*, or the assessment of the actual outcome of problem solving after a course of action has been carried out (D'Zurilla & Goldfried, 1971). This process requires the problem solver to obtain information about the actual consequences of his or her decision and compare it against expected goals or outcomes. If outcomes are acceptable, the problem-solving process can be discontinued, if they are not, the person can return to the initial stages of the process and continue to seek an acceptable solution.

The effects of the provision of instruction in interpersonal problem solving have been well studied in populations with and without disabilities. Studies of children without disabilities indicate that training in this area has a positive impact on social adjustment (Shure & Spivack, 1982) and teacher ratings of overall competence (Gesten et al., 1982). Research investigations with persons exhibiting a wide variety of disabilities, including mental retardation and learning disabilities, suggest that, with instruction, these groups are able to generate more effective planning and problem-solving responses, and show improvement in the quality and quantity of their responses, logical thinking, and ability to make critical judgements in interpersonal problem-solving situations (Castles & Glass, 1986; Ross & Ross, 1973, 1978; Tymchuk, Andron, & Rahbar, 1988).

Additional Individual Factors

Declarative and Procedural Knowledge In addition to possessing the basic skills necessary to exercise self-determination, it is also important for the individual to have available a working knowledge of the environment in which functioning will occur, as well as knowledge about his or her own competencies and skills (self-awareness). Chi (1987) and Whitman (1990a) specify two types of knowledge as important for self-determination. Declarative knowledge refers to the factual knowledge an individual possesses about his or her environment. If an individual has not had the opportunity to have a variety of experiences within a given context, it is likely that he or she does not have access to specific facts about the environment that would allow him or her to exert personal control. This would appear to be common among many persons with disabilities, especially those whose disabilities are of a severe nature (Shapiro, 1986; Zigler & Balla, 1982).

Procedural knowledge involves knowing how to engage one's environment (Whitman, 1990a). An understanding of how to effectively engage oneself in an ongoing conversation or how to interact with small children are two examples of this type of knowledge. The strategies most individuals use to accomplish engagement are quite varied, at least partially, because they have had a wide variety of experiences and have come to appreciate the importance of contextual cues. The situation for an individual with a disability may be quite different. In the absence of experience within specific environments, the individual may not be able to engage in the environment as effectively as others.

A third type of knowledge that would appear crucial for self-determination is self-knowledge, which refers to the individual's awareness of and ability to accurately assess his or her competencies and skills. In the absence of accurate information regarding one's levels of competence, it would be quite difficult to judge whether the course of action one has decided to take to solve a problem or make a decision is, in fact, feasible. While a degree of subjectively is inherent in the self-assessments of all individuals, the relative accuracy of these evaluations are likely to play an important role in whether the individual encounters success or failure in attempts to exercise self-determination.

Motivational Factors   While self-determination skills have the potential to aid an individual in gaining greater control over his or her life, they need to be used on a regular basis. Whether this takes place is at least partially a result of motivational factors. Until quite recently, researchers in disability-related fields paid little attention to these processes, focusing on cognitive and behavioral deficiencies instead. Two constructs that have been studied extensively by developmental psychologists may help to explain why, even when the prerequisite skills are available, some persons with disabilities make few attempts to exert personal control.

An individual's sense of self-efficacy refers to the degree to which he or she expects to successfully execute the behaviors necessary to achieve desired outcomes (Bandura, 1977). These expectations influence both the initiation and persistence of behavior and vary in magnitude, generality, and strength (Bandura, 1982). If one believes, for example, that he or she can successfully carry out the behaviors necessary to initiate social relationships, it is likely that he or she will persist in such behaviors even if initial attempts are not totally successful.

Sources of self-efficacy expectations include performance accomplishments (the experience of success/failure), vicarious experiences (observing others successfully carry out the behavior), verbal persuasion, and physiological states. If an individual does not believe that he or she can successfully engage in the behavioral sequence necessary to achieve a goal, it is likely that the sequence will never be initiated or will be discontinued when difficulties are encountered. In contrast, when a person believes that he or she can effectively execute the necessary behaviors, the probability of initiation and persistence are much higher (Bandura, 1982).

Closely related to the construct of self-efficacy is the notion that all individuals seek explanations or causal attributions for their behavior. If a person fails a science test, for example, he or she is likely to seek out the reasons for his or her failure. Was it due to a biased test, not enough studying, or lack of ability in the study of science? Two major dimensions of attributions have been identified: internal-external and stable-unstable (Lepper, 1981). If a person views failure as due to internal-stable causes (e.g., a lack of ability) or attributes success to external-unstable causes (e.g., luck), it is likely that the person will not be highly motivated to engage in similar behavior in the future. However, if success is perceived as due to internal-stable causes (e.g., high levels of competence or ability) and failure a result of external-unstable factors (the teacher just happened to write an extremely difficult test), the probability of such behavior continuing in the face of adversity is greatly enhanced.

The general consensus among developmental psychologists is that a person's beliefs, with respect to perceived control, arise from interactions with the environment. The individual's history of reinforcement (Rotter, 1966); frequent or prolonged exposure to noncontingent stimulation during infancy and childhood (Seligman, 1975); the opportunity (or lack thereof) to exert control over one's own world (Bandura, 1982); the quality of parent–child interactions (Buriel, 1981; Palmer, 1971); the child's past record of success and failure; attitudes conveyed by parents, teachers, and peers (Henkler, Whalen, & Hinshaw, 1980); and the encouragement of independence (Wichern & Nowicki, 1976) are all postulated to influence a child's developing sense of perceived control and self-efficacy.

During the 1970s and 1980s, research has conclusively linked various aspects of perceived control to a variety of outcomes. It has been associated with school failure (Borkowski, Estrada, Milstead, & Hale, 1991), achievement-oriented behavior (Dweck, 1975; Dweck & Wortman, 1982), unpopularity, and a variety of psychological disorders to include depression in both adults and children (Seligman, 1975). Little inference is necessary to recognize that perceived control and a person's sense of self-efficacy are also likely to have a profound effect on the exercise of self-determination. Individuals who often experience failure in multiple contexts are likely to develop belief systems that inhibit their attempts to exert control over their environment. If a person views behavior and outcomes as beyond personal control, it is unlikely they will engage in self-determined behavior.

Individuals with disabilities may also develop a second set of attributions, referred to as program-generated attributions (Henkler et al., 1980; Reid & Borowski, 1987), as a result of their encounters with the education and social service systems. During their lives these individuals learn that they differ from their peers, overhear diagnostic labels, and experience treatment that is different (Henkler et al., 1980; Reid & Borkowski, 1987). Experiences of this type are likely to produce specific attributions that will hinder the exercise of self-determination.

The impact of the attributions that persons with severe disabilities acquire with respect to their successes and failures and their sense of self-efficacy, which is developed through interactions with parents, family members, and significant others, can be expected to exert an important influence on self-determination. If an individual perceives outcomes as beyond his or her control or has a low sense of self-efficacy, it is less likely that he or she will engage in attempts to exercise personal control or initiate behavior that has the potential to lead to the fulfillment of goals. If experiences of failure are viewed as a result of stable-internal factors (lack of ability), the individual is less likely to exert effort in the face of difficulty, but rather, may decrease or cease to put forth the required effort.

THE IMPORTANCE OF ECOLOGICAL FACTORS

The Microsystem Level

Considerable research has been undertaken in recent years concerning the choice making, problem solving, and self-regulation skills of persons with disabilities. There has been little appreciation, to date, however, of the important role that the ecological contexts in which a person functions (e.g., family, community) play in the development and use of skills relevant to self-determination. In order to develop and refine competencies in these areas, an individual needs the *opportunity* to exert control over his or her life (i.e., practice). Unfortunately, in many instances, these opportunities are not provided, even when basic skills are present. Parents, siblings, residential staff, employment supervisors, teachers, and others often provide limited opportunities for the exercise of personal control (Houghton, Bronicki, & Guess, 1987). Without opportunities to practice necessary skills in a variety of environments, individuals with severe disabilities are unlikely to develop the self-determination needed for independent living in the community.

The Family System

The family system is the training ground in which individuals learn about empowerment, choice, and their strengths and weaknesses (Varela, 1988). The family plays an extremely important part in the acquisition of socially valued skills from infancy through adulthood, including those involved in self-determination. As early as the first few days after birth, the infant, through his or her behavior, begins to exert a controlling influence on his or her parents and the environment (Perry, 1980). The sensitivity of parents and other caregivers to expressions of preference are likely to play a major role in the development of a sense of self-esteem and autonomy, or feelings that desired outcomes are beyond one's control (Abramson, Garber, & Seligman, 1980). The opportunity to exert choice, engage in decision making, and regulate one's own behaviors in family relationships, provides individuals with the chance to practice skills and develop the belief systems that will eventually allow them to exert control over their lives.

Due to the characteristics inherent in many disabilities and the usually unfounded assumptions that members of society make about persons with disabilities, these persons often do not experience many opportunities for choice outside of the family setting. This magnifies the importance of the home environment in fostering the development of skills necessary for self-determination. If parents and other family members become highly skilled at recognizing and responding to unspoken preferences, provide few opportunities for choice making, or fail to allow the child to experience the consequences of their choices, the end result may be a person who rarely expresses preferences, has a difficult time making decisions, and cannot effectively problem-solve. While such an environment may alleviate short-term distress, it is often at odds with the desire of most families to facilitate full inclusion within the community.

Interactions with family members have the potential to facilitate self-determination and to prepare an individual with a developmental disability for life as an independent adult. Family life also has the potential to create numerous barriers to independent functioning. The family, however, is only one of the many behavioral contexts in which an individual develops. Interactions taking place in the school or work setting, peer group, and community at large also play an extremely important role.

The Community Context

School, Work, and Residential Environments In the past decade, professionals in the disability field have developed a greater appreciation of the importance that personal control plays in facilitating an enhanced quality of life (Klein & Babcock, 1979; Shevin & Klein, 1984; Williams, Vogelsburg, & Schutz, 1985). Instruction in the areas of choice making and self-regulation have been incorporated into programs developed by several leaders in the field (Guess & Helmsetter, 1986; Wuerch & Voeltz, 1982; Zeph, 1984). At the present time, however, it appears that this type of instruction is included in only a small number of education and residential programs. The work of Guess and his associates (Houghton et al., 1987), as well as others (Kishi et al., 1988; Rose, 1987; Shevin, 1984), suggests that teachers, residential staff, and their assistants respond at low rates to indications of preference and provide few opportunities for personal control within classroom, work, and residential contexts.

Just as persons with disabilities may have limited opportunities to exercise personal choice and autonomy on a daily basis, it is also quite unusual for them to be actively involved in the development of their service plans (e.g., educational, habilitation) programs (Abery & Eggebeen, 1993). The importance of the active participation of individuals with disabilities in service decision making increases dramatically as the person prepares for the transition from school and family to the community. Far too often, educational, residential, and vocational placements reflect the choice of well-meaning parents and staff rather than the preferences of the individual with the disability (Abery & Bruininks, 1990; Houghton et al., 1987). Without being given the opportunity to decide the type of educational program they will attend, where and with whom they live, and the nature of the employment they will undertake, persons with developmental disabilities have little control over the quality of life they will experience.

Peer Group Influences The neighborhood and the community are the settings for much of the social interaction that takes place among individuals. The manner in which skills important to self-determination are learned as a result of direct instruction from parents is fairly well-documented (Baumrind, 1967, 1977; Berndt, 1979; Brody & Stoneman, 1981; Grusec & Abramovitch, 1982). The impact of incidental, observational learning involving peers, however, has not been the focus of any studies. Interactions with members of a peer/friendship group have been found to play a role in the acquisition of many social skills and in the value systems developed by individuals (Hartup, 1983). Much of the learning that occurs in this context is not planned or intentional, but incidental in nature. Through observing other persons problem-solve, make decisions, and establish and work toward goals, individuals learn both the behaviors and outcomes that are acceptable and the processes through which to attain or work toward them. However, individuals with developmental disabilities often have limited opportunities to observe and interact with same-age peers without disabilities (Abery et al., 1989). Receiving their education and living and often working in segregated settings, they typically do not have the extensive opportunities of peers without disabilities to observe and model their behavior based on the actions of persons with higher levels of social competence. While this may not prevent the acquisition of skills and competencies essential to the exercise of self-determination, it does place individuals with developmental disabilities at a distinct disadvantage.

The Mesosystem Level

The mesosystem level of an individual's ecosystem consists of the linkages between two or more settings in which the individual participates (Bronfenbrenner, 1989). These linkages, more specifically their existence, strength, and valence, are likely to have a profound impact on self-determination. In a well-developed mesosystem, multiple, strong, positive contacts exist between the many contexts in which life takes place. These linkages allow for skills developed and refined in one setting to be practiced and adapted to others. For example, strong, positive connections between the family and residential setting are likely to facilitate in each context reinforcing behaviors, such as choice making and problem solving, that are being acquired in others. Linkages between settings will also provide the person with multiple opportunities to observe the positive manner in which setting participants interact with each other. An individual attending his or her individualized service plan (ISP) meeting, for example, may be able to observe parents and other family members actively contributing to the process, their comments valued by service personnel and incorporated into the final service plan designed. Contrast this situation to that of a person whose family has little to no contact with service providers and who may mistrust these staff. The family's lack of participation will send a message to the individual that the residential service context is one in which a person does not exercise personal control.

The Exosystem Level

The exosystem consists of the linkages between two or more settings, at least one of which does not ordinarily contain the individual in question, but in which events occur that influence processes in the immediate setting that does contain the person (Bronfenbrenner, 1989). Exosystem level factors that are likely to have an impact on self-determination include policies regarding the type of preservice and inservice training that professionals and paraprofessionals in disability-related fields receive; school board decisions regarding the curriculum offered to students (e.g., will the teaching of self-determination skills be included?); and the support that staff receive from administration and colleagues when attempting to enhance self-determination.

The quality and type of preservice training received by teachers and residential staff is likely to have a significant impact on the frequency with which opportunities for personal control are supported. Preservice training conducted in the traditional manner in which structure and control is emphasized and compliance with staff directives viewed as an index of success is unlikely to lead to the development of professionals who ensure that opportunities for personal control are available on a regular basis. In contrast, if decisions regarding preservice instruction are made in a manner such that professionals-in-training learn to respect the right of all persons to be self-determined, it is likely that greater opportunities will be available for persons with disabilities to learn and refine competencies in this area. At a more direct level, it can be assumed that without an administrative decision to support self-determination, efforts at ensuring that individuals with developmental disabilities actively participate in service planning are likely to be significantly more difficult.

In both of the aforementioned cases, decisions made in systems in which persons with disabilities do not typically participate (i.e., preservice training curriculum committees, school administrative committees) have an impact on the environments in which they do take part (i.e., school classrooms, residential settings). This may either facilitate or hinder the exercise of self-determination. If opportunities for enhanced self-determination are to be maximized, it is not sufficient to merely examine those environments in which an individual directly participates. Rather, decisions made in systems in which the individual may never take part must be considered and the impact of these decisions on opportunities for personal control examined.

The Macrosystem Level

The institutional and ideological patterns characteristic of a given culture are referred to as the *macrosystem* (Bronfenbrenner, 1989). How might these global factors have an impact on self-determination?

The manner in which society treats persons with disabilities has changed significantly over the last several decades. The passage of the Education for All Handicapped Children Act of 1975 (PL 94-142), the deinstitutionalization of persons with disabilities, and the recent implementation of the Americans with Disabilities Act of 1990 (PL 101-336) have served as legal mandates for persons with disabilities, affording them equal opportunities in society. If individuals with developmental disabilities are to function as self-determined adults, even further change at the macrosystem level will be necessary.

Presently, many parents and professionals remain reluctant to give up the control they exercise over the lives of persons with developmental disabilities. Why might this be the case? One could hypothesize a variety of reasons at the individual level. A more fruitful approach, however, would be to examine just how far societal attitudes toward persons with developmental disabilities have changed. Legislation itself does not guarantee changes in the manner in which individuals are perceived by society, as has clearly been experienced by persons of color despite the passage of civil rights legislation.

Many attitudinal barriers that affect individuals with disabilities still exist at the societal level and remain to be addressed. Although society has become more tolerant of persons with disabilities in the last several decades, this does not mean that we have universally come to accept such individuals as equals or as persons with capacities and skills. In many locations, neighborhood groups attempt to block the development of community residences for persons with developmental disabilities. More than 93% of children with mental retardation receive their education in segregated classrooms (Arc, 1992). The majority of individuals with disabilities still have little opportunity to participate in their own service planning (Abery & Eggebeen, 1993). Against this societal background, it is easy to understand why many family members and professionals are reluctant to give up the control they currently exercise over persons with severe disabilities. Most agencies at local, state, and federal levels continue to provide services in a manner that clearly implies that persons with developmental disabilities are not capable of controlling their own lives.

If the self-determination of children, youth, and adults with and without disabilities is a goal toward which society is committed, efforts to augment our understanding and the ability to develop instructional programs to enhance self-determination will also need to continue. First, changes will need to be made in the way that self-determination itself is conceptualized by society. Parents and professionals in education-related fields must understand that self-determination is more than just a transition issue. If persons with disabilities are to enjoy the rights and privileges of citizenship accorded to all members of society, efforts at providing them with opportunities to acquire, practice, and refine the competencies necessary for self-determination will need to begin at school entry and continue throughout life. Second, it must be realized that the exercise of personal control over one's life is not an all-or-nothing phenomenon. One by-product of this perspective is that persons with disabilities are often viewed as either totally capable or totally incapable of exercising complete control over their lives. The idea that an individual may possess the ability to control some aspects of their life, while not having the capacity to make decisions in others, is rarely encountered. This societal perception is reflected in current law regarding guardianship and conservatorship for persons with disabilities (see Flower, chap. 17, this volume). For many individuals with severe disabilities, this has resulted in a situation in which, despite the capacity to set goals for themselves, make decisions, and chart their own lives, they are denied this basic right.

Many individuals view self-determination as best developed through a trial-and-error process or as a set of competencies for which it is the family's responsibility to facilitate. As evidenced by the high numbers of high school dropouts, and the degree of chemical dependency, teenage pregnancy, and gang affiliation currently prevalent in the youth of American society, this perspective does not appear to have resulted in a generation of self-determined young adults.

Educators are just beginning to understand the complex process of self-determination. There is still little agreement regarding an operational definition of the construct or methods by which to assess a person's level of self-determination. The development and field-testing of instructional programs to enhance self-determination has only recently been initiated. Efforts in these areas will need to continue, not only to enhance the self-determination of individuals with disabilities, but to ensure that all citizens possess the competencies necessary to control their own lives.

Finally, it must be realized that many of the institutional and ideological changes necessary to enhance self-determination will be difficult to achieve until individuals with disabilities assume leadership roles and actively participate in decision-making processes. Only when persons with disabilities themselves acquire the power and authority to start defining the specific issues that need to be addressed, such as the residential services system, employment programs, education, and research and program development, will the institutional changes take place that facilitate self-determination at a systems level.

FACILITATING SELF-DETERMINATION

Facilitating the self-determination of persons with developmental disabilities is a complex process. Changes at all levels of the environment, as well as in the skills of the individual, are likely to be necessary. It would be pleasurable to be able to conclude this chapter with an overview of numerous instructional programs, legislation, and societal changes that have resulted in enhanced self-determination. Unfortunately, to this date, little legislation has been passed that has had such an effect, and few of the necessary changes at a societal level have occurred. In recent years, however, there has been considerable activity toward developing instructional programs to facilitate the skill development necessary for enhanced self-determination.

The development of instructional programs to enhance self-determination is a recent phenomenon, with field-testing yet to be completed. A number of researchers and practitioners, however, have become involved in the development and implementation of such programs. Some of these efforts, funded through the U.S. Department of Education Office of Special Education and Rehabilitative Services (OSERS), are currently in the process of being evaluated for their effectiveness. There are similarities, as well as differences, in the approaches taken by various groups in an attempt to enhance the self-determination of persons with developmental disabilities, an understandable state of affairs given the lack of basic research that has been conducted in this area. An examination of a few of these efforts gives the reader an idea as to the manner in which those in the field are beginning to conceptualize self-determination and respond to the need to enhance the personal control of individuals with developmental disabilities.

The Leadership ACTion Project
(Advocating Change Together, Inc. [ACT])

The Leadership ACTion Project consists of three independent training modules consisting of informational presentations and a series of active learning experiences developed by Advocating Change Together, Inc., a self-advocacy group.

The first module, Personal Advocacy, focuses on strengthening participants' abilities to speak for themselves, problem-solve and make effective decisions, enrich their knowledge of their rights and responsibilities, and foster participation in the community. Curriculum for the second module, Expressive Self-Advocacy, concentrates on enhancing self-esteem and interpersonal communication skills. In addition, it provides information on how to build effective teams and participate in meetings and on boards and committees. The third component of the Leadership

ACTion Project curriculum, Systems Advocacy, centers on enriching participants' understanding of citizenship and their ability to work with existing systems to create social change.

The Self-Determination Project
(Institute on Community Integration, University of Minnesota)

Staff at the University of Minnesota's Institute on Community Integration have developed and are field-testing a self-determination program for youth with mental retardation and physical disabilities. The program is based on an ecological model of self-determination (Abery & Bruininks, 1990) and contains four major components. The first component entails a modular skill-building curriculum that can be individualized to meet the needs of specific students. This curriculum focuses on skill development in the areas of self-awareness and self-efficacy, establishing and communicating preferences/goals, decision making, the self-regulation of behavior, creative problem solving, and personal advocacy. The second component of the program, which is educational and supportive in nature, focuses on the family. By taking part in a series of structured discussions, family members will have the opportunity to become better educated about self-determination, learn to create greater opportunities for personal control in the family for all members, and understand and use strategies to support the development of self-determination. The third component of the program is designed to increase opportunities for personal control in the school setting. Project staff provide ongoing technical assistance and consultation to teachers of students taking part in the project. This contact, in conjunction with materials developed by project staff, is designed to foster self-determination in the classroom on a daily basis as well as increased student involvement in both short and long-term educational planning.

While the programs that are described, and others like them, are promising approaches to enhancing the self-determination of persons with developmental disabilities, at the current time, they are unproven. Prior to widespread implementation, effectiveness evaluations that focus on long- as well as short-term outcomes and that deal with the generalization of skills from instructional settings to community environments will need to be completed. In addition, research will need to be conducted to establish whether specific aspects of these programs are more crucial than others in facilitating behavioral and attitudinal change. Finally, efforts will need to be made to establish the extent to which such programming is applicable to individuals with disabilities other than adolescents including children and adults.

CONCLUSION

During the 1970s and 1980s there has been a dramatic shift in the manner in which professionals, policymakers, and families view persons with disabilities. Legislation and shifts in public policy have also resulted in changes in the way in which services are provided to such individuals. The work of persons with disabilities themselves, both individually and through consumer organizations, has led to changes in societal attitudes, making it more possible that individuals with even the most severe disabilities will be able to lead meaningful lives in inclusive communities. As a result of this change in philosophy, or new way of thinking, greater emphasis has recently been given to providing opportunities for persons with developmental disabilities to exercise self-determination and exert greater control over their lives. Despite some promising research efforts in the area, little information currently exists about the nature of self-determination, the skills and competencies that are necessary to exercise personal control, the developmental processes that are involved in the acquisition of self-determination skills, or the most effective instructional techniques to facilitate the development of self-determined individuals. A review of the literature suggests that progress in this area has been impeded by the lack of an empirically tested conceptual framework of self-determination, satisfactory operational definitions of the competencies and skills necessary for the exercise of personal control, and adequate assessment procedures.

Since the early 1980s, there has been sufficient attitudinal change on the part of professionals and the general public to acknowledge that individuals with developmental disabilities are entitled to the same basic human rights as their counterparts without disabilities. The challenge for the decade of the 90s is to put this philosophy into practice by ensuring that opportunities are provided for individuals with severe disabilities to acquire, use, and refine those skills that will facilitate the personal control we often take for granted.

REFERENCES

Abery, B.H. (1988, April). *Family interaction and the school-based competence of children with Down syndrome*. Paper presented at the Annual Conference of the National Association of School Psychologists, Chicago, Illinois.

Abery, B.H. (manuscript in preparation). *An qualitative analysis of currently available self-advocacy programs*.

Abery, B.H., & Bruininks, R.H. (1990). *Enhancing the self-determination of youth with disabilities*. Minneapolis, MN: Institute on Community Integration.

Abery, B.H., Bruininks, R.H., Johnson, D.J., & Thurlow, M. (1989, December). *The social networks of young adults with moderate-severe mental retardation*. Paper presented at the Annual Conference of The Association of Persons with Severe Handicaps, San Francisco, California.

Abery, B.H., & Eggebeen, A. (1992). *The ecology of self-determination: Environmental opportunities for personal control*. Technical Report. Minneapolis, MN: University of Minnesota, Institute on Community Integration.

Abery, B.H., & Eggebeen, A. (1993, June). *A descriptive study of the self-determination skills and opportunities of youth with mental retardation*. Paper presented at the Annual Conference of the American Association on Mental Retardation, Washington, D.C.

Abramson, L.Y., Garber, J., & Seligman, M. (1980). Learned helplessness in humans: An attributional analysis. In J. Garber & M. Seligman (Eds.), *Human helplessness: Theory and application*. New York: Academic Press.

Allen, W.T. (1989). *Read my lips: It's my choice*. St. Paul, MN: Governor's Planning Council on Developmental Disabilities.

Arc. (1992). *Inclusive education report*. Arlington, TX: Author.

Bandura, A. (1977). Self-efficacy: Toward a unified theory of behavioral change. *Psychological Review*, *84*, 191–215.

Bandura, A. (1982). Self-efficacy mechanism in human agency. *American Psychologist*, *37*, 122–147.

Bauman, K.E., & Iwata, B.A. (1977). Maintenance of independent housekeeping skills using scheduling plus self-recording procedures. *Behavior Therapy*, *8*, 554–560.

Baumrind, D. (1967). Child care practices anteceding three patterns of preschool behavior. *Genetic Psychology Monographs*, *75*, 43–88.

Baumrind, D. (1977, March). *Socialization determinants of personal agency*. Paper presented at the biennial meeting of the Society for Research in Child Development. New Orleans, Louisianna.

Beatty, M.J. (1988). Increasing students' choice-making consistency: The effect of decision rule-use training. *Communication Education*, *37*, 96–105.

Berndt, T.J. (1979). Developmental changes in conformity to peers and parents. *Developmental Psychology*, *15*, 608–616.

Borkowski, J.G., Estrada, J.G., Milstead, M., & Hale, C.A. (1991). General problem-solving skills: Relations between meta-cognition and strategic processing. *Learning Disabilities Quarterly*, *12*, 159–171.

Bornstein, M., Bellack, A., & Werson, M. (1977). Social skills training for unassertive children: A multiple baseline analysis. *Journal of Applied Behavior Analysis*, *10*, 183–195.

Braddock, D., & Bachelder, L. (1990). *Comparative analysis of public support for mental retardation and mental health services in the United States* (Public Policy Monograph Series No. 48). Chicago, IL: University Affiliated Program in Developmental Disabilities, University of Illinois at Chicago.

Bregman, S. (1984). Assertiveness training for mentally retarded adults. *Mental Retardation*, *22*(1), 12–18.

Brody, G.H., & Stoneman, Z. (1981). Selective imitation of same-age, older, and younger peer models. *Child Development*, *52*, 717–720.

Bronfenbrenner, U. (1977). Toward an experimental ecology of human development. *American Psychologist*, 513–531.

Bronfenbrenner, U. (1979). *The ecology of human development: Experiments by nature and design*. Cambridge, MA: Harvard University Press.

Bronfenbrenner, U. (1989). Ecological systems theory. *Annals of Child Development*, *6*, 187–249.

Bronfenbrenner, U., Devereaux, E.C., Suci, G., & Rogers, R.R. (1965). *Adults and peers as sources of conformity and autonomy*. Paper presented at the Conference for Socialization for Competence, San Juan, Puerto Rico.

Browning, P., Rhoades, C., & Thorin, E. (1986). *The impact of nationwide training programs to promote self-advocacy for people with developmental disabilities*. Eugene: University of Oregon, Rehabilitation Research and Training Center in Mental Retardation.

Browning, P., Thorin, E., & Rhoades, C. (1984). A national profile of self-help/self-advocacy groups of people with mental retardation. *Mental Retardation*, *22*(5), 226–230.

Bruininks, R.H., Thurlow, M.L., & Lange, C. (1987). *Outcomes for students with moderate-severe handicaps in an urban school district*. Minneapolis, MN: University Affiliated Program.

Buriel, R. (1981). The relation of Anglo- and Mexican-American children's locus of control beliefs to parents' and teachers' socialization practices. *Child Development*, *52*, 104–113.

Castles, E.E., & Glass, C.R. (1986). Training in interpersonal and problem-solving skills for mildly and moderately retarded adults. *American Journal of Mental Deficiency*, *91*, 35–42.

Chadsey-Rusch, J., Rusch, F., & O'Reilly, M.F. (1991). Transition from school to integrated communities. *Remedial and Special Education*, *12*(6), 23–33.

Chi, M.T.H. (1987). Representing knowledge and metaknowledge: Implications for interpreting metamemory research. In F.E. Weinert & R.H. Kluwe (Eds.), *Metacognition, motivation and understanding* (pp. 239–266). Hillsdale, NJ: Erlbaum.

Deci, E.L., & Ryan, R.M. (1985). *Intrinsic motivation and self-determination in human behavior*. New York: Plenum Press.

Dweck, C.S. (1975). The role of expectations and attributions in the alleviation of learned helplessness. *Journal of Personality and Social Psychology*, *31*, 674–685.

Dweck, C.S., & Wortman, C.B. (1982). Learned helplessness, anxiety and achievement motivation: Neglected parallels in cognition, affect and coping responses. In H.W. Krohen & L. Laux (Eds.), *Achievement, stress and anxiety*. New York: Hemisphere.

D'Zurilla, T.J., & Goldfried, M.R. (1971). Problem-solving and behavior modification. *Journal of Abnormal Psychology*, *78*, 107–126.

Fisher, E. (1986). Behavioral weight reduction program for mentally retarded adult females. *Perceptual and Motor Skills*, *62*, 359–362.

Foster, S.L., & Ritchie, W.C. (1979). Issues in the assessment of social competence in children. *Journal of Applied Behavioral Analysis*, *12*, 625–638.

Franzini, L.R., Litrownik, A.J., & Magy, M.A. (1980). Training trainable mentally retarded adolescents in delay behavior. *Mental Retardation*, *18*, 45–47.

Garbarino, J. (1982). *Children and families in the social environment*. New York: Aldine Press.

Gardner, W.I., Clees, T.J., & Cole, C.L. (1983). Self-management of disruptive verbal ruminations by a mentally retarded adult. *Applied Research in Mental Retardation*, *4*, 41–58.

Gardner, W.I., & Cole, C.L. (1989). Self-management approaches. In E. Cipani (Ed.), *The treatment of severe behavior disorders: Behavior analysis approaches* (pp. 19–35). Washington, DC: American Association on Mental Retardation.

Gentile, C., & Jenkins, J.O. (1980). Assertive training with mildly mentally retarded persons. *Mental Retardation*, *18*, 315–317.

Gesten, E.L., Rains, M.H., Rapkin, B.D., Weissberg, R.P., Apocada, R.F., Cowen, E.I., & Bowen, R. (1982). Training children in social problem-solving competencies: A first and second look. *American Journal of Community Psychology*, *10*, 95–115.

Goode, D.A., & Gaddy, M.R. (1976). Ascertaining choice with alingual, deaf-blind, and retarded children. *Mental Retardation*, *14*, 10–12.

Grusec, J.E., & Abramovitch, R. (1982). Imitation of peers and adults in a natural setting. *Child Development*, *53*, 636–642.

Guess, D., Benson, H.A., & Siegel-Causey, E. (1985). Concepts and issues related to choice-making and autonomy among persons with severe handicaps. *Journal of The Association of Persons with Severe Handicaps*, *10*(2), 79–86.

Guess, D., & Helmsetter, E. (1986). Skill cluster instruction and the individualized curriculum sequencing model. In R. Horner, L. Meyer, & H.D. Fredericks (Eds.), *Education of learners with severe handicaps: Exemplary service strategies* (pp. 221–248). Baltimore: Paul H. Brookes Publishing Co.

Guess, D., & Siegel-Causey, E. (1985). Behavioral control and education of severely handicapped students: Who's doing what to whom? And why? In D. Bricker & J. Filler (Eds.), *Education of learners with severe handicaps: Exemplary service strategies* (pp. 230–244). Lancaster, PA: The Division on Mental Retardation of the Council for Exceptional Children, Lancaster Press.

Guralnick, M.J. (1976). Solving complex discrimination problems: Techniques for the development of problem-solving strategies. *American Journal of Mental Deficiency*, *81*(1), 18–25.

Hartup, W. W. (1983). Peer relations. In E. M. Hetherington (Ed.), *Handbook of child psychology socialization, personality, and social development* (Vol. 4, pp. 103–196). New York: Wiley.

Hasazi, S.B., Gordon, L.R., & Roe, C.A. (1985). Factors associated with the employment status of handicapped youth exiting high school from 1979 to 1983. *Exceptional Children*, *51*, 455–469.

Hayden, M.F., & Shoultz, B. (1991). *IMPACT*. Feature Issue on Self-Advocacy, *3*(4).

Henkler, B., Whalen, C.K., & Hinshaw, S.P. (1980). The attributional contexts of cognitive intervention strategies. *Exceptional Education Quarterly*, *1*(1), 17–30.

Holvoet, J., Brewer, M., Mulligan, M., Guess, D., Helmsetter, E., & Riggs, P. (1981). *Influence of activity choice on learning among students with severe handicaps*. Unpublished manuscript, University of Kansas, Lawrence, Kansas.

Horner, R.H., & Brigham, T.A. (1979). The effects of self-management procedures on the study behavior of two retarded children. *Education and Training of the Mentally Retarded*, *14*, 18–24.

Houghton, J., Bronicki, J.B., & Guess, D. (1987). Opportunities to express preferences and make choices among students with severe disabilities in classroom settings. *Journal of The Association of Persons with Severe Handicaps*, *12*(1), 18–27.

Hurst, J., Kinney, M., & Weiss, S.J. (1983). The decision-making process. *Theory and Research in Social Education*, *11*, 17–43.

Iceman, D.J., & Dunlap, W.R. (1984). Independent living skills training: A survey of current practices. *Journal of Rehabilitation*, 53–56.

Jackson, H.J., & Boag, P.G. (1981). The efficacy of self-control procedures as motivational strategies with mentally retarded persons: A review of the literature and guidelines for future research. *Australian Journal of Developmental Disabilities*, *7*(2), 65–79.

Jackson, H.J., & Patterson, C.P. (1979). Treatment of nail biting behavior in a moderately retarded female through the use of a self-recording procedure. *Special Education*, *14*, 7–13.

Jackson, H.J., & Patterson, C.P. (1980). Evidence for the long-term effectiveness of a self-recording procedure with a moderately retarded female. A one year follow-up. *Australian Journal of Developmental Disabilities*, *6*, 93–94.

Janis, I.L., & Mann, L. (1977). *Decision-making: A psychological analysis of conflict, choice and commitment*. New York: The Free Press, Division of MacMillan Publishing Co.

Joanning, H. (1976). Behavioral rehearsal in group treatment of socially nonassertive individuals. *Journal of College Student Personnel*, *17*, 303–318.

Johnston, M.B., Whitman, T.L., & Johnson, M. (1980). Teaching addition and subtraction to mentally retarded children: A self-motivational program. *Applied Research in Mental Retardation*, *1*, 141–160.

Kendall, P.D. (1990). Challenges for cognitive strategy training: The case of mental retardation [Commentary on Whitman, T.L., Self-regulation and mental retardation]. *American Journal on Mental Retardation*, *94*(4), 365–367.

Keogh, D.A., Whitman, T.L., & Maxwell, S.E. (1987). *Self-instruction versus didactic instructional training: A look at individual differences and how they relate to training*. Manuscript submitted for publication.

Keys C.B., & Foster-Fishman, P. (1991, April). *Advocacy in the United States: Content and process*. Paper presented at the International Conference on Mental Retardation: The way ahead. Hong Kong.

Kishi, G., Teelucksingh, B., Zollers, N., Seunghee, P., & Meyer, L. (1988). Daily decision-making in community residences: A social comparison of adults with and without mental retardation. *American Journal of Mental Retardation*, *92*(5), 430–435.

Klein, N.K., & Babcock, D. (1979). Assertiveness training for moderately retarded adults: A position. *Education and Training of the Mentally Retarded*, *14*, 232–234.

Krasnor, L.W., & Rubin, K.H. (1983). Preschool social problem-solving: Attempts and outcomes in naturalistic interaction *Child Development*, *54*, 1545–1558.

Lakin, K.C. (1988). *The Research and Training Center on Community Living*. Minneapolis, MN: Institute on Community Integration.

Lepper, M.R. (1981). Intrinsic and extrinsic motivation in children: Detrimental effects of superfluous social controls. In W.A. Collins (Ed.), *Minnesota Symposia on Child Psychology* (Vol. 14, pp. 155–214). Minneapolis: University of Minnesota Press.

Lerner, R.M., & Spanier, G.B. (1978). *Child influences on marital and family interaction*. New York: Academic Press.

Litrownik, A.J., Cleary, C.P., Lecklitner, G.L., & Franzini, L.R. (1978a). Self-regulation in retarded persons: Acquisition of standards for performance. *American Journal of Mental Deficiency*, *83*, 86–89.

Litrownik, A.J., Cleary, C.P., & Steinfield, B.I. (1978b). *Self-regulation in mentally retarded persons: Acquisition and effects of self-reinforcement*. Unpublished manuscript, San Diego State University, San Diego, California.

Litrownik, A.J., Franzini, L.R., Geller, S., & Geller, M. (1977). *American Journal of Mental Deficiency*, *82*(2), 149-154.

Litrownik, A.J., Freitas, J.L., & Franzini, L.R. (1978c). Self-regulation in retarded persons: Assessment and training of self-monitoring skills. *American Journal of Mental Deficiency*, *82*, 499–506.

Litrownik, A.J., Lecklitner, G.L., Cleary, C.P., & Franzini, L.R. (1978d). *Acquisition of self-evaluation and self-reward skills and their effects on performance*. Unpublished manuscript, San Diego State University, San Diego, California.

Litrownik, A.J., & Steinfield, B.I. (1982). Developing self-regulation in retarded children. *Advances in Child Behavior Analysis and Therapy*, *1*, 13–20.

Long, J.D., & Williams, R.L. (1976). The utility of self-management procedures in modifying the classroom behaviors of mentally retarded adolescents. *Adolescents*, *11*, 29–38.

MacPhail-Wilcox, B., & Bryant, H.D. (1988). A descriptive model of decision making: Review of idiographic influences. *Journal of Research and Development in Education*, *22*(1), 7–22.

Martin, J.E., Mithaug, D.E., Maxson, L., & Riley, M. (1992). *The missing transition factor: Self-determination*. Colorado Springs: University of Colorado.

Matson, J.L. (1978). Training socially appropriate behaviors to moderately retarded adults with contingent praise, instructions, feedback, and a modified self-recording procedure. *Scandinavian Journal of Behavior Therapy*, *7*, 167–175.

Matson, J.L. (1979). Decreasing inappropriate verbalizations of a moderately retarded adult by a staff assisted self-control program. *Australian Journal of Mental Retardation*, *5*, 242–245.

Matson, J.L., Ollendick, T.H., & Adkins, J. (1980). A comprehensive dining program for mentally retarded adults. *Behavior Research and Therapy*, *18*, 107–112.

Meichenbaum, D.H. (1977). *Cognitive behavior modification—An integrative approach*. New York: Plenum Press.

Meichenbaum, D. (1990). Cognitive perspective on teaching self-regulation [Commentary on Whitman, T.L., Self-regulation and mental retardation]. *American Journal on Mental Retardation*, *94*(4), 367–369.

Miller, R.J., LaFollette, M., & Green, K. (1990). Development and field-test of a transition planning procedure 1985–1988. *Career Development for Exceptional Individuals*, *13*(1), 45–55.

Mishel, M. (1978). Assertion training with handicapped persons. *Journal of Counseling and Psychology*, *25*, 238–241.

Mitchell, B. (1988). Who chooses? *Transition Summary*, *5*, 4–5.

Mithaug, D.E. (1991). *Self-determined kids*. Lexington, MA: Lexington Books.

Mithaug, D.E., & Hanawalt, D.A. (1978). The validation of procedures to assess prevocational task preferences in retarded adults. *Journal of Applied Behavioral Analysis, 11*(1), 153–162.

Mithaug, D.E., Horiuchi, C.N., & Fanning, P.N. (1985). A report on the Colorado state-wide follow-up survey of special education students. *Exceptional Children, 51*(5), 397–404.

Mithaug, D.E., Martin, J.E., Agran, M., & Rusch, F. (1988). *Why special education graduates fail: How to teach them to succeed.* Colorado Springs, CO: Ascent Publications.

Moody, P.E. (1983). *Decision-making: Proven methods for better decisions.* New York: McGraw-Hill.

Nezu, C.M., Nezu, A.M., & Arean, P. (1991). Assertiveness and problem-solving training for mildly mentally retarded persons with dual diagnosis. *Research in Developmental Disabilities, 12*, 371–386.

O'Brien, J. (1987). A guide to life-style planning: Using *The Activities Catalog* to integrate services and natural support systems. In B. Wilcox & G.T. Bellamy, *A comprehensive guide to The Activities Catalog: An alternative curriculum for youth and adults with severe disabilities* (pp. 175–189). Baltimore: Paul H. Brookes Publishing Co.

Onoda, L., & Bassert, L. (1978). Use of assertion training to improve job interview behavior. *Personnel and Guidance, 56*, 492–495.

Osborn, A.F. (1963). *Applied imagination: Principles and procedures for creative problem-solving* (3rd ed.). New York: Scribner's.

Pace, G.M., Ivancic, M.T., Edwards, G.L., Iwata, B.A., & Page, T.J. (1985). Assessment of stimulus preference and reinforcer value with profoundly retarded individuals. *Journal of Applied Behavior Analysis, 18*, 249–255.

Palmer, R.D. (1971). Parental perception and perceived locus of control in psychopathology. *Journal of Personality, 39*, 420–431.

Pearlman, J., & Mayo, M. (1977). Assertive training for women: A follow-up. *Journal of the National Association of Women Deans, Administrators and Counselors, 40*, 49–52.

People First of Washington. (1991). People First members teach transit. In M.F. Hayden & B. Shoultz (Eds.), Self-advocacy, *IMPACT, 3*(4), 9.

Percell, O., Berwick, P., & Beigel, A. (1974). The effects of assertion training on self-concept and anxiety. *Archives of General Psychiatry, 31*, 501–504.

Perry, J.C. (1980). Neonate and adult head movement: No and yes revisited. *Developmental Psychology, 16*, 245–250.

Peters, R., & Davies, K. (1981). Effects of self-instructional training on cognitive impulsivity of mentally retarded adolescents. *American Journal of Mental Deficiency, 85*, 377–382.

Platt, J., & Spivack, G. (1972). Problem-solving thinking of psychiatric patients. *Journal of Consulting and Clinical Psychology, 39*, 148–151.

Reid, M.K., & Borkowski, J.G. (1987). Causal attributions of hyperactive children: Implications for teaching strategies and self-control. *Journal of Educational Psychology, 79*(3), 296–307.

Robertson, S.J., Simon, S.J., Pachman, J.J., & Drabman, R.J. (1980). Self-control and generalization procedures in a classroom of disruptive retarded children. *Child Behavior Therapy, 1*, 347–362.

Rose, B.D. (1987). *Decision-making opportunities provided to moderately and severely intellectually limited students, ages 16–21 years within special education classrooms.* Unpublished doctoral dissertation, University of Maryland.

Ross, D.M., & Ross, S.A. (1973). Cognitive training for the EMR child: Situational problem-solving and planning. *American Journal of Mental Deficiency, 78*(1), 20–26.

Ross, D.M., & Ross, S.A. (1978). Cognitive training for EMR children: Choosing the best alternative. *American Journal of Mental Deficiency, 82*(6), 598–601.

Rotter, J.B. (1966). Generalized expectancies for internal versus external control of reinforcement. *Psychological Monographs*, *80*(1), No. 609.

Rupp, W. (1991). Self-advocates and the legislature: Making voices heard at the Capitol. In M.F. Hayden & B. Shoultz (Eds.), Self-advocacy, *IMPACT*, *3*(4), 6.

Sameroff, A.J., & Seifer, R. (1983). Familial risk and child competence. *Child Development*, *54*, 1254–1268.

Seligman, M.E.P. (1975). *Helplessness: On depression, death, and development*. San Francisco: Freeman.

Sengstock, W.L., & Kaufman, K.E. (1982). Guidelines for assertive training with mildly handicapped adolescents. *Childhood Education*, *52*, 106–115.

Shapiro, E.S. (1986). Behavior modification: Self-control and cognitive procedures. In R.P. Barrett (Ed.), *Severe behavior disorders in the mentally retarded: Non-drug approaches to treatment* (pp. 69–97). New York: Plenum Press.

Shapiro, E.S., & Klein, R.D. (1980). Self-management of classroom behavior with retarded/disturbed children. *Behavior Modification*, *4*, 83–97.

Shevin, M. (1984). *Choice-making in the classroom*. Paper presented at the Eleventh Annual Conference of The Association of Persons with Severe Handicaps, Chicago, Illinois.

Shevin, M., & Klein, N.K. (1984). The importance of choice-making skills for students who are severely disabled. *Journal of The Association of Persons with Severe Handicaps*, *9*(3), 159–166.

Shoultz, B. (1991). A short history of Amercian self-advocacy. In M.F. Hayden & B. Shoultz (Eds.), Self-advocacy, *IMPACT*, *3*(4), 2.

Shure, M.B., & Spivack G. (1972). Means-ends thinking, adjustment and social class among elementary school-age children. *Journal of Consulting and Clinical Psychology*, *38*, 348–353.

Shure, M.B., & Spivack G. (1982). Interpersonal problem-solving in young children: A cognitive approach to prevention. *American Journal of Community Psychology*, *10*(3), 341–356.

Sievert, A.L., Cuvo, A.J., & Davis, P.K. (1988). Training self-advocacy skills to adults with mild handicaps. *Journal of Applied Behavior Analysis*, *21*(3), 299–309.

Smith, D.L., Hamrick, M.H., & Anspaugh, D.J. (1981). Decision story strategy: A practical approach to teaching decision-making. *Journal of School Health*, *51*, 637-640.

Spivack, G., & Shure, M.B. (1974). *Social adjustment of young children*. San Francisco: Jossey-Bass.

Tymchuk, A.J. (1985). *Effective decision making for the developmentally disabled*. Portland, OR: EDNICK Communications, Inc.

Tymchuk, A.J., Andron, L., & Rahbar, B. (1988). Effective decision-making/problem-solving training with mothers who have mental retardation. *American Journal of Mental Retardation*, *92*(6), 510–516.

Urbain, E.S., & Kendall, P.C. (1980). Review of social-cognitive problem-solving interventions with children. *Psychological Bulletin*, *88*, 109–143.

Varela, R.A. (1988). Self-determination and normalization among adolescents: The family is a crucible of values. In NICHY National Information Center for Children and Youth with Disabilities, *Transition Summary*, 5, 6–7.

Ward, M.J. (1991). Self-determination revisited: Going beyond expectations. In *NICHY Transition Summary: Options after high school for persons with disabilities*, 7, 2–7.

Ward, M.J. (1988). The many facets of self-determination. In NICHY National Information Center for Children and Youth with Disabilities, *Transition Summary*, 5, 2–3.

Ward, N. (1989, January). *Self-determination*. Keynote address presented at the National Conference on Self-Determination, Arlington, VA. Minneapolis: University of Minnesota Research and Training Center on Community Living.

Weatherman, R.F., Stevens, L.J., & Krantz, G.C. (1986). *Passages to career: A framework for transition policy for mildly handicapped young adults.* Minneapolis: University of Minnesota, Department of Vocational and Technical Education and Department of Educational Psychology.

Wehman, P., & McLaughlin, P. (1981). *Program development in special education.* New York: McGraw-Hill.

Wehman, P., Schutz, R., Bates, P., Renzaglia, A., & Karan, O. (1978). Self-management programs with mentally retarded workers: Implications for developing independent vocational behavior. *British Journal of Social Clinical Psychology, 17,* 57–64.

Whitman, T.L. (1990a). Development of self-regulation in persons with mental retardation. *American Journal on Mental Retardation, 92*(4), 373–376.

Whitman, T.L. (1990b). Self-regulation and mental retardation. *American Journal of Mental Retardation, 92*(4), 347–362.

Whitman, T.L., & Johnston, M.B. (1983). Teaching addition and subtraction with regrouping to educable mentally retarded children: A group self-instructional training program. *Behavior Therapy, 14,* 127–143.

Whitman, T.L., Spence, B.H., & Maxwell, S.E. (1987). A comparison of external and self-instructional teaching formats with mentally retarded adults in a vocational training setting. *Applied Research in Developmental Disabilities, 8,* 371–388.

Wichern, R., & Nowicki, S. (1976). Independence training practices and locus of control orientation in children and adolescents. *Developmental Psychology, 12,* 77–87.

Williams, P., & Shoultz, B. (1982). *We can speak for ourselves.* Bloomington: Indiana University Press.

Williams, R.R. (1989, January). *Creating a new world of opportunity: Expanding choice and self-determination in the lives of Americans with severe disability by 1992 and beyond.* Keynote address presented at the National Conference on Self-Determination, Arlington, VA. Minneapolis: University of Minnesota, Research and Training Center on Community Living.

Williams, W., Vogelsburg, R., & Schutz, R. (1985). Programs for secondary age handicapped youth. In D. Bricker & J. Tiller (Eds.), *Severe mental retardation: From theory to practice* (pp. 97–118). Lancaster, PA: The Division of Mental Retardation of the Council for Exceptional Children.

Wuerch, B.B., & Voeltz, L.M. (1982). *Longitudinal leisure skills for severely handicapped learners: The Ho'onanea curriculum component.* Baltimore: Paul H. Brookes Publishing Co.

Zeph, L. (1984, November). *The model of CHOICE: A curriculum framework for incorporating choice-making into programs serving students with severe handicaps.* Paper presented at the Eleventh Annual Conference of The Association for Persons with Severe Handicaps, Chicago Illinois.

Zigler, E., & Balla, D. (1982). The developmental approach to mental retardation. In E. Zigler & D. Balla (Eds.), *Mental retardation: The developmental difference controversy.* Hillsdale, NJ: Lawrence Erlbaum.

— *Chapter 15* ——————————————

"A Home of Our Own"
Homes, Neighborhoods, and Personal Connections
Julie Ann Racino and Susan O'Connor

As the deinstitutionalization movement has unfolded into new frameworks of community membership, a growing number of organizations throughout the United States have changed the ways in which they support children and adults with disabilities as they live and participate in the community. For children, this has meant living with families, whether birth, adoptive, or foster (Center on Human Policy, 1987; Rosenau, 1990; Taylor, Lakin, & Hill, 1989). For adults, who had often been confined to agency facilities, this has meant living in their own home with the supports that they want and need to fully participate in community life (Center on Human Policy, 1989; Racino, Walker, O'Connor, & Taylor, 1993; Shoultz, 1992).

This chapter attempts to better understand the experiences of people with disabilities in their homes and neighborhoods and contrasts these experiences with the human service workers' perceptions. In addition to the literature review on housing and homes, this chapter is based primarily on in-depth participant observations (e.g., Taylor & Bogdan, 1984) of seven families as they lived in their homes and neighborhoods and as they interacted with workers within these settings. Supplemental data illustrative of these themes are from a national qualitative study research base of organizations supporting persons with disabilities in the community (for study results, see Racino, 1991b).

Preparation of this chapter was supported by a cooperative agreement between the National Institute on Disability and Rehabilitation Research (NIDRR); the Research and Training Center on Residential and Community Living at the University of Minnesota (College of Education) located within the Institute on Community Integration (UAP); and the Research and Training Center on Community Integration at the Center on Human Policy in Syracuse University, School of Education (Division of Special Education and Rehabilitation) (#H133B80048). Additional support was provided by a cooperative agreement between NIDRR and the Research and Training Center on Community Integration (#H133B00003-90). The opinions expressed herein are those of the authors.

The authors would like to thank Bonnie Shoultz, Pam Walker, Steve Taylor, and Rachael Zubal for their direct and indirect contributions to this chapter.

The purpose of this chapter is two-fold. The first purpose is to broaden the ways in which people in the human services field understand the complex meanings of home and neighborhood, both of which are necessary to promote community participation. The second is to present new research findings on the discrepancies between the experiences of persons with disabilities and the perceptions of those responsible for service planning and provision in order to reframe future discussion regarding community and personalized supports.

Homes

To understand the meaning of the research on homes as presented in this chapter, it is important to know that several trends characterize recent research, training, and program initiatives in this area. Only in the past few years has the meaning of the term "home," including its relationship to quality of life, been explored. In the 1980s, accompanied by an increase in regular housing initiatives, persons with disabilities also began to demand and experience more control over the places in which they live (Kennedy, 1993; Moore, 1993). In the area of services, supported living and supportive housing were more widely accepted (Carling, Randolph, Blanch, & Ridgway, 1988; Johnson, 1985; Karan & Granfield, 1990; Klein, 1992; Racino, 1988; Smith, 1990), although the mechanistic aspects that have characterized community living arrangements for persons with disabilities for more than a decade were retained.

Neighborhoods

Research relevant to neighborhoods is the second area presented in this chapter. Neighborhoods have traditionally been viewed by professionals in the disability field either in terms of the locations for group homes or in terms of the reactions of neighbors to persons with disabilities moving into what has been considered the neighbors' space or domain (Bradley, Knoll, Ellison, Freud, & Bedford, 1988; Community Integration Project, 1985; Community Residences Information Services Program, 1986; Mueller, 1985). In addition, the meanings of community regeneration (Lehman, 1988; Shoultz, 1991) and neighborhood revitalization (Racino, 1991a) have recently become topics of interest to such professionals. Yet, relatively little attention has been paid to the meaning of neighborhood as an extension of home. This is particularly true for certain social classes and cultural groups, especially in relation to elements of neighborhood connectedness, sense of place, and personal identity that may already exist for some persons and their families.

Supporting Home and Neighborhood Connections

The third area of qualitative research findings focuses on the development, maintenance, and function of the connections or linkages that are established within a neighborhood. In the past, personal connections or linkages were presented: 1) from the viewpoints of agencies and service providers (Minnesota Developmental Disabilities Planning Council, 1990; Walker & Racino, 1993); 2) as stories of friendships (Forest, 1989; Perske, 1988; Strully & Strully, 1985); or 3) from the framework of relationships and social networks (Lutfiyya, 1991). Although greater concern is being paid to the relationship between paid services and personal relationships (Bulmer, 1987; Dunst, Trivette, Gordon, & Pletcher, 1989; Hagner, Rogan, & Murphy, 1992; Mount, Beeman, & Ducharme, 1988; O'Brien & O'Brien, 1992; Traustadottir, 1991), little is known about how families and individuals with disabilities experience or understand the nature of support, the role of service providers, and the building of alliances.

THE MEANING OF HOME:
PHYSICAL SPACE, PERSONAL VALUES, AND SHARED LIVING

Many women, men, and children with disabilities wish to live in homes similar to those of their peers without disabilities (e.g., Covert, 1990). Expressing the desire to live in places where their lives are not controlled by agencies or others (e.g., Kennedy, 1993), persons with disabilities are seeking to create homes and home lives reflective of their culture, ethnicity, gender, and personal life-styles. Yet, the meanings of home for these persons, as expressed in the disability literature and in practice, contrast sharply with what home means for others in our society.

Literature Review on Homes

While conducting the qualitative research presented in this section, a literature review was completed on homes by one of the authors, including a review of leading texts and articles on community living for persons with disabilities, as well as a representative selection of historical, sociological, home design and living, and religious texts. Four of the basic findings were that: 1) the meaning of home is not a stagnant concept, but varies historically and societally; 2) the view of home as presented in disability texts of the 1970s and 1980s was very constricted compared to the view of homes for the population at large; 3) the concept of home in the disability field began to shift to become more personal and to have greater breadth in the 1980s; and 4) multiple dimensions of home were identifiable in the literature outside of the disability field. The following sections briefly highlight these findings.

Historical Meaning of Home In society, the meaning of home has shifted throughout the years as its relationships to work, social, and religious life and to political developments have changed. During the 1850s, for example, when women were generally relegated to the home, it was considered more central to our culture than it is today. More than 100 years later, some professionals still argue that the political, religious, social, and emotional meanings of home have diminished (Matthews, 1987), while greater emphasis is being placed on life outside the family home. Thus, homes for persons with disabilities must be understood in the context of these societal changes and the meaning of home in the popular domain.

Disability Perspectives on Homes During the 1970s and 1980s, homes for persons with developmental disabilities were typically viewed as physical sites—

places that fit a standardized criterion of appropriateness, with respect to both external and internal standards (Racino, 1990). Homes were equated with houses, thus placing an undue emphasis on the physical as opposed to the social, emotional, and spiritual meanings of a person's residence. Instead of possessing personal richness and diversity, descriptions of the people who lived in the residences seemed devoid of gender, age, ethnicity, and cultural background. To a large extent, professionals who did not personally know the residents of the home were viewed as having the right to control the home's location, its general appearance, and the home atmosphere.

In the disability literature, activities that traditionally took place in the homes of persons with disabilities, typically group home settings, centered around teaching homemaking skills, providing services, and guiding the functioning of residents. Rules predominated and issues such as visitation, decision making, and moving into or out of the homes were not under the control of the residents themselves. When options for choice existed, they were usually limited to choices of roommates, bedroom furnishings and decorations, and individual or group activities.

Changing Concepts in Homes for Persons with Disabilities   By the mid-1980s, the concept of home as it related to persons with disabilities began to be presented in the literature more broadly and personally. No longer perceived merely as physical structures, homes came to be viewed as bases for developing friendships and activities (O'Brien & O'Brien, 1989), for showing hospitality (Lutfiyya, 1991), and for marriage and parenting (Orlansky & Heward, 1981), and as environments that needed to be under the control of the individuals who lived there. This included the idea that persons with developmental disabilities should be able to choose where and with whom they live (Johnson, 1985), to have the right to limit access of service providers into the home (Raynes, Sumpton, & Flynn, 1987), and to use it as a place for rituals and celebrations (Taylor, Bogdan, & Racino, 1991).

Dimensions of Homes for Persons with and without Disabilities   The term home has a number of dimensions that distinguish it from the terms "housing" or "residential facilities," which are two common ways of describing community living for persons with disabilities. These dimensions (see Table 1) include: 1) the types of housing to which a person has access through rental, private, and cooperative ownership; 2) home as a physical place with social, personal, and control dimensions; and 3) the household unit, which reflects decision making across household members, and the establishment of the household. These dimensions are not particular to persons with disabilities, but instead reflect that of the broader population (O'Connor & Racino, 1993).

Participant Observations of Home Life

Based on the literature review, it was clear that the concept of home must be expanded in the field of disability if persons with disabilities are to achieve the opportunity to live in a home similar to others in society. The research findings presented in this section explore various dimensions of homes and home life of persons with developmental disabilities and their families. These dimensions are

Table 1. Dimensions of housing, home, and household

HOUSING

Legal Ownership/Tenancy
- Rental by person with disability
- Private ownership by person with disability
- Private ownership by parents or others on individual's behalf
- Cooperative ownership equity or nonequity
- Joint rental or ownership, including by person with disability
- Agency ownership on behalf of individual
- Disability agency ownership

Styles or Types
- Condominiums
- Duplexes
- Trailers/mobile homes
- Flats
- Apartments in complex
- Single-family home
- Apartments attached to houses
- Multiple family homes
- Cooperative sites

HOME

Physical Place
- Place of housework
- Place of leisure
- Place of learning
- Place of convalescence, death, and birth
- Place of courtship, marriage, and sexual experience
- Place to raise and nurture children and family
- Place of culture and education for family and visitors
- Place to practice religion and cultural traditions
- Place to promote health and daily routines

Social
- Feeling of belonging, love, and togetherness
- Companionship and social network
- Physical presence of others
- Relationship between social roles inside and outside of home
- Games, songs, and forms of home play
- Base for friendships and out-of-home activities
- Offer hospitality

Personal
- Privacy
- Personalized to one's tastes
- Self-identity
- Religious and cultural rituals
- Daily routines, styles, and interests
- Personal safety and comfort
- Home atmosphere, pace, and space preferences
- Personal values (e.g., stability)
- Respect and dignity
- Reflection of life-style
- Security

Control
- Home design and adaptation
- Finance management
- Home and household management and decision making
- Relationships with neighbors, kin, and others
- Support services and service providers
- Home location, ownership/tenancy
- Household members
- Access and departure
- Home rituals and routines
- Sense of ownership

(continued)

Table 1. (*continued*)

HOUSEHOLD

- Adequacy of household income
- Decency of housing and allocation of space
- Decision making across household members
- Household maintenance and routines
- Relationships among household members
- Transforming wages and goods into household use
- Household rhythms and task distribution
- Home atmosphere
- Negotiation of personal boundaries

Reprinted from O'Connor, S., & Racino, J.A. (1993). "A home of my own": Community housing options and strategies. In J.A. Racino, P. Walker, S. O'Connor, & S.J. Taylor (Eds.), *Housing, support, and community: Choices and strategies for adults with disabilities* (p. 140). Baltimore: Paul H. Brookes Publishing Co.

examined in order to expand the perceptions of service providers, planners, and researchers and influence the quality of life experienced by persons with disabilities in the community.

The Home as a Physical Place   As with other people in society, the ways in which persons with disabilities and their families use their home environment reflects personal tastes, their own and shared life-styles, space usage based on factors such as gender and age, and spaces that are shared with the public and those that are considered to be private. The following is one example taken from the research:

Sara Kelly[1], who is labeled as mentally retarded, and David Devers are both 20 years old. They have a long-standing relationship and have shared a number of apartments together during the past 6 years. They have organized their current home so that Sara can watch TV programs or videotapes, while David listens to his stereo. This gives the couple space to pursue their individual interests, while still spending time at home together. Similar to most people, they consider their bedrooms to be more private, and they seldom spend time there with people who are just acquaintances.

The image of Sara and David's apartment contrasts with the image of housing designed specifically for persons with disabilities in a number of ways. For example, nationwide, it is common to have strangers tour private places and to socialize in private bedroom areas in group homes and agency apartments (Racino, 1988–1991). In such settings, common standards of privacy are seldom recognized. In addition, David and Sara have "ownership" of their home and, thus, can use numerous rooms to organize their activities in ways that can enhance their relationship with each other.

[1]All names used in this chapter are pseudonyms; modifications have been made in case studies to further protect the research informants.

The use and organization of space is a negotiated process that can change depending on the layout of the physical environment and the role that the home plays in the lives of the individual residents. For some people, home is the central base in their lives, while for others it may be more insignificant. One of the factors people use in selecting a home is whether the home's layout supports the type of life-style they wish to lead. Persons with disabilities seldom have the luxury of considering these kinds of issues if they are receiving services from agencies.

The Home as a Site for Hospitality and Friendship   Homes are also organized to allow people to offer hospitality to friends, guests, and family members in their own ways or styles. Sally Jacobs, for example, is the mother of two children. Her one child, Tina, who is a teenager, has a progressive neurological disease, and her son, Ted, is at college in a neighboring state. Sally entertains in several places, including at the kitchen table, in the more formal living room, in front of the fireplace, and on the enclosed back patio overlooking the pool. Tina has one particular room where she spends a lot of her time watching videos; guests may be invited into this space. Tina also joins in for short periods of interaction in other areas of the home. Sally usually welcomes her guests with something to eat and drink.

In contrast, Sara entertains in her living room with the television set on in the background, sometimes pushing clothes or blankets to the side of the couch to make space for the visitor. She seldoms offers any food, which is at a premium, to people who stop by, yet she makes her guests welcome by focusing her full attention on them.

Though both have different styles and constraints, each of the women, one from an upper middle-class home and another from a lower socioeconomic class, is welcoming of their guests. As one participant observer experienced, however, hospitality tends to be evaluated on the basis of one's own familiarity, style, and standards. This can be problematic for persons such as Sara, whose socioeconomic background varies from that of the workers and visitors who are making judgments about her in this area.

Decorating the Home: Personal Values and Standards   The decorations that people select and display in their homes often reflect their personal values and interests, and are often influenced by ethnicity, culture, gender, and class. Sara, who loves horses, has a collection of statues of all shapes and sizes clustered on a table in the living room. A large ceramic black stallion, a present from David, adorns another table in the den area and a variety of framed and unframed pictures, many of which were presents to Sara, hang on the walls. David, in contrast, decorates and organizes around his stereo, his newest VCR, his summer "boom box," his latest TV, and other equipment that he periodically trades to bring in extra income.

Decorations are also used to mark events that a family or person has attended or plans to attend. In the Santiago family, wall hangings, such as a Spanish calendar, periodically change. The changing wall hangings mark the passage of events and time, as do the photos of children and family members in other homes.

These personal touches provide ways for people to get to know each other, as well as project peoples' images of themselves and the activities, values, and connections that are important in their lives. If a service provider does not know about the significance of horses in Sara's life or about how David understands and values his electronic equipment, he or she might be quick to prejudge both Sara and David. Similar to the Santiago family and others in society, persons with disabilities have a history and a future built on the past. Yet, persons with disabilities are often treated as if their history corresponds with that of their entry and exit into the life of an agency and a service provider.

Standards of Home Cleanliness   The standards for preparing a home for guests and for entertaining also vary from one household to another. For Sara, a clean house means washing all the floors and countertops by hand with a strong bleach. However, visiting service providers expect the dog to be put on the porch, and based on their concerns, getting as much of the dog hair off of the couch as possible. Therefore, if the smell of bleach dissipates, a new visitor would have difficulty noticing the intense effort that Sara had expended in preparing her home. Sara also periodically rearranges the living room furniture to provide variety for herself and visitors.

In contrast, the upper middle-class suburban home of the Sally Jacobs' family is orderly, with walls hand stenciled by Sally and with delicate handcrafted items and touches of brass and pewter scattered throughout. All toys are placed in cupboards, out of sight of any visitors, and counters are cleared of miscellaneous items. This house meets many of the standards of homes portrayed in home-life magazines.

Yet, both represent personal standards of a "clean home," although visitors, including service providers, typically use standards that reflect their own background and training in the evaluation of a home's cleanliness. For example, Sara's home tends to be described as "dirty," as if this is a statement of fact rather than one of perception.

The Home as a Social Site   The home is a place in which persons with various types of relationships live with each other. A home can be the site of a nuclear, two-parent family, or of an extended family in which brothers, sisters, or grandparents reside temporarily or continuously. A home can also be a place in which a couple shares their home with their children and, periodically, with boarders who pay for a room. Homes may also extend beyond an individual apartment or house, to include several places, as a larger extended network of family, friends, and neighbors. Even when two people share a home, it can sometimes be considered the home of one person who offers lodging to another, or a home in which both people have similar rights of ownership. Persons who live in a home define the home's membership, although the public presentation may vary, depending on the rules by which people abide in order to maintain income support and other assistance.

Within a home, people may vary in their support of one another, and this may be strengthened or harmed by different life events and people's reactions to them. For example, one mother was willing to wait for her boyfriend to return from an alcohol treatment facility because she genuinely believed he would change his habits. She regularly visited him during his stay, remained alone despite her fear of doing so, and stood up for him when others were critical. Since he has returned from the facility, they argue less and she says their relationship is much improved. Home life between them has undergone many changes.

Furthermore, persons who cohabitate often share certain customs and rituals. Religion may also influence home and home life through festivals, rituals and prayers, foods tied to religious customs, home decorations, home games and songs, gift exchanges, and changes in home routine. The Harris family, for example, regularly holds prayer meetings in their home, an important part of their home life. The Malicks, while not religious in orientation, plan their holiday celebrations far in advance and orient their conversation and activities around these events.

The Home as a Base for Friendship Development   Friendships can be fostered by exchanges and visits in one's home, by the sharing of meals, by becoming familiar with the personal touches in a home that reflect who people are, by learning about who else visits and telephones, by seeing how the house is structured for activities and life-styles, and by the simple invitation to share one's personal space with another.

Part of what professionals call a *support network* may also develop by using the home as the primary site for new relationships. Neighbors, who are part of such a network, can keep an eye on the other person's apartment or house, can trade babysitting, and sometimes socialize together in each other's homes, on porches, in backyards, or in buildings' hallways. Because these relationships may at first be unfamiliar to service providers, it is difficult for them to have the knowledge base necessary to interpret the meaning of or to support such connections.

THE MEANING OF NEIGHBORHOODS: MORE THAN FOUR WALLS

The meaning of home often goes beyond what occurs within the home. For many people, the concept of home and the sense of belonging that they receive from their home extends to the neighborhood in which they live. Expanding the typical service system view of housing and homes to include the role of neighborhoods can offer important insights into the lives of persons with disabilities. It can also demonstrate how service agency practices may need to change to better reflect the nature of neighborhood life and relationships.

Aspects of neighborhoods identified in these participant observations and discussed in the following section include: 1) a sense of movement, place, and familiarity; 2) ownership and belonging; 3) environmental control and choice; 4) safety and security; 5) personal and social identity; and 6) preserving traditions, history, and culture.

Neighborhoods as an Extension of Home

As the size of and mobility in our communities and neighborhoods have changed, fewer people hold onto the idealistic notion of connectedness, caring, and the sense of watching out for each other that pervaded people's thinking of neighbor-hoods and close communities in the past (Macionis, 1978; O'Connell, 1990). Even with the proliferation of suburban neighborhoods, with enhanced transportation, and with communication systems that allow people to keep in touch over long distances, some argue that communal bonds remain strong not only through prox-imity, but also through relationships (Bender, 1978; Schwartz, 1992).

Although changes have occurred in the nature of the neighborhood, there remain people who relate strongly to the sense of neighborhood as a place where they grew up, and to the size, people, habits, and rituals that go on within that setting. Due to such ties, some people may have a stronger desire to live in the country or in a particular area of a city (Hummon, 1986), thus choosing areas that reflect a style of living that mirrors their past or their hopes for the future.

In order to understand the meaning of home and neighborhood in people's lives, it is important to look at how the latter provides a sense of place for the individual. Ottensmann (1978) states that both street life and neighboring appear to be more prevalent in areas of high population density and among lower or work-ing class people. This could relate to finances and the resulting limited degree of mobility that is often found in lower or middle class populations. Elements of strong family and ethnic ties may also account for the degree of interconnectedness and neighboring that goes on for many people.

Neighborhoods and Children

In Arabic, Latino, and African-American cultures, the idea of neighborhood as an extension of the home has played an integral role in the sense of community for parents and their children. Neighbors watch out for one another and seem to know the events that are occurring in their neighborhood. During a visit to the Santiago family, for example, one author found no one at home, but the front door was open. Immediately, several of the neighborhood children ran up and asked the author what she wanted. They then proceeded to find one of the children who lived in the home, with the mother returning shortly thereafter (O'Connor, 1990). When these same practices occur in the lives of children with disabilities, parents may be con-sidered neglectful when, in fact, they are basing their judgments on a complex set of factors that include a knowledge of the neighborhood and the fact that neighbors watch out for one another.

Neighborhoods and Culture

For some people, including those with disabilities, the concept of neighborhood and the sense of belonging it creates remain strongly connected to a specific area or location. This sense of being part of a particular neighborhood often means stay-ing connected to traditions and language. As reflected in the research, this may include the idea of sharing with others and the expectation that children will leave home to play.

This was true for the Santiago family who lived in a neighborhood with people of a variety of backgrounds, as well as many Spanish-speaking people. Their neighborhood was described in local newspapers as having problems and as one in which drugs proliferated, yet for the Santiago family in which both the mother and a child were determined to have mental retardation, members moved about the neighborhood and children played in the streets with other neighborhood children, coming and going at will. While Ms. Santiago knew her way around, she did not drive or use public transportation. She did, however, live close to a number of local stores and, although she spoke no English, she was surrounded by other Spanish-speaking people. All of these elements were important to the Santiago family in maintaining a level of continuity and connection with their cultural identity and in developing a feeling of strength as well as a degree of mobility and socialization.

Neighborhoods and Persons with Disabilities

The type of neighborhood a person with a disability has lived in or wants to live in has not typically been a major factor in determining where they will, in fact, live. Type of disability and availability of space are often more instrumental in determining when and where a placement occurs rather than a person's experiences, his or her cultural identity, places he or she has lived in the past, and his or her friendships and connections.

This is the case for George Jarrar, a young Arab-American man with Down syndrome who lived and grew up in the same neighborhood until he reached young adulthood. For George, his sense of place was strong. He identified himself with his neighborhood and with the friends whom he had in it. He was described by his mother as:

> knowing everyone in the neighborhood. He knew people that we didn't and was invited to weddings of people we didn't even know. He would go out and ride his bicycle and guys would be out fixing cars and things and he would get to know them. (O'Connor, 1989)

Human services professionals in the local service system suggested that George move to a group home that was just ready to open. Although social service staff believed that they had found an appropriate placement for this young man, it is unclear whether he or his family were ready for him to move out. Eventually, George was moved to a group home in another area of the city. His three sisters, one of whom was older, remained at home, which was acceptable in their culture. George, unlike his sisters, did not have the option to remain in his own neighborhood.

The connections George had made in his neighborhood during his lifetime would now be left to the system to reconstruct. In his new residence, his friends were limited to the other six people living in the group home in contrast to the large, extended network of people he had known in his previous neighborhood. In addition, he was moved from a middle class neighborhood to an upper middle class neighborhood. As a result of the move, an important sense of place and ownership were no longer a part of his daily life merely because this did not fit in with the way in which the service system worked.

Neighborhood Familiarity

Familiarity in a neighborhood can help people, including those with disabilities, to decide what to do, where to go, and with whom they wish to interact. There is a sense of choice and control even in areas deemed dangerous by people unfamiliar with these neighborhoods based on their socioeconomic class and experience. For the persons with disabilities in these studies, especially those with limited resources, this sense of neighborhood familiarity was a key to their involvement, interaction, and control over their environment. They not only knew their way around but became acquainted and maintained ongoing contact with people in the neighborhood.

Often the service system's solution to the perceived needs of persons with disabilities was to place them according to the options that were available in the system, rather than first looking at the strengths that existed in their present situation. For James, an American Indian[2] living on the Pine Ridge reservation, his work consisted of his daily visits to the local post office where he would greet everyone who came to do business. He was referred to a nearby social service agency off the reservation and described by his service provider as having "nothing to do" in the referral. Yet the director of the agency states: "He could be trained to be a mailman. He knows everybody and they know him and talk with him . . . why should we take him out of that?" (O'Connor, 1991, p. 17). James was connected to and had a role in his community. His routine and role played a significant part in how he interacted with his neighborhood/community and how they, in turn, interacted with him. Yet, this important variable did not appear to be taken into account in planning.

Neighborhoods as Part of a Person's Identity

For many individuals, communities, neighborhoods, and the type of area in which they grew up have an impact on chosen likes, dislikes, and styles of living. Individual identities are diverse and affect personal experiences and the way people relate to the world. Professionals providing disability-related services, however, have done little to understand peoples' identities outside of their disability. A person's disability has typically been the sole focus of the service system, with little attention being paid to other salient elements of identity such as gender, color, class, or religion (O'Connor, 1993). Persons with disabilities often become their services histories and are related to accordingly.

John, for example, was labeled "dually diagnosed." When he was finally referred to an agency in a small community near his home, he had already been served by six different agencies around the state, including psychiatric institutions. He was described as having such severe behavioral problems that no one would accept him in their agencies.

---

[2]The term "American Indian" versus "Native American" is used here because that is what the Indians in this study called themselves.

At first, one of the service providers assigned to John explained that he "rebelled and didn't want to do anything. We gave him a lot of leeway, time and space, basically we just gave him support and that worked" (O'Connor, 1991, p. 19). Yet, giving support to John entailed more than making him fit into the traditional service plans developed by the agency. It meant stepping back, understanding his needs in relation to his cultural identity, and listening when he said that he wanted to go to a medicine man or do outdoor work. It meant taking time to get to know John, not as a "dually diagnosed trouble maker," but as a young man who had a strong cultural identity, who had his own ideas about what he felt would help him, and who wanted to remain connected to his culture (O'Connor, 1991).

Fortunately, the agency to which John was referred was culturally sensitive to the American Indians to whom they provided services and took into consideration the many aspects that compiled his identity.

Neighborhoods and Choice

Many people, including those with disabilities, have a limited range of choices as to where to live based on factors such as their ethnicity and socioeconomic class. While all persons with disabilities are not on low incomes, adults who live outside their family's home may be in a position to support themselves through low-paying jobs or government benefits. A person with a disability who is on low income faces many issues similar to their counterparts in the same income bracket. These factors appear to be more salient to their lives than the disability itself.

In one medium-size city, for example, two broad low-income areas on the west and north sides were common places for persons with disabilities to live. These areas were repeatedly selected, despite factors such as level of neighborhood safety and slum landlords, because the apartments were affordable and available at the time they were needed.

Individuals who have limited transportation and mobility may locate housing based primarily on its proximity to other important activities, people, and places in their lives. This appears to be particularly the case for persons with low incomes, including many who have disabilities. One redeeming feature of an apartment where Tom and Desiree lived, for example, was its closeness to the location where they visited their children who were placed in foster care.

A second reason that people continue to live in a neighborhood or decide to move are the relationships they have with people who live near them or the proximity of the home to family. When Desiree and Tom started to fight with their downstairs relatives, they immediately considered moving as one of their first options to respond to the situation, even though they loved everything else about their home.

Individuals who are limited to living in restricted sections of a city because of their income typically find their neighbors to be people whom they have known or lived next to at other times. Since residences are often located by word of mouth, these same neighbors are able to share concrete advice on landlords and available housing.

Neighborhood Safety

The vulnerability and safety of persons with disabilities is an issue that has drawn increasing attention in recent years. The place in which people live may put them in situations that others deem as unsafe, which in some cases is a matter of perception. The individual may feel that the neighborhood they live in, deemed dangerous by the media or by service providers, is better than where they lived before. Yet, many human service professionals entering such homes and neighborhoods tell parents that their children should be watched over more closely. Although not always evident to professionals, families may have their own standards on which they base safety (O'Connor, 1992). Typically, family members are aware of the dangers in the neighborhood their child faces, but create their own parameters of determining safety by implementing rules, such as no one outside after dark. These rules may be based on a delicate balance of precautions, practicalities, and aspirations regarding the growth and survival of the child.

SUPPORTING HOME, NEIGHBORHOOD, AND PERSONAL CONNECTIONS

The previous sections on homes and neighborhoods describe some of the essential elements that are critical to understanding the nature of the relationship of the person with a disability with an agency, service provider, or service system. In this final section, examples from the research are selected to illustrate the differences in perceptions among service providers and persons with disabilities when the service providers seek to support the development of home, neighborhood, and personal connections (see Table 2).

The concept of support can be viewed minimally as an act or set of actions, an attitude or set of values, a feeling or personal experience, a set of standards or expectations, a relationship descriptor, and an expected goal or accomplishment. In practice, it is most discernible at the level of person-to-person interactions, although other larger structures can influence and construct the boundaries of these interactions.

How Individuals with Disabilities and Families View Support

Individuals with disabilities and families do not tend to think in terms of the word "support," because this is not everyday language. People talk instead about being able to count on someone, being understood, coming through when needed, and having people who care, who agree with them, and who will take their side.

In these observations, persons with disabilities and their families expressed the desire to be listened to and heard from their perspective. This does not mean that other perspectives are not helpful or even welcome, but that a feeling of support appears connected with a confirmation that the situation, as a person experi-

Table 2. Differing perspectives on the meaning of support

	Support as personal/ family	Support as worker construction[a]
Actions	Source for tangible resources Being there Sounding board/opinion sharer Follows through on requests	Problem solver Facilitator/facilitation[b] Service coordinator/ broker/provider Accommodation[b] Interpretation[b]
Attitudes/values	Having one's own judgment and experience trusted Respect for persons with disability and family	Putting oneself in another's shoes
Feeling/personal experience	Being or feeling understood/validated Listened to/vouched for[c]	Caring Going beyond role limitations—more than a job
Relationship descriptor	Friends/like family Good service provider	Partnership Good family
Standard/ expectation	Personal/family member definition of success	Worker/agency standards of success (e.g., good parenting, good homes, good life-styles)
Goal/accomplishment	Concrete resources without strings Getting by/regaining normal lifestyle[d] Limiting family/personal intrusions Minimizing personal/family tension	Concrete assistance with required help in use Personal/family change Provision of services as agreed upon/hookup with services

[a]Also see Traustadottir, R. (1991, August). *Supports for community living: A case study.* Syracuse, NY: Center on Human Policy, Syracuse University, which illustrates some of these dimensions.

[b]Also see Lutfiyya, Z.M. (1991, February). Tony Santi and the bakery: The roles of facilitation, accommodation, and interpretation. In Z.M. Lutfiyya (Ed.), *Personal relationships and social networks: Facilitating the participation of individuals with disabilities in community life.* Syracuse, NY: Center on Human Policy, Syracuse University.

[c]Also see Taylor, S.J. (1991). *"You're not a retard, you're just wise": The social meaning of disability.* Syracuse, NY: Research and Training Center on Community Integration, Center on Human Policy, Syracuse University.

[d]Also see Traustadottir, R. (1990, April). *Constructing a normal family: Disability, gender, and family life.* Unpublished research apprenticeship, Syracuse University, Syracuse, New York.

ences it, is validated. Letting people know that they can count on someone and that there are people who are willing to vouch for them (i.e., support their viewpoint) are valued ways of relating to people.

Individuals often provide different forms of support to each other. The provision of information, instrumental/material aid, companionship, and emotional support are examples of the different types of support many persons take for granted. Sometimes just the remembrance of a birthday or a note on a holiday can be a sign of respect and caring. These forms of support and expression of caring can be provided, not only by loved ones, but also by human service professionals who work with persons with disabilities on a regular basis, and can do much to help sustain people in their day-to-day lives.

In these observations, many persons with disabilities and their families warmly acknowledge other individuals and places that have been a source of strength in their lives, including particular staff or agencies whom they believe care about them. In these situations, professional staff may take on a new identity in the people's eyes, such as that of a friend or family member. When asked about her family's strongest allies, one mother, for example, replied:

> people from Jasper Street School. They are probably our best friends. . . . If you're ever in the Jasper Street family, you're always a part of it. (Walker, 1991)

Attempts by others to describe the nature of a professional–client relationship solely in employment terms may be met by resistance from individuals with disabilities.

In many cases, persons with disabilities and family members take support for granted, except when it is no longer available to them. In these studies, the informants shared stories and experiences about friends, relatives, and service providers who let them down and of circumstances in which their personal and extended network of resources was just not enough to maintain what they considered a normal life-style.

In some cultures, such as Latino, African-American, and American Indian, extended family members play an important role in supporting family members with disabilities or who are elderly. It is only when the family members, including those with disabilities, move away from these close connections or when these relationships are disrupted that they may need assistance from nonfamiliar sources. In American Indian culture, giving up a family member to the service system because the family is no longer able to support him or her is viewed as losing that person (O'Connor, 1991). In other families, service providers coming into the home to provide support may be welcomed for a variety of reasons, including maintaining a family balance.

The Support Roles of Service Providers

Individuals with disabilities and family members often rely on service providers to intercede on their behalf because even a service provider who does not know them well is often perceived as having greater credibility by virtue of their role (e.g., Racino, O'Connor, Walker, & Taylor, 1991). Such individuals may also have concrete information and access to resources, such as financial aid, transportation, child care, or equipment, that may otherwise be inaccessible to an individual or family. When professional judgment deems that a request for service is appropriate, a family has the potential to enhance their access to tangible resources, including assistance with apartment-hunting, housing subsidies, home furnishings and appliances, and accessibility modifications that they might otherwise be denied based on their own judgment.

To some extent, in these observations, all workers were viewed as similar to each other, although specific explicit roles may vary from individual to individual (e.g., teaching the child, cleaning the house). Each worker was also personally assessed by persons with disabilities and family members as part of the development of a personal understanding of the nature of each service provider–client relationship (e.g., What will they do? Do they care about me? How do they go about things?). This contradicts the general perception that the service providers only complete the assessments during the initial phases of the relationship when persons with disabilities and families make their initial contact.

The informants noted that workers, regardless of their specific position, have certain jobs or roles they needed to fill and, at times, may need to take action that is against their personal values. The individuals with disabilities and family members seemed to give service providers leeway for their human mistakes and recognized their constraints. In these observations, any effort perceived as taken on their behalf was acknowledged and service providers were not blamed for things that the individuals and their families viewed as outside of the provider's prescribed role. When one family's service provider organized a meeting to talk about pressing legal issues, for example, one of the mothers said, "He didn't have to do that." From her perspective, the role of the support staff was to buy cribs for her children and to be there for the children once they came home. Anything that the service provider did beyond her understanding of his role was viewed as a personal contribution.

Contrasting Perspectives on Support:
Service Providers, Families, and Individuals with Disabilities

When people use paid services in order to get help, they usually become involved with support staff in a variety of ways. This involvement tends to be defined from the perspective of the service provider. A worker from child protective services, for example, has a checklist that indicates whether a person has a good home. Parents learn that to be perceived as "good" parents living in a "good" home, they must meet the criteria on the checklist. This is knowledge that is passed on among friends and family. Thus, before this service provider visits, efforts are made to meet these stated criteria, if the outcome is one in which the person is invested. A "good" service provider, in this circumstance, might be defined by the parent as an individual who simply believes the parent when they answer the questions on the checklist as opposed to an individual who insists on using more intrusive means to gather information (e.g., looking in the person's refrigerator or cupboards) (Racino, 1990–1991).

Service providers often get involved in determining where people will live and the types of persons with whom they should associate. Workers often share their judgments with other professionals, instead of with the individual or family member, using a person's friendship choice as evidence of their poor judgment. This may occur without any discussion of the differing perspectives and backgrounds of the persons involved. To service providers, the evidence is sometimes seen as clear-cut (e.g., the person has a criminal record), whereas from the point of view of a person with a disability, these transgressions may be less important than how the person has acted and treated them directly.

People may also be defined as good or bad families by service providers based on their ability or inability to meet certain standards, such as child rearing practices, distribution of income in the family, and other aspects of life that vary with social class and culture. Since these assumptions are often unstated, people with disabilities and their families are typically not in a position to defend themselves against unstated charges made among providers when they are not present (O'Connor, 1992).

Interactions between service providers and family members can also result in tension within the family or between friends. One mother, for example, explained that her boyfriend blames her for their children being kept in foster care and not being returned home. She says, "He blames me . . . they (their children) ain't coming home 'cause of what I said to the workers" (Racino, 1990–1991, p. 4). In this situation, the mother had honestly expressed the opinion that she did not want her children living in a bad neighborhood:

> She (the service provider) asked me if I wanted them to come back to this place with the people around here. They said the streets full of drugs and prostitutes. It's true, I don't want my kids around all that. (Racino, 1990–1991, p. 4)

This mother's boyfriend was angry because he believed that this comment might keep their children from coming home, whereas the mother saw her statement as an expression of wanting the best for her children. This did not mean, of course, that she did not want them to come home or thought the fact that she lived in this neighborhood should keep them from coming home. It was merely a sincere wish that life for all of them could include a home in a better place.

While service providers typically view services as supportive in nature, individuals with disabilities and their families may perceive that they intrude upon many areas of their lives and disrupt relationships (see McKnight, n.d.). One single-parent father, for example, explained that in order to obtain any services or financing, service providers were required, whether they were desired or not. Once the providers become involved with an individual or family, there is the possibility that they will expand their efforts into new areas. If the family or individual is unofficially labeled as "neglectful," "bad," or "incompetent," professionals might seek even more direct control over the individual's life.

The establishment of connections with supportive services can result in out-of-home placement, even though the explicit role of family support is to maintain the family. Another example of the disruption that services can cause is illustrated by the different implicit and explicit roles of services. Such supports can also become a way of socializing people into accepting a professional frame of reference as the right way to view a situation so that ordinary people come to think about their own lives, problems, and solutions in terms of the system (Racino et al., 1992).While professionals assume the human services delivery system operates as constructed in charts, policies, and procedures, individuals with disabilities and their families construct their own view of the system (see Wiseman, 1979) based on how the system can be used to meet their own purposes (Racino et al., 1991).

Personal Values of Researchers: Implications for Service Providers

To understand the issues that service providers face in meeting the relationship and service challenges of supporting persons with disabilities in homes and neighborhoods, the researchers reflected on their own experiences and the relevancy of these experiences for people in human services roles.

The researchers learned many things from the families and individuals with disabilities with whom they spent time—about their interactions with the service system and how they view and construct their lives, as well as about themselves. This included recognizing their ancestry as European Americans from middle class backgrounds with a history of work and roles in human services similar to those of the service providers. However, unlike the service providers, the researchers had the luxury in this situation to step back and to critically observe and reflect on their judgments as well as those of the informants in the settings.

Research is not value free (Becker, 1967; Ferguson, Ferguson, & Taylor, 1992; Harding, 1991; Kimmel, 1988) and personal values and beliefs must be taken into account. This is true for researchers, as well as for service workers, families, and persons with disabilities. In conducting the studies on which this chapter is based, the initial reactions of the authors were often much the same as the service providers in the study when they encountered situations that varied from their standards and values. A tendency to correct or intervene in a situation and to make negative judgments about situations that are based on different values is part of human nature.

One researcher, for example, observed service providers giving instructions to one family about their dog and how their children should interact with the dog. While the family listened without objection, they viewed this situation differently, and believed that the behavior of the dog and their children was fine. On several occasions when service providers were not present, the researcher, after observing similar interactions, felt prone to give suggestions about the way she felt things should go in this area of the family's life. Upon reflection, she realized that she was placing value judgments on the family as to how they should conduct themselves and interact with their own children, assuming her way was the proper response.

This realization that persons with disabilities and their family members make choices that all service providers would not approve of, and that they have the right to do so, is an essential starting point for genuine discussion, support, and alliance. If people with disabilities make different choices than the researcher or service provider, it is not necessarily wrong. People have different perspectives on how things should occur and service providers need to strive to respond in ways that do not assume that their set of values is the only correct one. This does not mean that the researchers espouse a totally relativistic approach to these issues, but that they come to better understand aspects of the relationship between the service provider and the person.

These experiences have made the observers much more aware of the importance of listening and assuming the validity of people's own unique situations. In many ways, the researchers learned to be more aware of their standards regarding homes and neighborhoods, to be more open in giving their opinion (instead of advice) in a way that invites exchange, and to develop a problem-solving stance with people about home and community participation issues. They learned that it is impossible to place oneself in other people's shoes or fully understand the nature of others' life experiences.

CONCLUSION

In the disability field today, there is a growing interest in the examination of how people can be supported to live in their own homes and participate in their neighborhoods, and how agencies and workers can better support families and individuals with disabilities. However, the context for these discussions tends to take one of two forms. Sometimes it is mechanistic or service-oriented (e.g., How should foster families be recruited? Should cash subsidies be set up?). In other situations, the primary focus is on relationships, community, and nonservice areas (e.g., What are barriers between people with or without disabilities? What is the nature of neighborhoods?). This chapter has begun to explore some of the areas between these two ends of the spectrum.

This chapter also looks at more typical ways in which persons approach homes and neighborhoods and examines situations that service providers typically encounter in their day-to-day interactions with individuals with disabilities and families. It also highlights the differing and often unexamined views of families and individuals with disabilities in their interactions with service providers and begins to develop and contrast various constructions of support. It is only with this kind of knowledge and information base that the meaning of home can be understood and that genuine dialogue can occur regarding how alliances can be formed and maintained between individuals with disabilities, families, and service providers.

REFERENCES

Becker, H. (1967). Whose side are we on? *Social Problems*, *14*, 239–247.

Bender, T. (1978). *Community and social change in America*. Baltimore: The Johns Hopkins University Press.

Bradley, V.J., Knoll, J.A., Ellison, M.L., Freud, E., & Bedford, S. (1988, March). *Becoming a neighbor: An examination of the placement of people with mental retardation in Connecticut communities*. Cambridge, MA: Human Services Research Institute.

Bulmer, M. (1987). *The social basis of community care*. Winchester, MA: Allen & Unwin.

Carling, P.J., Randolph, F.L., Blanch, A.K., & Ridgway, P. (1988). A review of the research on housing and community integration for people with psychiatric disabilities. *NARIC Quarterly*, *1*(3), 1, 6–18.

Center on Human Policy. (1987). *A statement in support of families and their children*. Syracuse, NY: Author.

Center on Human Policy. (1989). *In support of adults living in the community*. Syracuse, NY: Author.

Community Integration Project, Center on Human Policy. (1985). *Review of the literature on community integration: Report to NIDRR*. Syracuse, NY: Author.

Community Residences Information Services Program. (1986, March). *"There goes the neighborhood . . ."* White Plains, NY: Author.

Covert, S. (1990). *A facility is not a home: A report on a housing symposium*. Durham: University of New Hampshire.

Dunst, C., Trivette, C., Gordon, N., & Pletcher, L. (1989). Building and mobilizing informal family support networks. In G.H.S. Singer & K.L. Irvin (Eds.), *Support for caregiving families: Enabling positive adaptation to disability* (pp. 121–141). Baltimore: Paul H. Brookes Publishing Co.

Ferguson, P.M., Ferguson, D.L., & Taylor, S.J. (Eds.). (1992). *Interpreting disability: A qualitative reader*. New York: Teachers College Press.

Forest, M. (1989). *It's about relationships*. Toronto: Frontier College Press.

Hagner, D., Rogan, P., & Murphy, S. (1992). Facilitating natural supports in the workplace: Strategies for support consultants. *Journal of Rehabilitation*, *58*(1), 29–34.

Harding, S. (1991). *Whose science? Whose knowledge? Thinking from women's lives*. Ithaca, NY: Cornell University Press.

Hummon, D.M. (1986). City mouse, country mouse: The persistence of community identity. *Qualitative Sociology*, *9*(1), 3–25.

Johnson, T.Z. (1985). *Belonging to the community*. Madison, WI: Options in Community Living.

Karan, O.C., & Granfield, J.M. (1990, August). *Engaging people in life: A report on one supported living program in Connecticut*. East Hartford: A.J. Pappanikou Center on Special Education and Rehabilitation.

Kennedy, M.J. (1993). Turning the pages of life. In J.A. Racino, P. Walker, S. O'Connor, & S.J. Taylor (Eds.), *Housing, support, and community: Choices and strategies for adults with disabilities*. Baltimore: Paul H. Brookes Publishing Co.

Kimmel, A.J. (1988). *Ethics and values in applied research*. Newbury Park, CA: Sage Publications.

Klein, J. (1992). Get me the hell out of here: Supporting people with disabilities to live in their own homes. In J.A. Nisbet (Eds.), *Natural supports in school, at work, and in the community for people with severe disabilities* (pp. 277–339). Baltimore: Paul H. Brookes Publishing Co.

Lehman, K. (1988). Beyond Oz: The path to regeneration. *Social Policy*, *18*(4), 56–58.

Lutfiyya, Z.M. (1991). "A feeling of being connected": Friendships between people with and without learning difficulties. *Disability, Handicap & Society*, *6*(3), 233–245.

Lutfiyya, Z.M. (1991, February). Tony Santi and the bakery: The roles of facilitation, accommodation, and interpretation. In Z.M. Lutfiyya (Ed.), *Personal relationships and social networks: Facilitating the participation of individuals with disabilities in community life*. Syracuse, NY: Center on Human Policy, Syracuse University.

Macionis, J.J. (1978). The search for community in modern society: An interpretation. *Qualitative Sociology, 1*(2), 130–143.

Matthews, G. (1987). *"Just a housewife": The rise and fall of domesticity in America*. New York: Oxford University Press.

McKnight, J.L. (n.d.). *Do no harm: A policymaker's guide to evaluating human services and their alternatives*. Evanston, IL: Northwestern University.

Minnesota Developmental Disabilities Planning Council. (1990). *Friends: A manual for connecting persons with disabilities and community members*. St. Paul: Author.

Moore, C. (1993). Letting go, moving on: A parent's thoughts. In J.A. Racino, P. Walker, S. O'Connor, & S.J. Taylor (Eds.), *Housing, support, and community: Choices and strategies for adults with disabilities*. Baltimore: Paul H. Brookes Publishing Co.

Mount, B., Beeman, P., & Ducharme, G. (1988). *What are we learning about bridge-building? A summary of dialogue between people seeking to build community for people with disabilities*. Manchester, CT: Communitas, Inc.

Mueller, D. (1985, June). *The effects of group homes on neighboring property: An annotated bibliography*. Washington, DC: Mental Health Law Project.

O'Brien, J., & O'Brien, C. (1989). *Settling down: Creating effective personal supports for people who rely on the Residential Support Program of Centennial Developmental Services*. Lithonia, GA: Responsive Systems Associates.

O'Brien, J., & O'Brien, C. (1992). Members of each other: Perspectives on social support for people with severe disabilities. In J.A. Nisbet (Ed.), *Natural supports in school, at work, and in the community for people with severe disabilities* (pp. 17–63). Baltimore: Paul H. Brookes Publishing Co.

O'Connell, M. (1990). *Community building in Logan Square: How a community grew stronger with the contributions of people with disabilities*. Evanston, IL: Center for Urban Affairs and Policy Research.

O'Connor, S. (1989). [Field notes on families]. Syracuse, NY: Center on Human Policy, Syracuse University.

O'Connor, S. (1990). [Field notes on families]. Syracuse, NY: Center on Human Policy, Syracuse University.

O'Connor, S. (1991). *"I'm not Indian anymore": The challenge of providing culturally sensitive services to American Indians*. Syracuse, NY: Center on Human Policy, Syracuse University.

O'Connor, S. (1992). *"What would really help they can't do": The meaning of services and their cost to families of children with disabilities*. Boston: Federation of Children with Special Needs.

O'Connor, S. (1993). *Multiculturalism and disability: An annotated bibliography*. Syracuse, NY: Center on Human Policy.

O'Connor, S., & Racino, J.A. (1993). "A home of my own": Community housing options and strategies. In J.A. Racino, P. Walker, S. O'Connor, & S.J. Taylor (Eds.), *Housing, support, and community: Choices and strategies for adults with disabilities* (pp. 137–160). Baltimore: Paul H. Brookes Publishing Co.

Orlansky, M., & Heward, W. (1981). *Voices: Interviews with handicapped people*. Columbus, OH: Bell & Howell Co.

Ottensmann, J.R. (1978). Social behavior in urban space. *Urban Life, 7*(1), 3–22.

Perske, R. (1988). *Circles of friends: People with disabilities and their friends enrich the lives of one another*. Nashville, TN: Abingdon Press.

Racino, J. (1988). Supporting adults in individualized ways in the community. *TASH Newsletter, 14*(3), 4–5.

Racino, J. (1988–1991). *Field notes on organizations supporting people with disabilities*. Syracuse, NY: Center on Human Policy.

Racino, J.A. (1990, January). *Annotated bibliography: The meaning of home for women with disabilities*. Syracuse, NY: Author.

Racino, J.A. (1990–1991). [Field notes on families]. Syracuse, NY: Center on Human Policy, Syracuse University.

Racino, J.A. (1991a). *Madison Mutual Housing Association and Cooperative: "People and housing building communities."* Syracuse, NY: Center on Human Policy, Syracuse University.

Racino, J.A. (1991b). Organizations in community living: Supporting people with disabilities. *Journal of Mental Health Administration, 18*(1), 51–59.

Racino, J.A., O'Connor, S., Walker, P., & Taylor, S.J. (1991). *Innovations in family supports*. Unpublished confidential research report.

Racino, J.A., Walker, P., O'Connor, S., & Taylor S.J. (Eds.). (1993). *Housing, support, and community: Choices and strategies for adults with disabilities*. Baltimore: Paul H. Brookes Publishing Co.

Raynes, N., Sumpton, R., & Flynn, M. (1987). *Homes for the mentally handicapped*. London: Tavistock Publications.

Rosenau, N. (Ed.). (1990, October). *A child's birthright: To live in a family*. Mt. Clemens, MI: Macomb-Oakland Regional Center.

Schwartz, D.B. (1992). *Crossing the river: Creating a conceptual revolution*. Boston: Brookline Books.

Shoultz, B. (1991). Regenerating a community: Residential, Inc., Ohio. In S.J. Taylor, R. Bogdan, & J.A. Racino (Eds.), *Life in the community: Case studies of organizations supporting people with disabilities* (pp. 195–213). Baltimore: Paul H. Brookes Publishing Co.

Shoultz, B. (1992). *Community integration report: A home of one's own*. Arlington, TX: The Arc National Headquarters.

Smith, G.A. (1990, November). *Supported living: New directions in services to people with developmental disabilities*. Alexandria, VA: National Association of State Mental Retardation Program Directors.

Strully, J., & Strully, C. (1985). Friendship and our children. *Journal of The Association for Persons with Severe Handicaps, 10*(4), 224–227.

Taylor, S.J. (1991). *"You're not a retard, you're just wise": The social meaning of disability*. Syracuse, NY: Research and Training Center on Community Integration, Center on Human Policy, Syracuse University.

Taylor, S., & Bogdan, R. (1984). *An introduction to qualitative research methods*. New York: John Wiley.

Taylor, S.J., Bogdan, R., & Racino, J.A. (Eds.). (1991). *Life in the community: Case studies of organizations supporting people with disabilities*. Baltimore: Paul H. Brookes Publishing Co.

Taylor, S.J., Lakin, K.C., & Hill, B.K. (1989). Permanency planning for children and youth: Out-of-home placement decisions. *Exceptional Children, 55*(6), 541–549.

Traustadottir, R. (1990, April). *Constructing a normal family: Disability, gender, and family life*. Unpublished research apprenticeship, Syracuse University, Syracuse, New York.

Traustadottir, R. (1991, August). *Supports for community living: A case study*. Syracuse, NY: Center on Human Policy, Syracuse University.

Walker, P. (1991). *Case study of Anderson family*. Syracuse, NY: Author.

Walker, P., & Racino, J.A. (1993). Being with people: Support and support strategies. In J.A. Racino, P. Walker, S. O'Connor, & S.J. Taylor (Eds.), *Housing, support, and community: Choices and strategies for adults with disabilities* (pp. 81–106). Baltimore: Paul H. Brookes Publishing Co.

Wiseman, J.P. (1979). *Stations of the lost: The treatment of Skid Row alcoholics*. Chicago: University of Chicago Press.

Community Living
A Multicultural Perspective

Rannveig Traustadottir,
Zana Marie Lutfiyya, and Bonnie Shoultz

Human services professionals encounter individuals with disabilities from various ethnic, cultural, language, racial, religious, and economic backgrounds; however, most service delivery systems have assumed that these social and cultural dimensions are of little relevance, focusing narrowly on the medical and clinical aspects of disabilities. Therefore, persons with disabilities are traditionally thought of as *genderless, raceless, classless,* and without culture by human services professionals (Fine & Asch, 1988; Harry, 1992).

More recently, there is a growing number of attempts to examine and understand how social and cultural issues affect and are affected by disability. For example, instead of focusing primarily on white middle-class families, researchers have begun to account for the experiences of families of cultural or ethnic minorities and of low-income families of children with disabilities (Harry, 1992; Kalyanpur & Rao, 1991; Smith, Caro, & McKaig, 1987). Since the early 1980s, a substantial body of literature has examined the specific situations of women with disabilities (Deegan & Brooks, 1985; Fine & Asch, 1988; Traustadottir, 1990b) and the role of gender in family care of children with disabilities (Bright & Wright, 1986; Traustadottir, 1991).

Until recently, researchers have rarely focused on the relationship between disability, race, and poverty in the lives of persons with disabilities. Taylor (in preparation), for example, explores how poverty influences the life of a family in

---

Preparation of this chapter was supported by Cooperative Agreement #H33B89948 between the National Institute on Disability and Rehabilitation Research (NIDRR); the Research and Training Center on Residential Services and Community Living and the Institute on Community Integration (UAP) at the University of Minnesota; and the Research and Training Center on Community Integration at the Center on Human Policy in Syracuse University, School of Education (Division of Special Education and Rehabilitation).

The authors thank Bob Bogdan for his assistance with framing this chapter, Susan O'Connor for increasing our sensitivity to multicultural issues, Steve Taylor for his ongoing support, and Rachael Zubal for her assistance in preparing this chapter.

which all members are labeled as having disabilities. Studies have also compared employees of both minority and nonminority status in supported work programs (Wilson, O'Reilly, & Rusch, 1991). Other researchers have examined the residential placement patterns of adults with disabilities, including break down by racial background (Hill et al., 1989). Repeatedly, biases in the labeling of minority children and the education of students with disabilities have been demonstrated (Jones, 1976; Mercer, 1973; Ortiz & Ramirez, 1988; Tomlinson, 1982).

In the past, services for persons with disabilities were provided in segregated settings isolated from the larger society. Neither human services professionals nor the people they served had much contact with "natural" community environments. Today, most professionals in disability-related fields are in a new situation. For example, not only are they expected to provide services in the community, but they are also expected to facilitate the participation of persons with disabilities into a highly complex, multicultural society (Bradley & Knoll, n.d.; Hutchison, 1990; Knoll & Ford, 1987; Smull, 1989; Taylor, Bogdan, & Racino, 1991).

This chapter explores multiculturalism as it applies to the field of developmental disabilities. The first section introduces the concept of multiculturalism. Subsequent sections examine how gender, class, and race influence people with disabilities and the services they receive. These dimensions form a starting point for unraveling and mapping out the complex issues that influence service delivery to persons with disabilities, as well as for directing policymakers and service providers in a direction that does not require individuals to conform to the customs and assumptions of the dominant culture.

MULTICULTURALISM

Although the United States has always been a multicultural society, the nation's demographic characteristics are now rapidly changing toward increased cultural diversity (Yates, 1989). For example:

> The aging of the mainstream population and the influx of immigrants to the United States since the Immigration Reform Act of 1965 have resulted in a rapid rise in the percentage of ethnic, cultural, language, and religious minorities. . . . One out of three U.S. students will be an ethnic minority by the turn of the century. (Banks & McGee Banks, 1989 p. vi)

The trend toward increased cultural diversity poses a challenge to those who provide services for persons with disabilities. It can no longer be assumed that the needs and experiences of such persons are determined solely by the type and severity of disability. Through the adoption of a broad, multicultural approach, it is possible to focus on the interplay of a person's disability with a multitude of other social dimensions, including race, social class, culture, ethnicity, gender, and sexual orientation, in order to better understand the individuals and the contexts in which they live. Better understanding has implications for policy development and service provision.

Defining Multiculturalism

The term "multiculturalism" is used by a range of people in a variety of ways (Banks & McGee Banks, 1989; Gollnick & Chinn, 1990; Sleeter, 1991). In a review of how the term is used in connection with multicultural education, Sleeter and Grant (1987) found that the only meaning held in common by all authors reviewed referred to educational approaches aimed at benefiting people of color. While the characteristics most often referred to under the heading multiculturalism were race and ethnicity, some authors also included language, gender, and social class. Very few definitions of multiculturalism were found to include disability.

Multiculturalism, as used in this chapter, refers to the social dimensions of an individual's life, including race, ethnicity, culture, class, disability, and gender. A multicultural approach assumes that one must consider these broad social factors and issues to enhance community inclusion. Using a multicultural approach, researchers or practitioners might *ask*, for example, how and why different cultures attach different meanings to disability, and how disability affects family life in various cultures, ethnic, and racial groups. This approach to developmental disabilities differs from most approaches that currently exist within the human services system (Locust, 1988).

Multiculturalism and Disability Services

A primary assumption of a multicultural framework is that society consists of a shared, core culture, as well as many subcultures. Human services systems primarily operate within the shared, core culture—the mainstream or macroculture—and embody its values, norms, and characteristics. The diverse subcultures, or microcultures, are unfamiliar to the majority of service providers. An awareness and understanding of multicultural and multiple social dimensions along the lines of class, race, gender, culture, and ethnicity is needed in order to work effectively with individuals who have disabilities and who are from diverse backgrounds. Without this knowledge, service providers and policymakers are likely to assume that their own perspectives are universally held. Because of this assumption, they are unable to change policies and practices that violate the religious requirements or cultural expectations of those who are affected (Minow, 1990). The very identity of a person can be ignored and debased. A simple example would be an emphasis on the celebration of Christmas as the major religious holiday for everyone, rather than a recognition that people may celebrate a variety of holidays at that time of year, or that they may celebrate Christmas differently (e.g., for 12 days or on a day other than December 25).

A multicultural approach is perhaps most advanced in education where the term multicultural education has come to describe an educational approach that both accommodates and teaches about the diversity found in the general population (Banks & McGee Banks, 1989; Gollnick & Chinn, 1990). The emerging body of literature on multicultural education reflects a more comprehensive approach to education and provides one answer to the call for a more inclusive scholarship which accounts for the complexity in the experiences of people, their families, and their communities. Educational researchers have pointed out that there are some clear differences between the United States' emerging demographic characteristics and the demographics of professionals and persons who are served by the education system and other human services systems. For example, professionals within these systems tend to be white and middle-class, and administrators are most likely white, middle-class, and male. The training, research, and other activities of professionals generally focus on areas unrelated to the multicultural characteristics of the people who receive services. Increasingly, this has begun to be recognized by researchers and practitioners in disability-related fields. Yates (1989) discusses this issue in relation to special education:

> Issues such as ethnicity, minority status, bilingual education, second language acquisition, nonbiased assessment, socioeconomic status, and so forth are generally perceived by the special education profession as unrelated to special education as a discipline. (Yates, 1989, p. 3)

After more than two decades, community-based services stand at a crossroads. Growing demands for recognition of the diversity that exists among persons with disabilities, their families, and the communities in which they live can no longer be satisfied by token excursions into the lives of minority families or low-income neighborhoods. Instead, a different perspective on disability needs to be adopted.

In recent years, there has been a growing awareness of the importance of a multicultural approach to service delivery for persons with disabilities (Davila, 1991). A look at the changing professional vocabulary illustrates this well. The terms "cultural competence" (Cross, 1988); "ethnic-sensitive practice" (Devore & Schlesinger, 1981); "cross-cultural awareness" (Green, 1982); and "cross-cultural competence" (Lynch & Hanson, 1992) are different names for the organizational and professional policies that are being put into practice in attempts to work more effectively with individuals from diverse backgrounds.

GENDER AND DISABILITY

While both men and women with disabilities are subject to discrimination because of their disabilities, women with disabilities are at a further disadvantage because of the combined discrimination based on gender and disability (Deegan & Brooks, 1985; Fine & Asch, 1988). Both mainstream research and writing in disability-related fields have typically neglected issues related to gender, and professionals have yet to recognize the combined discrimination of gender and disability experienced by women with disabilities. Furthermore, disability policies and practices have not been designed to meet the specific needs of women with disabilities (Asch & Fine, 1988; Kutza, 1985; Mudrick, 1988). An example is the need for support with child rearing, which is largely ignored in policy and practice.

Although women with disabilities have historically been neglected by those concerned with disabilities and by feminist scholars, the past decade has been characterized by an increased interest in this group. However, much of the writing in this area has been done by women who have disabilities, and a substantial part of the writing consists of their personal accounts (Browne, Connors, & Stern, 1985; Campling, 1981; Hannaford, 1985; Matthews, 1983). Although research in this area is relatively new, the writings of the past decade have provided research-based information on the social, economic, and psychological circumstances of women with disabilities, along with theoretical analysis, providing a framework to understand their lives and experiences (Deegan & Brooks, 1985; Fine & Asch, 1988). Much of the literature has been devoted to identifying the barriers women with disabilities face in today's society and has documented that they fare more poorly than both men with disabilities and women without disabilities in education and employment, in receiving economic and social support, and in their access to sexuality and intimacy (Traustadottir, 1990b).

Multiple Minority Status

The major factor unifying scholarly writings about women with disabilities is the conceptualization of them as a group with a multiple minority status. This typically combines disability studies and feminist scholarship to explore discrimination based on both disability and gender (Deegan & Brooks, 1985; Fine & Asch, 1988).

Some authors have characterized women with disabilities as "roleless" because of the limited social roles available to them and the absence of structural and institutional means to achieve valued adult roles (Fine & Asch, 1981). Women with disabilities have limited opportunities to acquire even the most traditional female roles as nurturers, mothers, wives, homemakers, and lovers. While these roles may not be considered the best measure of a woman's social success, the limited access to this most traditional women's sphere clearly demonstrates the restricted social options that are available to these women.

Compared to both men with disabilities and women without disabilities, women with disabilities are less likely to marry, usually marry later, and are more likely to be divorced if they do get married (Asch & Fine, 1988; Hannaford, 1985; Simon, 1988). Compared to 60% of women without disabilities, only 49% of women with disabilities are married (Bowe, 1984). Fine and Asch (1988) report that only one group of women with disabilities is more likely to be married than men of the same disability group. This group is women with mental retardation. Asch and Fine (1988) suggest that this may be because women with mental retardation "may fit all too well the criteria of the 'good wife': one who is docile, passive, loyal, and dependent, and not likely to show her husband up" (p. 15).

Motherhood and Reproductive Rights

In North American society, women with disabilities are typically viewed as dependent and in need of care. It is therefore difficult for many to imagine how a mother with a disability can adequately fill the caring and nurturing mothering role (Shaul, Dowling, & Laden, 1985). The widespread belief that women with disabilities cannot and should not bear and raise children has made it difficult for pregnant women with disabilities to find doctors who will accept them as patients. They have also found it problematic to gain access to information and services related to their special needs with regard to birth control, pregnancy, and childbearing (Finger, 1985; Women and Disability Awareness Project, 1989).

Although society's fears that women with disabilities will produce defective children are for the most part groundless, these fears have resulted in severe discrimination against women with disabilities in general, especially those women with mental retardation (Wolfensberger, 1975). No group of women with disabilities has been as severely discriminated against in terms of their reproductive rights as women with mental retardation. Some of the myths surrounding women with mental retardation—such as their uncontrollable sexuality—are unfortunately still very much alive (Finger, 1985; Sank & Lafleche, 1981; Scheerenberger, 1987).

Sexual Abuse

Those who have studied sexual abuse (e.g., Cole, 1984; Longo & Gochenour, 1981) view sexual assault as having more to do with the oppressive use of power than with sex. Many abusers seem to look for and use vulnerability to create the opportunity to rape. This vulnerability is increased when people are marginalized, dependent, and in need of affection. Thus, the more vulnerable and powerless people are, the more they are at risk of being sexually abused.

The sexual abuse of women and children with disabilities is an area that has received growing attention in recent years (Sobsey, Gray, Wells, Pyper, & Reimer-Heck 1991; Watson, 1984). Much of the literature in this area is based on studies that show women with disabilities being at a much greater risk of being sexually abused than other women (Craine, Henson, Colliver, & McLelan, 1988; Musick, 1984; Senn, 1988). In fact, O'Toole (1990) reports that sexual assault and battering may be two to three times higher for women with disabilities than for other women. This is true in society in general and, particularly, within residential facilities. For example, additional research indicates that women in institutions are at a much greater risk of being sexually abused than other women (Musick, 1984; Stefan, 1987).

Professionals within the human services system continue to ignore this widespread abuse. These chilling realities have led Asch and Fine (1988) to wonder "how many of these same women have been sterilized to keep the effects of rape from the public eye" (p. 23).

Education

Women with disabilities are likely to have less education than both women without disabilities and men with disabilities. Women with disabilities are five times more likely than women without disabilities to have less than 8 years of formal education; 17.4% of all women with disabilities have less than 8 years of formal education as compared to 3.5% of women without disabilities. Only 16% of all women with disabilities are likely to have any college education compared to 31% of women without disabilities and 28% of men with disabilities (Bowe, 1984).

While all students, both male and female and those with and without disabilities, are subject to sex-biased assumptions in most schools and curricula, research indicates that sex-role stereotyping may be even more pervasive when students have disabilities. Gillespie and Fink (1974), for example, found that sex-role stereotyping seemed to be especially pervasive for children with mental retardation and behavioral problems. These students tended to be taught traditional sex-role modes of behavior because it would supposedly enable them to better adjust to society. Moreover, some authors report that school books for students with disabilities "include stories and illustrations that are deliberately stereotypical to foster this 'adjustment'" (Women and Disability Awareness Project, 1989, p. 12).

Employment

Adult males with disabilities have serious employment problems (Asch & Fine, 1988; Bowe, 1984); however, women with disabilities fare significantly worse (Disability Statistics Program, 1992; Russo & Jansen, 1988). This seems to hold true for all types and levels of disabilities. In fact, men with disabilities are almost twice as likely to have jobs than women with disabilities; that is, almost 42% of men with disabilities are in the labor force (meaning that they either work or are actively seeking work), compared to 24% of women with disabilities. In addition, while more than 30% of men with disabilities work full-time jobs, only 12% of women with disabilities have full-time employment (Bowe, 1984). Women with disabilities also receive considerably lower wages than their male counterparts. In 1990, mean annual earnings for men with work disabilities was close to $23,000, while it was under $16,000 for women with work disabilities. In contrast, men without work disabilities earned a mean income of $30,000, while women earned $18,000 (Disability Statistics Program, 1992). Most research on the employment of women with disabilities is not broken down by disability categories, and many studies seem to be based primarily on information about women with physical disabilities. As a result, it is hard to find information about employment of women with developmental disabilities.

Research and policy initiatives in the field of developmental disability have recently devoted increased attention to the importance of employment. A new federal initiative, supported employment, has been developed to assist those with even the most severe disabilities to get and hold a job. This emphasis recognizes the importance of productive work as a means to achieve social equality and financial independence. Supported employment programs are now being developed throughout the country (see Moon, Inge, Wehman, Brooke, & Barcus [1990] for descriptions of such programs). Despite a wealth of recent writings pertaining to the employment of persons with developmental disabilities, little attention has been devoted to the specific employment barriers faced by women, since most studies are not broken down by gender. Only a handful of studies have examined gender differences in supported employment. This research demonstrates that men are more likely than women to be placed in jobs through supported employment programs and more likely to retain their jobs. For example, in a study of a group of 186 individuals with mental retardation who had been placed in competitive jobs through supported employment programs, researchers found a "disproportionate representation of males (68% male to 32% female) in the population of placed consumers" (Kregel & Wehman, 1989, p. 265). A similar trend was found by Hill et al. (1985) in their study of a group of 155 people with mental retardation. They found that the majority of people placed through one supported employment program, or 66%, were men, while women represented only 34% of those who received jobs. These researchers also found that 70% of the men placed in such jobs achieved a retention rate of 6 months, or 70%, compared to 55% of the women. These studies seem to confirm that women with developmental disabilities are subject to the same employment barriers as women with other disabilities. Moreover, these studies indicate that the new approaches in the field of developmental disabilities retain the same pattern of gender discrimination as the older approaches they are intended to replace.

Service delivery to both men and women with disabilities has traditionally not taken into account the double discrimination against women with disabilities. In addition, policy and practices within the field have also not been designed to meet the specific needs of women with disabilities, whether the needs relate to marriage, childbearing, and parenting, or to education and employment. The situation of women with disabilities also has implications when it comes to community integration, flowing from the problematic nature of women's participation in the world outside the home (e.g., the worlds of work, academia, politics, and finance). If the woman has a disability, it will be even more difficult for her to gain full membership in society. Agencies and professionals need to be more sensitive to the specific barriers women with disabilities face when they attempt to become full participants in community life.

SOCIAL CLASS AND DISABILITY

This section examines the concept of social class and the problems in discussing social class in the United States, and briefly summarizes theories about class differences. It also identifies some ways in which social class affects persons with disabilities, their families, and the services they receive.

Discussion of social class differences is difficult because people continue to believe that this country is classless and that it offers equal opportunities to all. A concurrent belief is that anyone with talent who works hard enough can attain a higher standard of living. The reality, however, is that upward mobility is achieved by relatively few people (Gollnick & Chinn, 1990). In fact, current projections indicate that downward mobility will be much more common in the future; many sons and daughters of middle- and working-class families will have lower incomes than their parents (Kraus & Stoddard, 1989). Furthermore, evidence suggests that the middle class, defined by income level, is shrinking (Kraus & Stoddard, 1989; Rose, 1986). For example, of those who earned between $19,000 and $47,000 in 1978, only 2.8% are earning more than $47,000 in 1986, while 5.2% of the same group is earning less than $19,000 in 1986 (these figures have been adjusted to account for inflation). Nevertheless, the belief that the United States is a country that offers equal opportunity to all persons carries with it an implication that class position has to do with individual characteristics and is earned, rather than the result of societal structures and forces, such as inequitable access to unemployment, education, or health care, over which the individual has little power.

As a society, however, the United States is characterized by different socioeconomic levels or classes, distinguishable based on their members' access to power, status, and money, as well as on how their members live and relate to the means of production. The privileged upper class is made up of people and families who own and control corporations, banks, and other institutions that have power over the production of goods and services. The middle and working classes are comprised of families whose members sell their labor or the products thereof. There is also a poverty class who find it difficult or impossible to sell their labor for an adequate wage. This class is disproportionately filled with people with disabilities, single mothers, elderly people, and people of color (Kraus & Stoddard, 1989; Rose, 1986).

Effects of Class Position

Human service organizations, including those serving persons with disabilities, reflect middle-class expectations about how people should behave and how people should be treated. Their practices are typically based on middle-class assumptions about the families and individuals they serve. For example, while studies have shown that members of the middle and working class typically hold the same basic values, differences have been found in child-rearing patterns, community participation, clothing, hairstyles, foods, speech patterns and pronunciation, body language, style of homes, furnishings, numbers of people visible in the neighborhood, daily routines, music preferences, leisure time preferences, amount of community involvement, and level of involvement with extended family (Kerbo, 1983; Rubin 1976). The behavioral differences between the middle class and the poverty class are likely to be even more pronounced. People who are poor, however, share the values of the dominant culture and class (Taylor, in preparation).

The extent to which class-based differences are perceived and reacted to by human service providers can have major and lasting effects on people's lives. For example, a middle-class human services worker, hearing speech patterns and pronunciations that he or she has learned to associate with a lack of education or ability, may suspect that the person speaking lacks the capacity to raise children, work, or fill other valued societal roles. At the very least, such professionals must recognize and overcome their presumptions that people who speak differently are inferior. At worst, unconscious prejudices, triggered by hearing different speech patterns, can result in an unwarranted use of power over persons with disabilities or their families.

Differences in child-rearing patterns can provide another example. "Findings showing different socialization patterns by class do not suggest that working-class parents have less concern for their children or are harder on their children" (Kerbo, 1983, p. 285), but differences do exist. Kerbo also describes studies showing that middle-class fathers stress self-reliance for their children, while working-class fathers stress conformity to external rules. One explanation of these differences can be found in a major cross-national study, which contains data from 122 cultures (Ellis, Lee, & Peterson, 1978). This study found that the greater the supervision over parents in important aspects of life, such as their workplace, the greater the stress on conformity in child socialization.

In working with persons with disabilities and their families, service providers have traditionally tended to emphasize conformity (to the rules of the organization), achievement of independence, and self-reliance. Currently, some organizations are attempting to incorporate an emphasis on interdependence and on consumer control over services (Taylor et al., 1991). Both of these approaches are likely to be perceived and practiced differently by people raised in middle-class, working-class, and poverty-class families. These differences have the potential to create misunderstandings among service providers and the families with whom they interact. It is vital that providers' efforts to develop and implement community services must acknowledge and appreciate different ways of interpreting and responding to the values they promote.

Poverty and Disability

Kraus and Stoddard (1989) point to the clear link between "activity limitation" (a Census Bureau term that is broader than disability) and family income. More than 25% of the people in families whose annual income (in 1986 dollars) was under $10,000 have activity limitations. Many of these families have adult members with disabilities, who *if* unemployed, are likely to have no other income than a small monthly benefit through social security income (SSI) or social security disability income (SSDI). Children in low-income households also possess significantly higher proportions of limitations than those in higher income families. Low-income families may have difficulty obtaining food and shelter for their children, and rarely have the resources that middle-income families view as necessary for their children.

Members of racial minority groups are much more likely to be poor (U.S. Department of Commerce, 1992), and so there are many ways in which race, culture, and social class overlap. The effects of labeling practices (poor and nonwhite children are more likely to be diagnosed as disabled) and human services agency control mechanisms (e.g., removal of children from the home and judgments about a family's capacity to cooperate or benefit from services) are just two examples of the ways in which these overlaps affect families who are poor, nonwhite, and/or culturally different. In such situations, a family's perspective on what they really need is overridden or reframed by service providers based on prevailing middle-class perspectives (Harry, 1992). This occurs in the name of providing support, with little awareness by service providers that their own standards operate against families.

Adults with disabilities, especially those who have not had adequate or advanced education and training, are also likely to be poor, as they are limited to an income of government benefits and, possibly, very low wages (Disability Statistics Program, 1992; Wehman, 1993). For example, the 1990 census reveals that the mean income of persons with severe work limitations was $5,911 annually for the years 1989 and 1990. In comparison, for those with no work limitation, the mean income was $19,851 for the same years. Due to current policies regarding earned income, those who try to work may lose medical and other benefits; therefore, many people do not even look for employment. The poverty of adults with disabilities often results in living in low-income neighborhoods and substandard housing, as well as having less opportunity to participate in community life, to purchase personal items, or to spend time in ways they might prefer. An alternate result may be life under the roof of others, such as with parents, in group homes, in nursing homes, or in other residential settings. This type of life-style allows them little control over rules and limited access to the community. These limited alternatives are a direct result of the class position in which people with disabilities find themselves due to their poverty and lack of access to opportunities.

RACE AND DISABILITY

Members of racial minority groups with disabilities experience a double dose of discrimination. This section examines these experiences, which are now receiving more attention by researchers, policymakers, and professionals. Members of racial and ethnic minority groups encounter greater barriers to social services and to the protection of their rights than do individuals of nonminority status (Rosenthal & Carty, 1988). These barriers are "greatly compounded by systematic racism and the social and cultural factors that distance minorities from a public and social system primarily geared to—and run by—a middle-class, white Anglo culture" (Rosenthal & Carty, 1988, p. 1).

During the 1960s and 1970s, overall education and income levels rose for everyone, including members of racial minority groups. Government and public supports, such as scholarships for higher education, job training programs, family supports and other basic welfare provisions, housing subsidies, and public housing were available to a greater extent than before. Despite these supports, African-Americans, Native Americans, and Hispanics still experience far higher levels of poverty than do other Americans (Rose, 1986; Sterne, 1991; Trattner, 1984).

A conservative era dominated most of the 1980s, resulting in the curtailment of many social supports and services. Although welfare, Medicaid, and Medicare monies paid out by the federal government increased, educational and housing subsidies were decreased, causing less affordable housing and jobs to be available. Furthermore, in recent years, wages have not kept pace with cost of living increases. While these changes have affected all Americans, they have especially made an impact on those who are poor, disabled, and members of minority groups (U.S. Department of Commerce, 1992, pp. 456–460).

Those who analyze demographic information on race, ethnicity, and disability are faced with a methodological problem. There are no standard definitions of these terms and little record keeping of relevant demographic data (Czajka, 1984). Sterne (1991) suggests that one of the largest gaps in existing data is the health status of minority group members. For example, until 1983 persons of Hispanic origin may have been counted as Whites, Blacks, or members of a distinct category (U.S. Department of Commerce, 1992). Furthermore, no differentiation is made of populations that comprise the broad Hispanic group (e.g., Mexican-Americans, Puerto Ricans, Cubans, Central/South Americans). This practice of not delineating country of origin is maintained despite acknowledged differences in cultural traditions and identity (Schur, Bernstein, & Berk, 1987; Suazo, 1986). In addition, human services bureaucracies reduce racial and ethnic identity to an inadequate classification system and neglect the importance of people's backgrounds, as well as their strong sense of cultural identification.

Double Discrimination

The combined effects of race, poverty, and disability are not easy to disentangle and only a few attempts to do so exist in the literature (Baxter, Poonia, Ward, & Nadirshaw, 1990; Rosenthal & Carty, 1988). In their review of census data, Kraus and Stoddard (1989) found that "as household income rises, the proportion of children with no limitation also rises" (Kraus & Stoddard, 1989, p. 31). Those with less income also seek and receive less basic medical care and report worse health (Sterne, 1991).

These factors are associated with higher rates of disability and increases in the severity of disabling conditions. Thus, Native Americans and African-Americans report the highest levels of activity limitations.[1] Although Hispanics report lower levels of disability than whites, this has been attributed to inconsistent reporting of Hispanic persons and to the fact that many illegal residents in this country fail to be counted in the census (Kraus & Stoddard, 1989).

---

[1]A note about language: When selecting terms for various racial groups, we faced many difficulties. First, there is no consensus in the literature on what terms to use—different authors use different terms. Second, there is not a consensus within groups about how people refer to themselves. For example, some of the people who are indigenous to the United States call themselves "American Indians," while others prefer the term "Native Americans." Third, many people do not fall neatly into racial categories, and it is often unclear who is included in what category. Therefore, any terms used to label people according to racial categories tend to exclude certain groups of people. In selecting terms to use in this chapter we have attempted to use inclusive language that respects the preferences of individuals from diverse racial groups.

Access to Services

Individuals with disabilities who belong to minority groups receive differential access to social and human services. For instance, racial and ethnic minority groups are overrepresented in the human service system, including the areas of special education, vocational and residential services, and congregate care facilities. These groups are also overrepresented among individuals labeled as having developmental disabilities (or who are considered at risk of acquiring one) and individuals labeled as having mental illness (Maheady, Towne, Algozzine, Mercer, & Ysseldyke, 1983; Marcos, 1986; Mercer, 1973; Rosenthal & Carty, 1988; Sarason & Doris, 1979; Wilson et al., 1991).

The inclusion of persons with disabilities who are members of minority groups in disability-related service programs varies in different types of settings. Minority status persons with developmental disabilities are less likely to gain access to community-based or innovative programs, such as inclusive classrooms, family support services, supported employment, and outpatient support. Instead, members of minority groups are more likely to receive the most basic service provisions such as welfare, SSI checks, segregation, and institutionalization (Children's Defense Fund, 1974; Hodge & Edmonds, 1988; Jones, 1976; Rosenthal & Carty, 1988).

There appear to be some specific reasons for these patterns. First, fewer community-based services are located in neighborhoods with high concentrations of minority groups; that is, poor urban areas and certain rural areas, such as reservations (O'Connor, 1993; Rosenthal & Carty, 1988). Since services are generally not available in these areas, individuals must search for appropriate supports. As Kalyanpur (1988) points out, "Lack of information, financial, and transportation constraints further circumscribe the use of services outside of the reservation" (p. 46).

Second, certain misconceptions about the potential and capabilities of individuals who belong to minority groups further restrict the services made available to them (Marcos, 1986; Racino, O'Connor, Walker, & Taylor, 1991; Tomlinson, 1982). Harry (1992), for example, notes that in one urban school district, Puerto Rican children were placed into self-contained special education classrooms at a higher rate than white students, but at a much lower rate than African-American children. The realities of everyday existence mean that many minority families channel their energies into survival and not into the placement of their sons and daughters into schools and social service programs (Harry, 1992).

Ironically, there are some data to suggest that at least some individuals of minority groups who receive only cash payments may be better off than their white counterparts receiving significantly more services. Members of minority groups generally live within an extended family network. Depending on the circumstances, government subsidies may not be seen as devaluing and may represent a significant contribution to the family's income. They also provide the individual and his or her family with some degree of control. In contrast, more formalized service options (e.g., community residences or day treatment programs) impose restrictions upon individuals and their families. While clients of the human service system may be getting more programmatic supports, they and their families may lose personal autonomy and control (Kalyanpur & Rao, 1991; Racino et al., 1991).

Loss of Racial and Ethnic Identity

For individuals of racial and ethnic minority groups, the master status of "client" often has a more devastating effect than for individuals of white middle-class backgrounds (Goffman, 1963). To illustrate this point, Harry (1992) contrasts the different social definitions of childhood between white and Puerto Rican families. For the former, the basic social role available to children is that of a "student," one who will be taken care of by the nuclear family. However, in many Puerto Rican families, parents often quit school early in order to work and start their own families. In addition, to these families, poor academic performance does not tend to be equated with disability. However, these families do know that "the power of the school is such that to be stigmatized as a student is to be stigmatized as a whole person" (Harry, 1992, p. 246). Within these Hispanic families, Harry notes that the norms and values are not simply different from the dominant culture. "In the perspectives of these families, the parameters of 'normalcy' and acceptability are much wider than are those of the school, and the toleration for human difference much greater" (Harry, 1992, pp. 245–246). Yet within the larger, dominant culture, these same children are devalued.

The process of moving into clienthood and the subsequent loss of racial and ethnic identity means that the individual with a developmental disability who is of a minority status faces a number of "deculturing experiences." Staff members are typically not aware of, encouraged, or trained to appreciate the racial and ethnic identity of individuals with disabilities. As a result, people with disabilities from other cultural and racial backgrounds usually have little or no opportunity or support to express their cultural identities.

For example, O'Connor (1993) discusses the challenges of providing services to persons with disabilities in ways that respect their cultural backgrounds and identities. She describes efforts made by the staff of one agency serving members of the Lakota Sioux tribe who live on a South Dakota reservation. Staff learned the rudimentaries of the Lakota language and developed ways to determine the capabilities and backgrounds of individuals within their cultural context without having to resort to formal social histories or assessment tools that did not take into account the subtle meanings of certain behaviors and customs.

While this approach is encouraging, in order to receive programmatic support, individuals with disabilities on the reservation must move to a nearby town. For one woman, Anna[2], this meant that her contact with her family was severely curtailed, as was her opportunity to speak Lakota. In an attempt to assimilate into the community, Anna began wearing pants instead of dresses and had her hair cut, both of which were traditions found in the dominant culture. Staff, who had been

---

[2]All names of individuals who appear in this chapter are pseudonyms.

made aware of Anna's situation, introduced her to a woman who spoke Lakota, and the two developed a friendship. Despite this, when Anna visits the reservation, she is told that she has changed and is now different. As she said, ". . . I don't know . . . well, I'm not Indian anymore" (O'Connor, 1993, p. 327).

Individuals who speak languages other than English can face devastating consequences when staff members lack an awareness and appreciation of the person's situation. For example, Taylor, Lutfiyya, Racino, Walker, and Knoll (1986) describe how a Polish man who did not speak English was interpreted to be babbling and was consequently ignored. It was later determined that he spoke Polish and was much more competent than had been previously supposed.

Individuals with disabilities are often not enabled or supported to attend the relevant community or cultural centers, or to take part in typical activities related to their culture. Staff members may be oblivious of such considerations, or simply not able to support the individual to pursue these interests or activities. For individuals who have already been cut off from their racial and ethnic communities, staff members may not know how to obtain access to those communities in order to properly support the individual's potential participation.

To summarize, individuals with disabilities who are also members of minority groups face discrimination that is compounded by their doubly devalued status. These individuals face greater barriers to the full range of available social services and legal protection. These barriers must be addressed if individuals with disabilities who are members of minority groups are to become full members of society.

RACE, CLASS, GENDER, AND DISABILITY SERVICES

Social class, race, and gender are not isolated social forces; rather, they are interwoven and complex social relations. This makes it difficult to distinguish their impact independent of one another. It is particularly difficult to distinguish between the effects of social class and race. To illustrate the complexity of social relations and their embeddedness in the culture, this chapter concludes with a synthesis of the social dimensions previously addressed. Meanwhile, drawing on the research of one of the authors (Traustadottir, 1990a), the experiences and services offered to one African-American family are examined.

The African-American Family

Many scholars have criticized how the African-American family has been treated in the literature. Billingsley (1988) suggests that African-American families have been virtually ignored by those who have studied family life in America. On those rare occasions when African-American families have been studied, researchers have presented them as a social problem. As Billingsley (1988) points out, the majority of existing studies of the African-American family have compared them to the dominant white middle-class family. Based on this comparison, these studies concluded that African-American families, particularly the *poor* African-American families, are deviant, pathological, matriarchal, and broken. Walker

(1988) supports Billingsley's criticism and adds that, "the black American family is alternately a perplexing problem and an embarrassment to social researchers and policy makers alike" (Walker, 1988, p. 87). The fact that the patterns of family life expressed by African-Americans are different from those found among whites is not being criticized by this scholarship. Rather, the criticism is directed at how researchers have interpreted these differences and at the fact that "few attempts have been made to view black families as they actually are, recognizing the interpretations black people have of their own cultural patterns" (Stack, 1974, p. 22).

Differences between African-American and white families have received public attention because a large number of the former do not conform to the dominant patterns of marriage and family formation that exist within the white culture. This has been defined as a problem because, as Walker (1988) points out, it is widely assumed that life in the traditional nuclear family is an important prerequisite of social and economic success in American society. Scholars as well as policymakers have tended to define these differences as deviant and have joined forces to create social programs to reduce or eliminate these differences.

African-American Families and Disability Services

As part of the social programs established to "help" dependent populations, the disability service system has adopted the dominant view of the African-American family (Billingsley, 1988; Olion, 1989). This view, consciously or unconsciously, influences how disability services are provided to African-American families and is further reinforced by the fact that most professionals are white and middle-class (Hanson, 1992; Yates, 1989).

The story of Janet Lee and her 4-year-old son, Frank, demonstrates this view. Janet is a single African-American mother, and Frank has mental retardation, exhibits challenging behaviors, and has a communication disorder. At the time Janet and her son became involved in a family support program that provides them with in-home services, they were living with their extended family, which included Janet's parents, two brothers, a sister, and the sister's baby. Professionals from the family support program saw the collective efforts of the extended family as interfering with what the program was trying to accomplish. For example, staff complained about the way Frank's grandfather dealt with Frank's temper tantrums. The professionals wanted Frank to "work through" the tantrums. The grandfather did not agree because it would mean that the child would be left to cry on his own. Instead, he insisted on hugging Frank and comforting him. From the professionals' point of view, the grandfather's lack of cooperation with them was a problem. The professionals claimed that there was too much interference with the program they were trying to implement. They encouraged Janet to move away from her extended family and establish her own home with her son. Janet followed their advice and now lives alone with her son in what both she and the professionals describe as a "bad" inner-city neighborhood.

Janet's story highlights how the attitudes of white middle-class professionals can influence the way in which they relate to poor African-American families. The family support program operates with a definition of a family that led staff members to identify Janet and her son as "the family" with whom they should work. Instead of assisting Janet within the context of her existing family, these professionals attempted to make Janet conform to a family pattern that was based on white middle-class norms.

In her study of African-American family life, Willis (1992) has demonstrated how many poor African-American families form strong networks of cooperation, reciprocity, and support. Stack (1974) points out that these support networks are essential to the survival of the families. Her study highlights the importance of such kinship-based exchange networks in coping with poverty. In a service system dominated by the white middle-class culture there is a great probability that the system will fail to recognize and respect existing support networks and their importance. Interventions designed to help families may, in fact, damage these networks. An appreciation and knowledge of family diversity would allow human services professionals to build on and strengthen existing support networks, instead of replacing them with professional help, as was the case with Janet Lee and her son.

Issues of race seem to have had the greatest impact on the way the service system related to the Lee family. Although not as influential, issues of social class and gender also seemed to be at work. For example, the stereotype of women as the natural caregivers is pervasive in the dominant culture. This may be one of the reasons why professionals from the family support program did not view Frank's grandfather as an appropriate primary caregiver.

The social class differences between the Lee family and the professionals who served them may also have had an impact on the quality of services provided to the family. Besides being the "experts," the professionals were from a higher social class and had more education, as well as greater social, economic, and political resources. These factors resulted in their having a great deal of authority when they interacted with Janet Lee and her family.

Child rearing practices differ between social classes (Ellis et al., 1978; Kerbo, 1983). It can therefore be expected that middle-class professionals will have different ideas about raising children than families from lower socioeconomic groups. Instead of recognizing the possibility of class-based differences, the professionals judged the childrearing approaches used by Janet Lee and her family as "wrong." Moreover, because their training reflected the values of the dominant white middle-class culture, professionals have been reinforced in their belief that their views of raising children are correct. As a result, one major goal of professionals' work with the Lee family becomes that of correction. By virtue of their higher social class and training, these professionals influenced Janet Lee to conform to their perceptions of the way in which families should parent their children.

CONCLUSION

In this chapter, initial steps are taken toward unraveling some of the complex social forces that shape the lives of persons with disabilities and the services with which they are provided. The concept of multiculturalism offers the most inclusive framework for looking at these forces, as it is an approach that attempts to account for the multiple and complex social dimensions that shape our lives. Three of these dimensions—race, social class, and gender—and their association with disability and service delivery are addressed.

Those who work for community inclusion of persons with disabilities usually focus on the level of disability as the most critical factor in terms of a person's perceived ability to participate in community life. The social dimensions discussed in this chapter are equally important.

As the community-based approach to services for persons with developmental disabilities moves into its third decade, there are increasing signs of difficulties in how the system functions. This has led to calls for new approaches to service delivery (Meyer, Peck, & Brown, 1991; Taylor et al., 1991). At least some of the current problems in the service delivery system derive from a lack of understanding of the broader social forces that shape our society, the community-based service system, the workers within these services, and the persons who receive the services. Current approaches to community integration are typically based on an oversimplified view of the community as homogeneous, where "typical" people lead "ordinary lives." This view does not take into account the diversity of the American population or the complex social dimensions that shape our society. In order to effectively support a diverse population of individuals with disabilities in the community, the human services system must develop a better understanding and knowledge of the complexity of community life. Without such an understanding, it will be difficult to achieve the goal of full community inclusion.

REFERENCES

Asch, A., & Fine, M. (1988). Introduction: Beyond pedestals. In M. Fine & A. Asch (Eds.), *Women with disabilities: Essays in psychology, culture, and politics* (pp. 1–37). Philadelphia: Temple University Press.

Banks, J.A., & McGee Banks, C.A. (1989). Preface. In J.A. Banks & C.A. McGee Banks (Eds.), *Multicultural education: Issues and perspectives* (pp. xi–xiii). Boston: Allyn and Bacon.

Baxter, C., Poonia, K., Ward, L., & Nadirshaw, Z. (1990). *Double discrimination: Issues and services for people with learning difficulties from black and ethnic communities*. London: Kings Fund Centre/Commission for Racial Equality.

Billingsley, A. (1988). *Black families in white America* (20th anniversary ed.). New York: Simon & Schuster.

Bowe, F. (1984). *Disabled women in America: A statistical report drawn from census data*. Washington, DC: President's Committee on Employment of the Handicapped.

Bradley, V.J., & Knoll, J. (n.d.). *Shifting paradigms in services to people with developmental disabilities*. Cambridge, MA: Human Services Research Institute.

Bright, R.W., & Wright, J.M.C. (1986). Community-based services: The impact on mothers of children with disabilities. *Australia and New Zealand Journal of Development Disabilities, 12*(4), 223–228.

Browne, S.E., Connors, D., & Stern, N. (Eds.). (1985). *With the power of each breath: A disabled women's anthology*. Pittsburgh, PA: Cleis Press.

Campling, J. (Ed.). (1981). *Images of ourselves: Women with disabilities talking*. London: Routledge & Kegan Paul.

Children's Defense Fund. (1974). *Children out of school in America*. Cambridge, MA: Author.

Cole, S.S. (1984). Facing the challenges of sexual abuse in persons with disabilities. *Sexuality and Disability*, 7(3/4), 71–88.

Craine, L.S., Henson, C.E., Colliver, J.A., & McLelan, D.G. (1988). Prevalence of a history of sexual abuse among female psychiatric patients in a state hospital system. *Hospital and Community Psychiatry*, 39(3), 300–304.

Cross, T.L. (1988, Fall). Services to minority populations: Cultural competence continuum. *Focal Point*, 3(1), 1–4.

Czajka, J.L. (1984). *Digest of data on persons with disabilities*. Washington, DC: National Institute of Handicap Research, Office of Special Education and Research.

Davila, R.R. (1991, Spring). Goals for improving services to minority individuals with disabilities [Special Issue on Disability and People from Minority Backgrounds]. *OSERS News in Print*, 3(4), 2–5.

Deegan, M.J., & Brooks, N.A. (Eds.). (1985). *Women and disability: The double handicap*. New Brunswick, NJ: Transaction Books.

Devore, W., & Schlesinger, E.G. (1981). *Ethnic-sensitive social work practice*. St. Louis: C.V. Mosby.

Disability Statistics Program. (1992, May). People with work disability in the U.S. *Disability Studies Abstract*, No. 4, 1–4. San Francisco: University of California, San Francisco.

Ellis, G., Lee, G., & Paterson, L. (1978). Supervision and conformity: A cross-cultural analysis of parental socialization values. *American Journal of Sociology*, 84, 386–403.

Fine, M., & Asch, A. (1981). Disabled women: Sexism without the pedestal. *Journal of Sociology and Social Welfare*, 8(2), 233–248.

Fine, M., & Asch, A. (Eds.). (1988). *Women with disabilities: Essays in psychology, culture, and politics*. Philadelphia: Temple University Press.

Finger, A. (1985). Claiming all of our bodies: Reproductive rights and disability. In S.E. Brown, D. Connors, & N. Stern (Eds.), *With the power of each breath: A disability women's anthology* (pp. 292–307). Pittsburgh, PA: Cleis Press.

Gillespie, P., & Fink, A. (1974). The influence of sexism on education of handicapped children. *Exceptional Children*, 41(3), 159–162.

Goffman, E. (1963). *Stigma: Notes on the management of spoiled identity*. Englewood Cliffs, NJ: Prentice Hall.

Gollnick, D.M., & Chinn, P.C. (1990). *Multicultural education in a pluralistic society* (3rd ed.). New York: Macmillan.

Green, J.W. (1982). *Cultural awareness in the human services*. Englewood Cliffs, NJ: Prentice Hall.

Hannaford, S. (1985). *Living outside inside: A disabled woman's experience: Towards a social and political perspective*. Berkeley, CA: Canterbury Press.

Hanson, M.J. (1992). Ethnic, cultural, and language diversity in intervention settings. In E.W. Lynch & M.J. Hanson (Eds.), *Developing cross-cultural competence: A guide for working with young children and their families* (pp. 3–18). Baltimore: Paul H. Brookes Publishing Co.

Harry, B. (1992). *Cultural diversity, families, and the special education system: Communication and empowerment*. New York: Teachers College Press.

Hill, J.W., Hill, M., Wehman, P., Banks, P.D., Pendleton, P., & Britt, C. (1985). Demographic analysis related to successful job retention for competitively employed persons who are mentally retarded. In P. Wehman & J.W. Hill (Eds.), *Competitive employment for persons with mental retardation: From research to practice* (Vol. I). Richmond: Rehabilitation Research and Training Center, Virginia Commonwealth University.

Hill, B.K., Lakin, K.C., Bruininks, R.H., Amado, A.N., Anderson, D.J., & Copher, J.I. (1989). *Living in the community: A comparative study of foster homes and small group homes for people with mental retardation* (Report No. 28). Minneapolis: University of Minnesota, Center for Residential and Community Services.

Hodge, F., & Edmonds, R. (1988). *Socio-cultural aspects of disability: A three area survey of disabled American Indians*. Tucson, AZ: Native American Research and Training Center.

Hutchison, P. (1990). *Making friends: Developing relationships between people with a disability and other members of the community*. Toronto, Ontario, Canada: The G. Allan Roeher Institute.

Jones, R.L. (Ed.). (1976). *Mainstreaming and the minority child*. Reston, VA: The Council for Exceptional Children.

Kalyanpur, M. (1988). *"We look after our own": The impact of cultural differences on service delivery*. Unpublished research apprenticeship, Syracuse University, Division of Special Education and Rehabilitation, Syracuse, New York.

Kalyanpur, M., & Rao, S.S. (1991). Empowering low-income black families of handicapped children. *American Journal of Orthopsychiatry, 61*(4), 523–532.

Kerbo, H.R. (1983). *Social stratification and inequality: Class conflict in the United States*. New York: McGraw-Hill.

Knoll, J., & Ford, A. (1987). Beyond caregiving: A reconceptualization of the role of the residential service provider. In S.J. Taylor, D. Biklen, & J. Knoll (Eds.), *Community integration for people with severe disabilities* (pp. 129–146). New York: Teachers College Press.

Kraus, L.E., & Stoddard, S. (1989). *Chartbook on disability in the United States*. Washington, DC: U.S. National Institute on Disability and Rehabilitation Research.

Kregel, J., & Wehman, P. (1989). An analysis of the employment outcomes of young adults with mental retardation. In P. Wehman & J. Kregel (Eds.), *Supported employment for persons with disabilities: Focus on excellence* (pp. 257–267). New York: Human Sciences Press.

Kutza, E.A. (1985). Benefits for the disabled: How beneficial for women? In M.J. Deegan & N.A. Brooks (Eds.), *Women and disability: The double handicap* (pp. 68–86). New Brunswick, NJ: Transaction Books.

Locust, C. (1988). Wounding the spirit: Discrimination and traditional American Indian belief systems. *Harvard Educational Review, 58*(3), 315–330.

Longo, R.E., & Gochenour, C. (1981). Sexual assault of handicapped individuals. *Journal of Rehabilitation, 47*, 24–27.

Lynch, E.W., & Hanson, M.J. (Eds.). (1992). *Developing cross-cultural competence: A guide for working with young children and their families*. Baltimore: Paul H. Brookes Publishing Co.

Maheady, L., Towne, R., Algozzine, B., Mercer, J., & Ysseldyke, J. (1983). Minority overrepresentation: A case for alternative practices prior to referral. *Learning Disability Quarterly, 6*, 448–456.

Marcos, L.R. (1986, April). *Understanding ethnicity in serving Hispanic mentally disabled*. Paper presented at the Conference on Quality of Care, New York State Commission on Quality of Care for the Mentally Disabled, Albany, New York.

Matthews, G.F. (1983). *Voices from the shadows: Women with disabilities speak out*. Toronto, Ontario, Canada: The Women's Educational Press.

Mercer, J.R. (1973). *Labeling the mentally retarded: Clinical and social system perspectives on mental retardation*. Berkeley: University of California Press.

Meyer, L.H., Peck, C.A., & Brown, L. (Eds.). (1991). *Critical issues in the lives of people with severe disabilities*. Baltimore: Paul H. Brookes Publishing Co.

Minow, M. (1990). *Making all the difference: Inclusion, exclusion, and American law*. Ithaca, NY: Cornell University Press.

Moon, M.S., Inge, K.J., Wehman, P., Brooke, V., & Barcus, J.M. (1990). *Helping persons with severe mental retardation get and keep employment: Supported employment issues and strategies*. Baltimore: Paul H. Brookes Publishing Co.

Mudrick, N.A. (1988). Disabled women and public policies for income support. In M. Fine & A. Asch (Eds.), *Women with disabilities: Essays in psychology, culture, and politics* (pp. 245–268). Philadelphia: Temple University Press.

Musick, J.L. (1984). Patterns of institutional sexual abuse. *Response to Violence in the Family and Sexual Assault*, 7(3), 1–11.

O'Connor, S. (1993). "I'm not Indian anymore": The challenge of providing culturally sensitive services to American Indians. In J.A. Racino, P. Walker, S. O'Connor, & S.J. Taylor (Eds.), *Housing, support, and community: Choices and strategies for adults with disabilities* (pp. 313–331). Baltimore: Paul H. Brookes Publishing Co.

Olion, L. (1988). Enhancing the involvement of black parents of adolescents with handicaps. In A.A. Ortiz & B.A. Ramirez (Eds.), *Schools and the culturally diverse exceptional student: Promising practices and future directions* (pp. 96–103). Reston, VA: The Council for Exceptional Children.

Ortiz, A.A., & Ramirez, B.A. (Eds.). (1989). *Schools and the culturally diverse exceptional student: Promising practices and future directions*. Reston, VA: The Council for Exceptional Children.

O'Toole, C.J. (1990). Violence and sexual assault plague many disabled women. *New Directions for Women*, January/February, 19(17).

Racino, J.A., O'Connor, S., Walker, P., & Taylor, S.J. (1991). *Personalized supports project: Innovations in family support in New York State*. Unpublished confidential research report.

Rose, S.J. (1986). *The American profile poster: Who owns what, who makes how much, who works where, & who lives with whom*. New York: Pantheon Books.

Rosenthal, E., & Carty, L.A. (1988). *Impediments to services and advocacy for black and Hispanic people with mental illness*. Washington, DC: Mental Health Law Project.

Rubin, L.R. (1976). *Worlds of pain: Life in the working class family*. New York: Basic Books.

Russo, N.F., & Jansen, M.A. (1988). Women, work, and disability: Opportunities and challenges. In M. Fine & A. Asch (Eds.), *Women with disabilities: Essays in psychology, culture, and politics* (pp. 229–244). Philadelphia: Temple University Press.

Sank, C., & Lafleche, E. (1981). Special sisters: Health issues for mentally retarded women. *Off Our Backs*, 11(5), 26–27.

Sarason, S.B., & Doris, J. (1979). *Educational handicap, public policy, and social history: A broadened perspective on mental retardation*. New York: The Free Press.

Scheerenberger, R.C. (1987). *A history of mental retardation: A quarter century of promise*. Baltimore: Paul H. Brookes Publishing Co.

Schur, C.L., Bernstein, A.B., & Berk, M.L. (1987). The importance of distinguishing Hispanic subpopulations in the use of medical care. *Medical Care*, 35(7), 627–641.

Senn, C.Y. (1988). *Vulnerable: Sexual abuse and people with an intellectual handicap*. Toronto, Ontario, Canada: The G. Allan Roeher Institute.

Shaul, S., Dowling, P.J., & Laden, B.F. (1985). Like other women: Perspectives of mothers with physical disabilities. In M.J. Deegan & N.A. Brooks (Eds.), *Women and disability: The double handicap* (pp. 133–142). New Brunswick, NJ: Transaction Books.

Simon, B.L. (1988). Never-married old women and disability: A majority experience. In M. Fine & A. Asch (Eds.), *Women with disabilities: Essays in psychology, culture, and politics* (pp. 215–225). Philadelphia: Temple University Press.

Sleeter, C.E. (Ed.). (1991). *Empowerment through multicultural education*. Albany: State University of New York Press.

Sleeter, C.E., & Grant, C.A. (1987). An analysis of multicultural education in the United States. *Harvard Educational Review*, 57(4), 421–444.

Smith, M.J., Caro, F.G., & McKaig, K. (1987). *Caring for the developmentally disabled child at home: The experiences of low-income families*. New York: Community Service Society of New York.

Smull, M. (1989). *Crisis in the community*. Alexandria, VA: National Association of State Mental Retardation Program Directors, Inc.

Sobsey, D., Gray, S., Wells, D., Pyper, D., & Reimer-Heck, B. (1991). *Disability, sex-*

uality, and abuse: An annotated bibliography. Baltimore: Paul H. Brookes Publishing Co.

Stack, C.B. (1974). *All our kin: Strategies for survival in a black community*. New York: Harper & Row.

Stefan, S. (1987). Women in the mental health system. *Update: The Mental Health Law Project, 6*(4/5), 4–5.

Sterne, D. (1991). *Challenges in health care. A chartbook perspective, 1991*. Princeton, NJ: Robert Wood Johnson Foundation.

Suazo, A. (1986). The emerging role of the disabled Hispanics. In S. Walker, F.Z. Belgrave, A.M. Banner, & R.W. Nicholls (Eds.), *Equal to the challenge: Perspectives, problems, and strategies in the rehabilitation of the nonwhite disabled* (pp. 70–72). Washington, DC: Proceedings of the National Conference of the Howard University Model to Improve Rehabilitation Services to Minority Populations with Handicapping Conditions.

Taylor, S.J. (in preparation). *The other side of the tracks: Disability, poverty, and policy*. Unpublished manuscript.

Taylor, S.J., Bogdan, R., & Racino, J.A. (Eds.). (1991). *Life in the community: Case studies of organizations supporting people in the community*. Baltimore: Paul H. Brookes Publishing Co.

Taylor, S.J., Lutfiyya, Z.M., Racino, J.A., Walker, P., & Knoll, J. (1986). *An evaluation of Connecticut's training home program*. Syracuse, NY: The Center on Human Policy, Syracuse University.

Tomlinson, S. (1982). *A sociology of special education*. London: Routledge & Kegan Paul.

Trattner, W.I. (1984). *From poor law to welfare state* (3rd ed.). New York: The Free Press.

Traustadottir, R. (1990a). *Constructing a normal family: Disability and family life*. Unpublished research report, Center on Human Policy, Syracuse University, Syracuse, New York.

Traustadottir, R. (1990b). *Women with disabilities: Issues, resources, connections*. Syracuse, NY: Center on Human Policy, Syracuse University.

Traustadottir, R. (1991). Mothers who care: Gender, disability and family life. *Journal of Family Issues, 12*(2), 211–228.

U.S. Department of Commerce. (1992). *Statistical abstract of the United States 1992: The national data book*. Washington, DC: Author.

Walker, H.A. (1988). Black-white differences in marriage and family patterns. In S.M. Dornbusch & M.H. Strober (Eds.), *Feminism, children and the new families* (pp. 87–112). New York: Guilford Press.

Watson, J.D. (1984). Talking about the best kept secret: Sexual abuse and children with disabilities. *Exceptional Parent, 14*, 16–20.

Wehman, P. (1993). Employment opportunities and career development. In P. Wehman (Ed.), *The ADA mandate for social change* (pp. 45–68). Baltimore: Paul H. Brookes Publishing Co.

Willis, W. (1992). Families with African American roots. In E.W. Lynch & M.J. Hanson (Eds.), *Developing cross-cultural competence: A guide for working with young children and their families* (pp. 121–150). Baltimore: Paul H. Brookes Publishing Co.

Wilson, P.G., O'Reilly, M.F., & Rusch, F.R. (1991). Analysis of minority-status supported employees in relation to placement approach and selected outcomes. *Mental Retardation, 29*(6), 329–333.

Wolfensberger, W. (1975). *The origin and nature of our institutional models*. Syracuse, NY: Human Policy Press.

Women and Disability Awareness Project. (1989). *Building community: A manual exploring issues of women and disability*. New York: Educational Equity Concepts.

Yates, J.R. (1989). Demography as it affects special education. In A.A. Ortiz & B.A. Ramirez (Eds.), *Schools and the culturally diverse exceptional student: Promising practices and future directions* (pp. 1–5). Reston, VA: The Council for Exceptional Children.

— Chapter 17 ——————————

Legal Guardianship

The Implications of Law, Procedure, and Policy for the Lives of Persons with Developmental Disabilities

C. David Flower

———————————————————————

One of the primary ways of describing adulthood would be to say that adults are competent, self-determined individuals, who have the right to make their own life choices. These choices may be sensible, legal, ethical, and moral, or they may be destructive, ill-advised, or illegal. In either case, individual choice is a privilege of adulthood; it is assumed that adults are competent to choose, even to choose foolishly. In cases in which an adult may *not* be perceived as competent, the law provides for a relationship of *legal guardianship* to protect the best interests of that individual. *Legal guardianship* is a relationship in which an individual who is declared legally incompetent has all or some of his or her individual rights and decision-making authority removed and invested in a court-appointed guardian.

Citizens with developmental disabilities have long been perceived as lacking in some or all of the skills necessary for independent adult life (Beyer & Howell, 1988; Weeks, 1920). In the past, persons with cognitive disabilities, perceived to be "mentally deficient," were often declared legally incompetent at early ages, and a guardian (either a private individual or a state agency) was appointed. In the United States, such determination usually facilitated institutional placement (Levy, 1965; Parry, 1985b).

During the last three decades, there has been an increasing movement toward deinstitutionalization and community integration. More often, children with developmental disabilities are being raised by their natural families and educated in

Preparation of this chapter was supported by Cooperative Agreement #H33B89948 between the National Institute on Disability and Rehabilitation Research (NIDRR) and the Research and Training Center on Residential Services and Community Living and the Institute on Community Integration/UAP at the University of Minnesota.

community schools. Deinstitutionalization and community integration have resulted in a changing set of issues surrounding the legal status of individuals with developmental disabilities. When children reach the age of 18, they are assumed to be competent adults in the eyes of the law (Burge, 1991; Scott & Siuta, 1979). For parents of children with developmental disabilities, a legal determination of guardianship on or after their child's 18th birthday may be the only way to ensure that their child's best interests are protected in adulthood. If such a determination of guardianship is not made, adults with developmental disabilities may be taken advantage of by individuals who do *not* have their best interests in mind, and parents may find themselves with little legal authority concerning habilitational, residential, or medical decisions regarding their child (Beyer & Howell, 1988; Burge, 1991; Woody, 1974). In a society in which residential and community-based programs have proliferated, institutional placement is no longer attractive or readily available, and the extended family has eroded (Apolloni, 1987). A determination of legal guardianship after evaluating a person's adulthood has become almost a rite of passage for individuals with developmental disabilities. For example, Kritzer (1992) found that approximately 35% of the individuals with developmental disabilities who had guardianship hearings in Wisconsin were under age 25, and nearly 79% were under age 50.

The determination of incompetence and the appointment of a legal guardian can have an enormous impact on a person's life. Cases that involve parental decisions to withhold surgery, nourishment, or potentially life-saving treatment from infants with severe disabilities have focused much attention on *disputed* guardianship, as have cases involving limiting medical treatment for very elderly or permanently unconscious persons (Herr, 1983; Hudson, 1988; Kindred, 1976). In most instances in which a person is given a guardian, such dramatic, life-or-death decisions are not immediate. Rather, guardianship is a simple fact of life that—on a day-to-day basis—may not seem of great importance. It is, however, a serious step that has many moral, ethical, and social implications. Increasingly, services for individuals with developmental disabilities take as fundamental aims not just community integration, but also self-advocacy and self-determination (Wehmeyer & Berkobien, 1991). In light of this, any legal provision that may reinforce stereotypical views of persons with developmental disabilities as incompetent, incapable, and not likely to be self-determined individuals must be examined (Brechin & Swain, 1988; Hudson, 1988). As Kindred (1976) has noted:

> Important and appealing policy goals are in tension in the guardianship area. The first policy goal is protection against exploitation of mentally retarded citizens. The second goal is freedom of the mentally retarded citizen, with opportunity to develop as an independent member of the community. (p. 66)

Legal guardianship is an issue that is important on both individual and policy levels. For individuals, guardianship status makes legal claims about their competency and limits their right to self-determination. On a policy level, conceptions of competence and procedures for determining competency have had historical effects on the delivery of services. Rights of individual choice and self-determination are ultimately validated in any society only so far as they are legally *granted*. The facts, implications, and underlying beliefs of legal guardianship must, therefore, be examined if we are to be concerned with supporting all individuals in becoming self-active, self-advocating, self-determined citizens.

This chapter explores the tension that Kindred points out. Although not intended to be a comprehensive survey of current law and practice, some of the ethical issues and practical difficulties that arise out of contemporary guardianship law and policy are examined in this chapter. The discussion is divided into three sections. First, a description of the legal relationship of guardian and ward is provided. Topics discussed include types of guardianship, powers and duties of guardians, and implications of guardianship arrangements for the personal freedom and actions of persons with developmental disabilities. The second section describes legal procedures for determining guardianship, including petitioning the court, hearings, determination, restoration to capacity, and monitoring policies. The third section discusses the legal criteria for determining competency, particularly those criteria that relate to persons with cognitive disabilities. The chapter closes with a discussion of guardianship status and individual competency in light of changing knowledge and views of persons with developmental disabilities, and discusses changes to current guardianship policies that might more effectively support the unique needs of individuals while affirming the right to self-determination.

THE GUARDIAN AND WARD RELATIONSHIP

In the United States, guardianship law is a prerogative of the individual states; therefore, policies and procedures vary. Although the process by which competency is determined and guardianship assigned has varied both historically and regionally (Hurme, Parry, & Coleman, 1991; Parry, 1985b; Sales, Powell, & Van Duizend, 1982), the essential features of the guardian–ward relationship have remained remarkably consistent.

Guardianship practices have roots in medieval times, and were originally formulated to ensure that family estates would not be squandered by incompetent heirs (Parry, 1985b; Sales et al., 1982). In more recent times, an increasingly stated concern has been that guardians act on behalf of and advocate for the best interests of wards. Another concept of guardianship is that it is a process of "substitute decision making" or "substituted judgment," in which the guardian attempts to make choices that the ward would make if the ward was legally competent (Casasanto, Simon, & Roman, 1990; Zwyer, 1990).

Given these conceptions, guardianship should not be viewed as a removal of rights justified by a person's alleged incompetence, but rather, as a relationship that ensures that the civic and individual rights of the ward are competently protected by a surrogate decision maker. As Parry and Beck (1990) note:

We do not accept the validity of the argument that the substantive rights of competent and incompetent persons are different. We argue—and the current case law supports the view—that the rights are the same, but how the right is exercised differs. The key legal difference between self-determination for competent and incompetent persons is that competent individuals can make their own decisions, while incompetent persons need substitute decision-makers to help exercise their rights. (p. 103)

Therefore, it can be said that determination is vested in a guardian, and final legal authority for making *choices* is what a ward loses. Whether such a loss constitutes a loss of rights, *in fact*, is a question that is addressed in a subsequent section.

Official appointment of a legal guardian is not, of course, necessary for most individuals. In general, children are considered natural wards of their parents until they reach the age of 18 (Rodgers, 1984; Woody, 1974). Guardianship is typically determined for children only when custody is in dispute, or when an outside individual or agency believes that the parents are acting contrary to the best interests of their child and a change of guardianship is requested (Hudson, 1988). When children turn 18, they are assumed to be competent to retain their own guardianship and, unless a contrary claim is made before the court, are automatically conferred full civil and legal rights as adults. A determination of guardianship is made only if the parents, or some other party, petition the court, declaring that the individual is *not* capable of making all life decisions (Scott & Siuta, 1979).

Types of Guardianship

Most guardians are private individuals, often relatives of the proposed ward, who are deemed able and likely to protect the ward's best interests. Such guardianships are referred to as *private guardianships* (Scott & Siuta, 1979). An increasingly common form of private guardianship is *corporate guardianship*, in which a private agency provides guardianship services for individuals who have no otherwise qualified guardian. Guardianship may be provided by nonprofit social service agencies, profit-making agencies that exist solely to provide guardianship services, or individual professional guardians (Apolloni, 1987).

Approximately a dozen states have provisions for *public guardianship* for cases in which no suitable private individual or agency is willing to become guardian of the proposed ward (Parry, 1985b). In a public guardianship, guardianship authority is vested in a state agency. In Minnesota, for instance, public guardianships reside with the commissioner of the Department of Human Services, with actual day-to-day guardianship responsibilities carried out at the county level by case managers (Burge, 1991; Scott & Siuta, 1979). In most states in which there is public guardianship, such guardianships are only established for persons with mental illness or mental retardation (Burge, 1991; Hurme et al., 1991; Parry, 1985b). In a 1986 study authorized by the Minnesota legislature, approximately 6,800 adults with developmental disabilities were found to be wards of the state (Minnesota Guardianship Task Force, 1986). This represents about 40% of the estimated 17,000 adults with developmental disabilities who were receiving case management services in Minnesota at that time.

Whether a guardianship is private or public, the ward does not necessarily lose *all* rights of self-determination. In both past and current law, guardianship can be granted over the ward's *estate*, the ward's *person*, or over both the estate and the person. *Guardianship of the estate* grants to the guardian legal decision-making authority over the ward's property, assets, and finances (Parry, 1985b). A guardian of the estate (or guardian of the property) is assigned the authority to manage financial affairs of the ward, including bank accounts, investments, and property; enter into contracts for the ward; pay debts; make transactions, and so on (Parry, 1985b). Guardianships of estates have long been in use to protect the property of individuals deemed incompetent to manage their own affairs. In the past, such guardianships have been vested in family members of ill, young, or elderly persons who may function well in many life areas, but require protection from financial mismanagement or exploitation (Kindred, 1976; Parry, 1985a; Sales et al., 1982).

Guardianship of the person grants the guardian the authority to make everyday life decisions regarding the ward. Such authority is quite broad. It usually includes authority to make decisions about medical treatment, place of residence, educational programs, and virtually all other major and minor *personal* decisions that an individual might make (Parry, 1985b). Guardianship of the person implies that the ward is legally incompetent to make most personal decisions.

In about two-thirds of the states, guardianship confers to the guardian all decision-making authority over either the ward's person, estate, or both. Guardianships of this type are referred to as *plenary* guardianships (Sales et al., 1982). Plenary guardianship automatically invests in the guardian virtually all decision-making authority regarding the ward's person and/or property (Parry, 1985b).

Conservatorship and *limited guardianship* are less encompassing than plenary guardianship. These forms of guardianship have somewhat different meanings across states, but both are generally intended to be used for individuals who are perceived as competent to make decisions of particular kinds, but require a surrogate decision maker in other areas. Therefore, conservatorship and limited guardianship are less restrictive protective relationships in which the conservator or guardian is granted *limited* decision making authority in clearly specified domains (Maser, 1991; Parry, 1985b; Scott & Siuta, 1979). A person under conservatorship or limited guardianship may, for example, be quite capable of meeting his or her own daily living needs, but may not be able to make appropriate decisions regarding personal finances or medical needs. In other words, conservatorships and limited guardianships are typically used for individuals with good independent living skills who require assistance in *property*, rather than personal, decisions (Sales et al., 1982).

Conservatorship differs conceptually from both plenary and limited guardianships in that it does not usually imply legal incompetence of the conservatee. Rather, there is an assumption of *incapacity* that does not affect all life areas. The conservatee, therefore, typically retains certain civil and individual rights that a ward does not, such as the right to vote (Maser, 1991).

Authority and Obligations of Guardians

The conferral of guardianship of one individual to another has two effects: it takes away legal authority of the ward and it invests certain powers and responsibilities with the guardian. Although there has been an historical trend toward greater individualization of guardianship arrangements, limitations on powers of guardians, and more systematic monitoring (Parry, 1985b), the power of a guardian over a ward is still roughly comparable to that of a parent over a child (Kindred, 1976; Parry, 1985a). In fact, some states have historically defined the authority of guardians as identical to that of parents over minor children (Parry, 1985b).

Establishment of guardianship places clear restrictions on the civil rights of the ward. Wards, in contrast to conservatees, typically lose the right to vote in public elections (Parry, 1985a; Scott & Siuta, 1979) and may lose the right to marry (Scott & Siuta, 1979). Wards may also lose the right to enter into contracts and to obtain certain government licensures, such as driver's licenses (Parry, 1985a). In addition, unless stated otherwise in the court determination, a ward typically loses legal authority in making decisions about medical treatment, place of residence, and therapeutic or habilitational programming.

In the past, guardians often had the legal authority to order sterilization of wards (Kindred, 1976; Parry, 1985a), but now such a decision typically requires a hearing and a court order (Burge, 1991; Scott & Siuta, 1979). Even a court hearing, though, may not guarantee that a ward's best interests are being protected when sterilization is requested. Through interviews with legal and medical professionals, service providers, agency administrators, and educators, Brantlinger (1992) found that decisions regarding sterilization were often characterized by lack of information, lack of communication among involved parties, and personal attitudes about sexuality and disability.

Limits on wards' decision-making authority translate into certain obligations for guardians. Guardians of the person are expected to ensure that the ward is provided with an acceptable level of medical care, housing, clothing, and nourishment (Parry, 1985b; Scott & Siuta, 1979). They are also expected to represent the ward's best interests in educational or habilitational planning, and may be required to advocate for the ward and obtain assistance in legal proceedings. Guardians of the estate are expected to protect the ward's financial affairs and property faithfully and honestly and, typically, must account for any transactions or other financial dealings that they make in the ward's name (Parry, 1985b).

Implications of Guardianship

In general, the limitations of wards' authority and rights affect most decisions that require *informed consent*. Since a conferral of guardianship implies that the ward is not competent to make decisions, the right to make any choice or action that requires informed consent is potentially removed from the ward. Guardianship, then, is a serious step because it places restrictions on most actions that are typically thought of as *adult*. For adults with developmental disabilities, many of whom will, at some point, have a judicial determination of guardianship, rights of individual choice and self-determination are validated only so far as they are legally *granted*.

There are several potential problems with *public* guardianship, which has, in the past, been a frequent arrangement for individuals with developmental disabilities (Levy, 1965). If guardianship services can be seen as a continuum of more to less restrictive substitute decision-making relationships, public guardianship is the most restrictive alternative to complete self-determination. In public guardianships, authority to make very important life decisions is generally delegated to social workers, case managers, or other social services employees who may be considerably less knowledgeable about the desires, needs, and best interests of their wards than would a private guardian. Given the staff shortages and heavy caseloads in many social service agencies, caseworkers are often not able to be strong, knowledgeable advocates for the individual interests of the adults they serve (Scott & Siuta, 1979).

Further, agencies responsible for the guardianship of public wards may lack the resources and knowledge to provide effective guardianship services. A 1986 survey conducted by the Minnesota Guardianship Task Force, an investigative committee established by the Minnesota legislature, indicated that many county caseworkers lack effective training and monitoring. Two-thirds of Minnesota county social service agency directors who were surveyed reported that guardianship duties and responsibilities were not specified in caseworker job descriptions; 87% reported that training in guardianship functions was not provided within 90 days to new caseworkers with guardianship duties; 80% stated that staff guardianship performance was not regularly reviewed (Minnesota Guardianship Task Force, 1986).

Public guardianship also carries the potential for a very serious conflict of interest if, as is usually the case, the agency that retains guardianship is the same agency that provides, funds, or administers services (American Bar Association, 1989; Apolloni, 1987; Minnesota Guardianship Task Force, 1986; Scott & Siuta, 1979). In this case, advocacy for the best interests of the ward may conflict with agency policy, priorities, or funding allocations. If agency policies prevail, the best interests of the ward may not be protected.

For these reasons, public guardianship is generally seen as a last resort, to be sought only when no suitable person is willing to serve as a private guardian (Burge, 1991; Parry, 1985b; Sales et al., 1982). In fact, only 13 states have statutory provisions for public guardianship (Sales et al., 1982). This form of guardianship, by both law and policy, is the most restrictive option of a continuum of more or less restrictive alternatives for substitute decision making, even more so than private plenary guardianship, private limited guardianship or conservatorship, or no guardian at all.

States vary widely in the extent to which this continuum is readily available to adults with developmental disabilities who may require guardianship. Less than half of the states have guardianship statutes that explicitly call for limited guardianship where appropriate (Sales et al., 1982). Although most states allow judges to use their discretion to limit authority of guardians to only those areas in which the ward is incompetent, a 1978 American Bar Association study concluded that judges rarely order limited guardianships (Parry, 1985b). This implies that many adults, who may be well able to manage their own affairs in certain areas, may lack the *legal* authority to do so.

Limited guardianship may not always be perceived as an option by service providers or by parents. Mesibov, Conover, and Saur (1980) reported that, after institution of a limited guardianship law in North Carolina in 1978, fewer than 10 adults with developmental disabilities were granted limited guardianships by 1980. The authors reported that this was apparently due to a variety of informational and attitudinal problems. Parents of adult children with developmental disabilities expressed concern that limited guardianship would lessen their influence in making life decisions for their children. Court clerks, who conduct guardianship hearings in North Carolina, held generally negative views of limited guardianship, expressing that the law was "impractical" and that an adult could not be "partially competent" (Sales et al., 1982, p. 224). Finally, all groups interviewed (parents, clerks, residential staff, social service workers, mental retardation specialists, and adults with developmental disabilities) tended to express unwillingness to petition for limited guardianships.

A similar underuse of limited guardianship has recently been found in a study of private guardianship proceedings in Wisconsin (Kritzer, 1992). In a survey of court records in 12 counties, Kritzer found that in only 2.5% of guardianship orders were the powers of guardians limited in any way; wards were allowed to retain rights in only 7% of the orders. However, in very few cases did courts deny guardianship requests or modify requested guardian powers or responsibilities. It appeared that Wisconsin courts did little to tailor guardianship arrangements to the particular needs and abilities of proposed wards, and provided little screening and review of proposed guardianships.

Conservatorship is another potential option for adults who may need surrogate decision making in certain domains, but who are capable of exercising full individual and civil rights in other areas. Most states do provide for conservatorships for adults with developmental disabilities (Sales et al., 1982). As is the case with limited guardianships, it is not clear whether conservatorships are well-utilized in cases in which they are appropriate. Minnesota Department of Human Services data indicate that, in January 1992, less than 9% of 2,649 adults with developmental disabilities who received home or community-based waivered services in Minnesota had a private or public conservator. Approximately 34% of these persons were wards of the state (i.e., under public guardianship), approximately 37% were wards of their parents, and about 13.5% had neither a guardian or a conservator (Franczyk, 1992). It is, of course, difficult to say whether these figures accurately represent all adults in Minnesota who are receiving case management services, much less all of the more than 100,000 persons with developmental disabilities in the state. Nevertheless, it is clear that, for this particular sample, conservatorship was not frequently used as an alternative to full guardianship.

These findings indicate that in all likelihood, the continuum of least restrictive alternatives, theoretically available to provide surrogate decision making for adults with developmental disabilities, often fails to adequately address the balance between protection and freedom (Kindred, 1976). Less restrictive alternatives to full guardianship that may be appropriate for many adults with developmental disabilities apparently are not always readily used, and individual's rights may be restricted more than is necessary for their best interests. This is not to imply that this failure is due to bad intentions or the mistakes of parents, social service workers, or judges who hold competency hearings. Rather, it can be argued that the legal *procedures* for determining guardianship and the *criteria* for determining incompetency remain tied to an institutional model of service and inadequate conceptions of competency.

LEGAL PROCEDURES FOR DETERMINING GUARDIANSHIP

The determination of competency and the assignment of guardianship is a legal process, which operates by rules of evidence and due process. The legal procedures involved have remained remarkably consistent over time. In 1935, Taylor described the determination of public or private guardianship as a process involving the following steps: *petition, notice, hearing, appointment,* and *termination* or *restoration* (Taylor, 1935). This basic procedure is virtually identical to the one currently used in most states.

Petition

As noted previously, any person who is 18 years of age is assumed to be legally competent unless found by a court to be incompetent (Scott & Siuta, 1979). The first step in assigning guardianship is to petition in court (typically, the local probate court) that the individual is incompetent and requires a guardian (Sales et al., 1982). In almost all states, "any interested party" is allowed by statute to initiate guardianship proceedings (Parry, 1985b; Scott & Siuta, 1979). In recent years, cases of disputed guardianship have tested the meaning of any interested party. For example, in the 1983 "Baby Jane Doe" case in New York, the state Court of Appeals (the state high court) ruled that the attorney general's office (supported by the New York Civil Liberties Union and several advocacy groups for persons with disabilities) was not entitled to initiate guardianship proceedings for an infant born with spina bifida whose parents had decided to withhold potentially life-saving corrective surgery (Hentoff, 1991; Parry, 1985b). Guardianship proceedings for most *adults* with developmental disabilities, however, are typically initiated by parents or other relatives, usually to ensure that parents retain legal rights to make residential and habilitational decisions for their children (Beyer & Howell, 1988; Burge, 1991).

Hearing

Once a petition has been accepted, the court sets a hearing date and notifies the potential ward and, usually, his or her nearest relatives or current caregivers.

About two-thirds of the states require that the potential ward's competency be evaluated prior to the hearing. Evaluations of this type are typically conducted by one or more physicians, a psychiatrist or psychologist, and/or a social worker (Sales et al., 1982). Proceedings in the state of Minnesota are fairly typical. A formal evaluation is *not* a statutory requirement in cases of private guardianship proceedings, although individual courts may request evaluations. In cases in which the Minnesota Department of Human Services is asked to become public guardian, evaluation is required. Evaluations are conducted by a doctor, psychologist, and a social worker, who then make written recommendations to the commissioner which are introduced at the hearing (Scott & Siuta, 1979).

In almost all states, hearings are conducted by a judge, and potential wards are entitled to legal representation (Sales et al., 1982). Any evidence of incompetency is presented at the hearing. In most states, the potential ward is entitled to attend the hearing and, in some cases, to present contradictory evidence (i.e., evidence as to competency). In approximately half of the states the proposed ward is entitled to a jury trial (Parry, 1985b; Sales et al., 1982).

Determination

Guardianship is granted if, by the applicable standard of evidence, the proposed ward is found to be either "incompetent" or "incapacitated" and, therefore, unable to manage his or her own property or person. In making this determination, 41 states require some evidence of mental disability or illness in addition to evidence of incompetence (Hurme et al., 1991; Parry, 1985b). Only 13 states, however, have an established standard of evidence for determining incompetency (Parry, 1985b), while in 10 states, "clear and convincing" evidence must be presented that the proposed ward is incompetent. Other states require evidence "beyond a reasonable doubt," "that satisfies the judge," or has "the greater weight" (Maser, 1991; Parry, 1985b). The ordered guardianship typically becomes effective with the issuance of the determination.

Restoration to Capacity

Even though adults are assumed to be legally competent unless a petition is filed to the contrary, once a determination of incompetency is made, the ward is assumed incompetent unless a subsequent petition is filed to remove or modify the guardianship (Parry, 1985b; Scott & Siuta, 1979). The process of restoration to capacity typically resembles the original determination of incompetency. It is initiated by petition (which in most states may be initiated by any interested person, including the ward), followed by a hearing in which evidence is presented and a determination is made. Restoration may be either to full capacity, or to a less restrictive guardianship arrangement (Parry, 1985b).

Monitoring Procedures

Recently, increased attention has been paid to the supervisory role of courts after the granting of guardianship (Hurme et al., 1991). A primary concern in the past has been that guardians, because of the broad power they may have over the ward's property, be accountable for their management of that property (Hurme et al., 1991; Levy, 1965). Increasingly, guardians are also required to report periodically on how they have represented wards' *personal* interests (Hurme et al., 1991; Parry, 1985b).

Postdetermination monitoring is also important if the ward's needs change, or if a change in the guardianship arrangement is appropriate, such as a restoration to capacity or a lessening of restrictions on the ward's decision-making authority. More than 40 states require reports at least annually regarding the status of wards and court reviews of guardianship arrangements may be ordered as necessary, or, in some states, on a regular basis (Hurme et al., 1991).

Issues Concerning Guardianship Procedures

A number of issues are apparent in the procedures used to establish legal guardianship. The ostensible purpose of guardianship hearings is to determine the necessity of restricting the legal rights of particular individuals due to their particular incapacities or needs. Given this purpose, a hearing should ideally serve to evaluate evidence of both incapacity *and* of capabilities in order to fashion the most sensible, least restrictive guardianship arrangement. As noted above, however, many states do not even require comprehensive assessments of the needs and capabilities of proposed wards; nor do all states require the attendance of proposed wards, or make explicit provisions for wards to present evidence of competency. As Kritzer (1992) found in his survey of Wisconsin guardianship proceedings, there is little indication that courts use provided evidence to explore alternatives to full guardianship. In fact, it is questionable whether hearings actually serve as stringent reviews of proposals to limit individuals' rights through the establishment of guardianship.

Policies regarding follow-up and monitoring after the establishment of guardianship are also problematic. There is little evidence that courts are well-situated to actively monitor wards' needs. Even though most states require reports at least annually regarding the wards' guardianship needs, it is doubtful that county courts have the ability or resources to actively review such reports. It is unlikely that a monitoring system that acts primarily as a fulfillment of legal requirements, rather than as a proactive reassessment of the needs of individual wards, will be effective.

These procedural issues are *legal* questions that must be addressed by changes in state laws and by the adoption of standards for the provision of guardianship services. The need for changes in statutes and standards has been increasingly recognized and addressed by both government and private agencies (House of Representatives Select Committee on Aging, 1989; Hurme et al., 1991), as well as by advocacy groups for persons particularly likely to be perceived as incapacitated or incompetent, including those elderly who are suffering from dementia, individuals with mental illness, individuals who are chemically dependent, and adults with developmental disabilities (Hurme, 1990; Sales, Powell & Van Duizend, 1982). Unlike elderly persons with dementia, who also may require some form of guardianship, people with developmental disabilities have historically been assumed to *never* have been competent to live independently or to make or communicate personal decisions. Unlike persons with mental illness or chemical dependency, persons with developmental disabilities may be seen as basically "untreatable" rather than "temporarily incompetent." These issues point out a fundamental difficulty that faces persons with developmental disabilities in legal determinations of capacity: a legal rigidity in determining "competence" that may not reflect an individual's true or potential capacities. Clinical diagnostic criteria for mental retardation have increasingly reflected the interactive nature of disability, capability, and the nature of supports in an individual's environment, as well as growing knowledge that an individual's capabilities can change over his or her lifetime (American Association on Mental Retardation, 1992). However, as Anderer (1990) points out, determination of competency is a *legal* decision, not a clinical one, amd standards or criteria for legal capacity may well differ from clinical criteria for diagnosing specific disabilities. Any proposals for improvement of guardianship proceedings must take into account the legal criteria by which competency is judged. Procedural flaws are compounded by an all-or-nothing approach inherent in many of the legal standards for determining competency.

CRITERIA FOR DETERMINING COMPETENCY

One of the most fundamental changes in educational and habilitational services for individuals with developmental disabilities has been the recognition that cognitive impairment does not necessarily preclude learning, community participation, or personal growth. It is not clear, however, that criteria for determining legal competency have been particularly affected by this new understanding.

Historically, criteria for establishing incompetence reflected the belief that "mental deficiency" precluded self-determination and effective, competent action. For example, the original Minnesota Mental Retardation Protection Act of 1917, which codified private and public guardianship procedures, stated that guardianship was called for when a person was:

> so mentally defective as to be incapable of managing himself and his affairs, and to require supervision, control, and care for his own or the public welfare. (Weeks, 1920, p. 5)

There is little sense in the standard that people may be capable of managing *some* of their affairs or that they may require supervision or care in *some* life areas. Mental disability (or, in 1920, "feeble mindedness") is by this criteria an indicator of *global* incompetence. Criteria for determining legal competency were, by this standpoint, based largely on global indicators of mental disability, particularly IQ scores. Dr. F. Kuhlman, one-time director of a large public institution in Minnesota and an influential figure in the development of the 1917 Protection Act (Levy, 1965), wrote the following:

> There is no difference in opinion among experienced mental examiners who have used the mental test method together with other methods, concerning the reliability of the

mental test method as against all other methods. It is agreed that the former gives a far more reliable result than any other. A mistake very common in court procedure is the hearing of testimony by the defense to establish the fact that the case in question has not been regarded as feeble-minded by his associates, that he has been remuneratively employed and perhaps to the satisfaction of his employers, and so on. When all this has been established as a fact, as it sometimes can be, it proves nothing either in regard to the mental deficiency of the case, or the need of state guardianship. (Kuhlman, 1920, pp. 15–16)

Again, there is little room in this for partial competency—that is, competency to make decisions in some, but not all, life areas. These examples are cited not to disparage legislators and professionals who have worked with a different paradigm and knowledge-base concerning cognitive disability, but to pose the following questions: Have *legal* standards or criteria for determining incompetency changed greatly since 1920? Do current criteria represent our new understandings about the abilities of individuals with developmental disabilities, and do they afford room to determine guardianship arrangements that strike a sensible balance between protection from exploitation and undue restriction of freedom?

In fundamental ways, current criteria for determining legal competency do not, in fact, substantially differ in their focus on cognitive disability as an indicator of global incompetence. Parry (1985b) notes that current state guardianship statutes typically call for either a demonstrable, identifiable mental disability or illness, or a fairly general functional incompetency stemming from a mental impairment. The standard used in Nevada is fairly typical:

> "Incompetent" includes any person who, by reason of mental illness, mental deficiency, advanced age, weakness of mind or any other cause, is unable, without assistance, properly to manage and take care of himself or his property. (Nev. Stat. Ann. §159.019, cited in Hurme et al., 1991)

This standard is revealing because it equates mental disability with mental illness and age, and implies that such characteristics of an individual are likely to result in some degree of general inability to make responsible life choices. Similarly, Minnesota still uses, along with other criteria, a fairly rigid cut-off point, an IQ of 70, in determining whether to accept nominations for public guardianship of individuals with developmental disabilities (Levy, 1965; Minnesota Department of Human Services, 1990).

Legal standards for determining incompetency have, over time, become more concerned with defining and determining functional capacity. The current standard used in Minnesota's private guardianship statute defines an adult in need of guardianship of the person as:

> any adult person who is impaired to the extent of lacking sufficient understanding or capacity to make or communicate responsible personal decisions, and who has demonstrated deficits in behavior which evidence an inability to meet personal needs for medical care, nutrition, clothing, shelter, or safety. (Minnesota Statutes §525.24, Subd. 2)

With its functional competency orientation, this standard is a step in the right direction. It is important to note, though, that Minnesota's *public* guardianship statute, intended to be used only for adults with mental retardation, uses quite different criteria that do *not* strongly suggest a determination of functional capacity:

> The court shall order the appointment of the commissioner as guardian or conservator if it finds that: (1) the proposed ward or conservatee is a mentally retarded person . . . ; (2) the proposed ward is incapable of exercising specific legal rights . . . ; (3) the proposed ward or conservatee is in need of the supervision and protection of a guardian or conservator; and (4) no appropriate alternatives to public guardianship or public conservatorship exist that are less restrictive of the person's civil rights and liberties. . . . (Minnesota Statutes §252A.101, Subd.5)

These criteria, like the Nevada standard, do not appreciably differ from this Minnesota standard of 1917. "Competency" and "incompetency" are essentially defined as polar opposites, implying that there is some particular point at which a person, no matter what skills or abilities he or she may have, may be adjudicated as unable to manage his or her own affairs. Competence becomes an either-or affair. A legal determination of competence is not an evaluation of the areas in which a person may need help in making good decisions, but a referendum on a person's basic right to self-determination.

Even when legal standards for determining incompetency call for evidence of functional incapacity, there is little to indicate much statutory imperative to determine functional or decisional *capability*. It may be very easy to associate a label of mental retardation with an assumption of complete incompetency. Given an assumption of global incompetency, there may be little perceived need to explore less restrictive alternatives to full guardianship.

If this is the case, the unwillingness of court clerks in North Carolina to accept that a person with developmental disabilities could be "partially competent" is reasonable (Mesibov et al., 1980). Nor should it be surprising that less restrictive alternatives, such as limited guardianships and conservatorships, are apparently underutilized (Franczyk, 1992; Kritzer, 1992; Parry, 1985b). Current criteria for determining competence simply do not lend themselves to a determination of an appropriate, least restrictive guardianship arrangement for particular individuals. Competency is still determined based on criteria that serve an institutional model of service. In a time when community integration and the personal self-worth of individuals with developmental disabilities are increasingly part of the social conscience, such a legal anachronism is an unintended but effective vehicle for unduly restricting rights. The following exemplifies this point:

> Mentally disabled persons may be deprived of their rights of citizenship because they are labeled and categorized by terms that generally connote mental incapacity but which fail to reveal an individual's abilities—'incompetent,' 'idiot,' 'insane,' 'in need of guardianship,' 'institutional resident,' or 'mentally retarded'. Once the label is attached by the courts or the community, rights may be withheld en masse or simply presumed inapplicable. In this process, the logical step of matching the specific abilities of the individual with the functional capabilities society has determined as being necessary to exercise a particular right or privilege is eliminated or applied ignorantly, usually to the disadvantage of the mentally disabled person. (Parry, 1985a, p. 435)

Several authors have pointed out this fundamental discrepancy between *functional* competency and *legal* competency (Anderer, 1990; Beyer & Howell, 1988; Sales et al., 1982). In order to make determinations of guardianship that truly provide a *continuum* of alternatives to full guardianship, legal standards of competency need to be revised to reflect current knowledge that functional competency is a complex, individual phenomenon:

> Capacity cannot be determined in the abstract; a person is or is not incapacitated with respect to *do something*. A related principle is that a person may be incapacitated with respect to his or her ability to make one type of decision, while retaining capacity in other areas. . . . Furthermore, individuals are not completely proficient in performing tasks or completely unable to perform them. Rather, they perform tasks or make decisions with varying degrees of skill along a continuum. These principles dictate that legal decision-makers engage in a process of assessing areas and degrees of ability and disability. They should not seek at the outset to make global diagnoses of capacity or incapacity. (Anderer, 1990, p. 108)

Adoption of any *functional* criteria of competency would likely entail changes in the legal procedures involved in determining guardianship. A functional assessment would, for instance, require a thorough evaluation of a proposed ward's capabilities, rather than simple evidence of incompetence. Obviously, pre-hearing evaluations would have to carry more importance than they currently do—certainly in those states that do not require any assessment at all (Sales et al., 1982). Posthearing monitoring would also have to be systematized and thorough for, as we now recognize, individuals with developmental disabilities do acquire functional skills, thus having the ability to become increasingly independent.

A standard of competency based on functional abilities, rather than on some global conception of deficiency, creates the possibility that an individual may become competent both through growth of personal abilities *and* through the growth of a social or community environment that supports that person's capabilities. Beyer and Howell (1988) have noted that the ability to manage one's life—the very concern of hearings regarding legal competency—is *necessarily* improved by increasing functional competency. Conversely, building of *community* supports for individuals with developmental disabilities can effectively increase the ability of those individuals to live effectively and competently as members of those communities. Flexible and supportive systems of community-based social services is an essential step away from the institutional model and its accompanying conception of adults with developmental disabilities as incompetent (Kindred, 1976). Finally, legal structures to protect the interests of disadvantaged persons—for whatever reason they are disadvantaged—are only effective in a climate of social awareness, and individual and legal advocacy (Herr, 1983; Scott & Siuta, 1979). Without advocacy, laws for protection are sterile cages that separate people, rather than build communities.

The interrelationship of legal status, advocacy, and social support is clearly illustrated by a situation described by Levy in 1965. At that time, the only available public education and residential services for persons with developmental disabilities in Minnesota were acquired by way of institutional placement at state regional treatment centers (Levy, 1965; Scott & Siuta, 1979). By law, however, only wards of the state were eligible for placement in the regional centers (this provision was not changed until 1975) (Burge, 1991; Scott & Siuta, 1979). Because placements in the regional centers were limited and there were no alternative community-based services, placement was allotted on a waiting list basis. How was priority on the waiting list determined? In many areas, a person's place on the waiting list was determined by the date at which the individual became a ward of the state. Parents were therefore faced with a powerful incentive to relinquish custody of their children at an early age. In 1962 and 1963, 464 people became wards of the state and were subsequently institutionalized; 82% of those people were children under the age of 19. Of those children who became wards of the state during 1962–1963, 30% were under the age of five (Levy, 1965).

STEPS TO IMPROVE GUARDIANSHIP LAW AND POLICY

There are many legal and procedural changes that may be made to improve legal guardianship for persons with developmental disabilities. Several authors have made specific recommendations for model guardianship statutes. Anderer (1990) proposes a model based on a thorough and accurate determination of functional competencies of proposed wards. The American Bar Association's Commission on the Mentally Disabled has proposed a detailed, annotated model statute that incorporates determination of functional competencies, individualization of guardianship arrangements, and systematic monitoring (Sales et al., 1982). Specific legal and procedural needs include:

1. *The revision of legal standards of competency* Legal criteria need to reflect an assumption that adults with cognitive disabilities may have many functional skills. Standards should also more explicitly reflect that even a person who *lacks* certain skills necessary for independent living may be more than able to have and communicate his or her choices. Determination of competency should *never* be based on a person's need for support; standards should make it clear that need for assistance is not necessarily the same as need for supervision. Anderer (1990) has described a potentially useful model of legal competency that suggests that capacity be judicially determined by making inquiries in three areas: the existence of a specific disorder or disability; the ability of a person to care for self or property; and the ability of a person to make and communicate personal decisions. Anderer's model of capacity determination goes beyond typical current practice in that it calls for assessment of ways in which apparent deficits may be addressed by community support or services. In this model "capacity" is therefore an interaction between an individual's abilities and personal environment, rather than a personal trait. In this respect, Anderer's model of legal incapacity closely parallels the latest AAMR definition of mental retardation (American Association on Mental Retar-

dation, 1992). Legal criteria of competency should incorporate this same contextual perspective, in order to better insure that protective legal relationships, when truly necessary, are the least restrictive and most flexible arrangements possible.

2. *The increased use of guardianship hearings to determine individual needs, rather than to affirm previously made decisions* Comprehensive assessment of individuals' functional and decisional capabilities must be required components of all hearings. Furthermore, hearings need to more actively assess potential alternatives to full guardianship. It can be argued that judges are not trained to determine the needs of individuals with developmental disabilities, and that families and service providers do such assessment prior to guardianship hearings (Kritzer, 1992). This does not preclude, however, the establishment of standard procedures for judicial review of comprehensive evaluations and for assessment of proposed guardianship arrangements. Anderer's model of legal incapacity contains useful and concrete guidelines for courts to follow in evaluating evidence of incapacity and determining guardianship needs.

3. *The establishment of effective and responsive monitoring* Procedures for periodic and systematic re-evaluation of wards' needs for guardianship should be more thoroughly developed and implemented. As noted previously, courts may not be well-situated for effective monitoring through the review of written reports. Automatic monitoring procedures, such as mandatory expiration dates for guardianships, might compel periodic active review

4. *More effective training of guardians and the systematic establishment of standards for guardians* Even when legal procedures for establishing guardianship operate effectively and appropriately, there is no guarantee that the designated guardian will responsibly fulfill the duties of guardianship. In the case of public guardianships, staff with guardianship duties should receive prompt and systematic training. Agencies that administer public guardianships must be independent of agencies that provide direct service or allocate funding. Private guardians must be subject to standards that work to ensure responsible action on behalf of wards (House of Representatives Select Committee on Aging, 1989).

Revision of law, procedural changes, and establishment of standards for guardians are critical. Ultimately, though, such changes are impossible without the continued rethinking of the ethical and social implications of guardianship by service providers, policymakers, families, and society in general. Issues that must continue to be explored include:

The fundamental nature of guardianship It is not always clear what decisions or actions truly define best interests. What if a ward's preferences are not in his or her best interests as determined by the guardian? Should, for example, a ward's decision not to participate in physical therapy be confirmed by a guardian, or should the guardian determine that therapy is in the ward's best interests and act counter to the ward's preference? Is a decision that appears to counter a functional need necessarily reflective of an inability to choose appropriately? In New Hampshire, for example, a ward's choice that may appear "bad" or not in his or her best interest is nevertheless considered valid, provided the ward understands the consequences of the decision (Casasanto, Saunders, & Simon, 1986). This example points to a fundamental issue of guardianship: Should guardians act primarily to serve wards' best interest, or should they act as substitute decision makers and affirm wards' preferences regardless? The conflict between the best interest and substituted judgment conception of guardianship is an issue with which professionals in disability-related fields continue to wrestle (Casasanto et al., 1990; Zwyer, 1990).

Community integration and community supports foster increased capacity   Service providers must continue to foster the inclusion of persons with disabilities into communities. Through the establishment of supports for independent and assisted community living, individuals with developmental disabilities become more functionally capable by default. By establishing supportive and reciprocal social relationships with others, adults with developmental disabilities may become less dependent on, and less needful of, decisions made by a guardian. A guiding principal of both community integration and of guardianship should be *support*, not *supervision*.

Self-advocacy is the surest route to self-determination   It was stated at the beginning of this chapter that individual rights in a society are only truly validated to the extent that they are legally granted. It must also be affirmed that the extent to which autonomy is so granted can be greatly influenced by an expressed willingness to be autonomous. With the growing recognition that self-advocacy by persons with developmental disabilities is both possible and necessary, revisions to guardianship law and policy become more urgent and more likely. The increasing movement among these persons to chose, speak, and act on their *own* behalf can only result in a society that values their choices *and* supports their needs.

CONCLUSION

The purpose of this chapter is to explore some of the paradox inherent in the construct of legal guardianship—the apparent contradiction that a person's best interests as an individual must sometimes be protected by taking away some of his or her rights and freedoms as an adult in an ostensibly free society. It has not been an intention to cast doubt on the institution of legal guardianship itself. The ethical implications of guardianship have been increasingly attended to, and, more than ever, guardianship is fundamentally a compassionate response to society's need to offer protection to even its most vulnerable and marginalized members. Like any supportive service, guardianship should not be denied to those who may be better served by a guardianship arrangement (Woody, 1974). If, however, the legal procedures and assumptions of guardianship have actually served to sometimes *encourage* marginalization and undue restriction of citizens with developmental disabilities, this is due to outmoded and inadequate conceptions of competency, incompetency, and best interest. Such conceptions are being changed through research and advocacy, and the increased participation of citizens with developmental disabilities in their communities.

As these conceptions change, it is important that the laws do likewise. In particular, legal criteria for determining competency must be changed to reflect the functional competencies that most people with developmental disabilities *have*, rather than those they lack. A fully accessible continuum of guardianship services, including limited guardianships, conservatorships, and alternatives to public guardianship, such as the increasing number of corporate private guardianship agencies (Apolloni, 1988; Minnesota Guardianship Task Force, 1986), must be available for individuals who require surrogate decision makers for some life areas. Finally, and most important, changes in the law must be concurrent with a consistently more supportive social environment, in which individuals with developmental disabilities are advocated for and self-advocated, and in which they are able to participate and contribute as valued citizens. Hudson (1988), in a powerful discussion about the rights of individuals with mental disabilities, cites philosopher Errol E. Harris:

> The ultimate aim of the whole social way of life is the fullest possible development of the capacities of the individuals who make up the society concerned, giving the fullest possible satisfaction of the complete personality. This . . . can be realized only in persons, and it follows that each and every person is . . . of ultimate worth as the final source and vehicle of value. . . . The most important values can be enjoyed by any persons only if, and to the extent, they are enjoyed by all. (Harris, 1966, pp. 119–121)

Hudson goes on to say:

> Within such a framework, we may 'grade' people with a mental handicap according to their measured intelligence, personality traits, social competence, and so forth, but in respect of 'human worth', all [people] must get equal grades. 'Human worth' is simply not a grading concept, and the moral community is not a club from which members may be dropped. (Hudson, 1988, pp. 230–231)

These thoughts must not go unheeded as we consider the implications of legal guardianship for persons with developmental disabilities. It must be reaffirmed that the institutional, incompetency paradigm no longer serves, in communities or in the law.

REFERENCES

American Association on Mental Retardation. (1992). *Mental retardation: Definition, classification, and systems of supports (9th ed.).* Washington, DC: Author.

American Bar Association. (1989). Guardianship: An agenda for reform (Recommendations of the National Guardianship Symposium and policy of the American Bar Association). *Mental and Physical Disability Law Reporter, 13*(3), 271–314.

Anderer, S.J. (1990). A model for determining competency in guardianship proceedings. *Mental and Physical Disability Law Reporter, 14*(2), 107–114.

Apolloni, T. (1988). Guardianship: New options for parents. *Exceptional Parent, 17*(4), 24–28.

Beyer, H.A., & Howell, M.C. (1988). A question of competency. *Exceptional Parent, 18*(8), 52–57.

Brantlinger, E. (1992). Professionals' attitudes toward the sterilization of people with disabilities. *Journal of The Association for Persons with Severe Handicaps, 17*(1), 4–18.

Brechin, A., & Swain, J. (1988). Professional/client relationships: Creating a 'working alliance' with people with learning difficulties. *Disability, Handicap & Society, 3*(3), 213–226.

Burge, S. (1991). Public conservatorship and guardianship of adults. In Minnesota State Bar Association, *Minnesota conservatorships and guardianships: Vol. 1* (pp. 1–123). St. Paul: Minnesota State Bar Association.

Casasanto, M.D., Saunders, A.G., & Simon, M.M. (1986). Individual functional assessment: A guide to determining the need for guardianship under New Hampshire Law. *New Hampshire Bar Journal, 28*(1), 13–44.

Casasanto, M.D., Simon, M., & Roman, J. (1990). A model code of ethics for guardians. *National Guardianship Journal, 1*(1), 128–151.

Franczyk, J. (1992). [Guardianship status: DD home and community-based services recipients]. Minnesota Department of Human Services, Division for Persons with Developmental Disabilities. Unpublished raw data.

Harris, E.E. (1966). Respect for persons. In R.T. DeGeorge (Ed.), *Ethics and society: Original essays on contemporary moral problems* (pp. 111–132). Garden City, NY: Anchor Books.

Hentoff, N. (1991). Whatever happened to Baby Jane Doe? *TASH Newsletter, 16*(2), 3. (Reprinted from the *Washington Post,* December 11, 1990.)

Herr, S.S. (1983). *Rights and advocacy for retarded people.* Lexington, MA: Lexington Books.

House of Representatives Select Committee on Aging. (1989). *Model standards to ensure quality guardianship and representative payeeship services* (Comm. Publication No. 101–729). Washington, DC: U.S. Government Printing Office.

Hudson, B. (1988). Do people with a mental handicap have rights? *Disability, Handicap & Society, 3*(3), 227–237.

Hurme, S.B., Parry, J.W., & Coleman, N. (1991). *Steps to enhance guardianship monitoring.* Washington, DC: American Bar Association.

Kindred, M. (1976). Guardianship and limitations upon capacity. In M. Kindred, J. Cohen, D. Penrod, & T. Shaffer (Eds.), *The mentally retarded citizen and the law* (pp. 62–87). New York: The Free Press.

Kritzer, H.M. (1992). *Adult guardianship in Wisconsin: An empirical assessment* (Contract No. 90-12M-E-057). Madison, WI: The Center for Public Representation.

Kuhlman, F. (1920). *Determination of feeble-mindedness as related to the courts.* St. Paul, MN: State Board of Control.

Levy, R.J. (1965). Protecting the mentally retarded: An empirical survey and evaluation of the establishment of state guardianship in Minnesota. *Minnesota Law Review, 49,* 821–887.

Maser, K.L. (1991). Conservatorship and guardianship of adults. In Minnesota State Bar Association, *Minnesota conservatorships and guardianships* (Vol. 1). St. Paul: Minnesota State Bar Association.

Mesibov, G.B., Conover, B.S., & Saur, W.G. (1980). Limited guardianship laws and developmentally disabled adults: Needs and obstacles. *Mental Retardation,* 221–232.

Minnesota Department of Human Services, Guardianship Office. (1990). *Public conservatorship and guardianship in Minnesota* [video]. St. Paul: Minnesota Department of Human Services.

Minnesota Guardianship Task Force. (1986). *Report to the legislature: Public guardianship study.* Minneapolis: Author.

Parry, J. (1985a). Decision-making rights over persons and property. In S.J. Brakel, J. Parry, & B.A. Wiener (Eds.), *The mentally disabled and the law* (3rd ed.) (pp. 435–506). Chicago: American Bar Foundation.

Parry, J. (1985b). Incompetency, guardianship, and restoration. In S.J. Brakel, J. Parry, & B.A. Wiener (Eds.), *The mentally disabled and the law* (3rd ed.) (pp. 369–434). Chicago: American Bar Foundation.

Parry, J.W., & Beck, J.C. (1990). Revisiting the civil commitment/involuntary treatment stalemate using limited guardianship, substituted judgment and different due process consideration: A work in progress. *Mental and Physical Disability Law Reporter, 14*(2), 102–106.

Rogers, P.R. (1984). Understanding the legal concept of guardianship. In T. Apolloni & T.P. Cooke (Eds.), *A new look at guardianship: Protective services that support personalized living* (pp. 35–48). Baltimore: Paul H. Brookes Publishing Co.

Sales, B.D., Powell, D.M., & Van Duizend, R. (1982). *Disabled persons and the law: State legislative issues.* New York: Plenum Press.

Scott, S., & Siuta, P. (1979). *Legal rights of developmentally disabled persons: An advocacy manual for Minnesota.* Minneapolis: Legal Advocacy for Developmentally Disabled Persons in Minnesota.

Taylor, H.B. (1935). *Law of guardian and ward* (Social Service Monograph No. 35). Chicago: University of Chicago Press.

Weeks, C.L. (1920). *The law relating to the commitment of the feeble minded.* St. Paul, MN: State Board of Control.

Wehmeyer, M., & Berkobien, R. (1991). Self determination and self advocacy: A case of mistaken identity. *TASH Newsletter, 17*(7), 4.

Woody, R.H. (1974). *Legal aspects of mental retardation: A search for reliability.* Springfield, IL: Charles C Thomas.

Zwyer, D.A. (1990). A guardian's role in the Do Not Resuscitate (DNR) process. *National Guardianship Journal, 1*(1), 274–290.

_ *Chapter 18* _____

Supported Employment
Program Models, Strategies, and Evaluation Perspectives
David R. Johnson and Darrell R. Lewis

The recent emergence of supported employment programs in the United States has substantially raised expectations concerning the viability of employment in promoting the integration, productivity, and independence of persons with severe developmental disabilities. Traditionally, adults with severe disabilities were either provided access to habilitation and rehabilitation services in predominantly segregated settings or not at all. During the 1960s and 1970s, adult day activity centers and sheltered workshops became the primary service delivery models. Many of these programs offered individuals little more than token wages for performing menial tasks or simulated work. Such services were viewed, however, as essential in leading individuals through various stages of development to reach higher levels of job readiness and, ultimately, competitive employment. The actual movement of individuals with severe disabilities into competitive employment from sheltered workshops, work activity, and day activity programs simply did not occur (Loosemore, 1980; U.S. Department of Labor, 1979). In fact, individuals with severe disabilities experienced few opportunities for social and community integration through these programs.

More recently, a number of conceptual frameworks for competitive and supported employment have been put forth (Bates & Pancsofar, 1983; Mithaug, Hagmeier, & Harring, 1977; Rusch, 1983; Rusch & Mithaug, 1980; Vogelsberg, 1984; Wehman, 1981). These conceptual models apply learning and behavior principles to job training and employment for persons with severe disabilities, stressing the importance of job development and follow-up services as factors contributing to successful job placement and retention (Johnson, Warrington, & Mellberg, 1989).

Preparation of this chapter was supported by a cooperative agreement (#H133B80048) from the National Institute on Disability and Rehabilitation Research (NIDRR). The opinions expressed are those of the authors and do not necessarily reflect the position of NIDRR, the Center on Residential Services and Community Living, and the Institute on Community Integration.

449

The rapid evolution of supported employment during the 1980s was based, in large part, on responsive federal and state social policies and legislation, aggressive advocacy efforts, improvements in job placement and training strategies, expansions in the development of community-based services for persons with severe disabilities as a result of deinstitutionalization, and the increase in emphasis placed upon the potential benefits of supported employment in enabling individuals to achieve economic self-sufficiency and community integration. At last report, a total of 32,342 individuals were being served in supported employment programs in the United States, representing a 226% increase during the period of 1986 to 1988 (Wehman, Kregel, & Shafer, 1989).

Today, supported employment is being justified on the basis of two rationales: on its positive socioeconomic impact on individuals and on its economic benefit to society. The extent to which supported employment programs are fulfilling these individual and societal goals and outcomes remains the focus of deliberations regarding the expansion of such services in the United States. Questions concerning supported employment's costs, accountability, and effectiveness are increasingly being asked by policymakers and professionals. In addition to earnings and other related economic benefits, the efficacy of supported employment is being judged on its capacity to achieve employment integration for individuals served. It is believed by some that without a better understanding of the multidimensional nature of employment integration and its interrelatedness to other supported employment outcomes and costs, the current high levels of public and professional support for this program alternative may diminish.

The purpose of this chapter is four-fold. First, a brief introduction to supported employment, including its policy and legislative context, current program models, and service strategies, is offered. Second, contemporary perspectives on the social and economic goals and outcomes of this service delivery alternative are discussed. Third, selected outcome evaluation models and strategies are presented and described as a primary means of assessing the individual and societal impact of supported employment. Finally, alternative methods for improving current outcome evaluation practices from a multi-dimensional, multi-attribute, and cost perspective are explored. Developing improved methods for assessing supported employment's multiple goals and outcomes is definitely a critical area in need of further development in the United States.

SUPPORTED EMPLOYMENT: CURRENT POLICIES AND PRACTICES

Policy and Legislative Context

At the heart of the national supported employment initiative in the United States lies a shared federal and state commitment to incorporating individuals with developmental disabilities and other severe disabilities into our nation's work force (Kregel, Shafer, Wehman, & West, 1989). During the past three decades, public social policy and legislation have given increasing support to expanded employment opportunities for persons with severe disabilities. Throughout these years, one of the most striking features of federal policy development on behalf of individuals with disabilities has been its cross-agency support. Both federal and state agencies, based in the fields of vocational rehabilitation, special education, employment and training, developmental disabilities, and vocational education, have enacted legislation addressing the vocational training and employment needs of persons with disabilities.

The federal-state vocational rehabilitation program was among the first to initiate employment services. People who were disabled during World War I and employees who became disabled on the job were among the first recipients of rehabilitation services. During ensuing years, rehabilitation and related employment services expanded to a broader range of clientele, including individuals with severe and chronic disabilities. The passage of the Rehabilitation Act of 1973 (PL 93-112), in particular, emphasized the critical importance of extending rehabilitation services to persons with severe disabilities, and extended major constitutional protections regarding equal employment opportunity and nondiscrimination toward persons with disabilities in employment. Unquestionably, the 1973 act embodied the most sweeping changes in the federal-state rehabilitation system since its inception in 1918 (Shafer, 1988).

In 1984, Congress passed two key pieces of legislation: the Education of the Handicapped Act Amendments of 1983 (PL 98-199), which cited a lack of transitional services for special education students, and the Developmental Disabilities Assistance and Bill of Rights Act of 1984 (hereafter referred to as the Developmental Disabilities Act of 1984) (PL 98-527), which provided a mandate for addressing employment-related activities as a major priority (Rusch & Hughes, 1990). PL 98-199 specifically identified employment as the single most important outcome of a young person's cumulative special education experiences. In 1984, the Office of Special Education and Rehabilitative Services (OSERS) defined the transition from school to working life as an outcome-oriented process encompassing a broad array of services and experiences that lead to employment (Will, 1984, p. 2). Everson (1988), in her analysis of federal transition policy, suggested that the OSERS's definition of transition clearly applied two historically documented federal assumptions relating to employment: 1) employment is the desired outcome of education and transition planning and is consistent with the national work ethic for all Americans; and 2) employment is a cost-effective outcome that will increase an individual's productivity and worth to society, while decreasing dependence on social service programs.

The Developmental Disabilities Act of 1984 included supported employment as one of the employment-related activities underscored within the legislation. PL 98-527 defined supported employment as:

> paid employment which (i) is for persons with developmental disabilities for whom competitive employment at or above the minimum wage is unlikely and who, because of their disabilities, need ongoing support to perform in a work setting; (ii) is con-

ducted in a variety of settings, particularly work sites in which persons without disabilities are employed; and (iii) is supported by any activity needed to sustain paid work by persons with disabilities, including supervision, training, and transportation. (Developmental Disabilities Assistance and Bill of Rights Act of 1986, p. 2665)

The significance of the act is in its emphasis on the key concepts of integration in the workplace, pay for real work, and recognition of an individual's needs and requirements for a variety of ongoing support services. Based on these criteria, the outcomes of supported employment are broadly defined to include physical and social integration at the workplace (involvement at work sites where persons without disabilities are employed), paid work (at or above the minimum wage), and provision of support services (as such services relate to maintaining adequate levels of work performance and ensure job retention over time). The inception of supported employment as a national program was embraced within both a value-conscious and outcome-oriented policy context stemming from the initiatives of the U.S. Department of Education, OSERS, U.S. Department of Health and Human Services, and the Administration on Developmental Disabilities.

The Rehabilitation Act Amendments of 1986 (PL 99-506) further strengthened federal policy regarding supported employment. The re-authorized act included a new formula grant under Title VI, Part C, that permitted state vocational rehabilitation agencies to provide directly or purchase a variety of supported employment services (e.g., job development, job placement, job coaching). Under the authorizing legislation, supported employment is further defined as competitive work in integrated work settings for individuals with severe disabilities for whom competitive employment has not traditionally occurred, or for individuals for whom competitive employment has been interrupted or intermittent as a result of a severe disability, and who, because of their disability, need ongoing support services to perform such work (PL 99-506, Title 1, Sec. 103i). The 1986 amendments supplemented the earlier definition of supported employment included in the Developmental Disabilities Act of 1984.

The *Federal Register* (1987) published rules and regulations delineating minimum criteria for achieving compliance with the act amendments. Competitive employment means employment that averages at least 20 hours per week for each pay period. Integrated work settings are defined as settings where work groups of not more than eight individuals with disabilities are present and regular contact with nondisabled coworkers is attained. Finally, the regulations define ongoing support services as continuous or periodic job skill training services provided at least twice monthly at the job site. The exception to this is for individuals with chronic mental illness, who may or may not require job support services so frequently. The amendment specifically addresses individuals with severe disabilities for whom competitive employment has not traditionally occurred.

Supported employment continues to evolve as a multi-agency initiative, requiring extensive levels of federal, state, and local agency cooperation to fully achieve its mission and goals. As states and localities continue to grapple with the processes of implementation, more attention must be directed to defining and attaining consensus on the multiple individual goals, as well as societal goals and outcomes of this service alternative. Legislation enacted to date provides a useful starting point. In the long run, however, the richness of an individual's employment experiences in terms of personal, social, and economic opportunities, outcomes, and benefits, must be fully captured and agreement reached on the defining characteristics of these outcomes. This is necessary not only to promote the development and expansion of such services, but to facilitate a common and clear understanding of the nature of supported employment's mission and goals among policymakers, professionals, families, and individuals with disabilities themselves.

Program Models

Based on extensive research and demonstration activities over the past decade, supported employment programs are currently implemented under one of four primary models (Bates & Pancsofar, 1983; Bellamy, Rhodes, Mank, & Albin, 1988; Lagomarcino, 1986; Moon & Griffin, 1988; Rusch & Hughes, 1990; Trach & Rusch, 1989; Vogelsberg, 1990; Wehman, 1986). These models include: 1) individual placement model, 2) enclave model, 3) mobile work crew model, and 4) entrepreneurial model.

Individual Placement Model The individual placement approach relies on an employment specialist (the terms job coach or job training are often used synonymously with employment specialist) placing and training a worker in a community job and providing as much training and follow-along as is necessary to keep the individual in that position (Bellamy et al., 1988; Moon & Griffin, 1988; Rusch, Chadsey-Rusch, & Johnson, 1991; Wehman, 1981). Continuous on-site training is provided at the workplace until the new employee competently performs the job (Bellamy et al., 1988). It is assumed that, gradually, the type and amount of assistance provided by the trainer will be reduced, although some type of follow-along will be provided permanently (Moon & Griffin, 1988). Key features and outcomes of the individual placement model include: 1) the individual with a disability is typically hired directly by the community employer, and 2) hourly earnings received by workers tend to be at or above currently established minimum wage levels (Wehman et al., 1989). The individual placement model is by far the most widely used placement approach nationally (Kregel & Wehman, 1989). Persons with severe disabilities, however, tend to comprise only a very small percentage of individuals participating in this placement option (Wehman et al., 1989). This approach has been shown to be cost-effective in the use of limited case service dollars, as it emphasizes the delivery of placement and training services in real job environments, rather than more costly facility-based settings (Conley & Noble, 1990; Hill, Banks, et al., 1987; Vogelsberg, 1985).

Enclave Model Enclaves, or clustered placement, are group-supported employment options that typically provide permanent, on-site supervision to workers with disabilities. The enclave model differs from an individual job placement approach in that a group of persons with disabilities (usually three to eight workers) work in sufficient proximity to make coordinated training and supported services available at all times, not just during the initial training period (Bellamy et al., 1988; Rhodes & Valenta, 1985). As with the individual placement model, enclaves are established directly within community-based employment environments, where workers have opportunities to interact with coworkers who do not have disabilities.

Mobile Work Crew Model   Mobile work crews are essentially small businesses that commonly travel by way of van to a variety of work sites, most often performing janitorial, light assembly, groundskeeping, or other industry jobs. As with the enclave, the mobile work crew is a group-supported employment alternative, consisting of up to eight workers and one or more trainers. Mank, Rhodes, and Bellamy (1986) have argued that work crews are good options for communities such as rural areas or small towns with small service needs, towns without much industry, or in places where there is readily available short- or long-term contract work. Physical and social integration is presumed to occur through regular contacts with nondisabled persons at the various community work sites. In practice, however, it has been argued that the mobile work crew, as a result of its grouping of persons with disabilities, creates barriers to the integration objectives of supported employment (Bellamy et al., 1988). Since the actual employment of mobile crew workers remains under the auspices of a rehabilitation facility or day habilitation program, opportunities for establishing direct relationships with employers are lessened.

Entrepreneurial Model   This model, or the bench-work model, is designed to provide individuals with disabilities employment in light manufacturing and assembly work within a service agency that also functions as a business enterprise (Mank et al., 1986). As with the enclave and mobile work crew models, the entrepreneurial model is organized for small groups of individuals. The entrepreneurial or bench-work model was developed by the Specialized Training Program at the University of Oregon during the 1970s (Bellamy, Horner, & Inman, 1979). Although designed for persons with more severe disabilities, this model shares many features and constraints with traditional sheltered workshops (Mank et al., 1986). Work, typically subcontracted from an outside business, is performed in the rehabilitation or day program facilities, much as sheltered work and work activity programs have traditionally operated. Due to this limitation, opportunities for achieving physical and social integration are difficult at best. The entrepreneurial model, however, has been established to provide employment and work-related activities to persons with severe disabilities who continue to be denied access to community-based employment options.

Program Strategies

A variety of supported employment program strategies have evolved, focusing on two primary areas: participant skill acquisition and maintenance, and employment integration.

Skill Acquisition and Maintenance   Trach and Rusch (1989), in a review of supported employment model program strategies and components (see also

Kregel & Wehman, 1989; Lagomarcino, 1986; Vogelsberg, 1985; Wehman, 1981, 1986) identified the following program strategies and components of supported employment: 1) job survey and analysis, 2) job match, 3) job acquisition and maintenance, 4) conjunctive job services, 5) job fit, and 6) interagency coordination.

Conducting a job survey and analysis of local labor market conditions is generally the first step in the placement process. A variety of strategies have been advocated, including the use of mail surveys and telephone canvassing to secure job leads (Martin, 1986; Rusch & Mithaug, 1980; Wehman, 1981) and person-to-person contacts with employers (Garzan & Mansolo, 1981; Sands & Zalkind, 1972; Usdane, 1976; Vandergoot, 1976; Zadny, 1980). More recently, approaches in conducting community job surveys recommend mail, telephone, and in-person contacts in combination when securing job placement (Johnson et al., 1989; Roessler & Hiett, 1983). The principal purpose of the job survey and analysis is to identify primary job leads as well as the critical vocational and social skills required for specific jobs.

Successfully matching workers to jobs requires accurate and up-to-date information about individuals, as well as specific job criteria and requirements. Individual preferences and family perspectives must, however, be primary decision-making criteria. Basing placement decisions on this premise helps to ensure that workers with disabilities experience higher levels of job satisfaction, which should also positively influence job retention levels. In addition, no individual should be excluded from employment (a zero-reject feature), and the opportunity for increased wages and job advancement for each employee must also be considered (Rusch et al., 1991).

Job acquisition refers to procedures for training individuals with disabilities to perform on-the-job; *job maintenance* concerns procedures for assisting the individual in retaining the target job once he or she has learned the job (Trach & Rusch, 1989). Many of these vocational training procedures have grown out of prior research on the application of learning principles and behavior analytic approaches to training (Crosson, 1969; Evans & Spradlin, 1966; Gold, 1973, 1974; Rusch & Mithaug, 1980; Schutz, Vogelsberg, & Rusch, 1980; Wehman, 1981; Zimmerman, Stuckey, Garlick, & Miller, 1969).

Conjunctive job services include all necessary job-site training (e.g., job coaching, behavior analysis), related counseling and support services, job accommodations and modifications, coworker orientations and training, transportation, and other work-related support services viewed as essential for ensuring job acquisition, maintenance, and retention. This also includes the provision of follow-up services to ensure the long-term and successful assimilation of individuals with disabilities in the work environment. The provision of ongoing services remains one of the most distinguishing characteristics of supported employment programs from other employment and training programs. *Job fit* refers to the continuous re-assessment of consumer performance during and after training, validating the quality of job performance, and modifying efforts to meet the expectations of client, employer, and parent or guardian (Trach & Rusch, 1989). These reassessments of the environmental and behavioral attributes of the individual and the work setting are key components of comprehensive follow-up services.

Due to the multi-agency and often multiservice nature of supported employment, interagency cooperation and coordination are actively promoted. Persons with severe disabilities often require high levels of support from a variety of community service agencies to maintain employment. Interagency cooperation also continues to be of particular importance in ensuring that long-term funding is available to address an individual's need for ongoing support in the workplace.

Employment Integration A second major and emerging set of supported employment program strategies focuses on the physical and social integration of persons with disabilities in the work site. *Integration in the workplace* has been defined as participation of a worker in the operation of the work culture at both the environment's required level and the worker's desired level (Shafer & Nisbet, 1988). Recent research has investigated environmental factors that influence the successful integration of persons with severe disabilities in community-based employment (Chadsey-Rusch, 1985; Parent, Kregel, Twardzik, & Metzler, 1990; Schalock, 1985; Schalock, Harper, & Genung, 1981).

Other research on integration has focused on the development of a repertoire of social skills and positive behaviors that facilitate interactions between workers with disabilities and coworkers without disabilities (Chadsey-Rusch, 1986; Chadsey-Rusch, Gonzalez, & Tines, 1988; Chadsey-Rusch & Rusch, 1988; Lignugaris/Kraft, Salzberg, Rule, & Stowitschek, 1988). A variety of methods for achieving higher levels of social integration have been advocated, including maintaining close proximity between workers with and without disabilities, sharing job responsibilities, taking breaks and lunching together, attending social events with peers, receiving instructions from company supervisors, learning tasks from coworkers without disabilities, and developing other situational contexts that promote social interaction (Chadsey-Rusch, 1990; Nisbet & Callahan, 1987).

More recently, the use of natural supports (e.g., coworkers, mentors, volunteers) has been promoted as a means of achieving social integration in the workplace (Hughes, Rusch, & Curl, 1990; Nisbet & Callahan, 1987; Nisbet & Hagner, 1988). Advocates of this approach stress the importance of identifying stimuli in the work setting that promote independent work performance. Possible stimuli include clocks or whistles to prompt going to a workstation and beginning work, coworkers leaving a station to prompt going on breaks, or food scraps on tables to remind the employee to wipe the table's surface clean (Hughes et al., 1990; Lagomarcino, Hughes, & Rusch, 1989; Sowers, Rusch, Connis, & Cummings, 1980). Other researchers have argued that coworkers can provide much of the support needed by individuals with disabilities to maintain adequate levels of skill performance (Chadsey-Rusch et al., 1988; Nisbet & Hagner, 1988; Shafer, 1986). Shafer (1986) contends that coworkers can be effectively used as advocates, observers, and job trainers. Advocacy can take the form of helping individuals with disabilities complete particularly troublesome or new parts of jobs, speaking up for individuals, or shielding supported workers from antagonistic peers (Shafer, 1986). Coworkers can also assist workers with disabilities by observing and monitoring their levels of work performance (Rusch & Menchetti, 1981). These examples offer promising directions in the development of important strategies for promoting the social integration of individuals with disabilities in the workplace.

EVALUATING THE SOCIAL AND ECONOMIC GOALS OF SUPPORTED EMPLOYMENT

Collectively, the development of program models and strategies for supported employment programs has centered on maximizing opportunities for individuals with severe disabilities to experience the full social and economic benefits of employment. Developing meaningful ways to evaluate the multiple benefits and outcomes of supported employment has been an area of increasing interest among professionals, policymakers, and advocacy organizations. Evaluation methods and procedures vary extensively, however, depending on the focus of evaluation and the key evaluation questions to be addressed through the analysis. Evaluation foci, for example, differ depending on who the potential users of the information are and the ways the information will ultimately be used. Potential users include individuals with disabilities themselves, family members, program administrators and staff, taxpayers, advocacy groups, and federal and state policymakers. Program participants and family members share in the need to understand the program in terms of its direct impact on improving individual levels of economic self-sufficiency and quality of life. In contrast, professionals, policymakers, and the rest of society (i.e., other taxpayers) tend to be more interested in issues concerning program accountability, efficiency, and cost-containment.

Currently, supported employment is experiencing high levels of professional and public support. This has been predicated in large part on the virtually indisputable nature of the program's broad social and economic goals and claims made as to its potential positive impact on individuals with severe disabilities (and/or society in general). Nonetheless, professional attention must focus more directly on the program's long-term impact and benefits. The current political and economic climate of this country strongly suggests that we do so. This will require that present methods for evaluating supported employment's effectiveness and efficiency and its net individual and societal worth be substantially improved.

The goals and outcomes of supported employment programs are being evaluated from a variety of perspectives. The majority of these perspectives center on how well supported employment is meeting its asserted social policy intent to "achieve competitive work opportunities in integrated work settings for individuals with severe handicaps, for whom competitive employment has not occurred, or for whom competitive employment has been interrupted or intermittent" (*Federal Register*, 1987, p. 30,546). This perspective focuses on the "value base" of supported employment in achieving socially relevant outcomes for persons with disabilities. It also speaks to concerns about the extent to which employment creates meaningful social integration opportunities with nondisabled individuals. Many of the associated goals for integration also focus upon how we define quality of life (Goode, 1989; Mank & Buckley, 1989; Rusch et al., 1991; Schalock & Hill, 1986).

A second aspect of this perspective addresses the need for fiscal accountability in the operation and management of supported employment programs. Methods of cost-accounting are used to assess whether allocated funds have been used for their intended purposes. Also related to cost is the determination of whether supported employment itself is worth its cost (i.e., Does the program generates outcomes for individuals with disabilities that justify the costs of producing them?) (Lewis, Johnson, Bruininks, Kallsen, & Guillery, 1991). Recently, a variety of social benefit-cost models that calculate both the monetary and nonmonetary outcomes of employment programs have been employed in examining issues of program efficiency and equity (Conley & Noble, 1990; Hill, 1988; Johnston, 1987; Kregel, Wehman, Revell, & Hill, 1990; Lewis, Johnson, et al., 1991; Thornton & Maynard, 1989).

Overall, outcome evaluation approaches in supported employment should center on: 1) identifying and defining the multidimensional nature of supported employment's goals and outcomes; 2) determining the measurable attributes and characteristics of these outcomes; 3) examining these outcomes from multiple perspectives (i.e., individual, taxpayer, society); and 4) improving evaluation methods and procedures sufficiently to assess the full impact of supported employment in producing positive economic and social benefits for individuals and society as a whole. The remainder of this chapter examines these and other related issues.

Understanding the Multidimensional
Nature of Supported Employment Outcomes

To date, few efforts have been undertaken to develop an integrated perspective of supported employment's multiple outcomes and costs. During the past two decades, researchers based in the disciplines of rehabilitation and economics have offered broad conceptualizations of the outcomes and costs of employment services in the United States. Beginning in the early 1920s, vocational rehabilitation professionals adopted economic analysis to demonstrate that federal investment in the program was producing benefits and economic returns to society (Berkowitz & Berkowitz, 1983). At the time, rehabilitation programs wanted to show that taxpayers' money was being put to good use or, better yet, that the program would return more than it took from federal and state funds (Lewis, Johnson, Chen, & Erickson, 1992). This early form of benefit-cost analysis considered only limited economic criteria (i.e., increased individual earnings, fringe benefits, and taxes; costs of rehabilitation services; and other pecuniary values) in the analysis of state vocational rehabilitation programs. More sophisticated benefit-cost procedures were advanced in the field of economics and later applied in evaluations of federal training programs (Kerachsky, Thornton, Bloomenthal, Maynard, & Stephens, 1985; Long, Maller, & Thornton, 1981), but these procedures were not universally adopted by state vocational rehabilitation agencies. This practice continues today and has resulted in an insufficient understanding of the full economic and social impact of rehabilitation services on individuals with disabilities, employers, taxpayers, and society.

By the 1980s, economists were beginning to use more refined analytic frameworks and procedures to examine the economic as well as social outcomes of the federal-state rehabilitation program and related training programs (Cho & Schuermann, 1980; Conley, 1975; Kerachsky et al., 1985; Noble, 1977; Noble & Conley, 1987; Thornton, 1985). These approaches grew out of the recognition that there are many qualitative as well as quantitative outcomes implied in the goals of rehabilitation and related employment and training programs. Expanded cost-accounting frameworks were devised to illustrate the benefits and costs of employment services from multiple dimensions. For example, Thornton (1985) included estimations of program costs and benefits to account for the reduced use of alternative programs (i.e., residential services, medical care, transportation) and related social benefits (i.e., increased self-sufficiency, increased independence, and improved quality of life) resulting from participants' program participation. Despite the limitations of such data, the inclusion of these dimensions within economic analysis is argued on the grounds of providing a significantly improved estimate of the *true* costs of rehabilitation and related employment programs. (For a more detailed review of public and private cost-estimating procedures, see Conley, 1975; Kerachsky et al., 1985; Lewis et al., 1992; Long et al., 1981; Thornton, 1985.)

As the goals of employment services vis-à-vis supported employment for persons with disabilities broadened during the 1980s, nonmonetary outcomes were increasingly included in benefit-cost models to express the social benefits of such services. Nonmonetary outcomes such as increased independence, improved quality of life, increases in physical and social integration, and other indices of improved social well-being have continued to evolve as important considerations in outcome evaluations of employment programs. Evaluating employment programs is many times argued on the grounds that any outcome that increases social well-being is relevant to policy, program, and budgetary decision making and, as such, is the legitimate concern of benefit-cost analysis (Conley & Noble, 1989).

Definitional and methodological issues continue to limit analyses of the social benefits and outcomes of employment services. As supported employment emerged in the 1980s, growing attention turned to the socially relevant goals of employment in enabling individuals with severe disabilities to achieve social integration as an outcome of their participation in the workplace. Integration, in fact, may be the single most important purpose and quality of supported employment; and this important multifaceted outcome dimension of supported employment cannot be adequately accounted for in the routine analysis of monetary benefits and costs of programs (Lewis, Johnson, et al., 1991).

The justification of supported employment as a viable national program for persons with severe disabilities is inextricably focused on two broad premises, its cost-effectiveness and social value, and its contributions to individuals. Some (Parent et al., 1990; Rusch et al., 1991) have even argued that valuing supported employment strictly on the basis of its cost-effectiveness is illegitimate, and that the costs of supported employment should be considered only from the perspective of human costs associated with our failure to stimulate employment opportunities for persons who wish to work. Despite the appealing nature of this argument, few strategies have been marshalled to develop an integrated perspective of the multidimensional nature of supported employment costs and outcomes.

To date, evaluation studies in supported employment have investigated outcomes from a narrow and, often, singular perspective, such as postplacement earnings and related economic outcomes, attained levels of physical and social integration, or improvements in quality of life among program participants. From an efficiency point of view, the tendency is to examine cost and outcomes as a simple ratio of outcome to cost. From a program effectiveness perspective, the tendency has been to identify and attempt to measure an array of intangible social benefits, largely included within conceptual paradigms of integration and quality of life to express the socially desirable benefits and outcomes of supported employment. Rarely, if ever, are these multiple economic and social outcomes linked into an integrated or multidimensional perspective.

Evaluation studies continue to rely on unidimensional measurement systems and univariate statistical analyses to report on the impact of employment services. These procedures, however, fail to capture the complex, multivariate nature of the social benefits of supported employment. This situation has not only limited our understanding of supported employment's effectiveness in achieving its goals, but has prevented efforts to link multi-attribute program outcomes to costs. Attempting to find relationships between program costs and multiple effectiveness measures in supported employment has been especially problematic. No study to date has attempted to associate the multi-attributes of supported employment's effectiveness with actual related costs in an effort to derive meaningful cost-effectiveness measures. Such measures, however, are of critical importance in comparing alternative supported employment models and current service delivery options. Later in this chapter, an alternative evaluation strategy is presented and described for evaluating these multidimensional outcomes and linking multi-attribute program outcomes to costs. The following section provides an overview of outcome and cost evaluation procedures currently used in evaluating employment programs.

Outcome Evaluation

Increasing individual earnings and increasing employment integration opportunities are the principal aims of supported employment programs. Outcome evaluation should include strategies and procedures that provide managers and policymakers with an indication of the benefits and effects accruing for individuals, agencies, employers, and broader community-levels from a specific program. These multiple perspectives suggest that outcome evaluation strategies differ, depending on whether one focuses on the participant, the program, or the larger system (Schalock, 1988). Critical performance evaluation indicators are commonly established (e.g., postplacement earnings and related work benefits, employment in integrated environments, increased employment opportunities for persons with severe disabilities), against which programs and alternative service delivery strategies can be compared (DeStefano, 1990; Goode, 1989; Rockart, 1979; Schalock, 1988; Schalock & Hill, 1986; Schalock & Thornton, 1988).

Evaluation Models and Practices

Evaluation models and practices currently used in evaluating supported employment's effectiveness and efficiency can be grouped into four categories: 1) compliance monitoring, 2) process/progress evaluation, 3) outcome or impact evaluation, and 4) efficiency or benefit-cost analysis (DeStefano, 1990; Schalock & Hill, 1986; Schalock & Thornton, 1988). In broader terms, these evaluation models can be categorized as either formative or summative. Formative evaluation addresses the question of how well the program is doing in relation to its stated goals and to its required federal and state policy. Such evaluations are typically program-centered and focus on administrative needs in relation to program management, allocation of resources, personnel deployment, and reporting of information to external agencies. The compliance monitoring and process/progress evaluation models best characterize the formative approach.

Compliance Monitoring Compliance monitoring addresses whether or not a program adheres to certain regulations and operating standards required by federal, state, or local authorities. While compliance monitoring is often essential for accreditation and funding purposes, it is not always useful to program managers for decision making and program improvement (DeStefano, 1990). This model often has limited use in comparing the outcomes and costs of one program to another. Other useful program-level procedures for evaluating supported employment programs are described by Bellamy et al. (1988), Trach and Rusch (1989), and Wehman (1981).

Process/Progress Evaluation Progress/process evaluation is used to analyze program operations. It is intended to describe the program and the general environment in which it operates, including who is served, what services are provided, how much the service costs, and how the program could be replicated (Schalock & Hill, 1986). Similar to the compliance monitoring evaluation model, the process/progress model is also of limited use in comparing the outcomes and costs of one program to another. Due to this limitation, this chapter will focus on summative evaluation methods and procedures.

In contrast, summative evaluation is used in assessing outcomes in terms of the program's accomplishments, impact on individuals, and costs. It is this primary focus on the multiple economic and social outcomes of service delivery that is most critical when attempting to demonstrate the efficacy of supported employment and other social programs within today's political and economic climate.

Outcome of Impact Evaluation Outcome evaluation commonly entails several key activities and steps: 1) identifying key issues and information needs, 2) developing a conceptual framework to guide the process and subsequent analyses, 3) specifying the nature of comparisons to be made, 4) specifying and operationalizing outcome measures, and 5) collecting and analyzing outcome data appropriate to addressing earlier information needs and questions (DeStefano, 1990; DeStefano & Wagner, 1990; Lewis, Johnson, et al., 1991; Schalock, 1988; Schalock & Hill, 1986). A brief explanation of each of these key activities in the process of outcome evaluation is provided as follows.

Identifying Information Needs   This initial step involves stakeholders (i.e., individuals with disabilities, family members, professional staff, advisory board members) and others in a collaborative planning process to identify key evaluation questions and related outcome measures for study and analysis. This is advocated on the grounds that such participation is not only important in and of itself, but also improves the quality of the evaluation design and support for results obtained later. The importance of including participatory planning and consensus development techniques throughout the full duration of the evaluation process is also emphasized (DeStefano & Wagner, 1990).

Developing a Conceptual Framework   An example of a potentially useful conceptual framework for guiding outcome evaluations of supported employment programs is seen in Figure 1. The model is adapted, in part, from DeStefano (1990) and illustrates the interactive nature of individual, program, employment, and community variables related to supported employment outcomes. Depicted are the critical dependent and independent variables expected to influence outcomes in employment programs. The framework also sets the context for examining interrelationships among key variables (or variable clusters), along with the hypothesized path of influence. Such conceptualizations are important in determining later methods of analyses (i.e., univariate or multivariate procedures).

Specifying Comparisons   Several comparisons can be employed in outcome evaluations of supported employment programs: 1) intraprogram comparisons of differing supported employment models (i.e., individual placement, enclave, mobile work crew, and entrepreneurial models; sheltered work vs. supported employment); 2) comparisons by consumer characteristics (i.e., disability type and level, gender, disabled vs. nondisabled); 3) cross-program/agency comparisons; and 4) longitudinally based comparisons of the same individuals or programs over time. The reader is cautioned to consult other reviews that describe detailed procedures and techniques for establishing comparison groups for analyses (Attkisson, Hargreaves, Horowitz, & Sorenson, 1978; DeStefano & Wagner, 1990; Madaus, Scriven, & Stufflebeam, 1985; Posavac & Carey, 1980; Rossi, Freeman, & Wright, 1975). The principal caution is that for each type of comparison, alternative explanations commonly challenge the attribution, and the validity of such comparisons must be carefully assessed (DeStefano & Wagner, 1990).

Determining Outcome Measures   Identifying, selecting, and operationalizing relevant and measurable outcomes is one of the most pressing issues in conducting meaningful outcome evaluations of supported employment. As illustrated in Figure 1, outcome measures are typically defined from the perspective of the individual, employer, program or agency, and system or community levels. A dis-

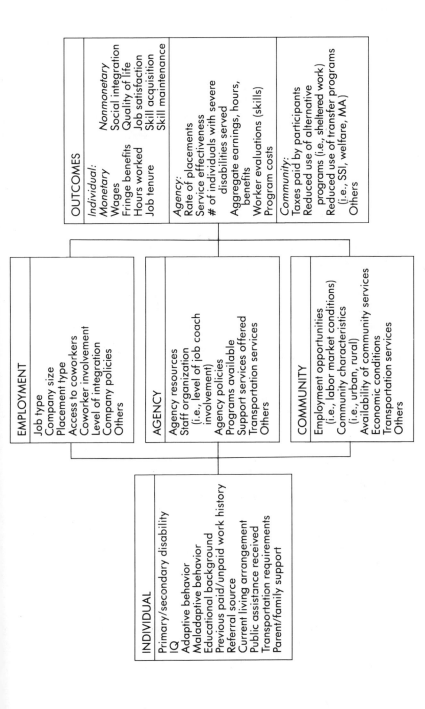

EMPLOYMENT

Job type
Company size
Placement type
Access to coworkers
Coworker involvement
Level of integration
Company policies
Others

AGENCY

Agency resources
Staff organization
(i.e., level of job coach
involvement)
Agency policies
Programs available
Support services offered
Transportation services
Others

COMMUNITY

Employment opportunities
(i.e., labor market conditions)
Community characteristics
(i.e., urban, rural)
Availability of community services
Economic conditions
Transportation services
Others

INDIVIDUAL

Primary/secondary disability
IQ
Adaptive behavior
Maladaptive behavior
Educational background
Previous paid/unpaid work history
Referral source
Current living arrangement
Public assistance received
Transportation requirements
Parent/family support

OUTCOMES

Individual:
Monetary   *Nonmonetary*
Wages   Social integration
Fringe benefits   Quality of life
Hours worked   Job satisfaction
Job tenure   Skill acquisition
                    Skill maintenance

Agency:
Rate of placements
Service effectiveness
# of individuals with severe
     disabilities served
Aggregate earnings, hours,
     benefits
Worker evaluations (skills)
Program costs

Community:
Taxes paid by participants
Reduced use of alternative
     programs (i.e., sheltered work)
Reduced use of transfer programs
     (i.e., SSI, welfare, MA)
Others

Figure 1. Conceptual model showing the interactive nature of individual, employment, agency, and community variables to produce outcomes in supported employment. (Adapted, in part, from DeStefano, L. [1990].)

463

cussion of these outcomes in relation to individuals with disabilities, supported employment programs, the system of community services, and society as a whole follows.

Individual Outcomes Individual-level outcomes are most often categorized in monetized and nonmonetized terms. Monetary outcomes include wages received per hour or week, fringe benefits (i.e., health insurance, sick leave, pension plans, life insurance), net annual earnings (less taxes paid), hours worked per week, and job tenure. These monetary-related outcomes are straightforward and measure the economic benefits and output of employment for individuals with disabilities. Importantly, supported employment has distinguished itself from other employment and training services in the United States by the fundamental nature of its broad qualitative, as well as quantitative, outcomes. Employment integration, quality of life, and skill acquisition and maintenance are critically important additional dimensions of supported employment's social benefits to individuals.

Outcomes associated with the qualitative dimensions or social benefits of supported employment cannot, however, be valued monetarily. Goode (1989) comments that because these outcomes are more difficult to operationalize and quantify than economic benefit data, they are often not included in outcome evaluations of supported employment programs, yet their relevance to job success, family involvement, and the philosophical mission of supported employment is unquestionable. As noted earlier in this chapter, employment integration and related quality of life issues are perhaps the most important attributes of supported employment programs, especially for persons with severe disabilities (Bellamy et al., 1988; Lewis, Johnson, et al., 1991; Mank & Buckley, 1989; Rusch et al., 1991).

Recently, researchers have evolved several alternative measurement strategies to address the need for improved measures and criteria on the social benefits and outcomes of employment. Chadsey-Rusch (1990) has suggested that employment integration includes both a physical and a social component. That is, "social integration implies that employees with and without disabilities are incorporated into and share equal membership in the same social network in the workplace" (Chadsey-Rusch, 1990, p. 161). The Vocational Integration Index (Parent et al., 1990) and the Employment Integration Index (Lagomarcino, 1989) are examples of instruments recently developed to evaluate the current status of employment integration for individual workers.

The concept of quality of life also continues to take on greater importance in evaluations of supported employment programs. Researchers have, however, found it difficult to reach consensus on the development of adequate social indicators (i.e., satisfaction level, increases in personal independence, mobility, social networks, and degree of environmental control) to objectively measure quality of life. Keith, Schalock, and Hoffman (1986) suggest that quality of community life is best operationalized by focusing on degree of environmental control, amount of social interaction, and variety of community utilization. Other dimensions, such as psychological well-being and personal satisfaction, can also be operationalized, through observations, questionnaires, or semistructured interviews. The Lifestyle Satisfaction Survey (Heal & Chadsey-Rusch, 1985), the Quality of Life Questionnaire (Schalock, 1986), and the Co-Worker Involvement Index (Rusch, Hughes, McNair, & Wilson, 1989) are several forms of such instrumentation now available. The acquisition and maintenance of job or community living skills is another associated outcome of supported employment. The positive impact of supported employment on the development of job-specific skills has been a subject of considerable interest among researchers during the past two decades (Gold, 1974; Rusch, Connis, & Sowers, 1978; Rusch & Mithaug, 1980; Wehman, 1981). Outcome criteria are established to determine whether or not performance requirements of the job are satisfactorily learned and mastered by individuals. These include tasks that the individual is expected to complete independently or with assistance. Eco-behavioral principles have recently been incorporated to help improve our understanding of the congruence or match between persons and their work environment (Krejc, Frankforter, & Schalock, 1986; Schalock & Jensen, 1986). Based on these principles, the quality of a person's employment (congruence) is enhanced through behavioral skill training, prosthetic usage, and/or environmental modification (Schalock & Koehler, 1984). Several instruments have been developed to measure skill gains and related performance outcomes among workers with disabilities. These include the Goodness of Fit Index (Krejc et al., 1986), Skill Acquisition Index (Schalock & Harper, 1982), Job/Person Compatibility Index (Wehman, Hill, & Hill, 1984), and the Skill Maintenance Index (Schalock, Gadwood, & Perry, 1984).

Involvement in employment programs also increases participants' independent living and community skills. Increases in adaptive behavior (or reductions in maladaptive behavior) must also be regarded as a valued outcome of supported employment programs. Standardized scales of adaptive behavior can be readily applied in evaluations of supported employment programs. For example, the Inventory for Client and Agency Planning (ICAP) (Bruininks, Hill, Weatherman, & Woodcock, 1986), can be used when collecting information on the adaptive and challenging behaviors of individuals served in supported employment. The ICAP is also useful in generating descriptive summary information on the characteristics and functional limitations of individuals with disabilities. Such descriptive information is important when analyzing differences among individuals served in supported employment programs (see, for example, Lewis, Johnson, et al., 1991; McGrew, Johnson, & Bruininks, 1992).

Despite the appeal and importance of evaluating these qualitative dimensions of supported employment, there remains a scarcity of empirical support as to how such outcome measures can uniformly and consistently be applied in service evaluations. The principal difficulties have stemmed from a lack of consensus on what constitutes and defines employment integration and quality of life, and from a lack of adequate instrumentation to measure these multi-attributes of employment.

Program-Level Outcomes

This area of outcome evaluation relates directly to the program's accomplishments in achieving its mission and goals. Here, too, monetary and nonmonetary outcomes can be measured. Many of these goals, however, are centered on individual outcomes and, therefore, need not be discussed in detail in this section. Summative information, such as program placement rates in community-based employment, average or mean earnings and related work benefits attained by program participants, degree or level of agency change-over from segregated to integrated employment, and a variety of other factors, can be developed to measure program effects. Nonmonetized outcomes may include levels of satisfaction expressed by consumers, family members, and employers with the quality and effectiveness of employment services provided by the program or agency. Most efforts to date have focused on evaluating program costs and related efficiency dimensions in achieving individual and programmatic outcomes. Benefit-cost analysis, discussed later in this chapter, has been a leading evaluation strategy in examining the social benefits and costs of alternative employment services.

System-Level and Societal-Level Outcomes

Evaluations of supported employment programs from the broader context of the service delivery system and society as a whole have recently been advocated (Schalock, 1988; Schalock & Hill, 1986; Schalock & Thornton, 1988; Wehman et al., 1989). Based on this view, networks of organizations dispensing a variety of social programs for individuals with disabilities also need clearly articulated goals and outcomes by which to judge the quality and effectiveness of their performance. System-level goals and outcomes are largely articulated in public social policy and legislation. For example, the evolution of public policy leading to the creation of services for individuals with severe disabilities has been influenced substantially by federal legislation. It is well-recognized, however, that the inherent intent of federal legislation is often expressed in broad goals and policy statements reflecting only a general course of action to be followed (Johnson, Bruininks, & Thurlow, 1987). The federal policy initiative on supported employment is stated in broad terms—"to provide competitive employment in integrated work settings for individuals with severe disabilities" (*Federal Register*, 1987, p. 30547). While the intent of this policy is generally understood, it does not answer specific questions concerning methods of program implementation, proportion of the total population of individuals with disabilities to be served, or what proportion of available resources should be expended on the development and delivery of these services.

Corwin (1974), in his analysis of goal formulation in public education, referred to these broad types of federal policy statements as nonoperational goals. He stressed that such goals are so abstract that it is difficult to dispute them and, because they are so abstract, they provide few clues as to what an agency should do to implement them. These broad official standards for practice must be translated into clearer, more concrete guides for planning and evaluating actions at the federal, state, and local levels (Johnson et al., 1987). State agencies in concert with local program operators must set about the task of defining clear goals and outcomes that can serve as the basis of ongoing evaluations of system-level effectiveness and efficiency.

Incorporating societal perspectives in outcome evaluations of supported employment services is also an area of growing interest among researchers. Benefit-cost analysis is being used as the primary evaluation strategy for determining whether the social and economic benefits of supported employment justify their costs.

Determining Methods of Analysis An extensive review of various approaches used in analyzing outcome data and information goes beyond the scope of this chapter. Decisions about how data are to be analyzed should be made early in the planning stages of an outcome assessment, in conjunction with decisions about information needs, variables and their measurement, data sources, and audiences (DeStefano & Wagner, 1990). Detailed discussions of appropriate data analysis strategies and techniques can be found in Bolton (1987); Borg and Gall (1983); Kleinbaum, Kupper, and Miller (1988); Rossi et al. (1975); and Walls and Tseng (1987).

Efficiency of Benefit-Cost Analysis

Efficiency evaluation, or benefit-cost analysis, is increasingly being used to assess the financial outcomes and related social benefits of supported employment services. Benefit-cost analysis addresses the fundamental questions of whether a particular program is worth its costs. To date, several studies have shown that supported employment does produce positive financial outcomes for individuals with disabilities, as well as for taxpayers. Supported employee earnings tend to be higher than similar persons' earnings who are participating in sheltered employment, work activity, or adult day habilitation programs (Hill et al., 1987; Noble & Conley, 1987). Others have concluded that supported employment does result in net monetary gains to society if examined over a long enough period of time (Hill et al., 1987; Lewis, Johnson, et al., 1991; Naeve, Allen, Harding, & Shea, 1990).

The use and application of benefit-cost analysis as a strategy for evaluating employment and other social programs has, however, been a subject of substantial controversy. This has been due, in large part, to insufficiencies of data concerning the benefits and costs of programs and to the extreme sensitivity of the results of benefit-cost models to their underlying assumptions relating to discount rates, earning streams, comparison groups, and the like (Lewis, Johnson, et al., 1991). Several excellent reviews of these and other related conceptual and methodological limitations of using benefit-cost analysis to evaluate employment programs for persons with disabilities can be found in Conley (1975), Conley and Noble (1990), Johnston (1987), Noble (1977), Noble and Conley (1987), and Thornton and Maynard (1989). Despite these limitations, benefit-cost analysis is increasingly being used and valued as a means of evaluating supported employment's efficiency and efficacy (Cho & Schuermann, 1980; Conley, Rusch, McCaughrin, & Tines, 1989; Hill, Wehman, Kregel, Banks, & Metzler, 1987; Lam, 1986; Lewis, Johnson, et al., 1991; Naeve et al., 1990; Noble, Conley, Banerjee, & Goodman, 1991).

The following section presents the reader an overview of the benefit-cost process. The discussion is based on earlier research work (Thornton, 1985; Thornton

& Will, 1988), as well as more recent conceptualizations and applications (Conley & Noble, 1990; Lewis, Johnson, et al., 1991). These analysts provide a useful description of the logical steps that make up this process.

Defining the Program and Its Alternatives

Benefit-cost analysis is essentially a structured comparison; thus, as the first step in a benefit-cost analysis, the analyst must specify the program or policy being evaluated and the program or option with which it will be compared (Lewis, Johnson, et al., 1991; Thornton & Will, 1988). The program itself must first be identified, and its tangible and intangible effects on individuals served must be understood. This also includes a clear depiction of the quantitative and qualitative dimensions of the program's goals and outcomes.

Determining the Analytical Perspective

The analytical perspectives of interest are commonly individuals with disabilities and their family members, taxpayers, and society. Issues of societal economic efficiency are centered directly on the perspective of taxpayers and society. In such social perspectives, benefit-cost analysis examines the net economic effect of the program on the total value of resources expended. Additional social and individual benefits are represented by the nonmonetized values and outcomes that individuals with disabilities directly experience as a result of program participation. These nonmonetary outcomes include the extent to which program participants experience increased levels of physical and social integration, improved quality of life, and so forth.

Listing the Benefits and Costs

Figure 1 identified the wide range of monetary and nonmonetary benefits and costs of supported employment programs. Many of these social and economic outcomes are also routinely factored into benefit-cost analyses. Table 1 illustrates a cost-accounting framework for a hypothetical supported employment program. Monetized and nonmonetized benefits and costs are conventionally listed and, in the present case, examined from the perspective of the individual and family, taxpayer, and society. Table 1 also illustrates how the anticipated impact of a supported employment program is expected to be perceived—as either benefits or costs—by the three groups. In the ideal analytic scenario, quantifiable measures (dollar values or other empirical weights) would be available for each benefit and cost dimension identified as a potential impact of supported employment in this table. In practice, however, dollar values or other quantitative measures are not always available. Due to this inavailability, other less tangible benefits, such as increased social integration and improved quality of life, are depicted symbolically as a net benefit (+), a net cost (−), or neither (0).

Table 1. Expected benefits and costs of a hypothetical supported employment program

Impacts	ANALYTICAL PERSPECTIVES		
	Social	Individual and Family	Other Taxpayers
INCREASED PRODUCTIVITY			
Additional earned income	+	+	0
Additional fringe benefits	+	+	0
Increased taxes	0	−	+
REDUCED USE OF ALTERNATIVE PROGRAMS			
Training-related services (e.g., sheltered work, work activity, day habilitation services)	+	0	+
Support services (e.g., transportation, healthcare, housing)	+	0	+
DECREASED GOVERNMENT SUBSIDIES			
Reductions in SSI/MA payments	0	−	+
Reductions in food stamps, welfare, others	0	−	+
Reduced administrative costs	+	0	+
OTHER BENEFITS			
Increased social integration	+	+	+
Improved quality of life	+	+	+
Increased job skills	+	+	+
Increased self-sufficiency	+	+	+
Increased job satisfaction	+	+	+
Others	+	+	+
COSTS *PROGRAM COSTS*			
Operating cost of program	−	0	−
Administrative cost	−	0	−
FOREGONE EARNINGS	−	0	−
INCREASED USE OF COMPLEMENTARY PROGRAMS (e.g., postsecondary training, competitive employment)	−	0	−

NOTE: Perspectives characterized as being a net benefit (+), a net cost (−), or neither (0).

Valuing Program Effects and Costs

Estimating the net present value of supported employment programs involves three general considerations: estimating the effects of the program itself, valuing the impacts of the program, and aggregating the valued benefits and costs (Thornton, 1985). Determining the magnitude of a program's effects on participants, taxpayers, and society is a difficult and challenging task. Factual data (i.e., actual program cost records, individual employment outcome data, and other actual cost and outcome data) are preferred for use in the analysis. Nonobservable program effects must, however, be estimated. This means that the analyst must infer, through observation, reliable sources, or best judgment, what the effects of the program would have been in the comparison situation. Placing values on the impact of the program is the next step. The analyst must value or measure, as best as possible, all costs and benefits for subsequent analyses. Since benefit-cost analysis attempts to assess all alternatives in terms of monetary values, pecuniary measurement becomes an obvious and challenging hurdle in this form of analysis (Lewis et al., 1988). When actual dollar values are unknown or unavailable, yet important to the analysis, estimations of monetary values (termed "shadow prices") are made. As discussed earlier, nonmonetized social benefits of supported employment are also identified as valued program effects and included in the analytic framework. The last step in estimating the program's net present value is the aggregation of the valued benefits and costs. This requires a detailed analysis of time-related problems associated with valuing the monetary effects (Thornton, 1985). These issues include developing adequate calculations and estimates of inflation, discounting, and extrapolation. A detailed description of these procedures can be found in Thornton (1985), Thornton and Dunstan (1986), and Thornton and Will (1988).

The hypothetical framework shown in Table 1 provides a useful method for presenting and interpreting benefits and costs of supported employment in monetary and nonmonetary terms. The benefit-cost analysis typically provides a detailed discussion of the monetary values expressed in the table and only inferred meanings (+ , − , or 0) are assigned to the nonmonetary benefits.

METHODOLOGICAL CONSIDERATIONS IN EVALUATING THE MULTI-ATTRIBUTE NATURE OF SUPPORTED EMPLOYMENT PROGRAMS

Several issues arise when professionals and analysts shift their focus to the assessment of outcomes in supported employment. There remains, for example, a lack of group consensus on the goals and outcomes of supported employment for individuals with severe disabilities. The question of whether to evaluate supported employment solely on the basis of economic criteria (i.e., cost efficiency, cost-benefit, or economic impact on individuals' earnings) or to focus on the social benefits to participants (i.e., social integration, quality of life, or increases in skill levels) continues with considerable debate among researchers and professionals.

Even if consensus can be reached on the multiple goals and outcomes of supported employment, there are continuing technical and methodological limitations in the assessment of these goals and, more so, in measuring the cost-effectiveness of programs. Suggested here are several methodological considerations for evaluating the multi-attribute nature of supported employment programs.

Evaluating the Multidimensional Nature of Employment Outcomes

A considerable base of research has now been assembled that provides valuable descriptive information on the social and economic outcomes and costs of supported employment. Unfortunately, much of this research has failed to adequately capture the multivariate complexity of the many dimensions conceptually argued as being associated with employment integration and related concepts of adult adjustment, quality of life, and social well-being. Ambiguity in current research findings on adult adjustment is often due to inadequate research designs (e.g., lack of comparison groups, single studies, inadequate conceptual frameworks, limited samples) and methodological weaknesses (e.g., reliance on single and, often, dichotomous variables; lack of multivariate perspectives) (Bruininks et al., 1990; McGrew & Bruininks, 1991; McGrew, Bruininks, Thurlow, & Lewis, 1992; Zetlin, 1987). Typically, evaluation studies in supported employment have focused on correlations of single outcomes (e.g., individual earning and related economic outcomes) or an analysis of narrow dimensions of social well-being (e.g., physical and social integration levels, improved quality of life, or increases in job and community living skills).

There are many qualitative, as well as quantitative, outcomes implied in supported employment's mission and goals. Due to this complexity, improved conceptual and analytic frameworks and methods are critically needed to understand the full impact of this program. There have been a number of investigations that have sought to improve upon the measurement of community adjustment through the development and validation of multidimensional outcomes measures. This research has, in large part, investigated community adjustment as a function of several broad dimensions—demographics; employment activities; education, job training, or day activities; living arrangements; family and friend social networks; community involvement; personal satisfaction levels; and financial independence (see Bruininks et al., 1990; Halpern, Nave, Close, & Nelson, 1986; Heal, 1985; McGrew et al., 1992; McGrew & Bruininks, 1991; Parmenter, 1987). A variety of factor analytic and other multivariate procedures to derive composite variables were employed in these studies.

The construction of composite variables, based on the reduction of many single outcome variables, helps to aid researchers and evaluators in several ways. First, the sheer number of variables included in outcome studies of employment and community services can be reduced. This not only saves valuable time during data collection and analysis, but reduces the tendency to misinterpret results when interrelationships among many variables must be explained. Second, the validation of multidimensional outcome measures may contribute to the development and empirical evaluation of comprehensive models of employment integration and related dimensions of community adjustment for individuals with severe disabilities. In relation to future research issues in employment services, Stark, Schalock, and Berland (1986) suggest that it is essential to realize that benefits and outcomes are multivariate and that the total outcome mosaic must be analyzed before making definitive statements. Considerable experimentation and research must ensue during the next few years to fully capture the complex, multifaceted nature of supported employment programs.

Linking Multi-Attribute Outcomes to Cost

Little attention has been directed to evaluating the cost-effectiveness of supported employment programs. For both public policy development and individual-level program planning, information about the relative cost-effectiveness of alternative employment programs for persons with disabilities is needed. Attempting to find relationships between program costs and effectiveness measures in supported employment has been difficult. Nevertheless, program alternatives sharing similar goals can be compared according to their relative costs and outcomes. Those alternatives with the lowest relative cost-effectiveness ratios would be considered to be the most promising with respect to the use of society's resources. Such choices would use the fewest resources to achieve the program's goals.

When the evaluation context is one in which multiple criteria and attributes must be considered, as in supported employment, the challenge to the evaluator or choice maker is how to convert these multiple outcomes into a single index that can be compared across several alternative programs or options (Lewis, Erickson, Johnson, & Bruininks, 1991). Determining appropriate and meaningful indices against which the relative cost-effectiveness of supported employment can be evaluated and compared with other service delivery alternatives (e.g., sheltered employment, work activity, day activity programs) is a highly challenging task. In addition, issues related to the cost-effectiveness of using alternative models of supported employment (e.g., individual placement, enclave, mobile work crew, or entrepreneurial models) and to whether individual or group placement models are more cost-effective, still remain unresolved. Such information is, however, important from the standpoint of both policy and program management, as efforts to expand supported employment services continue throughout the United States.

Even though a number of studies have attempted to link costs of supported employment with outcome information (Cho & Schuermann, 1980; Conley et al., 1989; Hill et al., 1987; Lam, 1986; Lewis, Johnson, et al., 1991; Noble et al., 1991), the analyses and the results of all these studies have focused on single dimensions of outcomes. So far, no study has attempted to associate the multi-attributes of supported employment effectiveness with actual related costs in an effort to derive meaningful cost-effectiveness measures for interprogram or cross-agency comparisons. Any comprehensive evaluation of effectiveness within supported employment must be sensitive not only to capture objectively verifiable outcomes of effectiveness, but also qualitative indicators that professionals, consumers, and family members value as important outcomes. This necessitates adopting measurement methodologies that are sensitive to both objective and subjective dimensions of the effectiveness of supported employment outcomes.

The use of multi-attribute utility (MAU) evaluation procedures may, at this juncture in supported employment's evolution, serve to provide important indices of the program's effectiveness. Such evaluation methodologies are essential for policymakers who must choose between alternative ways of delivering these services. MAU evaluation techniques have been used in the management sciences for a number of years for structuring decision making (Carroll & Johnson, 1990; Keeney & Raiffa, 1976; Poole & DeSanctis, 1990) and evaluating program alternatives (Edwards & Newman, 1982). MAU has also had extensive use in the private sector, and even some use in assessing social programs, especially in the field of public health (Kaplan, Atkins, & Wilson, 1988); in the criminal justice system (Edwards, 1980); and, recently, in making decisions about program alternatives in the field of education (Levin, 1983; Lewis, 1989; Lewis, Erickson, et al., 1991).

As an evaluation model, MAU is viewed as appropriate for assisting decision makers in operating supported employment programs. The multidimensional nature of goals and stakeholders in supported employment, for example, requires the unique methods and procedures of MAU analysis. Edwards, Guttentag, and Snapper (1975) have noted that MAU evaluation methods and procedures are most appropriately used in settings in which: 1) the evaluations are comparative; 2) programs normally serve multiple constituencies; 3) programs have multiple goals, not all equally important; 4) judgments are a required part of the evaluation; 5) judgments of magnitude can be assisted by numerical measurements; and 6) the evaluation is related to decisions. All of these characteristics are commonly found in the field of rehabilitation services, where decision makers need to make choices between alternative programs.

In the simplest terms, the MAU evaluation model structures the decision process for an individual, or a group of stakeholders, to make judgments about ranking several alternatives. It requires a comparison among two or more alternatives against two or more criteria. These criteria may also have several different dimensions (i.e., attributes) that need to be identified. After importance weights are attached to each of the criteria and attributes, a weighted importance value is assigned to each attribute within each criterion. Measured dimensions of each attribute are then assigned utility values for varying degrees of performance. Then, each of these alternatives is evaluated in the light of these criteria and attributes.

Based on the measure of performance of each attribute (either through actual measured performance or judgments about performance) within each alternative, utility scores are then computed and attached to each of the attributes. These attribute values are then multiplied by their importance weights and summed to derive a composite score for each alternative. If cost data are available, and if it was not one of the criteria or attributes in the evaluation model, cost per unit of utility can be estimated for determining the relative cost-effectiveness (i.e., internal technical efficiency) of each alternative. An extensive review of these techniques and procedures is beyond the scope of this chapter. (See Carroll & Johnson, 1990; Edwards et al., 1975; Edwards & Newman, 1982; Lewis, Johnson, et al., 1991 for detailed reviews.)

The unique quality of the MAU evaluation model is its ability to structure the evaluation decision into a weighted utility index for purposes of comparison. The term "utility" is used to measure the extent to which an alternative satisfies an attribute or criterion. It is a conventional way of expressing worth, psychological value, or satisfaction in a common numerical metric. The MAU model permits an evaluator to aggregate utility or satisfaction derived from each of the various attributes into a single measure of the overall utility of the multiattributed alternative.

In the past, comparisons of alternative rehabilitation programs (e.g., sheltered versus supported employment), as well as differing models of a similar service (i.e., supported employment with individual placement, enclave, mobile work crew, or entrepreneurial models), were either ignored or rested on idiosyncratic rationales unrelated to measures of effectiveness. Although these programs and service delivery models were assumed to have similar goals (i.e., employment outcomes for individuals with disabilities), comparative assessments were judged to be highly problematic because of the multiple nature of these goals and because of the presence of differing stakeholders. Through the use of MAU evaluation techniques, decision makers and policymakers now have an effective tool for assessing alternatives in the employment of individuals with disabilities. These procedures present considerable potential for improving consensus building, the evaluation of multiple outcomes, and the quality of decision making in supported employment.

CONCLUSION

Supported employment is fast becoming the preferred service delivery alternative for achieving broad social and economic goals and outcomes for individuals with severe disabilities, family members, and society as a whole. The richness of this service alternative is now enthusiastically embraced in public policy, for it acknowledges the value and importance of "competitive employment in an integrated work setting for individuals who, because of their handicaps, need ongoing support services to perform that work" (*Federal Register*, 1987, p. 30,546). This legacy of public policy may likely serve as part of the impetus for guaranteeing the future rights of individuals with severe disabilities in all areas of citizenship and community living.

Along with the evolution of supported employment, distinct service delivery models, strategies, and practices have emerged. A variety of individual and small group approaches have been developed, ensuring that irrespective of the severity of an individual's disability, employment is an attainable goal.

The focus of supported employment's short history has been the need for ongoing evaluations of its social and economic benefits and outcomes. Reliable and complete outcome and cost information are fast becoming an essential aspect of federal, state, and local decision making, and a necessity for planning and improving supported employment programs and services. The evaluation models described in this chapter address the difficulties and complexities involved in documenting the full individual and societal impact of supported employment. Cost and outcome evaluation methods and procedures developed to date are encouraging, yet replete with numerous conceptual and methodological limitations.

As a community of researchers and practitioners, we have reached a point, however, where the increasing demand for new and better information by policymakers, the general public, and consumers themselves necessitate that alternatives to current evaluation practices be examined. If community integration is valued, for example, and is viewed as the single most important outcome and attribute of supported employment for individuals with severe disabilities, more sophisticated methods to measure and communicate this important dimension will be needed. Thus far, this valued dimension has not been adequately accounted for in evaluations of program costs and outcomes. Two alternative evaluation strategies are proposed in this chapter that relate to the greater use of composite outcome indicators and multi-attribute evaluation techniques. Researchers are encouraged to experiment with their applicability and relevance in future evaluations of supported employment services.

REFERENCES

Attkisson, C.C., Hargreaves, W.A., Horowitz, M.J., & Sorenson, L.E. (Eds.). (1978). *Evaluation of human services programs*. New York: Academic Press.

Bates, P., & Pancsofar, E. (1983). Project EARN (Employment and Rehabilitation = Normalization): A competitive employment training program for severely disabled youth in the public schools. *British Journal of Mental Subnormality, 29*, 97–103.

Bellamy, G.T., Horner, R.H., & Inman, D.P. (1979). *Vocational habilitation of severely retarded adults: A direct service technology*. Baltimore: University Park Press.

Bellamy, G.T., Rhodes, L.E., Mank, D.M., & Albin, J.M. (1988). *Supported employment: A community implementation guide*. Baltimore: Paul H. Brookes Publishing Co.

Berkowitz, M., & Berkowitz, E.D. (1983). *Rehabilitation research review: Benefit-cost analysis*. Washington, DC: U.S. Department of Education, National Rehabilitation Information Center.

Bolton, B. (1987). Scores and norms. In B. Bolton (Ed.), *Handbook of measurement and evaluation in rehabilitation* (2nd ed.) (pp. 3–20). Baltimore: Paul H. Brookes Publishing Co.

Borg, W.R., & Gall, M.D. (1983). *Educational research: An introduction*. New York: Longman.

Bruininks, R.H., Hill, B.K., Weatherman, R.F., & Woodcock, R.W. (1986). *Inventory for client and agency planning*. Allen, TX: DLM Teaching Resources.

Bruininks, R.H., McGrew, K., Thurlow, M., & Lewis, D.R. (1990). Dimensions of community adjustment among young adults with intellectual disabilities. In W. Fraser (Ed.), *Key issues in mental retardation research* (pp. 435–448). London: Routledge.

Carroll, J.S., & Johnson, E.J. (1990). *Decision research: A field guide*. London: Sage.

Chadsey-Rusch, J.G. (1985). Community integration and mental retardation: The ecobehavioral approach to service provision and assessment. In R.H. Bruininks & K.C.

Lakin (Eds.), *Living and learning in the least restrictive environment* (pp. 245–260). Baltimore: Paul H. Brookes Publishing Co.

Chadsey-Rusch, J. (1986). Identifying and teaching valued social behaviors in competitive employment settings. In F.R. Rusch (Ed.), *Competitive employment issues and strategies* (pp. 273–287). Baltimore: Paul H. Brookes Publishing Co.

Chadsey-Rusch, J. (1990). Teaching social skills on the job. In F.R. Rusch (Ed.), *Supported employment: Models, methods, and issues*. Sycamore, IL: Sycamore Publishing Co.

Chadsey-Rusch, J., Gonzalez, P., & Tines, J. (1988). Social ecology of the workplace: A study of interactions among employees with and without mental retardation. In J. Chadsey-Rusch (Ed.), *Social ecology of the work place* (pp. 27–54). Champaign: University of Illinois at Urbana-Champaign, Secondary Transition Intervention Effectiveness Institute.

Chadsey-Rusch, J., & Rusch, F. (1988). Social ecology of the workplace. In R. Gaylord-Ross (Ed.), *Vocational education for persons with special needs* (pp. 234–256). Palo Alto, CA: Mayfield.

Cho, D.W., & Schuermann, A.C. (1980). Economic costs and benefits of private gainful employment of the severely handicapped. *Journal of Rehabilitation, 46*(3), 28–32.

Conley, R.W. (1975). Benefit-cost analysis and vocational rehabilitation. In M. Wersinger, I.P. Robinault, & E.C. Bennett (Eds.), *Program evaluation: Selected readings*. New York: ICD Rehabilitation and Research Center.

Conley, R.W., & Noble, J.H. (1989). The new supported employment program. In W.K. Kiernan & R.L. Schalock (Eds.), *Economics, industry, and disability: A look ahead* (pp. 207–222). Baltimore: Paul H. Brookes Publishing Co.

Conley, R.W., & Noble, J.H. (1990). Benefit-cost analysis of supported employment. In F.R. Rusch (Ed.), *Supported employment: Models, methods, and issues* (p. 271–287). Sycamore, IL: Sycamore Publishing Co.

Conley, R.W., Rusch, F.R., McCaughrin, W.B., & Tines, J. (1989). Benefits and costs of supported employment: An analysis of the Illinois Supported Employment Project. *Journal of Applied Behavior Analysis, 22*(4), 441–447.

Corwin, R.G. (1974). The formulation of goals in the public schools. In Y. Hasenfeld & R. English (Eds.), *Human service organizations: A book of readings*. Ann Arbor: University of Michigan Press.

Crosson, J. (1969). A technique for programming sheltered workshop environments for training severely retarded workers. *American Journal of Mental Deficiency, 73*, 814–818.

DeStefano, L. (1990). Designing and implementing program evaluation. In F.R. Rusch (Ed.), *Supported employment: Models, methods, and issues*. DeKalb, IL: Sycamore Publishing Co.

DeStefano, L., & Wagner, M. (1990). *Outcome assessment in special education: Lessons learned*. Rockville, MD: WESTAT.

Developmental Disabilities Assistance and Bill of Rights Act (PL 98–527) (1986).

Education of the Handicapped Act Amendments of 1983. PL 98–199. Title 20, U.S.C. 101 et seq: *U.S. Statutes at Large, 97*, 1357–1375.

Edwards, W. (1980). Multiattribute utility for evaluation. In M. Klein & K. Teilmann (Eds.), *Handbook of criminal justice evaluation*. Beverly Hills, CA: Sage.

Edwards, W., Guttentag, M., & Snapper, K. (1975). Effective evaluation: A decision theoretic approach. In C.A. Bennett & A. Lumsdaine (Eds.), *Evaluation and experiment: Some critical issues in assessing social programs*. New York: Academic Press.

Edwards, W., & Newman, J.R. (1982). *Multiattribute evaluation*. Beverly Hills, CA: Sage.

Evans, G., & Spradlin, J. (1966). Incentives and instructions as controlling variables in productivity. *American Journal of Mental Deficiency, 71*, 129–132.

Everson, J.M. (1988). An analysis of federal and state policy on transition from school to adult life for youth with disabilities. In P. Wehman & M.S. Moon (Eds.), *Vocational rehabilitation and supported employment* (pp. 67–78). Baltimore: Paul H. Brookes Publishing Co.

Federal Register. (1987, August 14). *52*(157), 30,546–30,552. Washington, DC: U.S. Government Printing Office.

Garzan, R., & Mansolo, R. (1981). Texas unit develops job opportunities for blind and visually impaired people. *American Rehabilitation, 7*, 25–26.

Gold, M.W. (1973). Vocational habilitation for the mentally retarded. In N.R. Ellis (Ed.), *International Review of Research in Mental Retardation, 6*, 97–147.

Gold, M.W. (1974). Redundant cue removal in skill training for the retarded. *Education and Training of the Mentally Retarded, 9*, 5–8.

Goode, D.A. (1989). Quality of life and quality of work life. In W.K. Kiernan & R.L. Schalock (Eds.), *Economics, industry, and disability: A look ahead* (pp. 337–349). Baltimore: Paul H. Brookes Publishing Co.

Halpern, A.S., Nave, G., Close, C., & Nelson, D. (1986). An empirical analysis of the dimensions of community adjustment for adults with mental retardation in semi-independent living programs. *Australia and New Zealand Journal of Developmental Disabilities, 12*(3), 147–157.

Heal, L. (1985). Methodology for community integration research. In R.H. Bruininks & K.C. Lakin (Eds.), *Living and learning in the least restrictive environment* (pp. 199–224). Baltimore: Paul H. Brookes Publishing Co.

Heal, L., & Chadsey-Rusch, J. (1985). Lifestyle Satisfaction Scale (LSS): Assessing individuals' satisfaction with residence, community setting, and associated services. *Applied Research in Mental Retardation, 6*, 475–490.

Hill, M.L. (1988). Supported competitive employment: An interagency perspective. In P. Wehman & M.S. Moon (Eds.), *Vocational rehabilitation and supported employment* (pp. 31–49). Baltimore: Paul H. Brookes Publishing Co.

Hill, M., Banks, P.D., Handrich, R., Wehman, P., Hill, J., & Shafer, M. (1987). Benefit-cost analysis of supported competitive employment for persons with mental retardation. *Research in Developmental Disabilities, 8*, 71–89.

Hill, M., Wehman, P., Kregel, J., Banks, P.D., & Metzler, H.M. (1987). Employment outcomes for people with moderate and severe disabilities: An eight-year longitudinal analysis of supported competitive employment. *Journal of The Association for the Severely Handicapped, 12*, 182–189.

Hughes, C., Rusch, F.R., & Curl, R.M. (1990). Extending individual competence, developing natural support, and promoting social acceptance. In F.R. Rusch (Ed.), *Supported employment: Models, methods, and issues* (pp. 181–197). DeKalb, IL: Sycamore Publishing Co.

Johnson, D.R., Bruininks, R.H., & Thurlow, M.L. (1987). Meeting the challenge of transition service planning through improved interagency cooperation. *Exceptional Children, 53*, 522–530.

Johnson, D.R., Warrington, G., & Mellberg, M. (1989). Job development, placement, and follow-up services. In D.E. Berkell & J.M. Brown (Eds.), *Transition from school to work for persons with disabilities* (pp. 161–186). New York: Longman.

Johnston, M.V. (1987). Cost-benefit methodologies in rehabilitation. In R. Fuhrer (Ed.), *Rehabilitation outcomes: Analysis and measurement* (pp. 99–113). Baltimore: Paul H. Brookes Publishing Co.

Kaplan, R.M., Atkins, C.J., & Wilson, D.K. (1988). The cost-utility of diet and exercise interventions in non-insulin–dependent diabetes mellitus. *Health Promotion, 2*, 331–340.

Keeney, R., & Raiffa, H. (1976). *Decisions with multiple objectives: Preferences and value tradeoffs*. New York: Wiley.

Keith, K.D., Schalock, R.L., & Hoffman K. (1986). *Quality of life: Measurement and programmatic implications*. Lincoln, NE: Region V Mental Retardation Services.

Kerachsky, S., Thornton, C., Bloomenthal, A., Maynard, R., & Stephens, S. (1985). *Impacts of transitional employment on mentally retarded young adults: Results of the STETS demonstration.* Princeton, NJ: Mathematica Policy Research.

Kleinbaum, D.G., Kupper, L.L., & Miller, K.E. (1988). *Applied regression analysis and other multi-variable methods.* Boston: PWS-KENT Publishing Co.

Kregel, J., Shafer, M., Wehman, P., & West, M. (1989). Policy development and public expenditures in supported employment: Current strategies to promote statewide systems change. *Journal for The Association of the Severely Handicapped, 14*(4), 283–292.

Kregel, J., & Wehman, P. (1989). Supported employment: Promises deferred for persons with severe disabilities. *Journal of The Association for Persons with Severe Handicaps, 14*, 293–303.

Kregel, J., Wehman, P., Revell, W.G., & Hill, M. (1990). Supported employment in Virginia. In F.R. Rusch (Ed.), *Supported employment: Models, methods, and issues* (pp. 15–29). DeKalb, IL: Sycamore Publishing Co.

Krejc, S., Frankforter, T., & Schalock, R.L. (1986). *Person-environmental and discrepancy analysis computer manual.* Hastings, NE: Mid-Nebraska Mental Retardation Services.

Lagomarcino, T.R. (1986). Community services: Using the supported work model within an adult service agency. In F.R. Rusch (Ed.), *Competitive employment issues and strategies* (pp. 65–76). Baltimore: Paul H. Brookes Publishing Co.

Lagomarcino, T.R. (1989). *Assessing integration in supported employment contexts.* Unpublished doctoral dissertation. Urbana: University of Illinois at Urbana-Champaign.

Lagomarcino, T.R., Hughes, C., & Rusch, F.R. (1989). Utilizing self-management to teach independence on the job. *Education and Training in Mental Retardation, 24*, 139–148.

Lam, C.S. (1986). Comparison of sheltered and supported work programs: A pilot study. *Rehabilitation Counseling Bulletin, 30*(2), 66–82.

Levin, H.M. (1983). *Cost-effectiveness: A primer.* Beverly Hills, CA: Sage.

Lewis, D.R. (1989, March). Use of cost-utility decision models in business education. *Journal of Education in Business, 64*, 275–278.

Lewis, D.R., Bruininks, R.H., Thurlow, M., & McGrew, K. (1988). Using benefit-cost analysis in special education. *Exceptional Children, 55*(3), 203–214.

Lewis, D.R., Erickson, R.N., Johnson, D.R., & Bruininks, R.H. (1991). *Using multiattribute utility evaluation techniques in special education.* St. Paul: Minnesota Department of Education, Unique Learner Needs Section.

Lewis, D.R., Johnson, D.R., Bruininks, R.H., Kallsen, L.A., & Guillery, R.P. (1991). *Costs and benefits of supported employment in Minnesota.* Minneapolis: University of Minnesota, College of Education, Institute on Community Integration (UAP).

Lewis, D.R., Johnson, D.R., Chen, T.H., & Erickson, R.N. (1992). On the use and reporting of benefit-cost analyses by state vocational rehabilitation agencies. *Evaluation Review, 16*(3), 266–287.

Lignugaris/Kraft, B., Salzberg, C.L., Rule, S., & Stowitschek, J.J. (1988). Social-vocational skills of workers with and without mental retardation in two community employment sites. *Mental Retardation, 26*(5), 297–305.

Long, D., Maller, C., & Thornton, C. (1981). Evaluating the benefits and costs of job corps. *Journal of Policy Analysis and Management, 1*(1), 55–76.

Loosemore, F. (1980). Surveys of sheltered workshops and activity therapy centres in Australia funded under the Handicapped Persons Assistance Act. *International Journal of Rehabilitation Research, 3*, 228–229.

Madaus, G., Scriven, M., & Stufflebeam, D. (1985). *Evaluation models: Viewpoints on educational and human services evaluation.* Boston: Kluwer-Nijhoff Publishing.

Mank, D.M., & Buckley, J. (1989). Strategies for integrated employment. In W.K. Kiernan

& R.L. Schalock (Eds.), *Economics, industry, and disability: A look ahead* (pp. 319–335). Baltimore: Paul H. Brookes Publishing Co.

Mank, D.M., Rhodes, L.E., & Bellamy, G.T. (1986). Four supported employment alternatives. In W.K. Kiernan & J.A. Stark (Eds.), *Pathways to employment for adults with developmental disabilities* (pp. 139–153). Baltimore: Paul H. Brookes Publishing Co.

Martin, J.E. (1986). Identifying potential jobs. In F.R. Rusch (Ed.), *Competitive employment issues and strategies* (pp. 165–185). Baltimore: Paul H. Brookes Publishing Co.

McGrew, K.S., & Bruininks, R.H. (1991, March). *Dimensions of personal competence and adjustment in the community*. A paper presented at the International Conference on Mental Retardation, Hong Kong.

McGrew, K., Bruininks, R.H., Thurlow, M., & Lewis, D.R. (1992). Empirical analysis of multi-dimensional measures of adjustment for young adults with retardation. *American Journal on Mental Retardation, 96*(5), 475–487.

McGrew, K., Johnson, D.R., & Bruininks, R.H. (1992). *Factor analysis of community adjustment outcome measures for young adults with mild to severe disabilities*. Minneapolis: University of Minnesota, Institute on Community Integration.

Mithaug, D.E., Hagmeier, L.D., & Harring, N.G. (1977). The relationship between training activities and job placement in vocational education of the severely and profoundly handicapped. *AAEPSH Review, 2*, 89–109.

Moon, M.S., & Griffin, S.L. (1988). Supported employment service delivery models. In P. Wehman & M.S. Moon (Eds.), *Vocational rehabilitation and supported employment* (pp. 17–30). Baltimore: Paul H. Brookes Publishing Co.

Naeve, L., Allen, W., Harding, F., & Shea, J. (1990). *Costs and outcomes study of individual supported employment placements by selected California Department of Rehabilitation funded employment service providers*. Sacramento: California Department of Rehabilitation.

Nisbet, J., & Callahan, M. (1987). Achieving success in integrated workplaces: Critical elements in assisting persons with severe disabilities. In S.I. Taylor, D. Biklen, & J. Knoll (Eds.), *Community integration for people with severe disabilities* (pp. 184–201). New York: Teachers College Press.

Nisbet, J., & Hagner, D. (1988). Natural supports in the workplace: A reexamination of supported employment. *Journal of The Association for Persons with Severe Handicaps, 13*, 260–267.

Noble, J.H. (1977). The limits of cost-benefit analysis as a guide to priority setting in rehabilitation. *Evaluation Quarterly, 1*(3), 347–379.

Noble, J.H., Jr., & Conley, R.W. (1987). Accumulating evidence on the benefits and costs of supported and transitional employment for persons with severe disabilities. *Journal of The Association of Persons with Severe Handicaps, 12*(3), 163–174.

Noble, J.H., Conley, R.W., Banerjee, S., & Goodman, S. (1991). Supported employment in New York State: A comparison of benefits and costs. *Journal of Disability Policy Studies, 2*(1), 39–7.

Parent, W.S., Kregel, J., Twardzik, G., & Metzler, H.M.D. (1990). Social integration in the workplace: An analysis of the integration activities of workers with mental retardation and their coworkers. In J. Kregel, P. Wehman, & M. Shafer (Eds.), *Supported employment for persons with severe disabilities: From research to practice* (Vol. III). Richmond: Virginia Commonwealth University Rehabilitation Research and Training Center.

Parmenter, T.R. (1987). An analysis of the dimensions of quality of life of people with physical disabilities. In R.I. Brown (Ed.), *Quality of life and handicapped people*. London: Croom Helm.

Poole, M.S., & DeSanctis, G. (1990). Understanding the use of group decision support systems. In C. Steinfeld & J. Fulk (Eds.), *Theoretical approaches to information tech-*

nologies in organizations. Beverly Hills, CA: Sage.

Posavac, E.J., & Carey, R.G. (1980). *Program evaluation: Methods and case studies.* Engelwood Cliffs, NJ: Prentice Hall.

Rehabilitation Act Amendments of 1986. (PL 99-506). Title 29, U.S.C. 701 et seq: *U.S. Statutes at Large, 100,* 1807–1846.

Rhodes, L.E., & Valenta, L. (1985). Industry-based supported employment: An enclave approach. *Journal of The Association for Persons with Severe Handicaps, 10,* 12–20.

Rockart, J.F. (1979). Chief executives define their own data needs. *Harvard Business Review, 79*(3), 81–93.

Roessler, R.T., & Hiett, A. (1983). *A comparison of job development strategies in rehabilitation.* Fayetteville: Arkansas University, Rehabilitation Research and Training Center.

Rossi, P.H., Freeman, H.E., & Wright, S.R. (1975). *Evaluation: A systematic approach.* Beverly Hills, CA: Sage Publications.

Rusch, F.R. (1983). Competitive vocational training. In M.E. Snell (Ed.), *Systematic instruction of the moderately and severely handicapped* (2nd ed.) (pp. 503–523). Columbus, OH: Merrill.

Rusch, F.R., Chadsey-Rusch, J., & Johnson, J.R. (1991). Supported employment: Emerging opportunities for employment integration. In L. Meyer, C. Peck, & L. Brown (Eds.), *Critical issues in the lives of people with severe disabilities* (pp. 145–169). Baltimore: Paul H. Brookes Publishing Co.

Rusch, F.R., Connis, R.T., & Sowers, J. (1978). The modification and maintenance of time spent attending to task using social reinforcement, token reinforcement and response cost in an applied restaurant setting. *Journal of Special Education Technology, 2,* 18–26.

Rusch, F.R., & Hughes, C. (1990). Historical overview of supported employment. In F.R. Rusch (Ed.), *Supported employment: Models, methods, and issues* (pp. 5–14). DeKalb, IL: Sycamore Publishing Co.

Rusch, F.R., Hughes, C., McNair, J., & Wilson, P.G. (1989). *Co-worker involvement scoring manual and instrument.* Champaign: University of Illinois, The Board of Trustees of the University of Illinois.

Rusch, F.R., & Menchetti, B.M. (1981). Increasing compliant work behaviors in a nonsheltered work setting. *Mental Retardation, 19,* 107–111.

Rusch, F.R., & Mithaug, D.E. (1980). *Vocational training for mentally retarded adults.* Champaign, IL: Research Press.

Sands, H., & Zalkind, S.S. (1972). Effects of an educational campaign to change employer attitudes toward hiring epileptics. *Epilepsia, 123,* 37–66.

Schalock, R.L. (1985). Comprehensive community services: A plea for interagency collaboration. In R.H. Bruininks & K.C. Lakin (Eds.), *Living and learning in the least restrictive environment* (pp. 37–63). Baltimore: Paul H. Brookes Publishing Co.

Schalock, R.L. (1986). *Defining and measuring the quality of work and outside life.* Paper presented at the 1986 Annual TASH Conference, San Francisco.

Schalock, R.L. (1988). Critical performance evaluation indicators in supported employment. In P. Wehman & M.S. Moon (Eds.), *Vocational rehabilitation and supported employment* (pp. 163–174). Baltimore: Paul H. Brookes Publishing Co.

Schalock, R.L., Gadwood, L.S., & Perry, P.G. (1984). Effects of different training environments on the acquisition of community living skills. *Applied Research in Mental Retardation, 5,* 425–438.

Schalock, R.L., & Harper, R.S., (1982). Skill acquisition and client movement indices: Implementing cost-effective analysis in rehabilitation programs. *Evaluation and Program Planning, 5,* 223–231.

Schalock, R.L., Harper, R.S., & Genung, T. (1981). Community integration of mentally retarded adults: Community placement and program success. *American Journal of Mental Deficiency, 85,* 478–488.

Schalock, R.L., & Hill, M. (1986). Evaluating employment services. In W.K. Kiernan & J.A. Stark (Eds.), *Pathways to employment for adults with developmental disabilities* (pp. 285–302). Baltimore: Paul H. Brookes Publishing Co.

Schalock, R.L., & Jensen, C.M. (1986). Assessing the goodness-of-fit between persons and their environments. *Journal of The Association for Persons with Severe Handicaps*, *11*(2), 103–109.

Schalock, R.L., & Koehler, B. (1984). *Ecobehavioral analysis and augmentative habilitation techniques.* Hastings, NE: Mid-Nebraska Mental Retardation Services.

Schalock, R.L., & Thornton, C. (1988). *Program evaluation: A field guide for program administrators.* New York: Plenum.

Schutz, R.P., Vogelsberg, R.T., & Rusch, F.R. (1980). A behavioral approach to community integration of mentally retarded persons. In A.R. Novak & L.W. Heal (Eds.), *Integration of developmentally disabled individuals into the community* (pp. 37–63). Baltimore: Paul H. Brookes Publishing Co.

Shafer, M.S. (1986). Utilizing co-workers as change agents. In F.R. Rusch (Ed.), *Competitive employment issues and strategies* (pp. 215–224). Baltimore: Paul H. Brookes Publishing Co.

Shafer, M.S. (1988). Supported employment in perspective: Traditions in the federal-state vocational rehabilitation system. In P. Wehman & M.S. Moon (Eds.), *Vocational rehabilitation and supported employment* (pp. 55–66). Baltimore: Paul H. Brookes Publishing Co.

Shafer, M., & Nisbet, J. (1988). Integration and empowerment in the workplace. In M. Barcus, S. Griffin, D. Mank, L. Rhodes, & S. Moon (Eds.), *Supported employment implementation issues.* Richmond: Virginia Commonwealth University Rehabilitation Research and Training Center.

Sowers, J., Rusch, F.R., Connis, R.T., & Cummings, L.E. (1980). Teaching mentally retarded adults to time manage in a vocational setting. *Journal of Applied Behavior Analysis*, *13*, 119–128.

Stark, J.A., Schalock, R.L., & Berland, B.J. (1986). Research demands of the future. In W.K. Kiernan & J.A. Stark (Eds.), *Pathways to employment for adults with developmental disabilities* (pp. 271–284). Baltimore: Paul H. Brookes Publishing Co.

Thornton, C. (1985). Benefit-cost analysis of social programs: Deinstitutionalization and education programs. In R.H. Bruininks & K.C. Lakin (Eds.), *Living and learning in the least restrictive environment* (pp. 225–243). Baltimore: Paul H. Brookes Publishing Co.

Thornton, C., & Dunstan, S.M. (1986). *The evaluation of the national long term care supplement, 1984–85.* Washington, DC: Social Security Administration.

Thornton, C., & Maynard, R. (1989). The economics of transitional employment and supported employment. In M. Berkowitz & M.A. Hill (Eds.), *Disability and the labor market.* Ithaca: Cornell University, New York State School of Industrial and Labor Relations, ILR Press.

Thornton, C., & Will, J. (1988). Benefit-cost analysis and special education programs. In R.H. Bruininks, D.R. Lewis, & M.L. Thurlow (Eds.), *Assessing outcomes, costs and benefits of special education programs.* Minneapolis: Minnesota University Affiliated Program on Developmental Disabilities, University of Minnesota.

Trach, J.S., & Rusch, F.R. (1989). Supported employment program evaluation: Evaluating degree of implementation and selected outcomes. *American Journal of Mental Retardation*, *94*, 134–139.

U.S. Department of Labor. (1979). *Study of handicapped clients in sheltered workshops* (Vol. 2). Washington, DC: Department of Labor.

Usdane, W. (1976). The placement process in the rehabilitation of the severely handicapped. *Rehabilitation Literature*, *37*, 162–165.

Vandergoot, D. (1976). A comparison of two mailing approaches attempting to generate the participation of businessmen in rehabilitation. *Rehabilitation Counseling Bulletin, 20,* 73–75.

Vogelsberg, R.T. (1984). Competitive employment programs for individuals with mental retardation in rural areas. In P. Wehman (Ed.), *Proceedings from the national symposium on employment of citizens with mental retardation.* Richmond: Virginia Commonwealth University.

Vogelsberg, R.T. (1985). Competitive employment in programs for individuals with mental retardation in rural areas. In S. Moon, P. Goodall, & P. Wehman (Eds.), *Critical issues related to supported competitive employment: Proceedings from the first RRTC symposium on employment for citizens who are mentally retarded* (pp. 57–81). Richmond: Virginia Commonwealth University, Rehabilitation Research and Training Center.

Vogelsberg, R.T. (1990). Supported employment in Pennsylvania. In F.R. Rusch (Ed.), *Supported employment: Models, methods, and issues* (pp. 45–64). DeKalb, IL: Sycamore Publishing Co.

Walls, R.T., & Tseng, M.S. (1987). Measurement of client outcomes in rehabilitation. In B. Bolton (Ed.), *Handbook of measurement and evaluation in rehabilitation* (2nd ed.) (pp. 183–201). Baltimore: Paul H. Brookes Publishing Co.

Wehman, P. (1981). *Competitive employment: New horizons for severely disabled individuals.* Baltimore: Paul H. Brookes Publishing Co.

Wehman, P. (1986). Competitive employment in Virginia. In F.R. Rusch (Ed.), *Competitive employment issues and strategies* (pp. 23–34). Baltimore: Paul H. Brookes Publishing Co.

Wehman, P., Hill, J., & Hill, M. (1984). *Employment opportunities for handicapped youth and adults: Enhancing transition.* Richmond: Virginia Commonwealth University, Rehabilitation Research and Training Center.

Wehman, P., Kregel, J., & Shafer, M.S. (1989). *Emerging trends in the national supported employment initiative: A preliminary analysis of twenty-seven states.* Richmond: Virginia Commonwealth University, Rehabilitation Research and Training Center.

Will, M. (1984). *Supported employment for adults with severe disabilities: An OSERS program initiative.* Washington, DC: U.S. Department of Education.

Zadny, J.J. (1980). Employer reactions to job development. *Rehabilitation Counseling Bulletin, 24,* 161–169.

Zetlin, A.G. (1987). Adult development of mildly retarded students: Implications for educational programs. In M.C. Wang, M.C. Reynolds, & H.J. Walberg (Eds.), *Handbook of special education: Research and practice* (Vol. 2, pp. 77–90). New York: Pargamon Press.

Zimmerman, J., Stuckey, T., Garlick, B., & Miller, M. (1969). Effects of token reinforcement on productivity in multiply handicapped clients in a sheltered workshop. *Rehabilitation Literature, 30,* 34–41.

Index

Page numbers followed by t and f denote tables and figures, respectively.

Abuse, 55, 208, 211–212
  sexual, 410
Accepting relationship, 52
Accessibility, 123
Accreditation agencies, outcome-based
  performance measures for, 77
Accreditation Council on Services for Peo-
  ple with Developmental Disabili-
  ties (ACDD), 209, 212
Acquaintance, definition of, 85
Action(s)
  individual, characteristics of, and chal-
    lenging behavior intervention, 163
  of social inclusion facilitator, 102, 103f
Action plan, development of, 100
Action research, 56
Activity limitations, 413, 416
ADA, *see* Americans with Disabilities Act
  of 1990
Adaptation studies, 27–28
Adaptive behavior, 346
  and social inclusion, 93
  and supported employment, 465
Advocacy
  and legal status issues, 441–442
  need for, 271
  and supported employment, 456–457
  see also Self-advocacy
African-American family
  and disability services, 419–421
  see also Race
After-school recreation programs, 122
Alternative, selection of, 363
Alternative choices, identification of, 356
Americans with Disabilities Act of 1990,
  9–10, 124, 281, 287, 369
Antecedent approach, to self-regulation,
  358
Applied qualitative research, 56–58

The Arc (Association for Retarded Cit-
  izens), 122, 174, 225–226, 268,
  279–280, 282, 307, 360
Architectural Barriers Act of 1968, 123
Assertiveness, 361
Associate of Arts degree, in mental retar-
  dation, 326
Attention-motivated behaviors, 150–151
Attribute values, 257
Attributions, program-generated, 365
Audio transcripts, 45–46
Autism, children with, recreational activi-
  ties for, 132–135
Autonomy, *see* Self-determination
Avoidance-motivated behavior, 151

Bachelor of Arts degree, in developmental
  disabilities, 326
Behavior
  attention-motivated, 150–151
  avoidance-/escape-motivated, 151
  form of, 149
  motivation of, 149–150
  object-motivated, 151
  self-regulation of, 357–359
Behavior disorders, *see* Challenging
  behavior
Behavior momentum, 156
Behavioral differences, and social class,
  413
Belief system, of social inclusion facilitator, 102, 103f
Beliefs, common, 95
Bench-work model, *see* Entrepreneurial
  model
Benefit(s), employee, 295, 301–303,
  306–307

Benefit-cost analysis, 244
  of supported employment, 458,
    467–470, 469t
Bias, experimental, 25–30
Body-rocking, 152
Bottom-up approach, 68
Bridgebuilder, see Social inclusion
  facilitator
Burt, Pattie, 52–53

Camping programs, 122
Capability, and guardianship issues, 440
Capital costs, 240, 245
Capital funding strategies, 284
CARF, see Commission on Accreditation
  of Rehabilitation Facilities
Case management, costs of, 272–273
Case management services, independent,
  271
Centers for Independent Living, 272,
  283–284
Chafee Bill, 285
Challenging behavior, 147–169
  communicative function of, 152–153
  definition of, 147
  and exclusion from community ser-
    vices, 186
  intervention strategies for
    selection of, 161–164
    types of, 153–161
  maintaining consequences of, 148,
    152–153
  motivations for
    distinguishing among, 149–153
    interrelatedness of, 152–153
    nonsocial, 151–152
    social, 150–151
  persons with, rights of, 10
Child-rearing patterns, and social class,
  413, 421
Choice(s)
  alternative
    analysis of, 356–357
    identification of, 356
  individual, promotion of, 219–221
Choice definition, 355–356
Choice-making process, 353–357
CIL, see Centers for Independent Living
Circle of friends, 109, 111
Class, see Social class

Classroom, integrated, qualitative research
  studies of, 54–55
Client satisfaction factor, 72
Clustered placement, see Enclave model
CMH centers, see Community mental
  health centers
COBRA, see Consolidated Omnibus Bud-
  get Reconciliation Act of 1987
Comfort, 4, 8–10
Commission on Accreditation of Rehabilitation Facilities, 209
Common values/beliefs, 95
Communicative function, of challenging
  behavior, 152–153
Community
  definition of, 4
  and development of self-determination
    skills, 350–353, 367–368
  persons living in
    and waiting for services/supports,
      190–192
    see also Home; Neighborhood
  shift from institutions to, see
    Deinstitutionalization
Community acceptance, 284–285
Community adjustment
  dimensions of, 73–74, 74f
  measurement of, 67–75
    multidimensional, 65–79
      implications of, 75–78
      reliability of, 66
  and personal competence, 76
Community assimilation/acceptance factor,
  73–74
Community benefactor, 91–92
Community development, 286–287
Community employment, planning and
  implementing, 281–282
Community guide, see Social inclusion
  facilitator
Community integration
  applied qualitative study of, 57–58
  and competency issues, 444
  and guardianship issues, 427–428
  levels of, and specific residential site, 91
Community living
  definition of, 4
  multicultural perspective on, 405–426
  options, and neighborhood housing pat-
    terns, 284–285
  overview of, 3–22
  supported, 7–8

transition from family living to, needs during, 194–195
Community living research, 23–41
  empirical tradition of, 24–33
  experiment and, 26–29
  functions of, 30–33
  multiple perspectives in, 33–36
  paradigm of, 29
  qualitative methods of, 43–63
Community mapping, 107–109, 111
  definition of, 108
Community mental health centers, 272, 281–283
Community participation, valued, 4, 13–14
Community presence, 4–8
  definition of, 4
Community provider organizations
  classification of, 269
  collaboration with state agencies, need for, 270
  financing provided by, 265–288
  study of
    experiences of, 271–284
    purpose and method of, 267–269
    recommendations of, 284–286
  missions and values of, 286
Community recreation services
  historical and legislative overview of, 122–124
  integrated, 124–129
Community residences
  costs of care in, 245–249
    versus institutions, 245
  persons living in
    versus residents of large institutions, 6
    social networks of, 90
Community resource use, 13
Community services
  access barriers to, 191, 195–197, 199
  demand for, 174, 210, 289
  financing of, 265–288
  legislative mandates for, need for, 270
  quality of, comprehensive approach to, 214–223, 215t
  underutilization of, 254–255
  waiting for, see Waiting
Community Service Training Program, 108
Companionship, 88–89
Compensation, of direct care staff,

250–252, 256, 266, 289–312
  improvement of, 308–309
  national survey of, 293–309
  research on, 292–293
Competency
  determination of, 437–438
  criteria for, 438–442
  functional versus legal, 441
  legal standards of, revision of, 442–443
  partial, 439
Competency-based training efforts, 328
Competitive employment, definition of, 452
Compliance monitoring, 461
Composite outcome measures, construction of, 69–71, 71f
Computerized system, for waiting list tracking, 177–181
Concepts, development of, with qualitative research, 50–52
Conditional discriminations, 158
Confirmatory factor analysis, 72–73
Conjunctive job services, 455
Connections
  personal, 381–403
  support of, 382–383, 394–400
  social, types of, 100, 101t
Consequence approach, to self-regulation, 358
Consequence manipulations, for challenging behavior, 159–161
Conservatees, civil rights of, 432
Conservatorship, 431
  underuse of, 434, 440
Consolidated Omnibus Budget Reconciliation Act of 1987, 187–189
Consumer choice, in services/vendors, 219–221
Consumer control, over home and resources, 220–221
Consumer monitoring, of quality assurance, 225–226
Consumer-owned housing, costs of, 279–280
Control
  perceived, 364–365
  see also Self-determination
Cooperative participation, 135
  in recreation activities, promotion of, 133–136
Cooperative peer interaction, promotion of, 136–137, 139–140

Cooperative structuring techniques,
130–132, 137–138
Corporate guardianship, 430
Cost(s), 231–263
linking with outcomes, 239, 255
problems of, 243–245
staff, see Compensation
Cost accounting
problems with, 240–243, 255
in supported employment programs,
458–459
Cost differences, factors accounting for,
249–255
Cost-effectiveness
evaluation of, 244
of supported employment programs,
472–474
of training programs, 327
Cost of living indices, 295, 306
Cost studies
findings, 245–249
methodological problems with,
232–245, 233t–238t, 255
County life service planning organization,
272
County-wide early childhood resource network, 274
Co-Worker Involvement Index, 465
Creaming, 185, 198
Credibility, of qualitative research study,
47
Crisis response activities, 223
Critical inquiry, 35–36
Critical outcome dimensions, delineation
of, 77–78
Crude separation rate, 295, 302,
304f–306f
Cultural diversity, see Multiculturalism
Cultural participation, see Community
participation

Daily life choices, 14
Data base, personal computer, for quality
assessment, 225
Data collection protocol
for community adjustment measures, 73
minimum indicator, 76
Data collection system
for estimation of waiting lists, 197–198
for qualitative research, 45–47
for quality assessment, 225

Daytime programs, waiting for, 174
Decentralization, and staffing, 314
Decision making, personal, 353–357
Declarative knowledge, 363
Deculturing experiences, 418–419
Deductive logic, 32
Deinstitutionalization, 4–5, 15
and challenging behavior, 147–148
and costs of community services,
231–232, 243–244, 255–256, 266
and guardianship issues, 427–428
and multiculturalism, 427–428
and self-determination, 346, 369
and social inclusion, 83
and supported living, 381
and waiting lists for community services, 173–174, 185–187, 198
Dental care, 8
Deprivational procedures, for challenging
behavior, 161
Descriptive data, qualitative research
based on, 45–47
Developmental disabilities, persons with
potential of, realization of, 11
quality services for, 207–230
social inclusion of, enhancement of,
83–119
social relationships/networks of, 90–92
social skills of, and social inclusion, 93
see also Mental retardation
Developmental Disabilities and Bill of
Rights Act of 1984, 451–452
Developmental disabilities councils, state,
268, 272, 280, 282, 284
Developmental equivalence, and self-
determination skills, 349, 352
Didactic training strategies, 324, 328
Differential reinforcement
of alternative behavior, 160
of incompatible behavior, 160
of other behavior, 159–160
Direct care staff
abuse of persons with disabilities by,
55, 208, 211–212
benefits for, 295, 301–303, 306–307
characteristics of, 316, 318t–319t
compensation of, 250–252, 256, 266,
289–312
improvement of, 308–309
national survey of, 293–309
research on, 292–293
development activities, 222–223

qualitative research studies of, 55
recruitment, training, and retention of,
    see Recruitment; Retention; Train-
    ing; Turnover
Direct care staffing, creative practices for
    and maintenance costs, 285
    recommendations for, 317–321
Direct service role, characteristics of, 315
Direct stimulation, and challenging behav-
    ior, 152
Disabilities
    severe, persons with, in community res-
        idences, 5–6, 185–186
    severity of, and costs, 250–251
    see also Developmental disabilities;
        Mental retardation
Discriminant analysis, 32
Discrimination
    and disability services, 419–421
    freedom from, 10
    gender, 408–412
    prohibition of, 123–124
    racial, 414–419
    social class, 412–414
Diversity, see Multiculturalism
Domestic involvement, 13–14
Double ABCX model, 32
DRA, see Differential reinforcement, of
    alternative behavior
DRI, see Differential reinforcement, of
    incompatible behavior
DRO, see Differential reinforcement, of
    other behavior
Dyadic network variables, 86–87

EAPs, see Employee Assistance Programs
Early childhood resource network, 274
Early intervention programs, costs of,
    274–275
Ecological factors, 154
    importance of, 365–371
    and perception of control, 364–365
    and self-determination skills, 350–353,
        351f, 365–371
    and social inclusion, 94
Ecological manipulations, 154–155
Economic integration factor, 73–74
Ecosystems framework, for self-
    determination skills development,
    350–353, 351f

Ecosystems model, of self-determination,
    353–365, 354f
Education
    multicultural approach to, 407–408
    of women with disabilities, 410–411
Education for All Handicapped Children
    Act of 1975, 123, 369
Education of the Handicapped Act
    Amendments of 1983, 451
Education of the Handicapped Act
    Amendments of 1986, Part H,
    272–274, 287
Education of the Handicapped Act
    Amendments of 1990, 123
Effective integration, 11
Elderly parents, adults living with, and
    waiting for community services,
    183
Elderly people, waiting for community
    services, 183–184
Eligibility, for services, determination of,
    197
Emergency procedures, for challenging
    behavior, 161
Emotional support, 88
Empirical tradition, of community living
    research, 24–33
Empiricism, 35–36
    concept of, 24–25
Employee(s), see Direct care staff
Employee Assistance Programs, 286
Employment
    community, planning and implement-
        ing, 281–282
    competitive, definition of, 452
    integration of, 456–457
    opportunities, need for, 270
    of women with disabilities, 411
    see also Supported employment
Employment integration factor, 73–74
Employment stability factor, 73–74
Empowerment, 14–15
    see also Self-determination
Enclave model, of supported employment,
    453–454
Entrepreneurial model, of supported
    employment, 454
Environmental factors, see Ecological
    factors
Escape-motivated behavior, 151
Estate, guardianship of, 431
Esteem support, 88

Ethnic identity, loss of, 418–419
Evaluation research, qualitative, 56
Exosystem, 351*f*, 352, 368–369
Experiment
alternative view of, 29–30
and community living research, 26–29
Experimental bias, 25–30
Experimental logic, 26
Exploratory factor analysis, 72–73
Eye-poking, 152

Facilitator, *see* Social inclusion facilitator
Facility
governmental certification of, requirements for, 252–253, 256
size of, and costs, 251–252
type of, and costs, 249, 255
see also specific type
Fact-finding, through research, 30–31
Factor analysis
confirmatory, 72–73
exploratory, 72–73
Family(ies)
basic right to live with, 9–10
qualitative research studies of, 55–56
Family care, costs of, 245–249
Family environment, and self-determination skills, 350–353, 366
Family income, and disability, 413–414
Family interviews, for waiting list study, 192–193
Family involvement
importance of, 12
in service planning, 216
Family members, relationships with, 12
Family support
costs of, 273–274
need for, 270
Federal constraints, on state agencies, 266, 269
Federal funding, state-by-state, variations in, 266
Federal government, collaboration with business and local communities, need for, 271
Feedback, and challenging behavior, 152
Field notes, 45
Financing
adequate, need for, 285–286
of community services, 265–288
flexibility in, 269–270, 285

study of
community provider experiences/recommendations, 271–286
purpose and method of, 267–269
state agency experiences/recommendations, 269–271
flexibility, 285
of service delivery systems, strategies for, 199–200
Finger-flicking, 152
Foster care, costs of, 246–248, 277
Friendships
definition of, 85
opportunity for, 111
between persons with and without disabilities, lack of, 91
between persons with disabilities, importance of, 92
promotion of, by recreational participation, 138–140
Functional service areas, 241, 242*t*

Gender, and disability, 408–412
Gender differences
in service delivery, 412
in support employment, 411–412
in wages, 290
Generic recreation programs
advantages of, 125
definition of, 124
disadvantages of, 125–126
integration of, 124–126
strategies for, 124–125
Government
leadership/technical assistance provided by, need for, 286
quality assurance provided by, 207–209
Governmental certification, of facilities, requirements for, 252–253, 256
Governmental constraints, on state agencies, 266, 269
Graduates, waiting for community services, 184–185
Grounded theory, 47–48
Group
restructuring of, 105–106, 107*f*
sociogram of, 105, 106*f*
Group homes, costs of, 246–248, 275–276
Growth and development, personal, 4
opportunity for, 10–12
Guardianship, *see* Legal guardianship

HCBS, *see* Home and Community Based Services
Head banging, 149–150, 152
Head Start, integration of, applied qualitative study of, 56–57
Health, 4, 8–9
Hearing, guardianship, 435–436, 443
Home, 381–403
  as base for friendship development, 389
  changing concepts of, 384
  cleanliness, standards of, 388
  decoration of, 387–388
  dimensions of, 384, 385*t*–386*t*
  disability perspectives on, 383–384
  environment, and self-determination skills, 350–353, 366
  historical meaning of, 383
  life, participant observations of, 384–389
  literature review on, 383–384
  meaning of, 383–389
  persons living at
    services/supports needed by, 193–194
    transition to community living by, needs during, 194–195
    and waiting for community services, 6–7, 182–183, 190–197
  as physical place, 386–387
  as site for hospitality and friendship, 387
  as social site, 388–389
  support of, 394–400
Home and Community Based Services Waiver Program, 9, 194, 210, 221, 225, 275–276, 322
Household tasks, participation in, 13–14
Housing
  affordable, costs of, 276–277
  consumer-owned, costs of, 279–280
Housing cooperative, 276
HUD, *see* U.S. Department of Housing and Urban Development
Hypothesis discovery analyses, 31

ICAP, *see* Inventory for Client and Agency Planning
ICC, *see* Interagency coordinating council
ICFs/MR, *see* Intermediate care facilities for persons with mental retardation
IDEA, *see* Individuals with Disabilities Education Act

IFSP, *see* Individualized family service plan
Immediate antecedent manipulations, 155–156
Inclusion, *see* Social inclusion
Incompetency, 427
  determination of, 439
  restoration to capacity after, 436
  global, 438
Independence, *see* Self-determination
Independent case management services, need for, 271
Independent living, costs of, 246–247
Individual actions, characteristics of, and challenging behavior intervention, 163
Individual assessment, and service planning, 215–217
Individual choice, promotion of, 219–221
Individual outcomes, supported employment, 464–465
Individual placement model, of supported employment, 453
Individual support, need for, 286
Individualized family service plan, 272
Individualized living, costs of, 277–278
Individualized outcome monitoring, 217–219
Individualized service plan, 272, 368
Individuals with Disabilities Education Act, 123
Inductive reasoning, in qualitative research, 47–48
Informal support network, *see* Social network
Informational support, 88
Informed consent, 432
Injurious forms, of challenging behavior, 149, 152
Inservice training, 325, 327
Instability rate, 295, 302–303
Institution(s)
  costs of care in, versus community settings, 245
  large
    persons living in, access to community services, 188–189
    residents of
      challenging behavior in, 148
      versus community facility residents, 6
  qualitative research studies of, 55
  shift to community from, *see*

Institution(s)—*continued*
    Deinstitutionalization
state
    persons living in, access to community services, 185–189
    residents of, 6
    challenging behavior in, 148
    wage rates at, versus private facilities, 296–301, 298*t*–299*t*
    total, concept of, 50–51
Institutional records, data collection from, 47
Instrumental support, 88
Integrated classroom, 54–55
Integrated preschool programs, costs of, 274–275
Integrated work settings, definition of, 452
Integration
    community, levels of, and specific residential site, 91
    of community recreation services, 124–129
    effective, 11
    employment, 456–457
    studies of, 27–28, 56–57
Interaction(s)
    environmental, and perception of control, 364–365
    social
        and peer programs, 134
        and self-determination skills, 349, 366–368
        between workers with and without disabilities, 54, 456
Interagency collaboration, need for, 285
Interdependence, 95
Intermediate care facilities for persons with mental retardation, 6, 175, 209, 215, 220, 285
    costs of, 247, 252–253
    federal reimbursements concerning, bias in, 266–267
    persons living in, access to community services, 187–190
Interpersonal problem solving, 361–363
Interpretative nature, of qualitative research, 44–45
Interpretive inquiry, 35–36
Interpretivist perspective, *see* Social constructionist perspective
Inventory for Client and Agency Planning, 250, 465
ISP, *see* Individualized service plan

Job
    acquisition, 455
    fit, 455–456
    loss, and social skill deficits, 93
    maintenance, 455
    services, conjunctive, 455
    surveys, 455
    see also Employment; Supported Employment
Job coaches, assigned to workers with disabilities, 54
Job Training Partnership Act (JTPA), 281

Kidspace study, of recreational participation, 130–131
Knowledge
    declarative, 363
    procedural, 363

Labor market conditions, analysis of, 455
Leadership ACTion Project, 371–372
Learning, as interactive process, 10
Least restrictive environment, 96–97, 123, 243, 346
Legal guardian(s)
    authority and obligations of, 432
    standards and training for, 443
Legal guardianship, 427–447
    concept of, 429–435
    definition of, 427
    determination of, 428, 430
        procedures for, 435–438
    disputed, 428
    fundamental nature of, 443–444
    implications of, 432–435
    law and policy, steps to improve, 442–444
    least restrictive forms of, underuse of, 434–435, 440
    monitoring of, 436–438, 441, 443
    types of, 430–431
Legal status issues, roles of social support and advocacy in, 441–442
Leisure activities, *see* Recreational program(s)
Leisure integration factor, 73–74
Leisure skills training, 134–135
Length of service, 295, 303
Life choices, daily, 14
Life histories, of persons with mental retardation, 52–53

Life service planning organization, 272
Life-Style Planning, 99
Lifestyle Satisfaction Survey, 464
Lights, gazing at, 152
Limited guardianship, 431
underuse of, 434, 440
Local government
collaboration with state agencies, need
for, 270
level of, difficulties at, 269
Logic
deductive, 32
by elimination, 26
experimental, 26
Logical intervention strategy, for challenging behavior, 157
LRE, see Least restrictive environment
LSP, see Life-Style Planning

Macrosystem, 351f, 352–353, 369–371
Maintenance costs, of services/supports, 285–286
Management Information System, 278, 280
Manual restraint, 161
Master of Science degree, in special education, 326
MAU, see Multi-attribute utility
McGill Action Planning System (MAPS), 99
McKinney Homeless Act, 284
Mechanical restraint, 161
Mediational model, 32
Medicaid, 189, 247–248, 267, 269, 283, 287
Home and Community Based Services Waiver Program, 9, 194, 210, 275–276, 322
Management Information System, 278, 280
personal care assistant reimbursement system, 278
reform, 285
Medical care, 8, 186
Mental retardation
applied research in, 56–58
definitions of, in social constructionist perspective, 48–49
as form of social deviance, 49
level of, and social inclusion, 93
persons with
experience in residential settings,

qualitative research on, 53–56
friendships between, importance of, 92
intermediate care facilities for, 6
life histories of, 52–53
potential of, realization of, 11
quality services for, 207–230
and social acceptance, 49–50
ways of thinking about, contribution of qualitative research to, 48–50
see also Developmental disabilities
Mesosystem, 351f, 352, 368
Meta-analytical study, of staff turnover, 330, 332
Microsystem, 350, 351f, 365–366
Middle class, 413
Minimum indicator data collection protocol, 76
Minnesota
Parents as Casemanagers program in, 223–224
public guardianship in, 430, 434, 436, 439–440
Minnesota Guardianship Task Force, 433
Minnesota Mental Retardation Protection Act of 1917, 438
Minority groups
poverty among, 413–414
see also Race
Minority status, multiple, 409, 416
MIS, see Management Information System
Mobile work crew model, of supported employment, 454
Model programs, 57
Monitoring
compliance, 461
of legal guardianship, 436–438, 441, 443
Motherhood, and disability, 409–410
Motivational factors, 364–365
Motor skills, and recreational activities, 132–133
Multiattribute evaluation techniques, for cost accounting, 257
Multi-attribute utility, 473–474
Multiculturalism, 406–408
and community living, 405–426
definition of, 407
and disability services, 407–408
Multidimensional measurement, of community adjustment, 65–79
implications of, 75–78

Multimodal training strategies, 324, 328
Multiple minority status, 409, 416
Multiple outcome measures, in community adjustment research, 67–68
Multiple perspectives, in community living research, 33–36
Multiple regression, in behavioral research, 28
Multivariate analyses
of staff turnover, 331–332
use of, 72–75

National Center on Educational Outcomes, conceptual model of outcome indicators, 69, 70f
National Institute on Mental Retardation, 209
National Longitudinal Transition Study of Special Education Students, 68
National Medical Expenditure Survey (1987), 6, 148
National Nursing Home Surveys, 187
National Recreation and Park Association, 122
National Study of Public Expenditures (1986), 189
NCEO, see National Center on Educational Outcomes
Neglect, of persons with disabilities, 211–212
Neighborhood, 381–403
and children, 390
and choice, 393
and culture, 390–391
as extension of home, 389–390
familiarity, 392
housing patterns, and community living options, 284–285
meaning of, 389–394
as part of person's identity, 391–392
and persons with disabilities, 391
safety, 394
support of, 394–400
Network, see Social network
Network variables, 86–87
Nonsocially motivated challenging behavior, 151–153
Normalization, 123, 346
North Dakota Career Ladder System, 326
Nursing aides
hourly wage for, 290
see also Direct care staff

Nursing homes, persons living in, access to community services, 187–188

Object consequences, 151
Object-motivated behavior, 151
Objectivity, 25
Occupation factor, 72
Office of Special Education and Rehabilitative Services, 282, 284, 347, 371, 451–452
Official documents, data collection from, 47
Ohio, quality assessment programs in, 225–226
Older adults, waiting for community services, 183–184
Opportunity
to choose services, 219–220
for employment, 270
for friendships, 111
for interaction, and social inclusion, 94–95
for personal growth and development, 10–12
Orientation, 325
OSERS, see Office of Special Education and Rehabilitative Services
Outcome(s)
critical dimensions of, delineation of, 77–78
of decisions, awareness of, 356
individualized monitoring of, 217–219
linking costs with, 239
problems of, 243–245
supported employment
evaluation of, 460–465, 463f
multidimensional nature of, 458–460
Outcome domains, identification of, 68–69
Outcome indicators, conceptual model of, 69, 70f
Outcome measures
of accreditation agencies, 77
benefits of, 217–218
composite, construction of, 69–71, 71f
multiple, in community adjustment research, 67–68
of quality assurance, 212, 217–219
single, in community adjustment research, 67
Overregulation, 285

Paradigm, of community living research, 29
Parents as Casemanagers program (Minnesota), 223–224
Partial competency, 439
Participation
  community, valued, 4, 13–14
  cooperative, 135
  in recreation activities, promotion of, 133–136
  in household tasks, 13–14
  part-time, in regular classes, by students with disabilities, 55
  productive, 11
  in recreational program
    benefits of, 121
    cooperatively structuring directions for, 130–132
Participatory action research, 56
Partners in Policymaking, 282, 360
Part-time participation, in regular classes, by students with disabilities, 55
Patterns, identification, through research, 31–32
Pay equity, 305
PCA, see Personal care assistant
Pedagogical research, 56
Peer acceptance, 85, 93
Peer interaction
  cooperative, promotion of, 136–137, 139–140
  and self-determination skills, 350–353, 367–368
Peer relations, 89
  definition of, 85
  in recreational activities, 131
Peer relationships
  in supported employment, 456
  vertical (tutoring) versus horizontal (socialization), 133–135
Peer socialization programs, 133
Peer tutoring programs, 133
People First, 359–360
Per diem rates, and cost accounting, 240, 245, 247–248
Performance evaluation indicators, 460–461
Permanency planning, 9–10
Person, guardianship of, 431
Person-centered planning
  and individual assessment, 215–216
  for social inclusion, 97–104, 111
    case study, 109–111

Person-centered planning groups, 100–102
Personal advocacy, see Self-advocacy
Personal autonomy, see Self-determination
Personal care assistant, 276, 287
  costs of, 278–279
Personal characteristics
  and self-determination skills, 350, 353–365
  and social inclusion, 93
Personal choice/decision making, 353–357
Personal competence, and community adjustment, 76
Personal computer data base, for quality assessment, 225
Personal connections, 381–403
  support of, 382–383, 394–400
Personal documents, data collection from, 46–47
Personal Futures Planning, 11, 99
Personal growth and development, 4
  opportunity for, 10–12
Personal satisfaction factor, 73–74
Personal values, of researchers, implications of, for service providers, 399–400
Personalization, 7
Personnel, see Direct care staff
Perspective, role of, 35–36
Petition, guardianship, 435
Physical proximity, versus social inclusion, 137
Placement decisions, supported employment, 455
Planning
  permanency, 9–10
  person-centered, 11
    and individual assessment, 215–216
    for social inclusion, 97–104, 111
      case study, 109–111
    service, and individual assessment, 215–217
Planning groups, person-centered, 100–102
Play, social components of, 132–133
Play skill training, 135
Poverty, 413
  and disability, 413–414
Poverty line statistics, 30–31
Practicum experiences, 327
Pre-experimental studies, 27
Preferences, awareness of, 355
Preschool programs, integrated, costs of, 274–275

Preservice training, 325, 327, 368–369
Prioritization, of waiting lists, for service
  delivery, 181
Private facilities, wage rates at, versus
  public institutions, 296–301,
  298t–299t
Private guardianship, 430
Private ownership, of residential facility,
  cost studies of, 253
Private sector level, difficulties at, 269
Problem solving
  definition of, 362
  interpersonal, 361–363
  process of, 362
Procedural knowledge, 363
Process/progress evaluation, of supported
  employment, 461
Productive participation, 11
Program directors, 322
Program-generated attributions, 365
Program-level outcomes, of supported
  employment, 465–466
Program planning/evaluation, implications
  of multidimensional measurement
  for, 77–78
Program support, 223
Progressivism, 207–208
Public expenditures, allocation of, 232
Public guardianship, 430
  potential problems with, 433
Public Law 90–480, see Architectural
  Barriers Act of 1968
Public Law 93–112, see Rehabilitation Act
  of 1973
Public Law 94–142, see Education for All
  Handicapped Children Act of 1975
Public Law 98–199, see Education of the
  Handicapped Act Amendments of
  1983
Public Law 98–527, see Developmental
  Disabilities and Bill of Rights Act
  of 1984
Public Law 99–457, see Education of the
  Handicapped Act Amendments of
  1986
Public Law 99–506, see Rehabilitation Act
  Amendments of 1986
Public Law 100–203, see Consolidated
  Omnibus Budget Reconciliation
  Act of 1987
Public Law 101–336, see Americans with
  Disabilities Act

Public Law 101-476, see Education of the
  Handicapped Act Amendments of
  1990
Public ownership, of residential facility,
  cost studies of, 253
Public records, data collection from, 47
Punishment procedures, for challenging
  behavior, 160

Qualitative research, 43–63
  applied, 56–58
  based on descriptive data, 45–47
  characteristics of, 44
  contributions of, 48–58
  credibility of, 47
  definition of, 44
  inductive nature of, 47–48
  interpretative nature of, 44–45
  recognition of, 44–48
Quality, definition of, 213
Quality assessment, 212–214
  practices in, 223–226
Quality assurance, 207–230
  approaches to, reliability and validity
    of, 211
  monitoring of, 211
  outcome-based measurement of, 212,
    217–219
  redesign of, 210–212
Quality Assurance Academy, 224
Quality enhancement, 212–214
  organizational development for, 222
  practices in, 223–226
Quality of care, and cost studies, 253
Quality of life
  aspects of, 4
  enhancement of, 213
  factors affecting, 313–314
  and supported employment evaluation,
    464–465
Quality of Life Questionnaire, 464–465
Quality of services
  definition of, 213–214
  from different vendors, providing infor-
    mation about, 220
Quantitative-qualitative distinction, 35

Race, and disability, 414–419
Racial identity, loss of, 418–419

Racial minority groups, poverty among, 413–414
Readiness model, 96
Realistic job previews, 332
Reality, social construction of, 44, 48–50
Recreational program(s), 14
  adult leader of
    crucial contribution of, 130–137
    direction provided by, effects on children's behavior, 136–137
  after-school, 122
  benefits of, 121, 137
  community
    historical and legislative overview of, 122–124
    integrated, 124–129
  generic, see Generic recreation programs
  integration in, facilitation of, 121–145
  intervention strategies for, 129–140
  and materials to promote socialization, 132–133
  neglect of, 121
Recreation integration factor, 73–74
Recruitment, staff, 11, 222–223, 291–292, 313–341
  factors influencing, 314–316
  impact of wages on, 315
  recommendations for, 317–321
  research related to, 316–321
  and retention, 333
Referent generality, 67
Regional variations, cost studies of, 253–254
Rehabilitation Act Amendments of 1986, 452
Rehabilitation Act of 1973, 283, 451
  Section 502, 123
  Section 504, 123
Reinforcement, time out from, 161
Reinforcement schedule, favorable, 158
Reinforcer-related considerations, with challenging behavior, 162
Relational content, 87
Relationship(s)
  accepting, concept of, 52
  with family members, 12
  see also Social relationships
Relativistic approach, 35–36
Replacement-based intervention strategies, for challenging behavior, 156–159
Reproductive rights, 409–410

Researchers, personal values of, implications of, for service providers, 399–400
Resident(s)
  characteristics of, and costs, 250–251, 255
  see also specific facility
Residential environment factor, 72
Residential facilities
  characteristics of, and staffing, 314–317
  persons living in, access to community services, 185–197
  private ownership of, cost studies of, 253
  public ownership of, cost studies of, 253
  site of, and level of community integration, 91
  staff of, see Direct care staff
  types of, and costs, 249–250
  see also Community residences
Resource components approach, to cost accounting, 256–257
Resource network, early childhood, 274
Respitality support, for families, 273
Restoration to capacity, after incompetency ruling, 436
Restraint, for challenging behavior, 161
Restructuring, of group, 105–106, 107f
Retention, staff, 11, 222–223, 291–292, 313–341
  factors influencing, 314–316
  impact of wages on, 315, 333
  innovative solutions for, 332
  recommendations for, 332–333
  research related to, 328–333
  see also Turnover
Reverse mainstreaming, 126–128
  advantages of, 127
  definition of, 126
  disadvantages of, 127–128
  process of, 126–127
Rights, basic, 9–10
RJPs, see Realistic job previews
RRTC, see Rehabilitation Research and Training Center

Safety, 4, 8–10
St. Louis County Community College Program, 326

School environment, and self-determination skills, 350–353, 367
Science, meaning of, 33–35
Segregation, supported by least restrictive environment principle, 96
Selection bias, in costs studies, 239–240, 255
Self-advocacy, 15, 259–361
    definition of, 259
    and guardianship issues, 428, 444
    need for, 271
    and staff interactions, 327
Self-advocacy movement, 359–360
Self-advocacy programs, 360–361
    costs of, 282–283
Self-determination, 4, 14–15, 345–380
    definition of, 346–348
    ecosystems model of, 353–365, 354f
    facilitation of, 371–372
    and guardianship issues, 428, 440, 444
    importance of, 345–347, 370
    research on
        alternative, 350–353, 351f
        traditional, 349–350
    skills, development of, 348–349
Self-determination project, University of Minnesota, 372
Self-efficacy, 345, 364–365
Self-esteem, 345
Self-injury, 149
Self-knowledge, 363–364
Self-regulation, of behavior, 357–359
Senior companion program, 283
Sensitizing concepts, 50
Separation rate, crude, 295, 302, 304f–306f
Service(s)
    access to, and racial discrimination, 417–418
    coordination of, effective, 216–217
    cost of, see Cost(s)
    opportunity to choose, 219–220
    planning, individual assessment and, 215–217
    quality of, see also Quality assurance
        definition of, 213–214
        from different vendors, providing information about, 220
    and social inclusion, 95–97, 111
    see also Community services
Service areas, functional, 241, 242t
Service delivery

alteration of, to resolve waiting list problems, 199
    discrimination in, 419–421
        gender, 412
        racial, 414–419
        social class, 412–414
    enhancement of, 221–223
    multicultural approach to, importance of, 408
    prioritization of waiting lists for, 181
    social class discrimination in, 413–414
Service providers
    characteristics of, and challenging behavior intervention, 163–164
    implications of research for, 399–400
    support roles of, 396–397
    see also Community provider organizations
SES, see Socioeconomic status
Severe disabilities, persons with, in community residences, 5–6, 185–186
Sex-role stereotyping, 411
Sexual abuse, of women with disabilities, 410
Single outcome measures, in community adjustment research, 67
Skill acquisition/maintenance, in supported employment, 454–456, 465
Skilled nursing facilities (SNFs), 187
Social acceptance, mental retardation and, 49–50
Social class
    and disability, 412–414, 421
    effects of, 413–414
Social companionship, 88–89
Social connections, types of, 100, 101t
Social construction, of reality, 44, 50
Social constructionist perspective, definitions of mental retardation in, 48–49
Social context, and qualitative research, 53–56
Social deviance, mental retardation as form of, 49
Social inclusion
    case study, 109–111
    definition of, 84, 86
    enhancement of, 83–119
    factors influencing, 92–95
    nature of, 84–85
    versus physical proximity, 137
    planning, person-centered approach to,

99–104
process of, 95–111
strategies for, 98–99
Social inclusion facilitator
beliefs and actions of, 102, 103f
and community mapping, 107–109
definition of, 107
recruitment of, 108
role of, 102–103, 111
and sociometric process, 104–106
Social initiation training, 135
Social integration factor, 73–74
Social interaction
and peer programs, 134
and self-determination skills, 349, 366–368
between workers with and without disabilities, 54
Social network
absence of, 91
characteristics of, 86
definition of, 86
function of, 87–90
of persons with developmental disabilities, 90–92
versus persons without disabilities, 90–91
types of relationships in, 89, 89f
Social network factor, 73–74
Social network structure, 86–92
definition of, 86
Social play, levels of, 132–133
Social processes, 86
Social reciprocity, 132
and peer programs, 133–134
Social relationships, 4, 12–13
definition of, 84
function of, 87–90
importance of, 83
nature of, 84–85
of persons with developmental disabilities, 90–92
provisions of, 89, 89f
quantity of, 86
within service system context, 95–96
structures of, 86
variety of, 85
Social Security Disability Insurance (SSDI), 283, 413
Social skill deficits, and social inclusion, 93
Social skills training, 134–135, 138

Social support
construct of, 88
definition of, 88
and legal status issues, 441–442, 444
provided by social network, 87–88
Social support/safety factor, 72
Socialization, materials to promote, and recreation activities, 132–133
Socially motivated challenging behavior, 149–153
Societal attitudes
negative, 315, 353, 369–370, 428
in popular media, data collection from, 47
positive, 137–138
and social inclusion, 93
toward direct care staff, 290, 315, 321
waiting lists as indicators of, 198
Societal-level outcomes, of supported employment, 466–467
Sociodramatic play, 131
Socioeconomic status, 32, see also Social class
Sociogram, of group, 105, 106f
Sociometry, 98–99, 104–107, 111
definition of, 104
rules for, 105
Solutions, possible, generation of, 363
Special education program graduates, waiting for community services, 184–185
Special Friends curriculum, 131, 134, 136
SSDI, see Social Security Disability Insurance
SSI, see Supplemental Security Income
Staff, see Direct care staff
Staff trainer, 322
Starting wages, direct care staff, 296–301, 303–306
Start-up costs, of services/supports, 284–285
State agencies, financing provided by, 265–288
study of
experiences and recommendations of, 269–271
purpose and method of, 267–269
variations in, 266
State developmental disabilities councils, 268, 272, 280, 282, 284
State government
collaboration with business and local

State government—*continued*
  communities, need for, 271
  level of, difficulties at, 269
State guardianship statutes, 433–434
State institutions
  persons living in, access to community
    services, 185–189
  residents of, 6
  challenging behavior in, 148
State-operated group homes, costs of, 247
State-operated regional centers, costs of,
  247
Statistical methods, multivariate, use of,
  72–75
Stereotyping
  sex-role, 411
  see also Societal attitudes
Sterilization, of wards, 432
Stigma, concept of, 51
The Structure of Science (Nagel), 34
Study Circles Resource Center, 103
Subculture, concept of, 51–52
Subjective experience, illumination of,
  with qualitative research, 52–53
Summer camps, 122
Supplemental Security Income (SSI),
  194–195, 278–279, 283, 413
Support
  meaning of, differing perspectives on,
    394–399, 395*t*
  of personal connections, 382–383,
    394–400
Support roles, of service providers,
  396–397
Supported employment, 13, 53–54, 286,
  449–482
  benefit-cost analysis of, 458, 467–470,
    469*t*
  benefits of, 450
  costs of, 280–281
  current policies and practices, 450–457
  definition of, 451–452
  gender differences in, 411–412
  justification of, 450, 459–460
  multiservice nature of, 452–453, 456
  number of individuals in, 450
  outcomes
    evaluation of, 460–465, 463*f*
    multidimensional nature of,
      458–460, 471–472
    program-level, 465–466
    system-level and societal-level,
      466–467

social and economic goals of, evalua-
    tion of, 457–470
Supported employment programs
  cost-effectiveness of, 472–474
  models for, 453–454
  multi-attribute nature of, 470–474
  strategies for, 454–457
Supported living, 7–8
  costs of, 277–278
System-level outcomes, of supported
  employment, 466–467

Task-related considerations, with challeng-
    ing behavior, 163
Tax incentives, for families and individ-
    uals with disabilities, need for, 286
Taxonomy
  of functional services, 241, 242*t*
  of vocational and training services, 243
Teacher instruction, effects on children's
    behavior, 136–137
Technical assistance, 223
  government, need for, 286
Theory
  grounded, 47–48
  implications of multidimensional mea-
    surement for, 77
Theory testing, 32–33
Time out from reinforcement, 161
Top-down approach, 68
Total institution, concept of, 50–51
Traditional models, creative use of, need
  for, 270
Training, staff, 11, 222–223, 291–292,
  313–341
  factors influencing, 314–316
  importance of, 321
  innovative solutions for, 325–326
  recommendations for, 326–328
  requirements for, 11–12, 322,
    323*t*–324*t*
  research related to, 321–328
  strategies for, 322–325
Training services, and cost accounting,
  243
Transcripts, 45–46
Transition
  from childhood to adulthood, 55–56,
    451
  from family living to community living,
    needs during, 194–195
Trust, 95

Trustworthiness, of qualitative research study, 47
Turning 22, 184
Turnover, staff, 11, 222, 251, 266, 285–286, 289–312
  national survey of, 293–309
  negative effects of, 308–309, 329
  research on, 292–293, 328–333

Upper class, 413
U.S. Department of Education, Office of Special Education and Rehabilitative Services, 282, 284, 347, 371, 451–452
U.S. Department of Health and Human Services, 284, 452
U.S. Department of Housing and Urban Development, loans/rent subsidies provided by, 276, 279, 284
U.S. General Accounting Office, 211
Utah, compliance and outcome monitoring programs in, 224–225

Valued community participation, 4, 13–14
Valued Outcomes Information Systems, 225
Vendors, opportunity to choose, 219–220
Verification, 363
Videotaping, data collection with, 46
Video transcripts, 45–46
VINE, see Volunteer interview network of employers
Vision
  creation of, 99–100
  definition of, 99
Vocational rehabilitation programs
  federal-state, 451
  see also Supported employment
Vocational services, and cost accounting, 243
VOIS, see Valued Outcomes Information Systems
Voluntary citizen monitoring, of quality assurance, 225–226

Volunteer interview network of employers, 280

Wage parity, need for, 285–286
Wage rate differences, 251–252, 256, 266, 290, 315
  and gender, 290
  by type of facility, national survey of, 296–297, 298t–299t, 303–306
Waiting, for community services, 6–7, 96, 173–206
  effects on persons with disabilities, 192–197
Waiting lists
  for community services
    average number on, 174
    current information and statistics on, 175–185, 178t–180t
    people on, characteristics of, 181–185
    resolution of, 199
  as indicators of societal attitudes, 198
Waiting list tracking systems, 177–181
Ward, civil rights of, 432
Ward–guardian relationship, 429–435
Women
  with disabilities, discrimination against, 408–412
  wage discrimination against, 290
Women, Infants, and Children (WIC) clinics, 274
Work environment
  integrated, definition of, 452
  and self-determination skills, 350–353, 367
  see also Supported employment
Working class, 413
Worst nightmare scenario, 100

Young adult graduates, waiting for community services, 184–185

Zero exclusion team approach, 128–129
  advantages of, 128–129
  components of, 128
  disadvantages of, 129